Lecture Notes in Computer Science   15651

Founding Editors

Gerhard Goos
Juris Hartmanis

AF167469

The series Lecture Notes in Computer Science (LNCS), including its subseries Lecture Notes in Artificial Intelligence (LNAI) and Lecture Notes in Bioinformatics (LNBI), has established itself as a medium for the publication of new developments in computer science and information technology research, teaching, and education.

LNCS enjoys close cooperation with the computer science R & D community, the series counts many renowned academics among its volume editors and paper authors, and collaborates with prestigious societies. Its mission is to serve this international community by providing an invaluable service, mainly focused on the publication of conference and workshop proceedings and postproceedings. LNCS commenced publication in 1973.

Abderrahmane Nitaj · Svetla Petkova-Nikova ·
Vincent Rijmen
Editors

Progress in Cryptology - AFRICACRYPT 2025

16th International Conference on Cryptology in Africa
Rabat, Morocco, July 21–23, 2025
Proceedings

 Springer

Editors
Abderrahmane Nitaj ⓘ
Université de Caen Normandie
Caen, France

Svetla Petkova-Nikova ⓘ
KU Leuven
Leuven-Heverlee, Belgium

Vincent Rijmen ⓘ
KU Leuven
Leuven-Heverlee, Belgium

University of Bergen
Bergen, Norway

ISSN 0302-9743   ISSN 1611-3349 (electronic)
Lecture Notes in Computer Science
ISBN 978-3-031-97259-1   ISBN 978-3-031-97260-7 (eBook)
https://doi.org/10.1007/978-3-031-97260-7

This Springer imprint is published by the registered company Springer Nature Switzerland AG
The registered company address is: Gewerbestrasse 11, 6330 Cham, Switzerland

If disposing of this product, please recycle the paper.

Preface

This volume contains the papers accepted for presentation at AFRICACRYPT 2025, the 16th International Conference on the Theory and Application of Cryptographic Techniques. The aim of this series of conferences is to provide an international forum for practitioners and researchers from industry, academia, and government agencies for a discussion of all forms of cryptography and its applications. The initiative of organizing AFRICACRYPT started in 2008 where it was first held in Morocco. Subsequent yearly events were held in Tunisia, South Africa, Senegal, Morocco, Egypt, and Cameroon. This year, AFRICACRYPT was organized in the ENSIAS College of Mohammed V University in Rabat, with the partnership of the General Directorate of Information Systems Security (DGSSI), Morocco, and in cooperation with the International Association for Cryptologic Research (IACR). It was held in Rabat, during July 21–23, 2025.

We received 45 submissions authored by researchers from countries from all over the world. After a double-blind reviewing process that included also online discussion and involved 46 Technical Program Committee members and 12 external reviewers, we decided to accept 21 papers. All submitted papers received at least 2 reviews. We thank the Program Committee and the external reviewers for their diligent work and fruitful discussions and we thank the authors of all submitted papers for supporting the conference. The authors of accepted papers are thanked again for revising their papers according to the suggestions of the reviewers. Apart from a few conditionally accepted papers, the revised versions were not checked again by the Program Committee, so authors bear full responsibility for their content.

The conference program featured three keynote speakers, Olivier Blazy from LIX, École Polytechnique Paris, France, Pascal Lafourcade, from LIMOS, Université Clermont Auvergne, France, and Jeongeun Park from NTNU, Norway. We were happy that they all agreed to attend and deliver their keynotes personally.

We heartily thank the Honorary Chairs, Mohammed Rhachi, President of Mohammed V University in Rabat, Morocco, Bouchaib Bounabat, Director of ENSIAS, Mohammed V University in Rabat, Morocco, and Mostafa Rabii, Brigadier General, Vice President of the ANCA Cybersecurity Authority Alliance, Morocco.

We thank the General Chairs, Mostafa Belkasmi from the ENSIAS College of University Mohammed V in Rabat, Morocco, and Said Eddahmani, from University of Paris VIII, France. Special thanks go to the local organizing committee who created and set up the conference website and executed all the updates almost instantly. We thank the staff at Springer for their help with the proceedings' production. The conference received generous support from the ENSIAS College of University Mohammed V in Rabat, the General Directorate of Information Systems Security (DGSSI), Morocco, Research group COSIC, KU Leuven, Belgium, LIX École Polytechnique Paris, France, and LIMOS, Université Clermont Auvergne, France.

Finally, we thank the organizing committee from the ENSIAS College of University Mohammed V in Rabat, Morocco, and the organizing committee from the General Directorate of Information Systems Security (DGSSI), Morocco.

Acting as program chairs for Africacrypt 2025 was a privilege and a great experience, thanks to all those people that helped us to make this conference a big success.

May 2025

Abderrahmane Nitaj
Svetla Petkova-Nikova
Vincent Rijmen

Organization

General Chairs

Mostafa Belkasmi   ENSIAS College, Mohammed V University in Rabat, Morocco

Said Eddahmani   University of Paris VIII, France

Program Chairs

Abderrahmane Nitaj   University of Caen Normandy, France

Svetla Petkova-Nikova   KU Leuven, Belgium

Vincent Rijmen   KU Leuven, Belgium and University of Bergen, Norway

Invited Speakers

Olvier Blazy   LIX, École Polytechnique Paris, France

Pascal Lafourcade   LIMOS, Université Clermont Auvergne, France

Jeongeun Park   NTNU, Norway

Honorary Committee

Mohammed Rhachi   Mohammed V University in Rabat, Morocco

Bouchaib Bounabat   ENSIAS, Mohammed V University in Rabat, Morocco

Mostafa Rabii   ANCA Cybersecurity Authority Alliance, Morocco

Organizing Committee

Ahmed Azouaoui   ESTK, Ibn Tofail University, Morocco

Driss Bouzidi   ENSIAS, Mohammed V University in Rabat, Morocco

Idriss Chana	ENSIAS, Mohammed V University in Rabat, Morocco
Moulay Ahmed Faqihi	ENSIAS, Mohammed V University in Rabat, Morocco
Ziad Akiirne	ENSIAS, Mohammed V University in Rabat, Morocco
Mohcine Baala	ENSIAS, Mohammed V University in Rabat, Morocco
Hamza Boualame	ENSIAS, Mohammed V University in Rabat, Morocco
Mahmoud Bouzid	ENSIAS, Mohammed V University in Rabat, Morocco
Ismail El Gaabouri	ENSIAS, Mohammed V University in Rabat, Morocco
Otmane El Mouaatamid	ENSIAS, Mohammed V University in Rabat, Morocco
Abdelhalim Houssaoui	ENSIAS, Mohammed V University in Rabat, Morocco
Zakaria Naji	ENSIAS, Mohammed V University in Rabat, Morocco

Program Committee

Gora Adj	Technology Innovation Institute, UAE
Riham Al Tawy	University of Victoria, Canada
Elena Andreeva	TU Wien, Austria
Ahmed Azouaoui	Ibn Tofail University, Morocco
Hatem M. Bahig	Ain Shams University, Egypt
Hussain Ben-Azza	Moulay Ismail University, Morocco
Olivier Blazy	École Polytechnique, France
Sébastien Canard	Télécom Paris, France
Céline Chevalier	Université Paris 2 Panthéon-Assas, France
Joan Daemen	Radboud University, The Netherlands
Luca De Feo	IBM Research Zürich, Switzerland
Christoph Dobraunig	Intel Corporation, Austria
Sylvain Duquesne	Université de Rennes, France
Betül Durak	Microsoft, USA
Laila El Aimani	Université Cadi Ayyad, Morocco
Nadia El Mrabet	Mines Saint-Étienne, France
Muhammad Elsheikh	National Institute of Standards, Egypt
Tony Ezome	ENS Libreville, Gabon
Georgios Fotiadis	nil; foundation

Emmanuel Fouotsa   University of Bamenda, Cameroon
Tako Boris Fouotsa   EPFL, Switzerland
Essam Ghadafi   Newcastle University, UK
Loubna Ghammam   ITK Engineering GmbH, Germany
Javier Herranz   Universitat Politècnica Catalunya, Spain
Sorina Ionica   Université de Picardie Jules Verne, France
Tetsu Iwata   Nagoya University, Japan
Samuel Jaques   University of Waterloo, Canada
Hervé Talé Kalachi   NASE, University of Yaoundé 1, Cameroon
Juliane Krämer   University of Regensburg, Germany
Péter Kutas   University of Birmingham, UK & Eötvös Loránd
                                    University, Hungary
Pascal Lafourcade   Université Clermont Auvergne, France
Xiangyu Liu   Purdue University & Georgia Tech, USA
Marine Minier   LORIA, Nancy, France
Mainack Mondal   IIT Kharagpur, India
Abderrahmane Nitaj   University of Caen Normandy, France
Yanbin Pan   Chinese Academy of Sciences, China
Christophe Petit   University of Birmingham, UK & Université
                                    Libre de Bruxelles, Belgium
Svetla Petkova-Nikova   KU Leuven, Belgium
Vincent Rijmen   KU Leuven, Belgium & University of Bergen,
                                    Norway
Yann Rotella   Paris-Saclay University, France
Simona Samardjiska   Radboud University, The Netherlands
Palsh Sarkar   Indian Statistical Institute, India
Ali Aydin Selçuk   TOBB University, Turkey
El Mamoun Souidi   Mohammed V University in Rabat, Morocco
Pantelimon Stanica   Naval Postgraduate School, USA
Yash Vasani   Intertek, USA
Fernando Virdia   NOVA Lisboa, Portugal

Additional Reviewers

Harrison Banda   Hengyi Luo
Rishiraj Bhattacharyya   Simon Merz
Chitchanok Chuengsatiansup   George O'Rourke
Valerio Cini   Carla Ràfols
Yansong Feng   Nicolas Resch
Andreas Hellenbrand   Roy Stracovsky

Invited Talks

Olivier Blazy	HQC and the Future of Code-Based Cryptography: From Foundations to Hybridization
Pascal Lafourcade	Proof of Behavior
Jeongeun Park	Fully homomorphic encryption; what, why, and how?

Abstracts of Invited Talks

HQC and the Future of Code-Based Cryptography: From Foundations to Hybridization

Olivier Blazy

Ecole Polytechnique, Inria, France

Abstract. The approval of HQC (Hamming Quasi-Cyclic) for standardization by NIST marks a major milestone for code-based cryptography in the post-quantum landscape. This talk will first revisit the evolution of code-based encryption, from the seminal McEliece scheme of 1978 to the pioneering work of Alekhnovich, who introduced a code-based encryption scheme with provable security with proper reduction — setting the stage for modern constructions. We will then delve into the design of HQC itself, emphasizing its reliance on quasi-cyclic structures and the hardness of decoding random errors, which underpin its security guarantees. Special attention will be given to the HHK transform, a refined framework that ensures an efficient full CCA-2 security (both in the ROM and the QROM), crucial for secure deployment in practice. In the final part of the talk, we will explore cryptographic agility through hybridization strategies, with a focus on a new technique inspired by the X-Wing framework.

This approach enables the combination of classical and post-quantum encryption schemes, preserving security guarantees while facilitating a smooth and secure transition to post-quantum infrastructures.

The presentation will offer both a historical perspective and a deep dive into the technical and practical innovations that lead to the selection of HQC.

Proof of Behavior

Pascal Lafourcade

Université Clermont Auvergne, LIMOS UMR 6158, Aubière, France

Abstract. Bitcoin was the beginning of a digital revolution and also the birth of blockchain technology. The security of this technology relies on the concept of Proof of Work (PoW). In order to validate a transaction, a miner needs to produce a PoW. In Bitcoin, a PoW is the computation of an objective of hash, which is finding a number that satisfies an inequation. Finding this number requires computation of thousands of hash functions. PoW is one of the main negative aspects of this technology since it is highly energy consuming. Moreover in the case of Bitcoin, the performed hash computations are really useless.

Our aim is to change the *Proof of Work* paradigm. Instead of wasting energy in dummy computations with hash computations, we propose a new approach based on the behavior of the users. We present the notion of PoB. The idea is to incentivize citizens to have responsible behaviors instead of doing useless computations as in PoW. Our idea is to design a mechanism that replaces the Proof of Work and that has a positive impact on the world and a social impact on the behaviors of the citizens. For this, we introduce the notion of *Proof of Behavior*.

We propose a first application to design a new cryptocurrency for mobility, called *EcoMobiCoin* for Ecological and Collaborative Mobility Coin. If you can prove that you are biking or walking or using public transportation to go somewhere instead of using your car, or if you can prove that you are using your car with some passengers to go somewhere, you are generating a Proof of Behavior for eco-responsible mobility and creating new *EcoMobiCoins*. This approach aims to facilitate the energy transition that is a key point of the next years.

Fully Homomorphic Encryption; What, Why, and How?

Jeongeun Park

NTNU, Norway

Abstract. This talk is about fully homomorphic encryption (FHE), which enables a computation over encrypted data without decrypting intermediate values. This talk will consist of the past, present, and the future of FHE. I will start with existing FHE schemes, focusing on how they have been developed over a decade. Also, the talk will focus on why it is important, and remaining challenges.

Contents

Side-channel Attacks

Designs

Cryptanalysis

Homomorphic Encryption

Convolution-Friendly Image Compression with FHE

Axel Mertens[1], Georgio Nicolas[1(✉)], and Sergi Rovira[2]

[1] COSIC, KU Leuven, Leuven, Belgium
{axel.mertens,georgio.nicolas}@esat.kuleuven.be
[2] Technology Innovation Institute (TII), Abu Dhabi, UAE
sergi.rovira@tii.ae

Abstract. During the past few decades, the field of image processing has grown to cradle hundreds of applications, many of which are outsourced to be computed on trusted remote servers. More recently, Fully Homomorphic Encryption (FHE) has grown in parallel as a powerful tool enabling computation on encrypted data, and transitively on untrusted servers. As a result, new FHE-supported applications have emerged, but not all have reached practicality due to hardware, bandwidth or mathematical constraints inherent to FHE. One example is processing encrypted images, where practicality is closely related to bandwidth availability. In this paper, we propose and implement a novel technique for FHE-based image compression and decompression. Our technique is a stepping stone towards practicality of encrypted image-processing and applications such as private inference, object recognition, satellite-image searching or video editing.

Inspired by the JPEG standard, and with new FHE-friendly compression/decompression algorithms, our technique allows a client to compress and encrypt images before sending them to a server, greatly reducing the required bandwidth. The server homomorphically decompresses a ciphertext to obtain an encrypted image to which generic pixel-wise processing or convolutional filters can be applied. To reduce the round-trip bandwidth requirement, we also propose a method for server-side post-processing compression.

Using our pipeline, we demonstrate that a high-definition grayscale image (1024×1024) can be homomorphically decompressed, processed and re-compressed in $\sim 8.1\,\mathrm{s}$ with a compression ratio of $100/34.4$ on a standard personal computer without compromising on fidelity.

Keywords: Secure Image Processing · Fully Homomorphic Encryption · Privacy-Enhancing Technologies

1 Introduction

Data compression is a crucial subfield within the domain of data science, playing a pivotal role in efficiently managing the flood of data generated and processed

A. Nitaj et al. (Eds.): AFRICACRYPT 2025, LNCS 15651, pp. 3–24, 2026.
https://doi.org/10.1007/978-3-031-97260-7_1

daily. Its significance is clear in diverse applications such as internet browsing, telecommunications, and data storage. Recent developments in Fully Homomorphic Encryption (FHE) have opened the door to new privacy-preserving applications which use data compression such as private satellite searching and object recognition. FHE allows us to perform additions and multiplications directly on ciphertexts without the need of the secret key. Unfortunately, using FHE has the inherent drawback of ciphertext expansion - a blow-up in the size of a plaintext when encrypted. Therefore, adding privacy to data compression and processing applications requires a robust data compression algorithm tailored for FHE.

This paper takes a big step in this direction, specifically for the homomorphic compression and processing of images. Possible applications of our work include satellite image-search, private object detection, facial recognition, etc. In this paper, we propose a compression scheme for the encryption of natural images in CKKS [11], that uses a modification of the method used in the JPEG-1 standard [21, 29]. Our pipeline is as in Fig. 1, where an image is compressed and encrypted before being sent to a server for processing. The server performs decompression, processing and compression all in the encrypted domain, before sending it back to the client for decryption. The suggested scheme is designed to be compatible with server-side image processing with convolutional filters and pixel-wise image processing.

The compression (decompression, resp.) algorithm is associative with encryption (decryption, resp.) algorithm, improving client-side performance.

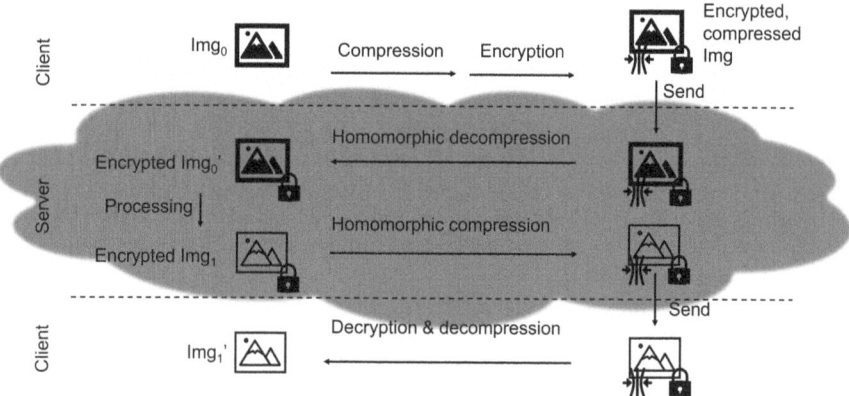

Fig. 1. Sketch of our pipeline.

1.1 Our Contributions

Our contributions can be summarized as follows:

1. We build the first end-to-end pipeline for efficient encrypted image compression and decompression based on FHE.

2. We demonstrate how to efficiently homomorphically apply a convolutional filter and pixel by pixel operations to a decompressed encrypted image.
3. We provide extensive reproducible benchmarks based on a proof-of-concept implementation of our framework.

In more detail, starting from the JPEG standard, we replace the entropy encoding with a constant cut-off. Not only is this cheap and efficient to perform, it also proves to be successful in practice. To the best of our knowledge, this technique is novel. We combine this compression scheme with the state-of-the-art FHE scheme CKKS [11], taking full advantage of its ciphertext packing technique and support for approximate arithmetic. We propose a trick that enables convolution-based image processing on images that are packed in this manner, avoiding a costly unpacking step. Together, this results in a homomorphic compression scheme that is fast and effective, while maintaining great image quality ($SSI \geq 0.95$).

Furthermore, our scheme is versatile and modular in the sense that all of its components not only complement each-other, but also can be used independently depending on the user's requirements. For instance, we can use the compression and decompression components to enable performing other kinds of processing.

It ultimately depends on the application whether the communication channel is the bottleneck, or if the server computation is the most costly. This paper tackles problem with privacy-preserving image processing which exists case when communication is expensive.

1.2   Related Work

Little research can be found on the topic of compression and decompression of encrypted images. There exists more work on the related topic of ciphertext compression, where the ciphertext is compressed in a manner that is agnostic to the structure of underlying plaintext data. Such techniques are independent of the scope of this work, and this could be combined with ours in certain cases. There also exists literature about homomorphic image processing, most notably a demo published by Zama [33] which we compare with in Sect. 4.4.

In 2017, Canard et al. [9] analyzed the execution of a run-length coding scheme in FHE. The authors came to the conclusion that homomorphic run-length coding is impractical, due to the large number of comparisons it requires. They further argue that lossless compression in FHE cannot be guaranteed, stating that any lossless compression algorithm has a lousy worst-case behavior. In FHE, every algorithm achieves its worst-case behavior. Other attempts at homomorphic compression, such as [17] and [31], are interesting but remain impractical due to this very issue. The authors of [27] attempt to tackle the problem of homomorphic Huffman decoding, but also remain far from practicality and proposing a solution for compression in the encrypted domain. We compare our results with theirs in Sect. 4.2.

In [25], the authors suggest an FHE-friendly homomorphic compression scheme. Unfortunately, they fall short of describing how to encode a compressed image or perform processing on it. Moreover, the method results in a high loss of image fidelity in comparison.

In [16], the authors suggest a technique using invertible Bloom filters to compress an encrypted sparse array, with a joint decompression - decryption function. This method is more general than the one we propose in this paper and only requires an additive homomorphic scheme. However, we still miss the discussion on encrypted decompression and find that our remains more effective for images. We require fewer operations overall and achieve a higher compression rate. The compression scheme of [34] remains versatile, as each pixel remains stored separately. Where our proposal loses versatility because of our packing method, their system loses in compression ratio.

In [24], the author studies information leakage in systems that combine both compression and encryption. A number of attacks that use only the compression ratio as a side-channel are listed. This study serves as a stern warning that for perfect privacy, a compression ratio should remain secret.

Related but less relevant work discusses homomorphic neural networks: [30] tackles related issues in limiting the memory required during homomorphic evaluation of a residual neural network. [3,23] and [26] describe methods for optimizing neural networks in FHE. While this is a very interesting and related topic, there remains not much consideration on how to limit the communication cost between client and server.

2 Preliminaries

In this section, we introduce some background on FHE, placing special emphasis on the CKKS scheme. We also provide the necessary background on image compression. We refer the interested reader to the references provided in this section for a more in-depth explanation of these topics.

2.1 Notation

We will denote by $\mathcal{R}$ and $\mathcal{R}_q$ the rings of polynomials $\mathbb{Z}[X]/(X^N + 1)$ and $\mathbb{Z}_q[X]/(X^N + 1)$ respectively, for positive integers q and N.

We use $x \leftarrow D$ to denote sampling x according to a distribution D. If D is finite, we assume the sampling is done uniformly at random.

The complex canonical embedding $\tau : \mathcal{S} \rightarrow \mathbb{C}^N$ is defined as $\tau(a) = (a(\eta^j))_{j \in \mathbb{Z}_M^*}$ for $\eta = \exp(2\pi i/M)$, where $M = 2N$ and $\mathbb{Z}_M^* = \{x \in \mathbb{Z}_M : \gcd(x, M) = 1\}$.

In CKKS, the maps $\tau_n' : \mathcal{S} \rightarrow \mathbb{C}^n$, a variant for $n \leq N/2$ of the canonical embedding τ, are used to encode and decode.

Let L be the maximum number of levels fixed in the CKKS setup and let q_i be the prime modulus for $i \in [L]$. Fix δ and set $\alpha = (L+1)/\delta$. Consider the products

$\tilde{Q}_j = \prod_{i=j\alpha}^{(j+1)\alpha-1} q_i$ for $j \in \{0, \ldots, \delta\}$. Given a level ℓ and $\delta' = \lceil (\ell+1)/\alpha \rceil$, we can decompose $a \in \mathcal{R}_\ell$ as follows:

$$\mathcal{WD}_\ell(a) = \left(\left[a \frac{\tilde{Q}_0}{Q_\ell} \right]_{\tilde{Q}_0}, \ldots, \left[a \frac{\tilde{Q}_{\delta'-1}}{Q_\ell} \right]_{\tilde{Q}_{\delta'-1}} \right) \in \mathcal{R}^{\delta'},$$

$$\mathcal{PW}_\ell(a) = \left(\left[a \frac{Q_\ell}{\tilde{Q}_0} \right]_{Q_\ell}, \ldots, \left[a \frac{Q_\ell}{\tilde{Q}_{\delta'-1}} \right]_{Q_\ell} \right) \in \mathcal{R}_{Q_\ell}^{\delta'}.$$

For any $(a, b) \in \mathcal{R}_\ell^2$, we have that

$$\langle \mathcal{WD}_\ell(a), \mathcal{PW}_\ell(b) \rangle \equiv a \cdot b \mod Q_\ell.$$

2.2 Background on Fully Homomorphic Encryption

A Fully Homomorphic Encryption (FHE) scheme allows us to perform arbitrary computations over encrypted inputs without decrypting them first. That is, given a ciphertext ct encrypting a plaintext m and an arbitrary function f, we can obtain a new ciphertext ct' encrypting $f(m)$ without decrypting ct.

Since the first FHE scheme [18], research in FHE has seen rapid growth, leading to a wide range of schemes built from different techniques and security assumptions [8,11,13,15].

It is important to remark that FHE schemes can only directly compute additions (XOR) and multiplications (AND) between ciphertexts. More complex functions are represented as arithmetic (boolean) circuits built from these two basic operations. The encryption function of most FHE schemes adds a random element to the message, commonly referred to as *error* or *noise* in the literature. When a multiplication or an addition is performed, this error increases. After a given number of operations, the error in a ciphertext may become too large, overwriting the encapsulated message. This leads to an inability of recovering the original message by the decryption algorithm. To solve this problem, an additional algorithm called *bootstrapping* is added to the scheme. This procedure reduces the noise of a ciphertext, allowing further operations. Unfortunately, bootstrapping is a costly operation. Therefore, it is common practice to set parameters of an FHE scheme in such a way that we can evaluate a function of our choice without the need for a bootstrapping operation. This approach is called *leveled* FHE and is the one that we take in this work.

Definition 1 (Homomorphic Encryption scheme). *A public-key homomorphic encryption scheme $\mathcal{E}$ consists of a set of probabilistic polynomial-time algorithms (KeyGen, Enc, Dec, Eval) such that:*

- KeyGen(1^λ): *outputs the secret key sk, the public key pk and the evaluation key evk given the security parameter λ. The evaluation key is also public, and it is used to perform the homomorphic operations over ciphertexts.*
- Enc$_{pk}(m)$: *Outputs a ciphertext ct encrypting m under the public key pk.*

- $\text{Dec}_{sk}(ct)$: *Outputs a message* m. *If the algorithm cannot recover* m *from* ct, *the output is* $\perp$.
- $\text{Eval}_{evk}(f; ct_1, \dots, ct_n)$: *Given a function* f *and a list of ciphertexts* $ct_1, \dots, ct_n$, *outputs a ciphertext* ct_f *such that* $\text{Dec}_{sk}(ct_f) = f(m_1, \dots, m_n)$, *where* $ct_i \leftarrow \text{Enc}_{pk}(m_i)$ *for all* $i \in \{1, \dots, n\}$.

Among the most popular FHE schemes available today [6,7,11,12,15], we consider CKKS [11] to be the best scheme for encrypted image processing for the following reasons:

- It allows us to compute directly on floating-point numbers, which is crucial for the fast evaluation of our compression and decompression algorithms. Furthermore, this allows us to work with non-integer kernels when performing image processing.
- The other key feature of CKKS is ciphertext packing, which allows us to encrypt multiple blocks of an image inside a single ciphertext. We expand on our use of ciphertext packing in Sect. 3.3.

We want to point out that very recently, floating-point operations have been added to TFHE [4], another rapidly growing FHE scheme. Nevertheless, CKKS remains the best option for encrypted image processing since TFHE does not support ciphertext packing, which is crucial for our application. Furthermore, the authors of [1] add functional bootstrapping to CKKS. This has direct implications to our framework, meaning that we can now apply a wider range of filters and transformations to the decompressed images on the server side. Unfortunately, we have not been able to test this extension since the technique of [1] has not yet been incorporated into OpenFHE, the FHE library we used to implement our proof of concept.

2.3   Background on CKKS

The CKKS scheme [11] is an approximate homomorphic encryption scheme. The key difference between CKKS and other schemes, such as BGV [7] or TFHE [12], is that the decryption function of CKKS does not remove the encryption noise. This makes the decryption structure to be $m+e \mod q$ where m is the encrypted message, e is the encryption error and q a suitable modulus. Intuitively, this approach simulates computer numerical errors. That is, if e is small enough compared to m, it only alters the least significant bits of m. Therefore, we can operate on $m + e$ knowing that only some portion of m has been altered and thus contains errors.

Another characteristic of CKKS is the native support for ciphertext packing, which allows for bundling multiple encrypted messages into a single ciphertext. More importantly, this provides the capability of performing computations between ciphertexts in a SIMD manner, reducing both effective memory requirements and computational complexity.

Below is a more rigorous definition of the main algorithms we employ from CKKS. We provide them to make the paper as self-contained as possible, the reader may skip these details if they are not interested in consulting the code from our proof-of-concept implementation.

- $\underline{\mathsf{Setup}(1^\lambda)}$. Fix $L \geq 0$ (largest ciphertext modulus level). Given the security parameter λ, output the ring dimension N. Set $\chi_{\mathsf{key}}, \chi_{\mathsf{err}}, \chi_{\mathsf{enc}}$ the secret, error and encryption distributions as follows. For an positive integer h, the secret key distribution χ_{key} follows a uniform distribution over the set of signed binary vectors in $\{0, \pm 1\}^N$ whose Hamming weight (the number of nonzero coefficients) is exactly h. The error distribution χ_{err} chooses a polynomial s by sampling its coefficients independently from the discrete Gaussian distribution of variance σ^2 for $\sigma > 0$. The encryption key distribution χ_{enc} draws each entry in the vector from $\{0, \pm 1\}$, with probability $1/4$ for each of $+1$ and -1, and probability being zero $1/2$.
- $\underline{\mathsf{KeyGen}}$. Sample $s \leftarrow \chi_{\mathsf{key}}$, $a \leftarrow \mathcal{R}_{Q_L}$, $e \leftarrow \chi_{\mathsf{err}}$. Set $\mathsf{sk} \leftarrow (1, s)$ and $\mathsf{pk} \leftarrow (b, a) \in \mathcal{R}_{Q_L}^2$, where $b = -as + e \mod Q_L$.
- $\underline{\mathsf{Encode}(\mathbf{x}, \Delta)}$. Given $\mathbf{x} \in \mathbb{C}^n$, output $m = \lfloor \tau_n'^{-1}(\Delta \cdot x) \rceil \in \mathcal{R}$.
- $\underline{\mathsf{Decode}(m, \Delta)}$. Given $m \in \mathcal{R}$, output $\mathbf{x} = \tau_n'(m/\Delta) \in \mathbb{C}^n$.
- $\underline{\mathsf{Enc}_{\mathsf{pk}}(m)}$. Given $m \in \mathcal{R}$, sample $v \leftarrow \chi_{\mathsf{enc}}$ and $e_0, e_1 \leftarrow \chi_{\mathsf{err}}$. Output $\mathsf{ct} = v\,\mathsf{pk} + (m + e_0, e_1) \mod Q_L$.
- $\underline{\mathsf{Dec}_{\mathsf{sk}}(\mathsf{ct})}$. Given $\mathsf{ct} = (b, a) \in \mathcal{R}_{Q_\ell}^2$, output $m = b + a \cdot s \mod Q_\ell$.
- $\underline{\mathsf{Rescale}(\mathsf{ct}, q_\ell)}$. Given $\mathsf{ct} \in \mathcal{R}_{Q_\ell}^2$, output $\mathsf{ct}' = \lfloor q_\ell^{-1} \cdot \mathsf{ct} \rceil \mod Q_{\ell-1}$.
- $\underline{\mathsf{CAdd}(\mathsf{ct}, \mathbf{x})}$. Given $\mathsf{ct} = (b, a) \in \mathcal{R}_{Q_\ell}^2$ with scaling factor $\Delta^{\ell'}$ and $\mathbf{x} \in \mathbb{C}^n$, encode $\mathbf{x}$ obtaining $m = \mathsf{Encode}(\mathbf{x}, \Delta^{\ell'})$, and output $\mathsf{ct}_{\mathsf{cadd}} \leftarrow (b + m, a) \mod Q_\ell$.
- $\underline{\mathsf{Add}(\mathsf{ct}_1, \mathsf{ct}_2)}$. Given $\mathsf{ct}_1, \mathsf{ct}_2 \in \mathcal{R}_{Q_\ell}^2$, output $\mathsf{ct}_{\mathsf{add}} = \mathsf{ct}_1 + \mathsf{ct}_2 \mod Q_\ell$.
- $\underline{\mathsf{CMult}(\mathsf{ct}, \mathbf{x})}$. Given $\mathsf{ct} = (c_0, c_1) \in \mathcal{R}_{Q_\ell}^2$ and $\mathbf{x} \in \mathbb{C}^n$, compute $m = \mathsf{Encode}(\mathbf{x}, \Delta)$ and output $\mathsf{ct}_{\mathsf{cmult}} = (c_0 \cdot m, c_1 \cdot m) \mod Q_\ell$.
- $\underline{\mathsf{KeySwitchGen}_{\mathsf{sk}}(s')}$. For auxiliary modulus $P = \prod_{i=0}^k p_i$, sample $a'_{\mathsf{pk}} \leftarrow \mathcal{R}_{PQ_L}$ and $e'_k \leftarrow \chi_{\mathsf{err}}$. For a predefined δ, output

$$\mathsf{swk} = (\mathsf{swk}_0, \mathsf{swk}_1) = (\{b'_k\}_{k=0}^{\delta-1}, \{a'_k\}_{k=0}^{\delta-1}) \in \mathcal{R}_{PQ_L}^{2\times\delta},$$

  where

$$b'_k = -a'_k \cdot s + e'_k + P \cdot \mathcal{PW}'(s')_k \mod PQ_L.$$

- $\underline{\mathsf{KeySwitch}_{\mathsf{swk}}(s')}$. Given $\mathsf{ct} = (c_0, c_1) \in \mathcal{R}_{Q_\ell}^2$, $\mathsf{swk} = (\mathsf{swk}_0, \mathsf{swk}_1)$, output

$$\left(c_0 + \left\lfloor \frac{\langle \mathcal{WD}_\ell(c_1), \mathsf{swk}_0 \rangle}{P} \right\rceil, \left\lfloor \frac{\langle \mathcal{WD}_\ell(c_1), \mathsf{swk}_1 \rangle}{P} \right\rceil \right) \mod Q_\ell$$

- $\underline{\mathsf{Mult}(\mathsf{ct}_1, \mathsf{ct}_2)}$. Given two ciphertexts ct_1 and ct_2, compute $\mathsf{ct}'_1 = \mathsf{Rescale}(\mathsf{ct}_1, q_\ell)$ and $\mathsf{ct}'_2 = \mathsf{Rescale}(\mathsf{ct}_2, q_\ell)$. Let $(d_0, d_1, d_2) = (b_1 \cdot b_2, a_1 \cdot b_2 + a_2 \cdot b_1, a_1 \cdot a_2) \mod Q_{\ell-1}$. Output

$$\mathsf{ct}_{\mathsf{mult}} \leftarrow (d_0, d_1) + \mathsf{KeySwitch}_{\mathsf{evk}}(0, d_2) \mod Q_{\ell-1}.$$

2.4   Background on Image Compression

When using lossy compression, data is represented more compactly, with the aim of retaining as much fidelity as possible to the original source before compression. When considering images, there are different methods to measure the level of fidelity or closeness. The measure closest to how the human eye perceives images is the Structural Similarity Index (SSI) [32]:

Definition 2 (Structural Similarity Index (SSI)). *SSI is defined as:*
$SSI(x,y) = \frac{(2\mu_x\mu_y+c_1)(2\sigma_{xy}+c_2)}{(\mu_x^2+\mu_y^2+c_1)(\sigma_x^2+\sigma_y^2+c_2)}$ *where μ_i is the pixel sample mean of image i,*
σ_i^2 is the variance of image i, σ_{xy}^2 is the covariance of images x and y,
$c_1 = (0.01L)^2$, $c_2 = (0.03L)^2$, with L the dynamic range of the pixel values.

It compares an imperfect image to its perfect version, and is a value between -1 and 1, where 1 is a perfect match, -1 is a perfectly negative correlation, and 0 means the two images are very different. The SSI is typically good at detecting structural deformations (stretching, rotation, etc.) and other forms of degradation such as blurriness or blockiness. Images with values of 0.95 are considered to be of very good quality [35].

Another important metric is the compression ratio:

Definition 3 (Compression ratio). *Let B_0 be the number of bytes needed to represent some data X, and let B_1 be the number of bytes needed for the same, compressed data X'. The compression ratio is then $\frac{B_0}{B_1}$, also written as B_0:B_1.*

An ideal compression scheme should have a high compression ratio, while maintaining an SSI that is close to 1.

3   Our Technique

Most traditional compression algorithms [19,20,28] used in the clear are unfit for FHE. They often contain comparisons and do not have a constant run-time. FHE inflicts its own special set of requirements upon an algorithm. The most important property of a homomorphic compression scheme is that no additional data or metadata about the image may leak, even through side-channels such as the compression ratio or running-time. This is precisely why implementing the JPEG standard as is in FHE would not be possible as we discuss later. Two more critical properties are efficient compression and decompression and that ciphertext packing should be done in a way that a ciphertext structurally reflects the compression of a plaintext. With some inefficient packing methods, the ciphertext length would not be influenced by a (slightly) shorter plaintext. And last but not least, the scheme should allow for both compression and decompression of the message without needing to decrypt it between the operations.

As an extra requirement for image processing, we also target having the encrypted, decompressed form of the message support efficient image processing. The type of image processing we choose to focus on is using convolutional filters, but we also look at pixel-wise processing methods. Furthermore, our technique can also handle colored images, both in the RGB format as in the YCbCr format, depending on the application. Without discussing this too far, it is clear to see how the proposed technique can be extended towards dealing with multi-channel images. Moreover, with the recent addition of functional bootstrapping to CKKS [1] our framework can be to support more complex image processing techniques.

3.1   Compression Algorithm

In this section we introduce our algorithms for compression and decompression. We want to emphasize that we present them in unencrypted format, as the client will run them. The reader should keep in mind that the server will execute them in the encrypted domain. Specifically, in the server side, the image data ($\mathbf{a}$, $\mathbf{A}$, $\mathbf{B}$) are encrypted, while the sizes of vectors and matrices (m, n, c) remain public. The algorithm we suggest is based on the JPEG-standard. For readability, we list our symbols and notations in Table 1.

As shown in Algorithm 2, we split the image into $m \times m$-sized blocks. We first center every pixel value in the $[-128, 128[$ interval. We call this operation $Level()$, while the inverse operation is called $Unlevel()$. Then, we apply a discrete cosine transform (DCT), which is done via two fixed-point matrix multiplications with DCT matrix T_m. This gives us representations of the frequency spectrum of each block of the image. The next step, still following the JPEG standard, is to apply a quantization, which scales each element of this frequency representation (lines 4–6 of Algorithm 2). The quantization matrix Q_m is defined through exhaustive testing and standardization. Hence, we are bound to the quantization matrices existing in prior research. We have only found a reliable matrix for $m = 8$ and a slightly less mature matrix for $m = 16$ [2].

The quantization matrix Q_m can be scaled to prioritize either quality or compression, by multiplying each element of Q_m with k:

$$k = \begin{cases} \frac{100-q}{50} & q > 50 \\ \frac{50}{q} & q < 50 \end{cases}$$

Table 1. List of Symbols

Symbol	Meaning
λ	Security Parameter
Q_m	Quantization Matrix
q	Quality Parameter
k	Quantization Matrix Scaling Factor
c, c_i	Cut-Off Value
$\mathbf{A}, \mathbf{B}$	Image Matrices
$\mathbf{a}_i, \mathbf{b}_i$	Image Blocks
m	Block Dimension
Π_i	FHE Parameter Set

If the quality level q is set to greater than 50, fidelity to the original image is prioritized over compression, whereas values under 50 compress the image more at the cost of losing some fidelity. q and c together define the compression-ratio and the lossiness of the reconstructed image. A lower q also lowers the risk of cutting off non-zero values. The more compression we enforce, the lower the quality will be.

Quantization results in a matrix with a large number of zeros, especially towards the bottom right corner of each matrix. To exploit this redundancy, a *Zigzag* traversal is applied, turning the matrix into a one-dimensional vector, with these zeroes at the end. The function $Inverse\_zigzag()$ turns a one-dimensional vector back into a matrix, following the same zigzag pattern.

The next step is where we really diverge from the JPEG standard. JPEG uses Huffman encoding [20] to represent this vector. Huffman coding, like other popular encoding schemes, relies on the principle that more frequent symbols should be represented with shorter codes compared to rarer symbols, resulting in an overall compression. This principle is unsuited for FHE, where consistency, constant-runtime, and input-agnosticism are desired above all.

The encoding we suggest (see Algorithm 1) is more simple: we only keep a constant number c of non-zero elements from each block, discarding all other elements. Ideally, this number should be determined independent of the image, such as not to reveal any information about the level of texture present in the data. However, in some applications, c might not leak much information about the image. For example, in simple portait photos, a busy background can greatly increase the necessary c, while this says nothing about the face in the image. In these cases, the client could pre-compute the ideal c. It should be noted that predetermining this c can result in non-zero values being discarded. This causes additional artifacts (blockiness) in the image, but the effect is usually minimal if the value is well selected. From our experiments, $c = 30$ seemed to be a good choice considering both the SSI and the compression ratio.

Using this encoding, we make sure that every block of the image undergoes the same compression ratio (see also Sect. 3.2). Furthermore, both compression and decompression become very simple actions, and can be efficiently performed under FHE. The encoding itself is lossless, but can be lossy for some highly textured or discrete-tone images. Granted, the data will be compressed less than it would using a more evolved coding scheme (Huffman, Golomb, ...). As discussed earlier, this approach is impractical with homomorphic encryption.

Decompression works very similarly to compression, knowing that in the decoding, we pad with encryptions of 0 until we reach the required size.

3.2   Non-constant Compression Ratio

As mentioned before, in regular JPEG, each block gets a different compression rate. This section will show why this is incompatible with FHE.

Consider the photo in Fig. 2a. The background of the image is blurry, which means that there is less information there. The foreground, the branches and the bird, contain more high-frequency data. In JPEG, these blocks in the foreground

---

Algorithm 1: Encode

Input: blocks $\mathbf{a} = [a_0, a_1, \ldots, a_{n-1}]$ with $|a_i| = l_a$
Input: Cut-off point $c < m^2$
Output: blocks $\mathbf{b} = [b_0, b_1, \ldots, b_{n-1}]$ with $|b_i| = l_b$ and $l_a \geq l_b$

1 **for** $i \in [0, n-1]$ **do**
2 $\quad$ $b_i \leftarrow a_i[0 : c]$;
3 **end**
4 **return b**

Algorithm 2: Compress

Input: Encrypted image $\mathbf{A}$: split into n $m \times m$ blocks: $\mathbf{A} = [A_0, A_1, \ldots, A_{n-1}]$
$\quad$ with $A_i \in \mathbb{Z}^{m \times m}$
Input: Cut-off point $c < m^2$
Output: Encrypted, compressed image $\mathbf{B} = [b_0, b_1, \ldots, b_{n-1}]$ with $b_i \in \mathbb{Z}^c$

1 **for** $l \in [0, n-1]$ **do**
2 $\quad$ $C_l \leftarrow Level(A_l)$;
3 $\quad$ $D_l \leftarrow T_m C_l T_m^\top$;
4 $\quad$ **for** $(i, j) \in \mathbb{N}_m^2$ **do**
5 $\quad\quad$ $E_{l,i,j} \leftarrow \lfloor (\frac{D_{l,i,j}}{Q_{m,i,j}}) \rceil$;
6 $\quad$ **end**
7 $\quad$ $b_l \leftarrow Zigzag(E_l)[0..c]$;
8 **end**
9 **return** $\{b_0, b_1, \ldots, b_{n-1}\}$

---

would be compressed less than the smoother blocks in the background. Say we implement this directly in FHE. The DCT transforms each block i to the frequency spectrum, representing the block based on the frequencies present in it. A smoother block with less high-frequency information in it would result in a lot of trailing zeros, whereas the DCT of a block with more high-frequency information would not have many zeros at all. In JPEG, the cutoff point c_i is determined by only cutting off zeros. This way, different blocks i get a different c_i. Encryption of these blocks mask the values, but does not hide that there are c_i values representing block i. An adversary listening in, who only knows the c_i, would then still learn some information about the encrypted image: if c_i is relatively large, it means block i contains high-frequency information, and is relatively "busy". If c_i is relatively small, it means block i is more "smooth", containing less high-frequency information, and hence it was possible to compress it more. While it may not seem like much information leaking, this is actually enough to make out for example the silhouette of an object or the presence of buildings on a satellite image. For our example bird photo, the leaked information translates to an image such as Fig. 2b, where we can clearly see the silhouette of the bird and the branches.

Algorithm 3: Decompress

Input: Block size m, which can be equal to either 8 or 16
Input: Encrypted, compressed image $\mathbf{B} = [b_0, b_1, \ldots, b_{n-1}]$ with $b_i \in \mathbb{Z}^c$
Output: Encrypted image $\mathbf{A} = [A_0, A_1, \ldots, A_{n-1}]$ with $A_i \in \mathbb{Z}^{m \times m}$

1 **for** $l \in [0, n-1]$ **do**
2   **for** $i \in [c, m^2[$ **do**
3 | $b_{l,i} \leftarrow Enc(0)$
4   **end**
5    $C_l \leftarrow Inverse\_Zigzag(b_l)$;
6   **for** $(i,j) \in \mathbb{N}_m^2$ **do**
7 | $D_{l,i,j} \leftarrow C_{l,i,j} \cdot Q_{l,i,j}$;
8   **end**
9    $E_l \leftarrow T_m^\top D_l T_m$;
10   $A_l \leftarrow Unlevel(E_l)$;
11 **end**
12 **return** $[A_0, A_1, \ldots, A_{n-1}]$

If an adversary were to try this method on our proposed compression scheme with constant block compression, they would see Fig. 2c, and not learn much.

 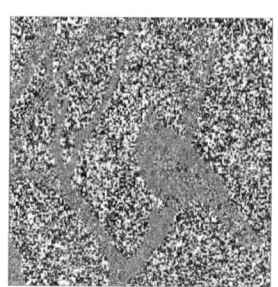 

(a) The original image

(b) Predicted image knowing only the compression rate of each block.

(c) Predicted image when every block is compressed equally.

Fig. 2. Example of the information leak caused by a variable block compression rate.

3.3 Ciphertext Packing

In order to make our algorithms more efficient we exploit the packing capabilities of CKKS [11]. Recall that ciphertext packing refers to the ability to encrypt multiple messages in a single ciphertext.

In our work, we use ciphertext packing as follows. First, the image is divided into blocks of size $m \times m$, after which each block separately undergoes compression. Then, each position in a block is encrypted in a separate ciphertext. We now have c ciphertexts, one for the first position in a block, one for the second, etc. Therefore, if $m = 8$ for example, a decompressed image is represented using 64 ciphertexts, regardless of the dimension of the image. Figure 3 illustrates this principle without compression (for clarity). Furthermore, with this design every block-wise operation becomes trivially parallelizable.

Observe that it is also possible to compress and process multiple images at a time. When compressing k images at once, we obtain the same number of ciphertexts, but they will be k times longer.

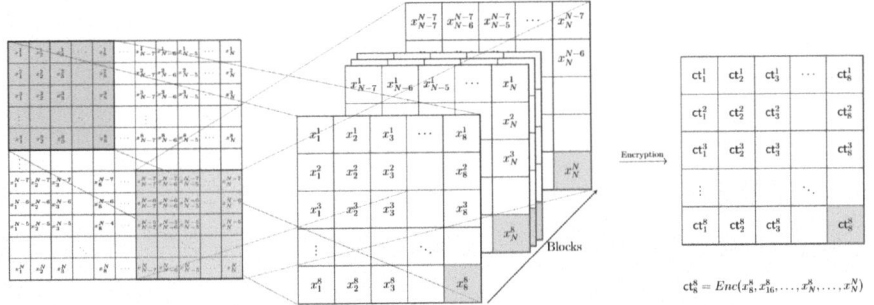

Fig. 3. Illustration of our ciphertext packing.

The packing method we opt for, using CKKS, is inspired by the method of [22]. The key difference between [22] and our packing method being the required number of ciphertexts. That is, in [22] one ciphertext is created per location/pixel in an image, needing as many ciphertexts as an image has pixels. In contrast, we create a ciphertext per frequency in a block, which is greatly fewer ciphertexts albeit longer ones. A similar packing technique is presented in CaReNets [10], where images are combined to completely fill the ciphertexts, and leave no slots empty. While this makes the ciphertext more compact, it is not suitable for our situation where the compression and the processing are highly parallelized per block.

3.4   Image Processing

A simple yet powerful and popular method of processing images is to apply convolutional filters on them: We apply filters or kernels on the image, by convolving the two. These kernels are small matrices, usually of size 3×3, containing integers or rational numbers. They are constructed for a specific purpose, be it blurring, sharpening, edge detection, etc. A convolution works by passing the kernel over the image and multiplying each value of the kernel with the overlapping value in the image. These products are summed, resulting in the new value for the pixel at the kernel's location.

In Fig. 4 we display some examples of kernels for horizontal and vertical edge detection: Prewitt kernels and Sobel kernels. These kernels may be applied for sharpening and blurring as well.

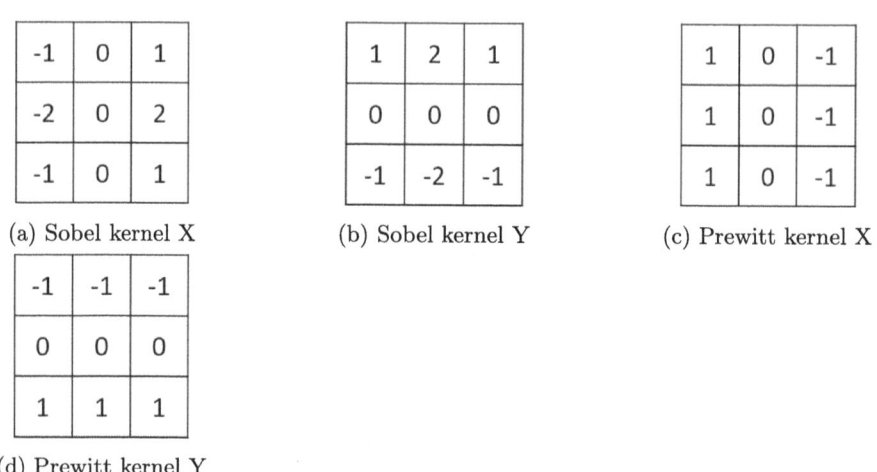

(a) Sobel kernel X   (b) Sobel kernel Y   (c) Prewitt kernel X

(d) Prewitt kernel Y

Fig. 4. Popular Edge Detection Kernels.

Our server needs to be able to perform convolutions on the encrypted (but decompressed) blocks of the image. This is hard to parallelize, as applying the convolution requires neighboring pixel values, regardless of block borders. We suggest the following solution: as the very first step, before the client even encrypts/compresses the image, the client can split the image into blocks of size $(m - 2) \times (m - 2)$. Then, these smaller blocks on the edges are padded with the neighboring cells, such that they end up with overlapping blocks of size $m \times m$. This system works for 3×3 kernels, which covers almost all convolutional filters used in practice. Recall that CKKS also provides supports for non-integer kernels.

This not only reduces the compression ratio, but also allows for efficient image processing on the server, and avoids costly server-side packing operations, where the ciphertexts would have to be reconfigured. It is also worth noting that while we strive for a good compression ratio, the goal of this paper is not to achieve the optimal compression ratio. It rather is to find a balance/trade-off between the compression ratio, fidelity and efficiency. We have found that for this setting, in order to maintain an SSI close to 0.95, most images require $c_8 = 30$ for $m = 8$, leading to a compression ratio of $100 : 83.3$. For $m = 16$, most images require $c_{16} = 70$, leading to a compression ratio of $100 : 35.7$. The simplest image processing actions, such as inversion and brightening, are pixel-based. Such operations do not require any knowledge of the values of neighboring pixels, and thus do not require our padding trick. In these cases, the client can simply split the image in blocks of size $m \times m$. Here, we find that most images require $c_8 = 22$ (respectively $c_{16} = 63$) to maintain an SSI ≥ 0.95, leading to a compression ratio of $100 : 34.4$ (respectively $100 : 24.6$).

In reality, the value of c can be determined for a specific image or a set of images by running the compression and decompression code in the clear, and verifying the image quality. The cut-off point could potentially be quite different after processing compared to before, depending on the operation that was performed.

Alternative Image Processing Techniques. Not all image processing techniques employ convolutional filters. Some operations can be done on individual pixels, without taking into account their neighbors. Think about inverting an image or changing its brightness. Our compression algorithm is compatible with this type of image processing without any modification. We can simply use 8×8 blocks and achieve a greater compression ratio.

Other image processing techniques are based in the frequency-domain: if we take a DCT of the entire image at once, we can increase or decrease the presence of certain frequencies. This is used in blurring or noise-cancellation. Our compression algorithm is not optimal for such techniques, as the server would need to merge the blocks together first, which can be quite costly for big images.

4   Experimental Results

All of our experiments for both client and server were run on a MacBook Pro with an M4 Pro (8P + 4E) CPU and 24 GB of RAM. Our implementation[1] has been moderately optimized, but could still be improved. Nonetheless, we think our numbers are promising as it would be safe to assume that the hardware setup we used is less powerful than a standard "server" and more powerful than a standard client.

4.1   Parameters

We ran tests for four different image dimensions, and four algorithms each. The four algorithms are:

1. Pixel-wise processing on 8×8 blocks.
2. Convolutional processing on 8×8 blocks.
3. Pixel-wise processing on 16×16 blocks.
4. Convolutional processing on 16×16 blocks.

---

[1] https://github.com/KULeuven-COSIC/img-processing-fhe.

Balancing performance, security, and bandwidth is always a challenge with FHE. The larger our parameters, the more we could pack in a ciphertext (Sect. 3.3) at the cost of larger ciphertext sizes and longer computation times. In an ideal world we would have a parameter set for every single image size and type of operation. However, for practicality, we prioritized fixing the security level at 128 bits for all cases and chose 3 different parameter sets for our experiments.

1. Π_1 for images smaller than or equal to 256×256.
2. Π_2 for images larger than 256×256 and smaller than or equal to 1024×1024.
3. Π_3 for images larger than 1024×1024.

We note that Π_2 is the most fine-tuned among our parameters.

4.2   Timing

Each timing in Table 2 is for one 8-bit grayscale image of mentioned dimensions. The values are averaged over a few randomly selected images: 3 images with dimensions 256×256, 7 images with 512×512 and 4 images with greater dimensions. The benchmarks are server-side timings, meaning that the compression and decompression are both done homomorphically. Server-side RAM Consumption varied between 1 GB and 13 GB based on the size of the image being processed.

The decompression is more costly than the compression, because the server needs to pad the compressed ciphertext with encryptions of zero and process them as well.

It is clear that the pixel-wise processing is highly efficient, but the 3×3 convolution as well is relatively fast. The largest image size we experimented on is considerably less fast, while the other image sizes are not as different. This has everything to do with the choices of CKKS-parameters. The parameter choices for 1024×1024 images do not allow for secure ciphertexts long enough to fit 2048×2048 images. Remember that the length of each ciphertext is equal to the number of blocks in the image.

We notice that the 8×8 techniques (1 and 2) are consistently faster, and keep the image quality the highest. This is expected, because these quantization matrices are more mature, and because smaller blocks have more efficient matrix multiplication. We do not include example images that have been put through our pipeline, because with SSI-values above 0.9, it is very hard to tell the difference.

When comparing with [27], we highlight that our numbers demonstrate a speedup rate between 173x and 1093x when decompressing the same 256×256 images, depending on the setting. It is also worth noting, however, that while their experiments were performed on a much more powerful machine, they also were run at least 7 years ago. We were unable to retrieve the source-code to run a fair benchmarking using a modern library.

Table 2. Experimental Timing Results (Server-Side)

Image Size	Setting	Decompression	Processing	Compression	Total	SSI	Compression Ratio
256×256	1	5.16 s	11 ms	3.24 s	8.41 s	0.95	100 : 34.4
256×256	2	6.47 s	2.02 s	4.58 s	13.07 s	0.935	100 : 83.3
252×252	3	26.40	68 ms	18.72 s	45.18 s	0.91	100 : 24.6
252×252	4	32.34 s	9.48 s	29.80 s	71.62 s	0.905	100 : 35.7
512×512	1	5.17 s	11 ms	3.23 s	8.41 s	0.95	100 : 34.4
512×512	2	6.40 s	2.00 s	4.57 s	12.97 s	0.935	100 : 83.3
504×504	3	26.22 s	69 ms	18.74 s	45.03 s	0.92	100 : 24.6
504×504	4	31.97 s	9.57 s	30.01 s	71.55 s	0.92	100 : 35.7
1024×1024	1	4.91 s	12 ms	3.18 s	8.10 s	0.98	100 : 34.4
1024×1024	2	6.12 s	1.98 s	4.53 s	12.63 s	0.975	100 : 83.3
1022×1022	3	25.68 s	73 ms	18.57 s	44.32 s	0.96	100 : 24.6
1022×1022	4	31.96 s	9.62 s	30.22 s	71.80 s	0.97	100 : 35.7
2048×2048	1	46.41 s	247 ms	30.49 s	77.14 s	0.98	100 : 34.4
2048×2048	2	46.22 s	16.31 s	35.32 s	97.85 s	0.98	100 : 83.3
2044×2044	3	67.87 s	260 ms	44.30 s	112.43 s	0.975	100 : 24.6
2044×2044	4	67.45 s	19.68 s	62.08 s	149.21 s	0.975	100 : 35.7

4.3   Bandwidth

In contrast to running time, the bandwidth required to send an image from client to server can be computed as a function of our selected parameters Π from Sect. 4.1 and our cut-off point c from Algorithm 2.

Moreover, since the server's ciphertexts that are intended to be sent back to the client for decryption contain less information by design (ref. Sect. 3.3), we can benefit from a reduced size on responses.

Table 3 demonstrates our bandwidth consumption, highlighting that Π_2 is our most versatile parameter set. We remind that tailor-made parameters per requirement, configuration and image size will always bring forth an improvement on the numbers below.

4.4   Comparison with the Current State of the Art

Zama's HuggingFace demo [33] is the only other public proof-of-concept implementation that works end-to-end. A comparison between our implementation and theirs is not a direct "apples-to-apples" comparison because of the following points:

-   They only support up images of up to 100×100 pixels in size.
-   The demo is built using TFHE, a different FHE scheme that has pros and cons compared to CKKS.

Table 3. Experimental bandwidth consumption for client requests ($\rightarrow$) and server responses ($\leftarrow$) given different parameter sets and settings

Parameter Set	$c_8 = 22$ (Setting 1)	$c_8 = 30$ (Setting 2)	$c_{16} = 63$ (Setting 3)	$c_{16} = 70$ (Setting 4)
Π_1	$\rightarrow$ 90.2 MB $\leftarrow$ 24.2 MB	$\rightarrow$ 123 MB $\leftarrow$ 33 MB	$\rightarrow$ 258 MB $\leftarrow$ 69.3 MB	$\rightarrow$ 287 MB $\leftarrow$ 77 MB
Π_2	$\rightarrow$ 123.2 MB $\leftarrow$ 24.2 MB	$\rightarrow$ 168 MB $\leftarrow$ 33 MB	$\rightarrow$ 352.8 MB $\leftarrow$ 69.3 MB	$\rightarrow$ 392 MB $\leftarrow$ 77 MB
Π_3	$\rightarrow$ 1034 MB $\leftarrow$ 134.2 MB	$\rightarrow$ 1410 MB $\leftarrow$ 183 MB	$\rightarrow$ 2961 MB $\leftarrow$ 384.3 MB	$\rightarrow$ 3290 MB $\leftarrow$ 427 MB

- Their experiments are run with RGB images whereas we ran our experiments with grayscale.
- They do not compress or encode images: a raw pixel-matrix is encrypted and sent to the server, therefore messages between client and server are equal in length and overall server running time will be lower in comparison to ours.
- Supported Convolution Operations (corr. our Setting 1): Blurring, Ridge Detection, Sharpening.
- Supported Pixel-Wise Operations (corr. our Setting 2): Identity, Rotation, Inversion.

In order to level out the comparison, we can assume that a 100×100 RGB image has an equivalent required bandwidth to a 300×300 grayscale image. We also cloned their code and ran it on the same machine we used for our experiments above. The results can be found in Table 4.

Table 4. Performance of Zama's TFHE-based Image Processing Demo for Colored 100×100 Images

Operation Type	Running Time	Bandwidth Consumed
Pixel-Wise	360 ms	$\rightarrow$ 177 MB $\leftarrow$ 177 MB
Convolution	650 ms	$\rightarrow$ 235 MB $\leftarrow$ 235 MB

Interpretation. When comparing Zama's running time with ours, they clearly stand at an overall advantage since no compression/decompression is taking place. If we perform a less rigorous comparison between their running time and only our processing time from the first two rows of Table 2, we can estimate that the numbers are comparable for performing convolutions while we seem to be at a disadvantage when it comes to pixel-wise processing.

However, the more interesting result emerges when we compare bandwidth: for us to transmit a single channel 1024×1024 image back and forth for convolutional processing, we require 147.4 MB whereas they require 470 MB for a 100×100 RGB image. This is approximately 3x more bandwidth for $\sim 30\%$ of the amount of pixels.

If Zama's TFHE solution scales to support higher-resolutions, it might eventually be practical in scenarios where only a predefined set of image-processing operations is interesting and the bandwidth cost between clients and server is negligible. Our solution for the time being natively supports generic operations, works for much higher resolutions, at a lower bandwidth-cost but higher-computational overhead which can be offset by a highly performing server, and more refined parameters.

5   Summary and Future Directions

In this work, we described a novel technique to homomorphically compress, process and decompress natural images. This is a fundamental step towards improved and more advanced privacy-preserving image manipulation, which is paramount in many important use-cases in computer vision such as biometric-based authentication and computer-aided medical diagnostics.

Prior to our work, the literature focused mainly on private image processing, leaving compression and decompression aside. We believe that providing the capability to compress and decompress images privately opens the door to the construction of more efficient, easy-to-use frameworks while reducing the bandwidth and memory requirements of the applications.

We discussed the two types of packing we use, depending on the kind of processing that should be applied (3×3 convolution or pixel-wise processing). Our implementation shows that the techniques using 8×8 blocks are more time-efficient, while the 16×16 blocks achieve more compression.

The next natural step would be to generalize our compression algorithm to make it compatible with more complex image processing, such as facial recognition and object detection.

Interesting orthogonal work could combine our results with the recent advancements on Zero Knowledge Proofs to support proofs of image provenance [5,14] or to certify the server's processing on the image.

Finally, an interesting question is whether it is possible to conclusively prove that entropy encoding is impractical in combination with FHE. If not, it should be possible to further improve the compression ratio we achieve.

Acknowledgements. This work was supported by the Flemish Government through the Cybersecurity Research Program with grant number: VOEWICS02 and by the FWO under an Odysseus project GOH9718N. This work was supported by the Spanish Ministry of Economy and Competitiveness with reference number RTI2018-102112-B-I00. Any opinions, findings and conclusions or recommendations expressed in this material are those of the authors and do not necessarily reflect the views of Cybersecurity Research Flanders, the FWO or the Spanish Ministry of Economy and Competitiveness.

References

1. Alexandru, A., Kim, A., Polyakov, Y.: General functional bootstrapping using CKKS. Cryptology ePrint Archive, Paper 2024/1623 (2024). https://eprint.iacr.org/2024/1623

2. Almohammad, A., Ghinea, G., Hierons, R.M.: JPEG steganography: a performance evaluation of quantization tables. In: 2009 International Conference on Advanced Information Networking and Applications, pp. 471–478 (2009). https://doi.org/10.1109/AINA.2009.67

3. Balla, S., Koushanfar, F.: Heliks: HE linear algebra kernels for secure inference. In: Meng, W., Jensen, C.D., Cremers, C., Kirda, E. (eds.) Proceedings of the 2023 ACM SIGSAC Conference on Computer and Communications Security, CCS 2023, Copenhagen, Denmark, 26–30 November 2023, pp. 2306–2320. ACM (2023). https://doi.org/10.1145/3576915.3623136

4. Bergerat, L., Chillotti, I., Ligier, D., Orfila, J.B., Tap, S.: TFHE gets real: an efficient and flexible homomorphic floating-point arithmetic. Cryptology ePrint Archive, Paper 2025/257 (2025). https://eprint.iacr.org/2025/257

5. Boneh, D., Grotto, A.J., McDaniel, P., Papernot, N.: Preparing for the age of deepfakes and disinformation. HAI Policy Brief (2020)

6. Brakerski, Z.: Fully homomorphic encryption without modulus switching from classical GapSVP. In: Safavi-Naini, R., Canetti, R. (eds.) CRYPTO 2012. LNCS, vol. 7417, pp. 868–886. Springer, Heidelberg (2012). https://doi.org/10.1007/978-3-642-32009-5_50

7. Brakerski, Z., Gentry, C., Vaikuntanathan, V.: (Leveled) fully homomorphic encryption without bootstrapping. In: Goldwasser, S. (ed.) ITCS 2012, pp. 309–325. ACM (2012). https://doi.org/10.1145/2090236.2090262

8. Brakerski, Z., Vaikuntanathan, V.: Lattice-based FHE as secure as PKE. In: Naor, M. (ed.) ITCS 2014, pp. 1–12. ACM (2014). https://doi.org/10.1145/2554797.2554799

9. Canard, S., Carpov, S., Kuate, D.N., Sirdey, R.: Running compression algorithms in the encrypted domain: a case-study on the homomorphic execution of RLE. Cryptology ePrint Archive, Report 2017/392 (2017). https://eprint.iacr.org/2017/392

10. Chao, J., et al.: Carenets: compact and resource-efficient CNN for homomorphic inference on encrypted medical images. CoRR abs/1901.10074 (2019). http://arxiv.org/abs/1901.10074

11. Cheon, J.H., Kim, A., Kim, M., Song, Y.: Homomorphic encryption for arithmetic of approximate numbers. In: Takagi, T., Peyrin, T. (eds.) ASIACRYPT 2017. LNCS, vol. 10624, pp. 409–437. Springer, Cham (2017). https://doi.org/10.1007/978-3-319-70694-8_15

12. Chillotti, I., Gama, N., Georgieva, M., Izabachène, M.: Faster fully homomorphic encryption: bootstrapping in less than 0.1 seconds. In: Cheon, J.H., Takagi, T. (eds.) ASIACRYPT 2016. LNCS, vol. 10031, pp. 3–33. Springer, Heidelberg (2016). https://doi.org/10.1007/978-3-662-53887-6_1

13. Chillotti, I., Gama, N., Georgieva, M., Izabachène, M.: TFHE: fast fully homomorphic encryption over the torus. J. Cryptol. **33**(1), 34–91 (2019). https://doi.org/10.1007/s00145-019-09319-x
14. Datta, T., Boneh, D.: Using ZK proofs to fight disinformation (2022). https://medium.com/@boneh/using-zk-proofs-to-fight-disinformation-17e7d57fe52f
15. Fan, J., Vercauteren, F.: Somewhat practical fully homomorphic encryption. Cryptology ePrint Archive, Report 2012/144 (2012). https://eprint.iacr.org/2012/144
16. Fleischhacker, N., Larsen, K.G., Simkin, M.: Compressing encrypted data over small fields. Cryptology ePrint Archive, Paper 2023/946 (2023). https://eprint.iacr.org/2023/946
17. Fu, W., Lin, R., Inge, D.: Fully homomorphic image processing. CoRR abs/1810.03249 (2018). http://arxiv.org/abs/1810.03249
18. Gentry, C.: Fully homomorphic encryption using ideal lattices. In: Mitzenmacher, M. (ed.) 41st ACM STOC, pp. 169–178. ACM Press (2009). https://doi.org/10.1145/1536414.1536440
19. Golomb, S.: Run-length encodings (coresp.). IEEE Trans. Inf. Theory **12**(3), 399–401 (1966). https://doi.org/10.1109/TIT.1966.1053907
20. Huffman, D.A.: A method for the construction of minimum-redundancy codes. Proc. IRE **40**(9), 1098–1101 (1952). https://doi.org/10.1109/JRPROC.1952.273898
21. International Organisation for Standardisation: Information technology – Digital compression and coding of continuous-tone still images - Requirements and guidelines. Standard, CCITT, Geneva, CH (1992)
22. Jain, N., Nandakumar, K., Ratha, N.K., Pankanti, S., Kumar, U.: Optimizing homomorphic encryption based secure image analytics. In: 23rd International Workshop on Multimedia Signal Processing, MMSP 2021, Tampere, Finland, 6–8 October 2021, pp. 1–6. IEEE (2021). https://doi.org/10.1109/MMSP53017.2021.9733620
23. Jiang, X., Kim, M., Lauter, K.E., Song, Y.: Secure outsourced matrix computation and application to neural networks. In: Lie, D., Mannan, M., Backes, M., Wang, X. (eds.) Proceedings of the 2018 ACM SIGSAC Conference on Computer and Communications Security, CCS 2018, Toronto, ON, Canada, 15–19 October 2018, pp. 1209–1222. ACM (2018). https://doi.org/10.1145/3243734.3243837
24. Kelsey, J.: Compression and information leakage of plaintext. In: Daemen, J., Rijmen, V. (eds.) FSE 2002. LNCS, vol. 2365, pp. 263–276. Springer, Heidelberg (2002). https://doi.org/10.1007/3-540-45661-9_21
25. Nokam Kuate, D., Canard, S., Sirdey, R.: Towards video compression in the encrypted domain: a case-study on the H264 and HEVC macroblock processing pipeline. In: Camenisch, J., Papadimitratos, P. (eds.) CANS 2018. LNCS, vol. 11124, pp. 109–129. Springer, Cham (2018). https://doi.org/10.1007/978-3-030-00434-7_6
26. Lee, E., et al.: Low-complexity deep convolutional neural networks on fully homomorphic encryption using multiplexed parallel convolutions. In: Chaudhuri, K., Jegelka, S., Song, L., Szepesvári, C., Niu, G., Sabato, S. (eds.) International Conference on Machine Learning, ICML 2022, 17-23 July 2022, Baltimore, Maryland, USA. Proceedings of Machine Learning Research, vol. 162, pp. 12403–12422. PMLR (2022). https://proceedings.mlr.press/v162/lee22e.html
27. Ma, X., Liu, C., Cao, S., Zhu, B.: JPEG decompression in the homomorphic encryption domain. In: Boll, S., et al. (eds.) 2018 ACM Multimedia Conference on Multimedia Conference, MM 2018, Seoul, Republic of Korea, 22–26 October 2018, pp. 905–913. ACM (2018). https://doi.org/10.1145/3240508.3240672

28. Nithya, P., Sathya, M., Vengattaraman, T.: Survey on image compression algorithms and their efficiencies under different types of files. In: 2023 6th International Conference on Recent Trends in Advance Computing (ICRTAC), pp. 238–246 (2023). https://doi.org/10.1109/ICRTAC59277.2023.10480806

29. Pennebaker, W.B., Mitchell, J.L.: JPEG still image data compression standard. Van Nostrand Reinhold, New York (N.Y.) (1993)

30. Rovida, L., Leporati, A.: Encrypted image classification with low memory footprint using fully homomorphic encryption. Int. J. Neural Syst. **34**(5), 2450025:1–2450025:16 (2024). https://doi.org/10.1142/S0129065724500254

31. Vengadapurvaja, A., Nisha, G., Aarthy, R., Sasikaladevi, N.: An efficient homomorphic medical image encryption algorithm for cloud storage security. Procedia Comput. Sci. **115**, 643–650 (2017). https://doi.org/10.1016/j.procs.2017.09.150. https://www.sciencedirect.com/science/article/pii/S1877050917319798, 7th International Conference on Advances in Computing & Communications, ICACC-2017, 22-24 August 2017, Cochin, India

32. Wang, Z., Simoncelli, E., Bovik, A.: Multiscale structural similarity for image quality assessment. In: The Thirty-Seventh Asilomar Conference on Signals, Systems & Computers, vol. 2, pp. 1398–1402 (2003). https://doi.org/10.1109/ACSSC.2003.1292216

33. Zama: Image filtering on encrypted data using fully homomorphic encryption (2023). https://huggingface.co/spaces/zama-fhe/encrypted_image_filtering

34. Zheng, P., Huang, J.: An efficient image homomorphic encryption scheme with small ciphertext expansion. In: Jaimes, A., et al. (eds.) ACM Multimedia Conference, MM 2013, Barcelona, Spain, 21–25 October 2013, pp. 803–812. ACM (2013). https://doi.org/10.1145/2502081.2502105

35. Zinner, T., Hohlfeld, O., Abboud, O., Hossfeld, T.: Impact of frame rate and resolution on objective QoE metrics. In: 2010 Second International Workshop on Quality of Multimedia Experience (QoMEX), pp. 29–34 (2010). https://doi.org/10.1109/QOMEX.2010.5518277

Leveled Homomorphic Encryption over Composite Groups

Mahdi Mahdavi[1], Ehsan Meamari[2(✉)], Emad Heydari Beni[3], and Maryam Sheikhi[4]

[1] Universitat Oberta de Catalunya (UOC), Barcelona, Spain
m_mahdavi@uoc.edu
[2] University of Delaware, Newark, USA
ehsan@udel.edu
[3] COSIC, KU Leuven & Nokia Bell Labs, Leuven, Belgium
emad.heydaribeni@esat.kuleuven.be
[4] University of Hamburg, Hamburg, Germany
maryam.sheikhi.garjan@uni-hamburg.de

Abstract. Homomorphic encryption is a powerful tool that enables computation on encrypted data without requiring decryption. While many Fully Homomorphic Encryption schemes, supporting arbitrary computations on encrypted data, have been developed using lattice-based and AGCD-based approaches, progress in composite groups has been limited to Partial Homomorphic Encryption schemes, which only support either addition or multiplication. This paper introduces the first ℓ-leveled homomorphic encryption schemes over composite groups, based on factoring problem, that achieve both multiplicative and additive homomorphic properties. Our novel design eliminates the need for relinearization operation, which is common in LWE-based HE schemes, and removes the requirement for the circular security assumption. For applications where the traffic must be indistinguishable as encrypted, a scrambled scheme is designed using a labeling technique. While the initial schemes offer an expanded message space, the introduction of the double-sized Message technique enables the encryption of messages up to twice the size without increasing the ciphertext size. Implementation results show that our schemes significantly outperform existing solutions, particularly in multiplication operations, achieving speeds up to 1000 times faster than well-known schemes such as BFV, BGV, CKKS, and TFHE.

Keywords: Homomorphic Encryption · Leveled Homomorphic Encryption · Composite Group · Factoring · Bézout's coefficients

1 Introduction

Homomorphic Encryption (HE) is a robust cryptographic technique that enables computations on encrypted data. Consequently, sensitive information can be

© The Author(s), under exclusive license to Springer Nature Switzerland AG 2026
A. Nitaj et al. (Eds.): AFRICACRYPT 2025, LNCS 15651, pp. 25–50, 2026.
https://doi.org/10.1007/978-3-031-97260-7_2

processed and analyzed without being exposed, ensuring a high level of confidentiality. This capability makes HE particularly valuable for numerous applications in privacy and security. In machine learning [CJP20] and image processing [MNR24], HE allows for secure computation on encrypted data, enabling companies to collaborate on sensitive datasets without revealing the underlying information. In cloud computing [LATV12a], HE can potentially facilitate secure outsourcing of computations to untrusted servers, maintaining the confidentiality of the data being processed. Despite its valuable applications, designing a HE scheme capable of evaluating complicated functions on encrypted data is not straightforward. The concept of homomorphic encryption began with the first class, Partially Homomorphic Encryption (PHE), which supports either addition or multiplication operations on encrypted data, but not both. GM [GM82] and RSA [RSA78] are two PHE schemes that support addition or multiplication. The next class of HE, Somewhat Homomorphic Encryption (SHE), extends the capabilities of PHE by allowing both addition and multiplication operations on encrypted data, but with certain limitations. [BGN05] proposed a SHE scheme which supports one multiplication but unlimited addition operations.

Leveled Homomorphic Encryption (LHE) extends the capability to handle computations up to a certain complexity or depth, defined by the number of multiplicative as level ℓ. [Bra12, FV12] proposed an LHE scheme which supports maximum of ℓ multiplication, but unlimited addition operations. Gentry et al. [Gen09] made significant breakthroughs in the development of the first Fully Homomorphic Encryption (FHE) which provides an unlimited number of multiplications and additions. This breakthrough demonstrated that it is possible to create a cryptographic system capable of arbitrary computation on encrypted data with confidentiality preserving.

1.1   Mathematical Foundations in HE

There are various mathematical techniques used to design Homomorphic Encryption schemes, each offering distinct properties such as security, efficiency, and so on. The different approaches can be classified as follows:

- **Pairing and Multi-linear Maps:** This technique, first introduced in [BGN05], utilizes pairings and supports unlimited additions along with a single multiplication. Although [GGH13] later developed ℓ-Multilinear maps, which allow for ℓ multiplications, this approach did not gain wide adoption due to the non-standard nature of multilinear assumptions in cryptography.
- **Ideal-Lattice:** Gentry's HE scheme [Gen09], based on Ideal-Lattices, introduced bootstrapping techniques, enabling the first FHE. Although efforts were made by schemes such as [SS10] to enhance the efficiency of this category, the proposed methods remained extremely slow, preventing this approach from gaining much traction.
- **LWE-based:** This category, typically derives from the Regev encryption system [Reg09], utilizes Learning with Errors (LWE) and its variant, the Ring Learning with Errors (RLWE) problems [BGV12, Bra12, FV12, CGGI17, GIKV23, MHWW24].

- **NTRU-based:** NTRU is a lattice-based problem utilized in the design of HE schemes, such as LTV [LATV12a] and YASHE [BLLN13]. This area has demonstrated notable progress, with several recent publications [JMPP24] and [Klu22] contributing to its development.
- **AGCD:** Another direction for proposed HE schemes utilizes the Approximate Greatest Common Divisor (AGCD) problem, which operates over integers [vDGHV10, Per20, BBL17, Per21].
- **Composite Group:** This direction, which is based on the factoring problem, is initially explored by the RSA [RSA78], and then GM [GM82], and Paillier [Pai99] schemes.

Among the listed categories, some are well-researched, while others are not. The "LWE-based" category is regarded as the most prominent and thoroughly investigated class, while the "AGCD" category is also well-studied. In contrast, categories such as "Pairing and Multi-linear Maps" and "Composite Group" exhibit limited progress. Specifically, the schemes within the "Composite Group" category have made minimal advancements, resulting in only partial homomorphic encryption schemes. For example, RSA [RSA78] supports only multiplication, and GM [GM82] supports only addition. The most notable scheme in this category is Paillier [Pai99], which supports addition and scalar multiplication. To the best of our knowledge, despite numerous attempts, there is currently no known scheme that provides at least somewhat homomorphic encryption over composite groups. This paper aims to overcome prior obstacles and advance this area by introducing l-Leveled Homomorphic Encryption in composite groups.

One advantage of the Composite Group is its potential to support a larger message space compared to other approaches.[1] As a result, the ratio of ciphertext space to a single message is smaller than in other schemes, leading to lower communication overhead.[2].

1.2   Design Techniques in HE

Other than the mathematical foundation of an HE scheme, there are different design techniques that matter while designing an HE scheme.

Relinearization, which decreases the size of the resulting ciphertext after each multiplication back into a fresh ciphertext, is required in schemes such as BGV [BGV12] and BFV [Bra12, FV12]. However, the relinearization key comprises an encrypted version of the secret key. Publishing this key as a public parameter relies on circular security which is potentially a security concern.

---

[1] Although LWE-based schemes like TFHE [CGGI17] can support homomorphism over large messages, they require additional computations or modifications.

[2] While other schemes utilize Batching and Single Instruction Multiple Data (SIMD) techniques to pack more data items into a single ciphertext, these techniques are ineffective for applications that require encrypting a single data item. Our schemes offer an alternative for such use cases.

The decomposition technique, utilized in LWE-based [GSW13, ASP14, CGGI17] and AGCD-based schemes [BBL17, Per20], transforms the exponential growth of noise during multiplication into an additive growth pattern. Additionally, noise reduction can be achieved through another technique that involves switching the modulus of the ciphertext space, as applied in [BV14, BGV12, Bra12, FV12, CNT12].

Algebraic operations, such as addition and multiplication in ciphertext space, could be computed simply in evaluation. However, maintenance operations such as bit decomposition, bit-wise operations, real division, and rounding are complicated in evaluation computation. Most of practical FHE schemes, such as BGV [BGV12] and BFV [Bra12, FV12] schemes, require some of the maintenance operations for evaluation of an inquired function.

While relinearization, decomposition, modulus switching, and maintenance operations are powerful techniques essential for most HE schemes, they significantly increase the complexity and inefficiency of implementing the FHE systems. In contrast, our designs do not require these techniques, resulting in a less complex design and more efficiency compared to other HE schemes.

Beyond designing new FHE schemes, several areas of improvement aim to enhance their practicality, performance, and adaptability. These improvements include performance optimization, application-specific optimizations, and parallelism and distributed computing. Existing FHE schemes typically generate ciphertexts that appear random-like at first glance. However, an eavesdropper analyzing multiple ciphertexts may detect patterns in the traffic. While this does not compromise the confidentiality of the data, it enables the identification of traffic flows containing encrypted messages. In applications such as steganography, ensuring that traffic patterns remain indistinguishable from randomness is vital to avoid detection.

1.3   Our Contributions

The contributions are detailed as follows:

- This paper introduces the Straw-Man (SM) LHE scheme using composite groups. Then, the Labeled Scrambled Ciphertext (LSC) scheme is introduced to make the SM's ciphertext more scrambled. Eventually, a modified Rothblum's transformation technique is introduced to convert the symmetric schemes into public key versions.
- To enhance the performance of the schemes, a double-sized Message technique is introduced, allowing the encryption of a message with up to 2τ-bit without increasing the value of η.
- Implementation results demonstrate that our designed schemes can perform evaluation algorithms significantly faster, particularly for multiplication—the most computationally expensive operation in LHE schemes—achieving speeds up to 1000 times faster than well-known schemes like BFV, BGV, CKKS, and TFHE.

1.4 Paper Organization

The paper proceeds in Sect. 2 with the preliminaries. Section 3 introduces two leveled homomorphic schemes: Straw-Man and Labeled Scrambled Ciphertext, followed by their public key versions. A performance enhancement technique, called doubling, is proposed in Sect. 4 to improve the efficiency of the schemes. Section 5 provides the implementation results of the schemes and compares them with the most well-known homomorphic encryption schemes. Finally, the conclusion in Sect. 6 summarizes the results of the paper.

2 Preliminaries

This section introduces notation, presents supporting mathematical lemmas, and provides an overview of homomorphic encryption.

2.1 Notation

Operations within a modulus x are denoted by $[.]_x$. The signs of $\lfloor x \rfloor$, $\lceil x \rceil$, and $\lfloor x \rceil$ represent the floor, ceiling, and rounding of x to the nearest integer, respectively.

$y \leftarrow \mathcal{A}(x)$ indicates that y is the output of algorithm (or attacker) $\mathcal{A}$ when run with x as the input.

The security parameter is shown by λ; ρ is the bit length of the noise where $\rho > \lambda$ to protect the scheme against exhaustive search. Messages are selected from $\mathbb{Z}_t$; while τ is the bit length of the message space (i.e., $\tau = \lceil \log_2 t \rceil$). The ciphertext is in modulo N, which is 2η-bit. Specifically, $N = p \cdot q$, where p and q are prime numbers with η-bit of size[3].

2.2 Supporting Mathematical Lemmas

Lemma 1. *Let $N = p \cdot q$, where p and q are prime numbers. For an integer $r \in \mathbb{Z}_N$, the equations $[qr]_N = q[r]_p$ and $[pr]_N = p[r]_q$ hold.*

Proof. We only prove $[pr]_N = p[r]_q$, and the proof of $[qr]_N = q[r]_p$ follows similarly. The Euclidean division concludes:

$$pr = \alpha N + r_N \tag{1}$$

where $r_N < N$, and

$$r = \beta q + r_q \tag{2}$$

where $r_q < q$. Equation 1 represents the division of pr by N, while Eq. 2 corresponds to the division of r by q. Equation 2 concludes $p \cdot r = \beta pq + pr_q$. Since $r_q < q$, it follows that $pr_q < pq$. The uniqueness property of Euclidean division concludes that $pr_q = r_N$, implying that $p[r]_q = [pr]_N$. □

---

[3] The complexity of the factoring problem is at least 2^λ using the best-known practical factoring algorithm known as the number field sieve (NFS). Quantum algorithms for factoring, e.g., Shor algorithm, are not taken into account.

Remark 1. The Lemma 1 shows that if the value of pr overflows from N, the result remains in the form of a multiple of p, specifically $p[r]_q$. The proposed lemma suggests that computations modulo N are equivalent to computations modulo p or q.

Lemma 2. *Let p and q be two odd primes and $N = p \cdot q$. For any number $c \in \mathbb{Z}_N$, a unique pair $(a, b) \in \mathbb{Z}_p \times \mathbb{Z}_q$ exists such that $aq + bp = c$. In other words, the equation $qx + py = c$ has a unique answer for x and y.*

Proof. Suppose there are two pairs (a_1, b_1) and (a_2, b_2) such that $a_1 q + b_2 p = a_2 q + b_2 p = c$, which can be written as $(a_1 - a_2)q = (b_2 - b_1)p$. Since p and q are primes, it follows that $a_1 - a_2 = \alpha p$ and $b_2 - b_1 = \alpha q$. Therefore, it can be concluded that $a_1 \equiv a_2 \mod p$, and $b_1 \equiv b_2 \mod q$. This implies that if the equation $a \cdot q + b \cdot p = c$ has a solution, the solution is unique. Next, it will be shown that the equation indeed has a solution.

Given the uniqueness of values for a and b, and since there are p possible values for a and q possible values for b, there are pq possible pairs (a, b) that cover all representations of $\mathbb{Z}_N$. This implies that such an equation has a unique solution. $\square$

Lemma 3. *Let p and q be two odd primes, and let $N = p \cdot q$. It follows that $[p^q]_N = p$ and $[q^p]_N = q$.*

Proof. According to Lemma 1, for $r = [q^{p-1}]_N$ it can be concluded that $[q \cdot q^{p-1}]_N = q[q^{p-1}]_p$. This can be rewritten as $[q^p]_N = q[1]_p$. Similarly, the other equation holds. $\square$

Remark 2. Let p and q be two primes and $N = pq$. Consider $\hat{p} = [p^{q-1}]_N = \alpha p = \alpha' q + 1$ and $\hat{q} = [q^{p-1}]_N = \beta q = \beta' p + 1$. For any i, the relations $[\hat{p}^i]_N = \hat{p}$ and $[\hat{q}^i]_N = \hat{q}$ are hold, means that the order of $\hat{p}$ and $\hat{q}$ are equal to one.

2.3   Overview of Homomorphic Encryption

Instead of computing the function f on the message m, Homomorphic Encryption allows for the computation of a function f' on the encrypted data $\mathtt{ct}$ such that decrypting the output of f' yields the same result as applying f to m. Therefore, HE can ensure data confidentiality during computation. HE schemes typically comprise four fundamental algorithms: Key Generation, Encryption, Evaluation, and Decryption, denoted as KeyGen, Enc, Eval, and Dec, respectively. In this section, we present the symmetric-key HE algorithms, which are transformable to the public-key version using Rothblum's transformation [Rot11]. The functionality of each algorithm is as follows:

- $\mathsf{KeyGen}(1^\lambda, t, \ell)$: This algorithm takes security parameter λ, space of messages t, and maximum depth ℓ as input, and outputs the secret key sk, public parameters pp, and the evaluation key evk.
- $\mathsf{Enc}(m, \mathsf{sk}, \mathsf{pp})$: This algorithm utilizes the secret key sk and public parameters pp to generate a ciphertext ct corresponding to the input message m.

– $\mathtt{Eval}(\overrightarrow{\mathtt{ct}}, \mathtt{evk}, f)$: This algorithm takes a set of ciphertexts $\overrightarrow{\mathtt{ct}}$, evaluation key $\mathtt{evk}$, and an evaluation function f as input, and outputs $\mathtt{ct}_f$, which is the encryption of $f(m_1, m_2, ..., m_k)$. The evaluation algorithm is valid for any function f that the number of multiplications is less than ℓ, and consists of two sub-algorithms as follows:
  - $\mathtt{Add}$: represents addition evaluation function.
  - $\mathtt{Mult}$: represents multiplication evaluation function.
– $\mathtt{Dec}(\mathtt{ct}, \mathtt{sk})$: This algorithm takes a ciphertext $\mathtt{ct}$ and secret key $\mathtt{sk}$ as inputs and generates the plaintext message.

Definition 1 (Correct Homomorphic Encryption). *The scheme* $\mathcal{E} = \{\mathtt{KeyGen}, \mathtt{Enc}, \mathtt{Eval}, \mathtt{Dec}\}$ *is correct if, for any key pair* $(\mathtt{sk}, \mathtt{evk})$ *generated by* $\mathtt{KeyGen}$, *and any* l *ciphertexts* $\overrightarrow{c} = \langle c_1, c_2, ..., c_l \rangle$ *encrypted with* l *messages* $m_1, ..., m_l$, *for a given* l-*input function* f, *the following relation holds:*

$$\mathtt{Dec}(\mathtt{sk}, \mathtt{Eval}(\overrightarrow{c}, \mathtt{evk}, f)) = f(m_1, ..., m_l)$$

3 Proposed HE Schemes

This section introduces three LHE schemes: the Straw-Man (SM), the Labeled Scrambled Ciphertext (LSC), and the public key version of LSC. The Straw-Man scheme designs an LHE using composite groups. However, the ciphertext is placed near to a multiple of the secret key. This pattern makes the traffic of the Straw-Man scheme identifiable as encrypted, such as other schemes like [vDGHV10], which is undesirable in applications like steganography. To address this issue, the Labeled Scrambled Ciphertext scheme makes the ciphertext more indistinguishable. Eventually, the public key version of the LSC scheme is designed using a revised Ron Rothblum's technique.

3.1 Straw-Man LHE

The Straw-Man scheme works as follows:

– $\mathtt{SM.KeyGen}(1^\lambda, \ell, t)$: Based on the security parameters λ, select two η-bit prime numbers p and q, set the secret key as $\mathtt{sk} := p$, and publish $\mathtt{evk} := N = p \cdot q$ as evaluation key. For $\tau = \lceil \log_2 t \rceil$, set noise length $\rho > \lambda^4$ such that $p > 2^{\ell \cdot (\rho + \tau)}$, where ℓ is the level (maximum number of multiplication). This algorithm also defines the public parameters as $\mathtt{pp} := \{\lambda, \rho, \tau, \ell, t\}$ and publishes them along with $\mathtt{evk}$, both of which serve as inputs for the subsequent algorithms.
– $\mathtt{SM.Enc}(m, \mathtt{sk})$: For $m \in \mathbb{Z}_t$ as a message, select a ρ-bit random integer e as an error (or noise) and compute the plaintext in form of $\mu = t \cdot e + m^5$. Next, select a random number $r \in \mathbb{Z}_q$ and return

$$\mathtt{ct} = p \cdot r + \mu$$

---

[4] To protect against exhaustive search.

[5] This means that, μ is a $(\rho + \tau)$-bit random coding of message m, such that $m = [\mu]_t$.

as the ciphertext[6].

- SM.Eval($ct_1, ct_2, \cdots, ct_k, f$): Consist of the two addition and multiplication sub-algorithms:
  - SM.Add(ct_1, ct_2, N): Addition algorithm computes $ct_+ = [ct_1 + ct_2]_N$.
  - ST.Mult(ct_1, ct_2, N): Multiplication algorithm computes $ct_\times = [ct_1.ct_2]_N$.
- SM.Dec(ct, sk): Return $m = [[ct]_p]_t$.

Remark 3. Since the Eval algorithm does not use any maintenance operation, so that it can compute $ct_f = [f(ct_1, ct_2, \cdots, ct_k)]_N$ to compute the encryption of the $[f(m_1, m_2, \cdots, m_k)]_t$.

Remark 4. Scalar addition (adding a constant $c \in \mathbb{Z}_t$ with ciphertext ct) and scalar multiplication (multiplying a constant $c \in \mathbb{Z}_t$ with ciphertext ct) can be computed as $[ct + c]_N$ and $[c.ct]_N$, respectively.

Remark 5. The Enc algorithm encodes the message m into the LSB part of μ. Although the LSB mode of the scheme is discussed, because of simplicity and efficiency, the MSB mode for the schemes could be designed similarly.

Remark 6. Our proposed schemes support ℓ multiplications, with the value of ℓ being increased by utilizing larger public parameters. Specifically, the relationship $\ell = \lfloor \frac{\eta-1}{\rho+\tau} \rfloor$ governs the interaction between these parameters. This relationship guarantees the requirement $p > 2^{\ell.(\rho+\tau)}$. The number of additions is significantly greater than ℓ, and therefore, it is not discussed further in this document.

Remark 7. In the proposed schemes, the value of noise e is chosen from a uniform distribution, which is less complex than other schemes based on Lattice, such as vDGHV, BGV, BFV, etc., where the noise is chosen from a Gaussian distribution.

Correctness. The proof of correctness is as follows:

$$[[ct]_p]_t = [[pr + \mu]_p]_t = [[p.r + \mu]_p]_t = [[\mu]_p]_t = [\mu]_t = m \tag{3}$$

The correctness condition in Eq. 3 holds as long as $\mu < p$. For fresh ciphertexts, μ remains below p since $\mu < 2^{\rho+\tau} < p$. While μ increases after evaluation, particularly during multiplication, the growth is manageable, and addition does not significantly increase μ. After ℓ multiplications, for the resulting μ_ℓ, it holds that $\mu_\ell < 2^{\ell(\rho+\tau)}$. Setting the parameter as $\ell = \lfloor \frac{\eta-1}{\rho+\tau} \rfloor$ ensures that $\mu_\ell < 2^{\ell(\rho+\tau)} \leq 2^{\eta-1} < p$. Therefore, as long as the evaluation function depth does not exceed ℓ, the correctness is preserved.

---

[6] Since $r \leq q - 1$ and $\mu < p$, it follows that $pr + \mu < p(q - 1) + p$, which implies that $ct < N$. Therefore, the ciphertext is given by $ct = [pr + \mu]_N$, ensuring that the fresh ciphertext never exceeds the value of N.

Homomorphism. The homomorphic property of addition can be validated as follows.

$$\mathsf{ct}_+ = [pr_1 + \mu_1 + pr_2 + \mu_2]_N = [p(r_1 + r_2) + te_1 + m_1 + te_2 + m_2]_N$$

According to Lemma 1, term $[p(r_1 + r_2)]_N$ can be written to $p[(r_1 + r_2)]_q$. If $(r_1 + r_2)$ exceeds from q, equivalently $p(r_1 + r_2)$ exceeds from N, the result also is in the same format, i.e., multiplication of p. So, the ciphertext can be simplified as

$$\mathsf{ct}_+ = [pr_+ + te_+ + m_+]_N$$

where $r_+ = r_1 + r_2$, $e_+ = e_1 + e_2 + cr$, and cr represents the carry value of $m_1 + m_2$, and $m_+ = [m_1 + m_2]_t$.

With similar explanation about the homomorphic property of addition, the homomorphic property of multiplication can be validated as follows.

$$\begin{aligned}
\mathsf{ct}_\times &= [(pr_1 + \mu_1).(pr_2 + \mu_2)]_N \\
&= [p.(\mu_1 r_2 + r_1\mu_2 + pr_1 r_2) + \mu_1\mu_2]_N \\
&= [p.(\mu_1 r_2 + r_1\mu_2 + pr_1 r_2) + m_1 m_2 + t(m_1 e_2 + te_1 e_2 + e_1 m_2)]_N \\
&= [pr_\times + m_\times + te_\times]_N
\end{aligned}$$

Note that $te_\times = t^2 e_1 e_2 + t(m_1 e_2 + e_1 m_2 + cr)$, where cr represents the carry of $m_1 + m_2$.

A similar discussion can represent the correctness of scalar addition and multiplication homomorphism.

3.2   Labeled Scrambled Ciphertext LHE

In the SM scheme, such as the vDGHV scheme, given a closer exploration of the ciphertext ct in the Straw-Man version, it is concluded that an eavesdropper can infer ct is nearly (in comparison to the size of N) equal to a multiple of the secret key p. If an eavesdropper intercepts network traffic, they may notice a consistent pattern in the data[7], leading them to conclude that the traffic contains encrypted messages. However, in applications such as steganography, the sender seeks to conceal this pattern. To protect the encrypted data from such threats, it is preferable to design a cryptographic scheme that produces scrambled ciphertexts. This paper introduces a labeling technique to enhance the scrambling of the SM scheme, which can also be applied to the DGHV scheme [vDGHV10].

This section describes the Labeled Scrambled Ciphertext (LSC) scheme in which the output of the encryption algorithm is more scrambled away from the multiplications of the secret key. In other words, the ciphertext generated by the SM scheme is predictable and follows a unique pattern, but the LSC scheme scrambled the distribution pattern in ciphertext space (i.e., $[0, N - 1]$).

---

[7] This paper does not discuss detection techniques, but it can be observed that the ciphertexts generated by the SM scheme exhibit a consistent pattern.

The LSC scheme requires that the labels of ciphertexts be attached and updated after each (multiplication) operation. Additionally, an equalizer algorithm is designed to *equalize* the labels of ciphertexts, which is necessary for the addition evaluation. The equalizer is a concept that can be used in any scheme which works with labels.

Definition 2 (Equalizer). *This algorithm takes as input two ciphertexts,* $\mathtt{ct}_1$ *and* $\mathtt{ct}_2$ *with labels* l_1 *and* l_2*, respectively. The algorithm updates the input ciphertexts to* $\mathtt{ct}_i^* = \mathtt{Eq}^{(l_m - l_i)} \cdot \mathtt{ct}_i$*, for* $i \in \{0,1\}$ *and* $l_m = max(l_1, l_2)$*, equalizing its label to* l_m *without affecting the included message[8]. Here,* $\mathtt{Eq}$ *is the equalizer parameter (i.e., encryption of* 1*,* $\mathtt{Enc}(1)$*)[9].*

Remark 8. In general, for a function $f(\mathbf{x}) = \sum_{i=1}^{v} a_i \prod_{j=1}^{w} x_j^{k_j}$ which is required to be evaluated, the algorithm computes the level for each term i as $l_i = \sum_{j}^{w} l_j \cdot k_j$, where l_j is the label of the ciphertext $\mathtt{ct}_j$. Then, the algorithm rewrites the function as $f'(\mathtt{Eq}; \mathbf{x}) = \sum_{i=1}^{v} a_i \prod_{j=1}^{w} \mathtt{Eq}^{(l_m - l_i)} x_j^{k_j}$, where l_m is the maximum of levels. Eventually, all terms of the rewritten function have the equalized label l_m.

Remark 9. Using an equalizer does not introduce new security concerns, as it is essentially the encryption of 1, and its security is tied to the scheme itself, rather than to other assumptions, such as circular security.

The LSC scheme's algorithms are as follows:

- $\mathtt{LSC.KeyGen}(1^\lambda, \ell, t)$: Based on the security parameters λ, select two η-bit prime numbers p and q. Then, choose a random integer $D \in \mathbb{Z}_p^*$, consider secret key as $\mathtt{sk} := (p, D)$, and publish $\mathtt{evk} := N = p \cdot q$ as evaluation key and equalizer $\mathtt{Eq} = \mathtt{LSC.Enc}(1, \mathtt{sk})$. For $\tau = \lceil \log_2 t \rceil$, set noise length $\rho > \lambda$ such that $p > 2^{\ell \cdot (\rho + \tau)}$. The algorithm then defines the public parameters as $\mathtt{pp} := \{\lambda, \rho, \tau, \ell, t\}$ and publishes them along with $\mathtt{evk}$, which both serve as inputs for the subsequent algorithms.
- $\mathtt{LSC.Enc}(m, \mathtt{sk})$: For a message $m \in \mathbb{Z}_t$, select a ρ-bit random integer e as an error (or noise) and set the plaintext to $\mu = t.e + m$. Furthermore, select a random number $r \in \mathbb{Z}_q$ and return

$$\mathtt{ct} = [pr + D\mu]_N$$

  as the ciphertext. In addition, the label l, which shows the power of D and is 1 for fresh ciphertexts, should be attached to the ciphertext.
- $\mathtt{LSC.Eval}(\mathtt{ct}_1, l_1, \mathtt{ct}_2, l_2, \cdots, \mathtt{ct}_k, l_k, N, f)$: Consists of two sub-algorithms as follow:

---

[8] Note that, the equalizer does not changes the ciphertext with maximum label. Without losing of generality, if $l_2 \geq l_1$, this algorithm only changes the ciphertext $\mathtt{ct}_1$.

[9] The values of $\mathtt{Eq}^{(i)}$ for $1 \leq i \leq \ell$ can be pre-computed and stored to reduce computation overhead.

- LSC.Add($\mathsf{ct}_1, l_1, \mathsf{ct}_2, l_2$): Update the two ciphertexts using the Equalizer algorithm to equalize the label of them. Then return $\mathsf{ct}_+ = [\mathsf{ct}_1 + \mathsf{ct}_2]_N$ with the updated label.
- LSC.Mult($\mathsf{ct}_1, l_1, \mathsf{ct}_2, l_2$): Compute $\mathsf{ct}_\times = [\mathsf{ct}_1.\mathsf{ct}_2]_N$, and update label using $l_\times = l_1 + l_2$.
- LSC.Dec($\mathsf{ct}, l, \mathsf{sk}$): Compute $\mu = [D^{-l}.\mathsf{ct}]_p$, and then return $m = [\mu]_t{}^{10}$.

Remark 10. Since the Eval algorithm does not use any maintenance operation, so that it can call equalizer in general and receive the rewritten function f' and compute $\mathsf{ct}_f = [f'(\mathsf{ct}_1, \mathsf{ct}_2, \cdots, \mathsf{ct}_k)]_N$ to calculate the encryption of $[f(m_1, m_2, \cdots, m_k)]_t$. Note that the function f is computed modulo t on the plaintext, but f' is computed modulo N on the ciphertext.

Remark 11. For scalar multiplication and scalar addition, the scheme treats with the constant $c \in \mathbb{Z}_t$ like a ciphertext with label 0. Therefore, scalar multiplication for ciphertext ct with label l can be computed straightforward as $[c.\mathsf{ct}]_N$ without changing the label value. For scalar addition, the scheme calls equalizer, computes $[c \cdot \mathsf{Eq}^l]_N$ and then returns $[\mathsf{ct} + c \cdot \mathsf{Eq}^l]_N$.

Correctness. The correctness of decryption in LSC could be validated, as follows:

$$[D^{-1} \cdot \mathsf{ct}]_p = [D^{-1}[pr + D\mu]_N]_p = [D^{-1}(pr + D\mu)]_p$$
$$= [D^{-1}D\mu]_p = [\mu]_p = \mu \qquad (4)$$

Clearly, $[\mu]_t = m$, with the same explanation about the correctness of the SM scheme.

Homomorphism. The addition homomorphism property can be proved for two ciphertexts with the equalized labels l as follows:

$$\mathsf{ct}_+ = [\mathsf{ct}_1 + \mathsf{ct}_2]_N = [pr_1 + (D)^l \mu_1 + pr_2 + (D)^l \mu_2]_N = [p(r_1 + r_2) + (D)^l(\mu_1 + \mu_2)]_N$$
$$= [p(r_1 + r_2) + (D)^l(te_1 + m_1 + te_2 + m_2)]_N$$
$$= [pr_+ + (D)^l(te_+ + m_+)]_N$$

The multiplication homomorphism property of the scheme could be validated as follows:

$$\mathsf{ct}_\times = [\mathsf{ct}_1.\mathsf{ct}_2]_N = [(pr_1 + (D)^{l_1}\mu_1)(pr_2 + (D)^{l_2}\mu_2)]_N$$
$$= [p^2(r_1 r_2) + p(D)^{l_2}\mu_2 r_1 + p(D)^{l_1}\mu_1 r_2 + (D)^{l_1 + l_2}(\mu_1 \mu_2)]_N$$
$$= [pr_\times + (D)^l(te_\times + m_\times)]_N$$

---

[10] Since the label l is limited by ℓ, the values of $\{D^{-1}, D^{-2}, \cdots, D^{-\ell}\}$ and $\{\mathsf{Eq}^{-1}, \mathsf{Eq}^{-2}, \cdots, \mathsf{Eq}^{-\ell}\}$ can be pre-computed and stored.

The correctness of the equalizer algorithm can be simply approved similar to the correctness of multiplication.

The correctness of the scalar addition and multiplication homomorphism can be discussed similarly.

Remark 12. It can be observed that the ciphertexts produced by the LSC scheme are more scrambled than those generated by the SM scheme, which does not employ the labeling technique. This technique can also be similarly applied to the DGHV scheme [vDGHV10] to enhance its scrambling.

3.3   Public Key LHE

This section introduces the public key version of the LSC scheme. Usually, the Ron Rothblum's technique [Rot11] is used to transform a symmetric HE scheme to a public-key one, defined as follows:

$$Enc_{pk}(m) = \left[\sum_{i \in [k]} b_i \cdot \mathbf{p}_i + m \right]_N$$

where $b_i \in \{0, 1\}$, and $\mathbf{p}_i = \texttt{Enc}(0)$, which is defined as the public key pk. However, this technique does not work for the LSC scheme, so that, a modified version of Rothblum's technique is defined as follows:

$$Enc_{pk}(m) = \left[\sum_{i \in [k]} b_i \cdot \mathbf{p}_i + m \cdot \texttt{Eq} \right]_N \tag{5}$$

Note that, in Eq. 5, since the message m is multiplied by $\texttt{Eq}$, the noise in $\texttt{Eq}$ increases. This should be considered when defining the bounds of ℓ and p.

4   Optimization

This section investigates techniques to improve the performance of the proposed schemes.

4.1   Double Sized Straw-Man

Recalling the SM scheme from Sect. 3.1, the decryption algorithm can compute the value of the random integer r from the ciphertext $\texttt{ct} = [p.r + \mu]_N$. However, the random integer r could be substituted with a plaintext. This capability is used to propose a technique to encrypt a message with up to 2τ-bit without increasing the value of η. Consider the message space in $\mathbb{Z}_t$ where $t = \acute{t} \cdot \ddot{t}$, and $\gcd(\acute{t}, \ddot{t}) = 1$. Assume $\acute{t}$ and $\ddot{t}$ are τ_1 and τ_2-bit long, respectively. For simplicity, let $\tau_1 = \tau_2 = \tau$. Given a message $m \in \mathbb{Z}_t$, we can split it into two components: $\acute{m} = [m]_{\acute{t}}$ and $\ddot{m} = [m]_{\ddot{t}}$. Knowing $\acute{m}$ and $\ddot{m}$, the Chinese Remainder Theorem (CRT) could be used to recover m as:

$$m = \dot{m} \cdot \dot{t} \cdot [\ddot{t}^{-1}]_{\dot{t}} + \ddot{m} \cdot \dot{t} \cdot [\dot{t}^{-1}]_{\ddot{t}}$$

With doubling the space of m, two decryption keys are needed where each of them retrieves one of the messages.

By this introduction, this subsection proposes a Double-sized Straw-Man (DSM) scheme which provides the possibility of encryption of double-sized messages over composite message space, using Remark 2. The Algorithms of the DSM scheme works as follows.

– DSM.KeyGen($1^\lambda, \ell, t$): Select two η-bit prime numbers p and q and compute $N = p \cdot q$ as evaluation key evk. The space of the message is $\mathbb{Z}_t$ (or $\mathbb{Z}_{\dot{t}} \times \mathbb{Z}_{\ddot{t}}$) where $t = \dot{t}.\ddot{t}$ and $\gcd(\dot{t}, \ddot{t}) = 1$. Then, compute $(\hat{p}, \hat{q}) = ([p^{q-1}]_N, [q^{p-1}]_N) \in \mathbb{Z}_N^2$, and set the secret key as sk $:= (p, q, \hat{p}, \hat{q})$. We should have $2^{\ell(\rho+\tau)} < p$ and $2^{\ell(\rho+\tau)} < q$. This algorithm also defines public parameters as pp $:= \{\lambda, \rho, \tau, \ell, t, \dot{t}, \ddot{t}\}$ and publish them with evk to be inputs to the next algorithms.

– DSM.Enc(m, sk): For $\dot{m} = [m]_{\dot{t}}$, $\ddot{m} = [m]_{\ddot{t}}$, select two ρ-bit random integers $\dot{e}, \ddot{e}$ and define two plaintexts $\dot{\mu} = \dot{t}.\dot{e} + \dot{m}$ and $\ddot{\mu} = \dot{t}.\ddot{e} + \ddot{m}$, and then return

$$ct = [\hat{p}\dot{\mu} + \hat{q}\ddot{\mu}]_N$$

as ciphertext[11].

– DSM.Eval($ct_1, ct_2, \cdots, ct_k, f$): two sub-algorithms are as follows:
  • DSM.Add(ct_1, ct_2, N): Compute $ct_+ = [ct_1 + ct_2]_N$.
  • DSM.Mult(ct_1, ct_2, N): Compute $ct_\times = [ct_1.ct_2]_N$.
– DSM.Dec(ct, sk): Compute $\dot{m} = [[ct]_q]_{\dot{t}}$ and $\ddot{m} = [[ct]_p]_{\ddot{t}}$, and then return $m = \dot{m}\ddot{t}.[\ddot{t}^{-1}]_{\dot{t}} + \ddot{m}\dot{t}.[\dot{t}^{-1}]_{\ddot{t}}$.

Remark 13. Similar to the previous schemes, scalar multiplication is straightforward in this scheme too. For scalar addition, the DSM scheme returns $ct + c \cdot E_1$, where E_1 is the encryption of one, $E_1 = $ DSM.Enc(1, sk), which is like an equalizer in the LSC scheme.

Remark 14. In the DSM scheme, let assume $\gcd(\dot{t}, \ddot{t}) = t_g \neq 1$. For two double-sized messages $m_1 = (\dot{m}_1, \ddot{m}_1) = (0, 1)$ and $m_2 = (\dot{m}_2, \ddot{m}_2) = (1, 0)$, an adversary could query the encryption and receive ciphertexts ct_1 and ct_2. The adversary can then compute $[ct_1]_{t_g}$, revealing $[gp]_{t_g}$, and $[ct_2]_{t_g}$, revealing $[dq]_{t_g}$. This is why the condition $\gcd(\dot{t}, \ddot{t}) = 1$ is necessary.

Correctness. The correctness of the decryption algorithm for a message $\dot{m}$ can be verified by considering Remark 2 as follows.

$$[ct]_q = [[\hat{p}\dot{\mu} + \hat{q}\ddot{\mu}]_N]_q = [[(\alpha'.q + 1)\dot{\mu} + \beta.q\ddot{\mu}]_N]_q$$
$$= [[\dot{\mu} + q(\alpha'.\dot{\mu} + \beta.\ddot{\mu})]_N]_q = [\dot{\mu} + q(\alpha'.\dot{\mu} + \beta.\ddot{\mu})]_q = [q\dot{r} + \dot{\mu}]_N = [\dot{\mu}]_q = \dot{\mu}$$

Note that $\dot{m} = [\dot{\mu}]_{\dot{t}}$, with considering the same explanation about the correctness of the SM scheme. The correction of the decryption for a message $\ddot{m}$ is similar.

---

[11] The ciphertext of the DSM scheme could be rewritten as $[p\ddot{r} + \ddot{\mu}] = [q\dot{r} + \dot{\mu}]$, which is similar to the ciphertext of the SM scheme. For more details, see the correctness.

Homomorphism. The addition homomorphism property can be proved as follows:

$$\mathsf{ct}_+ = [\mathsf{ct}_1 + \mathsf{ct}_2]_N = [(\hat{p}.\dot{\mu}_1 + \hat{q}.\ddot{\mu}_1) + (\hat{p}.\dot{\mu}_2 + \hat{q}.\ddot{\mu}_2)]_N = [\hat{p}.(\dot{\mu}_1 + \dot{\mu}_2) + \hat{q}.(\ddot{\mu}_1 + \ddot{\mu}_2)]_N$$
$$= [\hat{p}.(\dot{t}\dot{e}_1 + \dot{m}_1 + \dot{t}\dot{e}_2 + \dot{m}_2) + \hat{q}.(\ddot{t}\ddot{e}_1 + \ddot{m}_1 + \ddot{t}\ddot{e}_2 + \ddot{m}_2)]_N$$
$$= [\hat{p}.(\dot{t}\dot{e}_+ + \dot{m}_+) + \hat{q}.(\ddot{t}\ddot{e}_+ + \ddot{m}_+)]_N$$

The multiplication homomorphism property can be proved as follows:

$$\mathsf{ct}_\times = [\mathsf{ct}_1.\mathsf{ct}_2]_N = [(\hat{p}.\dot{\mu}_1 + \hat{q}.\ddot{\mu}_1).(\hat{p}.\dot{\mu}_2 + \hat{q}.\ddot{\mu}_2)]_N$$
$$= [(\hat{p}^2.(\dot{\mu}_1.\dot{\mu}_2) + \hat{p}\hat{q}(\dot{\mu}_1\ddot{\mu}_2 + \dot{\mu}_2.\ddot{\mu}_1) + \hat{q}^2.(\ddot{\mu}_1.\ddot{\mu}_2))]_N$$
$$= [\hat{p}^2.(\dot{\mu}_1.\dot{\mu}_2) + \hat{q}^2.(\ddot{\mu}_1.\ddot{\mu}_2))]_N$$
$$= [\hat{p}.\dot{\mu}_\times + \hat{q}.\ddot{\mu}_\times]_N = [\hat{p}.(\dot{t}\dot{e}_\times + \dot{m}_\times) + \hat{q}.(\ddot{t}\ddot{e}_\times + \ddot{m}_\times)]_N$$

The correctness of the scalar addition and multiplication homomorphism can be approved similarly.

4.2   Double-Sized Labeled Scrambled Ciphertext

With a similar discussion about the idea of the DSM scheme, this subsection describes the Double-sized Labeled Scrambled Ciphertext (DLSC) scheme which works as follows.

- DLSC.KeyGen(1^λ): For the space of the message $\mathbb{Z}_t$ (or $\mathbb{Z}_{\dot{t}} \times \mathbb{Z}_{\ddot{t}}$), where $t = \dot{t}.\ddot{t}$ and $\gcd(\dot{t}, \ddot{t}) = 1$, select two η-bit prime numbers p and q and publish evk $:= N = p \cdot q$ as evaluation key. Then, select random pair $(d, g) \in \mathbb{Z}_p \times \mathbb{Z}_q$, and let $D = dq$ and $G = gp$. Eventually, set the secret key as sk $:= (p, q, D, G)$ and equalizer as Eq $=$ DLSC.Enc$(1, \mathsf{sk})$. Two requirements must be satisfied: $2^{\ell(\rho+\tau)} < p$ and $2^{\ell(\rho+\tau)} < q$. Eventually, the algorithm define public parameters as pp $:= \{\lambda, \rho, \tau, \ell, t, \dot{t}, \ddot{t}\}$ and publish them with evk as inputs to the next algorithms.
- DLSC.Enc(m, sk): For $\dot{m} = [m]_{\dot{t}}$ and $\ddot{m} = [m]_{\ddot{t}}$, select two η-bit random integers $\dot{e}$ and $\ddot{e}$ and set the plaintexts as $\dot{\mu} = \dot{t}.\dot{e} + \dot{m}$ and $\ddot{\mu} = \ddot{t}.\ddot{e} + \ddot{m}$. Return

$$\mathsf{ct} = [G.\dot{\mu} + D.\ddot{\mu}]_N = [gp.\dot{\mu} + dq.\ddot{\mu}]_N$$

  as the ciphertext. In addition, the label value l, which is 1 for fresh ciphertexts, should be attached to the ciphertext.
- DLSC.Eval$(\mathsf{ct}_1, l_1, \mathsf{ct}_2, l_2, \cdots, \mathsf{ct}_k, l_k, N, f)$: Consists of two sub-algorithms as follow:
  - DLSC.Add$(\mathsf{ct}_1, l_1, \mathsf{ct}_2, l_2)$: Update the two ciphertexts using the Equalizer algorithm to equalize the label of them. Then return $\mathsf{ct}_+ = [\mathsf{ct}_1 + \mathsf{ct}_2]_N$ with the updated label.
  - DLSC.Mult$(\mathsf{ct}_1, l_1, \mathsf{ct}_2, l_2)$: Compute $\mathsf{ct}_\times = [\mathsf{ct}_1.\mathsf{ct}_2]_N$, and update label using $l_\times = l_1 + l_2$.

- DLSC.Dec(ct, sk): Compute $\dot{\mu} = [G^{-1} \cdot ct]_q$ and $\ddot{\mu} = [D^{-1} \cdot ct]_p$, then return $[\dot{\mu}]_{\dot{t}} = \dot{m}$ and $[\ddot{\mu}]_{\ddot{t}} = \ddot{m}$. The message m can be recovered by CRT as $m = m_1 \dot{t} [\dot{t}^{-1}]_{\ddot{t}} + m_2 \ddot{t} [\ddot{t}^{-1}]_{\dot{t}}$.

Remark 15. The scalar multiplication can be computed straightforward as $[c.ct]_N$ without changing the label value. For the scalar addition of the constant c with the ciphertext ct with label l, the scheme treats the constant like a ciphertext with label 0. So it computes $[c \cdot Eq^l]_N$ using equalizer, and then returns $[ct + c \cdot Eq^l]_N$.

Remark 16. Alternatively, plaintexts can be computed through $\dot{\mu} = \frac{[ct.g^{-1}p^{q-1}]_N}{p}$ and $\ddot{\mu} = \frac{[ct.d^{-1}q^{p-1}]_N}{q}$ for decryption.

Remark 17. Clearly, if $D = \hat{q}$ and $G = \hat{p}$, the DLSC scheme is simplified to the DSM scheme. So the DSM scheme is a special case of the DLSC.

Remark 18. Values $\dot{m}$ and $\ddot{m}$ could be two separate messages instead of parts of a single message m. In this situation, the two separate messages are effectively batched together.

Correctness. The correctness of the decryption methods can be verified similar to the correctness of the LSC scheme in Sect. 3.2.

$$[G^{-1} \cdot ct]_q = [G^{-1}[gp\dot{\mu} + dq\ddot{\mu}]_N]_q = [G^{-1}(G\dot{\mu} + dq\ddot{\mu})]_q$$
$$= [G^{-1}G\dot{\mu}]_q = [\dot{\mu}]_q = \dot{\mu}$$

The correctness holds with considering the same explanation about the correctness of SM scheme. The decryption of the second part, $\ddot{\mu}$, also can be proved similarly.

The correctness of the alternative decryption algorithm can be validated as follows.

$$\frac{[ct.f^{-1}p^{q-1}]_N}{p} = \frac{[(fp.\dot{\mu} + dq.\ddot{\mu}).f^{-1}p^{q-1}]_N}{p} = \frac{[p^q.\dot{\mu} + dq.f^{-1}p^{q-1}\ddot{\mu}]_N}{p}$$
$$= \frac{[p.\dot{\mu}]_N}{p} = \frac{p.[\dot{\mu}]_q}{p} = [\dot{\mu}]_q = \dot{\mu}$$

The equations are valid because of Lemma 3 and Lemma 1, and the same explanation about the correctness of the SM scheme. The decryption of the second part, $\ddot{\mu}$, also can be proved similarly.

Homomorphism. The addition homomorphism property can be proved as follows:

$$\text{ct}_+ = [\text{ct}_1 + \text{ct}_2]_N = [(G\dot{\mu}_1 + D\ddot{\mu}_1) + (G\dot{\mu}_2 + D\ddot{\mu}_2)]_N = [G(\dot{\mu}_1 + \dot{\mu}_2) + D(\ddot{\mu}_1 + \ddot{\mu}_2)]_N$$
$$= [G(\dot{te}_1 + \dot{m}_1 + \dot{te}_2 + \dot{m}_2) + D(\ddot{te}_1 + \ddot{m}_1 + \ddot{te}_2 + \ddot{m}_2)]_N$$
$$= [G(\dot{te}_+ + \dot{m}_+) + D(\ddot{te}_+ + \ddot{m}_+)]_N$$

The multiplication homomorphism property can be proved as follows:

$$\text{ct}_\times = [\text{ct}_1.\text{ct}_2]_N = [(G.\dot{\mu}_1 + D.\ddot{\mu}_1).(G.\dot{\mu}_2 + D.\ddot{\mu}_2)]_N$$
$$= [g^2 p^2.(\dot{\mu}_1.\dot{\mu}_2) + gdpq(\dot{\mu}_1\ddot{\mu}_2 + \dot{\mu}_2.\ddot{\mu}_1) + d^2 q^2.(\ddot{\mu}_1.\ddot{\mu}_2)]_N$$
$$= [g^2 p^2.(\dot{\mu}_1.\dot{\mu}_2) + d^2 q^2.(\ddot{\mu}_1.\ddot{\mu}_2)]_N$$
$$= [G^2.(\dot{te}_\times + \dot{m}_\times) + D^2.(\ddot{te}_\times + \ddot{m}_\times)]_N$$

Since G and D have the power of two, the resulting ciphertext is labeled 2.

A similar discussion can prove the correctness of scalar addition and multiplication homomorphism.

Remark 19. The proposed doubling technique can be extended to increase the message size by more than double, k. In the k-sized technique, the evaluation key should be updated to $N = p_1 \cdot p_2 \cdots p_k$, where each p_i is a large prime number. The ciphertext would be defined as $\text{ct} = \mu_1 \frac{N}{p_1} + \mu_2 \frac{N}{p_2} + \cdots + \mu_k \frac{N}{p_k}$, and Bézout's coefficients are then used to decrypt the ciphertext into k parts.

4.3   Removing Label

Recall that the labels in the LSC and DLSC schemes are necessary when using the addition algorithm to equalize the labels of two ciphertexts. However, these labels introduce additional communication and computation costs, so that removing the labels can improve performance. In other words, the propose of this section is providing a scrambled ciphertext without using labeling.

Initially, fresh ciphertexts have a label of one, which increases after each multiplication. Therefore, to eliminate the label attached to a ciphertext, the label must be reduced to one after each multiplication. So, a *reducer* is defined as an extra part of evaluation key as $\text{Re} = [p \cdot r + D^{-1}]_N$ for LSC scheme, and $\text{Re} = [g^{-1} \cdot p^{q-2} + d^{-1} \cdot q^{p-2}]_N$ for DLSC scheme. Therefore, multiplication algorithm should be changed to $\text{ct}_\times = [\text{ct}_1.\text{ct}_2.\text{Re}]_N$. With this changes, the addition algorithm does not need equalizer, and the labels of ciphertexts could be removed.

However, for a ciphertext ct of the LSC/DLSC scheme, the eavesdropper can compute $\text{ct}' = [\text{ct} \cdot \text{Re}]_N$ to convert ct into a ciphertext of the SM/DSM scheme, ct', sacrificing the security advantages of the LSC and DLSC schemes. In addition, this approach relies on circular security which is not ideal from security perspectives. As a result, the proposed idea of removing labels is not realistic, but it is discussed to provide insights for future research.

5   Performance Evaluation and Comparison

This section first evaluates the performance of the LSC scheme, as the main contribution, and then compares it with the most well-known homomorphic schemes; BGV, BFV, TFHE, and CKKS. Implementations are executed on a MacBook Pro with an Apple M1 Pro chip, featuring 10 cores (8 performance and 2 efficiency) and 16 GB of memory, and the times, reported in the tables, represent the average of 5–10 runs.

5.1   Implementation Results

We have implemented the SM and LSC schemes in Rust[12]. The current implementation operates in single-threaded mode, but performance improvements are possible with a multi-threaded optimization. Table 1 presents the timing results for four algorithms: KeyGen, Enc, Eval (Add and Mult), and Dec, with varying values of λ set to 80, 92, 112, and 128, where η is the size of secret key (2η is the size of N). As expected, higher security levels associated with larger λ values result in an increase in the size of N, leading to longer execution times for all algorithms.

Table 1. Timing results for four algorithm; ($t = 256$)

λ	η	KeyGen (s)	Enc (μs)	Add (μs)	Mult (μs)	Dec (μs)
80	512	0.21	4.0	0.22	2.54	4.1
92	768	0.43	4.9	0.34	3.5	6.8
112	1024	1.0	7.2	0.4	4.5	11.5
128	1536	3.39	8.2	0.45	8.7	14.5

Table 2 presents the timing results for four algorithms as the multiplicative depth (ℓ) varies. For simplicity, the values of t are chosen as powers of 2 ($t = 2^\tau$); however, the scheme also supports other values. Row 2 indicates that for $\tau = 1$, the scheme can support up to 11 multiplications with an N size of 3072 bits. If the evaluation function requires 50 or 100 multiplications for the same value of τ, the size of N would need to increase accordingly to 13102, and the timing values increase as reported in row 3. If the value of τ increases (row 8), while keeping N constant at 3072 bits, the value of ℓ decreases. Meanwhile, increasing the size of N allows for a greater number of multiplications. For computing ℓ, we used the relationship $\ell = \lfloor \frac{\eta-1}{\rho+\tau} \rfloor$, while $\rho = \lambda + 2$.

---

[12] The implementation is available at https://github.com/Lhecg/LHECG-Labeled.

Table 2. Timing results for four algorithm; ($\lambda = 128$)

τ	ℓ	η	KeyGen (s)	Enc (μs)	Add (μs)	Mult (μs)	Dec (μs)
1	11	1536	3.39	8.2	0.45	8.7	14.5
1	50	6551	537.8	28.2	1.3	185.6	132.2
1	100	13101	12824	40.4	2.27	405.8	221
8	11	1536	4.71	9.2	0.57	8.8	6.2
8	50	6901	978.28	40.1	1.8	229.7	159.2
8	100	13801	13729	62.2	2.3	627.4	422.3
16	10	1536	1.18	19.4	1.8	19.4	15.4
16	50	7301	1924	17.8	1.85	298.3	67.4
16	100	14601	17870	93.2	2.9	733.8	615.4
32	9	1536	2.38	20.4	3.04	21.54	19.4
32	50	8101	1712	25.9	1.04	152.7	111
32	100	16201	18207	102.9	5.3	1112.3	738.1

5.2   Comparison

This section compares the implemented LSC scheme with some of the most well-known schemes, including BGVrns, BFVrns, CKKSrns[13], and TFHE[14], in security of 128 bits, and for $\ell = 10^{15}$. Although these schemes are fully homomorphic, while LSC is leveled, the comparison is limited to leveled evaluations.

Table 3 presents the implementation times. Since the equalizer is a multiplication operation, if addition requires equalization using pre-computed values of $Eq^{(i)}$, the time required for addition will increase by approximately one additional multiplication. Consequently, such an addition will take nearly as long as a multiplication. Given this, the addition and decryption times for the LSC scheme are comparable to the best times among the other four schemes. However, the LSC scheme performs multiplication approximately 1,000 times faster than the established schemes. Additionally, the Encryption algorithm of the LSC scheme is 100 times faster than that of the other four schemes.[16] Although the KeyGen algorithm of the LSC scheme is longer than that of the other four schemes, this is acceptable since it only needs to be run once.

---

[13] For BGV, BFV and CKKS, we used the implementation at https://github.com/openfheorg/openfhe-development.

[14] For TFHE, we used the implementation at https://github.com/zama-ai/tfhe-rs.

[15] TFHE can support each level since it runs programmable bootstrapping after each multiplication.

[16] It is important to note that our scheme is in its early stages of development, whereas the other schemes have undergone years of refinement. Therefore, we anticipate that further optimizations will make our scheme even more efficient over time.

Table 3. Performance results for different schemes; ($\lambda = 128$)

Scheme	τ	ℓ	KeyGen (ms)	Enc (μs)	Add (μs)	Mult (μs)	Dec (μs)
BGVrns	16	10	2.434	1686	32	19771	226
BFrns	16	10	1.906	2405	23	15783	324
CKKSrns	16	10	2.627	1697	43	23368	107
TFHE	16	NA	546.5	285.72	107111	382582	6.06
LSC	16	10	1180	19.4	1.8	19.4	15.4

While the compared schemes offer quantum security, our schemes provide significant performance advantages in non-quantum settings. In many practical applications where quantum resistance is not yet a critical requirement, our schemes deliver a highly efficient and favorable solution.

6   Conclusion

We have proposed the first leveled homomorphic encryption schemes over integers within composite groups. Specifically, we designed a Straw-Man scheme that supports ℓ multiplications, and then to make the traffic of ciphertexts indistinguishable as encrypted, the Labeled Scrambled Ciphertext scheme is designed using the labeling technique. Additionally, we introduced a modified version of the Rothblum transformation to create a public key version of the symmetric schemes. Furthermore, we presented double-sized message schemes to enhance efficiency. Implementation results demonstrate that our schemes significantly outperform well-known homomorphic schemes, particularly in multiplication. For future work, we aim to explore the use of SIMD to further improve performance and investigate the potential of bootstrapping to transform these leveled homomorphic encryption schemes into fully homomorphic encryption schemes.

Acknowledgments. The firs author was supported by the Spanish Ministry of Science and Innovation through the PID2021-125962OB-C31 "SECURING" project. Additional funding was provided by the ARTEMISA International Chair of Cybersecurity (C057/23) and the DANGER Strategic Project of Cybersecurity (C062/23), both funded by the Spanish National Institute of Cybersecurity through the European Union—NextGenerationEU and the Recovery, Transformation, and Resilience Plan. We also thank Jeongeun Park from NTNU and Hilder Vitor Lima Pereira from Unicamp for their valuable comments.

Appendix 1: Security Assumptions

This appendix defines two security assumptions and discusses their hardness.

Definition 3 (Double Modulus Problem). *Let $N = pq$, where p and q are two η-bit prime numbers such that factoring of N is λ-bit secure. The computation of $[[r]_p]_t$ for any integer $r \in \mathbb{Z}_N$ and a known integer $t \ll p, q$ is referred to as the Double Modulus (DM) Problem.*

Theorem 1. *Let $N = pq$ where p and q are two η-bit prime numbers such that factoring of N is λ-bit secure. For any attacker $\mathcal{A}$ that can solve the Double Modulus Problem (Definition 3), there exists an attacker $\mathcal{B}$ that can factor N.*

Proof. To factor N, the attacker $\mathcal{B}$ can run Algorithm 1 as follow.

Algorithm 1: Factoring with DM attacker

Input: $\mathcal{A}$, and $N \in [2^{2\eta-1}, 2^{2\eta})$
Output: $p \in [2^{\eta-1}, 2^{\eta})$
1 Select $I' \in \mathbb{Z}_N$;
2 Query I' from $\mathcal{A}$; $(z' = [[I']_p]_t \leftarrow \mathcal{A}(I'))$
3 Set $I = I' - z'$, and $F = I + 2^\eta$;
4 **if** $F > N$ **then**
5 $\quad$ ⌊ go to step 1
6 $k = 2^8$;
7 **while** $k < F - I$ **do**
8 $\quad$ $r = [\lfloor \frac{I+F}{2} \rfloor]$;
9 $\quad$ $z = [[r]_p]_t \leftarrow \mathcal{A}(r)$
10 $\quad$ **if** $z = [r - I]_t$ **then**
11 $\quad\quad$ ⌊ $I = r - z$
12 $\quad$ **else**
13 $\quad\quad$ ⌊ $F = r$
14 $p = 1$
15 **while** $p = 1$ **do**
16 $\quad$ **for** $i = I : F$ **do**
17 $\quad\quad$ ⌊ $p = \gcd(i, N)$
18 **return** p;

Considering I and F defined in line 3, since $F - I = 2^\eta$, and $p < 2^\eta$, so there exists an integer T such that $I < T < F$ and $[T]_p = 0$. If $I' = \alpha \cdot p + te + z'$, then $I = \alpha \cdot p + te$, and the target point that the algorithm aims to find can be defined as $T = (\alpha + 1)p$, and then extract $p = \gcd(T, N)$.

Even though the probability of line 4's condition being true is negligible, we consider it to maintain accuracy. This is because if $F > N$, the target point T becomes equivalent to N, which is not helpful for factoring. Additionally, in each step of the proposed algorithm, I is set such that $[[I]_p]_t = 0$.

While $I = \alpha p + te$, and r defines as line (8), if $p > r$, the value of r definitely equals $\alpha p + te' + z$, and then $[r - I]_t = [t(e' - e) + z]_t = z$. This value would be equal to the value of z received from attacker $\mathcal{A}$, line (9). Then I should be substituted with the new value $r - z$; otherwise, $p < r$ and the value of r definitely equals $(\alpha + 1)p + te' + z$, and then $[r - I]_t = [p + t(e' - e) + z]_t \neq z$, so the value of F should be substitute by r (line 13). During this process, the target point would be between I and F and always $[[I]_p]_t = 0$. By repeating the process, the attacker $\mathcal{B}$ reaches to a searchable space, such as $k = 2^8$, which includes the target point T. Eventually, the attacker $\mathcal{B}$ can search to find p through computing $gcd(T, N)$.

The complexity of Algorithm 1 is $O(\log N)$, indicating its efficiency in factoring N. □

Remark 20. Algorithm 1 is effective when the attacker $\mathcal{A}$ can solve the DM problem with a probability of 1. However, if the attacker $\mathcal{A}$ solves the DM problem with a probability of $\frac{1}{t} + \epsilon$, where ϵ is non-negligible, attacker $\mathcal{B}$ can still factorize N with high probability. To do this, for each specific r, attacker $\mathcal{B}$ queries $(2j+1)$ times, where $r_j = r + i$ and $-j \leq i \leq j$, where j is much smaller than 2^λ. Then, the attacker $\mathcal{A}$ returns $z_i = [[r_i]_p]_t$ and attacker $\mathcal{B}$ computes the possible values of $z = [[r]_p]_t$ by calculating $z^{(i)} = z_i - i$. The final answer is determined by selecting the most frequent value from the set $\vec{Z} = \langle z^{(-j)}, \ldots, z^{(-1)}, z^{(0)}, z^{(1)}, \ldots, z^{(j)} \rangle$.

Definition 4 (Decisional Modified Double Modulus Problem). *Let $N = pq$, where p and q are two η-bit prime numbers such that factoring of N is λ-bit secure. Given a random vector $\vec{x} = \langle x_0, \ldots, x_{k-1} \rangle \in \mathbb{Z}_N^k$ such that $[[x_i]_p]_t = 0$ for $0 \leq i \leq k - 1$, and a challenge pair $(x, z) \in \mathbb{Z}_N \times \mathbb{Z}_t$, where $|x - x_i| \gg 2^\eta$, deciding about $z = [[x]_p]_t$ is defined as the Decisional Modified Double Modulus (DMDM) Problem[17].*

Unlike the previous discussion, which proved the hardness of the DM problem, the following explanation offers a discussion aimed at providing insights into the hardness of the DMDM problem.

The DMDM problem is similar to the AGCD (and noise-free AGCD) problem. Below, a comparison between these two problems is discussed. In the DMDM problem, the x_is are 2η-bit integers that can be expressed as $x_i = pr_i + te$, where p and r_i are η-bit integers, and noise e is a ρ-bit integer in the level 1 version. In contrast, for the AGCD problem, $x_i = pr_i + e$ is typically a λ^5-bit integer, where p is about λ^2-bit, r_i is about λ^3-bit, and noise e is about λ-bit[18]. For both DMDM and AGCD problems, it is evident that the larger the noise compared to the given number x_i, the more difficult it becomes to find p. To have a better comparison between the two problems, the ratio of the noise size to the given number size should be defined. Specifically, this ratio is equal to the ratio of the noise size to the size of x_0 in AGCD ($\frac{\rho}{|x_0|}$), and the ratio of the noise size to the size of N in DMDM problem ($\frac{\rho}{|N|}$), where $\frac{\rho}{|N|} > \frac{\rho}{|x_0|}$. For instance, for $\lambda = 128$, in the AGCD problem, $\frac{\rho}{|x_0|} = \frac{\rho}{\lambda^5} \approx \frac{1}{\lambda^4} = 2^{-28}$, whereas in DMSM problem, $\frac{\rho}{|N|} = \frac{\rho}{2\eta} \approx \frac{128}{3072} = \frac{1}{24} \approx 2^{-5}$. It is evident that as this ratio increases, the security of the assumption strengthens, leading to the conclusion that the proposed attacks on the AGCD and noise-free AGCD problems are less likely to succeed against the DMDM problem.

---

[17] The level 1 version of the DMDM problem is defined as $t \cdot 2^\rho \leq [x_i]_p < t^2 \cdot 2^{2\rho}$, where $\rho > \lambda$, and the level l version is defined as $t^l \cdot 2^{l\rho} \leq [x_i]_p < t^{l+1} \cdot 2^{(l+1)\rho}$.

[18] Note that in noise-free AGCD, x_0 is defined as $x_0 = pr_0$. For a better understanding of the definition of x_0, refer to [vDGHV10, CP19].

Remark 21. The DMDM problem for (x, z) can be solved if there exist x_i such that $\delta = |x - x_i| < 2^\lambda$. Specifically, x and x_i can be rewritten as $\alpha'p + te + z'$ and $\alpha p + te_1$ respectively, and then $|x - x_i| = |(\alpha' - \alpha)p + t(e - e_1) + z'|$. Since $|x - x_i| < 2^\lambda$, with hight probability $\alpha' = \alpha$. So the value of z' can be computed as $z' = [x - x_i]_t$, then it can be compare with the given z. If $z = z'$, it can be concluded that $z = [[x]_p]_t$; otherwise, z is not a valid value for $[[x]_p]_t$.

Lemma 4. *Let $N = pq$, where p and q are prime numbers. Finding $x \in \mathbb{Z}_p$, or $y \in \mathbb{Z}_p$, for any integer $c \in \mathbb{Z}_N$ such that $qx + py = c$ is equivalent to factoring N.*

Proof. Let an algorithm $\mathcal{A}$ find x for any equation $qx + py = c$, where $c \in \mathbb{Z}_N$. Then, assume that $x = a$ is a solution for $qx + py = c$ and $x' = a'$ for $qx' + py' = c'$. This leads to the equations $[q + pya^{-1}]_N = [ca^{-1}]_N$ and $[q + py(a')^{-1}]_N = [c'(a')^{-1}]_N$. Therefore, $[q + pya^{-1} - (q + py(a')^{-1})]_N = [ca^{-1} - c'(a')^{-1}]_N$, which simplifies to $[pya^{-1} - py(a')^{-1}]_N = [ca^{-1} - c'(a')^{-1}]_N$. Consequently, it can be concluded that $\gcd(N, [ca^{-1} - c'(a')^{-1}]_N) = p$.[19]   □

Appendix 2: Security Proofs for the Schemes

The following discusses the security proofs for the proposed SM and LSC schemes.

Theorem 2. *If an attacker $\mathcal{A}$ can win the Ind-CPA game for the proposed SM scheme, there is an attacker $\mathcal{B}$ who can solve the DMDM problem.*

Proof. Let $\mathcal{A}$ be an attacker that can break the proposed SM scheme with a non-negligible advantage ϵ. So, an attacker $\mathcal{B}$ can be simulated that solves DMDM problem[20]. Suppose that the challenger generates the inputs of DMDM problem as $\{N, \vec{x}\}$ where $\vec{x} = \langle x_0, x_1, ..., x_{k-1} \rangle$, and $[[x_i]_p]_t = 0$. The challenger flips a fair coin ν and sets $z^\star = [[x^\star]_p]_t$ if $\nu = 1$; otherwise, $z^\star \in \mathbb{Z}_t$ such that $z^\star \neq [[x^\star]_p]_t$. The attacker $\mathcal{B}$ aims to distinguish if $z^\star = [[x^\star]_p]_t$ or not and return his guess ν', with non-negligible advantage. The security game works as follows.

- *Initialization.* The attacker $\mathcal{B}$ receives $\{N, \vec{x}\}$, and challenge pair $(x^\star, z^\star)$ as a DMDM problem inputs.
- *Setup.* The attacker $\mathcal{B}$ sets N as an evaluation key and sends it to the attacker $\mathcal{A}$.

---

[19] Note that the proof can be extended such that the algorithm $\mathcal{A}$ computes only $x = a$ for $qx + py = c$ without computing $x' = a'$ for $qx' + py' = c'$.

[20] To be more precise, we should consider DMDM with level 1 version to guarantee evaluation and computation over encrypted data.

- *Query 1.* The attacker $\mathcal{A}$ queries for encryption of the message m. For any received query m, the attacker $\mathcal{B}$ simulates the encryption algorithm through $\text{ct} = [x_i + m]_N$, where x_i is a random element of the vector $\vec{x}$, and forwards the ciphertext ct to the attacker $\mathcal{A}$[21].
- *Challenge.* The attacker $\mathcal{A}$ selects two messages (m_0, m_1) and sends them to the attacker $\mathcal{B}$. Then attacker $\mathcal{B}$ selects a random bit $b \in \{0, 1\}$ and a ρ-bit random noise e, and computes $\text{ct}^* = x^* - z^* + m_b$ and sends it to the attacker $\mathcal{A}$.
- *Query 2.* The query 1 phase is repeated.
- *Guess.* The attacker $\mathcal{A}$ forwards its guess about b as b' to the attacker $\mathcal{B}$. If $b' = b$, the attacker $\mathcal{B}$ outputs $\nu' = 1$, indicating that $z^* = [[x^*]_p]_t$ in the given DMDM problem instance; otherwise, it outputs $\nu' = 0$ indicating that z^* is a random.

Note that if $z^* = [[x^*]_p]_t$, then ct^* is the encryption of m_b. Because, by running decryption algorithm, m_b can be achieved (i.e. $[[\text{ct}]_p]_t = m_b$). In this case, attacker $\mathcal{A}$ can distinguish with probability $\frac{1}{2} + \epsilon$. On the other hand, if $z^* = [[x^*]_p]_t$ does not hold, $\text{ct} = x^* - z^* + m_b$ seems as a random number and the probability of success for the attacker $\mathcal{A}$ is equal to $\frac{1}{2}$. The overall advantage of the attacker $\mathcal{B}$ for DMDM problem is:

$$\mathbf{Adv}_{\mathcal{B}}^{DMDM} = \frac{1}{2}Pr[\nu' = \nu | \nu = 0] + \frac{1}{2}Pr[\nu' = \nu | \nu = 1] - \frac{1}{2}$$
$$= \frac{1}{2} \cdot (\frac{1}{2} + \epsilon) + \frac{1}{2} \cdot \frac{1}{2} - \frac{1}{2} = \frac{\epsilon}{2} \qquad (6)$$

In Eq. 6, the value of $\frac{\epsilon}{2}$ is non-negligible, so the probability of solving the DMDM problem is non-negligibly greater than $\frac{1}{2}$. □

Remark 22. In the SM scheme, if the value of the evaluation key, N, is not published, the risk of computing the secret key using a (quantum) factoring algorithm will be eliminated. However, under such circumstances, the ciphertext size is not constant and tends to increase with each subsequent evaluation.

Remark 23. According to Remark 21, if an attacker has two ciphertexts, ct and ct', such that $|\text{ct} - \text{ct}'| \ll 2^\eta$, and one of the associated messages, m or m', they may attempt to retrieve the other message. Suppose $\text{ct} = pr + te + m$ and $\text{ct}' = pr' + te' + m'$. Given that $|p(r - r') + t(e - e') + (m - m')| \ll 2^\eta$, it follows that $r = r'$ with high probability. The attacker can then compute $m - m'$ via $[t(e - e') + (m - m')]_t$. If the attacker knows one of m or m', they can compute the other message. This attack becomes practical if $[r]_q = [r']_q$ holds. However, the probability of this condition being satisfied is approximately $\frac{1}{q}$, which is considered negligible.

---

[21] The value of k is big enough, but if the number of encryption query is greater than k, attacker $\mathcal{B}$ can select a ρ-bit random noise e and a random set $S \subset \{0, 1, ..., k\}$, and then compute $\text{ct} = \sum_{i \in S} x_i + m + te$.

Theorem 3. *The security of the proposed LSC scheme is at least as strong as the security of SM scheme. Therefore, if an attacker $\mathcal{D}$ can break the LSC scheme, then there exists an attacker $\mathcal{A}$ who can break the SM scheme.*

Proof. Let $\mathcal{D}$ be an attacker that can break the LSC scheme. We simulate an attacker $\mathcal{A}$ that can break the SM scheme. The SM scheme oracle sends the public parameters and evaluation key to the attacker $\mathcal{A}$. The attacker $\mathcal{A}$ request the encryption of 1 from the SM oracle and receive $E_1 = SM.Enc(1) = pr + te + 1$. The attacker $\mathcal{A}$ selects an η-bit integer D as a part of secret key in the LSC scheme and computes $D \cdot E_1 = pr' + D(te + 1)$ and defines it as equalizer Eq. The attacker $\mathcal{A}$ forwards the public parameters, evaluation key, and the equalizer Eq to the attacker $\mathcal{D}$. Then the attacker $\mathcal{D}$ queries the encryption of message m. The attacker $\mathcal{A}$ forwards the query to SM oracle and receives ciphertext $\mathsf{ct_{SM}}$. The attacker $\mathcal{A}$ forwards $\mathsf{ct_{LSC}} = D \cdot \mathsf{ct_{SM}}$ to the attacker $\mathcal{D}$. Suppose $\mathsf{ct_{SM}^\star} = pr^\star + te^\star + m^\star$ is a challenge ciphertext of the SM scheme. Attacker $\mathcal{A}$ computes $[D \cdot \mathsf{ct_{SM}^\star}]_N$ with label 1 and sends it to the attacker $\mathcal{D}$. In the viewpoint of attacker $\mathcal{D}$, this value equals to $\mathsf{ct_{LSC}^\star}$ as follows:

$$[D \cdot \mathsf{ct_{SM}^\star}]_N = [D(pr^\star + te^\star + m^\star)]_N$$
$$= [pr + D(te + m^\star)]_N = \mathsf{ct_{LSC}^\star}$$

Since $\mathsf{ct_{LSC}^\star}$ is the encryption of the challenge message $m^\star$ under the LSC scheme, the attacker $\mathcal{D}$ can retrieve $m^\star$ and sends it to attacker $\mathcal{A}$, which means that the attacker $\mathcal{A}$ breaks the SM scheme.   □

References

[ASP14] Alperin-Sheriff, J., Peikert, C.: Faster bootstrapping with polynomial error. In: Garay, J.A., Gennaro, R. (eds.) CRYPTO 2014. LNCS, vol. 8616, pp. 297–314. Springer, Heidelberg (2014). https://doi.org/10.1007/978-3-662-44371-2_17

[BBL17] Benarroch, D., Brakerski, Z., Lepoint, T.: FHE over the integers: decomposed and batched in the post-quantum regime. In: Fehr, S. (ed.) PKC 2017. LNCS, vol. 10175, pp. 271–301. Springer, Heidelberg (2017). https://doi.org/10.1007/978-3-662-54388-7_10

[BGN05] Boneh, D., Goh, E.-J., Nissim, K.: Evaluating 2-DNF formulas on ciphertexts. In: Kilian, J. (ed.) TCC 2005. LNCS, vol. 3378, pp. 325–341. Springer, Heidelberg (2005). https://doi.org/10.1007/978-3-540-30576-7_18

[BGV12] Brakerski, Z., Gentry, C., Vaikuntanathan, V.: (Leveled) fully homomorphic encryption without bootstrapping. In: Proceedings of the 3rd Innovations in Theoretical Computer Science Conference, ITCS 2012, pp. 309–325. Association for Computing Machinery, New York (2012)

[BLLN13] Bos, J.W., Lauter, K., Loftus, J., Naehrig, M.: Improved security for a ring-based fully homomorphic encryption scheme. In: Stam, M. (ed.) IMACC 2013. LNCS, vol. 8308, pp. 45–64. Springer, Heidelberg (2013). https://doi.org/10.1007/978-3-642-45239-0_4

[Bra12]   Brakerski, Z.: Fully homomorphic encryption without modulus switching from classical GapSVP. In: Annual International Cryptology Conference (2012)

[BV14]   Brakerski, Z., Vaikuntanathan, V.: Efficient fully homomorphic encryption from (standard) LWE. SIAM J. Comput. **43**(2), 831–871 (2014)

[CGGI17] Chillotti, I., Gama, N., Georgieva, M., Izabachène, M.: Faster packed homomorphic operations and efficient circuit bootstrapping for TFHE. In: International Conference on the Theory and Application of Cryptology and Information Security (2017)

[CJP20]   Chillotti, I., Joye, M., Paillier, P.: New challenges for fully homomorphic encryption. In: Privacy-Preserving Machine Learning (PPML-PriML 2020) NeurIPS 2020 Workshop (2020)

[CNT12]   Coron, J.-S., Naccache, D., Tibouchi, M.: Public key compression and modulus switching for fully homomorphic encryption over the integers. In: Pointcheval, D., Johansson, T. (eds.) EUROCRYPT 2012. LNCS, vol. 7237, pp. 446–464. Springer, Heidelberg (2012). https://doi.org/10.1007/978-3-642-29011-4_27

[CP19]   Coron, J.-S., Pereira, H.: On Kilian's randomization of multilinear map encodings. In: Galbraith, S.D., Moriai, S. (eds.) ASIACRYPT 2019. LNCS, vol. 11922, pp. 325–355. Springer, Cham (2019). https://doi.org/10.1007/978-3-030-34621-8_12

[FV12]   Fan, J., Vercauteren, F.: Somewhat practical fully homomorphic encryption. IACR Cryptology ePrint Archive 2012:144 (2012)

[Gen09]   Gentry, C.: Fully homomorphic encryption using ideal lattices. In: Proceedings of the Forty-First Annual ACM Symposium on Theory of Computing, STOC 2009, pp. 169–178. Association for Computing Machinery, New York (2009)

[GGH13]   Garg, S., Gentry, C., Halevi, S.: Candidate multilinear maps from ideal lattices. In: Johansson, T., Nguyen, P.Q. (eds.) EUROCRYPT 2013. LNCS, vol. 7881, pp. 1–17. Springer, Heidelberg (2013). https://doi.org/10.1007/978-3-642-38348-9_1

[GIKV23] Geelen, R., Iliashenko, I., Kang, J., Vercauteren, F.: On polynomial functions modulo p^e and faster bootstrapping for homomorphic encryption. In: Annual International Conference on the Theory and Applications of Cryptographic Techniques, pp. 257–286. Springer, Cham (2023)

[GM82]   Goldwasser, S., Micali, S.: Probabilistic encryption & how to play mental poker keeping secret all partial information. In: Proceedings of the Fourteenth Annual ACM Symposium on Theory of Computing, STOC 1982, pp. 365–377. Association for Computing Machinery, New York (1982)

[GSW13]   Gentry, C., Sahai, A., Waters, B.: Homomorphic encryption from learning with errors: conceptually-simpler, asymptotically-faster, attribute-based. IACR Cryptology ePrint Archive 2013:340 (2013)

[JMPP24] Jadoul, R., Mertens, A., Park, J., Pereira, H.V.L.: NTRU-based FHE for larger key and message space. In: Australasian Conference on Information Security and Privacy, pp. 141–160. Springer, Cham (2024)

[Klu22]   Kluczniak, K.: NTRU-V-UM: secure fully homomorphic encryption from NTRU with small modulus. In: Proceedings of the 2022 ACM SIGSAC Conference on Computer and Communications Security, pp. 1783–1797 (2022)

[LATV12a] López-Alt, A., Tromer, E., Vaikuntanathan, V.: On-the-fly multiparty computation on the cloud via multikey fully homomorphic encryption. In: Proceedings of the Forty-Fourth Annual ACM Symposium on Theory of Computing, pp. 1219–1234 (2012)

[MHWW24] Ma, S., Huang, T., Wang, A., Wang, X.: Accelerating BGV bootstrapping for large p using null polynomials over $\mathbb{Z}_{p^e}$. In: Annual International Conference on the Theory and Applications of Cryptographic Techniques, pp. 403–432. Springer, Cham (2024)

[MNR24] Mertens, A., Nicolas, G., Rovira, S.: Convolution-friendly image compression in FHE. Cryptology ePrint Archive, Paper 2024/559 (2024). https://eprint.iacr.org/2024/559

[Pai99] Paillier, P.: Public-key cryptosystems based on composite degree residuosity classes. In: International Conference on the Theory and Applications of Cryptographic Techniques, pp. 223–238. Springer, Cham (1999)

[Per20] Pereira, H.: Efficient AGCD-based homomorphic encryption for matrix and vector arithmetic. In: Conti, M., Zhou, J., Casalicchio, E., Spognardi, A. (eds.) ACNS 2020. LNCS, vol. 12146, pp. 110–129. Springer, Cham (2020). https://doi.org/10.1007/978-3-030-57808-4_6

[Per21] Pereira, H.: Bootstrapping fully homomorphic encryption over the integers in less than one second. In: Garay, J.A. (ed.) PKC 2021. LNCS, vol. 12710, pp. 331–359. Springer, Cham (2021). https://doi.org/10.1007/978-3-030-75245-3_13

[Reg09] Regev, O.: On lattices, learning with errors, random linear codes, and cryptography. J. ACM (JACM) **56**(6), 1–40 (2009)

[Rot11] Rothblum, R.: Homomorphic encryption: from private-key to public-key. In: Ishai, Y. (ed.) TCC 2011. LNCS, vol. 6597, pp. 219–234. Springer, Heidelberg (2011). https://doi.org/10.1007/978-3-642-19571-6_14

[RSA78] Rivest, R.L., Shamir, A., Adleman, L.: A method for obtaining digital signatures and public-key cryptosystems. Commun. ACM **21**(2), 120–126 (1978)

[SS10] Stehlé, D., Steinfeld, R.: Faster fully homomorphic encryption. In: Abe, M. (ed.) ASIACRYPT 2010. LNCS, vol. 6477, pp. 377–394. Springer, Heidelberg (2010). https://doi.org/10.1007/978-3-642-17373-8_22

[vDGHV10] van Dijk, M., Gentry, C., Halevi, S., Vaikuntanathan, V.: Fully homomorphic encryption over the integers. In: International Conference on the Theory and Application of Cryptographic Techniques (2010)

Activate Me!: Designing Efficient Activation Functions for Privacy-Preserving Machine Learning with Fully Homomorphic Encryption

Nges Brian Njungle$^{(\boxtimes)}$ ⓘ and Michel A. Kinsy ⓘ

STAM Center, Ira A. Fulton Schools of Engineering, Arizona State University,
Tempe 85281, USA
{nnjungle,mkinsy}@asu.edu

Abstract. The rapid integration of machine learning into applications in sensitive domains like healthcare and defense raises serious privacy and security concerns. These applications require strong privacy protections, as they rely on large amounts of sensitive data for both training and inference. Fully Homomorphic Encryption (FHE) offers a promising solution by allowing computations on encrypted data, thereby preserving confidentiality throughout the entire machine-learning pipeline. However, FHE only supports linear operations natively. This makes it hard to implement non-linear activation functions - an essential component of modern machine learning applications - under FHE constraints.

In this study, we design, implement, and evaluate activation functions optimized for FHE-based machine learning applications. We focus on two widely used functions: the Square function and the Rectified Linear Unit (ReLU). Our experiments utilize the LeNet-5 and ResNet-20 architectures implemented with the CKKS scheme from the OpenFHE library. For ReLU, we compare two approaches. First, we explore the popular low-degree polynomial approximation approach. Second, we introduce a novel scheme-switching technique that also securely evaluates ReLU under FHE constraints. Our results show that the square function is highly effective in shallow models like LeNet-5, achieving 99.4% accuracy with an inference time of 128 s per image. In deeper networks like ResNet-20, ReLU is more appropriate. The FHE-based ResNet-20 model implemented with ReLU polynomial approximation resulted in an accuracy of 83.8% and an inference time of 1,145 s per image. Further, our proposed scheme-switching algorithm achieved a higher accuracy of 89.8%, with an increased inference time of 1,697 s per image on a ResNet-20 model as well. These results highlight the key trade-off to be considered when selecting activation functions for FHE-based machine learning applications. The activation functions that reduce computation time tend to significantly lower accuracy, while those that preserve accuracy incur higher computational costs.

Keywords: Privacy Preserving Machine Learning · Fully Homomorphic Encryption · Activation Functions · ReLU · Square Function · CKKS

ⓒ The Author(s), under exclusive license to Springer Nature Switzerland AG 2026
A. Nitaj et al. (Eds.): AFRICACRYPT 2025, LNCS 15651, pp. 51–73, 2026.
https://doi.org/10.1007/978-3-031-97260-7_3

1   Introduction

Machine learning (ML) has emerged as a cornerstone of Artificial Intelligence (AI) and is often regarded a key driver for the Fourth Industrial Revolution [MJKEG22, VGT+24]. Over the past decade, it has experienced unprecedented growth, becoming an essential asset to technology across various sectors, including healthcare, finance, and defense. The ability of ML to derive insights from vast datasets has proven invaluable in critical systems such as medical diagnostics, predictive healthcare, and military decision making [VGT+24]. In defense, for example, ML is used in high-stakes applications such as autonomous weapon systems, threat detection, cybersecurity, and intelligence analysis [ASMB23]. These capabilities enable faster, data-driven decision making while significantly enhancing operational efficiency and mission effectiveness. However, the successful deployment of ML in these critical applications is highly dependent on access to large volumes of sensitive data for both training and inference. This dependency also presents serious privacy and security challenges. The privacy and security of data are particularly acute in military applications, since the data involved are often classified or highly confidential. Unauthorized access, leakage, or misuse of these data could compromise national security, operational plans, or strategic assets. As a result, ensuring the security and privacy of data in ML workflows in military systems is not only a technical necessity but a matter of national importance [TMA+20].

Traditional cryptographic methods, although effective at securing data during storage or transmission, fall short when it comes to protecting data during processing. In most cases, data must be decrypted before it can be processed, potentially exposing it to unauthorized access [SMK19]. Fully Homomorphic Encryption (FHE) has emerged as a promising solution to this drawback by enabling computations directly on encrypted data [TEK16]. It ensures that privacy and security are maintained throughout the entire life cycle of data, making it particularly valuable for privacy-preserving machine learning (PPML) applications, where data security and privacy are paramount. Despite its potential, the application of FHE in ML models presents two key challenges: a very high computational cost of evaluating models and the inability to efficiently evaluate non-linear functions [PGTCM+21]. Artificial neural networks are the dominant sub-field of ML today. These networks depend on non-linear activation functions to introduce complexity and enable effective learning. However, the FHE schemes of today typically support only linear operations. This limitation severely restricts the size and practical application of artificial neural networks under FHE constraints [NJW+25].

Prior research on the intersection of ML and FHE has centered on enhancing computational efficiency through various optimizations in the design of FHE-based models. In contrast, this work is focused on the design and implementation of activation functions tailored for FHE-based ML models. We examine two commonly used activation functions in FHE-based neural networks architectures: the square function and the Rectified Linear Unit (ReLU). Early FHE-compatible models predominantly employed simple polynomial activations, with the square function being the most widely used. However, recent advancements in the field have shifted FHE-based models toward the adoption of polynomial approximations of the ReLU activation function [BMPJ19]. While the approximation of ReLU approach resulted in performance improvements, there have been little systematic investigation regarding the contexts and model architectures where different activation functions perform best under FHE constraints. This work bridges that gap by implementing FHE-based neural networks using various activation functions and rigorously evaluating their effectiveness.

We evaluate the performance of these different activation functions using the LeNet-5 and ResNet-20 architectures. These architectures represent shallow and deep artificial neural network models, respectively. For the non-linear ReLU activation function, we implement the widely adopted polynomial approximation technique. We also introduced a novel algorithm that leverages FHE scheme-switching capabilities to enable a high precision evaluation of ReLU under FHE constraints. We compare the approaches based on inference latency and accuracy, emphasizing the trade-offs involved in designing activation functions for FHE-based ML models. Our results indicate that the square function is highly effective for shallow networks like LeNet-5, while ReLU proves more suitable for deeper architectures like ResNet-20. The polyapproximation-based approach delivers relatively low inference latency but introduces a higher accuracy degradation. In contrast, our scheme-switching method achieves a higher accuracy with minimal loss, albeit at the cost of increased computational overhead. These findings provide important insights into the design of FHE-compatible activation functions and contribute to the development of more practical yet efficient PPML solutions. Our main contributions in this work are as follows:

– Design and Implementation of Activation Functions for FHE-based ML models namely, the square and ReLU activation functions.
– Introduction of a novel algorithm using the scheme-switching capabilities of FHE to evaluate the ReLU activation function in the encrypted domain.
– Conduction of a comprehensive evaluation of the square function, polynomiL approximation of ReLU, and the proposed scheme-switching ReLU evaluation approach using LeNet-5 and ResNet-20 models under FHE constraints. We illustrate the trade-offs of these approaches in terms of accuracies and inference latencies of the different models.

2   Related Works

Artificial neural networks have become the dominant approach in modern machine learning applications. They are generally composed of interconnected linear layers and activation functions. Activation functions play a crucial role in these models as they enable them to capture complex, non-linear patterns in data [SSA17]. In recent years, artificial neural network models incorporating FHE for enhanced security and privacy have made significant advancements. However, research has predominantly focused on enhancing the efficiency of encrypted inference. While notable advancements have been achieved in this direction, training artificial neural networks under FHE constraints remains an open challenge. This is because of the substantial computational overhead and inherent accuracy loss of models when trained in the encrypted domain. The high computational cost and accuracy loss associated with FHE-based training arises from the complexity of operations like backpropagation, which must be executed on large amounts of encrypted data while maintaining high precision. Thus, making the process a very expensive and challenging computational task [PTH+22].

PPML applications utilizing FHE are generally categorized into two generations. The first-generation approaches are characterized by limited model depth and high computational overhead. The second-generation methods introduced advanced cryptographic optimizations including approximation of ReLU and Bootstrapping. These advancements significantly improved efficiency and enabling more practical applications of FHE in machine learning applications. There are other existing FHE-based ML applications which leverage other privacy preserving techniques like multi-party computation [CCDC+05] to facilitate the evaluation of non-linear activation functions with examples being; Gazelle [JVC18], MiniONN [LJLA17], and XONN [RSC+19]. However, these works are generally considered as hybrid due to their integration of multiple techniques to provide privacy and security thus we do not employ this approach in this work. In this work, we focus on strict FHE-based ML applications specifically artificial neural networks.

The first generation of FHE-based neural networks began with CryptoNets from Microsoft Research in 2016. The framework achieved a 99% accuracy on the MNIST dataset using a neural network custom architecture designed specifically for this task [GBDL+16]. CryptoNets main adjustment to neural network architectures was the use of the square function as their activation function which removed the complexity involved with non-linear activation functions. In 2017, Ehsan et al. proposed CryptoDL, which shitted from the simple square to a more complex low degree polynomial as the activation function [HTG17]. Another notable contribution came from Al Badawi et al. who accelerated HE inference using GPUs with a custom AlexNet-like architecture [ABJL+20] still utilizing the square activation function. Other works in this generation such as; E2DM [JKLS18], and DiNN [BMMP17] have also adopted the approach of using simple low-degree polynomial functions as activation functions.

The second generation of FHE-based neural networks introduced more sophisticated architectures with significant performance improvements. These works employed sophisticated techniques like bootstrapping which enables computations of arbitrary depth networks. They also introduced the evaluation of non-linear activation functions using polynomial approximation methods to enable privacy-preserving computation in complex and deep neural networks under FHE constraints. During training, non-linear functions are utilized (specifically the ReLU activation function). For encrypted inference, the non-linear functions are replaced with their polynomial approximations. A primary focus of various works in this generation has been optimizing resource usage and performance in HE-based neural networks. Works in this generation generally adopt the CKKS or TFHE homomorphic encryption schemes. The TFHE scheme is known for its fast and efficient bootstrapping after every multiplication called programmable bootstrapping [CGGI18]. This approach enables the evaluation of binary neural networks of arbitrary depth circuits while maintaining small ciphertext sizes with minimal precision loss. The most recent and most efficient of these works is the work of Benamira et al. [BP23], which proposed a TFHE-based architecture that achieved 74.1% accuracy on the CIFAR-10 dataset using a custom TFHE-CNN friendly architecture. The main limitation of these works stems from the fact that TFHE is inherently slow in large-scale data processing compared to other FHE schemes, like CKKS and BGV. This is due to its lack of support for parallel data processing. Also, the TFHE scheme operates on bit-wise data, which contrasts the floating-point arithmetic generally used in modern machine learning models applications. These limitations make TFHE not very tractable for processing complex or deep neural network architectures [NGEG17]. On the other-hand, the CKKS scheme has emerged as the most compatible FHE scheme for ML works given that it is the only mainstream FHE scheme that supports floating-point arithmetic and parallel data processing [CKKS16, LKL+22]. These capabilities significantly accelerate computations while providing a possible direct mapping of functionalities with unencrypted ML works. In 2022, Lee et al. proposed an FHE inference system that achieved 91.31% accuracy on the CIFAR-10 dataset in 2,271 s [LKL+22] using the polynomial approximation of the ReLU activation function. Building on this, Kim et al. introduced a more efficient approach, achieving 92.04% accuracy on CIFAR-10 with a single image inference time of 255 s [KG23]. Most recently, Rovida et al. proposed an optimized implementation of Kim et al.'s work, achieving 91.53% accuracy on the CIFAR-10 dataset in 260 s while using only 15.1 GB of memory [RL24]. All works mentioned have used the polynomial approximation of the ReLU activation function to evaluate ResNet-20 models.

Unlike most FHE-based ML works today, which primarily focus on optimizing FHE inference while applying the approximation of ReLU or using low-degree polynomials like the square function, our work takes a different approach. We focus on evaluating different activation functions suitable for PPML solutions under FHE constraints. By analyzing different methods, we identify where the different activation functions are most effective in constructing FHE-based models. Through a comprehensive analysis of results, this work provides insights that will assist in selecting activation functions that best fit the privacy preserving needs of different applications.

3 Background

3.1 Fully Homomorphic Encryption

Homomorphic Encryption (HE) is a cryptographic paradigm that enables direct computations on encrypted data without requiring decryption. This concept was originally introduced in 1978 under the term *Privacy Homomorphism* [BY88], shortly after the introduction of the RSA public key encryption scheme [TEK16].

The introduction of HE marked a significant advancement in secure computation, allowing encrypted data to be manipulated while preserving confidentiality. A major breakthrough in this domain occurred in 2009 when Craig Gentry introduced the first Fully Homomorphic Encryption (FHE) scheme [Gen09]. FHE enables an arbitrary number of computations on encrypted data, overcoming the limitations from earlier HE schemes that only supported a restricted set of operations and only very limited depth circuits. Gentry's work laid the foundation for practical FHE by introducing two fundamental techniques: *bootstrapping* and *squashing*. These innovations provided a structured approach to extending somewhat homomorphic encryption schemes to fully homomorphic ones. Gentry's scheme was based on ideal lattices, that inherently support homomorphic addition and multiplication. However, a critical challenge in lattice based HE schemes is noise accumulation within ciphertexts. As computations proceed, the noise level increases, and if it surpasses a certain threshold, the ciphertext becomes undecipherable thus rendering the encrypted message to be irretrievable. To address this issue, Gentry used an expensive computational operation called bootstrapping. It is a mechanism that periodically reduces noise within a ciphertext, thereby enabling indefinite computations on encrypted data. This approach established a foundation for subsequent improvements in FHE schemes, making them increasingly efficient and practical for real-world applications.

While other mainstream FHE schemes such as BGV [AGS14], BFV [FV12], and TFHE [CGGI18] exist, the CKKS scheme [CKKS16] is the most suitable for machine learning applications. It is the only mainstream FHE scheme that supports both approximate arithmetic and parallel data processing, therefore being the only scheme that aligns perfectly well with the needs of modern machine learning workflows and workloads. Figure 1 illustrates a scenario of privacy preserving outsourced ML inference utilizing HE. In this setup, a user is seeking to perform inference on an encrypted model stored in the cloud. First, they encrypt their input data using their public key and transmit it to the cloud. The cloud server processes the encrypted data using the encrypted model without ever decrypting it. Once the processing is completed, it returns the encrypted inference result to the user. Upon receiving the encrypted result, the user then decrypts it using their private key to gain access to the model's inference output. It is important to note that, at no point in this process did the cloud provider or anyone else gain access to the input data or inference result except for the user. Also, the cloud provider cannot extract any information from the encrypted model, since they do not have access to the private key. Furthermore, even in the event of a cloud breach, the user data and model stay protected, since all information is maintained in its encrypted form. This mechanism upholds confidentiality of both the user's data and the model, making HE a robust solution for secure cloud-based inference.

3.2   Cheon-Kim-Kim-Song (CKKS) Scheme

In 2016, Cheon, Kim, Kim, and Song introduced the CKKS scheme, a HE scheme specifically designed for approximate arithmetic [CKKS16]. Its security is based

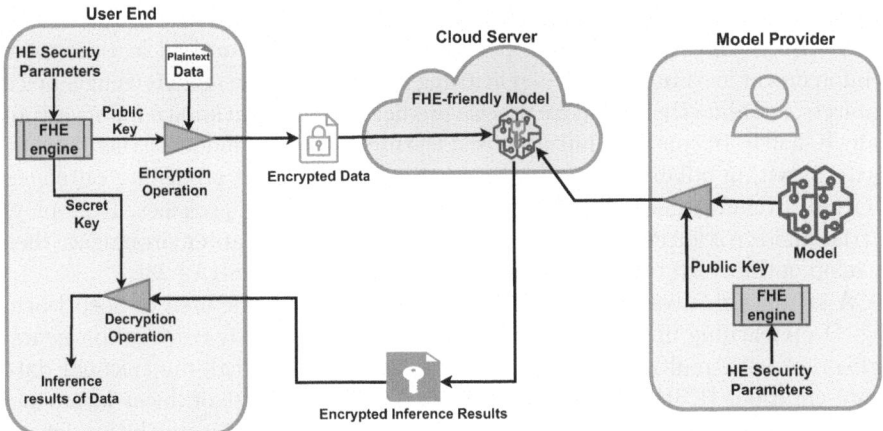

Fig. 1. Privacy-preserving machine learning inference in an outsourced cloud scenario showing a user inferring encrypted data over an encrypted model.

on the Ring Learning with Errors (RLWE) problem, a structured extension of the Learning with Errors (LWE) problem proposed by Regev in 2005 [Reg05] and later refined for polynomial rings by Lyubashevsky et al. [LPR12]. The LWE problem involves recovering a hidden vector from noisy linear equations generated using random samples. Formally, given a matrix $A \in \mathbb{Z}_q^{m \times n}$ and a vector $b \in \mathbb{Z}_q^m$, the goal is to find an unknown vector $s \in \mathbb{Z}_q^n$ satisfying:

$$As + e = b \bmod q, \tag{1}$$

where e is a noise vector sampled from a predefined error distribution, and q is a large prime modulus.

Expanding on this, the RLWE problem generalizes LWE to polynomial rings, leveraging their algebraic properties for computational efficiency. A key advantage of CKKS is its ability to encode multiple plaintext values into a single polynomial through a technique known as "slot packing". This feature enables efficient parallel computations using the Single Instruction Multiple Data (SIMD) paradigm, significantly accelerating homomorphic operations through batch processing of data. The CKKS scheme defines a range of homomorphic operations, including addition, subtraction, multiplication, rotation, and bootstrapping. These operations enable users to build a wide range of applications that support encrypted data processing with CKKS making it well-suited for PPML and other critical applications that require privacy computations on real-valued data.

3.3 Machine Learning

Machine learning (ML) is a sub-field of artificial intelligence that empowers computers to recognize patterns within data and generate predictions or decisions without requiring explicit programming [ARC19]. The field of ML is broadly cat-egorized into three paradigms: supervised learning, unsupervised learning, and reinforcement learning. Supervised learning involves training models using labeled datasets, enabling them to make precise predictions based on known input-output pairs [Gha04]. In contrast, unsupervised learning identifies hidden structures and patterns within unlabeled data, uncovering insights without predefined outcomes [JGR20]. Reinforcement learning is distinct from these approaches. It employs a trial-and-error mechanism where models interact with an environment, then develop optimal strategies through rewards and penalties [SRA+23].

A significant advancement within the field of ML is the area of deep learn-ing. Deep learning utilizes artificial neural networks (mainly convolution neural networks) with multiple layers to process complex and high-dimensional data representations [KSH12]. These networks typically comprise of linear layers and activation functions. The linear layers generally include the convolution layers, the pooling layers, and the fully connected layers. These linear layers have been widely studied under FHE constraints as they generally account for the bulk of the computational cost of FHE-based models. For this reason, we will not discuss them in this work. Instead, we will focus on activation functions since they have not been systematically studied under FHE constraints. Activation functions are particularly interesting as they introduce nonlinearity in learning, allowing the model to capture intricate relationships within data. Commonly used activation functions in modern ML applications include the Rectified Lin-ear Unit (ReLU), Sigmoid, and Hyperbolic Tangent (Tanh), each contributing uniquely to model efficiency and performance. Deep learning techniques can be applied across all three ML paradigms, enhancing supervised learning with highly accurate models, enabling advanced clustering in unsupervised learning, and improving decision-making capabilities in reinforcement learning.

4   FHE-Based Activation Functions

Activation functions play a fundamental role in ML models. Particularly in artifi-cial neural networks, they introduce non-linearity and enabling complex pattern learning [DSC22]. This non-linearity allows networks to learn complex patterns and relationships in data that linear models cannot capture. By determining how neurons process and transmit signals through layers, activation functions fundamentally shape a network's ability to learn and generalize from data. Tra-ditional activation functions like the sigmoid and hyperbolic tangent (tanh) were widely used in early neural networks due to their smooth, differentiable prop-erties. However, they often suffered from vanishing gradient issues, which made training deep networks difficult [RGSW20,HHAL18]. In response, more recent advancements have favored the Rectified Linear Unit (ReLU) and its variants because they provide faster convergence, reduce the gradient-related problems, and encourage sparse activations [GBJ20,HLXZ18].

While activation functions are relatively straightforward to implement in the plaintext domain, they present significant challenges in PPML settings, particu-larly when using FHE. For instance, ReLU, is non-polynomial and non-smooth, making it incompatible with the algebraic operations supported by most FHE schemes. To address this issue, researchers have proposed FHE-based alternatives based on low-degree polynomial functions including simple square functions and polynomial approximations of ReLU. In this section, we examined the design and implementation of these activation functions in the FHE context, highlighting their algorithms, benefits, and the trade-offs they entail.

4.1 Square Activation Function

Popular activation functions used in ML, such as the ReLU and sigmoid functions, involve non-polynomial operations that are difficult to compute under FHE constraints. In contrast, the square function is inherently polynomial, making it well-suited for homomorphic evaluation. Its algebraic simplicity aligns naturally with the linear structures supported by most FHE schemes, making it both easy to understand and straightforward to implement. Due to these advantages, the square activation function gained significant attention in the context of FHE-based PPML solutions. As a low-degree polynomial, it was the first activation function adopted for encrypted neural networks computation. Among other low-degree polynomials, it is valued for its simplicity, computational efficiency, and compatibility with homomorphic operations. Mathematically, the square activation function is defined in Eq. 2.

$$f(x) = x^2 \tag{2}$$

where x is the input to the function f.

The implementation of the square activation function using the CKKS scheme is outlined in Algorithm 1.

Algorithm 1. The Square Function Algorithm in FHE

1: **Input:** x (input ciphertext)
2: **Output:** y
3: $y \leftarrow CKKSmultiply(x, x)$
4: **return** y

The square activation function is smooth and differentiable everywhere, which facilitates stable gradient propagation during training. However, its derivative, given by $f'(x) = 2x$, is also a linear function. Unlike non-linear activation functions whose gradients exhibit non-linear behavior—promoting piecewise non-linearity and sparsity—the square function's linear derivative introduces certain optimization challenges. In particular, the lack of saturation regions and the absence of a thresholding mechanism reduce the network's capacity to capture complex hierarchical features effectively. Another key limitation of the square function is its inherent non-negativity. By squaring all inputs, it eliminates sign information and produces only non-negative outputs without any accumulations. This behavior can lead to redundancy in activation patterns and increase the correlation among neuron outputs, which may negatively affect the model's ability to generalize. Moreover, the unbounded nature of the derivative $2x$ for large input magnitudes can cause gradient instability during training. This is especially problematic in deep architectures, where the accumulation of large gradients can result in exploding gradient phenomena, ultimately destabilizing the learning process.

These challenges make it difficult to train deep neural networks effectively using the square activation function. Modern architectures like ResNet-20, rely on residual connections that perform best when activation functions maintain controlled gradient norms. The unbounded growth of the square function's derivative disrupts this balance, leading to unstable weight updates. As a result, while the square function is computationally efficient and works well in shallow FHE-based models, it is not suitable for deeper architectures. For instance, training the ResNet-20 model with the square activation function was proved infeasible due to instability during backpropagation. The exploding gradients prevented effective learning and completely hindered the network's ability to generalize.

4.2   ReLU Activation Function

Rectified Linear Unit (ReLU) is the most widely adopted activation function in ML today due to its simplicity and effectiveness [HLXZ18]. ReLU applies a threshold operation where all negative values are set to 0. This non-linearity accelerates convergence and helps reduce the vanishing gradient problem in training. Equation 3 shows the mathematical representation of the ReLU activation function.

$$f(x) = max(0, x) \tag{3}$$

Unlike traditional activation functions such as sigmoid and tanh, that suffer from vanishing gradient problems, ReLU preserves gradient flow for positive inputs, allowing for faster convergence and improved performance in deep architectures. By setting all negative inputs to zero, ReLU introduces sparsity in activations, reducing computational complexity and enhancing model generalization by mitigating unnecessary neuron activations. This sparsity also contributes to an implicit form of regularization, preventing over-fitting in large networks.

Polynomial Approximation of ReLU. In FHE-based ML models, the implementation of ReLU poses challenges due to its non-polynomial nature, making direct computation on encrypted data inefficient especially in the CKKS scheme. Previous FHE-based neural networks implementations have focused on Polynomial approximation of the ReLU activation function mainly using the Chebyshev's Polynomial Approximation.

Chebyshev polynomials form a family of orthogonal polynomials defined on the interval $[-1, 1]$. They are highly effective in approximating complex, non-linear functions with both efficiency and precision [GAC12]. These polynomials are denoted by $T_n(x)$ and are defined recursively as follows:

$$T_0(x) = 1, \tag{4}$$
$$T_1(x) = x, \tag{5}$$
$$T_n(x) = 2xT_{n-1}(x) - T_{n-2}(x), \quad \text{for } n \geq 2. \tag{6}$$

A distinctive feature of Chebyshev polynomials is the distribution of their roots. A polynomial of degree n has exactly n roots, all of which are located within the interval $[-1, 1]$. These roots are expressed in the following form:

$$x_k = \cos\left(\frac{k\pi}{n}\right), \quad \text{for } 0 \leq k < n. \tag{7}$$

The Chebyshev polynomials offer an efficient way to express non-linear functions as a sum of polynomials. This approach proves especially useful in FHE applications as polynomials seamlessly integrate with the underlining data representations. By employing Chebyshev polynomial approximations, the ReLU function can be approximated securely within the encrypted domain.

To correctly apply Chebyshev approximations, it is important to normalize the input data to lie within the interval $[-1, 1]$. We achieved this by introducing a scaling factor β that adjusts the input vector accordingly. The input vector is scaled by multiplying it with $\frac{1}{\beta}$, as shown in Eq. 8:

$$x_{\text{s}} = \frac{1}{\beta} \cdot x \tag{8}$$

The parameter β is selected through an analysis of values across different datasets and networks. This process ensures that the data is accurately normalized while maintaining the representational integrity of the ReLU activation function under FHE constraints. When $\beta > 1$, a scaling mask is applied to the input vector $\mathbf{x}$ to ensure proper scaling of data before processing. Once scaled, the modified input is passed to the Chebyshev approximation function. The results are then scaled back by multiplying them by β, as shown in Algorithm 2.

Algorithm 2. Secure ReLU Using Homomorphic Encryption

1: **Input:** x, β
2: **Output:** y
3: **Initialization:** $D, v \leftarrow x$
4: **if** $\beta > 1$ **then**
5:     $v \leftarrow \text{CKKSMultiply}(x, \beta)$
6: **end if**
7: Define $f(z) : f(z) \leftarrow 0$ if $z < 0$; $f(z) \leftarrow \beta \cdot z$ otherwise
8: $y \leftarrow \text{ChebyshevFunction}(f(z), v, D)$
9: **return** y

In Algorithm 2, D is the degree of the Chebyshev polynomial used for approximating the function. The value of D determines the accuracy of the Chebyshev

Approximation of the ReLU function. The higher the degree, the better the approximation but the higher the computational cost. To determine the right value of D to use, we conducted an experiment with varying values for the polynomial degree between 10 and 100. We studied how well the function approximated the results of the ReLU function. We determined that when D is equal 50, we obtain a good balance between accuracy and the resources used for the polynomial approximation of the ReLU activation function. This value of D consumes a noise budget equivalent to that of eight multiplications thus efficient for use in applications with FHE parameters that can lead to a multiplication depth after bootstrapping to still be greater than eight.

4.3   Secure ReLU Evaluation via Scheme Switching

FHE schemes exhibit varying degrees of efficiency and computational capabilities, making them suitable for different types of encrypted computations and operations. The CKKS scheme, in particular, is well-suited for approximate arithmetic and supports efficient parallel computation. These properties make CKKS the optimal choice for evaluating linear operations in FHE-based ML applications. However, CKKS is inherently limited in its ability to perform non-linear operations, such as the comparison operation required for thresholding in the ReLU activation function.

In contrast, the FHEW [CGGI16] and TFHE schemes [CGGI18] are specifically designed for efficient evaluation of boolean gates. They enable precise computation of non-linear functions such as comparisons, sign determination, and the floor function [CGGI18]. These functions are expressed as boolean circuits which are then constructed from basic logic gates such as; AND, OR, NOR, and XOR defined in these schemes. This gate-based approach allows for accurate discrete computation of functions under FHE constraints. While FHEW and TFHE offer high accuracy in such boolean computations, they do not support SIMD-style parallelism. Consequently, they introduce significant computational overhead when applied to large-scale data processing tasks like those commonly encountered in ML applications.

To leverage the strengths of both encryption schemes, we adopt a scheme-switching approach that integrates CKKS with TFHE. Specifically, CKKS is used to efficiently evaluate all linear layers in the model, while TFHE is employed in the evaluation of non-linear activation functions. During inference, ciphertexts are switched back and forth between the two schemes depending on the type of layer and operation been evaluated. This hybrid strategy enables efficient computation while maintaining compatibility with the constraints of FHE and capitalizing on the complementary strengths of both schemes. The concept of scheme switching between different homomorphic encryption schemes was first introduced by Christina et al. in 2018 under the name CHIMERA [BGGJ18]. This technique is feasible between CKKS and TFHE because both schemes are rooted in the LWE problem. As a result, ciphertexts in either scheme share the same foundational algebraic structures, making translation between schemes mathematically viable. In essence, scheme switching involves transforming the underlying representation of ciphertexts from one scheme to another while preserving the encrypted data and its semantic integrity.

In this method of evaluating the ReLU activation function, we first determine the sign of each encrypted value within a CKKS SIMD ciphertext by switching to the TFHE scheme, which supports precise comparison operations. Once the signs are computed in TFHE, we switch back to CKKS and use the resulting ciphertext to construct a binary mask. This mask is then homomorphically multiplied with the original CKKS ciphertext, effectively zeroing out the negative values and thereby implementing a more precise, secure, and privacy-preserving ReLU activation function. This algorithm consumes just a single multiplication depth in the noise budget of ciphertext. The complete procedure is outlined in Algorithm 3.

This proposed scheme-switching technique effectively integrates the strengths of CKKS and TFHE, enabling efficient and secure ReLU activation in encrypted neural networks. CKKS provides high throughput in evaluating linear layers, while TFHE assist in a precise computation of the comparison operation needed to effectively evaluate the non-linear ReLU activation function. This hybrid approach allows for the construction of high-precision PPML models under FHE constraints. Although the scheme-switching process of ReLU still results in some errors, the resulting errors are much smaller than those incur in the approximation when using low-degree polynomials.

Algorithm 3. Secure Scheme-Switching ReLU Algorithm

1: **Input:** c_{enc} (encrypted input vector), c_{sec} (second ciphertext), vector_size
2: **Output:** c_{result}
3: Set slots of c_{enc} to vector_size
4: $tc_{enc} \leftarrow$ CKKSSwitchToTFHEW(c_{enc})
5: $tc_{sec} \leftarrow$ CKKSSwitchToTFHEW(c_{sec})
6: $c_{comp} \leftarrow$ TFHECompare(tc_{enc}, tc_{sec}, vector_size)
7: mask $\leftarrow$ GenerateCKKSPlaintextMask(1, vector_size)
8: $c_{sign} \leftarrow$ CKKSSubtract(mask, c_{comp})
9: $c_{result} \leftarrow$ CKKSMultiply(c_{sign}, c_{enc})
10: **return** c_{result}

---

5 Experiment and Results

All experiments in this study were performed on a AMD Ryzen 9 5900X 12-core processor with 64 GB of RAM. We build all our models on OpenFHE v1.2.3 which is the most stable version of the library at the time of development. We chose OpenFHE because it is the most advanced FHE library available to the development community. Additionally, it is the only FHE library that supports implementations for both CKKS and FHEW/TFHE gates [BBB+22, ABBB+22].

5.1   Network Architectures

To comprehensively evaluate the performance of these different activation function implementations under FHE, we evaluate two distinct neural network architectures: LeNet-5 and ResNet-20. These models differ significantly in complexity and application domains, making them ideal candidates for assessing the trade-offs between efficiency and accuracy in privacy-centric applications.

LeNet-5 is a relatively simple and shallow artificial neural network originally designed for grayscale image classification tasks such as handwritten digits recognition [LBBH98]. Despite its simplicity, LeNet-5 remains one of the most widely studied architectures in ML literature, making it an excellent baseline for evaluating activation functions in FHE settings. For this study, we trained two versions of LeNet-5 on the MNIST dataset using the ReLU activation function and using the square activation function. The training process was conducted in PyTorch, and the learned model weights were exported as CSV files which were then loaded into the encrypted models for inference. Within the encrypted domain, we implemented three different evaluation models. Our first model used the square activation function with equivalent weights exported from the model trained on the square activation function. Our second model used the polynomial approximation of ReLU activation function while our third model used the scheme-switching evaluation of ReLU activation function. The last two FHE-based LeNet-5 models used the weights from the model trained with the ReLU activation functions. Each encrypted model was evaluated using 750 images from the MNIST validation set. Figures 2 illustrate the detailed architectures of the LeNet-5 models used in this study including the input channels, output channels, kernel, padding, and striding configurations.

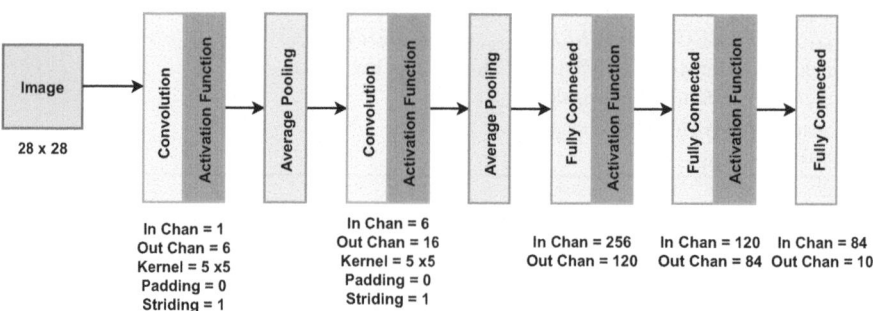

Fig. 2. The LeNet-5 Architecture used in this work: In Chan = input channels, Out Chan = output channels

The ResNet models are some of the most widely adopted deep learning models for complex image classification tasks today [HZRS15]. The core innovation in ResNets is the introduction of residual connections, which mitigate the vanishing gradient problem and enable efficient training of deeper networks. Due to its balance of depth and computational feasibility, ResNet-20 has been commonly employed in prior FHE research and serves as an ideal benchmark for our study.

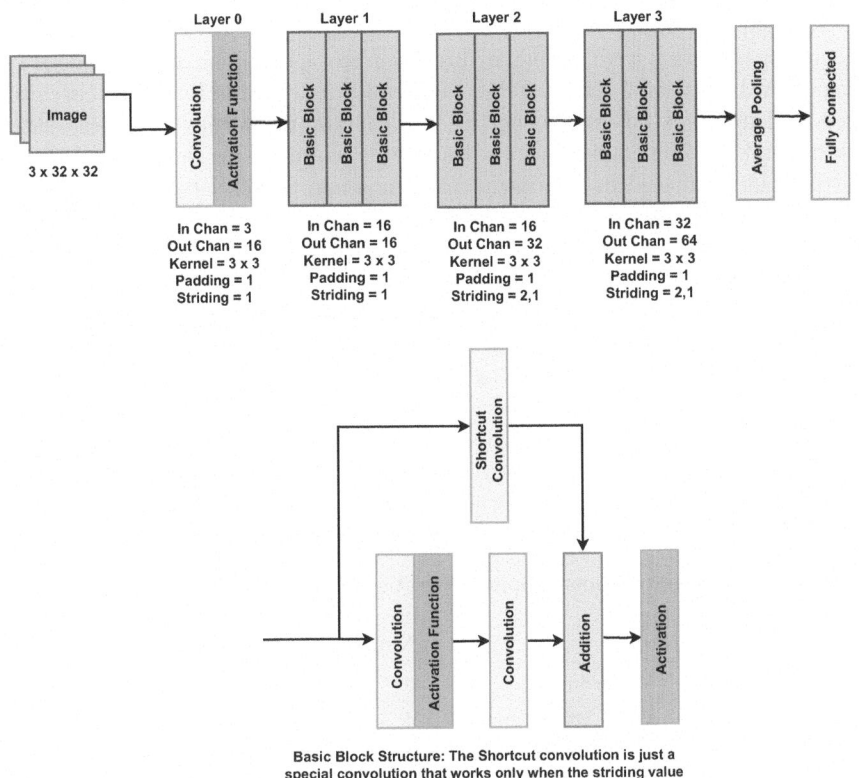

Fig. 3. ResNet-20 Architecture. The Blocks show the ResNet blocks. The Block Structure shows the details and how the convolutions are connected

For our evaluation, we trained a ResNet-20 model on the CIFAR-10 dataset using the ReLU activation function. In contrast to LeNet-5, we found that training ResNet-20 with the square activation function was infeasible due to its limited capacity to approximate non-linear behaviors in deep architectures (see Sect. 4). This result highlights a fundamental limitation of low-degree polynomial activation functions in privacy-preserving deep learning, as their expressive power diminishes with increasing network depth.

After training the ResNet-20 model with ReLU activation functions, the resulting model weights were also exported as CSV files for use with the FHE-based models to inference on encrypted data. Within the encrypted domain, we implemented two evaluation models: one utilizing a polynomial approximation of ReLU and the other employing the scheme-switching approach introduced in Algorithm 3. We conducted encrypted inference on both models on a subset of 250 images from the CIFAR-10 validation set. The key metrics evaluated were accuracy retention and inference latency for the two ReLU implementation approaches. To achieve fast inference for accuracy evaluation, we utilized the SOL supercomputer at Arizona State University [JLK+23]. Latency measurements, however, were collected directly from a local consumer-grade setup using an AMD Ryzen 9 5900X CPU. Figures 3 illustrate the ResNet-20 architectures used in this study including the input channels, output channels, kernel, padding and striding configurations. Its residual connections show the additional convolutions evaluated in the down-sampling stage of ResNets.

Furthermore, since noise accumulation is a critical challenge in FHE, we incorporated bootstrapping operations at necessary points to preserve computational integrity. Table 1 summarizes the number of bootstrapping operations required for each model to ensure accurate and efficient encrypted inference. The placement of bootstraps within the models were carefully determined based on the estimated noise levels at various stages of the inference process. These estimates were derived from a detailed analysis of ciphertext modulus consumption throughout the computation pipeline. By strategically applying bootstrapping only when the noise threatened to exceed the decryption threshold, we minimized overhead while maintaining correctness in the encrypted domain.

Table 1. Number of Bootstrapping Operations required in Encrypted Models

Architecture	Number of Bootstraps used
LeNet-5 With Square	0
LeNet-5 with Approximation	4
LeNet-5 with Scheme Switch	0
ResNet-20 with Approximation	18
ResNet-20 with Scheme Swith	8

Table 2 provides an overview of the security parameters used in our encrypted inference experiments. These parameters were carefully chosen to maintain a security level around 128 bits of security with maximum throughput within the models, ensuring robustness against cryptographic attacks while optimizing computational efficiency.

Table 2. The CKKS Parameter sets used to evaluate the LeNet-5 and ResNet-20

Parameter	LeNet-5	ResNet-20
Polynomial Degree	16384	32768
Number of Slots	8192	16384
Multiplications after Bootstrap	10	10

5.2   Results

Table 3 presents the accuracy of the evaluated neural network models under both plaintext and under FHE constraints, as well as the latency measurements in the encrypted domain. The primary objective of this evaluation was to investigate the trade-offs between computational overhead and model accuracy associated with different methods for evaluating activation functions under FHE constraints. Our analysis compares the three activation function evaluation approaches in the encrypted domain: the low-degree polynomial square function, polynomial approximations of the ReLU function, and the scheme-switching ReLU evaluation method. The results show the inherent trade-offs between accuracy retention and computational efficiency in FHE-based PPML solutions.

For the LeNet-5 architecture, all three activation function methods achieve comparable performance, exhibiting minimal accuracy loss between plaintext and encrypted inference. Notably, the square activation function achieves the highest encrypted accuracy of 99.4%, with only a 0.2% degradation from its plaintext counterpart. However, it offers latency performance higher than that of the ReLU polynomial approximations which significantly outperforms the scheme-switching method in terms of runtime. A key advantage of the square function lies in its seamless compatibility with the CKKS scheme, which allows it to be implemented using a single homomorphic multiplication—thereby eliminating the need for bootstrapping and further improving computational efficiency in shallow architectures like LeNet-5.

The ReLU approximation method shows a modest accuracy degradation of 0.3% in the encrypted LeNet-5 model while maintaining the best latency across all evaluations. Meanwhile, the scheme-switching ReLU approach also incurs a 0.3% accuracy loss but introduces significant computational overhead. Specifically, it requires approximately 168 s to inference a single image—about 1.7× the latency of the approximation-based method. This increased cost arises from the additional operations required to switch between CKKS and TFHE schemes, along with the inherently higher computational complexity of TFHE operations. Despite its slower performance, the scheme-switching method still offers latency that is practical for many real-world applications.

In deeper architectures like ResNet-20, the choice of activation function plays a critical role in determining the model's performance. Residual networks, in particular, rely on non-linear activations to enable effective feature transformation across layers. Consequently, the selection of an appropriate activation function directly affects the model's expressiveness and accuracy. When employing polynomial approximations of the ReLU function within the CKKS framework, we observed an 8.4% accuracy degradation relative to the plaintext model. This substantial drop in performance can be attributed to the limited capacity of low-degree polynomials to accurately approximate the non-linear behavior of ReLU, thereby leading to suboptimal feature transformations during inference. Nevertheless, this method remains computationally efficient, as it avoids the need for scheme-switching or bootstrapping, making it well-suited for latency-sensitive applications where minor accuracy compromises are acceptable. In contrast, the scheme-switching ReLU evaluation method achieves significantly higher accuracy, incurring only a 2.4% drop from the plaintext baseline. This demonstrates the effectiveness of leveraging TFHE's precise operations capabilities to reconstruct the ReLU function more efficiently within the encrypted domain. However, the improved accuracy comes at the cost of increased computational complexity. The scheme-switching model required approximately 1,697 seconds for inference, representing a 1.5× increase in runtime compared to the polynomial approximation approach.

Table 3. Accuracy Comparison Between Plaintext and FHE Settings as well as the latency in the FHE setting for the LeNet-5 models and ResNet-20 models

Architecture	Plaintext (%)	Encrypted (%)	Latency (s)
LeNet-5 Square	99.6	99.4	128
LeNet-5 Approximation	99.2	98.9	95
LeNet-5 Scheme Switch	99.2	98.9	168
ResNet-20 Approximation	92.2	83.8	1,145
ResNet Scheme Switch	99.2	89.8	1,697

These results highlight a fundamental trade-off in PPML applications that rely on FHE. While polynomial approximations of ReLU activation functions substantially accelerate encrypted inference, they introduce notable accuracy degradation, particularly in deeper network architectures. Conversely, our introduced scheme-switching methods offer a more faithful representation of ReLU, preserving model accuracy at the cost of increased computational overhead.

With shallow neural networks like LeNet-5, polynomial activation functions—particularly the square function—offer an optimal balance between accuracy and computational efficiency under FHE constraints. This function aligns well with the CKKS encryption scheme and avoids costly bootstrapping operations in this model, making it especially suitable for real-time applications in resource-limited settings. ReLU-based LeNet-5 models also performed well, with the approximation approach achieving the lowest latency in the FHE-based LeNet-5 models. For deeper architectures like ResNet-20, the optimal activation function strategy depends heavily on application-specific requirements. If accuracy preservation is paramount, the scheme-switching ReLU approach provides a robust solution with minimal degradation. However, if inference latency and computational resources are the primary constraints, ReLU approximation methods offer a practical alternative, albeit with a slight compromise in accuracy. Ultimately, these findings underscore that activation function selection in PPML is not a one-size-fits-all decision. Researchers and practitioners must carefully evaluate their deployment requirements in other to balance accuracy, latency, and model depth when selecting an appropriate activation function strategy for FHE-based neural networks.

6   Conclusion

In this work, we explored the impact of activation functions on the efficiency and accuracy of privacy-preserving neural networks under Fully Homomorphic Encryption (FHE) constraints. We also introduce a novel algorithm for high precision evaluation of the ReLU activation function based on scheme-switching between the TFHE and CKKS schemes. Our results, highlight the trade-offs between the square activation function, ReLU approximation, and our proposed scheme-switching ReLU activation functions in both shallow and deep neural network architectures. For shallow networks like LeNet-5, the square activation function proved to be the most efficient choice, offering the best accuracy with a comparable latency. Additionally, its implementation allowed us to completely eliminate the need for bootstrapping. This further enhance computational efficiency of models like LeNet-5 in scenarios where bootstrapping implementation is not possible. On the other hand, the challenges that come with low degree polynomial activation functions makes it difficult to adopt the square activation function in deep models. For deeper architectures like ResNet-20, the choice of activation function had a more pronounced effect. The polynomial approximation approach for evaluating ReLU was computationally efficient but resulted in a notable accuracy drop of 8.4%. In contrast, the scheme-switching method preserved accuracy with only a 2.4% degradation, though it came at the cost of increased latency.

These findings highlight a fundamental trade-off in the selection of activation functions for privacy-preserving machine learning application based on FHE. Polynomial activations like the square activation function are computationally efficient and well-suited for shallow models such as LeNet-5, whereas the scheme-switching method is better aligned with deep architectures where maintaining precision is critical. In performance sensitive applications, the ReLU approximation approach emerges as the most practical choice, underscoring the importance of fine-grained tuning to reduce accuracy degradation. In high precision settings, our proposed scheme-switching approach of evaluating the ReLU activation function is the most appropriate though it comes with a higher computational cost compared to the approximation approach. Thus, the choice between activation functions in FHE-based machine learning applications should be guided by the specific accuracy and efficiency requirements of the target application. Future research should prioritize optimizing scheme-switching mechanisms to reduce inference latency without compromising accuracy as well as fine-tuning of the polynomial approximation technique to reduce their accuracy degradation rates. These advancements will enhance the feasibility and scalability of FHE-based solutions in modern machine learning applications.

References

[ABBB+22] Al Badawi, A., et al.: OpenFHE: open-source fully homomorphic encryption library. In: Proceedings of the 10th Workshop on Encrypted Computing & Applied Homomorphic Cryptography, WAHC 2022, pp. 53–63. Association for Computing Machinery, New York (2022)

[ABJL+20] Al Badawi, A., et al.: Towards the alexnet moment for homomorphic encryption: HCNN, the first homomorphic CNN on encrypted data with GPUs. IEEE Trans. Emerg. Topics Comput. **9**(3), 1330–1343 (2020)

[AGS14] Aggarwal, N., Gupta, C.P., Sharma, I.: Fully homomorphic symmetric scheme without bootstrapping (2014)

[ARC19] Al-Rubaie, M., Morris Chang, J.: Privacy-preserving machine learning: threats and solutions. IEEE Secur. Priv. **17**(2), 49–58 (2019)

[ASMB23] Suárez, E., Baeza, V.M.: Evaluating the role of machine learning in defense applications and industry. Mach. Learn. Knowl. Extraction **5**(4), 1557–1569 (2023)

[BBB+22] Al Badawi, A., et al.: OpenFHE: open-source fully homomorphic encryption library. Cryptology ePrint Archive, Paper 2022/915 (2022). https://eprint.iacr.org/2022/915

[BGGJ18] Boura, C., Gama, N., Georgieva, M., Jetchev, D.: CHIMERA: combining ring-LWE-based fully homomorphic encryption schemes. Cryptology ePrint Archive, Paper 2018/758 (2018)

[BMMP17] Bourse, F., Minelli, M., Minihold, M., Paillier, P.: Fast homomorphic evaluation of deep discretized neural networks. Cryptology ePrint Archive, Paper 2017/1114 (2017)

[BMPJ19] Banerjee, C., Mukherjee, T., Pasiliao, E., Jr.: An empirical study on generalizations of the relu activation function. In: Proceedings of the 2019 ACM Southeast Conference, pp. 164–167 (2019)

[BP23] Al Badawi, A., Polyakov, Y.: Demystifying bootstrapping in fully homomorphic encryption. Cryptology ePrint Archive, Paper 2023/149 (2023)

[BY88] Brickell, E.F., Yacobi, Y.: On privacy homomorphisms (extended abstract). In: Chaum, D., Price, W.L. (eds.) EUROCRYPT 1987. LNCS, vol. 304, pp. 117–125. Springer, Heidelberg (1988). https://doi.org/10.1007/3-540-39118-5_12

[CCDC+05] Catalano, D., et al.: Multiparty computation, an introduction. Contemp. Cryptol. 41–87 (2005)

[CGGI16] Chillotti, I., Gama, N., Georgieva, M., Izabachène, M.: Faster fully homomorphic encryption: bootstrapping in less than 0.1 seconds. Cryptology ePrint Archive, Paper 2016/870 (2016)

[CGGI18] Chillotti, I., Gama, N., Georgieva, M., Izabachène, M.: TFHE: fast fully homomorphic encryption over the torus. Cryptology ePrint Archive, Paper 2018/421 (2018). https://eprint.iacr.org/2018/421

[CKKS16] Cheon, J.H., Kim, A., Kim, M., Song, Y.: Homomorphic encryption for arithmetic of approximate numbers. Cryptology ePrint Archive, Paper 2016/421 (2016)

[DSC22] Dubey, S.R., Singh, S.K., Chaudhuri, B.B.: Activation functions in deep learning: a comprehensive survey and benchmark. Neurocomputing **503**, 92–108 (2022)

[FV12] Fan, J., Vercauteren, F.: Somewhat practical fully homomorphic encryption. IACR Cryptology ePrint Archive 2012:144 (2012)

[GAC12]   Gil-Alana, L.A., Cuestas, J.C.: A non-linear approach with long range dependence based on Chebyshev polynomials (2012)

[GBDL+16]   Gilad-Bachrach, R., Dowlin, N., Laine, K., Lauter, K., Naehrig, M., Wernsing, J.: Cryptonets: applying neural networks to encrypted data with high throughput and accuracy. In: International Conference on Machine Learning, pp. 201–210. PMLR (2016)

[GBJ20]   Gupta, N., Bedi, P., Jindal, V.: Effect of activation functions on the performance of deep learning algorithms for network intrusion detection systems. In: Singh, P.K., Panigrahi, B.K., Suryadevara, N.K., Sharma, S.K., Singh, A.P. (eds.) Proceedings of ICETIT 2019. LNEE, vol. 605, pp. 949–960. Springer, Cham (2020). https://doi.org/10.1007/978-3-030-30577-2_84

[Gen09]   Gentry, C.: A fully homomorphic encryption scheme. Ph.D. thesis, Stanford University (2009). http://crypto.stanford.edu/craig

[Gha04]   Ghahramani, Z.: Unsupervised Learning, pp. 72–112. Springer, Heidelberg (2004)

[HHAL18]   Hu, Y., Huber, A., Anumula, J., Liu, S.-C.: Overcoming the vanishing gradient problem in plain recurrent networks. arXiv preprint arXiv:1801.06105 (2018)

[HLXZ18]   He, J., Li, L., Xu, J., Zheng, C.: Relu deep neural networks and linear finite elements. arXiv preprint arXiv:1807.03973 (2018)

[HTG17]   Hesamifard, E., Takabi, H., Ghasemi, M.: CryptoDL: deep neural networks over encrypted data. arXiv preprint arXiv:1711.05189 (2017)

[HZRS15]   He, K., Zhang, X., Ren, S., Sun, J.: Deep residual learning for image recognition (2015)

[JGR20]   Jiang, T., Gradus, J.L., Rosellini, A.J.: Supervised machine learning: a brief primer. Behav. Ther. 51(5), 675–687 (2020)

[JKLS18]   Jiang, X., Kim, M., Lauter, K., Song, Y.: Secure outsourced matrix computation and application to neural networks. Cryptology ePrint Archive, Paper 2018/1041 (2018)

[JLK+23]   Jennewein, D.M., et al.: The sol supercomputer at Arizona state university. In: PEARC 2023, pp. 296–301. Association for Computing Machinery, New York (2023)

[JVC18]   Juvekar, C., Vaikuntanathan, V., Chandrakasan, A.: GAZELLE: a low latency framework for secure neural network inference. In: 27th USENIX Security Symposium (USENIX Security 2018), pp. 1651–1669. USENIX Association, Baltimore (2018)

[KG23]   Kim, D., Guyot, C.: Optimized privacy-preserving CNN inference with fully homomorphic encryption. IEEE Trans. Inf. Forensics Secur. 18, 2175–2187 (2023)

[KSH12]   Krizhevsky, A., Sutskever, I., Hinton, G.E.: Imagenet classification with deep convolutional neural networks. In: Pereira, F., Burges, C.J., Bottou, L., Weinberger, K.Q. (eds.) Advances in Neural Information Processing Systems, vol. 25. Curran Associates, Inc. (2012)

[LBBH98]   Lecun, Y., Bottou, L., Bengio, Y., Haffner, P.: Gradient-based learning applied to document recognition. Proc. IEEE 86(11), 2278–2324 (1998)

[LJLA17]   Liu, J., Juuti, M., Lu, Y., Asokan, N.: Oblivious neural network predictions via minionn transformations. In: Proceedings of the 2017 ACM SIGSAC Conference on Computer and Communications Security, pp. 619–631 (2017)

[LKL+22] Lee, J.-W., et al.: Privacy-preserving machine learning with fully homo-morphic encryption for deep neural network. IEEE Access **10**, 30039–30054 (2022)

[LPR12] Lyubashevsky, V., Peikert, C., Regev, O.: On ideal lattices and learning with errors over rings. Cryptology ePrint Archive, Paper 2012/230 (2012)

[MJKEG22] Magd, H., Jonathan, H., Khan, S.A., El Geddawy, M.: Artificial intelligence—the driving force of industry 4.0. A roadmap for enabling industry 4.0 by artificial intelligence, pp. 1–15 (2022)

[NGEG17] Narumanchi, H., Goyal, D., Emmadi, N., Gauravaram, P.: Performance analysis of sorting of FHE data: integer-wise comparison vs bit-wise comparison. In: 2017 IEEE 31st International Conference on Advanced Information Networking and Applications (AINA), pp. 902–908. IEEE (2017)

[NJW+25] Njungle, N.B., Jahns, E., Wu, Z., Mastromauro, L., Stojkov, M., Kinsy, M.: GuardianML: anatomy of privacy-preserving machine learning techniques and frameworks. IEEE Access (2025)

[PGTCM+21] Pulido-Gaytan, B., et al.: Privacy-preserving neural networks with homomorphic encryption: C hallenges and opportunities. Peer-to-Peer Netw. Appl. **14**(3), 1666–1691 (2021)

[PTH+22] Podschwadt, R., Takabi, D., Peizhao, H., Rafiei, M.H., Cai, Z.: A survey of deep learning architectures for privacy-preserving machine learning with fully homomorphic encryption. IEEE Access **10**, 117477–117500 (2022)

[Reg05] Regev, O.: On lattices, learning with errors, random linear codes, and cryptography. In: Proceedings of the Thirty-Seventh Annual ACM Symposium on Theory of Computing (2005)

[RGSW20] Roodschild, M., Gotay Sardiñas, J., Will, A.: A new approach for the vanishing gradient problem on sigmoid activation. Progress Artif. Intell. **9**(4), 351–360 (2020). https://doi.org/10.1007/s13748-020-00218-y

[RL24] Rovida, L., Leporati, A.: Encrypted image classification with low memory footprint using fully homomorphic encryption. Cryptology ePrint Archive, Paper 2024/460 (2024)

[RSC+19] Sadegh Riazi, M., Samragh, M., Chen, H., Laine, K., Lauter, K., Koushan-far, F.: {XONN}:{XNOR-based} oblivious deep neural network inference. In: 28th USENIX Security Symposium (USENIX Security 2019), pp. 1501–1518 (2019)

[SMK19] Salavi, R.R., Math, M.M., Kulkarni, U.P.: A survey of various crypto-graphic techniques: from traditional cryptography to fully homomorphic encryption. In: Saini, H.S., Sayal, R., Govardhan, A., Buyya, R. (eds.) Innovations in Computer Science and Engineering. LNNS, vol. 74, pp. 295–305. Springer, Singapore (2019). https://doi.org/10.1007/978-981-13-7082-3_34

[SRA+23] Sivamayil, K., Rajasekar, E., Aljafari, B., Nikolovski, S., Vairavasun-daram, S., Vairavasundaram, I.: A systematic study on reinforcement learning based applications. Energies **16**(3) (2023)

[SSA17] Sharma, S., Sharma, S., Athaiya, A.: Activation functions in neural net-works. Towards Data Sci. **6**(12), 310–316 (2017)

[TEK16] Tourky, D., ElKawkagy, M., Keshk, A.: Homomorphic encryption the "holy grail" of cryptography. In: 2016 2nd IEEE International Conference on Computer and Communications (ICCC), pp. 196–201 (2016). Accessed 06 Mar 2024

[TMA+20] Tariq, M.I., et al.: A review of deep learning security and privacy defensive techniques. Mob. Inf. Syst. **2020**(1), 6535834 (2020)

[VGT+24] Virmani, D., Ghori, Md.A.S., Tyagi, N., Ambilwade, R.P., Patil, P.R., Sharma, M.K.: Machine learning: the driving force behind intelligent systems and predictive analytics. In: 2024 International Conference on Trends in Quantum Computing and Emerging Business Technologies, pp. 1–6. IEEE (2024)

One-Way Homomorphic Encryption: A Composite Group Approach

Mahdi Mahdavi[1,2] and Helena Rifà-Pous[1(✉)]

[1] Internet Interdisciplinary Institute (IN3), Universitat Oberta de Catalunya (UOC),
Barcelona, Spain
{m_mahdavi,hrifa}@uoc.edu
[2] Shahid Beheshti University (SBU), Tehran, Iran

Abstract. Homomorphic Encryption (HE) is a fundamental Privacy-Enhancing Technology (PET) that enables computations on encrypted data without decryption. Despite its utility, designing an efficient and secure HE scheme is highly complex, requiring sophisticated cryptographic techniques. This paper introduces a novel approach to achieving homomorphic properties—supporting either one addition or one multiplication—within composite groups. While the proposed technique exhibits one-wayness, it has a good potential to serve as a foundational building block for constructing indistinguishable cryptosystems. This work contributes to the advancement of homomorphic encryption by providing a new perspective on secure computation within structured algebraic settings.

Keywords: Homomorphic Encryption · One way function · Composite group · Rabin Cryptosystem · Quadratic residue

1 Introduction

Fully Homomorphic Encryption (FHE) is a fundamental cryptographic tool that ensures data confidentiality during computation, allowing operations on encrypted data without requiring decryption. Several FHE schemes have been developed based on different hardness assumptions, including Ideal Lattices [8,15], Learning with Errors (LWE) [2–5,7], and Approximate Greatest Common Divisor (AGCD) [6,12].

In contrast, homomorphic encryption schemes within composite groups generally provide only partial homomorphism, with the exception of the Boneh-Goh-Nissim (BGN) scheme [1]. The BGN scheme supports the evaluation of any 2-DNF (Disjunctive Normal Form) function, but it relies on pairings over composite-order groups, which involve computationally intensive operations. Moreover, the BGN scheme restricts the message size to a single bit or a short-length message, rather than allowing messages of the size of the composite-order group. Other cryptosystems, such as Paillier [11], GM [9], Rabin [13], and RSA [14], also operate within composite groups but provide limited homomorphic properties.

A. Nitaj et al. (Eds.): AFRICACRYPT 2025, LNCS 15651, pp. 74–88, 2026.
https://doi.org/10.1007/978-3-031-97260-7_4

The Rabin cryptosystem [13] stands out for its simplicity and efficiency among composite-group schemes. Grounded in the hardness of the factoring problem, it provides a one-way encryption mechanism where the ciphertext is computed as the square of the plaintext modulo a composite integer.

This paper presents a novel homomorphic encryption scheme that builds upon the Rabin cryptosystem to achieve one-way homomorphic properties within composite groups. Its key contributions include a new encryption framework that efficiently encrypts two messages within a single ciphertext, the definition and validation of four homomorphic operations (scalar multiplication, scalar addition, ciphertext multiplication, and ciphertext addition), a security analysis linking the scheme's one-wayness to the factoring problem, and the establishment of a foundational approach that paves the way for constructing more advanced, potentially Indistinguishability under Chosen-Plaintext Attack (IND-CPA) secure cryptosystems.

2 Background

This section introduces the key mathematical tools that facilitate our scheme's design and analysis, setting the stage for understanding its operation within composite groups.

2.1 Quadratic Residue

Quadratic residues play a significant role in cryptosystems based on composite groups, such as the Rabin cryptosystem. If p is an odd prime, then half of the residue classes that are relatively prime to p are called *quadratic residues*; these correspond to the integers that are *perfect squares modulo* p. Since $a^2 \equiv (-a)^2$ (mod p) and $a \not\equiv -a$ (mod p) for $a \neq 0$, each non-zero quadratic residue has exactly *two square roots modulo* p, differing only in sign.

The structure becomes more intricate when considering a composite modulus $N = pq$, where p and q are two distinct odd primes. Let $k \in \mathbb{Z}_N$ be an integer such that:

$$k_p \equiv k \quad (\text{mod } p), \quad k_q \equiv k \quad (\text{mod } q)$$

By the *Chinese Remainder Theorem (CRT)*, k can be reconstructed using the formula:

$$k = \text{CRT}(k_p, k_q) = k_p \cdot q \cdot q' + k_q \cdot p \cdot p' \quad (\text{mod } N)$$

where $q' \equiv q^{-1}$ (mod p) and $p' \equiv p^{-1}$ (mod q) are modular inverses. Furthermore, defining:

$$k_1 = \text{CRT}(k_p, k_q), \quad k_2 = \text{CRT}(k_p, -k_q), \quad k_3 = \text{CRT}(-k_p, k_q), \quad k_4 = \text{CRT}(-k_p, -k_q),$$

it follows that:

$$k_1^2 \equiv k_2^2 \equiv k_3^2 \equiv k_4^2 \quad (\text{mod } N).$$

Thus, every *quadratic residue modulo* N, when relatively prime to N, has exactly *four square roots modulo* $N = pq$.

2.2   Rabin Cryptosystem

Rabin's scheme requires selecting prime numbers p and q such that $p \equiv q \equiv 3 \pmod 4$, enabling efficient computation of square roots in $\mathbb{Z}_N$, where $N = p \cdot q$. In the Rabin cryptosystem, encryption is performed by squaring the plaintext message m, producing the ciphertext:

$$c = m^2 \pmod N$$

Decryption involves computing the square root of c modulo N using the following equations:

$$m_p = \pm\sqrt{c} \equiv \pm c^{\frac{p+1}{4}} \pmod p \tag{1}$$

$$m_q = \pm\sqrt{c} \equiv \pm c^{\frac{q+1}{4}} \pmod q \tag{2}$$

The plaintext message m is then recovered using CRT as $m = \mathrm{CRT}(m_p, m_q)$.

Since the decryption process results in four possible values, only one of which corresponds to the original plaintext, the probability of successful decryption is $\frac{1}{4}$ in the Rabin cryptosystem. Additionally, Rabin encryption satisfies one-way security but is not IND-CPA secure, making it vulnerable to chosen-plaintext attacks.

3   Proposed Scheme

In this section, we introduce a homomorphic encryption scheme adapted from the Rabin cryptosystem [13]. The scheme consists of four core algorithms: KeyGen, Enc, Dec, and Eval, corresponding to *key generation*, *encryption*, *decryption*, and *evaluation*, respectively. The Eval algorithm will be detailed in the next section, while the KeyGen, Enc, and Dec algorithms are defined as follows:

- KeyGen: Generate two large, distinct prime numbers p and q such that $p \equiv q \equiv 3 \pmod 4$, and compute the public key $pk = N = p \cdot q$. The private key is $sk = (p, q)$, enabling factorization of N for decryption.
- Enc: For a (nonzero) message $m \in \mathbb{Z}_N$, select a random integer $r \in \mathbb{Z}_N$ and generate the ciphertext as

$$ctx = \{S, \ P\} \equiv \{m + r, \ mr\} \pmod N.$$

- Dec: Given a fresh ciphertext $ctx = \{S, \ P\}$, decrypt by solving the quadratic equation:

$$x^2 - Sx + P = 0 \pmod N.$$

To solve this equation, first compute:

$$\delta = \sqrt{\Delta} = \sqrt{S^2 - 4P} \pmod N$$

which yields four possible roots $\delta_i; i \in [1, 4]$. Then compute:

$$x_i = \frac{S + \delta_i}{2}; i \in [1, 4]$$

Among these roots, x_1 corresponds to the original message m, x_2 corresponds to the random integer r, and x_3 and x_4 are additional roots. As a result, the probability of successful decryption is $\frac{1}{4}$.

Remark 1. Since the random integer r can be recovered in the same way as the message m, it can be treated as a second message. As a result, the ciphertext effectively encrypts two messages simultaneously, forming what is known as a Double Message Ciphertext.

3.1 Evaluation

This section introduces four primary evaluation operations: *scalar multiplication, scalar addition, ciphertext multiplication,* and *ciphertext addition.* While scalar operations do not affect the ciphertext size or the decryption probability, ciphertext operations lead to an increase in ciphertext size and a decrease in decryption probability. The following formally define these operations and establish their homomorphic properties.

Scalar Operations

1. Scalar Multiplication. For a ciphertext $ctx = \{S, P\} = \{m + r, mr\}$ and a constant $c \in \mathbb{Z}_N$, the scalar multiplication SMult is computed as:

$$ctx_{SM} = \text{SMult}(c, ctx) = \{cS,\ c^2 P\} = \{cm + cr,\ (cm)(cr)\} \tag{3}$$

Since $cr \in \mathbb{Z}_N$ is a random integer, the result is equivalent to $Enc(cm)$.

2. Scalar Addition: For the same ctx and constant $c \in \mathbb{Z}_N$, compute the scalar addition SAdd as:

$$\begin{aligned} ctx_{SA} = \text{SAdd}(c, ctx) &= \{S + 2c,\ P + cS + c^2\} \\ &= \{m + r + 2c,\ mr + cm + cr + c^2\} \\ &= \{(m + c) + (r + c),\ (m + c)(r + c)\} \end{aligned} \tag{4}$$

Since $r + c \in \mathbb{Z}_N$ is a random integer, the result is equivalent to $Enc(m + c)$.

Ciphertext Operations

1. Ciphertext Multiplication. For two ciphertexts $ctx_1 = \{m_1 + r_1, \ m_1 r_1\}$ and $ctx_2 = \{m_2 + r_2, \ m_2 r_2\}$, multiplication, which is shown by `Mult`, is done as follows:

$$ctx_{CM} = \texttt{CMult}(ctx_1, ctx_2) = \{ \ S_1 S_2 \ , \ (S_1^2 - 2P_1)P_2 + (S_2^2 - 2P_2)P_1 \ , \ P_1 P_2 \ \}$$

The result is a *nested ciphertext* with three components:

$$ctx_{CM} = Enc_\times^2(m_1.m_2) = \{S_\times + r, S_\times \cdot r, P_\times\},$$

where

$$S_\times = m_1 m_2 + r_1 r_2, \quad r = m_1 r_2 + m_2 r_1, \quad P_\times = m_1 m_2 r_1 r_2.$$

Following, the correctness of the first component of ctx_{CM} is demonstrated.

$$S_1 S_2 = (m_1 + r_1)(m_2 + r_2) = m_1 m_2 + m_1 r_2 + r_1 m_2 + r_1 r_2$$
$$= (m_1 m_2 + r_1 r_2) + (m_1 r_2 + m_2 r_1) = S_\times + r$$

The correction of the second part is also as follows:

$$(S_1^2 - 2P_1)P_2 + (S_2^2 - 2P_2)P_1$$
$$= ((m_1 + r_1)^2 - 2m_1 r_1)m_2 r_2 + ((m_2 + r_2)^2 - 2m_2 r_2)m_1 r_1$$
$$= (m_1^2 + r_1^2)m_2 r_2 + (m_2^2 + r_2^2)m_1 r_1$$
$$= (m_1 m_2 + r_1 r_2)(m_1 r_2 + m_2 r_1) = S_\times \cdot r \tag{5}$$

The third component of ctx_{CM} is as follows:

$$P_1 P_2 = (m_1 r_1)(m_2 r_2) = (m_1 m_2)(r_1 r_2) = P_\times \tag{6}$$

To decrypt a nested ciphertext $Enc_\times^2(m_1, m_2)$, begin by parsing the first two components as a fresh ciphertext $Enc(S_\times) = \{S_\times + r, \ S_\times \cdot r\}$, where $r = m_1 r_2 + m_2 r_1$ is a random integer. Run the decryption algorithm on $Enc(S_\times)$ to obtain $S_\times$. Then construct the fresh ciphertext $\{S_\times, P_\times\} = \{m_1 m_2 + r_1 r_2, m_1 m_2 r_1 r_2\}$, which is equivalent to $Enc(m_1 m_2)$ because $r_1 r_2$ is also a random integer. Finally, run the decryption algorithm on $Enc_\times(m_1, m_2)$ to obtain the plaintext $m_1 m_2 = m_\times$.

Note that the size of the ciphertext grows with each evaluation operation, and the probability of successful decryption for the nested ciphertext decreases to $(\frac{1}{4})^2 = \frac{1}{16}$.

2. Ciphertext Addition. For two ciphertexts $ctx_1 = \{m_1 + r_1, \ m_1 r_1\}$ and $ctx_2 = \{m_2 + r_2, \ m_2 r_2\}$, the addition operation, denoted by `CAdd`, is computed as:

$$ctx_{CA} = \texttt{CAdd}(ctx_1, ctx_2) \tag{7}$$
$$= \{ S_1 + S_2,$$
$$S_1 \cdot S_2 + 2(P_1 + P_2),$$
$$(P_1 + P_2)(S_1 S_2) + (P_1 + P_2)^2 \quad + (S_1^2 - 2P_1)P_2 + (S_2^2 - 2P_2)P_1 \}$$

Like in the ciphertext multiplication evaluation, the result is a *nested cipher-text* with three components:

$$ctx_{CA} = Enc_+^2(m_1 + m_2) = \{ S_+, P_+ + r, P_+ \cdot r \}$$

where:

$$S_+ = (m_1 + m_2) + (r_1 + r_2), \quad P_+ = (m_1 + m_2)(r_1 + r_2), \quad r = (m_1 + r_2)(m_2 + r_1).$$

In the following, the investigation and the correctness of each of these components are demonstrated.

$$S_1 + S_2 = (m_1 + r_1) + (m_2 + r_2) = (m_1 + m_2) + (r_1 + r_2)$$

The correction of the second part also as follows:

$$2(P_2 + P_1) + S_1.S_2 = 2(m_1 r_1 + m_2 r_2) + (m_1 + r_1)(m_2 + r_2)$$
$$= 2m_1 r_1 + 2m_2 r_2 + m_1 m_2 + m_1 r_2 + r_1 m_2 + r_1 r_2$$
$$= (m_1 r_1 + m_1 m_2 + m_2 r_2 + m_2 r_1) + (m_1 r_1 + m_2 r_2 + m_1 m_2 + r_1 r_2)$$
$$= (m_1 + m_2)(r_1 + r_2) + (m_1 + r_2)(m_2 + r_1) = P_+ + r$$

Third component of ctx_{CA} is as follows:

$$P_+ \cdot r = (P_1 + P_2)(S_1 S_2) + (P_1 + P_2)^2 + (S_1^2 - 2P_1)P_2 + (S_2^2 - 2P_2)P_1$$
$$= (m_1 r_1 + m_2 r_2)(m_1 + r_1)(m_2 + r_2) + (m_1 r_1 + m_2 r_2)^2$$
$$+ (m_1^2 + r_1^2)m_2 r_2 + (m_2^2 + r_2^2)m_1 r_1$$
$$= \cdots = (m_1 + m_2)(r_1 + r_2) \cdot (m_1 + r_2)(m_2 + r_1) = P_+ \cdot r$$

To decrypt a nested ciphertext $Enc_+^2(m_1 + m_2)$, begin by parsing the last two components as a fresh ciphertext $Enc(P_+) = \{ P_+ + r, \ P_+ \cdot r \}$, where $r = (m_1 + r_2)(m_2 + r_1)$ is a random integer. Next, run the decryption algorithm to obtain P_+. Then construct the fresh ciphertext $\{ S_+, P_+ \} = \{ (m_1 + m_2) + (r_1 + r_2), \ (m_1 + m_2)(r_1 + r_2) \}$, which is equivalent to $Enc(m_1 + m_2)$ because $r_1 + r_2$ is also a random integer. Finally, run the decryption algorithm on $Enc(m_1 + m_2)$ to obtain the plaintext $m_1 + m_2 = m_+$.

4 Improvements

This section presents several enhancements to the homomorphic encryption scheme, focusing on improving the decryption success probability and expanding evaluation capabilities. These improvements address the limitations of the basic scheme, which supports only one addition or one multiplication per fresh ciphertext and has a decryption success probability of $\frac{1}{4}$.

4.1 Probability Enhancement

Efforts to improve decryption success probabilities in the Rabin cryptosystem, such as those in [10,16], could potentially be adapted to our scheme. However, these techniques typically apply only to fresh ciphertexts, losing effectiveness after evaluation operations. To address this, we introduce modifications designed to elevate the probability of successful decryption across both fresh and nested ciphertexts.

Fresh Ciphertext. Let a fresh ciphertext be represented as $ctx = \{S, P\} = \{m + r, mr\}$, where $m \in \mathbb{Z}_N$ is the message and $r \in \mathbb{Z}_N$ is a random integer. To enhance decryption reliability, we select r such that $m - r$ is a perfect square. Specifically, given m, we choose a random integer $\sigma \in \mathbb{Z}_N$, such that $\sigma^2 < N$, so $\sigma^2 = \sigma \cdot \sigma \mod N$ is a perfect square, and set $r = m - \sigma^2 \mod N$. This preserves the randomness of r due to the random selection of σ. The discriminant δ is then computed as:

$$\delta = \sqrt{\Delta} = \sqrt{S^2 - 4P} = \sqrt{(m + r)^2 - 4mr} = \sqrt{(m - r)^2} \tag{8}$$

Since $m - r = \sigma^2$, this implies $\delta = \sqrt{(\sigma^2)^2} = |\sigma^2| \mod N$, and thus two of the four possible roots, δ_1 and δ_2, are $\pm \sigma^2$. The other two roots, δ_3 and δ_4, depend on the modulo N structure and are typically not perfect squares.

The decryption algorithm examines all four potential roots, $\delta_1, \delta_2, \delta_3$, and δ_4, and identifies which are perfect squares modulo N. Since σ^2 is a perfect square by construction, $\delta_1 = \sigma^2$ satisfies this condition. With high probability, the other roots (including $\delta_2 = -\sigma^2$) are not perfect squares, as -1 is not a quadratic residue modulo N when N's factors p and q satisfy $p, q \equiv 3 \mod 4$ (per Sect. 2.2)[1]. The message can then be recovered as follows:

$$m = \frac{S + \sigma^2}{2} = \frac{(m + r) + \sigma^2}{2} = \frac{m + (m - \sigma^2) + \sigma^2}{2} \tag{9}$$

This modification raises the decryption success probability to approximately 1. Regarding the security of this technique, an adversary capable of exhaustively searching all integers $\mathbb{Z}_N$ satisfying $\sigma^2 < N$ and ensuring $\sigma^2 \pmod{N}$ is a perfect square could compromise the scheme. The number of such σ is approximately $2^{\eta/2}$ for an η-bit modulus N, rendering the attack computationally infeasible for sufficiently large η to resist factoring. A formal security analysis is presented in Theorem 2. The impact on nested ciphertexts is discussed in the next subsection.

Multiplied Nested Ciphertext. Consider two ciphertexts:

$$ctx_1 = \{S_1, P_1\} = \{m_1 + r_1, m_1 r_1\}, \quad r_1 = m_1 - \sigma_1^2$$

---

[1] Note that in our setting, $-\sigma^2$ is not a perfect square. One of the two other roots is a quadratic residue in $\mathbb{Z}_N$, but this does not necessarily mean that it is a perfect square integer.

$$ctx_2 = \{S_2, P_2\} = \{m_2 + r_2, m_2 r_2\}, \quad r_2 = m_2 - \sigma_2^2$$

For the encryption of their product, $E_\times(m_1 m_2)$, the following holds:

$$\{S_\times + r, \ S_\times \cdot r, \ P_\times\} = \{S_1 S_2, \ (S_1^2 - 2P_1)P_2 + (S_2^2 - 2P_2)P_1, \ P_1 P_2\}$$
$$= \{(m_1 m_2 + r_1 r_2) + (m_1 r_2 + m_2 r_1),$$
$$(m_1 m_2 + r_1 r_2)(m_1 r_2 + m_2 r_1), \ (m_1 m_2)(r_1 r_2)\}$$

To decrypt this nested ciphertext, we first treat $\{S_\times + r, S_\times \cdot r\}$ as a fresh ciphertext and proceed with decryption. The decryption algorithm computes the following:

$$\sqrt{(S_\times + r)^2 - 4(S_\times \cdot r)} = \sqrt{(S_\times - r)^2} \quad \mod N$$
$$= \sqrt{((m_1 m_2 + r_1 r_2) - (m_1 r_2 + m_2 r_1))^2}$$
$$= \sqrt{(m_1 m_2 + (m_1 - \sigma_1^2)(m_2 - \sigma_2^2) - m_1(m_2 - \sigma_2^2) - m_2(m_1 - \sigma_1^2))^2}$$
$$= \sqrt{(m_1 m_2 + m_1 m_2 - m_1 \sigma_1^2 - m_2 \sigma_1^2 + \sigma_1^2 \sigma_2^2 - m_1(m_2 - \sigma_2^2) - m_2(m_1 - \sigma_1^2))^2}$$
$$= \sqrt{(2 m_1 m_2 - m_1 \sigma_1^2 - m_2 \sigma_1^2 + \sigma_1^2 \sigma_2^2 - m_1 m_2 + m_1 \sigma_2^2 - m_2 m_1 + m_2 \sigma_1^2))^2}$$
$$= \sqrt{(\sigma_1^2 \sigma^2)^2} \quad \mod N$$

Thus, one of the solutions to the above equation is $\sigma_1^2 \sigma_2^2 \mod N$. However, it is important to note that $\sigma_1^2 \sigma_2^2 \mod N$ is not necessarily a perfect square integer. This is because $\sigma_1^2 \sigma_2^2$ may exceed N, leading to an overflow. Nevertheless, it is always a quadratic residue modulo N.

Since the result of $\sqrt{(\sigma_1^2 \sigma_2^2)^2} \mod N$ has two quadratic residue roots, the probability of correctly determining $\sigma_1^2 \sigma_2^2$ is $\frac{1}{2}$.

Added Nested Ciphertext. Consider two ciphertexts:

$$ctx_1 = \{S_1, P_1\} = \{m_1 + r_1, m_1 r_1\}, \quad r_1 = m_1 - \sigma_1^2$$

$$ctx_2 = \{S_2, P_2\} = \{m_2 + r_2, m_2 r_2\}, \quad r_2 = m_2 - \sigma_2^2$$

For the encryption of their summation, $E_+(m_1 + m_2)$, the following holds:

$$\{S_+, \ P_+ + r, \ P_\times \cdot r\} = \{S_1 + S_2, \ S_1 S_2 + 2(P_2 + P_1),$$
$$(P_1 + P_2)(S_1 S_2) + (P_1 + P_2)^2 + (S_1^2 - 2P_1)P_2 + (S_2^2 - 2P_2)P_1\}$$
$$= \{(m_1 + m_2) + (r_1 + r_2),$$
$$(m_1 + m_2)(r_1 + r_2) + (m_1 + r_2)(m_2 + r_1),$$
$$(m_1 + m_2)(r_1 + r_2) \cdot (m_1 + r_2)(m_2 + r_1) \ \}$$

To decrypt this nested ciphertext, we first treat $\{P_+ + r, \; P_\times \cdot r\}$ as a fresh ciphertext and proceed with decryption. The decryption algorithm computes the following:

$$
\begin{aligned}
\sqrt{(P_+ + r)^2 - 4(P_+ \cdot r)} &= \sqrt{(P_+ - r)^2} \quad \mod N \\
&= \sqrt{((m_1 + m_2)(r_1 + r_2) - (m_1 + r_2)(m_2 + r_1))^2} \\
&= \sqrt{(m_1 r_1 + m_1 r_2 + m_2 r_1 + m_2 r_2 - (m_1 m_2 + m_1 r_1 + m_2 r_2 + r_1 r_2))^2} \\
&= \sqrt{(m_1 r_2 + m_2 r_1 - m_1 m_2 - r_1 r_2)^2} = \sqrt{((m_1 - r_1)(r_2 - m_2))^2} \\
&= \sqrt{(m_1 - r_1)^2 (r_2 - m_2)^2} = \sqrt{(\sigma_1^2 \sigma_2^2)^2} \quad \mod N
\end{aligned}
$$

Thus, one of the solutions to the above equation is $\sigma_1^2 \sigma_2^2 \mod N$. However, it is important to note that $\sigma_1^2 \sigma_2^2 \mod N$ is not necessarily a perfect square integer. This is because $\sigma_1^2 \sigma_2^2$ may exceed N, leading to an overflow. Nevertheless, it is always a quadratic residue modulo N.

Since the result of $\sqrt{(\sigma_1^2 \sigma_2^2)^2} \mod N$ has two quadratic residue roots, the probability of correctly determining $\sigma_1^2 \sigma_2^2$ is $\frac{1}{2}$.

Scalar Operations. The proposed technique is not effective for scalar operations, i.e., scalar multiplication and scalar addition. However, if the constant c in scalar multiplication is a quadratic residue, the decryption probability grows to $\frac{1}{2}$. This is because of the following property for a ciphertext $\{cS, \; c^2 P\}$.

$$
\delta = \sqrt{\Delta} = \sqrt{c^2 S^2 - 4c^2 P} = \sqrt{c^2 (m + r)^2 - 4c^2 mr} = \sqrt{c^2 (m - r)^2} = \sqrt{(c\sigma^2)^2}
$$

This means that one of the roots is $c\sigma^2$ which is quadratic residue by assumption. Therefore, the probability of detecting this value is $\frac{1}{2}$, as there is another root that is also a quadratic residue.

4.2 Interactive Evaluation

The proposed scheme supports either one multiplication or one addition operation using ciphertext multiplication and ciphertext addition, respectively. However, this is insufficient for evaluating more complex functions. To address this limitation, this section introduces an interactive evaluation technique that enables the evaluation of more complex functions. In this approach, the data user (i.e., the destination party holding the secret key) must be online and collaborate with the evaluator, while ensuring that intermediate data remains hidden from the data user.

Consider a nested ciphertext of the form:

$$
E_\times(m_1 m_2) = \{S_\times + r, \; S_\times \cdot r, \; P_\times\}
$$

The evaluator treats $\{S_\times + r, \; S_\times \cdot r\}$ as a fresh ciphertext. To facilitate secure interactive decryption, the evaluator performs the following steps:

1. Randomization: The evaluator selects a random integer $c \in \mathbb{Z}_N$ and performs a scalar multiplication on the ciphertext:

$$\{c(S \times +r), \ c^2 \cdot S_\times \cdot r\}$$

This randomized ciphertext is then sent to the data user.

2. Decryption by the Data User: The data user applies the decryption algorithm to recover $cS_\times$ and forwards this value to the evaluator, who can then compute cr. To preserve security, the data user must not reveal other possible decryption solutions, as this could allow the evaluator to factor N.

3. Recovery of $S_\times$: Upon receiving $cS_\times$, the evaluator removes the random scalar c and computes $S_\times$. The ciphertext is then updated to $S_\times, P_\times$, which serves as a fresh ciphertext, allowing the evaluation process to continue.

It is important that the data user sends the same value of $S_\times$ consistently, which occurs with a probability of $\frac{1}{4}$. This probability can be increased to $\frac{1}{2}$ if the encryption algorithm follows the technique described in Sect. 4.1 and the evaluator ensures that the chosen constant c is a quadratic residue. To guarantee this, the evaluator selects a random integer $t \in \mathbb{Z}_N$ and computes $c = t^2 \mod N$.

A similar interactive decryption process can be applied to a nested ciphertext of the form:

$$E_+(m_1 + m_2) = \{S_+, \ P_+ + r, \ P_\times \cdot r\}$$

In this case, the evaluator extracts $\{S_+, \ P_+ + r\}$ and performs the following steps:

1. Randomization: The evaluator selects a random integer $c \in \mathbb{Z}_N$ and performs a scalar multiplication on the ciphertext:

$$\{c(P + +r), c^2 \cdot P_+ \cdot r\}$$

This randomized ciphertext is then sent to the data user.

2. Decryption by the Data User: The data user applies the decryption algorithm to recover cP_+ and forwards this value to the evaluator.

3. Recovery of P_+: Upon receiving cP_+, the evaluator removes the random scalar c and computes P_+. The ciphertext is then updated to S_+, P_+, which serves as a fresh ciphertext, allowing the evaluation process to continue.

The probability of returning the correct value cP_+ is $\frac{1}{4}$, which can be increased to $\frac{1}{2}$ by following the technique described in Sect. 4.1 and ensuring that c is a quadratic residue, computed as $c = t^2 \mod N$.

5   Analysis

This section provides an analysis of the proposed scheme, focusing on its decryption probability and security properties. Key remarks and a formal theorem establish the scheme's strengths and limitations, linking its security to established cryptographic assumptions.

First, the decryption probability of nested ciphertexts, such as $Enc_\times^2(m_1, m_2)$ or $Enc_+^2(m_1+m_2)$, is $\frac{1}{16}$. This is because two sequential decryptions are required: one to recover the intermediate value (e.g., $S_\times$ or P_+) and the other to obtain the final result (e.g., $m_1 m_2$ or $m_1 + m_2$). Since these steps are independent and each one has a success probability of $\frac{1}{4}$, the total probability of successful decryption is $\frac{1}{4} \times \frac{1}{4} = \frac{1}{16}$. Moreover, even an adversary with knowledge of the secret key or the ability to factor N cannot recover the original messages m_1 and m_2 from the nested ciphertext. For a detailed explanation, see Remark 3 in the appendix.

Remark 2. For any adversary $\mathcal{A}$ capable of breaking the Rabin cryptosystem [13], there exists an adversary $\mathcal{N}$ who can factor the public key $N = p \cdot q$.

Theorem 1. *For any adversary $\mathcal{A}$ who can break the proposed cryptosystem, there exists an adversary $\mathcal{B}$ who can break the Rabin cryptosystem.*

Proof. Let c be a ciphertext in the Rabin cryptosystem, computed as $c = m^2 \mod N$, with public key N. Adversary $\mathcal{B}$ constructs a ciphertext in the proposed scheme as follows: select a random integer $S \in \mathbb{Z}_N$, compute

$$P = \frac{S^2 - c}{4} \mod N,$$

and form $ctx = \{S, P\}$. This ctx satisfies the structure of the proposed encryption, since $S = x_1 + x_2$ and $P = x_1 x_2$ for roots x_1 and x_2 of the equation

$$x^2 - Sx + P = 0 \mod N,$$

where

$$(x_1 - x_2)^2 = S^2 - 4P = c.$$

Adversary $\mathcal{B}$ submits ctx to $\mathcal{A}$, who, if capable of breaking the proposed scheme, returns

$$x_i = \frac{S + \delta_i}{2} \quad \text{for} \quad i \in [1, 4],$$

where

$$\delta_i = \sqrt{S^2 - 4P} = \sqrt{c} \mod N.$$

From this, $\mathcal{B}$ computes

$$\delta_i = 2x_i - S,$$

recovering a square root of c. Since computing square roots modulo N in the Rabin cryptosystem is equivalent to factoring N, $\mathcal{B}$ succeeds whenever $\mathcal{A}$ does, establishing the reduction.

Theorem 2. *For any adversary $\mathcal{A}$ who can break the proposed enhanced cryptosystem, there exists an adversary $\mathcal{R}$ who can recover any perfect squares messages encrypted by the Rabin cryptosystem [13].*

Proof. Let c be a ciphertext in the Rabin cryptosystem, computed as $c = m^2$ mod N, where N is the public key and the message m is a perfect square, i.e., $m = \sigma^2$ for some integer σ. An adversary $\mathcal{B}$ constructs a ciphertext for the enhanced scheme by choosing a random $S \in \mathbb{Z}_N$ and computing

$$P = \frac{S^2 - c}{4} \mod N,$$

then forms $ctx = \{S, P\}$.
Substituting $c = m^2$, we obtain:

$$P = \frac{(S + m)(S - m)}{4} \mod N,$$

This construction satisfies the structure of the proposed encryption scheme, where $S = x_1 + x_2$ and $P = x_1 x_2$, with

$$x_1 = \frac{S + m}{2} \ , \ x_2 = \frac{S - m}{2}.$$

This implies that ctx is a valid encryption of x_1 under the enhanced scheme, with x_2 acting as the random component, since $x_2 = x_1 - m = x_1 - \sigma^2$.

Adversary $\mathcal{B}$ submits ctx to $\mathcal{A}$, who, if capable of breaking the proposed enhanced scheme, returns x_1. From this, $\mathcal{B}$ computes

$$m = 2x_1 - S,$$

recovering the message m, which is a square root of c. Thus, $\mathcal{B}$ breaks the Rabin cryptosystem for perfect square messages, implying that the security of the proposed scheme reduces to that of the Rabin cryptosystem.

In other words, this proof says that if the Rabin cryptosystem can securely encrypt a perfect square integer as a message, then the proposed enhanced scheme is also safe.

6   Conclusion

This paper introduces a novel cryptosystem that employs innovative techniques to achieve homomorphic properties for four fundamental operations: scalar multiplication, scalar addition, ciphertext multiplication, and ciphertext addition. Building on the Rabin cryptosystem, the proposed scheme supports either a single ciphertext multiplication or a single ciphertext addition, with the ciphertext size increasing by a factor of 1.5 after each such operation. This approach strikes a compelling balance between computational efficiency and functional versatility, offering a new lens on secure computation within composite groups.

While the current design is limited to operations involving two ciphertexts, the proposed techniques have the potential to be extended to support multiple ciphertext multiplications and additions. Additionally, although the current construction only achieves one-way security, we believe it opens avenues for further development toward achieving IND-CPA security through the introduction of randomness and additional structure.

These findings contribute to advancing homomorphic encryption by balancing efficiency, functionality, and security, paving the way for further improvements and practical implementations.

Acknowledgments. This work was supported by the Spanish Ministry of Science and Innovation through the PID2021-125962OB-C31 "SECURING" project. Additional funding was provided by the ARTEMISA International Chair of Cybersecurity (C057/23) and the DANGER Strategic Project of Cybersecurity (C062/23), both funded by the Spanish National Institute of Cybersecurity through the European Union—NextGenerationEU and the Recovery, Transformation, and Resilience Plan.

Appendix

Remark 3. Recovering the original messages m_1 and m_2 from a nested ciphertext—whether $Enc_\times^2(m_1 \cdot m_2)$ or $Enc_+^2(m_1 + m_2)$—is information-theoretically impossible, even if the adversary has access to the secret key or can factor N. This follows from Shannon's entropy bound on ciphertexts.

Proof. Consider the nested ciphertext $Enc_\times^2(m_1 \cdot m_2) = \{S_\times + r, \ S_\times \cdot r, \ P_\times\}$, where:

$$S_\times = m_1 m_2 + r_1 r_2, \quad r = m_1 r_2 + m_2 r_1, \quad P_\times = m_1 m_2 r_1 r_2.$$

This ciphertext consists of three components in $\mathbb{Z}_N$, totaling approximately $3 \log N$ bits of information for an η-bit modulus N.

However, these components depend on four unknowns: $(m_1, m_2, r_1, r_2) \in \mathbb{Z}_N^4$. Since only three independent algebraic relations are available, it is impossible to uniquely recover even two of the unknowns.

Moreover, the message pair (m_1, m_2) and the randomness pair (r_1, r_2) are structurally symmetric due to *isochronism*: recovering (m_1, m_2) and (r_1, r_2) are equivalent and (m_1, m_2) inherently reveals (r_1, r_2) and vice versa. Thus, any adversary capable of extracting the messages must also recover the full set (m_1, m_2, r_1, r_2), which requires $4 \log N$ bits of information.

From an information-theoretic standpoint, a ciphertext encoding only $3 \log N$ bits cannot carry $4 \log N$ bits of information. Doing so would violate Shannon's entropy bound, which states that the entropy of the ciphertext must not be less than the entropy of the encoded message.

Therefore, recovering both m_1 and m_2 from the nested ciphertext is information-theoretically impossible.

This argument applies analogously to the additive case $Enc_+^2(m_1 + m_2) = \{S_+, \ P_+ + r, \ P_+ \cdot r\}$, which exhibits the same dependency structure.

Note that Remark 3 is not specific to the composite group setting in which our scheme operates. The impossibility of solving for four variables from three equations is a general limitation that holds in any algebraic group, including over the integers or other structures.

References

1. Boneh, D., Goh, E.-J., Nissim, K.: Evaluating 2-DNF formulas on ciphertexts. In: Kilian, J. (ed.) TCC 2005. LNCS, vol. 3378, pp. 325–341. Springer, Heidelberg (2005). https://doi.org/10.1007/978-3-540-30576-7_18
2. Brakerski, Z.: Fully homomorphic encryption without modulus switching from classical GapSVP. In: Annual International Cryptology Conference (2012). https://api.semanticscholar.org/CorpusID:9156246
3. Brakerski, Z., Gentry, C., Vaikuntanathan, V.: (Leveled) fully homomorphic encryption without bootstrapping. In: Proceedings of the 3rd Innovations in Theoretical Computer Science Conference, ITCS 2012, pp. 309–325. Association for Computing Machinery, New York (2012). https://doi.org/10.1145/2090236.2090262
4. Cheon, J.H., Kim, A., Kim, M., Song, Y.: Homomorphic encryption for arithmetic of approximate numbers. In: International Conference on the Theory and Application of Cryptology and Information Security (2017). https://api.semanticscholar.org/CorpusID:3164123
5. Chillotti, I., Gama, N., Georgieva, M., Izabachène, M.: Faster packed homomorphic operations and efficient circuit bootstrapping for TFHE. In: International Conference on the Theory and Application of Cryptology and Information Security (2017). https://api.semanticscholar.org/CorpusID:40718273
6. van Dijk, M., Gentry, C., Halevi, S., Vaikuntanathan, V.: Fully homomorphic encryption over the integers. In: International Conference on the Theory and Application of Cryptographic Techniques (2010). https://api.semanticscholar.org/CorpusID:5627147
7. Fan, J., Vercauteren, F.: Somewhat practical fully homomorphic encryption. IACR Cryptol. ePrint Arch. **2012**, 144 (2012). https://api.semanticscholar.org/CorpusID:1467571
8. Gentry, C.: Fully homomorphic encryption using ideal lattices. In: Proceedings of the Forty-First Annual ACM Symposium on Theory of Computing, STOC 2009, pp. 169–178. Association for Computing Machinery, New York (2009). https://doi.org/10.1145/1536414.1536440
9. Goldwasser, S., Micali, S.: Probabilistic encryption & how to play mental poker keeping secret all partial information. In: Proceedings of the Fourteenth Annual ACM Symposium on Theory of Computing, STOC 1982, pp. 365–377. Association for Computing Machinery, New York (1982). https://doi.org/10.1145/800070.802212
10. Mahad, Z., Asbullah, M., Ariffin, M.: Efficient methods to overcome Rabin cryptosystem decryption failure. Malaysian J. Math. Sci. **11**, 9–20 (2017)
11. Paillier, P.: Public-key cryptosystems based on composite degree residuosity classes. In: Stern, J. (ed.) EUROCRYPT 1999. LNCS, vol. 1592, pp. 223–238. Springer, Heidelberg (1999). https://doi.org/10.1007/3-540-48910-X_16
12. Pereira, H.: Efficient AGCD-based homomorphic encryption for matrix and vector arithmetic. In: Conti, M., Zhou, J., Casalicchio, E., Spognardi, A. (eds.) ACNS 2020. LNCS, vol. 12146, pp. 110–129. Springer, Cham (2020). https://doi.org/10.1007/978-3-030-57808-4_6
13. Rabin, M.O.: Digitalized signatures and public-key functions as intractable as factorization (1979)
14. Rivest, R.L., Shamir, A., Adleman, L.: A method for obtaining digital signatures and public-key cryptosystems. Commun. ACM **21**(2), 120–126 (1978)

15. Stehlé, D., Steinfeld, R.: Faster fully homomorphic encryption. In: Abe, M. (ed.) ASIACRYPT 2010. LNCS, vol. 6477, pp. 377–394. Springer, Heidelberg (2010). https://doi.org/10.1007/978-3-642-17373-8_22
16. Williams, H.: A modification of the RSA public-key encryption procedure (corresp.). IEEE Trans. Inf. Theory **26**(6), 726–729 (1980)

Cryptanalysis of RSA

A Novel Partial Key Exposure Attack on Common Prime RSA

Mengce Zheng[1]([✉])[iD] and Abderrahmane Nitaj[2][iD]

[1] Zhejiang Wanli University, Ningbo, China
mczheng@zwu.edu.cn
[2] Normandie Univ, UNICAEN, CNRS, LMNO, 14000 Caen, France
abderrahmane.nitaj@unicaen.fr

Abstract. We propose a novel partial key exposure attack on common prime RSA by leveraging lattice-based techniques. In common prime RSA, the primes p and q are defined as $p = 2ga + 1$ and $q = 2gb + 1$ for a common prime g. Recently, Zheng introduced the first partial key exposure attack on this scheme; however, it is limited to instances where $g > N^{1/4}$. In contrast, our work investigates deeper into partial key exposure attacks by presenting a unified generic case that targets one consecutive unknown block of the private key. By employing a lattice-based solving strategy for trivariate integer polynomials, we can effectively identify additional weak private keys that are vulnerable to partial exposure. Extensive numerical experiments validate the correctness and practicality of our proposed attack on common prime RSA.

Keywords: Common Prime RSA · Cryptanalysis · Lattice · Partial Key Exposure Attack · Trivariate Integer Polynomial

1 Introduction

The RSA cryptosystem, originally introduced by Rivest, Shamir, and Adleman [24], remains one of the most prominent public key encryption schemes. To reduce the high computational overhead associated with the original RSA, several variants have been developed, including CRT-RSA [22], multi-prime RSA [6], prime-power RSA [27], and common prime RSA [11]. In this paper, we focus on partial key exposure attacks against the common prime RSA variant by employing a lattice-based solving strategy, which serves as an effective tool to assess cryptanalytic vulnerabilities in RSA and its variants.

Consider an RSA instance with a public key (N, e) and a private key (p, q, d), where the modulus is defined as $N = pq$ with p and q being balanced primes. In the original RSA scheme [24], the exponents e and d are selected as mutual inverses modulo Euler's totient function $\varphi(N) = (p - 1)(q - 1)$. However, it has become customary to define these exponents modulo Carmichael's lambda function [8], i.e.,

$$\lambda(N) = \mathrm{lcm}(p - 1, q - 1),$$

© The Author(s), under exclusive license to Springer Nature Switzerland AG 2026
A. Nitaj et al. (Eds.): AFRICACRYPT 2025, LNCS 15651, pp. 91–112, 2026.
https://doi.org/10.1007/978-3-031-97260-7_5

which represents the least common multiple of $p - 1$ and $q - 1$. In the case of common prime RSA—a variant first suggested by Wiener [31] and later refined by Hinek [11]—the balanced primes p and q possess a special structure that enhances resistance against small private key attacks.

We now delve into the mathematical underpinnings of common prime RSA as described in [11]. In Hinek's design, the balanced primes are defined as

$$p = 2ga + 1, \quad q = 2gb + 1, \tag{1}$$

where g is a common prime and a, b are positive integers. These primes p, q are subject to two constraints: $\gcd(a, b) = 1$, which ensures that $\gcd(p{-}1, q{-}1) = 2g$, and the requirement that $h = 2gab + a + b$ is prime, so that $(pq - 1)/2 = gh$ is a semiprime with a bit-length comparable to that of the RSA modulus N. A modified version of the common prime generation algorithm from [11] is provided in Algorithm 1 in Appendix A.

Within the common prime RSA framework, the public and private exponents e and d are defined modulo

$$\lambda(N) = \lambda(pq) = \mathrm{lcm}(p - 1, q - 1) = \mathrm{lcm}(2ga, 2gb) = 2gab.$$

According to Hinek's construction, the modulus can be expressed as

$$N = pq = (2ga + 1)(2gb + 1) = 2g(2gab + a + b) + 1 = 2gh + 1. \tag{2}$$

Moreover, the key congruence

$$ed \equiv 1 \pmod{2gab}, \tag{3}$$

can be equivalently written as

$$ed = 2gabk + 1, \tag{4}$$

where k is an unknown positive integer relatively prime to $2g$.

Throughout this paper, we use the symbol $\simeq$ to indicate asymptotic equivalence with respect to a certain power of the RSA modulus N. In particular, we assume that the large prime satisfies $g \simeq N^\gamma$ and that the private exponent obeys $d \simeq N^\delta$. Since balanced primes yield $\gcd(p - 1, q - 1) = 2g$, it follows that $0 < \gamma < 1/2$. Furthermore, by assuming that the bit-length of e is approximately that of N/g, we have $e \simeq N^{1-\gamma}$.

The security of common prime RSA has been extensively analyzed in the literature [11, 14, 17, 21, 26, 35]. Notably, partial key exposure attacks—wherein an adversary obtains a fraction of the private key bits—are particularly pertinent in resource-constrained environments such as the Internet of Things [21]. These attacks exploit side-channel information acquired through methods including cold boot attacks [10] and various other side-channel analysis techniques [15, 23, 25]. Therefore, a rigorous investigation of partial key exposure attacks on common prime RSA is of considerable importance.

Partial key exposure attacks on RSA, which rely on the leakage of partial information about the private key, were initially introduced by Boneh et al. [5]. Such attacks typically exploit the knowledge of either the most significant bits (MSBs) or the least significant bits (LSBs) of the private exponent d, information that may be obtained via side-channel attacks. Subsequently, Blömer and May [2] refined these techniques using Coppersmith's lattice-based techniques [7], demonstrating that RSA becomes vulnerable even for larger public exponents when some private key bits are exposed. Ernst et al. [9] further proposed attacks applicable to full-size exponents (i.e., $e \simeq N$ or $d \simeq N$) based on three theorems under a common heuristic assumption. The most effective partial key exposure attack on standard RSA to date was proposed by Takayasu and Kunihiro [29], which achieves Boneh-Durfee's bound [4] for small private key attacks. In addition, similar attack techniques have been extended to other RSA variants [13,20,32]. However, research focusing on partial key exposure attacks for the common prime RSA scheme is rare, with Zheng's work [33,34] being an exception.

1.1   Related Work

Recently, Zheng [33,34] presented the first dedicated investigation of partial key exposure attacks on common prime RSA. His study begins by the congruence $ed \equiv 1 \pmod{2gab}$. To address the small private key attack scenario on common prime RSA, his method focuses on solving the congruence $ex - 1 \equiv 0 \pmod{g}$, where $x = d$ is treated as the small root.

To extend the analysis to partial key exposure attacks, Zheng formalized several attack scenarios. These include cases where the MSBs of the private key, the LSBs, or both are leaked. Accordingly, the attack scenarios are classified into three cases: the MSB case, the LSB case, and the MSB-LSB case. In each scenario, the private key d assumes a different form based on the leaked information. By substituting the corresponding form of d into the congruence $ex - 1 \equiv 0 \pmod{g}$ and applying a modular inverse, a new modular univariate linear equation is derived for each scenario. To solve these equations, Zheng employs the lattice-based method introduced by Coppersmith [7].

Furthermore, an auxiliary modular univariate linear equation can be derived from the identity $(p-1)(q-1) = 2ga \cdot 2gb = 4g^2ab$, which implies $pq-p-q+1 \equiv 0 \pmod{g^2}$. Thus, one seeks to solve $x + N + 1 \equiv 0 \pmod{g^2}$, with $x = -(p+q)$ as the small root. In this way, the problem reduces to solving two simultaneous modular univariate linear equations. The following proposition summarizes the first demonstration of the MSB-LSB case partial key exposure attack on common prime RSA.

Proposition 1 ([34]). *Let $N = pq$ be an ℓ-bit common prime RSA modulus with balanced primes p and q of equal bit-length. Let $e \simeq N^{1-\gamma}$ and $d \simeq N^\delta$ be the public and private exponents satisfying*

$$ed \equiv 1 \pmod{\mathrm{lcm}(p - 1, q - 1)},$$

with $\gcd(p-1, q-1) = 2g$ for a common prime $g \simeq N^\gamma$. Suppose an approximation of d is available, where the most significant bits d_M form a $(\delta_M \ell)$-bit block and the least significant bits d_L form a $(\delta_L \ell)$-bit block, such that

$$d = d_M M + \bar{d} L + d_L,$$

with $M = 2^{(\delta - \delta_M)\ell}$, $L = 2^{\delta_L \ell}$, and the unknown component $\bar{d}$ satisfying $|\bar{d}| \leq N^{\delta - \delta_M - \delta_L}$. Then, N can be efficiently factored in time polynomial in ℓ if

$$\delta_M + \delta_L < \delta < 4\gamma^3 + \delta_M + \delta_L, \quad \frac{1}{4} \leq \gamma < \frac{1}{2}.$$

The aforementioned work explores a novel domain in which partial leakage of private key bits is assumed. Zheng [34] proposed three distinct attacks corresponding to the MSB, LSB, and MSB-LSB cases. His results demonstrate new advancements in assessing the security of common prime RSA relative to previous small private key attacks. Moreover, Zheng noted that several enhancements, such as the adoption of more efficient lattice-based strategies, could further improve the primary results. This observation leaves ample room for future work to generalize partial key exposure attacks on common prime RSA.

1.2 Our Contribution

Although Zheng's work represents a seminal contribution to partial key exposure attacks on common prime RSA, it is subject to the limitation that $1/4 \leq \gamma < 1/2$. Hence, there is a need to develop attacks for scenarios where the prime g is smaller (i.e., $\gamma < 1/4$). Inspired by the small private key attack on common prime RSA [14], we propose a novel partial key exposure attack based on solving trivariate integer polynomial equations, where the desired root is related to the secret parameters inherent in common prime RSA. Moreover, in contrast to the three separate scenarios presented in [34], our approach unifies them into a generic case that considers only one consecutive unknown block in the private key.

Our main contributions are summarized as follows:

- We extend the seminal partial-key-leakage attack on common-prime RSA [34] from the regime $1/4 \leq \gamma < 1/2$ down to *any* $\gamma < 1/2$, in particular covering $\gamma < 1/4$.
- We introduce a generic trivariate-polynomial based formulation that simultaneously handles MSB, LSB, and MSB-LSB exposures of the private key.
- We derive attack bounds on the maximum exploitable exponent size δ as a function of $(\gamma, \delta_M, \delta_L)$, improving previous limits.
- We validate the proposed attack in `SageMath` with 1024-bit and 2048-bit moduli experiments and publish our detailed implementation under an open-source license on `GitHub`[1].

---

[1] https://github.com/MengceZheng/CPRSA_PKEA

1.3 Organization

The remainder of this paper is organized as follows. In Sect. 2 we introduce key mathematical lemmas and fundamental facts pertinent to the lattice-based solving strategy. Section 3 details our new partial key exposure attack on common prime RSA. In Sect. 4 we present numerical experimental results to substantiate the correctness and effectiveness of the proposed attack. Finally, Sect. 5 concludes the paper.

2 Preliminaries

This section reviews the fundamental concepts and techniques employed in our cryptanalysis, including lattice reduction—mostly the LLL algorithm [16]—and Coppersmith's lattice-based method [7], which was later refined via Howgrave-Graham's lemma [12]. For a more comprehensive understanding, readers are referred to [18,19,36]. We begin by defining a lattice as a discrete additive subgroup of $\mathbb{R}^n$.

Definition 1. *A* lattice Λ *is the set of all integer linear combinations of ω linearly independent vectors $\boldsymbol{b}_1, \ldots, \boldsymbol{b}_\omega \in \mathbb{R}^n$, i.e.,*

$$\Lambda = \left\{ \sum_{i=1}^{\omega} z_i \boldsymbol{b}_i : z_i \in \mathbb{Z} \right\}.$$

The *determinant* of a lattice, denoted $\det(\Lambda)$, is defined as $\sqrt{\det(BB^\mathsf{T})}$, where B is the basis matrix whose rows are the basis vectors $\boldsymbol{b}_1, \ldots, \boldsymbol{b}_\omega$ and B^T denotes its transpose. In the case of a full-rank lattice (i.e., $\omega = n$), the determinant simplifies to $\det(\Lambda) = |\det(B)|$. The integers n and ω are referred to as the *dimension* and the *rank* of the lattice, respectively.

The LLL algorithm [16] is a widely used tool for efficiently obtaining an approximately short basis for a lattice. As shown in [18], the LLL algorithm produces a reduced basis $(\boldsymbol{v}_1, \boldsymbol{v}_2, \ldots, \boldsymbol{v}_\omega)$ satisfying the following bound.

Lemma 1 ([16,18]). *Let Λ be an ω-dimensional lattice. The LLL algorithm returns a reduced basis $(\boldsymbol{v}_1, \boldsymbol{v}_2, \ldots, \boldsymbol{v}_\omega)$ such that, for each $1 \leq i \leq \omega$,*

$$\|\boldsymbol{v}_1\|, \ldots, \|\boldsymbol{v}_i\| \leq 2^{\frac{\omega(\omega-1)}{4(\omega+1-i)}} \det(\Lambda)^{\frac{1}{\omega+1-i}}.$$

The running time of the LLL algorithm is polynomial in ω and in the logarithm of the maximal input vector component.

Howgrave-Graham's lemma [12] provides a criterion to decide when a root of a modular polynomial equation is also a root over the integers. Consider an integer polynomial

$$g(x_1, \ldots, x_n) = \sum a_{i_1, \ldots, i_n} x_1^{i_1} \cdots x_n^{i_n}$$

with the norm defined by

$$\|g(x_1,\ldots,x_n)\| := \sqrt{\sum |a_{i_1,\ldots,i_n}|^2}.$$

The following lemma is instrumental in our analysis.

Lemma 2 ([12]). *Let* $g(x_1,\ldots,x_n) \in \mathbb{Z}[x_1,\ldots,x_n]$ *be an integer polynomial comprising at most* ω *monomials. Let* $R, X_1,\ldots,X_n$ *be given positive integers. If there exists a tuple* $(x_1^\star,\ldots,x_n^\star)$ *with* $|x_i^\star| \leq X_i$ *for* $1 \leq i \leq n$ *such that*

$$g(x_1^\star,\ldots,x_n^\star) \equiv 0 \pmod{R},$$

and if

$$\|g(x_1 X_1,\ldots,x_n X_n)\| < \frac{R}{\sqrt{\omega}},$$

then $g(x_1^\star,\ldots,x_n^\star) = 0$ *over the integers.*

By combining the output of the LLL algorithm with Howgrave-Graham's lemma, one can effectively solve modular or integer polynomial equations. In practice, if one computes the first ℓ reduced vectors of the lattice, successful application of the lattice-based solving strategy is achieved provided that

$$2^{\frac{\omega(\omega-1)}{4(\omega+1-\ell)}} \det(\Lambda)^{\frac{1}{\omega+1-\ell}} < \frac{R}{\sqrt{\omega}}.$$

This condition can be rearranged as

$$\det(\Lambda) < R^{\omega+1-\ell} 2^{-\frac{\omega(\omega-1)}{4}} \omega^{-\frac{\omega+1-\ell}{2}}.$$

Since $\ell < \omega \ll R$, this further implies, up to a small error term, that $\det(\Lambda) < R^{\omega-\epsilon}$, which asymptotically leads to the condition

$$\det(\Lambda) < R^{\omega}. \qquad (5)$$

This inequality forms the basis for effectively solving the targeted modular or integer polynomial equations.

A critical aspect of the lattice-based solving strategy is the construction of an appropriate lattice. Several works (e.g., [3,14,28]) have focused on designing lattices with optimized solving conditions. In our approach, we adopt the strategy proposed by Jochemsz-May [14], which constructs a lattice with a triangular basis matrix so that the determinant is easily computed as the product of its diagonal elements.

In our setting, we seek a small root of a trivariate integer polynomial of the form

$$f(x,y,z) = a_1 x^2 + a_2 xy + a_3 xz + a_4 yz + a_5 x + a_6 y + a_7 z + a_0.$$

We now describe in detail the lattice-based strategy to solve for the small root $(x^\star, y^\star, z^\star)$ of $f(x,y,z)$.

Polynomial Target: Suppose $f(x, y, z)$ is an irreducible trivariate polynomial with the property that $f(x^\star, y^\star, z^\star) = 0$ for some unknown triple $(x^\star, y^\star, z^\star)$ satisfying the bounds $|x^\star| \leq X$, $|y^\star| \leq Y$, and $|z^\star| \leq Z$. Define

$$U = \|f(xX, yY, zZ)\|_\infty, \tag{6}$$

which represents the maximum absolute value of the coefficients when the variables are scaled by their bounds. An additional integer parameter R is then introduced as a useful modulus. If the constant term $a_0 \neq 1$, one may rescale the polynomial via $f(x, y, z) \leftarrow a_0^{-1} f(x, y, z) \pmod{R}$ to ensure the constant term equal to 1.

Shift Construction: Using $f(x, y, z)$, one constructs a family of *shift polynomials* $g_{[i,j,k]}(x, y, z)$ such that each satisfies

$$g_{[i,j,k]}(x^\star, y^\star, z^\star) \equiv 0 \pmod{R}.$$

A standard method is to define two monomial sets:

$$\mathcal{M}_\uparrow = \bigcup_{0 \leq l \leq t} \{x^{i+l} y^j z^k : x^i y^j z^k \in \text{monomial}(f^{m-1})\},$$

$$\mathcal{M}_\downarrow = \bigcup_{0 \leq l \leq t} \{x^{i+l} y^j z^k : x^i y^j z^k \in \text{monomial}(f^m)\},$$

where m is a suitably chosen positive integer and $t \geq 0$ is an integer. These sets yield the corresponding index sets $\mathcal{I}_\uparrow$ and $\mathcal{I}_\downarrow$. Let μ_x, μ_y, and μ_z denote the maximum degrees in x, y, and z, respectively, appearing in $\mathcal{M}_\uparrow$. Then, set

$$R := U\, X^{\mu_x} Y^{\mu_y} Z^{\mu_z}.$$

The shift polynomials $g_{[i,j,k]}(x, y, z)$ are defined by

$$\begin{cases} x^i y^j z^k\, f(x, y, z)\, X^{\mu_x - i} Y^{\mu_y - j} Z^{\mu_z - k}, & \text{if } x^i y^j z^k \in \mathcal{M}_\uparrow, \\ x^i y^j z^k\, R, & \text{if } x^i y^j z^k \in \mathcal{M}_\downarrow \setminus \mathcal{M}_\uparrow. \end{cases}$$

By construction, each $g_{[i,j,k]}(x, y, z)$ vanishes modulo R at $(x^\star, y^\star, z^\star)$.

Lattice Generation: Ordering the monomials and polynomials according to a chosen term order (e.g., ascending graded lexicographic order), one can form a lattice Λ by mapping the coefficient vectors of the scaled shift polynomials $g_{[i,j,k]}(xX, yY, zZ)$, for $[i, j, k] \in \mathcal{I}_\downarrow$, into row vectors $\boldsymbol{b}_1, \ldots, \boldsymbol{b}_\omega$ of a basis matrix B, where $\omega = |\mathcal{M}_\downarrow|$. Under the chosen order, this matrix is full-rank and triangular, making the determinant easy to compute as the product of its diagonal entries.

Lattice Reduction: Applying the LLL algorithm to the basis matrix B, one obtains a sequence of reduced vectors $(\boldsymbol{v}_1, \ldots, \boldsymbol{v}_\ell)$ (with $\ell \geq 2$). These vectors correspond to integer polynomials $h_i(x, y, z)$, each being a linear combination of the $g_{[i,j,k]}(x, y, z)$, and satisfying

$$h_i(x^\star, y^\star, z^\star) \equiv 0 \pmod{R}, \quad 1 \leq i \leq \ell.$$

By Lemma 1 and Lemma 2, if the parameters involved satisfy the condition in (5), then the small root $(x^\star, y^\star, z^\star)$ is guaranteed to be a correct integer solution.

Root Extraction: Provided that at least two of the derived polynomials, say $h_1(x, y, z)$ and $h_2(x, y, z)$, are algebraically independent, the system

$$\mathcal{V} = \{f(x, y, z), h_1(x, y, z), h_2(x, y, z)\}$$

can be solved using techniques such as resultant or Gröbner basis computations [1] to recover the unique small root $(x^\star, y^\star, z^\star)$. The overall running time is dominated by the lattice reduction and the subsequent root recovery, both of which can be performed in polynomial time relative to the input size.

It is important to note that the lattice-based solving strategy is heuristic in nature, as there is no absolute guarantee that the constructed integer polynomials will always be algebraically independent. In practice, however, it is commonly assumed in lattice-based attacks that the polynomials derived via the LLL algorithm exhibit algebraic independence.

Assumption 1. *The derived integer polynomials by the LLL reduction algorithm are algebraically independent, ensuring that their common root can be efficiently recovered.*

In most prior Coppersmith-style attacks on RSA variants (e.g. Boneh-Durfee [4], Jochemsz-May [14]) and in our own extensive experiments (see Sect. 4), the reduced vectors always yielded independent polynomials whose common small root was recovered with negligible failure rate.

3   Novel Partial Key Exposure Attack

We present a new partial key exposure attack on common prime RSA by applying the lattice-based solving strategy outlined in Sect. 2. Our main result is summarized in the following proposition.

Proposition 2. *Let $N = pq$ be an ℓ-bit common prime RSA modulus with balanced primes p and q of equal bit-length. Let $e \simeq N^{1-\gamma}$ and $d \simeq N^{\delta}$ be the public and private exponents satisfying*

$$ed \equiv 1 \pmod{\mathrm{lcm}(p-1, q-1)},$$

with $\gcd(p-1, q-1) = 2g$ for a common prime $g \simeq N^{\gamma}$. Suppose an approximation of d is available, where the most significant bits d_M form a $(\delta_M \ell)$-bit block and the least significant bits d_L form a $(\delta_L \ell)$-bit block, such that

$$d = d_M M + \bar{d} L + d_L,$$

where $M = 2^{(\delta - \delta_{\mathrm{M}})\ell}$, $L = 2^{\delta_{\mathrm{L}}\ell}$, and the unknown component $\bar{d}$ satisfies $|\bar{d}| \leq N^{\delta - \delta_{\mathrm{M}} - \delta_{\mathrm{L}}}$. Then, N can be efficiently factored in time polynomial in ℓ if

$$\begin{cases} \delta < \gamma + 1 - \dfrac{\sqrt{4(\gamma - \delta_{\mathrm{M}} - \delta_{\mathrm{L}})^2 + 20(\gamma - \delta_{\mathrm{M}} - \delta_{\mathrm{L}}) + 13}}{4}, & \text{if } \gamma \leq \delta_{\mathrm{M}} + \delta_{\mathrm{L}} + \dfrac{3}{10}, \\ \delta < \dfrac{4\gamma + 7\delta_{\mathrm{M}} + 7\delta_{\mathrm{L}} + 1}{11}, & \text{if } \gamma > \delta_{\mathrm{M}} + \delta_{\mathrm{L}} + \dfrac{3}{10}. \end{cases}$$

Proof. Recall that common prime RSA satisfies the key equation $ed = 2gabk+1$, where k is an unknown positive integer. By substituting $2ga = p - 1$ and $2gb = q - 1$ into (4), we obtain

$$ed = (p - 1)bk + 1, \quad ed = (q - 1)ak + 1.$$

These equations imply

$$ed - 1 + bk = pbk, \quad ed - 1 + ak = qak.$$

Multiplying the two equations yields

$$\big(ed - 1 + bk\big)\big(ed - 1 + ak\big) = (pbk)(qak) = ak \cdot bk \cdot N.$$

Substitute the decomposition

$$d = d_{\mathrm{M}} M + \bar{d} L + d_{\mathrm{L}}$$

and treat $\bar{d}$, ak, and bk as unknowns. Then, the above relation becomes

$$\Big(e(d_{\mathrm{M}} M + \bar{d} L + d_{\mathrm{L}}) - 1 + bk\Big)\Big(e(d_{\mathrm{M}} M + \bar{d} L + d_{\mathrm{L}}) - 1 + ak\Big) - ak \cdot bk \cdot N = 0.$$

Let $x = \bar{d}$, $y = ak$, and $z = bk$. Then, the above equation can be written as a trivariate integer polynomial

$$f(x, y, z) = a_1 x^2 + a_2 xy + a_3 xz + a_4 yz + a_5 x + a_6 y + a_7 z + a_0 = 0, \qquad (7)$$

with the coefficients given by

$$a_0 = e^2 d_{\mathrm{M}}^2 M^2 + 2e^2 d_{\mathrm{M}} d_{\mathrm{L}} M + e^2 d_{\mathrm{L}}^2 - 2ed_{\mathrm{M}} M - 2ed_{\mathrm{L}} + 1,$$

$$a_1 = e^2 L^2,$$

$$a_2 = a_3 = eL,$$

$$a_4 = -N + 1,$$

$$a_5 = 2e^2 d_{\mathrm{M}} ML + 2e^2 d_{\mathrm{L}} L - 2eL,$$

$$a_6 = a_7 = ed_{\mathrm{M}} M + ed_{\mathrm{L}} - 1.$$

Thus, the task reduces to finding the small root $(x^\star, y^\star, z^\star) = (\bar{d}, ak, bk)$ of the polynomial (7).

Using the estimates $e \simeq N^{1-\gamma}$ and $d \simeq N^{\delta}$, and from (4) we deduce that

$$ak \simeq N^{\delta-\gamma+1/2} \quad \text{and} \quad bk \simeq N^{\delta-\gamma+1/2}.$$

Thus, we set the upper bounds:

$$|x^{\star}| \leq X = N^{\delta-\delta_{\mathrm{M}}-\delta_{\mathrm{L}}}, \quad |y^{\star}| \leq Y = N^{\delta-\gamma+1/2}, \quad |z^{\star}| \leq Z = N^{\delta-\gamma+1/2}. \quad (8)$$

In the lattice-based solving strategy, the maximal coefficient is defined by

$$U = \|f(xX, yY, zZ)\|_{\infty},$$

which can be estimated as

$$
\begin{aligned}
U &= \max\left\{|a_1|X^2, |a_2|XY, |a_3|XZ, |a_4|YZ, |a_5|X, |a_6|Y, |a_7|Z, |a_0|\right\} \\
&= \max\left\{N^{2\delta-2\gamma-2\delta_{\mathrm{M}}+2}, N^{2\delta-2\gamma-\delta_{\mathrm{M}}+3/2}, N^{2\delta-2\gamma+2}, \right. \\
&\qquad\qquad \left. N^{2\delta-2\gamma-\delta_{\mathrm{M}}+2}, N^{2\delta-2\gamma+3/2}, N^{2\delta-2\gamma+2}\right\} \\
&= N^{2\delta-2\gamma+2}.
\end{aligned}
$$

Since X is smaller than both Y and Z, we apply an extra shift in the x-variable during the shift construction stage. For a chosen positive integer m and a non-negative integer $t = \tau m$, we define the monomial sets

$$\mathcal{M}_{\uparrow} = \bigcup_{0 \leq l \leq t} \{x^{i+l}y^j z^k : x^i y^j z^k \in \mathrm{monomial}(f^{m-1})\},$$

$$\mathcal{M}_{\downarrow} = \bigcup_{0 \leq l \leq t} \{x^{i+l}y^j z^k : x^i y^j z^k \in \mathrm{monomial}(f^{m})\}.$$

That is, if we denote by $\mathcal{I}_{\uparrow}$ and $\mathcal{I}_{\downarrow}$ the corresponding integer index sets, then:

$$x^i y^j z^k \in \mathcal{M}_{\uparrow} \iff \begin{cases} 0 \leq j \leq m-1, \\ 0 \leq k \leq m-1, \\ 0 \leq i \leq 2m-2+t-j-k; \end{cases}$$

$$x^i y^j z^k \in \mathcal{M}_{\downarrow} \iff \begin{cases} 0 \leq j \leq m, \\ 0 \leq k \leq m, \\ 0 \leq i \leq 2m+t-j-k. \end{cases}$$

Accordingly, the maximal degrees in $\mathcal{M}_{\uparrow}$ are $\mu_x = 2m-2+t$, $\mu_y = \mu_z = m-1$, and we set

$$R = U X^{2m-2+t} Y^{m-1} Z^{m-1}.$$

Then, the shift polynomials $g_{[i,j,k]}(x, y, z)$ are defined as

$$\begin{cases} x^i y^j z^k f(x, y, z) X^{2m-2+t-i} Y^{m-1-j} Z^{m-1-k}, & \text{if } x^i y^j z^k \in \mathcal{M}_{\uparrow}, \\ x^i y^j z^k R, & \text{if } x^i y^j z^k \in \mathcal{M}_{\downarrow} \setminus \mathcal{M}_{\uparrow}. \end{cases}$$

To be specific, the monomials of $\mathcal{M}_\downarrow \setminus \mathcal{M}_\uparrow$ are related to $[i, j, k]$ triples in $\mathcal{I}_\downarrow \setminus \mathcal{I}_\uparrow$ with

$$\begin{cases} j = m, \\ k = 0, \ldots, m - 1, \\ i = 0, \ldots, m - 2 + t - k. \end{cases} \quad \begin{cases} j = 0, \ldots, m - 1, \\ k = m, \\ i = 0, \ldots, m - 2 + t - j. \end{cases} \quad \begin{cases} j = m, \\ k = m, \\ i = 0, \ldots, t. \end{cases}$$

and

$$\begin{cases} j = 0, \ldots, m - 1, \\ k = 0, \ldots, m - 1, \\ i = 2m - 1 + t - j - k, 2m + t - j - k. \end{cases}$$

The polynomial order $\prec_p$ (resp. the monomial order $\prec_m$) related to the row order (resp. the column order) of B are specified as follows. The rule is to arrange the shift polynomials $g_{[i,j,k]}$ in the ascending graded lexicographic order. The polynomial order $\prec_p$ is defined as $g_{[i,j,k]} \prec_p g_{[i',j',k']}$ if $i + j + k < i' + j' + k'$, or $i + j + k = i' + j' + k'$, $i > i'$, or $i + j + k = i' + j' + k'$, $i = i'$, $j > j'$. The monomial order $\prec_m$ is defined as $x^i y^j z^k \prec_m x^{i'} y^{j'} z^{k'}$ similarly. For instance, Table 1 provides a toy example of the lattice basis matrix B for $m = 1$ and $t = 1$, where "$*$" denotes a nonzero off-diagonal entry and other off-diagonal entries are 0.

Table 1. A toy example of lattice basis matrix B with $m = 1$ and $t = 1$.

$g_{[i,j,k]}$	$x^i y^j z^k$											
	1	x	y	z	x^2	xy	xz	yz	x^3	$x^2 y$	$x^2 z$	xyz
$g_{[0,0,0]}$	X	$*$	$*$	$*$	$*$	$*$	$*$	$*$				
$g_{[1,0,0]}$		X			$*$	$*$	$*$		$*$	$*$	$*$	$*$
$g_{[0,1,0]}$			YR									
$g_{[0,0,1]}$				ZR								
$g_{[2,0,0]}$					$X^2 R$							
$g_{[1,1,0]}$						XYR						
$g_{[1,0,1]}$							XZR					
$g_{[0,1,1]}$								YZR				
$g_{[3,0,0]}$									$X^3 R$			
$g_{[2,1,0]}$										$X^2 YR$		
$g_{[2,0,1]}$											$X^2 ZR$	
$g_{[1,1,1]}$												XYZR

The coefficient vectors of the scaled shift polynomials $g_{[i,j,k]}(xX, yY, zZ)$ are then used as the rows of a lattice basis matrix B regarding a lattice Λ. The respective diagonal elements of $g_{[i,j,k]}(xX, yY, zZ)$, i.e., the leading terms of $g_{[i,j,k]}(xX, yY, zZ)$ are

$$\begin{cases} X^{2m-2+t} Y^{m-1} Z^{m-1}, & \text{if } x^i y^j z^k \in \mathcal{M}_\uparrow, \\ X^i Y^j Z^k R, & \text{if } x^i y^j z^k \in \mathcal{M}_\downarrow \setminus \mathcal{M}_\uparrow. \end{cases}$$

Since $R = UX^{2m-2+t}Y^{m-1}Z^{m-1}$, the determinant $\det(\Lambda)$ can be expressed (after appropriate grouping) in the form

$$\left(\frac{R}{U}\right)^{s_\uparrow} X^{s_X} Y^{s_Y} Z^{s_Z} R^{s_R},$$

where

$$s_\uparrow = |\mathcal{M}_\uparrow|, \quad s_R = |\mathcal{M}_\downarrow \setminus \mathcal{M}_\uparrow|, \quad \omega = |\mathcal{M}_\downarrow| = s_\uparrow + s_R,$$

and

$$s_X = \sum_{[i,j,k]\in\mathcal{I}_\downarrow\setminus\mathcal{I}_\uparrow} i, \quad s_Y = \sum_{[i,j,k]\in\mathcal{I}_\downarrow\setminus\mathcal{I}_\uparrow} j, \quad s_Z = \sum_{[i,j,k]\in\mathcal{I}_\downarrow\setminus\mathcal{I}_\uparrow} k.$$

Invoking the lattice condition (5) with $\omega = |\mathcal{M}_\downarrow| = |\mathcal{M}_\uparrow| + |\mathcal{M}_\downarrow \setminus \mathcal{M}_\uparrow| = s_\uparrow + s_R$ leads to

$$X^{s_X} Y^{s_Y} Z^{s_Z} < U^{s_\uparrow}. \tag{9}$$

By calculating $s_\uparrow$, s_X, s_Y, s_Z and representing them as functions of dominated terms through the above deduction, we obtain

$$s_\uparrow = |\mathcal{M}_\uparrow| = \sum_{j=0}^{m-1}\sum_{k=0}^{m-1}\sum_{i=0}^{2m-2+t-j-k} 1 = m^3 + m^2 t + o(m^3),$$

$$s_X = \sum_{[i,j,k]\in\mathcal{I}_\downarrow\setminus\mathcal{I}_\uparrow} i$$

$$= \sum_{j=0}^{m}\sum_{k=0}^{m}\sum_{i=0}^{2m+t-j-k} i - \sum_{j=0}^{m-1}\sum_{k=0}^{m-1}\sum_{i=0}^{2m-2+t-j-k} i = \frac{7m^3}{3} + 3m^2 t + mt^2 + o(m^3),$$

$$s_Y = \sum_{[i,j,k]\in\mathcal{I}_\downarrow\setminus\mathcal{I}_\uparrow} j$$

$$= \sum_{j=0}^{m}\sum_{k=0}^{m}\sum_{i=0}^{2m+t-j-k} j - \sum_{j=0}^{m-1}\sum_{k=0}^{m-1}\sum_{i=0}^{2m-2+t-j-k} j = \frac{5m^3}{3} + \frac{3m^2 t}{2} + o(m^3),$$

$$s_Z = \sum_{[i,j,k]\in\mathcal{I}_\downarrow\setminus\mathcal{I}_\uparrow} k$$

$$= \sum_{j=0}^{m}\sum_{k=0}^{m}\sum_{i=0}^{2m+t-j-k} k - \sum_{j=0}^{m-1}\sum_{k=0}^{m-1}\sum_{i=0}^{2m-2+t-j-k} k = \frac{5m^3}{3} + \frac{3m^2 t}{2} + o(m^3).$$

Letting m go to infinity with $t = \tau m$ (omitting its rounding) and ignoring lower-order terms $o(m^3)$ gives

$$s_\uparrow = (1+\tau)m^3, \quad s_X = \left(\frac{7}{3} + 3\tau + \tau^2\right)m^3, \quad s_Y = s_Z = \left(\frac{5}{3} + \frac{3\tau}{2}\right)m^3. \tag{10}$$

Substituting the upper bounds from (8) and $U = N^{2\delta-2\gamma+2}$ with (10) into (9), and equating the exponents (with respect to N), we obtain the inequality

$$(\delta - \delta_{\mathrm{M}} - \delta_{\mathrm{L}})\left(\frac{7}{3} + 3\tau + \tau^2\right) + 2\left(\delta - \gamma + \frac{1}{2}\right)\left(\frac{5}{3} + \frac{3\tau}{2}\right)$$
$$< (2\delta - 2\gamma + 2)(1 + \tau).$$

After further simplification, this reduces to

$$\delta\left(\frac{11}{3} + 4\tau + \tau^2\right) < (\delta_{\mathrm{M}} + \delta_{\mathrm{L}})\left(\frac{7}{3} + 3\tau + \tau^2\right) + \gamma\left(\frac{4}{3} + \tau\right) + \frac{1}{3} + \frac{\tau}{2}.$$

Rearranging yields

$$\delta < \delta_{\mathrm{M}} + \delta_{\mathrm{L}} + \frac{8\gamma - 8\delta_{\mathrm{M}} - 8\delta_{\mathrm{L}} + 2 + (6\gamma - 6\delta_{\mathrm{M}} - 6\delta_{\mathrm{L}} + 3)\tau}{22 + 24\tau + 6\tau^2}. \tag{11}$$

Optimizing the right-hand side with respect to τ, define

$$\eta := \gamma - \delta_{\mathrm{M}} - \delta_{\mathrm{L}} \quad \text{and} \quad \xi := \frac{8\eta + 2 + (6\eta + 3)\tau}{22 + 24\tau + 6\tau^2}.$$

It can be shown that the maximal value of ξ is achieved at

$$\tau_0 = \frac{\sqrt{4\eta^2 + 20\eta + 13} - 8\eta - 2}{3(2\eta + 1)},$$

which leads to

$$\xi \le \eta + 1 - \frac{\sqrt{4\eta^2 + 20\eta + 13}}{4}.$$

Substituting back $\eta = \gamma - \delta_{\mathrm{M}} - \delta_{\mathrm{L}}$, we deduce that

$$\delta < \gamma + 1 - \frac{\sqrt{4(\gamma - \delta_{\mathrm{M}} - \delta_{\mathrm{L}})^2 + 20(\gamma - \delta_{\mathrm{M}} - \delta_{\mathrm{L}}) + 13}}{4}, \tag{12}$$

which holds when $\gamma \le \delta_{\mathrm{M}} + \delta_{\mathrm{L}} + \frac{3}{10}$ (so that $\tau_0 \ge 0$ and hence $\eta \le \frac{3}{10}$).

For the case $\gamma > \delta_{\mathrm{M}} + \delta_{\mathrm{L}} + \frac{3}{10}$, one should set $\tau_0 = 0$, and (11) then directly implies

$$\delta < \frac{4\gamma + 7\delta_{\mathrm{M}} + 7\delta_{\mathrm{L}} + 1}{11}. \tag{13}$$

Collecting (12) and (13) yields the final attack bound:

$$\begin{cases} \delta < \gamma + 1 - \dfrac{\sqrt{4(\gamma - \delta_{\mathrm{M}} - \delta_{\mathrm{L}})^2 + 20(\gamma - \delta_{\mathrm{M}} - \delta_{\mathrm{L}}) + 13}}{4}, & \gamma \le \delta_{\mathrm{M}} + \delta_{\mathrm{L}} + \dfrac{3}{10}, \\ \delta < \dfrac{4\gamma + 7\delta_{\mathrm{M}} + 7\delta_{\mathrm{L}} + 1}{11}, & \gamma > \delta_{\mathrm{M}} + \delta_{\mathrm{L}} + \dfrac{3}{10}. \end{cases}$$

Once the integer polynomial (7) is solved, we can recover the common root $(x^\star, y^\star, z^\star) = (\bar{d}, ak, bk)$. Since $\gcd(a, b) = 1$, we can compute

$$k = \gcd(y^\star, z^\star),$$

from which it follows that $a = y^\star/k$ and $b = z^\star/k$. With the recovered $\bar{d}$ (and hence d), the equation $ed = 2gabk + 1$ (with known a, b, and k) yields

$$g = \frac{ed - 1}{2abk}.$$

Finally, the primes are given by

$$p = 2ga + 1, \quad q = 2gb + 1,$$

which furnishes the factorization of N. All these steps, including lattice reduction and root extraction, are executable in time polynomial in ℓ. □

Remark 1. It is interesting to note that when $\delta_M = \delta_L = 0$, our proposed attack reduces to the small private key attack on common prime RSA as described in [14] (i.e., in the absence of any partial key exposure). In contrast, when a fraction of the most or least significant bits is leaked, our attack extends and strengthens the small private key attack, thereby enlarging the vulnerable bound on the private key.

Remark 2. Our attack would be easier to understand if defining $\delta = \delta_U + \delta_K$ with expressions $\delta_U = \delta - \delta_M - \delta_L$ and $\delta_K = \delta_M + \delta_L$. This makes the dependence on known (i.e., δ_K) vs. unknown (i.e., δ_U) bits explicit. One may readily see that the attack bound on δ increases as the attacker knows more bits, and that it is irrelevant whether MSBs or LSBs are known.

Remark 3. The bounds of Proposition 2 can be reproduced from the small private key attack on Common Prime RSA in [35, Proposition 1] by substituting $\delta' = \delta - \delta_K$ and $\gamma' = \gamma - \delta_K$.

4   Experimental Results

In order to assess the practicality and effectiveness of our proposed partial key exposure attack on common prime RSA (as formalized in Proposition 2), we carried out a series of numerical experiments. All experiments were performed using SageMath [30] on a system configured with a 64-bit Windows 10 platform (running Ubuntu 22.04 via WSL 2). The common prime RSA instances were generated with parameters chosen at random.

Initially, we generated RSA moduli of bit-length ℓ (equaling $1024, 2048, 4096$ to demonstrate practicality on modern key sizes) by varying the parameter γ (which governs the size of g). For each instance, a private exponent d with a predetermined bit-length was produced, with specified segments of its most significant bits (MSBs) and/or least significant bits (LSBs) exposed. The corresponding public exponent e was then computed from the relation $ed \equiv 1 \pmod{\text{lcm}(p-1, q-1)}$. By gradually increasing the bit-length of d, we were able to achieve larger values of δ that fall within the vulnerable range predicted by our theoretical analysis. The open-source implementation of the proposed attacks is available at https://github.com/MengceZheng/CPRSA_PKEA.

To implement the attack, we selected appropriate lattice parameters m and t to construct a lattice tailored for our instance. Table 2 summarizes the experimental outcomes. In this table, the γ column specifies the size of g, while $\delta_\mathrm{M}\ell$ and $\delta_\mathrm{L}\ell$ denote the number of exposed bits in the MSB and LSB portions, respectively. The column δ_t lists the theoretical upper bound for δ, and δ_e shows its experimentally determined value. The lattice parameters m and t determine the lattice dimension, given in the ω column, and the overall computational time—comprising both the LLL reduction and subsequent Gröbner basis computations—is recorded in the Time column (in seconds).

Table 2. Experimental results of the proposed partial key exposure attack

ℓ	γ	$\delta_\mathrm{M}\ell$	$\delta_\mathrm{L}\ell$	δ_t	δ_e	m	t	ω	Time
1024	0.10	51	0	0.164	0.083	2	0	27	0.93 s
1024	0.15	92	0	0.207	0.124	2	0	27	0.95 s
1024	0.20	122	0	0.244	0.166	2	0	27	0.91 s
1024	0.25	153	0	0.280	0.209	2	0	27	0.96 s
2048	0.17	200	0	0.219	0.145	2	0	27	2.39 s
2048	0.22	250	0	0.252	0.164	2	0	27	2.24 s
4096	0.20	491	0	0.244	0.166	2	0	27	7.82 s
1024	0.15	0	40	0.174	0.112	2	0	27	0.92 s
1024	0.20	0	102	0.230	0.169	2	0	27	0.86 s
1024	0.25	0	163	0.287	0.224	3	0	64	36.39 s
1024	0.30	0	225	0.344	0.272	3	1	80	182.25 s
2048	0.17	0	200	0.219	0.145	2	0	27	2.21 s
2048	0.22	0	250	0.252	0.164	2	0	27	2.17 s
4096	0.25	0	655	0.287	0.211	2	0	27	7.43 s
1024	0.25	92	51	0.274	0.208	2	0	27	1.06 s
1024	0.30	102	102	0.330	0.249	2	0	27	0.96 s
1024	0.35	153	81	0.367	0.287	3	0	64	35.72 s
1024	0.40	40	256	0.424	0.333	3	0	64	37.46 s
2048	0.35	280	150	0.353	0.225	2	0	27	2.15 s
2048	0.40	100	400	0.393	0.291	3	0	64	123.23 s
4096	0.25	327	327	0.287	0.205	2	0	27	7.68 s

For each experiment, we generated a sufficient number of shift polynomials whose corresponding integer polynomial equations shared a common root. As observed in Table 2, the computational time grows with the lattice dimension, which is largely influenced by both the dimension itself and the magnitude of the matrix entries. The derived vectors were then converted into integer polynomials that satisfy the conditions for successful root recovery.

The root extraction process was implemented as follows. After obtaining the reduced vectors, we recovered the unknown component $\bar{d}$ and the products ak and bk. These values were derived from a Gröbner basis algorithm for extracting the common root. With $\bar{d}$, ak, and bk in hand, the factorization of the RSA modulus N was completed by computing $k = \gcd(ak, bk)$, determining a and b, and finally recovering g via the key equation. Although the recovered experimental bounds were below the theoretical insecure bound—primarily due to hardware limitations—we expect that further improvements in lattice construction (e.g., using higher-dimensional lattices) can bridge this gap.

To illustrate the procedure concretely, we present a toy example with a small ℓ below.

Example 1. Consider a toy instance in which we set $\gamma = 0.1$ and use two 256-bit balanced primes, so that the composite modulus N has a bit-length of $\ell = 512$. Suppose the private exponent d is 79 bits long, and that 20 MSBs and 25 LSBs of d are known. The specific parameters for this instance are:

$$N = 94401588121449406276513274312243007927987702798776098745020461080587811411650767972528097968298225859599369086559413926836307186426880985959478260566055595,$$

$$e = 15807761233746011952961936756443818455052108197790787506301757219824089762823704780335979983995094370758599655433016753725293112516788607,$$

$d_{\mathrm{M}} = 585670$ (i.e., 10001110111111000110),

$d_{\mathrm{L}} = 856799747$ (i.e., 111101001000110011000101111).

In this example, we derived parameters a_i for $0 \le i \le 7$ and then generated the target trivariate integer polynomial $f(x, y, z)$. By setting $m = 3$ and $t = 1$, we constructed a lattice of dimension $\omega = 80$. After approximately 56 seconds of computation, the desired root $(x^\star, y^\star, z^\star)$ was successfully extracted:

$x^\star = 7600455243$,

$$y^\star = 470719931192695442899091272918982120932401559897714908818003951733486605098620174 80,$$

$$z^\star = 6409806934405779647513217563049686192197232084751943894588374023080646664051466782 0.$$

Using $y^\star$ and $z^\star$, we computed $k = \gcd(y^\star, z^\star)$ as

$$k = 2908377569207397435020,$$

and hence

$$a = 16184966359817508199533906423147448480943318821053062250566374,$$

$$b = 22039115561438625728027143037476181391585030854211092058691641.$$

Finally, we derived the common prime g as

$$g = 2572211484787583,$$

which enabled the factorization of N into

$p = 8326231270324655019133886021862948606088499348310561912263026$
$93267053665068085,$

$q = 1133785323233863468200675903029273550935734413892496282175999$
$51023731565387407.$

One may readily verify that $N = pq$, confirming the validity of the partial key exposure attack as dictated by Proposition 2. We provide more toy numerical examples when only MSBs or LSBs is leaked in Appendix B. One may find additional numerical examples for common prime RSA modulus of larger bit-length at https://github.com/MengceZheng/CPRSA_PKEA.

5   Concluding Remarks

In this work, we introduced a new partial key exposure attack on common prime RSA that employs a lattice-based strategy to solve trivariate integer polynomial equations. By generalizing the traditional small private key attack, our approach accommodates attack scenarios in which only a fraction of the private key's bits (from both its most and least significant parts) is exposed. We derived the attack bounds under which the RSA modulus can be factored in polynomial time and provided a detailed demonstration.

Our experimental results demonstrate that even partial leakage of key bits can significantly compromise the security of common prime RSA. Although the overall efficiency is influenced by the lattice dimension and the specific parameters chosen for the lattice construction, the experiments affirm the theoretical predictions and the practical viability of the proposed attack.

Future work mainly includes interpolating smoothly between common prime variant and standard RSA by analyzing the case $\gamma = \delta_M = \delta_L = 0$ and closing the gap to Boneh-Durfee's bound $\delta < 0.292$.

Acknowledgments. Mengce Zheng gratefully acknowledges the financial support for academic visiting provided by the China Scholarship Council (CSC No. 202308330390). This work was partially supported by the National Natural Science Foundation of China (No. 62002335), and Ningbo Young Science and Technology Talent Cultivation Program (No. 2023QL007).

Disclosure of Interests. The authors have no competing interests.

A   Algorithm

Algorithm 1: Common Prime Generation

   Input: Modulus bit-length n and γ
   Output: Common primes p and q
1 $g \leftarrow$ a random $\lceil \gamma n \rceil$-bit prime;
2 **while** p, q, h *are not primes* **do**
3   **while** $\gcd(a, b) \neq 1$ **do**
4        $a, b \leftarrow$ two random $[(1/2 - \gamma)n - 1]$-bit positive integers;
5   **end**
6     $p \leftarrow 2ga + 1$;
7     $q \leftarrow 2gb + 1$;
8     $h \leftarrow 2gab + a + b$;
9 **end**
10 **return** p and q

B   Numerical Examples

B.1   Leaked MSBs

We provide a toy instance with $\ell = 512$, $\gamma = 0.1$, $\delta = 0.078$, $\delta_{\mathrm{M}} = 0.05$, and $\delta_{\mathrm{L}} = 0$. The related parameters for this instance are as follows.

$N = 107374379172778170604042854989720956959647738164874913130348$
$31384532360359960163100659769395285746303611633611335926 7089$
$17283884604777889614028444748003231,$

$e = 637379973709147474567304848439405742212285325607597220554721$
$35614599123545484863607446598092930881588878289065446292523154$
$365624952198774619,$

$d_{\mathrm{M}} = 23771926$ (i.e., **10110101010111011100010110**),

$d_{\mathrm{L}} = 0.$

By setting $m = 2$ and $t = 0$, we constructed a lattice of dimension $\omega = 27$. After approximately one second of computation, the desired root $(x^\star, y^\star, z^\star)$ was successfully extracted:

$x^\star = 22319,$

$y^\star = 453636671427988818041955360188029006589199434541165041486855$
$8350955140946,$

$z^\star = 506077047772035316087132283751430055048494040424060822364528$
$1919443543507.$

Using $y^\star$ and $z^\star$, we computed $k = \gcd(y^\star, z^\star) = 255411358841$, and hence

$a = 1776102180758487976184939168666473969966107872930491682959190 6,$

$b = 1981419503300481702976682703155432507017856668778384412810282 7.$

Finally, we derived the common prime $g = 2761837656493103$, which enabled the factorization of N into

$p = 9810611769196624095778697825226250347766308162459385382114 30$
$\quad 07014069187248637,$

$q = 1094471799505026110311197401744290937964490809550177553417 50$
$\quad 304679506800604363.$

B.2   Leaked LSBs

We provide a toy instance with $\ell = 512$, $\gamma = 0.1$, $\delta = 0.082$, $\delta_M = 0$, and $\delta_L = 0.03$. The related parameters for this instance are as follows.

$N = 10051113455690792020588618623417018308338952476138681628580 3$
$\quad 46527682750224273543863760544224264478337129910654883601335 5$
$\quad 71366090682251104126216944003749205,$

$e = 93935345107046344066672473222446122700625861892439104256634 7$
$\quad 25066655361949961083687951828417938811846804877246275643246 6$
$\quad 655875310607167825,$

$d_M = 0,$

$d_L = 27707$ (i.e., 110110000111011).

By setting $m = 2$ and $t = 0$, we constructed a lattice of dimension $\omega = 27$. After approximately one second of computation, the desired root $(x^\star, y^\star, z^\star)$ was successfully extracted:

$x^\star = 52225948,$

$y^\star = 14888661532401302169044039092175866551643762295940032947366 8$
$\quad 14846114761143,$

$z^\star = 17268745380919756730533030526443988398534270599406656540181 1$
$\quad 78673022718021.$

Using $y^\star$ and $z^\star$, we computed $k = \gcd(y^\star, z^\star) = 1130627741929$, and hence

$a = 1527359071470951194056001314199466134417201621684855994943154 9,$

$b = 1316849125513166918927272138756191051445176545337776462817116 7.$

Finally, we derived the common prime $g = 3534585632619791$, which enabled the factorization of N into

$p = 93090319987335513096179523849007923352738645216411173770252174863062759532195$,

$q = 107971628597454572042992767201154273826212457211419268840416370965044194372519$.

References

1. Becker, T., Weispfenning, V., Kredel, H.: Gröbner Bases - A Computational Approach to Commutative Algebra. Graduate Texts in Mathematics, vol. 141. Springer (1993)
2. Blömer, J., May, A.: New partial key exposure attacks on RSA. In: Boneh, D. (ed.) CRYPTO 2003. LNCS, vol. 2729, pp. 27–43. Springer, Heidelberg (2003). https://doi.org/10.1007/978-3-540-45146-4_2
3. Blömer, J., May, A.: A tool kit for finding small roots of bivariate polynomials over the integers. In: Cramer, R. (ed.) EUROCRYPT 2005. LNCS, vol. 3494, pp. 251–267. Springer, Heidelberg (2005). https://doi.org/10.1007/11426639_15
4. Boneh, D., Durfee, G.: Cryptanalysis of RSA with private key d less than $N^{0.292}$. In: Stern, J. (ed.) EUROCRYPT 1999. LNCS, vol. 1592, pp. 1–11. Springer, Heidelberg (1999). https://doi.org/10.1007/3-540-48910-X_1
5. Boneh, D., Durfee, G., Frankel, Y.: An attack on RSA given a small fraction of the private key bits. In: Ohta, K., Pei, D. (eds.) ASIACRYPT 1998. LNCS, vol. 1514, pp. 25–34. Springer, Heidelberg (1998). https://doi.org/10.1007/3-540-49649-1_3
6. Collins, T., Hopkins, D., Langford, S., Sabin, M.: Public key cryptographic apparatus and method. U.S. Patent 5848159 (1998)
7. Coppersmith, D.: Small solutions to polynomial equations, and low exponent RSA vulnerabilities. J. Cryptol. **10**(4), 233–260 (1997). https://doi.org/10.1007/s001459900030
8. Erdos, P., Pomerance, C., Schmutz, E.: Carmichael's lambda function. Acta Arith **58**(4), 363–385 (1991)
9. Ernst, M., Jochemsz, E., May, A., de Weger, B.: Partial key exposure attacks on RSA up to full size exponents. In: Cramer, R. (ed.) EUROCRYPT 2005. LNCS, vol. 3494, pp. 371–386. Springer, Heidelberg (2005). https://doi.org/10.1007/11426639_22
10. Halderman, J., et al.: Lest we remember: cold-boot attacks on encryption keys. Commun. ACM **52**(5), 91–98 (2009). https://doi.org/10.1145/1506409.1506429
11. Hinek, M.J.: Another look at small RSA exponents. In: Pointcheval, D. (ed.) CT-RSA 2006. LNCS, vol. 3860, pp. 82–98. Springer, Heidelberg (2006). https://doi.org/10.1007/11605805_6
12. Howgrave-Graham, N.: Finding small roots of univariate modular equations revisited. In: Darnell, M. (ed.) Cryptography and Coding 1997. LNCS, vol. 1355, pp. 131–142. Springer, Heidelberg (1997). https://doi.org/10.1007/BFb0024458
13. Jiang, Z., Zhou, Y., Liu, Y.: Partial key exposure attacks on prime power RSA with non-consecutive blocks. Theor. Comput. Sci. **1019**, 114845 (2024). https://doi.org/10.1016/J.TCS.2024.114845

14. Jochemsz, E., May, A.: A strategy for finding roots of multivariate polynomials with new applications in attacking RSA variants. In: Lai, X., Chen, K. (eds.) ASIACRYPT 2006. LNCS, vol. 4284, pp. 267–282. Springer, Heidelberg (2006). https://doi.org/10.1007/11935230_18

15. Kocher, P.C.: Timing attacks on implementations of Diffie-Hellman, RSA, DSS, and other systems. In: Koblitz, N. (ed.) CRYPTO 1996. LNCS, vol. 1109, pp. 104–113. Springer, Heidelberg (1996). https://doi.org/10.1007/3-540-68697-5_9

16. Lenstra, A., Lenstra, H., Lovász, L.: Factoring polynomials with rational coefficients. Math. Ann. **261**(4), 515–534 (1982)

17. Lu, Y., Zhang, R., Peng, L., Lin, D.: Solving linear equations modulo unknown divisors: revisited. In: Iwata, T., Cheon, J.H. (eds.) ASIACRYPT 2015. LNCS, vol. 9452, pp. 189–213. Springer, Heidelberg (2015). https://doi.org/10.1007/978-3-662-48797-6_9

18. May, A.: New RSA vulnerabilities using lattice reduction methods. Ph.D. thesis, University of Paderborn (2003). http://ubdata.uni-paderborn.de/ediss/17/2003/may/disserta.pdf

19. May, A.: Using LLL-reduction for solving RSA and factorization problems. In: Nguyen, P.Q., Vallée, B. (eds.) The LLL Algorithm - Survey and Applications. Information Security and Cryptography, pp. 315–348. Springer (2010). https://doi.org/10.1007/978-3-642-02295-1_10

20. May, A., Nowakowski, J., Sarkar, S.: Partial key exposure attack on short secret exponent CRT-RSA. In: Tibouchi, M., Wang, H. (eds.) ASIACRYPT 2021. LNCS, vol. 13090, pp. 99–129. Springer, Cham (2021). https://doi.org/10.1007/978-3-030-92062-3_4

21. Mumtaz, M., Luo, P.: Remarks on the cryptanalysis of common prime RSA for IoT constrained low power devices. Inf. Sci. **538**, 54–68 (2020). https://doi.org/10.1016/j.ins.2020.05.075

22. Quisquater, J.J., Couvreur, C.: Fast decipherment algorithm for RSA public-key cryptosystem. Electron. Lett. **18**(21), 905–907 (1982). https://doi.org/10.1145/359340.359342

23. Ristenpart, T., Tromer, E., Shacham, H., Savage, S.: Hey, you, get off of my cloud: exploring information leakage in third-party compute clouds. In: Al-Shaer, E., Jha, S., Keromytis, A.D. (eds.) Proceedings of the 2009 ACM Conference on Computer and Communications Security, CCS 2009, Chicago, Illinois, USA, 9–13 November 2009, pp. 199–212. ACM (2009). https://doi.org/10.1145/1653662.1653687

24. Rivest, R., Shamir, A., Adleman, L.: A method for obtaining digital signatures and public-key cryptosystems. Commun. ACM **21**(2), 120–126 (1978). https://doi.org/10.1145/359340.359342

25. Sarkar, S., Maitra, S.: Side channel attack to actual cryptanalysis: breaking CRT-RSA with low weight decryption exponents. In: Prouff, E., Schaumont, P. (eds.) CHES 2012. LNCS, vol. 7428, pp. 476–493. Springer, Heidelberg (2012). https://doi.org/10.1007/978-3-642-33027-8_28

26. Sarkar, S., Maitra, S.: Cryptanalytic results on 'dual CRT' and 'common prime' RSA. Des. Codes Cryptogr. **66**(1–3), 157–174 (2013). https://doi.org/10.1007/s10623-012-9675-5

27. Takagi, T.: Fast RSA-type cryptosystem modulo $p^k q$. In: Krawczyk, H. (ed.) CRYPTO 1998. LNCS, vol. 1462, pp. 318–326. Springer, Heidelberg (1998). https://doi.org/10.1007/BFb0055738

28. Takayasu, A., Kunihiro, N.: Better lattice constructions for solving multivariate linear equations modulo unknown divisors. In: Boyd, C., Simpson, L. (eds.) ACISP

2013. LNCS, vol. 7959, pp. 118–135. Springer, Heidelberg (2013). https://doi.org/10.1007/978-3-642-39059-3_9

29. Takayasu, A., Kunihiro, N.: Partial key exposure attacks on RSA: achieving the Boneh-Durfee bound. Theor. Comput. Sci. **761**, 51–77 (2019). https://doi.org/10.1016/j.tcs.2018.08.021

30. The Sage Developers: SageMath, the Sage Mathematics Software System (Version 9.5) (2025). https://www.sagemath.org

31. Wiener, M.: Cryptanalysis of short RSA secret exponents. IEEE Trans. Inf. Theory **36**(3), 553–558 (1990). https://doi.org/10.1109/18.54902

32. Yuan, S., Yu, W., Wang, K., Li, X.: Partial key exposure attacks on RSA with moduli $N = p^r q^s$. In: IEEE International Symposium on Information Theory, ISIT 2022, Espoo, Finland, 26 June–1 July 2022, pp. 1436–1440. IEEE (2022). https://doi.org/10.1109/ISIT50566.2022.9834542

33. Zheng, M.: Partial key exposure attack on common prime RSA. In: Ge, C., Yung, M. (eds.) Inscrypt 2023, Part II. LNCS, vol. 14527, pp. 407–410. Springer, Cham (2023). https://doi.org/10.1007/978-981-97-0945-8_27

34. Zheng, M.: Partial key exposure attack on common prime RSA. IACR Cryptol. ePrint Arch. 61 (2024). https://eprint.iacr.org/2024/061

35. Zheng, M.: Revisiting small private key attacks on common prime RSA. IEEE Access **12**, 5203–5211 (2024). https://doi.org/10.1109/ACCESS.2024.3349633

36. Zheng, M., Kang, H.: Lattice-based cryptanalysis of RSA-type cryptosystems: a bibliometric analysis. Cybersecur. **7**(1), 74 (2024). https://doi.org/10.1186/S42400-024-00289-7

Improved Cryptanalysis of an RSA Variant Based on Cubic Pell Curve

Mohammed Rahmani[1] and Abderrahmane Nitaj[2(✉)]⑩

[1] Sciences Faculty, Department of Mathematics and Computer Science, ACSA Laboratory, Mohammed First University, 60000 Oujda, Morocco
mohammed.rahmani@ump.ac.ma
[2] Normandie Univ, UNICAEN, CNRS, LMNO, 14000 Caen, France
abderrahmane.nitaj@unicaen.fr

Abstract. In 2024, based on the cubic Pell curve, Nitaj and Seck proposed a variant of the RSA cryptosystem where the modulus is in the form $N = p^r q^s$, and the public key e and private key d satisfy the equation $ed \equiv 1 \pmod{(p-1)^2(q-1)^2}$. They showed that N can be factored when d is less than a certain bound that depends on r and s in the situation $rs \geq 2$, which is not extendable to $r = s = 1$. In this paper, we propose a cryptanalysis of this scheme in the situation $r = s = 1$, and give an explicit bound for d that makes the scheme insecure. The method is based on Coppersmith's method and lattice reduction.

Keywords: RSA Cryptosystem · Factorization · Coppersmith's method · Lattice reduction · RSA Variant

1 Introduction

In 1978, the RSA cryptosystem was introduced by Rivest, Shamir, and Adleman [18]. It is still one of the most widely used public-key cryptosystems. Its security is based on the computational challenge of factoring large composite numbers. In this framework, the modulus, denoted by N, is defined as the product of two large primes, p and q, of equal bit-length. A public exponent e is chosen with $e < N$ and $\gcd(e, (p-1)(q-1)) = 1$, guaranteeing the existence of an integer d satisfying the equation $ed \equiv 1 \pmod{(p-1)(q-1)}$. The public key is the pair (N, e), while the private key is the pair (N, d). To encrypt a plaintext message m where $m < N$, the ciphertext c is computed as $c \equiv m^e \pmod{N}$. For decryption, the original message m is recovered by computing $m \equiv c^d \pmod{N}$.

In practical implementations, both encryption and decryption can be computationally costly. A widely adopted strategy to accelerate decryption involves selecting small private exponents. However, Wiener [22] demonstrated in 1990 that RSA becomes insecure when $d < \frac{1}{3}N^{1/4}$. This bound was later refined by Boneh and Durfee [1], who extended the attack to cases where $d < N^{0.292}$. These vulnerabilities have motivated research aimed at strengthening RSA while maintaining efficiency, giving rise to several variants. Noteworthy examples include

A. Nitaj et al. (Eds.): AFRICACRYPT 2025, LNCS 15651, pp. 113–125, 2026.
https://doi.org/10.1007/978-3-031-97260-7_6

CRT-RSA [16] and others [7,22], all of which preserve the conventional modulus structure $N = pq$. Other methods, such as Prime-Power RSA [20] and others [2,21], alter the modulus to investigate different formulations. Additional variants involve the complete substitution of the standard Euler function with alternative expressions.

In 1995, Kuwakado et al. [8] introduced an alternative approach to the RSA cryptosystem based on singular cubic curves described by the equation $y^2 \equiv x^3 + bx^2 \pmod{N}$, where $N = pq$ represents an RSA modulus and $b \in \mathbb{Z}/N\mathbb{Z}$. Their method involved selecting a public exponent e such that $\gcd(e, \theta(N)) = 1$, with $\theta(N) = (p^2 - 1)(q^2 - 1)$. The secret exponent d was determined through the modular equation $ed \equiv 1 \pmod{(p^2 - 1)(q^2 - 1)}$. Subsequent cryptanalytic efforts on this scheme were presented in [4,17].

In 2018, Murru and Saettone [11] introduced a variant of the RSA cryptosystem that relies on the cubic Pell equation $x_1^3 + \alpha x_2^3 + \alpha^2 x_3^3 - 3\alpha x_1 x_2 x_3 = 1$ in $\mathbb{Z}/N\mathbb{Z}$, where α is a cubic nonresidue modulo N. In this scheme, the modulus is given by $N = pq$, and the exponents e and d are constrained by the modular relation $ed \equiv 1 \pmod{(p^2 + p + 1)(q^2 + q + 1)}$.

In 2024, Nitaj and Seck [14] proposed a cryptosystem using encoding functions and the cubic Pell curve defined by the equation

$$x_1^3 + \alpha x_2^3 + \alpha^2 x_3^3 - 3\alpha x_1 x_2 x_3 \equiv 1 \pmod{N},$$

with $N = p^r q^s$. In this scheme, the encryption and decryption exponents fulfill the modular equation $ed \equiv 1 \pmod{\psi(r, s, N)}$, where

$$\psi(r, s, N) = p^{2(r-1)} q^{2(s-1)} (p - 1)^2 (q - 1)^2.$$

Beyond Wiener's well-known attack and its refinement by Boneh and Durfee, numerous attacks have been devised against alternative RSA variants, as noted in [4,13,19,23]. In the same work by Nitaj and Seck [14], a continued fraction-based attack on the variant with the key equation

$$ed \equiv 1 \pmod{\psi(r, s, N)},$$

is presented. They showed that if $N = p^r q^s$ and $d < N^\delta$ with $\delta < 2 - \frac{2(3r+s)}{(r+s)^2}$, then the factorization of N can be done in polynomial time.

We observe in the former attack that if the modulus takes the classical form $N = pq$, that is $r = s = 1$, the attack of Nitaj and Seck [14] does not work since their condition becomes $\delta < 0$ which is not possible. In this paper, we fill this gap by presenting a Coppersmith-based approach. We show that if $N = pq$, $e = N^\alpha$, and $d < N^\delta$, then we can break the scheme whenever $1 < \alpha < 4$ and $\delta < 2 - \sqrt{\alpha}$.

The rest of the paper is structured as follows. Section 2 covers preliminaries. Section 3 applies a variant of Coppersmith's method for breaking the scheme of Nitaj and Seck. Section 4 offers a detailed numerical experiment to validate the proposed attack. Finally, Sect. 5 concludes the paper.

2 Preliminaries

2.1 Useful Lemmas

The following result from [12] establishes explicit bounds for p and q using the public value N, given that $N = pq$ with $q < p < 2q$.

Lemma 1. *Each pair of primes p and q such that $N = pq$ with $q < p < 2q$ satisfy the following inequalities*

$$\frac{\sqrt{2}}{2}\sqrt{N} < q < \sqrt{N} < p < \sqrt{2}\sqrt{N}.$$

The subsequent result yields a lower bound for $(p-1)^2(q-1)^2$.

Lemma 2. *If $N = pq$ and $q < p < 2q$, then*

$$(p-1)^2(q-1)^2 > \frac{N^2}{4}.$$

Proof. We have $(p-1)(q-1) = N - p - q + 1$. According to Lemma 1, we get $p + q < 3\sqrt{N}$, yielding for $N > 6$

$$(p-1)(q-1) > N - 3\sqrt{N} + 1 > \frac{N}{2}.$$

This implies that

$$(p-1)^2(q-1)^2 > \frac{N^2}{4},$$

which concludes the proof. □

2.2 The Scheme of Nitaj and Seck

The scheme of Nitaj and Seck [14] is based on the following cubic Pell curve

$$\mathcal{C}_\alpha(N) \quad : \quad x_1^3 + ax_2^3 + \alpha^2 x_3^3 - 3\alpha x_1 x_2 x_3 \equiv 1 \pmod{N},$$

where α is a cubic residue modulo N. In the encryption and decryption processes, an encoding function $\mathcal{E}$ is used to map $(m_{x_1}, m_{x_2}) \in \mathbb{Z}/N\mathbb{Z} \times \mathbb{Z}/N\mathbb{Z}$ to

$$\mathcal{E}\left((m_{x_1}, m_{x_2}), \beta, N\right) = (x_1, x_2, x_3) \in \mathcal{C}_\alpha(N),$$

such that $\alpha \equiv \beta^3 \pmod{N}$. Similarly, a decoding function $\mathcal{D}$ is used to reverse $(x_1, x_2, x_3) \in \mathcal{C}_\alpha(N)$ with $\alpha \equiv \beta^3 \pmod{N}$ to

$$\mathcal{D}\left((x_1, x_2, x_3), \beta, N\right) = (m_{x_1}, m_{x_2}) \in \mathbb{Z}/N\mathbb{Z} \times \mathbb{Z}/N\mathbb{Z}.$$

The cryptosystem of Nitaj and Seck can be described as follows.

Key Generation

1. Choose a security parameter ρ along with two small positive integers r and s.
2. Randomly choose two prime numbers p and q, both of size ρ, such that $p \equiv q \equiv 1 \pmod 3$.
3. Compute $N = p^r q^s$ and $\psi(r, s, N) = p^{2(r-1)} q^{2(s-1)} (p-1)^2 (q-1)^2$.
4. Randomly select an integer $\beta < N$ and compute $\alpha \equiv \beta^3 \pmod N$, such that α is a nonzero cubic residue modulo p and modulo q.
5. Pick an integer $e < N$ such that $\gcd(e, pq(p-1)(q-1)) = 1$.
6. Compute

$$d \equiv \frac{1}{e} \pmod{\psi(r, s, N)}.$$

7. The public key consists of (N, β, e), while the private key comprises (N, β, d).

Encryption

1. Express a plaintext as an ordered pair $M = (x_M, y_M)$ within the set $\mathbb{Z}/N\mathbb{Z} \times \mathbb{Z}/N\mathbb{Z}$.
2. Compute $\alpha \equiv \beta^3 \pmod N$.
3. Compute the triplet (x_1, x_2, x_3) using the function $\mathcal{E}$ applied to (x_M, y_M), along with β and N.
4. Derive $C = (x_C, y_C, z_C)$ by applying the exponent e to (x_1, x_2, x_3) over the curve $\mathcal{C}_\alpha(N)$.
5. The encrypted output is given by $(c_{x_1}, c_{x_2}) = \mathcal{D}(C, \beta, N)$.

Decryption. To recover the plaintext we follow the steps

1. Consider the ciphertext as an ordered pair (c_{x_1}, c_{x_2}) within the set $\mathbb{Z}/N\mathbb{Z} \times \mathbb{Z}/N\mathbb{Z}$.
2. Compute $\alpha \equiv \beta^3 \pmod N$.
3. Compute the triplet (x_C, y_C, z_C) using the function $\mathcal{E}$ applied to (c_{x_1}, c_{x_2}), along with β and N.
4. Obtain (x_1, x_2, x_3) by applying the exponent d to (x_C, y_C, z_C) over the curve $\mathcal{C}_\alpha(N)$.
5. The plaintext is retrieved by $(x_M, y_M) = \mathcal{D}((x_1, x_2, x_3), \beta, N)$.

2.3   Lattice Theory

A subset $\mathcal{L} \subset \mathbb{R}^n$ is defined as a lattice if it forms a finitely generated free abelian subgroup of $\mathbb{R}^n$, generated by $\omega \leq n$ linearly independent vectors in $\mathbb{R}^n$. In other words, it can be expressed as

$$\mathcal{L} = \mathbb{Z}u_1 + \mathbb{Z}u_2 + \cdots + \mathbb{Z}u_\omega.$$

The lattice $\mathcal{L}$ can be represented by a matrix M, whose rows consist of the basis vectors $u_1, u_2, \ldots, u_\omega$. The lattice dimension is n, its rank is ω, and an associated determinant is given by

$$\det(\mathcal{L}) = \sqrt{\det(M \cdot M^t)},$$

where M^t denotes the transpose of M. In the special case where $\omega = n$, the lattice $\mathcal{L}$ is said to be of full rank, and its determinant becomes $\det(\mathcal{L}) = |\det(M)|$.

A lattice $\mathcal{L}$ possesses an infinite number of possible bases when $\omega \geq 2$. However, every basis of $\mathcal{L}$ consists of the same number of vectors and maintains an identical determinant. Finding a basis consisting of short vectors becomes computationally challenging as the dimension increases. In 1982, Lenstra, Lenstra, and Lovász [9] proposed the LLL algorithm, which efficiently computes an approximate short basis in polynomial time. The following result [10] is frequently used to analyze the output of the basis produced by the LLL algorithm.

Theorem 1. *Consider a lattice $\mathcal{L}$ generated by a basis $\{u_1, u_2, \ldots, u_\omega\}$. The LLL algorithm outputs a reduced basis $\{w_1, w_2, \ldots, w_\omega\}$ that satisfies the following*

$$\|w_1\| \leq \cdots \leq \|w_i\| \leq 2^{\frac{\omega(\omega-1)}{4(\omega+1-i)}} \det(\mathcal{L})^{\frac{1}{\omega+1-i}}, \quad \text{for } i = 1, \ldots, \omega.$$

2.4   Coppersmith's Approach

In 1996, Coppersmith [3] introduced an algorithm that operates in polynomial time to find small solutions to a univariate polynomial congruence of the form $p(x) \equiv 0 \pmod{R}$, where R is an integer with an unknown factorization. This method has been extended to handle multivariate polynomials, particularly those of the form

$$p(x_1, x_2, \ldots, x_n) = \sum_{i_1, i_2, \ldots, i_n} n_{i_1, i_2, \ldots, i_n} x_1^{i_1} x_2^{i_2} \cdots x_n^{i_n},$$

where the coefficients $n_{i_1, i_2, \ldots, i_n}$ are integers. The Euclidean norm for such polynomials is given by

$$\|p(x_1, x_2, \ldots, x_n)\| = \sqrt{\sum n_{i_1, i_2, \ldots, i_n}^2}.$$

In 1997, Howgrave-Graham [5] refined Coppersmith's technique, simplifying the process of finding small roots, as demonstrated in the following result.

Theorem 2 (Howgrave-Graham). *If $p(x_1, x_2, \ldots, x_n) \in \mathbb{Z}[x_1, x_2, \ldots, x_n]$ is a multivariate polynomial containing at most ω monomials, and R is a positive integer with the two statements*

1. *$p(y_1, y_2, \ldots, y_n) \equiv 0 \pmod{R}$.*
2. *$\|p(x_1 Y_1, x_2 Y_2, \ldots, x_n Y_n)\| < \frac{R}{\sqrt{\omega}}$, with $|y_i| < Y_i$ for $i = 1, \ldots, n$,*

then, it follows that $p(y_1, y_2, \ldots, y_n) = 0$ holds true in $\mathbb{Z}$.

When more than two variables are considered, approaches based on Coppersmith's method are heuristic in nature. In this study, we rely on the following assumption [1, 6, 15, 23].

Assumption 1. *The polynomials $h_1, h_2, \ldots, h_\omega$ reduced by the LLL algorithm are algebraically independent.*

Under this assumption, the shared solution $(y_1, y_2, \ldots, y_n)$ to the system of polynomial equations $h_i(y_1, y_2, \ldots, y_n) = 0$ for $i = 1, \ldots, \omega$ can be obtained using approaches like the Gröbner basis technique or resultants.

3   Attacking the Scheme of Nitaj and Seck

In this section, we propose a new attack on the scheme of Nitaj and Seck when the modulus takes the standard form $N = pq$.

3.1   The New Method

Theorem 3. *Let N be an RSA modulus such that $N = pq$, where $q < p < 2q$. Let $e = N^\alpha$ and $d < N^\delta$ represent the public and private exponents, respectively, such that $ed \equiv 1 \pmod{\Lambda(N)}$, where $\Lambda(N) = (p-1)^2(q-1)^2$. Assume that both α and δ satisfy*

$$1 < \alpha < 4 \quad and \quad \delta < 2 - \sqrt{\alpha},$$

then the recovery of the RSA primes can be done in polynomial time.

Proof. The first point is to reformulate the modular equation $ed \equiv 1 \pmod{\Lambda(N)}$ into $ed - k\Lambda(N) = 1$ for some integer k. By expressing $\Lambda(N)$ as

$$\Lambda(N) = (p+q)^2 - 2(N+1)(p+q) + (N+1)^2,$$

the former equation can be rewritten as a modular one of the form

$$h(x_1, x_2) \equiv 0 \pmod{e},$$

with $h(x_1, x_2) = x_1(x_2^2 + a_1 x_2 + a_0) + 1$ for $x_1 = k$, $x_2 = p+q$, $a_1 = -2(N+1)$, and $a_0 = (N+1)^2$. In order to solve this modular equation, one can use Coppersmith's approach. To this end, we define $x_3 = x_1 x_2^2 + 1$. So $h(x_1, x_2) = H(x_1, x_2, x_3)$ where

$$H(x_1, x_2, x_3) = x_3 + x_1(a_1 x_2 + a_0).$$

Consider a positive parameter $t > 0$ to be optimized. Let μ be a positive integer and w an integer such that $0 \le w \le \mu$. Define the following set of polynomials

$$A_{w,a,b}(x_1, x_2, x_3) = x_1^a x_2^b H(x_1, x_2, x_3)^w e^{\mu-w}, \quad (w, a, b) \in \mathcal{E} \cup \mathcal{F},$$

where

$$\mathcal{E} = \{(w, a, b) \mid b = 0, 1, \ w = 0, \ldots, \mu, \ a = 1, \ldots, \mu - w\},$$

$$\mathcal{F} = \left\{(w, a, b) \mid b = 0, \ldots, \lfloor t \rfloor, \ w = \left\lfloor \frac{\mu}{t} \right\rfloor b, \ldots, \mu, \ a = 0\right\},$$

and during each computation, replace the term $x_1 x_2^2$ with $x_3 - 1$.

As the pair (x_1, x_2) satisfies the equation $h(x_1, x_2) \equiv 0 \pmod{e}$, then also the tuple (x_1, x_2, x_3) fulfills the equation $H(x_1, x_2, x_3) \equiv 0 \pmod{e}$, implying

$$A_{w,a,b}(x_1, x_2, x_3) \equiv 0 \pmod{e^{\mu}},$$

for all $(w, a, b) \in \mathcal{E} \cup \mathcal{F}$. In accordance to Coppersmith's technique, we must try to find bounds X_1, X_2 and X_3 so that

$$|x_1| \leq X_1, \quad |x_2| \leq X_2, \quad |x_3| \leq X_3.$$

By Lemma 2, we get $\Lambda(N) > \frac{N^2}{4}$. This implies that

$$|x_1| = \left| \frac{ed - 1}{\Lambda(N)} \right| < 4edN^{-2} \leq 4N^{\alpha + \delta - 2}.$$

Also, according to Lemma 1, we can set $|x_2| = p + q < 3\sqrt{N}$, so we can apply the following bounds

$$X_1 = 4N^{\alpha + \delta - 2}, \quad X_2 = 3N^{0.5}, \quad X_3 = X_1 X_2^2.$$

Afterwards, we generate the basis matrix of the lattice $\mathcal{L}$ by taking the coefficient vectors from the polynomials $A_{w,a,b}(X_1 x_1, X_2 x_2, X_3 x_3)$. The rows of this matrix are arranged following the rule

$$A_{w,a,b}(X_1 x_1, X_2 x_2, X_3 x_3) \prec A_{w',a',b'}(X_1 x_1, X_2 x_2, X_3 x_3),$$

if $w < w'$, or if $w = w'$ and $a < a'$, or if $w = w'$, $a = a'$, and $b < b'$. For the monomials, we establish the ordering as

$$x_1^a x_2^b x_3^w \prec x_1^{a'} x_2^{b'} x_3^{w'},$$

based on the same criteria. An example of the lattice basis matrix for $\mu = 2$, $t = 2$, and the polynomial

$$h(x_1, x_2) = x_1(x_2^2 + a_1 x_2 + a_0) + 1,$$

with $x_1 x_2^2 = x_3 - 1$, is shown in Table 1. Non-zero entries are denoted by $\star$.

The lattice is constructed in such a way that the resulting basis matrix is left triangular, with each diagonal element having the form $X_1^a X_2^b X_3^w e^{\mu - w}$ for a combination (w, a, b) in $\mathcal{E} \cup \mathcal{F}$. As a result, the determinant of the lattice takes the form

$$\det(\mathcal{L}) = X_1^{\lambda_{X_1}} X_2^{\lambda_{X_2}} X_3^{\lambda_{X_3}} e^{\lambda_e}, \tag{1}$$

Table 1. The lattice basis matrix for $\mu = 2$ and $t = 2$.

$A_{w,a,b}$	1	x_1	x_1x_2	x_1^2	$x_1^2x_2$	x_3	x_2x_3	x_1x_3	$x_1x_2x_3$	x_3^2	$x_2x_3^2$	$x_2^2x_3^2$
$A_{0,0,0}$	e^2	0	0	0	0	0	0	0	0	0	0	0
$A_{0,1,0}$	0	e^2X_1	0	0	0	0	0	0	0	0	0	0
$A_{0,1,1}$	0	0	$e^2X_1X_2$	0	0	0	0	0	0	0	0	0
$A_{0,2,0}$	0	0	0	$e^2X_1^2$	0	0	0	0	0	0	0	0
$A_{0,2,1}$	0	0	0	0	$e^2X_1^2X_2$	0	0	0	0	0	0	0
$A_{1,0,0}$	0	$\star$	$\star$	0	0	eX_3	0	0	0	0	0	0
$A_{1,0,1}$	$\star$	0	$\star$	0	0	$\star$	eX_2X_3	0	0	0	0	0
$A_{1,1,0}$	0	0	0	$\star$	$\star$	0	0	eX_1X_3	0	0	0	0
$A_{1,1,1}$	0	$\star$	0	0	$\star$	0	0	$\star$	$eX_1X_2X_3$	0	0	0
$A_{2,0,0}$	0	$\star$	0	$\star$	$\star$	0	0	$\star$	$\star$	X_3^2	0	0
$A_{2,0,1}$	0	$\star$	$\star$	0	$\star$	$\star$	0	$\star$	$\star$	$\star$	$X_2X_3^2$	0
$A_{2,0,2}$	$\star$	$\star$	$\star$	0	0	$\star$	$\star$	$\star$	$\star$	$\star$	$\star$	$X_2^2X_3^2$

with $\lambda_{X_1} = \mathcal{B}(a)$, $\lambda_{X_2} = \mathcal{B}(b)$, $\lambda_{X_3} = \mathcal{B}(w)$, $\lambda_e = \mathcal{B}(\mu - w)$, and

$$\mathcal{B}(u) = \sum_{b=0}^{1}\sum_{w=0}^{\mu}\sum_{a=1}^{\mu - w} u + \sum_{b=0}^{\lfloor t \rfloor}\sum_{w=\lfloor \frac{\mu}{t} \rfloor b}^{\mu}\sum_{a=0}^{0} u.$$

For simplicity in the calculations, we approximate $\lfloor t \rfloor \approx t$ and $\lfloor \frac{\mu}{t} \rfloor \approx \frac{\mu}{t}$. Set $t = \mu\tau$ for some $\tau \geq 0$, then, the main components of the exponents λ_{X_1}, λ_{X_2}, λ_{X_3}, λ_e, and the lattice dimension $\omega = \mathcal{A}(1)$ satisfy

$$\lambda_{X_1} = \frac{1}{3}\mu^3 + o(\mu^3)$$

$$\lambda_{X_2} = \frac{1}{6}\tau^2\mu^3 + o(\mu^3)$$

$$\lambda_{X_3} = \frac{1}{3}(\tau + 1)\mu^3 + o(\mu^3) \tag{2}$$

$$\lambda_e = \frac{1}{6}(\tau + 4)\mu^3 + o(\mu^3)$$

$$\omega = \frac{1}{2}(\tau + 2)\mu^2 + o(\mu^2).$$

The matrix M undergoes reduction via the LLL algorithm, resulting in a new matrix M' that retains the same determinant. From this reduced matrix, we derive ω polynomials $g_i(x_1, x_2, x_3)$, for $i = 1, \ldots, \omega$, each of which satisfies the congruence

$$g_i(x_1, x_2, x_3) \equiv 0 \pmod{e^\mu}.$$

To obtain the root, we connect Theorem 2 with Theorem 1, specifically considering the case where $j = 3$. As a result, we fix

$$2^{\frac{\omega(\omega-1)}{4(\omega-2)}} \det(\mathcal{L})^{\frac{1}{\omega-2}} < \frac{e^{\mu}}{\sqrt{\omega}}.$$

By combining with (1), this simplifies to

$$e^{\lambda_e - \mu(\omega-2)} X^{\lambda_X} Y^{\lambda_Y} Z^{\lambda_Z} < \frac{1}{2^{\frac{\omega(\omega-1)}{4}} (\sqrt{\omega})^{\omega-2}} < 1. \tag{3}$$

Along with the dominant parts (2) and the corresponding bounds

$$X_1 = 4N^{\alpha+\delta-2}, \quad X_2 = 3N^{0.5}, \quad X_3 = 36N^{\alpha+\delta-1}, \quad e = N^{\alpha},$$

and by disregarding some smaller values, we obtain that

$$\tau^2 + 4(\delta - 1)\tau + 4\alpha + 8\delta - 12 < 0, \tag{4}$$

for which the optimal value of τ is determined by $\tau_0 = -2\delta + 2$. To guarantee that $\tau_0 > 0$, the parameter δ must meet

$$\delta < 1. \tag{5}$$

Plugging τ_0 into (4), we get

$$-\delta^2 + 4\delta + \alpha - 4 < 0.$$

By solving the previous inequality for δ, we obtain

$$\delta < 2 - \sqrt{\alpha}.$$

Together with $\alpha > 1$ and (5), we obtain

$$\delta < \min\left(2 - \sqrt{\alpha}, 1\right) = 2 - \sqrt{\alpha}.$$

Furthermore, since $\delta \geq 0$, the inequality

$$2 - \sqrt{\alpha} > 0,$$

is satisfied if $\alpha < 4$.

In addition to the given conditions, we select three reduced and algebraically independent polynomials $g_i(x_1, x_2, x_3)$ where $1 \leq i \leq 3$. From these, we can extract $(x_1, x_2) = (k, p + q)$ by solving the system of equations $g_i(x_1, x_2, x_3) = 0$ for $i = 1, 2, 3$ over the integers, either using the Gröbner basis method or resultant computations.

Finally, combining $N = pq$ with $x_2 = p + q$ leads to the recovery of the prime factors p and q. This completes the proof.

4   A Numerical Example

This section provides a detailed numerical example demonstrating that our app-roach can break a specific RSA variant where an earlier method proves inef-fective. The computations were carried out using SageMath 10.4 on a PC run-ning Ubuntu 22.04.3 LTS, equipped with an Intel(R) Core(TM) i5-4460 CPU @ 3.20GHz × 4 and 8.00 GB of RAM.

Let the public key $(N, e) \approx (2^{401}, 2^{799})$ be given by

$$N = 4535759871339515314032145788812400834826384175859926240543089976\backslash$$
$$9734049096326468429965626286880195320622174625836395532811,$$
$$e = 2377749886904916499289158774158963845613907677286828363920649 13\backslash$$
$$360397419378303801406650377684568885674443669610749224500466777\backslash$$
$$33571176547374191298900694486972402492997080844069280375450338 1\backslash$$
$$01988217377135633662596006092159462203515340980 68381.$$

This gives that $e = N^{\alpha}$ with $\alpha \approx 1.9922$.

Write

$$\Lambda(N) = (p-1)^2(q-1)^2 = x_2^2 + a_1 x_2 + a_0,$$

with

$$x_2 = p + q,$$
$$a_1 = -2(N+1),$$
$$a_0 = (N+1)^2.$$

Specifically, we have

$$a_1 = -\ 9071519742679030628064291577624801669652768351719852481086\backslash$$
$$17953946809819265293685993125257376039064124434925167279 1065\backslash$$
$$624,$$
$$a_0 = 2057311761045385651506921079429620347871069845858587976110328\backslash$$
$$606844444415531602899423743067694294982751615314499328276 64\backslash$$
$$39402290424183880869819767073929975427507216457164089014610\backslash$$
$$6934928379878596835249680347952479871645933752007830786936 8\backslash$$
$$627344.$$

Our aim is to find a small solution of the equation

$$x_1(x_2^2 + a_1 x_2 + a_0) + 1 \equiv 0 \pmod{e}.$$

To implement the method outlined in Theorem 3, the attacker, who does not know d, p, and q can experiment with different values of δ. Let $\delta = 0.4$. With these parameters, the inequalities specified by Theorem 3 are satisfied, namely $1 < \alpha < 4$ and $\delta < 2 - \sqrt{\alpha} \approx 0.58854$. Setting then the bounds

$$X_1 = \lfloor 4N^{\alpha+\delta-2} \rfloor = 84593556141243703579182074721876233752894924390 4,$$

$$X_2 = \lfloor 3N^{1/2} \rfloor = 6389197042043361322138375200782704203704726102304 8\backslash$$
$$35914929866,$$

$$X_3 = X_1 X_2^2 = 345326451587423645853837092839042523966132410123681 45\backslash$$
$$624120071897255100245523084047348927768868448893619713884826\backslash$$
$$617771376908934878829058672996296095928566635098982580224.$$

To build the lattice $\mathcal{L}$, we select $\mu = t = 3$ and utilize the coefficient vectors of the polynomials $A_{w,a,b}(X_1x_1, X_2x_2, X_3x_3)$, where

$$A_{w,a,b}(x_1, x_2, x_3) = x_1^a x_2^b H(x_1, x_2, x_3)^w e^{\mu-w}, \quad (w,a,b) \in \mathcal{E} \cup \mathcal{F},$$

$$\mathcal{E} = \{(w,a,b) \mid b = 0,1, \ w = 0,\ldots,\mu, \ a = 1,\ldots,\mu - w\},$$
$$\mathcal{F} = \left\{(w,a,b) \mid b = 0,\ldots,\lfloor t \rfloor, \ w = \left\lfloor \frac{\mu}{t} \right\rfloor b,\ldots,\mu, \ a = 0\right\},$$

and the expression $x_1 x_2^2$ is substituted with $x_3 - 1$.

The lattice $\mathcal{L}$ has dimension $\omega = 22$. Upon performing lattice reduction through the LLL algorithm, 22 polynomials are generated. Using the Gröbner basis technique, we select three of these polynomials and solve them in the integer domain, yielding

$$x_1 = 8366983861354768178122228725184063071 8621177,$$

$$x_2 = 43729319177064667909487203755587688736787015817332356098724 20,$$

$$x_3 = 1599979296587634659276648348291272111541107140730522861667008 93928\backslash$$
$$944004387447490658162717809050679598364098132358986952729411524946\backslash$$
$$9761448544704651264932554592582801.$$

Using the values of both $x_2 = p + q$ and $N = pq$ gives

$$p = 26813129229587778457294914208173935339589918982609560846827 27,$$
$$q = 16916189947476889452192289547413753397197096834722795251896 93.$$

Notice that the LLL algorithm and the Gröbner basis calculations were finished in under 1 s.

The private exponent d can be calculated via the rule

$$d \equiv \frac{1}{e} \pmod{((p-1)^2(q-1)^2)}.$$

This implies that

$$d = 72394049505544374240447202369395218697349109,$$

and $d = N^{\delta_0}$ for $\delta_0 \approx 0.3718$.

Observe that the condition for breaking the scheme of Nitaj and Seck [14] when $N = p^r q^s$ and $d < N^{\delta_0}$ is given by

$$0 < \delta_0 < 2 - \frac{2(3r + s)}{(r + s)^2}.$$

To compare this with our case, consider setting $r = s = 1$. In this scenario, their bound becomes

$$2 - \frac{2 \times 4}{4} = 0.$$

This result indicates that their method fails to break the scheme in this case.

5   Conclusion

In this paper, we introduced a novel approach to compromising the scheme proposed by Nitaj and Seck when an RSA modulus $N = pq$ is employed. We transformed the key equation $ed - k(p-1)^2(q-1)^2 = 1$ into a modular equation and applied Coppersmith's method along with lattice basis reduction techniques to solve it, allowing for the recovery of the prime factors in polynomial time.

References

1. Boneh, D., Durfee, G.: Cryptanalysis of RSA with private key d less than $N^{0.292}$. In: Stern, J. (ed.) EUROCRYPT 1999. LNCS, vol. 1592, pp. 1–11. Springer, Heidelberg (1999). https://doi.org/10.1007/3-540-48910-X_1
2. Boudabra, M., Nitaj, A.: A new generalization of the KMOV cryptosystem. J. Appl. Math. Comput. **57**(12), 229–245 (2018)
3. Coppersmith, D.: Small solutions to polynomial equations, and low exponent RSA vulnerabilities. J. Cryptol. **10**(4), 233–260 (1997)
4. Feng, Y., Nitaj, A., Pan, Y.: Partial prime factor exposure attacks on some RSA variants. Theor. Comput. Sci. **999**, 114549 (2024)
5. Howgrave-Graham, N.: Finding small roots of univariate modular equations revisited. In: Darnell, M. (ed.) Cryptography and Coding 1997. LNCS, vol. 1355, pp. 131–142. Springer, Heidelberg (1997). https://doi.org/10.1007/BFb0024458
6. Jochemsz, E., May, A.: A strategy for finding roots of multivariate polynomials with new applications in attacking RSA variants. In: Lai, X., Chen, K. (eds.) ASIACRYPT 2006. LNCS, vol. 4284, pp. 267–282. Springer, Heidelberg (2006). https://doi.org/10.1007/11935230_18
7. Koyama, K., Maurer, U.M., Okamoto, T., Vanstone, S.A.: New public-key schemes based on elliptic curves over the ring Z_n. In: Feigenbaum, J. (ed.) CRYPTO 1991. LNCS, vol. 576, pp. 252–266. Springer, Heidelberg (1992). https://doi.org/10.1007/3-540-46766-1_20
8. Kuwakado, H., Koyama, K., Tsuruoka, Y.: A new RSA-type scheme based on singular cubic curves with equation $y^2 \equiv x^3 + bx^2 (\bmod N)$. IEICE TRANS. Fundam. Electron. Commun. Comput. Sci. **78**(1), 27–33 (1995)
9. Lenstra, A.K., Lenstra, H.W., Lovász, L.: Factoring polynomials with rational coefficients. Math. Ann. **261**, 513–534 (1982)

10. May, A.: New RSA vulnerabilities using lattice reduction methods. Ph.D. thesis, University of Paderborn (2003)
11. Murru, N., Saettone, F.M.: A novel RSA-like cryptosystem based on a generalization of the Rédei rational functions. In: Kaczorowski, J., Pieprzyk, J., Pomykała, J. (eds.) NuTMiC 2017. LNCS, vol. 10737, pp. 91–103. Springer, Cham (2018). https://doi.org/10.1007/978-3-319-76620-1_6
12. Nitaj, A.: Another generalization of Wiener's attack on RSA. In: Vaudenay, S. (ed.) AFRICACRYPT 2008. LNCS, vol. 5023, pp. 174–190. Springer, Heidelberg (2008). https://doi.org/10.1007/978-3-540-68164-9_12
13. Nitaj, A., Arrifin, M.R.K., Adenan, N.N.H., Abu, N.A.: Classical attacks on a variant of the RSA cryptosystem. In: LatinCrypt 2021 (2021)
14. Nitaj, A., Seck, M.: A new public key encryption scheme based on the cubic pell curve using encoding functions. Moroccan J. Algebra Geom. Appl. (2024). https://ced.fst-usmba.ac.ma/p/mjaga/wp-content/uploads/2024/12/NitajSeck_MJAGA-2.pdf
15. Peng, L., Hu, L., Lu, Y., Wei, H.: An improved analysis on three variants of the RSA cryptosystem. In: Chen, K., Lin, D., Yung, M. (eds.) Inscrypt 2016. LNCS, vol. 10143, pp. 140–149. Springer, Cham (2017). https://doi.org/10.1007/978-3-319-54705-3_9
16. Quisquater, J.J., Couvreur, C.: Fast decipherment algorithm for RSA public-key cryptosystem. Electron. Lett. **18**(21), 905–907 (1982)
17. Rahmani, M., Nitaj, A., Ziane, M.: Further cryptanalysis of some variants of the RSA cryptosystem. J. Appl. Math. Comput. 1–31 (2024)
18. Rivest, R., Shamir, A., Adleman, L.: A Method for Obtaining digital signatures and public-key cryptosystems. Commun. ACM **21**(2), 120–126 (1978)
19. Shi, G., Wang, G., Gu, D.: Further cryptanalysis of a type of RSA variants. In: Susilo, W., Chen, X., Guo, F., Zhang, Y., Intan, R. (eds.) ISC 2022. LNCS, vol. 13640, pp. 133–152. Springer, Cham (2022). https://doi.org/10.1007/978-3-031-22390-7_9
20. Takagi, T.: A fast RSA-type public-key primitive modulo $p^k q$ using Hensel lifting. IEICE Trans. Fundam. Electron. Commun. Comput. Sci. **87**(1), 94–101 (2004)
21. Collins, T., Hopkins, D., Langford, S., Sabin, M.: Public key cryptographic apparatus and Method. US Patent #5,848,159 (1997)
22. Wiener, M.: Cryptanalysis of short RSA secret exponents. IEEE Trans. Inf. Theory **36**(3), 553–558 (1990)
23. Zheng, M., Kunihiro, N., Yao, Y.: Cryptanalysis of the RSA variant based on cubic Pell equation. Theor. Comput. Sci. **889**, 135–144 (2021)

A New Generalized Attack on RSA-Like Cryptosystems

Michel Seck[1]($\boxtimes$), Oumar Niang[1], Djiby Sow[2], Abderrahmane Nitaj[3], Mengce Zheng[4], and Boudabra[5]

[1] LTISI, CRISIN'2D, Ecole Polytechnique de Thies, Thies, Senegal
{mseck,oniang}@ept.edu.sn
[2] Department of Mathematics and Computer Science, FST, UCAD, Dakar, Senegal
djiby.sow@ucad.edu.sn
[3] Normandie Univ, UNICAEN, CNRS, LMNO, 14000 Caen, France
abderrahmane.nitaj@unicaen.fr
[4] Zhejiang Wanli University, Ningbo, China
mczheng@zwu.edu.cn
[5] Department of Mathematics, King Fahd University of Petroleum and Minerals,
Dhahran, Saudi Arabia

Abstract. Rivest, Shamir, and Adleman published the RSA cryptosystem in 1978, which has been widely used over the last four decades. The security of RSA is based on the difficulty of factoring large integers $N = pq$, where p and q are prime numbers. The public exponent e and the private exponent d are related by the equation $ed - k(p-1)(q-1) = 1$. Recently, Cotan and Teşeleanu (NordSec 2023) introduced a variant of RSA, where the public exponent e and the private exponent d satisfy the equation $ed - k(p^n - 1)(q^n - 1) = 1$ for some positive integer n. In this paper, we study the general equation $eu - (p^n - 1)(q^n - 1)v = w$ with positive integers u and v, and $w \in \mathbb{Z}$. We show that, given the public parameters N and e, one can recover u and v and factor the modulus N in polynomial time by combining continued fractions with Coppersmith's algorithm which relies on lattice reduction techniques, under specific conditions on u, v, and w. Furthermore, we show that if the private exponent d in an RSA-like cryptosystem is either small or too large, then N can be factored in polynomial time. This attack applies to the standard RSA cryptosystem.

Keywords: RSA · Continued fractions · Cryptanalysis · Coppersmith's method · Generalized Wiener attack

1 Introduction

The RSA cryptosystem [18], published in 1978 by Ron Rivest, Adi Shamir, and Leonard Adleman, is a widely used cryptographic primitive over the past four decades that enables secure data transmission over insecure channels. Its security relies on the computational difficulty of factoring an integer $N = pq$ which is

A. Nitaj et al. (Eds.): AFRICACRYPT 2025, LNCS 15651, pp. 126–144, 2026.
https://doi.org/10.1007/978-3-031-97260-7_7

a product of two large prime numbers, a problem believed to be intractable for classical computers when N is big. The public key $\mathsf{pk} = (N, e)$ and the private key $\mathsf{sk} = (N, d)$ are related by the equation $ed - k(p-1)(q-1) = 1$ for some positive integer k. To obtain a safe private key, the public exponent e, the private exponent d and the parameter k should be chosen carefully. It is well known that if these parameters are too small, then RSA cryptosystem is vulnerable. For instance, Håstad [9] has showed that when the same message m is encrypted with multiple public keys $(e, N_1), (e, N_2), \ldots, (e, N_s)$ sharing a same small public exponent e (e.g. $e = 3$) and broadcast to multiple recipients, then m can be recovered in polynomial time given only the public information. Wiener [20] showed in 1990 that if the private exponent $d < \frac{1}{3}N^{\frac{1}{4}}$, then the modulus N can be factored in polynomial time by using continued fractions [15] by exploiting the equation

$$ed - k(p-1)(q-1) = 1 \tag{1}$$

This bound was later improved by Boneh and Durfee [2] who proved that the primes p and q can be recovered in polynomial time if $d < N^{0.292}$. Their attack is based on Coppersmith's method [11,14] which is based on lattice reduction techniques, especially the LLL algorithm [13]. Recently, Cotan and Teşeleanu [5] (NordSec 2023) have proposed a variant of RSA cryptosystem where the public exponent e and the private exponent d are related by the equation

$$ed - k(p^n - 1)(q^n - 1) = 1, \tag{2}$$

where n is a positive integer. Notice that the RSA equation is a special case of this generalized equation $(n = 1)$.

In this paper, we are mainly interested to the cryptanalysis the Cotan-Teşeleanu cryptosystem. More specifically, we study the generalized equation

$$eu - (p^n - 1)(q^n - 1)v = w \tag{3}$$

where u and v are positive integers and $w \in \mathbb{Z}$. The key ingredients of our attack is combining continued fractions and Coppersmith's method to successfully recover u, v, and the factors p and q in polynomial time under specific conditions on u, v and w.

1.1   Related Works

We summarize the generalized Wiener attack on some RSA-like cryptosystems combining the continued fractions and Coppersmith's method.

Blömer and May attack [1]. In 2004, Blömer and May proposed, to our knowledge, the first generalized Wiener attack combining continued fractions and Coppersmith's method. They proved that, for an RSA modulus $N = pq$, if the public exponent e satisfies the equation

$$ex + y = (p-1)(q-1)k \tag{4}$$

with $0 < x < \dfrac{1}{3}\sqrt{\dfrac{(p-1)(q-1)}{e}}\,\dfrac{N^{3/4}}{p-q}$ and $|y| < \dfrac{p-q}{(p-1)(q-1)\cdot N^{3/4}}\cdot ex$. Then one can factor N in polynomial time in $\log(N)$.

Nitaj attack [16]. In 2008, Nitaj [16] proposed another generalized attack on RSA cryptosystem. He showed that if the public exponent e is related to the equation

$$eX - (p-u)(q-v)Y = 1 \tag{5}$$

with integers X, Y, u, v such that

$$1 \le X < Y < 2^{-1/4}N^{1/4}, |u| < N^{1/4}, v = \left[-\dfrac{qu}{p-u}\right]$$

with the extra condition on $p - u$ and $(q - v)$ yields the factorization of $N = pq$.

Another Nitaj attack [17]. In 1991, Koyama, Maurer, Okamoto and Vanstone [12] introduced a new public key cryptosystem on elliptic curves over the ring $\mathbb{Z}/N\mathbb{Z}$, with $N = pq$, called KMOV, where e and d are related to the equation $ed - (p+1)(q+1)k = 1$. Nitaj has proposed a generalized Wiener attack on their scheme. He showed that if the public exponent e satisfies an equation

$$ex - (p+1)(q+1)y = z \tag{6}$$

where x and y are positive integers with $\gcd(x, y) = 1$ and

$$|z| < \dfrac{(p-q)N^{1/4}y}{3(p+q)} \text{ and } xy < \dfrac{\sqrt{2N}}{12}$$

Then one can recover p and q in polynomial time.

Bunder et al. attack [3]. In 2002, Elkamchouchi, Elshenawy and Shaban [7] adapted RSA to the Gaussian domain by using a modulus of the form $N = PQ$ where P and Q are two Gaussian primes. their exponents e and d are related to the equation $ed - (p^2 - 1)(q^2 - 1)k = 1$. In 2017, Bunder et al. [3] proposed an attack that factors the modulus $N = pq$ in their schemes by using the generalized equation

$$ex - (p^2 - 1)(q^2 - 1)y = z \tag{7}$$

by combining the continued fraction algorithm and Coppersmith's method.

1.2 Our Contributions

In this paper, we study a generalized Wiener attack for RSA-like cryptosystems whose their public exponent e and the private exponent d satisfy the generalized equation

$$eu - (p^4 - 1)(q^4 - 1)v = w \tag{8}$$

We get the following results:

- Combining continued fractions and Coppersmith's method, we show that one can recover u, v and the primes p and q in polynomial time in $\log(N)$ if $uv < (2N^4 - 49N^2 + 2)/(4N + 170N^2)$ and $|w| < vN$.
- We have also proposed a generic attack for some RSA-like cryptosystems when e is related to the equation

$$ex - y\psi(p,q) = z \text{ with } |z| \leq \mathcal{B}_2, \ \mathcal{B}_2 \geq 1 \tag{9}$$

We show that if there is an algorithm $\mathcal{A}$ that is able to factor N in polynomial time given N and a public exponent $0 < e < \psi(p,q)$ such that there exist positive integers x and y with $xy < \mathcal{B}_1 \in \mathbb{R}^+$ (resp. $x < \mathcal{B}_1 \in \mathbb{R}^+$) satisfying Eq. 9, then using $\mathcal{A}$, one can factor N in polynomial time given N and a public exponent $0 < e' < \psi(p,q)$ such that the corresponding private exponent $d' = \psi(p,q) - d$ for some $d < \sqrt{\mathcal{B}_1}$ (resp. $d < \mathcal{B}_1$).

- A consequence of the previous result is that for many RSA-like cryptosystems, including standard RSA and the Cotan-Teşeleanu cryptosystem [5], if the private key d, $0 < d < \psi(p,q)$ is too large, then one can factor N in polynomial time. Notice that a similar result was proved by Hinek [10].
- We give an algorithm that is able to generate weak RSA public key instances (N, e) in polynomial time such that (N, e) is vulnerable to our attack but safe for classical Wiener-like attacks. We provide a proof-of-concept implementation[1] in SageMath [6] for this algorithm and for our generalized attack.

1.3 Paper Organization

The rest of this paper is organized as follows. Section 2 is devoted to the preliminaries on continued fractions, Coppersmith's method and the Cotan-Teşeleanu cryptosystem [5]. In Sect. 3, we detail our generalized Wiener attack on Cotan-Teşeleanu cryptosystem [5]. In Sect. 4, we show how to recover p and q in polynomial time if the private exponents d of RSA-like cryptosystems are large. We conclude our work in the final Sect. 5.

2 Preliminaries

In this section, we recall useful properties on continued fractions expansion and Legendre's Theorem. We also summarize the Coppersmith's method for factoring integers $N = pq$ given an approximation $\widehat{p}$ of p such that $|p - \widehat{p}| < N^{1/4}$. We terminate by presenting the algorithms of Cotan-Teşeleanu cryptosystem [5].

---

[1] https://github.com/mseckept/generalized-wiener-attack.

2.1   Continued Fractions

Definition 1 (continued fraction [8,15]). *A continued fraction is an expression of the form:*

$$a_0 + \cfrac{1}{a_1 + \cfrac{1}{a_2 + \cfrac{1}{a_3 + \ddots}}}$$

where a_0 is an integer and $a_1, a_2, a_3, \ldots$ are positive integers. This representation is often denoted as $[a_0; a_1, a_2, a_3, \ldots]$.

Notice that every real number α can be expressed as a continued fraction; and α is a rational number if and only if it has a finite continued fraction representation i.e.

$$\alpha = \frac{a}{b} = [a_0; a_1, a_2, \ldots, a_k]$$

Definition 2 (Computation of a_i). *Let $\lfloor \alpha \rfloor$ denote the greatest integer less than or equal to α. Let $\alpha_0 = \alpha$ and $a_0 = \lfloor \alpha_0 \rfloor$. Then the other a_i, $i \geq 1$ are computed as follows.*

$$a_{i+1} = \lfloor \alpha_{i+1} \rfloor \text{ where } \alpha_{i+1} = \frac{1}{\alpha_i - a_i}$$

Notice that this procedure terminates only if $a_i = \alpha_i$ for some $i \geq 0$.

Definition 3 (convergent, [8,15]). *The convergents of a continued fraction $[a_0; a_1, a_2, \ldots]$ are the rational numbers obtained by truncating the continued fraction at each step. The n-th convergent is given by:*

$$C_n = [a_0; a_1, a_2, \ldots, a_n] = \frac{p_n}{q_n}$$

where p_n and q_n are the numerator and denominator of the n-th convergent, respectively. These can be computed recursively using the relations:

$$p_n = a_n p_{n-1} + p_{n-2}, \quad q_n = a_n q_{n-1} + q_{n-2}$$

with initial conditions $p_{-2} = 0$, $p_{-1} = 1$, $q_{-2} = 1$, and $q_{-1} = 0$.

We denote the set of the convergents of a rational number $r := [a_0; a_1, a_2, \ldots, a_m]$ by

$$\text{Convergents}(r) := \left\{ (u, v) \in \mathbb{N}^2 : \frac{v}{u} = C_n, \gcd(u, v) = 1, n = 1, 2, \ldots, m \right\} \quad (10)$$

In the following, we recall the Legendre's theorem which provides a criterion for a rational number to be a convergent of a real number's continued fraction.

Theorem 1 (Legendre). *Let α be a real number, and let $\frac{a}{b}$ be a rational number where a and b are positive integers such that $\gcd(a, b) = 1$. If*

$$\left| \alpha - \frac{a}{b} \right| < \frac{1}{2b^2},$$

then $\frac{a}{b}$ is a convergent of the continued fraction expansion of α.

It is well known that if α is a rational number, then the sequence of convergents of its continued fraction expansion can be computed in polynomial time in $\log(\max(a, b))$.

2.2 Coppersmith's Method

Coppersmith [4] presented, in 1996, an algorithm to find small integer roots of univariate modular polynomials. His method is based on lattice reduction techniques such as the well known LLL algorithm [13]. A lattice is a discrete additive subgroup of $\mathbb{R}^n$ and is generated by a basis of linearly independent vectors $\mathbf{b}_1, \mathbf{b}_2, \ldots, \mathbf{b}_m$, forming integer linear combinations:

$$\mathcal{L} = \left\{ \sum_{i=1}^{m} a_i \mathbf{b}_i \mid a_i \in \mathbb{Z} \right\}$$

The rank of a lattice is the number of basis vectors. If the rank is equal to the ambient space dimension n, the lattice is full-rank. The determinant (or covolume) of a lattice is $\det(\mathcal{L}) = \sqrt{\det(B^T B)}$ where B is the $n \times m$ matrix whose columns are the basis vectors. If the lattice is full-rank ($m = n$), the determinant simplifies to $\det(\mathcal{L}) = |\det(B)|$. In a lattice, short vectors refer to nonzero lattice points with relatively small Euclidean norm. Finding such vectors is crucial in many computational problems, including cryptanalysis and integer factorization. Efficient approximation of short vectors is achieved using lattice reduction techniques like LLL [13] and BKZ [19], which are widely used in cryptographic attacks (e.g. Coppersmith-like algorithms [4]) and post-quantum cryptography.

Theorem 2 (Coppersmith [11,14]). *Let $N = pq$ be an RSA modulus, where p and q have the same bit size. Suppose we are given an approximation of p with additive error at most $N^{1/4}$. Then N can be factored in time polynomial in $\log(N)$.*

For the sake of completeness, we summarize in the following, the Coppersmith's algorithm (see [14] for more details) to find a factor p of N given N and an approximation $\widehat{p}$ of p.

Algorithm 1. Coppersmith's algorithm for finding a factor p of N

Input: $N = pq$ (unknown factorization), an approximation $\widehat{p}$ of p, a positive real β for lower bound $p > N^\beta$, a positive real ϵ such that $|p - \widehat{p}| < N^{\frac{1}{2}-\epsilon}$.

Output: A factor p of N or $\perp$

1: Define the polynomial $f_p(x) = (x - \widehat{p})$.

2: Choose the smallest integer m such that $m \geq \max\left\{\frac{\beta^2}{\epsilon}, 7\beta\right\}$.

3: Compute $t = \left\lfloor m\left(\frac{1}{\beta} - 1\right)\right\rfloor$.

4: Compute the shift polynomials

$$g_i(x) = N^i f_p^{m-i}(x), \quad \text{for } i = 0, 1, \ldots, m,$$
$$h_i(x) = x^i f_p^m(x), \quad \text{for } i = 0, 1, \ldots, t-1.$$

5: Compute the bound $X = \lceil N^{\beta^2 - \epsilon}\rceil$.

6: Construct the lattice basis B, where the basis vectors of B are the coefficient vectors of $g_i(xX)$ and $h_i(xX)$.

7: Apply the LLL-algorithm to B. Let v be the shortest vector in the LLL-reduced basis.

8: Construct $f(x)$ from v.

9: Find the set $\mathcal{R}$ of all roots of $f(x)$ over the integers. For every root $x_0 \in \mathcal{R}$, check whether $\gcd(N, f_p(x_0)) \geq N^\beta$. If this condition is not satisfied then remove x_0 from $\mathcal{R}$.

10: **If** $\widehat{p} + x_0$ divides N; $p := \widehat{p} + x_0$ **else** $p := \perp$.

11: **Return** p

2.3   Cotan and Teşeleanu Scheme

In NordSec 2023, Cotan and Teşeleanu [5] introduced a new RSA-like cryptosystem using the key equation

$$ex - k(p^n - 1)(q^n - 1) = 1 \text{ for some positive integer } n$$

Notice that for $n = 1$, we have the standard RSA [18] equation and for $n = 2$, the Elkamchouchi, Elshenawy and Shaban scheme proposed in 2002 [7].

In the Cotan and Teşeleanu public key encryption scheme, the computations are done in the set $\dfrac{\mathbb{Z}/N\mathbb{Z}[t]}{t^n - r}$ instead of $\mathbb{Z}/N\mathbb{Z}$.

Let p be a prime number, n a positive integer and $r \in \dfrac{\mathbb{Z}}{p\mathbb{Z}}$ such that $t^n - r$ is an irreducible polynomial over $\dfrac{\mathbb{Z}}{p\mathbb{Z}}[t]$. Define the set

$$\mathbb{A}_n(p) = \frac{\mathbb{Z}/p\mathbb{Z}[t]}{t^n - r}$$

Notice that $\mathbb{A}_n(p)$ is a finite field of order p^n and can be represented as follows:

$$\mathbb{A}_n(p) = \left\{ a(t) = a_0 + a_1 t + \ldots + a_{n-1} t^{n-r} : a_0, a_1, \ldots, a_{n-1} \in \frac{\mathbb{Z}}{p\mathbb{Z}} \right\}$$

Let $a(t)$ and $b(t)$ be two elements in $\mathbb{A}_n(p)$, then the quotient field induces a natural product $\circ$

$$a(t) \circ b(t) = \sum_{i=0}^{n-2} \left(\sum_{j=0}^{i} a_j b_{i-j} + r \sum_{j=0}^{i+n} a_j b_{i-j+n} \right) t^i + \sum_{j=0}^{b-1} a_j b_{n-1-j} t^{n-1}.$$

$\mathbb{A}_n^\star(p)$ is a cyclic group of order $\phi_n(p) = p^n - 1$. Let $a(t) \in \mathbb{A}_n^\star(p)$ and e an integer, we define

$$[a(t)]^e = a(t) \circ a(t) \circ \ldots \circ a(t) \ (e \ \text{times})$$

The key generation, encryption and decryption algorithms are given as follows.

Key Generation: Let λ be a security parameter and $n \geq 1$ an integer.
- Randomly generate two distinct large prime numbers p, q such that $p, q \geq 2^\lambda$ and compute the modulus $N = pq$.
- Choose an integer $r \in \mathbb{Z}/N\mathbb{Z}$ such that $t^n - r$ is an irreducible polynomial over $\frac{\mathbb{Z}}{p\mathbb{Z}}[t]$ and $\frac{\mathbb{Z}}{q\mathbb{Z}}[t]$. Let $\phi_n = (p^n - 1)(q^n - 1)$.
- Select a positive integer $e < \phi_n$ such that $\gcd(e, \phi_n) = 1$.
- Compute $d = e^{-1} \pmod{\phi_n}$. The public key is $pk = (N, e, n, r)$ and the secret key is $sk = (N, d, n, r)$.

Encryption process: To encrypt a message $m = (m_0, m_1, \ldots, m_{n-1}) \in (\mathbb{Z}/N\mathbb{Z})^n$ with the public key $pk = (N, e, n, r)$,
- Represent the message m as $m(t) = m_0 + m_1 t + \ldots + m_{n-1} t^{n-1} \in \mathbb{A}_n^\star(N)$.
- The ciphertext is $c(t) = [m(t)]^e \pmod{N}$.

Decryption process: To decrypt a ciphertext $c(t) \in \mathbb{A}_n^\star(N)$ with the secret key $sk = (N, d, n, r)$, Compute

$$m(t) = [c(t)]^d \pmod{N}$$

Lemma 1 [3]. *Let $N = pq$ be an RSA modulus with $q < p < 2q$. The following holds:*

$$2\sqrt{N} < p + q < 3\frac{\sqrt{2}}{2}\sqrt{N} < 3\sqrt{N}$$

Wlog, we can assume, in the rest of this paper that $p - q > N^{\frac{1}{4}}$; otherwise N can be factored in polynomial time [14].

3   Our New Attack

In this section, we present our new attack to factor N by combining two techniques: the continued fractions and Coppersmith's algorithm. More precisely, we show how to obtain p and q by solving the general equation

$$eu - (p^4 - 1)(q^4 - 1)v = w$$

3.1   The New Attack

Lemma 2. *Let $N = pq$ be a balanced RSA modulus ($q < p < 2q$). Let u and v be two coprime positive integers. Let e a public exponent satisfying $eu - (p^4 - 1)(q^4 - 1)v = w$ such that $|w| < vN$. Given e, N, u and v, one can find p and q in polynomial time.*

Proof. Suppose that we know e, N, u and v such that $eu - (p^4 - 1)(q^4 - 1)v = w$ with $|w| < vN$. To show that one can factor N in polynomial time, we will first find an approximation $\widehat{p}$ of the prime p such that $|p - \widehat{p}| < N^{1/4}$. Afterwards, we apply the Coppersmith's algorithm as stated in Theorem 2 to find p; and finally get $q = N/p$.

First, let us find an approximation of $p + q$ and $p - q$.

i) **Approximation of $p+q$:** In the one hand, $\phi_4 = \dfrac{eu}{v} - \dfrac{w}{v}$ since $eu - \phi_4 v = w$. In the other hand,

$$\begin{aligned}
\phi_4 &= (p^4 - 1)(q^4 - 1) \\
&= N^4 - (p^4 + q^4) + 1 \\
&= N^4 - (p+q)^4 + 4N(p+q)^2 - 2N^2 + 1 \\
&= -(p+q)^4 + 4N(p+q)^2 + (N^2 - 1)^2
\end{aligned}$$

Then $p + q$ satisfies the following equation:

$$\left((p+q)^2\right)^2 - 4N(p+q)^2 - \left((N^2-1)^2 - \frac{eu}{v} + \frac{w}{v}\right) = 0$$

By computing the discriminant, we get

$$\Delta = 16N^2 + 4\left((N^2-1)^2 - \frac{eu}{v} + \frac{w}{v}\right) \geq 0$$

This implies that

$$(p+q)^2 = \frac{4N + 2\sqrt{\left((N^2+1)^2 - \dfrac{eu}{v} + \dfrac{w}{v}\right)}}{2}$$

Thus

$$p+q = \sqrt{2N + \sqrt{(N^2+1)^2 - \frac{eu}{v} + \frac{w}{v}}}$$

We then approximate $p + q$ as follows.

$$\widehat{p+q} = \sqrt{2N + \sqrt{(N^2 + 1)^2 - \frac{eu}{v}}}$$

Using the fact that $\sqrt{a} - \sqrt{b} < \sqrt{a \pm b} < \sqrt{a} + \sqrt{b}$ for positive integers $a > b > 0$, then the following holds.

$$\left| (p + q) - \widehat{p+q} \right| < \sqrt{\sqrt{\frac{|w|}{v}}} = N^{1/4}$$

ii) **Approximation of $p - q$:** We have

$$\phi_4 = N^4 - (p^4 + q^4) + 1 = (N^2 - 1)^2 - (p - q)^4 - 4N(p - q)^2$$

Then $p - q$ satisfies the following equation

$$\left((p - q)^2 \right)^2 + 4N(p - q)^2 - \left((N^2 - 1)^2 - \frac{eu}{v} + \frac{w}{v} \right) = 0$$

The discriminant of the previous equation is

$$\Delta' = 16N^2 + 4 \left((N^2 - 1)^2 - \frac{eu}{v} + \frac{w}{v} \right) \geq 0$$

Thus

$$p - q = \sqrt{-2N + \sqrt{(N^2 + 1)^2 - \frac{eu}{v} + \frac{w}{v}}}$$

And we approximate $p - q$ as follows.

$$\widehat{p-q} = \sqrt{-2N + \sqrt{(N^2 + 1)^2 - \frac{eu}{v}}}$$

Notice that $\widehat{p-q}$ is well defined since we have supposed that $p - q > N^{1/4}$.
One can check that $\left| (p - q) - \widehat{p-q} \right| < \sqrt{\sqrt{\frac{|w|}{v}}} = N^{1/4}$.

Combining the approximation of $p + q$ and $p - q$, we have

$$\left| p - \frac{1}{2} \left(\widehat{p+q} + \widehat{p-q} \right) \right| \leq \frac{1}{2} \left| (p + q) - \widehat{p+q} \right| + \frac{1}{2} \left| (p - q) - \widehat{p-q} \right|$$

$$< \frac{1}{2} N^{1/4} + \frac{1}{2} N^{1/4} = N^{1/4}$$

Now applying the Coppersmith's algorithm for input N and the approximation $\widehat{p} = \frac{1}{2} \left(\widehat{p+q} + \widehat{p-q} \right)$, we get p, and then we compute $q = N/p$.   □

Theorem 3. *Let $N = pq$ be an RSA modulus where p and q have the same bit size $(q < p < 2q)$. Let e be a public exponent satisfying*

$$eu - (p^4 - 1)(q^4 - 1)v = w$$

with coprime positive integers u and v. If $uv < (2N^4 - 49N^2 + 2)/(4N + 170N^2)$ and $|w| < vN$, then one can find p and q in polynomial time in $\log(N)$.

Proof. Suppose that $N = pq$ and $q < p < 2q$ and the public exponent e satisfies the general equation $eu - (p^4 - 1)(q^4 - 1)v = w$ with $u, v > 0$ and $\gcd(u, v) = 1$.

$$\phi_4 = (p^4 - 1)(q^4 - 1)$$
$$= N^4 - 2N^2 + 1 - (p + q)^4 + 4N(p + q)^2$$

This implies that

$$eu - \phi_4 v = w$$
$$\Longleftrightarrow eu - \left[N^4 - 2N^2 + 1 - (p+q)^4 + 4N(p+q)^2\right]v = w$$
$$\Longleftrightarrow eu - \left(N^4 - \frac{49}{2}N^2 + 1\right)v - \left[-(p+q)^4 + 4N(p+q)^2 + \frac{45}{2}N^2\right]v = w$$
$$\Longleftrightarrow eu - \left(N^4 - \frac{49}{2}N^2 + 1\right)v = w + \left[-(p+q)^4 + 4N(p+q)^2 + \frac{45}{2}N^2\right]v.$$

Then we divide both side by $(N^4 - \frac{49}{2}N^2 + 1)u$ and we obtain

$$\frac{2e}{2N^4 - 49N^2 + 2} - \frac{v}{u} = \frac{w + \left[-(p+q)^4 + 4N(p+q)^2 + \frac{45}{2}N^2\right]v}{(N^4 - \frac{49}{2}N^2 + 1)u}$$

The absolute value of the left hand side is bounded as follows

$$\left|\frac{2e}{2N^4 - 49N^2 + 2} - \frac{v}{u}\right| \le \frac{|w| + \left|-(p+q)^4 + 4N(p+q)^2 + \frac{45}{2}N^2\right|v}{(N^4 - \frac{49}{2}N^2 + 1)u}$$
$$< \frac{2N + 2\left|-(p+q)^4 + 4N(p+q)^2 + \frac{45}{2}N^2\right|}{2N^4 - 49N^2 + 2} \times \frac{v}{u}$$
$$= \frac{2N + 2|A|}{2N^4 - 49N^2 + 2} \times \frac{v}{u}$$

with $A = -(p+q)^4 + 4N(p+q)^2 + \frac{45}{2}N^2$. Let us now find an upper bound of $|A|$. By Lemma 1, we have $2\sqrt{N} < p+q < 3\sqrt{N}$. This implies that $4N < (p+q)^2 < 9N$ and $16N^2 < (p+q)^4 < 81N^2$. Then we have the following bound

$$16N^2 - 36N^2 - \frac{45}{2}N^2 < (p+q)^4 - 4N(p+q)^2 - \frac{45}{2}N^2 < 81N^2 - 16N^2 - \frac{45}{2}N^2$$

Therefore $|A| = |(p+q)^4 - 4N(p+q)^2 - \frac{45}{2}N^2| < \frac{85}{2}N^2.$

Then we get

$$\left| \frac{2e}{2N^4 - 49N^2 + 2} - \frac{v}{u} \right| < \frac{2N + 85N^2}{2N^4 - 49N^2 + 2} \times \frac{v}{u}$$

Since $uv < \dfrac{2N^4 - 49N^2 + 2}{4N + 170N^2}$ then $\dfrac{2N + 85N^2}{2N^4 - 49N^2 + 2} < \dfrac{1}{2uv}.$

Thus

$$\left| \frac{2e}{2N^4 - 49N^2 + 2} - \frac{v}{u} \right| < \frac{1}{2uv} \times \frac{v}{u} = \frac{1}{2u^2}$$

Hence, by Lemma 2, the fraction $\dfrac{v}{u}$ appears among the convergents of the continued fraction expansion of $\dfrac{2e}{2N^4 - 49N^2 + 2}$ which can be computed in polynomial time in $\log(N)$. Thus once we obtain u and v, one can compute p and q in polynomial time by Lemma 2. $\qquad\square$

Corollary 1. *Let $N = pq$ be an RSA modulus with $q < p < 2q$. Let $e < (p^4 - 1)(q^4 - 1)$ be a public exponent. If the private exponent d satisfies the following bound*

$$d < \sqrt{(2N^4 - 49N^2 + 2)/(4N + 170N^2)}$$

then one can find p and q in polynomial time in $\log(N)$.

Proof. Suppose that $q < p < 2q$ and $e < (p^4 - 1)(q^4 - 1)$. Suppose that the private exponent $d < \sqrt{(2N^4 - 49N^2 + 2)/(4N + 170N^2)}$. We know that the private exponent d satisfies the equation

$$ed - (p^4 - 1)(q^4 - 1)k = 1$$

for some positive integer k. Then to show that one can factor N in polynomial time in $\log(N)$, it is enough to show that $kd < (2N^4 - 49N^2 + 2)/(4N + 170N^2)$ by Theorem 3. We have

$$k = \frac{ed - 1}{(p^4 - 1)(q^4 - 1)} < \frac{e}{(p^4 - 1)(q^4 - 1)d} < d$$

Therefore $kd < d^2 < (2N^4 - 49N^2 + 2)/(4N + 170N^2)$. This ends the proof. $\square$

We summarize in the following algorithm our attack to factor N.

Algorithm 2. Our Attack to factor a modulus N

Input: The modulus N and the public exponent e.
Output: The factors (p, q) of N or $\bot$.
1: $r := (2e)/(2N^4 - 49N + 2)$.
2: convs := Convergents(r) ▷ Defined in Eq. 10
3: **For** (u, v) in convs **do**

4:    $\widehat{p+q} := \left\lfloor \sqrt{\left| 2N + \sqrt{\left|(N^2+1)^2 - \dfrac{eu}{v}\right|} \right|} \right\rfloor.$

5:    $\widehat{p-q} := \left\lfloor \sqrt{\left| -2N + \sqrt{\left|(N^2+1)^2 - \dfrac{eu}{v}\right|} \right|} \right\rfloor.$

6:    $\widehat{p} := \left\lfloor \frac{1}{2}\left(\widehat{p+q} + \widehat{p-q}\right) \right\rfloor.$
7:    $p := \text{Coppersmith}(N, \widehat{p})$ ▷ See Algorithm 1
8:    **If** $p \neq \bot$ **then**
9:        $q := N/p$.
10:        Return (p, q) and stop the loop.
11:    **end If**
12: **end For**
13: Return $\bot$.

3.2 A Numerical Example

In this section, we give a detailed numerical example to explain the different steps of our attack as presented in Algorithm 2. Let us consider the following public parameters where N is a 192 bit integer:

$N = 3489655588599196597998727781564283681960038261038493763731$

$e = 1212645714005236502130003207845392219550914289421579542876\backslash$
$2747588869937066452764958707247235073835137336084401036 3123\backslash$
$2696543804656879163494807215473923870631948211710169000 3224\backslash$
$8592826620643450055808148570038313973227958484483674761$

We get

$2N^4 - 49N^2 + 2 = 2965925659251282249852609285737277526349331 9435631\backslash$
$228113422881048895189176448539116661868758 36941574\backslash$
$772595490809626658037224782060803377911228 330289331\backslash$
$027312229395683785037068498150661534674700 219693407\backslash$
$915803297056579985444 01042955$

The continued fraction expansion of $\dfrac{2e}{2N^4 - 49N^2 + 2}$ is given as follows.

$$\frac{2e}{2N^4 - 49N^2 + 2} = [0; 1, 4, 2, 17, 2, 1, 2, 4, 1, 2, 1, 2, 1, 1, 3, 2, 11, 3, 2, 13, 10, \backslash$$
$$1, 1, 1, 1, 9, 6, 3, 1, 2, 2, 15, 4, 2, 2, 29, 20, 1, 1, 2, 13, 3, 14, \backslash$$
$$1, 2, 2, 1, 1, 7, 1, 4, 1, 2, 44, 3, 1, 8, 5, 1, 232, 1, 3, 1, 6, 2, 1, 5, \ldots]$$

For the 101st convergent C_{101} (note that $C_1 = 1$, $C_2 = \frac{4}{5}$, and $C_3 = \frac{9}{11}$) of the continued fraction expansion of $\dfrac{2e}{2N^4 - 49N^2 + 2}$, we obtain

$$u = 10916466211227234644455523378824814295237746951904 0396359$$
$$v = 89265932352933203808239549339516537133049722059157965712$$

One can check that $uv < (2N^4 - 49N^2 + 2)/(4N + 170N^2) \approx 1.43 \times 10^{113}$. We obtain the approximation of $p + q$ and $p - q$ (see Algorithm 2) as follows.

$$\widehat{p+q} = 158666848432062407414462565131$$
$$\widehat{p-q} = 105908198157490520315381810349$$

From the approximation of $p + q$ and $p - q$, we compute the approximation of p and obtain

$$\widehat{p} = \left\lfloor \frac{\widehat{p+q} + \widehat{p-q}}{2} \right\rfloor = 132287523294776463864922187740$$

By applying Coppersmith's algorithm, we find

$$p = 132287523294776463864922187741$$

which is a divisor of N. Finally, we compute the other factor as $q = N/p = 263793251372859435495403 77391$.

One can verify that:

$$w = eu - (p^4 - 1)(q^4 - 1)v = -1.$$

The private exponent is

$$d = 14829628296256411249263046428686387631746659717815 61405671144\backslash$$
$$05244475945882242695583309343791847078738629774540481 32452157\backslash$$
$$42907511231313767882786768557366673854820521856655651 95204905\backslash$$
$$57995174944057273302393639166519405059596609 3241$$

which is large but

$$\phi_4 - d = 1091646621122723464445552337882481429523774695190 40396359$$

Notice that the parameter k such that $ed - k(p^4 - 1)(q^4 - 1) = 1$ is also too large.

$$k = 14829628296256411249263046428686387631746659717815614056711\backslash$$
$$44052444759458822426955833093437918470787386297745404813245\backslash$$
$$21574290751123131376788278676855736667385482052185665565195\backslash$$
$$20490557995174944057273302393639166519405059596609093241$$

4   A Generalized Wiener Attack for RSA-Like Cryptosystems

In the following Theorem, we prove that if the private exponent of an RSA-like cryptosystem is too large, then one can factor N in polynomial time given the public parameters (N, e).

Theorem 4. *Let $N = pq$ be an RSA modulus. Let $\psi : \mathbb{N} \times \mathbb{N} \to \mathbb{N}$. Suppose $\mathcal{A}$ is an algorithm that is able to factor N in polynomial time given N and a public exponent $0 < e < \psi(p, q)$ such that there exist positive integers x and y with $xy < \mathcal{B}_1 \in \mathbb{R}^+$ satisfying*

$$ex - y\psi(p, q) = z \text{ with } |z| \leq \mathcal{B}_2, \ \mathcal{B}_2 \geq 1$$

Then, using $\mathcal{A}$, one can factor N in polynomial time given N and a public exponent $0 < e' < \psi(p, q)$ such that the corresponding private exponent $d' = \psi(p, q) - d$ for some $d < \sqrt{\mathcal{B}_1}$.

Proof. Suppose $\mathcal{A}$ is able to factor N in polynomial time given N and a public exponent $0 < e < \psi(p, q)$ such that there exist positive integers x and y with $xy < \mathcal{B}_1$, $ex - y\psi(p, q) = z$ with $|z| \leq \mathcal{B}_2$, $\mathcal{B}_2 \geq 1$. Let e', $0 < e' < \psi(p, q)$ a public exponent such that $(e')^{-1} \mod \psi(p, q) = d' = \psi(p, q) - d$ for some $d < \sqrt{\mathcal{B}_1}$. To show that one can factor N in polynomial time, we will show that there exist positive integers x_0 and y_0 such that $e'x_0 - y_0\psi(p, q) = -1$ with $x_0 y_0 < \mathcal{B}_1$ and afterwards use the algorithm $\mathcal{A}$ to factor N. We have $(e')^{-1} \mod \psi(p, q) = \psi(p, q) - d$, then there exists a positive integer k such that

$$e'(\psi(p, q) - d) - k\psi(p, q) = 1 \iff e'(-d) + (\psi(p, q) - k)\psi(p, q) = 1$$
$$\iff e'd - (\psi(p, q) - k)\psi(p, q) = -1$$

We have $\psi(p, q) - k = \dfrac{e'd + 1}{\psi(p, q)} > 0$. This implies that

$$(\psi(p, q) - k) - \frac{1}{\psi(p, q)} = \frac{e'd}{\psi(p, q)} < d \text{ since } 0 < e' < \psi(p, q)$$

Therefore $\psi(p, q) - k < d + \dfrac{1}{\psi(p, q)}$. Since $\psi(p, q) - k \in \mathbb{N}$, then $\psi(p, q) - k \leq d \Rightarrow$ $d(\psi(p, q) - k) < d^2 < \mathcal{B}_1$. We have showed that $e'd - (\psi(p, q) - k)\psi(p, q) = -1$ with $d(\psi(p, q) - k) < \mathcal{B}_1$, then using algorithm $\mathcal{A}$, one can factor N in polynomial time.   □

Notice that if the private exponent d' is big then so is the positive integer k such that

$$e'd' - k\psi(p,q) = 1$$

since $\psi(p,q) - k \leq d$.

Corollary 2. *Let $N = pq$ be an RSA modulus with $q < p < 2q$. Let $e < (p^4 - 1)(q^4 - 1)$ be a public exponent. If the private exponent d satisfies the following bound*

$$d > (p^4 - 1)(q^4 - 1) - \sqrt{\frac{2N^4 - 49N^2 + 2}{4N + 170N^2}}$$

then one can find p and q in polynomial time in $\log(N)$.

Proof. It follows from Theorem 3 and Theorem 4.   □

This corollary tells us if the private exponent d is too large, i.e.

$$|\phi_4 - d| < \sqrt{\frac{2N^4 - 49N^2 + 2}{4N + 170N^2}}$$

then we can factor the modulus N in polynomial time.

Using the result of Bunder et al. [3] (Theorem 3) and Theorem 4, we get the following result.

Corollary 3. *Let $N = pq$ be an RSA modulus with $q < p < 2q$. Let $e < (p^2 - 1)(q^2 - 1)$ be a public exponent. If the private exponent d satisfies the following bound*

$$d > (p^2 - 1)(q^2 - 1) - \sqrt{2N - 4\sqrt{2}N^{\frac{3}{4}}}$$

then one can find p and q in polynomial time in $\log(N)$.

The following Theorem is a variant of Theorem 4.

Theorem 5. *Let $N = pq$ an RSA modulus. Let $\psi : \mathbb{N} \times \mathbb{N} \to \mathbb{N}$. Suppose $\mathcal{A}$ is an algorithm that is able to factor N in polynomial time given N and a public exponent $0 < e < \psi(p,q)$ such that there exist positive integers x and y with $x < \mathcal{B}_1 \in \mathbb{R}^+$ satisfying*

$$ex - y\psi(p,q) = z \text{ with } |z| \leq \mathcal{B}_2, \ \mathcal{B}_2 \geq 1$$

Then, using $\mathcal{A}$, one can factor N in polynomial time given N and a public exponent $0 < e' < \psi(p,q)$ such that the corresponding private exponent $d' = \psi(p,q) - d$ for some $d < \mathcal{B}_1$.

Proof. Similarly to the proof of Theorem 4, we have

$$e'(\psi(p,q) - d) - k\psi(p,q) = 1 \iff e'd - (\psi(p,q) - k)\psi(p,q) = -1$$

This shows that if $d < \mathcal{B}_1$, one can factor N in polynomial time using the algorithm $\mathcal{A}$.   □

Combining the result of Blömer and May [1] (Theorem 2) and the previous theorem, we get the following result.

Corollary 4. *Let $c \le 1$ and let (N, e) be an RSA public key tuple with $N = pq$ and $p - q \ge c\sqrt{N}$. If the private exponent d verifies*

$$d > (p-1)(q-1) - \frac{1}{3}N^{\frac{1}{4}}$$

Then N can be factored in polynomial time.

We summarize in the following Fig. 1, the vulnerable areas for the private exponent d.

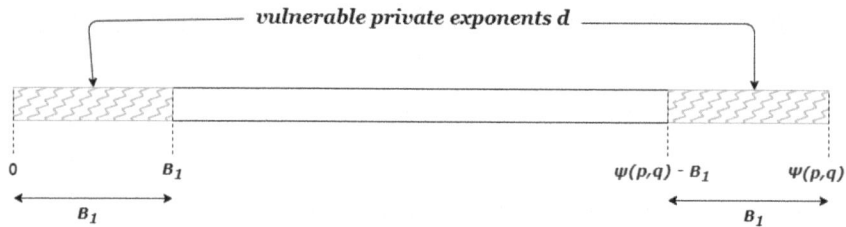

Fig. 1. Vulnerable areas for the private exponent d

Notice that in our generalized attack,

$$\psi(p, q) = (p^4 - 1)(q^4 - 1) \text{ and } \mathcal{B}_1 \ge \sqrt{\frac{2N^4 - 49N^2 + 2}{4N + 170N^2}}$$

From Theorem 4, we build an algorithm that takes as input a security parameter λ and outputs a weak RSA public key (N, e).

Algorithm 3. GenWeakRSAInstance

Input: A security parameter λ.
Output: A weak RSA public key (N, e).
 1: Generate randomly a prime p of size $\lambda/2$ bits.
 2: Generate randomly a prime q of size $\lambda/2$ bits with $q < p < 2q$.
 3: Compute $N = pq$ and $\psi(p, q) = (p^4 - 1)(q^4 - 1)$.
 4: Generate randomly an integer d with $0 < d < \sqrt{\dfrac{2N^4 - 49N^2 + 2}{4N + 170N^2}}$ such that

$$\gcd(\psi(p, q) - d, \psi(p, q)) = 1$$

 5: Compute $e = (\psi(p, q) - d)^{-1} \pmod{\psi(p, q)}$.
 6: Return (N, e).

Notice that this algorithm runs in polynomial time and can be easily adapted for other RSA-like cryptosystems. The weak instances (N, e) outputted by Algorithm 4 are:

- vulnerable for the generalized Wiener attack presented in Algorithm 2;
- safe for classical Wiener-like attacks because the corresponding private exponents d' are very large.

We have provided a proof-of-concept implementation[2] in SageMath [6] of our attack presented in Algorithm 2 as well as an implementation of the previous Algorithm 4 that generates weak instances in polynomial time.

5 Conclusion

In this paper, we have investigated the equation $eu - (p^n - 1)(q^n - 1)v = w$, which is a generalization of the key equation of some variants of the RSA cryptosystem. We have showed that, for the specific case $n = 4$, by combining the continued fraction algorithm, and the Coppersmith's method, one can find (u, v) and factor the modulus N in polynomial time when $uv < (2N^4 - 49N^2 + 2)/(4N + 170N^2)$ and $|w| < vN$. We have adapted our method and proved that a sufficiently small private exponent d in the RSA variants with the key equation $ed - (p^n - 1)(q^n - 1)v = 1$ can be recovered in polynomial time, leading to the factorization of N.

References

1. Blömer, J., May, A.: A generalized Wiener attack on RSA. In: International Workshop on Public Key Cryptography, pp. 1–13. Springer (2004)
2. Boneh, D., Durfee, G.: Cryptanalysis of RSA with private key d less than $N^{0.292}$. In: Advances in Cryptology—EUROCRYPT 1999: International Conference on the Theory and Application of Cryptographic Techniques Prague, Czech Republic, 2–6 May 1999, Proceedings 18, pp. 1–11. Springer (1999)
3. Bunder, M., Nitaj, A., Susilo, W., Tonien, J.: A generalized attack on RSA type cryptosystems. Theoret. Comput. Sci. **704**, 74–81 (2017)
4. Coppersmith, D.: Finding a small root of a univariate modular equation. In: International Conference on the Theory and Applications of Cryptographic Techniques, pp. 155–165. Springer (1996)
5. Cotan, P., Teşeleanu, G.: Small private key attack against a family of RSA-like cryptosystems. In: Nordic Conference on Secure IT Systems, pp. 57–72. Springer (2023)
6. Developers, T.S.: SageMath, the Sage Mathematics Software System (Version 10.4). SageMath (2024). https://www.sagemath.org
7. Elkamchouchi, H., Elshenawy, K., Shaban, H.: Extended RSA cryptosystem and digital signature schemes in the domain of Gaussian integers. In: 2002 the 8th International Conference on Communication Systems, ICCS 2002, vol. 1, pp. 91–95. IEEE (2002)

---

[2] https://github.com/mseckept/generalized-wiener-attack.

8. Hardy, G., Wright, E.M.: An Introduction to the Theory of Numbers. Oxford University Press (1979)
9. Chan, A.H., Games, R.A.: On the linear span of binary sequences obtained from finite geometries. In: Odlyzko, A.M. (ed.) CRYPTO 1986. LNCS, vol. 263, pp. 405–417. Springer, Heidelberg (1987). https://doi.org/10.1007/3-540-47721-7_29
10. Hinek, M.J.: (Very) large RSA private exponent vulnerabilities. Technical report CACR 2004-01, Centre for Applied Cryptographic Research, University of Waterloo (2004)
11. Howgrave-Graham, N.: Finding small roots of univariate modular equations revisited. In: IMA International Conference on Cryptography and Coding, pp. 131–142. Springer (1997)
12. Koyama, K., Maurer, U.M., Okamoto, T., Vanstone, S.A.: New public-key schemes based on elliptic curves over the ring Z_n. In: Feigenbaum, J. (ed.) CRYPTO 1991. LNCS, vol. 576, pp. 252–266. Springer, Heidelberg (1992). https://doi.org/10.1007/3-540-46766-1_20
13. Lenstra, A.K., Lenstra, H.W., Lovász, L.: Factoring polynomials with rational coefficients. Math. Ann. **261**, 515–534 (1982)
14. May, A.: New RSA vulnerabilities using lattice reduction methods. Ph.D. thesis, University of Paderborn, Paderborn, Germany. Citeseer (2003)
15. Moore, C.G.: An Introduction to Continued Fractions. National Council of Teachers of Mathematics, Washington, D.C. (1964)
16. Nitaj, A.: Another generalization of Wiener's attack on RSA. In: International Conference on Cryptology in Africa, pp. 174–190. Springer (2008)
17. Nitaj, A.: A new attack on the KMOV cryptosystem. Bull. Korean Math. Soc. **51**(5), 1347–1356 (2014). https://doi.org/10.4134/BKMS.2014.51.5.1347
18. Rivest, R., Shamir, A., Adleman, L.: A method for obtaining digital signatures and public-key cryptosystems. Commun. ACM (1978)
19. Schnorr, C.P.: A hierarchy of polynomial time lattice basis reduction algorithms. In: Proceedings of the 30th Annual Symposium on Foundations of Computer Science (FOCS), pp. 179–185. IEEE Computer Society (1991). https://doi.org/10.1109/FSCS.1991.185380
20. Wiener, M.J.: Cryptanalysis of short RSA secret exponents. IEEE Trans. Inf. Theory **36**(3), 553–558 (1990)

Cryptography Arithmetic

An Improvement of the Congruence Solver of Lattice Isomorphism Problem over Totally Real Number Fields and Applications

Nour-eddine Rahmani$^{(\boxtimes)}$ [ID], Taoufik Serraj, and Moulay Chrif Ismaili

ACSA Laboratory, Faculty of Sciences, Mohammed I University, BV Mohammed VI,
60000 Oujda, Morocco
`nour-eddine.rahmani@ump.ac.ma`

Abstract. The Module Lattice Isomorphism Problem (Module-LIP) is one of the lattice building blocks of the post-quantum cryptographic schemes, in particular HAWK signature scheme. In 2024, Mureau et al. introduced an algorithm to solve the lattice isomorphism problem of rank 2 Module-lattices over a totally real number field. In this paper, we revisit this algorithm and suggest an improvement making the algorithm more than 40% faster and we give some perspectives for future cryptanalysis works. As an application, we propose a partial-key exposure attack and demonstrate the impact of our study on exploiting side-information from leaks on the HAWK signature scheme.

Keywords: Lattices · Cryptanalysis · Digital Signature ·
Improvements · Lattice Isomorphism Problem · Side channel attacks

1 Introduction

The purpose of post-quantum cryptography is to develop cryptographic primitives that remain secure against cryptanalytic attacks even in the presence of a quantum computer. Several post-quantum cryptographic schemes have been developed to ensure secure communications in the presence of quantum adversaries. Lattice-based cryptographic schemes have emerged as promising candidates due to their conjectural resistance to quantum attacks. Such schemes leverage the hardness of lattice problems. Among these, CRYSTALS-Kyber [7] which is standardised by the National Institute of Standards and Technologies (NIST) in 2023 under the name **M**odule-**L**attice **K**ey **E**ncapsulation Mechanism (ML-KEM [20]) and the digital signature scheme CRYSTALS-Dilithium [10] is standardized as **M**odule **L**attice **D**igital **S**ignature **A**lgorithm (ML-DSA [21]), both of the schemes are based on Module Lattice (ML) structures. Additionally, Falcon, which stands for **F**ast-**F**ourier **L**attice-Based **Co**mpact Signatures over **NTRU**, operates as a Module Lattice Signature based on the hardness of NTRU [15] also selected by the NIST to be standardized and is noted for its compact

© The Author(s), under exclusive license to Springer Nature Switzerland AG 2026
A. Nitaj et al. (Eds.): AFRICACRYPT 2025, LNCS 15651, pp. 147–163, 2026.
https://doi.org/10.1007/978-3-031-97260-7_8

signature size and fast verification times [13]. These algorithms represent significant advancements in the field of cryptography, providing secure alternatives in a landscape increasingly threatened by the potential of quantum computing [23,24].

The algorithmic Lattice Isomorphism Problem (LIP) was introduced in the field of cryptography by Ducas et al. in [11]. The search variant of LIP is to find an isometry that is, a linear map that preserves distance and maps a lattice $\mathfrak{L}_1$ onto an isomorphic lattice $\mathfrak{L}_2$ [6,11].

In [19], Mureau et al. introduced an efficient algorithm that solves the two-squares sum problem for a prime integer in a totally real subfield of a CM-number field L, using the later algorithm as a subroutine to solve LIP. This method allows finding all possible solutions C in $\mathbf{GL}_2(\mathcal{O}_K)$, where $\mathcal{O}_K$ is the ring of integers of K. Specifically, given a quadratic form Q such that $Q = C^*C = C^tC$, such that C^* denotes the conjugate transpose of C, the algorithm identifies the possible transformations, when the coefficients of C are from a real number field, i.e. C^* equals C^t. The work of [19] provided a new framework for analysing constructions based on LIP. On October 25th 2024, the National Institute of Standards and Technology (NIST) announced the list of candidates advanced to round two of the additional post quantum digital signatures standardization process[1]. The digital signature HAWK is the only lattice based candidate passed to this round, whose security is relying on the assumed hardness of LIP.

In this work, we propose an improvement of the congruence solver of lattice isomorphism problem over totally real number fields in general, the theory behind this improvement leads us to mount attacks on HAWK scheme, in the presence of side information.

Our improvement is based on algebraic relations between Q and C which we give simpler proof for. It can be seen as a particular case of the works [18] and [3,8]. While these works share some structural similarities, our contribution was developed independently and prior to awareness of these papers [3,8,18].

The rest of the paper is organised as follows: Sect. 2 recalls some notions on lattices and module lattice isomorphism problem and briefly reviews the congruence solver algorithm introduced by Mureau et al. to solve the lattice isomorphism problem of rank 2 Module-lattices over a totally real number field. Our enhanced algorithm is presented and discussed in Sects. 3 and 4, a partial information exposure attack on HAWK scheme is proposed in Sect. 5. Finally, a conclusion is provided.

2   Preliminaries and Notations

In this section, we provide all the definitions and theorems related to the previous work [19]. In order for our arguments to continue being comprehensible and consistent, especially when dealing with algebraic, lattice-structured, and cryptographic structures, this initial work is crucial. Prior to venturing into the

---

[1] https://csrc.nist.gov/News/2024/pqc-digital-signature-second-round-announcement.

notational conventions to be used in later sections, we start by summarising important mathematical properties that are applicable to our problem domain. This will give a common framework to make our suggested approach and findings more comprehensible. Most of the preliminaries are taken and reformulated from [19] since we suggest an improvement to their work.

Notations. We follow the same notation and definitions from [19]. A number field $L := \mathbb{Q}[X]/(P(X))$ for a monic irreducible polynomial P in $\mathbb{Q}[X]$, $\mathcal{O}_L$ denotes its ring of integers. Let K be a subfield of L then the relative norm is denoted by $\mathcal{N}_{L/K}$. For a ring R, $R^\times$ its set of units, and $\mathrm{GL}_n(R)$ is the set of all $n \times n$ matrices of a unit determinant in $R^\times$.

2.1 Lattices

A lattice is defined as $\mathfrak{L} = \sum_{1 \leq i \leq r} \mathbb{Z} \mathbf{b}_i$ such that the $\mathbb{R}$-linearly independent vectors $\mathbf{b}_1, \mathbf{b}_2, \ldots, \mathbf{b}_n$ are elements of $\mathbb{R}^m$. It constitutes a discrete additive subgroup of the real vector space of dimension m. The natural number n is called the rank; the lattice is said to have full rank whenever $m = n$. The basis of L is the matrix constituted by the columns $\mathbf{b}_i$ and denoted by B.

Every lattice $\mathfrak{L}$ of rank greater than 2, has infinitely many bases, and if B is such a basis, then we can change it by multiplying B on the right by U to construct another basis $C = BU$ such as U is a unimodular matrix, which belongs to the general linear group $GL_n(\mathbb{Z})$. To specify the lattice for one of its bases, instead of writing $\mathfrak{L}$ we write $\mathfrak{L}(B)$ to represent $\mathfrak{L}$ by the basis B. The real value $\det(\mathfrak{L}) = \sqrt{B^\top \cdot B}$ defines *the volume of the lattice.*

2.2 Lattice Isomorphism Problem

Now we state the Lattice Isomorphism Problem as shown in [11]. In the following, Let $\mathfrak{L}_1(B_1)$ and $\mathfrak{L}_2(B_2)$ be two lattices.

Definition 1 ([5,11]). $\mathfrak{L}_1(B_1)$ *and* $\mathfrak{L}_2(B_2)$ *are isomorphic as lattices if* $\mathfrak{L}_2 = O \cdot \mathfrak{L}_1$ *for an orthonormal transformation* $O \in O_n(\mathbb{R})$.

Equivalently, in matrix form, $B_2 = OB_1U$, *where* O *is an orthogonal matrix and* $U \in GL_n(\mathbb{Z})$ *is unimodular.*

The search variant of lattice isomorphism problem is finding O or U given B and B'.

Definition 2 (wc-sLIP$_{B_1}$ [19]). *The* **worst-case search** *variant of* **Lattice Isomorphism Problem** *of parameter* B_1 *(denoted by wc-sLIP$_{B_1}$) is given* B_1 *and* B_2 *such that* B_2 *defines an isomorphic lattice to* $\mathfrak{L}(B_1)$, *and the goal is to find* O *in* $O_n(\mathbb{R})$ *or* U *in* $GL_n(\mathbb{Z})$ *such that* $B_2 = OB_1U$.

The LIP is defined also in terms of quadratic forms. The definite positive quadratic form $Q_1 = B_1^\top B_1 \in S_n^>(\mathbb{R})$ is called the Gram matrix associated with a basis $B_1 \in \mathrm{GL}_n(\mathbb{R})$.

Definition 3 (wc-sLIP$_{Q_1}$ [19]). *The worst-case search problem with the parameter Q_1 of a lattice isomorphism* (denoted by wc-sLIP$_{Q_1}$) *for a given quadratic form $Q_1 \in S_n^>(\mathbb{R})$, for any other $Q_2 \in S_n^>(\mathbb{R})$ such that Q_1 and Q_2 are congruent, and the goal is to find $U \in GL_n(\mathbb{Z})$ that satisfies $Q_2 = U^\top Q_1 U$.*

By using the Cholesky decomposition, it is be possible to show that the two problems are polynomial-time equivalent. [11,19]

2.3   Module Lattice Isomorphism Problem

For efficiency reasons, it becomes a habit in lattice-based cryptography to consider structured variant of lattice hard problems, this is a trade-off between security and efficiency. In this subsection we recall the definitions related to Module-lattice Isomorphism Problem as defined in [19].

Before we state the module variant, we need the two following definitions. We start by reciting the definition of pseudo-Gram matrix [19].

Definition 4 ([19]). *For a pseudo-basis $\mathbf{B} = (B, \{I_i\}_i)$ of a module $M \subseteq K^r$, the pseudo-Gram matrix associated with $\mathbf{B}$ is defined as $\mathbf{G} = (B^*B, \{I_i\}_i)$, wher $\{I_i\}_i$ are fractional ideals and B is of coefficients in K.*

After extending the definition of Gram matrices to modules over a ring of integers of a number field K, [19] gave the following definition of the congruence of two pseudo-Gram matrices.

Definition 5 ([19]). *Let $\mathbf{G} = (G, \{I_i\}_i)$ and $\mathbf{G}' = (G', \{J_i\}_i)$ be two pseudo-Gram matrices, then $\mathbf{G}$ and $\mathbf{G}'$ are congruent if $G' = U^*GU$ for a matrix $U \in GL_r(K)$ and U respects the ideal structure, i.e., $u_{ij} \in I_i J_j^{-1}$ for matrix elements u_{ij}.*

This allows the module variant of two isomorphic lattices to be defined as isomorphic module-lattices over a given number field K.

Definition 6 (Isomorphic Module-lattices [19]). *Two modules $M, M' \subseteq K^\ell$ of rank ℓ are isomorphic as module lattices if there exists a unitary transformation $O \in U_\ell(K_\mathbb{R})$ where $M' = O \cdot M$. This means that M' can be obtained by applying an orthogonal transformation that respects the structure of the number field K to M. [19]*

The worst-case module lattice isomorphism problem definitions in its both versions for basis and quadratic form are defined as follows.

Definition 7 (wc-smodLIP$_K^B$ [19]). *The worst-case search module-Lattice Isomorphism Problem with parameters K and $\mathbf{B}$, denoted by wc-SmodLIP$_B^K$, is the following: For any given pseudo-Gram matrix $\mathbf{G}'$ congruent to $\mathbf{G}$, the task is to determine a congruence matrix between $\mathbf{G}$ and $\mathbf{G}'$. In this case, the congruence matrix $U \in GL_\ell(K)$ such that $G' = U^*GU$.*

Definition 8 (wc-smodLIP$_K^Q$ [19]). *For a quadratic form $Q \in S_{>0}^\ell(K)$, **the worst-case search module-Lattice Isomorphism Problem with parameter** Q, denoted by wc-SmodLIP$_Q^K$, is as follows: For any quadratic form $Q' \in S_{>0}^\ell(K)$ that is congruent to Q, find a matrix $U \in GL_\ell(K)$ such that $Q' = U^*QU$. This problem is about finding the transformation matrix between two congruent quadratic forms over a number field K.*

2.4   Congruence Solver

Now after given all the required mathematical concepts, we move to define the Congruence solver. Before we describe the `CongruenceSolver` from [19], and since we do not modify the algorithms `NormEquation`, `GaussianGram` and `TwoSquares` we refer the reader to [19]. The authors shown the following theorem:

Theorem 1 ([19]). *Let $L|K$ be a CM extension of number fields and $q \in \mathcal{O}_K$. Given as input a basis of $\mathcal{O}_K$, a basis of $\mathcal{O}_L$, the element $q \in \mathcal{O}_K$, and the factorization of $|\mathcal{N}_K(q)|$ over $\mathbb{Z}$, the algorithm `NormEquation` (Algorithm 2.1 in [19]) computes the list of all elements $z \in \mathcal{O}_L$ such that $\mathcal{N}_{L|K}(z) = q$. Moreover, the algorithm runs in time $\mathsf{poly}(\log \Delta_L, \log |\mathcal{N}_K(q)|) \cdot (1 + \log |\mathcal{N}_K(q)|)^r$, where r is the number of distinct prime factors of the ideal $q \cdot \mathcal{O}_K$.*

Lemma 1 ([19]). *There is a probabilistic polynomial time algorithm `GaussianGram` such that the following holds. Let $\boldsymbol{B} = (B, (I_i)_{1 \leq i \leq l})$ be a pseudo-basis of a rank l module M in $K_{\mathbb{R}}^l$, and $\boldsymbol{G} = (G, (I_i)_{1 \leq i \leq l})$ be the pseudo-Gram matrix of $\boldsymbol{B}$. Let $s > 0$ be a real number satisfying*

$$s \geq \sqrt{\frac{d \cdot \log(2dl + 4)}{\pi}} \cdot 2^d \cdot \Delta_K^{\frac{3}{2d}} \cdot \max(\|\sigma(g_{j,j})^{\frac{1}{2}}\mathcal{N}(I_j)^{\frac{1}{d}}),$$

where $G = (g_{i,j})_{1 \leq i,j \leq l}$ and the square-root is applied coordinate-wise to $\sigma(gj, j) \in \mathbb{C}^d$. On input $\boldsymbol{G}$ and s, `GaussianGram`($\boldsymbol{G}, s$) outputs $z \in I_1 \times \cdots \times I_l$ such that $v := B \cdot z$ follows a discrete Gaussian distribution of parameter s in M (i.e. $\sigma(v) \sim D_{\sigma(M),s}$).

Lemma 2 ([19]). *Let K be a totally real number field and $q \in \mathcal{O}_K$. Given as input a basis of $\mathcal{O}_K$, the element $q \in \mathcal{O}_K$ and the factorization of $|N_K(q)|$. the Algorithm 4.1 `TwoSquares` (in [19]) computes all $(x, y) \in \mathcal{O}_K^2$ such that $q = x^2 + y^2$. Moreover, the algorithm runs in time $\mathsf{poly}(\log \Delta_K, (\log |N_K(q)|)^r)$, where r is the number of distinct prime factors of the ideal $q\mathcal{O}_K$.*

The Algorithm 1 runs in polynomial time as stated in [19] (Corollary 4.8). This algorithm runs in expected time relative to its input size and

$$(\mathsf{poly}(\rho_K, \log \Delta_K, \mathsf{size}(\boldsymbol{G}')))^r + T_{\mathrm{factor}}(N(\mathrm{RG}(M))),$$

where r is the number of distinct prime ideals dividing the relative Gram ideal $\mathrm{RG}(M)$ [19].

Algorithm 1 . "Finding all congruence matrices for integer rank-2 modules(`CongruenceSolver`) [19]"

1: **Input:** A basis B_K of $\mathcal{O}_K$, a pseudo-basis $\mathbf{B} = (B, (I_1, I_2))$ of $M \subset \mathcal{O}_K^2$ with pseudo-Gram matrix $\mathbf{G}$, and $\mathbf{G}' = (G', (I_1', I_2')) \sim \mathbf{G}$ an instance of wc-smodLIP$_\mathbf{B}^K$.

2: **Output:** All congruence matrices between G and G'.

3: $I \leftarrow G(M)$; $\alpha = \rho_K \cdot P(d)$ (with $P(d)$ from Assumption 1)

4: Factor $N(I) = \prod_j q_j^{f_j}$

    Generating two "nice" instances of TwoSquares:

5: $q \leftarrow 0$; $(u, v) \leftarrow (0, 0)$; $s \leftarrow 4d \cdot \Delta_K^{3/(2d)} \cdot \max_{1 \leq j \leq 2}(\|\sigma(g_{j,j}')^{1/2}\| \cdot N(I_j')^{1/d})$

6: **while** $\sqrt{\|\sigma(q)\|_1} > s \cdot \sqrt{8d + \log(4\alpha \log(s))}$ **or** $q \cdot I^{-1}$ is not a prime idea

7:     $(u, v)^T \leftarrow$ `GaussianGram`(G', s)

8:     $q \leftarrow (u, v) \cdot G' \cdot (u, v)^T$ **do**

9: **end while**

10: $q' \leftarrow 0$; $(u', v') \leftarrow (0, 0)$; $s' \leftarrow 144 \cdot d \cdot \Delta_K^{1/d} \cdot \max(\alpha^2, 1) \cdot s^4$

11: **while** $(u', v') \in \mathrm{Span}_K((u, v))$ **or** $\sqrt{\|\sigma(q)\|_1} > s' \cdot \sqrt{8d + \log(4\alpha \log(s'))}$ **or** $q' \cdot I^{-1}$ is not a prime ideal

12:     $(u', v')^T \leftarrow$ `GaussianGram`(G', s')

13:     $q' \leftarrow (u', v') \cdot G' \cdot (u', v')^T$ **do**

14: **end while**

    Solving the two instances of TwoSquares:

15: Factor $N(qI^{-1}) = p^e$ and $N(q'I^{-1}) = (p')^f$

16: $S_1 \leftarrow$ `TwoSquares`$(B_K, q, p^e \cdot \prod_j q_j^{f_j})$

17: $S_2 \leftarrow$ `TwoSquares`$(B_K, q', (p')^f \cdot \prod_j q_j^{f_j})$

    Recovering the congruence matrices from the solutions to TwoSquares:

18: $S \leftarrow \emptyset$

19: **for** $(t_1, t_2), (t_1', t_2') \in S_1 \times S_2$ **do**

20:     $D \leftarrow \begin{pmatrix} t_1 & t_1' \\ t_2 & t_2' \end{pmatrix} \cdot \begin{pmatrix} u & u' \\ v & v' \end{pmatrix}^{-1}$

21:     $V \leftarrow B^{-1} \cdot D$

22:     **if** V is a congruence matrix between G and G' **then**

23:         $S \leftarrow S \cup \{V\}$

24:     **end if**

25: **end for**

26: **return** S

Theorem 2 (Assumption 1 [19]). *Let K be a totally real number field and $M \subset K^2$ a module lattice of rank 2 with pseudo-basis $\mathbf{B} = (\mathbf{B}, I_1, I_2)$ and associated pseudo-Gram matrix $\mathbf{G}$. There exists a probabilistic algorithm (Algorithm 1) that takes as input a basis of $\mathcal{O}_K$, the pseudo-basis $\mathbf{B}$, and $\mathbf{G}' = (\mathbf{G}', I_1', I_2')$, an instance of wc-smodLIP$_\mathbf{B}^K$, and finds all congruence matrices between $\mathbf{G}$ and $\mathbf{G}'$.*

3   Improving the Congruence Solver

3.1   Linear Dependence

In this section we prove the relationship between B and Q over $\mathcal{O}_L$, the ring of integers of the CM-number field L, then we restrict it to the ring of integers $\mathcal{O}_K$ of the totally real number subfield K of L to improve the congruence solver in the next section.

Proposition 1. *Let* $C = \begin{pmatrix} u & r \\ v & t \end{pmatrix}$ *be a matrix in* $\mathbf{GL}_2(\mathcal{O}_L)$, $d_C = \det(C)$ *and let*

$Q = \begin{pmatrix} a & \bar{b} \\ b & c \end{pmatrix} = C^*C$, *then*

$$r = \frac{u\bar{b} - \bar{v}d_C}{a} \ and \ t = \frac{\bar{u}d_C + v\bar{b}}{a}$$

Proof. The proof is similar for r and t, so we prove it only for r. Substituting in the numerator of right hand side of $b = u\bar{r} + v\bar{t}$ and $d_C = ut - vr$, we get

$$u\bar{b} - \bar{v}d_C = u\bar{u}r + u\bar{v}t - \bar{v}ut + \bar{v}vr = (u\bar{u} + v\bar{v})r = ar.$$

The fact that the above-mentioned formulas were not found by chance, but finding the previous formulas (of r and t) required starting from the expressions we know (of a, b, c and $ut - vr = 1$) finding those we listed in the previous proposition, but in the proof we did the opposite for the sake of brevity. If the coefficients of C are in the maximal totally real number field then the conjugation acts like identity. Note that computationally we can retrieve the value of d_C in polynomial time from the determinant of Q by computing using two square sum solver, and if we know that the coefficients of C are in K then by computing the determinant square root, which in both cases can be done in polynomial time. For the signature scheme HAWK we already know that d_C is equal to 1 so this step is unnecessary.

Corollary 1. *Under the same notation of the previous proposition, if C is in* $\mathbf{GL}_2(\mathcal{O}_K)$ *then:*

$$r = \frac{ub - vd_C}{a} \ and \ t = \frac{ud_C + vb}{a}$$

From now on, we assume that C has coefficients in $\mathcal{O}_K$ until we mention if not.

3.2   The Proposed Algorithm

The previous Corollary 1 reveals two significant insights regarding the congruence solver. First, the problem of finding algebraic integers u and v in $\mathcal{O}_K$ such that $u^2 + v^2 = a$ can be reformulated into a problem of finding a solution to the equation $r^2 + t^2 = c$, where the conditions $ut - rv = d_C$ and $ur + vt = b$ must also hold. This transformation indicates a more efficient pathway to obtaining the desired results. Specifically, it implies that we can invoke the `TwoSquares` algorithm just once, obtaining the values for r and t from the resultant solutions of $u^2 + v^2 = a$ (or vice versa). This is a significant optimization compared to the original algorithm, which required the `TwoSquares` algorithm to be called twice, thereby enhancing the computational efficiency.

The second key insight allows us to eliminate the second while loop found in the original algorithm, specifically the lines numbered 10 through 14, as well as line 17. Since the most computationally intensive part of the congruence solver is indeed the execution of the `TwoSquares` algorithm, as documented by Mureau et al. in [19] (refer to Sect. 5: Implementation of the algorithm), we can expect a substantial reduction in the overall running time of the congruence solver, potentially halving it. The algorithm's enhanced efficiency derives from the streamlined process of combining and solving the equations, making it significantly faster and more suitable for practical applications in cryptographic contexts.

The modified algorithm described below 2 is based on these principles, and its correctness, as well as its ability to terminate properly, is assured through the findings presented in [19] and the implications of the previously discussed corollary. By relying on the newly derived insights and adjustments, we aim to enhance the practical usability of the congruence solver, facilitating quicker computations without compromising accuracy or reliability.

This approach not only simplifies the overall structure of the algorithm but also enhances the ability to perform congruence checks in scenarios relevant to cryptographic applications, such as those encountered in the HAWK signature scheme. The connections drawn between the modified algorithm and the underlying mathematical principles reinforce the importance of efficient computation in cryptographic algorithms, particularly as the complexity of the problems at hand continues to grow.

4   Experimental Results and Comparison

We modified the original code from [19], which is available at:

https://gitlab.inria.fr/capsule/code-for-module-lip,

and our enhanced implementation can be found at:

https://github.com/latticefun1/improved_tot_real_lip.

The experiments were conducted on the HPC-MARWAN cluster, utilizing a single core with 64 GB of RAM. Both the original `CongruenceSolver` and our modified version were executed on the same set of inputs, with each algorithm being run five times for each parameter m to ensure the reliability of the results.

The following table summarizes the differences in running time (in seconds) between the two implementations:

From the table, we can conclude that our modifications resulted in a reduction of the running time by more than 40% compared to the original implementation.

Algorithm 2. Our modified version

1: **Input:** Same as 1
2: **Output:** Same as 1
3: $I \leftarrow G(M); \alpha = \rho_K \cdot P(d)$ (with $P(d)$ from Assumption 1)
4: Factor $N(I) = \prod_j q_j^{f_j}$

      Generating one "nice" instance of TwoSquares:
5: $q \leftarrow 0; (u,v) \leftarrow (0,0); s \leftarrow 4d \cdot \Delta_K^{3/(2d)} \cdot \max_{1 \le j \le 2}(\|\sigma(g'_{j,j})^{1/2}\| \cdot N(I'_j)^{1/d}$
6: **while** $\sqrt{\|\sigma(q)\|_1} > s \cdot \sqrt{8d + \log(4\alpha \log(s))}$ **or** $q \cdot I^{-1}$ is not a prime idea
7:    $(u,v)^T \leftarrow \texttt{GaussianGram}(G', s)$
8:    $q \leftarrow (u,v) \cdot G' \cdot (u,v)^T$ **do**
9: **end while**

      Solving one instance of TwoSquares:
10: Factor $N(qI^{-1}) = p^e$
11: $S_1 \leftarrow \texttt{TwoSquares}(B_K, q, p^e \cdot \prod_j q_j^{f_j})$

      Recovering the congruence matrices from the solutions to TwoSquares:
12: $S \leftarrow \emptyset$
13: $U \leftarrow \begin{pmatrix} u & 0 \\ v & 1 \end{pmatrix}$
14: $Q' \leftarrow U^t Q U$
15: $\alpha \leftarrow Q'[0,0], \beta \leftarrow Q'[0,1], \gamma \leftarrow Q'[1,1],$
16: **for** $(t_1, t_2) \in S_1$ **do**
17:    $t'_1 = \dfrac{t_1\beta - t_2 u}{\alpha}$
18:    $t'_2 = \dfrac{t_1 u + t_2 \beta}{\alpha}$
19:    $D \leftarrow \begin{pmatrix} t_1 & t'_1 \\ t_2 & t'_2 \end{pmatrix} \cdot U^{-1}$
20:    **if** D is a congruence matrix between G and G' **then**
21:       $S \leftarrow S \cup \{D\}$
22:    **end if**
23: **end for**
24: **return** S

Table: Comparison of CongruenceSolver and Modified CongruenceSolver

Algorithm	32	64	128	256
CongruenceSolver	0.7449	4.6576	57.532	1826
CongruenceSolver (modified)	0.3573	2.3798	31.054	1001.0
Improvement (%)	52%	48%	46%	45%

This improvement can be attributed to the strategic elimination of unnecessary computational steps, particularly the second invocation of the TwoSquares algorithm and the removal of redundant loops.

The observed performance gains underscore the importance of optimizing algorithms in lattice-based cryptography, particularly as the complexity of problems continues to grow. This improvement may facilitate faster computations in key recovery attacks against signature schemes like HAWK over totally real number field.

5   Partial Information Exposure Attack

5.1   HAWK Signature Scheme

HAWK [12] is a digital signature scheme that extends the use of LIP to a more practical setting by incorporating a module structure over lattices and simplifying key generation and signing procedures. It was introduced as a candidate in the additional call for digital signature schemes by NIST, focusing on post-quantum cryptographic security. HAWK builds on the initial ideas of LIP-based signatures, aiming for both efficiency and robustness.

The core security of HAWK relies on the search module-LIP (smLIP) and the one-more Shortest Vector Problem (omSVP), which are foundational to both the key generation and the signature verification processes. The transition from earlier LIP-based approaches to HAWK involved simplifying the sampling methods and reducing computational overhead, especially during signature generation.

HAWK comes with three parameters sets, one as a challenge with number field degree 256 and the two other sets of parameters, HAWK-512 and HAWK-1024, targeting different levels of security, corresponding to Level-I and level-V. These parameter sets ensure that HAWK provides strong security guarantees while remaining computationally feasible for a wide range of devices, from high-performance servers to constrained embedded systems. We give only an overview description of HAWK to present the attack.

HAWK Keys. Recalling that the number field degree n used in HAWK is $n \in \{256, 512, 1024\}$. The coefficient of the algebraic integers f and g are sampled from the centred binomial distribution of parameter $\eta = \frac{n}{128}$ and then used to solve the NTRU equation $fG - gF = 1$ to construct the signing key B:

$$B = \begin{bmatrix} f & F \\ g & G \end{bmatrix},$$

The verification key $Q = \bar{B} \cdot B$, where $\bar{B}$ is the adjoint matrix of B, i.e., it is the matrix resulting from computing the transpose B and conjugating each of its components.

HAWK Signature Generation. To sign a message m, HAWK signature generation proceeds as follow:

1. the message m is hashed to a vector $\mathbf{h} \in \mathcal{O}_L^2$,
2. a target binary vector is computed $\mathbf{t} = B\mathbf{h} \mod 2$,
3. a vector $\mathbf{x}$ is sampled from a distribution approximating the Gaussian on $2\mathbb{Z}^{2n} + \mathbf{t}$, with standard deviation $2\sigma_{sign}$,
4. compute $\mathbf{w} = B^{-1}\mathbf{x}$,
5. the signature is $\mathbf{s} = \frac{1}{2}(\mathbf{h} - \mathbf{w})$.

HAWK Signature Verification. To verify **s** using the verification key Q, the verifier computes **h** and then reconstructs **w**, and computes $\|\mathbf{w}\|_Q = \|\mathbf{x}\|$, accepts if it is small, otherwise he rejects.

After giving an overview of HAWK, we present some implications of our study on the cryptanalytic side.

5.2 Two Known Algebraic Coefficient of HAWK Attack

In this subsection we present an attack on HAWK scheme when the attacker knows two of the coefficients of B such that B is in $\mathbf{GL}_n(\mathcal{O}_L)$, without loss of generality say u, v^2.

Corollary 2. *Let f, g, F and G from $\mathcal{O}_L$, $B = \begin{bmatrix} f & F \\ g & G \end{bmatrix}$, such that $\det(B) = 1$ and $Q = \bar{B} \cdot B$. Given Q and given u and v from $\{f, g, F, G\}$ and $u \neq v$, then we can construct B in polynomial time.*

Proof. Apply 1 to compute r, s then reconstruct B.

Since the NTRU equation is linear, knowing f and g using an NTRU solver to get back F and G, we can also solve this equation by knowing Q without an NTRU solver, although in other situations we could obtain, for instance, if we obtain f and G, in this case, $fG - gF = 1$ is not an NTRU equation, hence our attack, with the knowledge of Q is more straightforward than solving the supplied NTRU equation $fG - gF = 1$ given one of the following (f, F) or (f, g) or (G, g) or (G, F) (the cases of the NTRU equation). On the one hand, we have the additional information from the public key Q for verification. On the other hand, we can easily recover the other two coefficients if we know Q and are given any two of B's coefficients, for example, F and g by computing f and G as follows:

$$f = \frac{aF + \bar{g}}{\bar{b}} \quad \text{and} \quad = \frac{a\bar{F} + g + g b\bar{b}}{ab}.$$

The other cases can be handled by the same approach, and reconstruct the valid signing key.

5.3 Side Channel Attacks on HAWK

In their paper [14], Guerreau and Rossi gave a framework for a side-channel attack on HAWK. They must retrieve two vectors x, y from side-channel leakage of signatures to recover the key using linear algebra and only one vector to recover the key using hints strategy[3] of [9] to retrieve the signing key. Our observations could improve the attack by requiring only one extra vector $\mathbf{x} = \begin{bmatrix} x_1 \\ x_2 \end{bmatrix} = B\mathbf{w}$. In this section, we prove how to achieve this goal.

---

[2] it is an easy linear algebra exercise to retrieve any two unknown coefficients of B from two other coefficients of B and the quadratic matrix Q.

[3] This strategy uses lattice reduction techniques.

Recall that in HAWK setting for $B = \begin{bmatrix} u & r \\ v & t \end{bmatrix}$ we have $\det(B) = 1$ and $B^{-1} = \begin{bmatrix} t & -r \\ -v & u \end{bmatrix}$. We prove the following proposition:

Proposition 2. *Assume we are given $Q = \begin{pmatrix} a & \bar{b} \\ b & c \end{pmatrix}$ in HAWK setting, and given $\mathbf{x} = B\mathbf{w}$ for known $\mathbf{w} = \begin{bmatrix} w_1 \\ w_1 \end{bmatrix}$ from valid signature, and let $M = \begin{bmatrix} \bar{x}_1 & \bar{x}_2 \\ x_2 & -x_1 \end{bmatrix}$. If $\det(M) \neq 0$ then we have:*

$$\begin{bmatrix} u \\ v \end{bmatrix} = M^{-1} \begin{bmatrix} a\bar{w}_1 + b\bar{w}_2 \\ w_2 \end{bmatrix}$$

Proof. Start from $\mathbf{x} = B\mathbf{w}$ and compute $\bar{x}_1 u, \bar{x}_2 v$ those adds to $a\bar{w}_1 + b\bar{w}_2$ then compute $x_2 u, x_1 v$ those adds to w_2.

The previous Proposition 2 combined with the Proposition 1 tell that we can get the whole B given Q and $\mathbf{x}$ using linear algebra only, while in the paper of Guerreau and Rossi [14] they require using hints framework [9] to get the whole signing key. This open the question that how really do hints affects the security of HAWK. We do not handle this question in this paper and let it as an open problem.

A demonstrative code of our attack can be found in the following link:

https://github.com/latticefun1/hawk_secret_exposure_attack.

The code shows a proof of concept of the attack by given the secret factors Q, w_1, w_2, x_1 and x_2. We tested the attack on HAWK parameters for the degrees $\{256, 512, 1024\}$. The following table summarises the average running time on 5 instances for each degree:

Table: Running Time of the attack on parameters of HAWK

degree	256	512	1024
Running time	3 s	21 s	2 min 40 s

From the previous table, we see that the attack has a low running time even for the degree 1024. the attack also doesn't use techniques of lattice reduction as in [14], which makes more faster in practice. We also tried to lower the requirement by providing only one of the coefficients x_1 or x_2 but failed to complete the attack, so we left this as an open problem for the future.

We implemented this attack on SageMath as follows:

```
load("https://raw.githubusercontent.com/ludopulles/hawk-aux/refs/heads/main/
    ↪ code/hawk.sage")

#HAWK 256 parameters

N=256
Sig = SignatureScheme(n=N,sigma_kg=1.042, sigma_sig=1.010, sigma_ver=1.042)
L = Sig.CT.top_K
m = 2*N #L.conductor()

sk, pk = Sig.KGen()

f,g,F,G = sk
a,b,c = pk
m = L.degree() *2

h=h0,h1 = ([randint(0, 1) for _ in range(N)], [randint(0, 1) for _ in range(N)
    ↪ ])
s0,s1 = Sig.Sign(sk,h)
w0,w1 = L(h0) - 2 * s0, L(h1) - 2 * s1

#B = matrix([[f,F],[g,G]])
#Q = B.C.T*B

x0 = f*w0 + F*w1
x1 = g*w0 + G*w1



#x1 = B*vector([w0,w1]) # Suppose we got the x0,x1 from Side channels as in
    ↪ the paper

Delta = x0*x0.conjugate() + x1*x1.conjugate() # ((matrix(L,[x0,x1]).C* matrix(
    ↪ L,[x0,x1]).T)[0,0])

#w* Q w
wQw = w0.conjugate()*w0 * a + w0 .conjugate()*w1*b + w1.conjugate()*w0*b.
    ↪ conjugate() + w1.conjugate()*w1*c #
bool(vector(Delta).norm() == vector(wQw).norm()), bool(vector(wQw[0]).norm().n
    ↪ () <Sig.verif_bound.n())
#print(Delta)
assert x0 *(w0.conjugate()*a +(w1*b).conjugate()) + x1.conjugate()*w1 == f*
    ↪ Delta
assert x1 *(w0.conjugate()*a +(w1*b).conjugate()) - x0.conjugate()*w1 == g*
    ↪ Delta

# HAWK 512 parameters
N=512
Sig = SignatureScheme(n=N,sigma_kg=1.425, sigma_sig=1.278, sigma_ver=1.425)
L = Sig.CT.top_K
m = 2*N #L.conductor()

sk, pk = Sig.KGen()
```

```
f,g,F,G = sk
a,b,c = pk
m = L.degree() *2

h=h0,h1 = ([randint(0, 1) for _ in range(N)], [randint(0, 1) for _ in range(N)
    ↪ ])
s0,s1 = Sig.Sign(sk,h)
w0,w1 = L(h0) - 2 * s0, L(h1) - 2 * s1

#B = matrix([[f,F],[g,G]])
#Q = B.C.T*B


#x1 = B*vector([w0,w1]) # Suppose we got the x0,x1 from Side channels as in
    ↪ the paper

x0 = f*w0 + F*w1
x1 = g*w0 + G*w1

Delta = x0*x0.conjugate() + x1*x1.conjugate() # ((matrix(L,[x0,x1]).C* matrix(
    ↪ L,[x0,x1]).T)[0,0])

#w* Q w
wQw = w0.conjugate()*w0 * a + w0 .conjugate()*w1*b + w1.conjugate()*w0*b.
    ↪ conjugate() + w1.conjugate()*w1*c #
bool(vector(Delta).norm() == vector(wQw).norm()), bool(vector(wQw[0]).norm().n
    ↪ () <Sig.verif_bound.n())
assert x0 *(w0.conjugate()*a +(w1*b).conjugate()) + x1.conjugate()*w1 == f*
    ↪ Delta
assert x1 *(w0.conjugate()*a +(w1*b).conjugate()) - x0.conjugate()*w1 == g*
    ↪ Delta


# HAWK 1024 parameters

N=1024
Sig = SignatureScheme(n=N,sigma_kg=1.974, sigma_sig=1.299, sigma_ver=1.571)
L = Sig.CT.top_K
m = 2*N #L.conductor()

sk, pk = Sig.KGen()

f,g,F,G = sk
a,b,c = pk
m = L.degree() *2


h=h0,h1 = ([randint(0, 1) for _ in range(N)], [randint(0, 1) for _ in range(N)
    ↪ ])
s0,s1 = Sig.Sign(sk,h)
w0,w1 = L(h0) - 2 * s0, L(h1) - 2 * s1

#B = matrix([[f,F],[g,G]])
```

```
#Q = B.C.T*B

x0 = f*w0 + F*w1
x1 = g*w0 + G*w1


#x1 = B*vector([w0,w1]) # Suppose we got the x0,x1 from Side channels as in
    ↪ the paper

Delta = x0*x0.conjugate() + x1*x1.conjugate() # ((matrix(L,[x0,x1]).C* matrix(
    ↪ L,[x0,x1]).T)[0,0])

#w* Q w
wQw = w0.conjugate()*w0 * a + w0 .conjugate()*w1*b + w1.conjugate()*w0*b.
    ↪ conjugate() + w1.conjugate()*w1*c #
bool(vector(Delta).norm() == vector(wQw).norm()), bool(vector(wQw[0]).norm().n
    ↪ () <Sig.verif_bound.n())
```

6   Conclusion

In this paper, we revisited the smodLIP over totally real number fields and presented improvements to the algorithm originally proposed by Mureau et al., successfully decreasing the running time by over 40%. Our proposed enhancements reflect a deeper understanding of the mathematical principles underlying the problem, demonstrating that thoughtful algorithmic adjustments can lead to significant performance improvements. Moreover, the strategies employed in our proposal may also indicate that solving the four squares sum problem over totally real number fields can effectively lead to solving the wc-smodLIP over CM-number fields using only one call to a solver of the four squares sum problem over totally real number fields. This insight has substantial implications, suggesting potential key recovery attacks against the digital signature scheme HAWK. As the reliance on lattice-based cryptography increases, especially in post-quantum contexts, our findings contribute to the ongoing discourse around the robustness and efficiency of such schemes. Lastly, we have demonstrated, on the one hand, a partial attack on HAWK; on the other hand, we have shown an impact of our analysis on side-channel attacks.

Acknowledgements. We would like to express our gratitude to the anonymous referees for their insightful suggestions, which have greatly contributed to improving the presentation of this paper.

Nour-eddine Rahmani acknowledges the support of *the Institut Henri Poincaré* (UAR 839 CNRS-Sorbonne Université) and *LabEx CARMIN* (ANR-10-LABX-59-01).

References

1. Albrecht, M.R., Gheorghiu, V., Postlethwaite, E.W., Schanck, J.M.: Estimating quantum speedups for lattice sieves. In: Moriai, S., Wang, H. (eds.) ASIACRYPT 2020. LNCS, vol. 12492, pp. 583–613. Springer, Cham (2020). https://doi.org/10.1007/978-3-030-64834-3_20

2. Alkim, E., Ducas, L., Pöppelmann, T., Schwabe, P.: Post-quantum key exchange - a new hope. In: USENIX Security Symposium, pp. 327–343. USENIX Association (2016)

3. Allombert, B., Pellet-Mary, A., van Woerden, W.: Cryptanalysis of rank-2 module-LIP: a single real embedding is all it takes. In: Fehr, S., Fouque, PA. (eds.) EURO-CRYPT 2025. LNCS, vol. 15602, pp. 184–212. Springer, Cham (2025). https://doi.org/10.1007/978-3-031-91124-8_7

4. Babai, L.: On Lovász' lattice reduction and the nearest lattice point problem. In: Proceedings of the 18th Annual ACM Symposium on Theory of Computing (STOC), pp. 13–20. ACM (1986). https://doi.org/10.1145/12130.12134

5. Benčina, B., Budroni, A., Chi-Domínguez, JJ., Kulkarni, M.: Properties of lattice isomorphism as a cryptographic group action. In: Saarinen, MJ., Smith-Tone, D. (eds.) PQCrypto 2024. LNCS, vol. 14771, pp. 170–201. Springer, Cham (2024). https://doi.org/10.1007/978-3-031-62743-9_6

6. Bennett, H., Ganju, A., Peetathawatchai, P., Stephens-Davidowitz, N.: Just how hard are rotations of $\mathbb{Z}^n$? Algorithms and cryptography with the simplest lattice. In: Hazay, C., Stam, M. (eds.) EUROCRYPT 2023. LNCS, vol. 14008, pp. 252–281. Springer, Cham (2023). https://doi.org/10.1007/978-3-031-30589-4_9

7. Bos, J., et al.: CRYSTALS - Kyber: a module-lattice-based KEM. In: 2018 IEEE European Symposium on Security and Privacy (EuroS&P), pp. 353–367. IEEE (2018). https://doi.org/10.1109/EuroSP.2018.00032

8. Chevignard, C., Mureau, G., Espitau, T., Pellet-Mary, A., Pliatsok, H., Wallet, A.: A reduction from hawk to the principal ideal problem in a quaternion algebra. In: Fehr, S., Fouque, PA. (eds.) EUROCRYPT 2025. LNCS, vol. 15602, pp. 154–183. Springer, Cham (2025). https://doi.org/10.1007/978-3-031-91124-8_6

9. Dachman-Soled, D., Ducas, L., Gong, H., Rossi, M.: LWE with side information: attacks and concrete security estimation. In: Micciancio, D., Ristenpart, T. (eds.) CRYPTO 2020. LNCS, vol. 12171, pp. 329–358. Springer, Cham (2020). https://doi.org/10.1007/978-3-030-56880-1_12

10. Ducas, L., Lepoint, T., Lyubashevsky, V., Schwabe, P., Seiler, G., Stehlé, D.: Crystals-Dilithium: digital signatures from module lattices (2018)

11. Ducas, L., van Woerden, W.: On the lattice isomorphism problem, quadratic forms, remarkable lattices, and cryptography. In: Dunkelman, O., Dziembowski, S. (eds.) EUROCRYPT 2022. LNCS, vol. 13277, pp. 643–673. Springer, Cham (2022). https://doi.org/10.1007/978-3-031-07082-2_23

12. Ducas, L., Postlethwaite, E.W., Pulles, L.N., van Woerden, W.: Hawk: module LIP makes lattice signatures fast, compact, and simple. In: International Conference on the Theory and Application of Cryptology and Information Security, pp. 65–94. Springer (2022)

13. Fouque, P.-A., et al.: Falcon: fast-Fourier lattice-based compact signatures over NTRU. Submission NIST's Post-Quantum Cryptogr. Stand. Process **36**(5), 1–75 (2018)

14. Guerreau, M., Rossi, M.: A not so discrete sampler: power analysis attacks on HAWK signature scheme. IACR Trans. Cryptogr. Hardw. Embed. Syst. **2024**(4),

156–178 (2024). https://doi.org/10.46586/tches.v2024.i4.156-178 https://doi.org/10.46586/tches.v2024.i4.156-178

15. Hoffstein, J., Pipher, J., Silverman, J.H.: NTRU: a ring-based public key cryptosystem. In: Buhler, J.P. (ed.) ANTS 1998. LNCS, vol. 1423, pp. 267–288. Springer, Heidelberg (1998). https://doi.org/10.1007/BFb0054868

16. Langlois, A., Stehlé, D.: Worst-case to average-case reductions for module lattices. Des. Codes Crypt. **75**(3), 565–599 (2014). https://doi.org/10.1007/s10623-014-9938-4

17. Lenstra, A.K., Lenstra, H.W., Lovász, L.: Factoring polynomials with rational coefficients. Math. Ann. **261**(4), 515–534 (1982). https://doi.org/10.1007/BF01457454

18. Luo, H., Jiang, K., Pan, Y., Wang, A.: Cryptanalysis of rank-2 module-LIP with symplectic automorphisms. In: Chung, K.M., Sasaki, Y. (eds.) ASIACRYPT 2024. LNCS, vol. 15487, pp. 359–385. Springer, Singapore (2024). https://doi.org/10.1007/978-981-96-0894-2_12

19. Mureau, G., Pellet-Mary, A., Pliatsok, G., Wallet, A.: Cryptanalysis of rank-2 module-LIP in totally real number fields. In: Joye, M., Leander, G. (eds.) EUROCRYPT 2024. LNCS, vol. 14657, pp. 226–255. Springer, Cham (2024). https://doi.org/10.1007/978-3-031-58754-2_9

20. National Institute of Standards and Technology. Module-Lattice-Based Key Encapsulation Mechanism Standard. Federal Information Processing Standards Publication (FIPS) NIST FIPS 203. Washington, D.C. (2024). https://doi.org/10.6028/NIST.FIPS.203

21. National Institute of Standards and Technology. Module-Lattice-Based Digital Signature Standard. Federal Information Processing Standards Publication (FIPS) NIST FIPS 204. Washington, D.C. (2024). https://doi.org/10.6028/NIST.FIPS.204

22. National Institute of Standards and Technology. Stateless Hash-Based Digital Signature Standard. Federal Information Processing Standards Publication (FIPS) NIST FIPS 205. Washington, D.C. (2024). https://doi.org/10.6028/NIST.FIPS.205

23. Regev, O.: An efficient quantum factoring algorithm. J. ACM **72**(1), 1–13 (2025). https://doi.org/10.1145/3708471. Article 10

24. Shor, P.W.: Algorithms for quantum computation: discrete logarithms and factoring. In: Proceedings of the 35th Annual Symposium on Foundations of Computer Science, pp. 124–134. IEEE (1994). https://doi.org/10.1109/SFCS.1994.365700

25. The PARI Group: PARI/GP version 2.15.4. Univ. Bordeaux (2023). http://pari.math.u-bordeaux.fr/

26. The Sage Developers: SageMath, the Sage Mathematics Software System (Version 10.4) (2024). https://www.sagemath.org

27. Washington, L.C.: Introduction to Cyclotomic Fields. Graduate Texts in Mathematics, vol. 83. Springer (1997). 978-0387947628

PMNS Arithmetic for Elliptic Curve Cryptography

Fangan Yssouf Dosso[1], Sylvain Duquesne[2]($\boxtimes$), Nadia El Mrabet[1], and Emma Gautier[2]

[1] SAS Laboratory, École des Mines de Saint-Étienne, Gardanne, France
{fanganyssouf.dosso,nadia.el-mrabet}@emse.fr
[2] Univ Rennes, CNRS, IRMAR - UMR 6625, 35000 Rennes, France
{sylvain.duquesne,emma.gautier}@univ-rennes.fr

Abstract. We show that using the polynomial modular number system (PMNS) can be relevant for real-world cryptographic applications even in terms of performance. More specifically, we consider elliptic curves for cryptography when pseudo-Mersenne primes cannot be used to define the base field (e.g. Brainpool standardized curves, JubJub curves in the zkSNARK context, pairing-friendly curves). All these primitives make massive use of the Montgomery reduction algorithm and well-known libraries such as GMP or OpenSSL for base field arithmetic. We show how this arithmetic can be replaced by PMNS, a number system with very high parallelisation capability, no carry propagation, which allows efficient arithmetic randomization. We provide good PMNS bases in the cryptographic context mentioned above, together with a C implementation that is competitive with GMP and OpenSSL for performing basic operations in the base fields considered. We also integrate this arithmetic into the Rust reference implementation of elliptic curve scalar multiplication for Zero-knowledge applications, and achieve better practical performances for such protocols. This shows that PMNS is an attractive alternative for the base field arithmetic layer in cryptographic primitives using elliptic curves or pairings.

Keywords: Polynomial Modular Number System · Cryptography · Elliptic curves · Pairings · Brainpool · JubJub

1 Introduction

Elliptic curve cryptography is widely used nowadays: Internet communications make use of it through TLS [27], and several standards include it since the 2000s [48,51]. Additionally, the NIST (National Institute of Standard and Technology) has standardized several curves for cryptography. Let $\mathbb{F}_p$ be the finite field of characteristic p. An elliptic curve $E(\mathbb{F}_p)$ can be briefly defined by its Weierstrass equation as $E(\mathbb{F}_p) := \{(x,y) \in \mathbb{F}_p \times \mathbb{F}_p;\ y^2 = x^3 + ax + b,\ \text{for } a,b \in \mathbb{F}_p\}$. By construction, elliptic curve cryptography involves arithmetic over finite

© The Author(s), under exclusive license to Springer Nature Switzerland AG 2026
A. Nitaj et al. (Eds.): AFRICACRYPT 2025, LNCS 15651, pp. 164–191, 2026.
https://doi.org/10.1007/978-3-031-97260-7_9

fields and the most popular ones (NIST curves, Curve25519) were chosen such that the modular arithmetic over $\mathbb{F}_p$ is very efficient.

More generally, modular arithmetic is one of the most important operations in asymmetric cryptography. Indeed, whether for RSA or ECC but also for more recent post-quantum primitives (Kyber, Dilithium, SqiSign for example), the efficiency of implementations relies on the efficiency of modular operations, and in particular modular multiplication. When p can be chosen in a specific form, the modular multiplication can be performed as a classical multiplication followed by a modular reduction that is not expensive because of the sparsity of p. When possible, the shape of p is then constructed as pseudo-Mersenne (or even Mersenne) primes [53]. This is for example the case of the elliptic curves standardised by the NIST P-224, P-256, P-384 and P-521. However, after the discovery of a trapdoor in the elliptic curve used for the DUAL ECB DRBG standard of the NIST [14,17], the scientific community has proposed other elliptic curves for the standards, generated in a more random way and ensuring the right level of security [11]. Some of these curves are defined on finite fields whose binary decomposition of the characteristic is not sparse [5,16,41]. Modular arithmetic is then more expensive and more generic algorithms like Montgomery multiplication [46] or Barrett reduction [7] must be used in order to ensure efficient implementation.

These methods are based on the classical binary number system; an element of $\mathbb{F}_p$ is an integer between 0 and $(p-1)$ or between $\frac{-(p-1)}{2}$ and $\frac{(p-1)}{2}$. To further improve modular arithmetic, alternative number systems have been proposed. A famous one is the Residue Number System (RNS) [29], which has been widely studied and implemented. It is an efficient number system which has a very high parallelisation capability. Another one is the Polynomial Modular Number System (PMNS) [2], proposed by Bajard et al. for modular arithmetic modulo a prime number p. In this system, elements are represented by polynomials with small coefficients. Like the RNS, it offers a very high parallelisation capability but also additional properties like the possibility of randomising the arithmetic. Many works have shown the efficiency of PMNS for both software [20,23,44] and hardware [50] implementations considering random prime numbers but without consideration for their cryptographic use. Our purpose in this paper is to show, and illustrate on concrete examples, that this way to represent numbers is interesting for cryptographic applications, even in terms of performance and for relatively small primes as the ones used in elliptic curve cryptography, which was not evident a priori.

Cryptographers have been working on developing open source libraries for finite fields and elliptic curves. There are two mainstream libraries for cryptography: GMP and OpenSSL. Since 1991, the GMP library manages large numbers (among others functionalities) for the C implementation language [31]. GMP is designed for maximum speed for large operands. Its efficiency comes from state-of-the-art arithmetic optimizations, fast algorithms, and highly optimized assembly code. GMP is continuously improved, with a new release every year. OpenSSL is another free to use software library for general-purpose cryptography and secure communication [40]. It includes implementations for standardised elliptic curves. These two libraries are considered to be a reliable resource and are used by cryptographers to compare the effectiveness of new software implementations. That is the reason why we decided to compare our results with these libraries.

Our Contributions: In this article we want to answer the question: can PMNS be advantageously used for real-world cryptography? To do this, we generate PMNS basis for the base fields of some popular elliptic curves that cannot be defined over pseudo-Mersenne primes. More precisely we study the Brainpool elliptic curves, pairing-friendly elliptic curves such as BN, BLS12 and KSS16, and the JubJub elliptic curve used in the cryptocurrency Zcash. We implement the PMNS arithmetic for each type of elliptic curve, and compare as fairly as we can the number of clock cycles for performing a modular multiplication between our implementation of PMNS without any assembly code and the two state-of-the-art versions of GMP [31] and OpenSSL [40]. As a result, our implementation is competitive with the reference ones at the finite field arithmetic level, sometimes better and sometimes slightly worse depending on the context (bit-size, use of assembly code for example).

Concerning the JubJub elliptic curve, we provide a comparison with the reference library of Zcash written in Rust both at the finite field level (modular multiplication) and at the elliptic curve level (scalar multiplication). In both cases, we show that using a PMNS arithmetic is significantly more efficient than using the reference arithmetic.

Note that the theoretical complexity in terms of word multiplications is better for the Montgomery arithmetic but there are many factors that can influence practical comparisons (carry propagation, impact of the cost of additions and other ancillary instructions, quality of the implementation and compilation, level of adaptation to specific field sizes,...). As a consequence, this paper does not prove that the PMNS always provides better efficiency for elliptic curve based cryptography but that, despite a higher theoretical complexity in terms of word multiplications, it is sufficiently competitive to be used in practice (especially if one could take advantage of its additional properties).

Organization of the Paper: In Sect. 2 we recall elementary definitions of the PMNS, with the description of efficient algorithms. In particular, in Sect. 2.9, we recall the advantages and drawbacks of PMNS arithmetic. Our first comparison is made on the Brainpool elliptic curves in Sect. 3, we compare our implementation with the OpenSSL implementation. We then work on pairing-friendly elliptic curves in Sect. 4 and on the JubJub curve for Zcash in Sect. 5. We conclude our work and open new perspectives in Sect. 6.

2 PMNS

Let us first introduce and explain the Polynomial Modular Number System (PMNS) as well as its advantages and drawbacks in the cryptographic context. Let us start with some notations that we will be using throughout this paper.

2.1 Notations

For consistency, we assume that $p \geqslant 3$ and $n \geqslant 2$.

- $\mathbb{Z}_{n-1}[X]$ is the set of polynomials in $\mathbb{Z}[X]$ with degrees lower than or equal to $n-1$:

$$\mathbb{Z}_{n-1}[X] = \{C \in \mathbb{Z}[X] \mid \deg(C) \leqslant n-1\}.$$

- Let $A \in \mathbb{Z}_{n-1}[X]$ be a polynomial. We assume that:
  - $A(X) = a_0 + a_1 X + \cdots + a_{n-1} X^{n-1}$
  - A can equivalently be represented as the vector $A = (a_0, \ldots, a_{n-1}) \in \mathbb{Z}^n$.
- Also, $\|A\|_\infty = \max\limits_{0 \leqslant i \leqslant n-1} |a_i|$.
- Let $\mathcal{W} \in \mathbb{Z}^{n \times n}$ be a matrix. $\|\mathcal{W}\|_1 = \max\limits_{0 \leqslant j \leqslant n-1} \sum_{i=0}^{n-1} |w_{ij}|$.

2.2 Definition and Example

The PMNS has been introduced by Bajard et al. [2]. It is a non-positional number system for modular arithmetic modulo a prime integer p. A PMNS is defined by a tuple (p, n, γ, ρ, E), where p, n, γ and ρ are positive non-zero integers and $E \in \mathbb{Z}_n[X]$ is a monic polynomial such that $E(\gamma) \equiv 0 \pmod{p}$. In this system, elements are represented by polynomials. More precisely, we have the following definition.

Definition 1. *A polynomial modular number system (PMNS) is defined by a tuple $\mathcal{B} = (p, n, \gamma, \rho, E)$, such that for each integer $y \in \mathbb{Z}/p\mathbb{Z}$ there exists a polynomial $V(X) = v_0 + v_1.X + \cdots + v_{n-1}.X^{n-1}$ such that:*

$$y = V(\gamma) \pmod{p},$$

where $|v_i| < \rho$ and $2 \leqslant \rho$, $\gamma < p$. In this case, we say that $V(X)$ (or equivalently the vector $V = (v_0, \ldots, v_{n-1})$) is a representation of y in $\mathcal{B}$.
The parameter E is a monic polynomial in $\mathbb{Z}[X]$ of degree n, having γ as a root modulo p, i.e. $E(\gamma) \equiv 0 \pmod{p}$.

Remark 1. From the definition above, we say that a polynomial $A \in \mathbb{Z}[X]$ is in the PMNS $\mathcal{B} = (p, n, \gamma, \rho, E)$ if and only if:

$$\deg(A) < n \text{ and } \|A\|_\infty < \rho,$$

where $\|A\|_\infty = \max\limits_{0 \leqslant i \leqslant n-1} |a_i|$.

Example 1. Let us take $p = 19$. For this prime, we have the PMNS $\mathcal{B} = (9, 3, 7, 2, E)$, with $E(X) = X^3 - 1$. Table 1 gives an example of representation for each elements of $\mathbb{Z}/19\mathbb{Z}$.

Table 1. Example of representations for the elements of $\mathbb{Z}/19\mathbb{Z}$ in $\mathcal{B} = (19, 3, 7, 2, X^3 - 1)$

0	1	2	3	4
0	1	$-X^2 - X + 1$	$X^2 - X - 1$	$X^2 - X$

5	6	7	8	9
$X^2 - X + 1$	$X - 1$	X	$X + 1$	$-X^2 + 1$

10	11	12	13	14
$X^2 - 1$	X^2	$X^2 + 1$	$-X + 1$	$-X^2 + X - 1$

15	16	17	18
$-X^2 + X$	$-X^2 + X + 1$	$X^2 + X - 1$	-1

In this table, one can observe that the polynomial $X^2 - 1$ is a representation of 10, since we have $10 = 7^2 - 1 \pmod{19}$.

2.3 Arithmetic Operations in the PMNS

Like most number systems, the main operations in the PMNS are the addition and the multiplication. Let $\mathcal{B} = (p, n, \gamma, \rho, E)$ be a PMNS, and $A, B \in \mathcal{B}$.

The addition is the simple polynomial addition, i.e. $C = A + B$. However, there is no guarantee that $C \in \mathcal{B}$, since we only have $\|C\|_\infty < 2\rho$. To guarantee the result in $\mathcal{B}$, we need to perform an operation called **internal reduction**. This operation is equivalent to the modular reduction in the classical representation. In Sect. 2.5 we describe it, and in Sect. 2.6 we explain why it is not interesting to perform this operation after a simple polynomial addition, and we present the parameter δ which has been introduced to deal with this "problem".

The multiplication is the polynomial multiplication, i.e. $C = A \times B$. Here also, there is no guarantee that $C \in \mathcal{B}$. In fact, we only have:

$$\deg(C) < 2n - 1 \ and \ \|C\|_\infty < n\rho^2.$$

Here, we first reduce the degree of C. That is, we compute a polynomial $R \in \mathbb{Z}_{n-1}[X]$ such that:

$$R(\gamma) \equiv C(\gamma) \pmod{p}.$$

This operation is called the **external reduction**. It is done using the polynomial E, which is thus called the external reduction polynomial.

The external reduction is the operation:

$$R = C \bmod E.$$

Remember that E is a monic polynomial, with $\deg(E) = n$ and $E(\gamma) \equiv 0$ (mod p). This thus guarantees that $\deg(R) < n$ and $R(\gamma) \equiv C(\gamma)$ (mod p).

In practice, we want this reduction to be very fast. So, the parameter E is chosen very sparse, with very small coefficients. For example, $E(X) = X^n - \lambda$, where $|\lambda|$ is a very small non-zero integer.

Let us assume that $E(X) = X^n + e_{n-1}X^{n-1} + \cdots + e_1 X + e_0$. To optimise the external reduction, the external reduction matrix $\mathcal{E}$ in introduced in [23]. It is the $(n-1) \times n$ matrix defined as follows:

$$\mathcal{E} = \begin{pmatrix} -e_0 & -e_1 & \cdots & -e_{n-1} \\ \cdots & \cdots & \cdots & \cdots \\ \vdots & \vdots & & \vdots \\ \cdots & \cdots & \cdots & \cdots \end{pmatrix} \begin{matrix} \leftarrow X^n \bmod E \\ \leftarrow X^{n+1} \bmod E \\ \\ \leftarrow X^{2n-2} \bmod E \end{matrix}. \tag{1}$$

Let us assume that $C = A \times B = c_0 + c_1 X + \cdots + c_{2n-2}X^{2n-2}$. With the external reduction matrix $\mathcal{E}$, the authors show:

$$R = C \bmod E = (c_0, \ldots, c_{n-1}) + (c_n, \ldots, c_{2n-2})\mathcal{E} \tag{2}$$

So for very efficient external reduction, we want the external reduction matrix $\mathcal{E}$ to be very sparse with very small coefficients. This is achieved with polynomials $E(X) = X^n - \lambda$ having $|\lambda|$ very small. Moreover, [23, Table 1] gives several additional polynomials E that achieve this goal.

Let us now look at an example of modular multiplication in the PMNS.

Example 2. Let us consider the PMNS $\mathcal{B} = (9, 3, 7, 2, X^3 - 1)$ given in Example 1. Let $a = 10$ and $b = 15$. In Table 1, $A(X) = X^2 - 1$ is a representation of 10, while $B(X) = -X^2 + X$ is a representation of 15.

Let us multiply A by B. We have:

$$C(X) = A(X) \times B(X) = -X^4 + X^3 + X^2 - X.$$

One can verify that: $C(7) \equiv 17$ (mod 19) and $10 \times 15 \equiv 17$ (mod 19). However, $C \notin \mathcal{B}$, since $\deg(C) > 2$. So, we perform the external reduction:

$$R(X) = C(X) \bmod E(X) = X^2 - 2X + 1.$$

We have $\deg(R) < 3$, however $R \notin \mathcal{B}$, because $\|R\|_\infty \not< \rho$.

Now let us consider the polynomial $T(X) = 3X - 2$, which is such that $T(\gamma) \equiv 0$ (mod p). Let us compute the polynomial $S = R + T$.

We have $S(X) = X^2 + X - 1$. So,

$$S(\gamma) \equiv C(\gamma) \pmod{p} \ and \ S \in \mathcal{B}.$$

Thus, the polynomial S is the result of $A \times B$ in the PMNS $\mathcal{B}$.

The question then is: given $R \in \mathbb{Z}_{n-1}[X]$, how does one compute such a polynomial T? This is the **internal reduction** we present in Sect. 2.5.

Before presenting the internal reduction, we discuss the Euclidean lattice that comes with every PMNS.

2.4 PMNS and Euclidean Lattices

A PMNS $\mathcal{B} = (p, n, \gamma, \rho, E)$ is associated with the n-dimensional full-rank Euclidean lattice $\mathcal{L}_\mathcal{B}$, defined as follows:

$$\mathcal{L}_\mathcal{B} = \{A \in \mathbb{Z}_{n-1}[X] \quad A(\gamma) \equiv 0 \pmod{p}\}. \tag{3}$$

This lattice is the set of all the polynomials with degrees strictly less than n and with γ as a root modulo p. A basis of $\mathcal{L}_\mathcal{B}$ is the $n \times n$ matrix $\mathbf{B}$, defined as follows:

$$\mathbf{B} = \begin{pmatrix} p & 0 \ 0 \ldots 0 \ 0 \\ t_1 & 1 \ 0 \ldots 0 \ 0 \\ t_2 & 0 \ 1 \ldots 0 \ 0 \\ \vdots & \quad \ddots \quad \vdots \\ t_{n-2} & 0 \ 0 \ldots 1 \ 0 \\ t_{n-1} & 0 \ 0 \ldots 0 \ 1 \end{pmatrix} \begin{matrix} \leftarrow p \\ \leftarrow X + t_1 \\ \leftarrow X^2 + t_2 \\ \\ \leftarrow X^{n-2} + t_{n-2} \\ \leftarrow X^{n-1} + t_{n-1} \end{matrix} \tag{4}$$

where $t_i = (-\gamma^i) \bmod p$.

In [21], the following result gives a condition on the parameter ρ for $\mathcal{B}$ to be a PMNS.

Lemma 1 [21]. *Let $\mathcal{L}$ be a sub-lattice of $\mathcal{L}_\mathcal{B}$, having a matrix $\mathcal{G}$ as a basis. A tuple $\mathcal{B} = (p, n, \gamma, \rho, E)$ defines a PMNS if:*

$$\rho > \frac{1}{2}\|\mathcal{G}\|_1.$$

2.5 The Internal Reduction

Let $\mathcal{B} = (p, n, \gamma, \rho, E)$ be a PMNS. Let $R \in \mathbb{Z}_{n-1}[X]$ be a polynomial, with possibly $\|R\|_\infty \geqslant \rho$. The internal reduction consists in computing a polynomial S such that $\|S\|_\infty < \rho$ and $S(\gamma) \equiv R(\gamma) \pmod{p}$.

Many approaches have been proposed to perform this operation [1,2,44,47].

In [47], the authors propose a Montgomery-like method. This method has been proven efficient for both software [20,23] and hardware [50] implementations.

In [21], the authors show that this Montgomery-like method works on a particular sub-lattice $\mathcal{L}(\mathcal{M})$ of $\mathcal{L}_\mathcal{B}$ (see [21, Equation 9] which gives the basis $\mathcal{M}$ used). They then generalise the Montgomery-like method to any basis $\mathcal{G}$ of any sub-lattice $\mathcal{L}$ of $\mathcal{L}_\mathcal{B}$. In this paper, we focus on this extended Montgomery-like method, which they call **GMont-like**.

Let $\mathcal{L}$ be a sub-lattice of $\mathcal{L}_\mathcal{B}$. **GMont-like** requires three parameters: a basis $\mathcal{G}$ of $\mathcal{L}$, an integer $\phi \geqslant 2$ such that $\gcd(\phi, \det(\mathcal{G})) = 1$, and the matrix $\mathcal{G}' = -\mathcal{G}^{-1}$ (mod ϕ). In Sect. 2.8, we discuss the choice of $\mathcal{G}$ and ϕ. Algorithm 1 describes **GMont-like**.

Algorithm 1. Coefficients reduction for PMNS (**GMont-like**) [21]

Require: $C \in \mathbb{Z}^n$, $\phi \in \mathbb{N} \setminus \{0, 1\}$, and the matrices $\mathcal{G}$ and $\mathcal{G}'$.
Ensure: $S(\gamma) = C(\gamma)\phi^{-1}$ (mod p), with $S \in \mathbb{Z}^n$
  1: $Q = (c_0, \ldots, c_{n-1})\mathcal{G}'$ (mod ϕ)
  2: $T = (q_0, \ldots, q_{n-1})\mathcal{G}$
  3: $S \leftarrow (C + T)/\phi$
  4: return S

Remark 2. Note that **GMont-like** introduces a factor ϕ^{-1} on the output. So, similar to the classical Montgomery method, elements in the PMNS are placed in a Montgomery domain to ensure consistency of operations in the system. That is, an integer $a \in \mathbb{Z}/p\mathbb{Z}$ is represented in the PMNS $\mathcal{B}$ by a polynomial A such that $A(\gamma) \equiv (a\phi)$ (mod p). This is done during the integer to PMNS conversion, as proposed in [20]. In Sect. 2.7 we recall the conversion processes.

With **GMont-like**, Algorithm 2 describes the modular multiplication in the PMNS.

Algorithm 2. Modular multiplication for PMNS (**ModMult**)[21]

Require: $A, B \in \mathbb{Z}_{n-1}[X]$, $\phi \in \mathbb{N} \setminus \{0, 1\}$, and the matrices $\mathcal{G}$, $\mathcal{G}'$ and $\mathcal{E}$.
Ensure: $S(\gamma) = A(\gamma)B(\gamma)\phi^{-1}$ (mod p), with $S \in \mathbb{Z}_{n-1}[X]$
  1: $C = A \times B$
  2: $R = (c_0, \ldots, c_{n-1}) + (c_n, \ldots, c_{2n-2})\mathcal{E}$
  3: $S \leftarrow$ **GMont-like**(R)
  4: return S

2.6   The Parameter δ and Bounds

Recall that the addition in the PMNS is the simple polynomial addition, which is quite simple. In comparison, the internal reduction (Algorithm 1) is very expensive. Thus, it is not interesting to perform this reduction after an addition (to guarantee the result in $\mathcal{B}$). To solve this "issue", the authors in [20] introduce a parameter δ. It is the maximum number of consecutive additions of elements in $\mathcal{B}$ that we want to compute before doing a multiplication (**ModMult**: Algorithm 2). Its value is chosen according to the target application.

Let A and B each be the result of such successive additions. Then, we have: $\|A\|_\infty, \|B\|_\infty < (\delta + 1)\rho$. If $S = $ **ModMult**(A, B), we want $S \in \mathcal{B}$.

This is achieved by taking the parameters ρ and ϕ such that [22]:

$$\rho = \|\mathcal{G}\|_1 - 1 \quad \text{and} \quad \phi \geqslant 2w(\rho - 1)(\delta + 1)^2, \qquad (5)$$

where:

$$w = \|(1, 2, \ldots, n) + (n - 1, n - 2, \ldots, 1)\mathcal{E}'\|_\infty,$$

with $\mathcal{E}'$ being the $(n - 1) \times n$ matrix such that $\mathcal{E}'_{ij} = |\mathcal{E}_{ij}|$.

Remark 3. In this paper we are not interested in redundancy control or equality test within the PMNS. If redundancy control in the PMNS and/or equality testing within the system is desired, the parameters ρ and ϕ should instead be chosen as proposed in [21]:

$$\rho = \|\mathcal{G}\|_1 + 1 \quad \text{and} \quad \phi \geqslant 2\lceil w(\delta + 1)^2 \|\mathcal{G}^{-1}\|_1 \|\mathcal{G}\|_1^2 \rceil.$$

2.7   Conversion Operations

This section briefly presents the conversion operations to and from the PMNS. Two methods have been proposed for conversion to PMNS. One is slow (Algorithm 3) and is used for pre-computation. The other one (Algorithm 4), which is fast, requires pre-computed polynomials. It also performs the conversion to the Montgomery domain mentioned in Remark 2. The polynomials P_i required by Algorithm 4 are computed using Algorithm 3.

Conversion from PMNS is a simple polynomial evaluation modulo p. One must also not forget the conversion from the Montgomery domain. That is, let $A \in \mathcal{B}$, we compute: $a = A(\gamma)\phi^{-1} \pmod{p}$. An easy way to perform this operation is to use the classical Horner's scheme [39], or it can be done more efficiently by pre-computing $\gamma^i \phi^{-1} \pmod{p}$, for $i = 0, \ldots, n - 1$, for very fast polynomial evaluation modulo p.

Algorithm 3. Exact Conversion to PMNS

Require: $a \in \mathbb{Z}/p\mathbb{Z}$, $\mathcal{B} = (p, n, \gamma, \rho, E)$ and the matrices $\mathcal{G}$, $\mathcal{G}'$.
Ensure: $A \in \mathcal{B}$ with $A(\gamma) \equiv a \pmod{p}$.
1: $\tau \leftarrow a \times \phi^{n-1} \pmod{p}$
2: $A \leftarrow (\tau, 0, \ldots, 0)$ # a vector of dimension n
3: **for** $i = 0 \ldots (n-1)$ **do**
4:     $A \leftarrow$ **GMont-like**(A)
5: **end for**
6: **return** A

Algorithm 4. Fast Conversion to PMNS

Require: $a \in \mathbb{Z}/p\mathbb{Z}$, $\mathcal{B} = (p, n, \gamma, \rho, E)$ and the matrices $\mathcal{G}$, $\mathcal{G}'$,
        β the smallest power of 2 such that $\beta^n > p$, and $P_i \in \mathcal{B}$ such that $P_i(\gamma) \equiv \beta^i \phi^2$
        $\pmod{p}$ for $i = 0 \ldots (n-1)$.
Ensure: $A \in \mathcal{B}$, such that $A \equiv (a\phi)_\mathcal{B}$
1: $t = (t_{n-1}, \ldots, t_0)_\beta$ # radix-β decomposition of a
2: $U \leftarrow \sum_{i=0}^{n-1} t_i P_i(X)$
3: $A \leftarrow$ **GMont-like**(U)
4: return A

2.8 Generating PMNS Basis in Practice

This section describes the steps to generate PMNS for a given modulus p.

Before generating the PMNS, we need to chose the value of δ according to the target application (see Sect. 2.6). Additionally, for **GMont-like** to be efficient, the parameter ϕ must be taken as a power of two. Let us assume that the target hardware is a h-bit architecture. As suggested in [20], a good choice for efficient internal reduction is to take $\phi = 2^h$. Thus, implying the parameter n to be such that:

$$n \geqslant \left\lfloor \frac{\lceil \log_2(p) \rceil}{h} \right\rfloor + 1 \,.$$

Depending on the value of δ, the value of n will be increased as much as necessary in order to find a suitable PMNS. As mentioned in Sect. 2.3, we want a polynomial E which allows very efficient external reduction. Table 2 gives some examples of such polynomials E. Algorithm 5 describes PMNS generation process.

Table 2. Example of polynomials E for efficient external reduction and small memory cost.

$E(X)$	n	w
$X^n - \lambda$, with $|\lambda|$ very small	–	$1 + (n-1)|\lambda|$
$X^n \pm X^{\frac{n}{2}} + 1$	even	$3n/2$
$X^n + X^{n-2} + X^{n-4} + \cdots + X^2 + 1$	even	$2n - 2$
$X^n - X^{n-1} + X^{n-2} - X^{n-3} + \cdots - X + 1$	even	$2n - 1$
$X^n - X^{n-1} + X^{n-2} - X^{n-3} + \cdots + X - 1$	odd	$2n - 1$
$X^n \pm X \pm 1$	–	$2n - 1$
$X^n + X^{n-1} + \cdots + X + 1$	–	$2n - 1$

Algorithm 5. PMNS generation

Require: p, δ, $\phi = 2^h$, and $\lambda_{\max}$ the maximum for $|\lambda|$ in Table 2.
Ensure: $\mathcal{B}$ is a PMNS
1: $n = \left\lfloor \frac{\lceil \log_2(p) \rceil}{h} \right\rfloor + 1$
2: found = False
3: **while** not found **do**
4:     Randomly (or iteratively) choose a polynomial E in Table 2 having a root γ modulo p.
5:     Compute the basis **B** of $\mathcal{L_B}$ (see Eq. 4)
6:     $\mathcal{G} \leftarrow$ LLL(**B**) # or use BKZ, HKZ, ...
7:     $\rho \leftarrow \|\mathcal{G}\|_1 - 1$
8:     **if** $\phi < 2w(\rho - 1)(\delta + 1)^2$ **then**
9:         **if** all the polynomials E have been checked **then**
10:             $n \leftarrow n + 1$
11:         **end if**
12:         Choose another polynomial E (i.e. go back to step 4)
13:     **end if**
14:     found = True
15:     $\mathcal{B} \leftarrow (p, n, \gamma, \rho, E, \mathcal{G}, \phi, \delta)$
16: **end while**
17: return $\mathcal{B}$

Remark 4. At line 6 of Algorithm 5, a lattice basis reduction is performed using the LLL algorithm. Here the goal is to have a basis $\mathcal{G}$ with the smallest possible 1-norm. Indeed, the parameter ρ, which is the upper bound on the infinity norm of PMNS elements, is computed with $\|\mathcal{G}\|_1$ (see line 7). Since we want to use as little memory as possible to represent elements in the PMNS, we want the $\mathcal{G}$ 1-norm to be as small as possible. In addition, the smaller ρ is, the more likely it is that the **if** statement on line 8 will not be satisfied, thus giving more chance of finding PMNS with smaller of n, which is better for efficiency.

To sum up, if you have a better basis reduction algorithm/implementation than LLL (i.e. that leads to a basis $\mathcal{G}$ with a smaller 1-norm), you must use it instead.

2.9 Advantages and Drawbacks

Elements in PMNS are polynomials. This has many advantages. Here, we highlight some of them:

- Since polynomial coefficients are independent, there is no carry propagation to deal with when performing arithmetic operations, unlike the classical representation where one has to deal with this propagation.
- Arithmetic and conversion operations have no conditional branching. This property is an advantage for efficiency and is also very helpful against side channel attacks.
- As the coefficients are independent, they can be computed simultaneously. As a consequence, PMNS is well fitted for a parallel implementation. Note that in this paper we only present results for sequential implementations. We do not take advantage of the high parallelisation capability of PMNS, which should lead to much better efficiency. Parallel hardware implementations of PMNS have been studied and compared to classical Montgomery modular multiplication in [50].
- PMNS is a redundant number system. This redundancy can easily be used to randomise arithmetic and conversion operations. This can be used to protect some cryptographic protocols against side-channel attacks, as shown in [19].
- Finally, thanks to the parameter δ, it is possible to add PMNS elements without having to perform an internal reduction (which is in comparison very expensive). In the classical representation, this is not possible when the modulus size is $h \times n$ (e.g. when $\lceil \log_2(p) \rceil = 256 = 64 * 4$, with $h = 64$).

Compared to the classical representations, PMNS has two main disadvantages:

- The first one is the generation process. For applications where new moduli need to be generated many times, Algorithm 5 may be too expensive, mainly because of the lattice basis reduction at line 6. Note, however, that in practice the modulus size is in most cases small enough to make this reduction very efficient. This is the case, for example, with ECC moduli and moduli used in post-quantum cryptographic schemes. In fact, with our experiments using the SageMath library [54], we observe that for modulus sizes smaller than 2048 bits, this reduction is fast and efficient.
- The second one is the number of coefficients (i.e. the value of n). The PMNS generation process presented in Sect. 2.8 requires to take $n \geqslant \left\lfloor \frac{\lceil \log_2(p) \rceil}{h} \right\rfloor + 1$. In practice, this often results in PMNS having one more coefficient than the classical representation. However, thanks to the polynomial structure of its elements, PMNS may still remain very competitive in this case, as will be

shown in the next application sections. Of course, when the modulus size leads to the same number of coefficients than the classical representation, PMNS will be more efficient. This is for example the case for the modulus of the parings `KSS16-330` and `BN-462` (see Sect. 4.3).

3   Application to Elliptic Curves Defined over Random Prime Fields

3.1   The Brainpool Curves

For efficiency reasons, Mersenne or pseudo-Mersenne primes are very often used for base fields in classical elliptic curve cryptography. This is for example the case of the standard NIST curves such as the P256 curve [49] defined over the prime field of order $2^{256} - 2^{224} + 2^{192} + 2^{96} - 1$ which has been extensively used in cybersecurity during the last decades. However it is not satisfying for several reasons:

- this parameter is not randomly generated which can be considered as a potential weakness. In particular, there has been some debate about whether the NSA introduced a backdoor in the P256 curve because the seed for generating it has not been published by the NIST,
- this may yield to use patented algorithm for efficient modular arithmetic specific to these primes (even if these patents have now expired),
- for hardware devices, specific and not flexible designs must be deployed to benefit of such an efficient modular arithmetic which may be very expensive [52],
- sparse prime field (as well as sparse order of the curve because of the Hasse-Weil bound) requires larger blinding factors for its randomization to protect against side-channel attacks [52].

To address these problems, the ECC Brainpool consortium suggested to use only pseudo-random numbers to generate ECC parameters and introduced rigidity in the process thanks to the notion of verifiable pseudo-random [16]. For example, they propose to use natural constants (as the digits of $e = exp(1)$) in place of random seeds. Even if the so-called Brainpool curves have not been defined following this procedure, the idea remains the same and is described in an RFC [45]. The Brainpool initiative was the first open work aiming to produce a fully transparent and verifiable pseudo-random elliptic curve generation process.

For example the `BrainpoolP256r1` curve is defined by the short Weierstrass equation

$$y^2 = x^3 + Ax + B$$

over the prime field $\mathbb{F}_p$ with

$p = 76884956397045344220809746629001649093037950200943055203735601445$
     031516197751

$A = 56669818760532611004362722839617834607712061453947521410938682818$
     8763884139993

$B = 17577232497321838841075697789794520262950426058923084567046852300$
     633325438902

As a consequence of its randomizing, the base field $\mathbb{F}_p$ do not have any specificity so that only generic modular arithmetic can be used. It may then be interesting to generate a PMNS basis for this prime and compare the PMNS representation arithmetic in this field with more classical ones such as Montgomery [46] or Barrett [7].

Recently (November 2023), OpenSSL 3.2.0 integrated the Brainpool curves. This shows that, even if Curve25519 [12] is more and more popular for its efficiency, the need for randomly generated alternative is still relevant. As OpenSSL is clearly a recognised reference in cryptographic implementations, we decided to compared it with our PMNS arithmetic for the 256, 384 and 512-bits prime fields of Brainpool.

3.2   PMNS Parameters

As mentioned above, we consider the moduli of Brainpool P256r1, P384r1 and P512r1 curves. This section gives the parameters of the PMNS generated for these moduli, using Algorithm 5 of Subsect. 2.8.

Let us start with brainpoolP256r1 modulus. We get the following parameters:

$p = 76884956397045344220809746629001649093037950200943055203735601$
     445031516197751

$n = 5$

$\gamma = 69419170576495936951229257827200835275135500751173168338114307$
     7761123131575941

$\rho = 5798424837117361$

$E = X^5 - 5$

$\phi = 2^{64}$

$\delta = 7$

The parameters for brainpoolP384r1 modulus are:

$p = 2165927077011931617306923684233260497979611638701764860008161850382108993402596182223656198284453408844070841797331$

$n = 7$

$\gamma = 111227304978670824267037748985863892145549721362390042341626137227824698035112321114839360848927435875637067797889250$

$\rho = 92143305512072319$

$E = X^7 - 2$

$\phi = 2^{64}$

$\delta = 1$

The parameters for `brainpoolP512r1` modulus are:

$p = 894896220765023255165660281515915342216260964409835451134459718720005701041355243991793430419195694276544653038642734593796389430992392853607053460781694731$

$n = 9$

$\gamma = 20670140623632241292106902112791444395638356376389137152957073973914031952411388598133886529587536136669343079369256892137492508555078458075711180903933371$

$\rho = 92143305512072319$

$E = X^9 - 2$

$\phi = 2^{64}$

$\delta = 0$

3.3 Measurement Procedure

Before presenting our comparison results, we first describe our measurement procedure for C language implementations. Measurements were performed on a HP EliteBook laptop, with:

- Processor: Intel 11th Gen Intel Core $i5$-1135G7@$2.40GHz \times 8$
- Memory: 16 GiB of RAM
- OS: Ubuntu 20.04.6 LTS (64 bits)

The compiler is `gcc` version 9.4.0, the compiler options are as follows: `-Wall -O3 -lgmp -lcrypto`.

The test procedure is as follows:

- the *Turbo-Boost*® is deactivated during the tests;

- 1001 runs are executed in order to "heat" the cache memory, i.e. we ensure that the cache memory (data and instruction) is in an enough stabilized state in order to avoid untimely cache faults;
- one generates 51 random data sets, and for each data set the minimum of the execution clock cycle numbers over a batch of 1001 runs is recorded;
- the performance is the average of all these minimums;
- this procedure is run on console mode, to avoid system perturbations, and obtain the most accurate cycle counts.

The clock cycle number is obtained using the `rdtsc` instruction which loads the current value of the processor's time-stamp counter into a 64-bit register. The processor monotonically increments the time-stamp counter every clock cycle. Hence calling this instruction before and just after a sequence of instructions allows to obtain the number of elapsed cycles.

Our C implementations of PMNS presented in this paper can be found in this GitHub repository:

https://github.com/PMNS-APPLICATION/C-code-brainpool-pairing

3.4   PMNS Arithmetic vs OpenSSL library

In this section, we compare PMNS to OpenSSL for modular multiplication with the moduli of the Brainpool curves. We made this choice because Brainpool curves are now officially included in OpenSSL. Table 3 gives clock cycle numbers for PMNS, for the standard modular multiplication provided in OpenSSL (Std in the table) and for its implementation of Montgomery modular multiplication (Bloc-Mont in the table). Note that the latter is the most relevant element of comparison since PMNS uses a Montgomery-like reduction method, and both approaches require some pre-computation and conversion in a Montgomery domain. It can be seen that PMNS is faster for `brainpoolP256r1` and `brainpoolP384r1`, but slower for `brainpoolP512r1`. For the latter, we checked the OpenSSL library and found that it uses the Karatsuba method of integer multiplication for this size of integer and above. Due to time constraints, we have not yet done this for PMNS. This will be done in a future work and we expect to outperform the OpenSSL implementation again. Also note that, as mentioned in Sect. 2.9, we are presenting a sequential implementation here, while PMNS is well suited for parallel implementation. So these PMNS should be expected to perform much better with a parallel implementation.

Table 3. Clock cycle number comparisons of Modular Multiplication for **brainpool** curve moduli.

Modulus	PMNS	OpenSSL	
		Bloc-Mont	Std
brainpoolP256r1	177	181	718
brainpoolP384r1	267	294	1071
brainpoolP512r1	405	347	1385

4   Application to Pairing-Friendly Base Fields

4.1   Pairing-Friendly Base Fields

Pairings are interesting in cryptography because of the large number of protocols they can be used for; as identity-based cryptography, multiple signature schemes, attribute-based cryptography, or hierarchical encryption... [24,25]. Pairing-based cryptography is based on the arithmetic of finite fields $\mathbb{F}_p$, for p a large prime number, extensions of finite fields $\mathbb{F}_{p^k}$, and the arithmetic of an elliptic curve defined over these two finite fields [25]. There are different constructions of pairing curves [28]. Some are called pairing-friendly elliptic curves because they allow efficient pairing calculations. Among the pairing-friendly elliptic curves, the BN [6], BLS [5], and KSS [41] curves present a good trade off between the size of $\mathbb{F}_p$ and $\mathbb{F}_{p^k}$. The BN and BLS curves are recommended by the Internet Engineering Task Force [51] at 128 and 194 bit security level.

Such pairing-friendly elliptic curves are determined by a polynomial expression for the number p defining the finite field $\mathbb{F}_p$. This expression depends on a parameter often noted u, such that $p(u)$ is a prime of predetermined size in bits. The size of p depends on the level of security. The most effective discrete logarithm attack for pairing-friendly elliptic fields and curves is Kim and Barbulescu's TNFS attack [42]. It has a different impact on families of pairing-friendly elliptic curves [3,4]. Construction of pairing-friendly elliptic curve relies on the Complex Multiplication [25]. The value of p is randomly generated during the construction. Although the expression of p obtained for a pairing-friendly elliptic curve is polynomial in u, the prime numbers allowing correct parameters for pairing-friendly elliptic curve have no structure allowing efficient modular arithmetic [51]. We recall in Table 4 the parametric definition of the large prime p for the BN, BLS, and KSS families. The BN-462 curve is standardised at the 128 bits security level [51]; the two others families are the ones that allow efficient pairing computation in terms of operation complexity, arithmetic on finite fields and elliptic curves, and execution time [51]. The BLS12 curve is implemented in the cryptocurrencies Zcash [57] and Ethereum [26]. The KSS curve does not seem to be used in practice, but it has good properties for efficient implementations [3].

Table 4. Expression of p according to the pairing-friendly family of curve

Family	Expression of p
BN	$p(u) = 36u^4 + 36u^3 + 24u^2 + 6u + 1$
BLS12	$p(u) = \frac{1}{3}(u-1)^2(u^4 - u^2 + 1) + u$
KSS16	$p(u) = \frac{1}{980}\left(u^{10} + 2u^9 + 5u^8 + 48u^6 + 152u^5 \right.$ $\left. 240u^4 + 625u^2 + 2398u + 3125\right)$

4.2 PMNS Parameters

Section 3.4 presents a comparison between PMNS and the GMP library for modular multiplication with the moduli used in pairing-based cryptography. More precisely, we consider the moduli of the base fields defining the pairing-friendly curves BN-462, BLS12-381 and KSS16-330.

This section gives the parameters of the PMNS generated for these moduli.

Let us start with BLS12-381 modulus. Thanks to Algorithm 5 given in Subsect. 2.8, we get the following parameters:

$p = 4002409555221667393417789825735904156556882819939007885332058136124031650490837864442687629129015664037894272559787$

$n = 7$

$\gamma = 8439523423486319150638028379657090639981335620567352002001654235297606413082346297697287941199117717482560648925 58$

$\rho = 68257199819371999$

$E = X^7 + X + 1$

$\phi = 2^{64}$

$\delta = 2$

The parameters for KSS16-330 modulus are:

$p = 2122170134488686779110065285098201491111393711817963402400071851758703670191428860638477993139881 09$

$n = 6$

$\gamma = 6080816996612077797296361989198721754750095433268475254194921731177814573678895869896472138478851 14$

$\rho = 81242268367433855$

$E = X^6 + X + 1$

$\phi = 2^{64}$

$\delta = 2$

The parameters for BN-462 modulus are:

$p = 6701817056313037086248947066310538444882082605308124576230408038843357549886356779857393336996701076480254100579671144035575350370105632360$

$n = 8$

$\gamma = 5509829180826187139291015819800185267441357388380712197477923518196116089573433646450554434397321515192859927217396118149703736444512082942$

$\rho = 789727156710839423$

$E = X^8 - X - 1$

$\phi = 2^{64}$

$\delta = 0$

4.3 PMNS Arithmetic vs GMP library

In this section, we compare PMNS to GMP for modular multiplication with the moduli presented above. We use exactly the same procedure described in Sect. 3.3 with the same hardware. Table 5 gives clock cycle numbers for PMNS, for the standard modular multiplication provided in GMP (Std in the table), for its implementation of Montgomery modular multiplication (Bloc-Mont in the table). GMP also allows the use of some low-level functions that are slightly faster than the standard ones. The corresponding function for modular multiplication is called Low-lvl in Table 5. Similar to the OpenSSL library, note that Bloc-Mont is the most relevant element of the comparison, since PMNS uses a Montgomery-like reduction method, and both approaches require some pre-computation and conversion in a Montgomery domain.

Table 5. Clock cycle number comparisons of Modular Multiplication for pairing-friendly base fields

Modulus	PMNS	GMP		
		Bloc-Mont	Low-lvl	Std
KSS16-330	225	248	494	541
BN-462	349	368	709	762
BLS12-381	275	249	496	547

First, one can observe in Table 5 that our PMNS implementation is always faster than GMP standard and low-level implementations. Regarding GMP implementation of Montgomery modular multiplication (i.e. GMP Bloc-Mont in the table), it can be seen that PMNS is also faster, except for BLS12-381.

This is because, for KSS16-330 and BN-462, PMNS and GMP use the same number of coefficients to represent their elements. As mentioned in Sect. 2.9, PMNS is faster in this case. For BLS12-381, the corresponding PMNS uses one more coefficient than GMP ($n = 7$ instead of 6).

Remark 5. As mentioned earlier, we are comparing sequential implementations here, whereas PMNS is much more suited to parallel implementation. In addition, GMP uses assembly code to optimise its operations, whereas our implementation of PMNS is standard C code without any assembly code. With equivalent optimisation (perhaps in future work), we expect our PMNS implementation to always outperform the GMP implementation of Montgomery modular multiplication.

5   Application to Elliptic Curves for Zero-Knowledge Protocols

Most of today's digital services use centralized systems, which implies a trusted authority. For some years now, there has been growing interest in decentralised systems, such as blockchains, which avoid the need for a central authority to certify data. However, most existing systems require parties to publish all their computations and recalculate those published by other parties to ensure that they are correct. This is expensive, especially in terms of memory storage. For example, the size of the bitcoin chain reached 600 GigaBytes in September 2024. To deal with this problem (and not only in the blockchain context), it is convenient to use proof systems [32], where a prover convinces a verifier that a given statement is correct. More specifically, zk-SNARK (zero-knowledge Succinct Non-interactive ARgument of Knowledge) provides a proof (that is short and easy to verify) of the correct execution of the computation [8] and is very useful in decentralised systems. Such systems are not trivial to construct, and it is not the aim of this paper to describe such construction but the interesting point for our purpose is that the most popular ones are using pairing-friendly elliptic curves [30,33–37]. Elliptic curves and base fields involved have specific constraints so that base field providing efficient reduction (such as pseudo-Mersenne prime) cannot be used in this context. As a consequence, using efficient alternative reduction algorithm as the PMNS must be considered. There are many zk-SNARK construction depending on the use-case. For example if one wants to use proof of proofs, it is necessary to find chains of pairing-friendly elliptic curves such that the prime order of the first has to be chosen to define the base field of the second one [18]. Indeed, in pairing-based SNARK, the verification is usually made in the base field while the proof is made in the field defined by the prime order of the considered elliptic curve subgroup (usually called the scalar field). This illustrate the fact that at least one of the base field cannot be chosen in a specific form. This is for example used in the MINA protocol [15] which is a very light blockchain thanks to the use of zk-SNARK (fixed size of 22 KiloBytes). But there is no need to choose such advanced protocols to meet a base field that cannot be chosen in the blockchain context.

5.1   The JubJub Elliptic Curve

To illustrate the interest of using PMNS arithmetic in the zk-SNARK context, we will focus on Zcash which is a cryptocurrency based on bitcoin and where anonymity is ensured thanks to zk-SNARK. The zk-SNARK is made on the BLS12-381 pairing-friendly elliptic curve already introduced in Subsect. 4 to prove an Elliptic Curve Diffie-Hellman (ECDH) key exchange following the CØCØ construction [43]. As the proof is made on the scalar field, the cardinality of the prime subgroup involved in the pairing must be used to define the base field of the elliptic curve where the ECDH key exchange is performed. As a consequence, the JubJub curve used in [56] is defined over $\mathbb{F}_p$ with

$$p = 5243587517512619047944774050818596583769055250052763782260365\,8\\699938581184513$$

for which no specific reduction algorithm is known. Indeed, as it comes from the cardinality of the BLS12-381 curve, it has no specific form. The JubJub curve is then defined as a twisted Edwards curve in a deterministic way following the SafeCurve recommendations [13]

$$E_J : -u^2 + v^2 = 1 + du^2 v^2 \tag{6}$$

with $d = -(10240/10241)$
$$= 1925703803668094935975031266978687799194943540225412028618\,41\\96891950884077233$$

It has cofactor 8 and we can use $G = (80762466406628849098818017587\,04\\306714\ \ 0346099874558698045205220918555166029\,23, 1326237469369891070192\\9044844\ \ 60046583141312281844735959452740019467527406045\,8)$ as a base point.

5.2   Efficient Group Law on the JubJub Elliptic Curve

The most efficient coordinate system for this curve is the extended projective one [9,38]. In this case, a point on the curve E_J is given by 4 coordinates (U, V, Z, T) in $\mathbb{F}_p$ such that $u = \frac{U}{Z}, v = \frac{V}{Z}$ are satisfying the defining equation of E_J 6 and $T = \frac{UV}{Z}$.

For doubling a point in this form, the following formulas are used [38]

$$
\begin{array}{ll}
T_2 = V^2 + U^2 & T_2' = V^2 - U^2 \\
T_1 = (U+V)^2 - T_2 & J = 2Z^2 - T_2' \\
U = T_1 J & V = T_2' T_2 \\
Z = T_2' J & T = T_1 T_2
\end{array}
$$

These formulas require 4 multiplications and 4 squarings in the base field $\mathbb{F}_p$. Note that many additions or subtractions are also involved in these formulas, so that the use of the δ parameter introduced in Subsect. 2.6 is crucial in order to avoid internal reduction after each addition/subtraction operation. More precisely, there is 1 non-reduced addition in the expressions of T_2, T_2' so that it is sufficient to have $\delta = 1$ in order to compute $V = T_2'T_2$ without intermediate internal reduction. However $T_1 = (U + V)^2 - T_2$ and $J = 2Z^2 - T_2'$ are made of respectively 2 and 3 additions assuming that T_2 and T_2' have not been reduced. As a consequence we need to have a δ value equal to 3 in order to compute efficiently U and Z.

We do not give the mixed addition formulas for this system of coordinates here (they can be find in [38] or on [10]) because they do not provide any additional information or constraint on the choice of δ.

5.3   PMNS Parameters for JubJub Arithmetic

We then apply the method described in Subsect. 2.8 to generate a PMNS basis for the modulus used to construct the JubJub elliptic curve. In this specific context, as explained in the previous section, we also have to choose a parameter δ at least equal to 3 to avoid internal reductions after addition/subtraction operations involved in the group law. The parameters of the PMNS generated for this modulus are given by:

$$p = 5243587517512619047944774050818596583769055250052763782260365869993581184513$$

$$n = 5$$

$$\gamma = 17165118212817083565366397558045145856414930757760865323558718474655557272360$$

$$\rho = 5216921637660971$$

$$E = X^5 - 2$$

$$\phi = 2^{64}$$

$$\delta = 13$$

5.4   Comparison of Efficiency

For safety reasons many cryptocurrency protocols are using Rust libraries. This is a nice opportunity to compare our PMNS arithmetic with classical ones in another language than C. We chose the Zcash official library [55] to make this comparison. We first compare the cost of basic modular multiplication (which is classically done using Montgomery reduction in the Zcash library) as in the other sections of this paper.

All the measurments of this section were performed on a Legion by Lenovo laptop, with:

- Processor: Intel 7th Gen Intel Core $i5$-$7300HQ$ @ $2.50GHz \times 4$
- Memory: 8 GiB of RAM
- OS: Ubuntu 20.04.5 LTS (64 bits)

The compiler used is `cargo` version 1.84.1 . The test procedure for the Modular Multiplication is as follows:

- 10000 runs are executed. For each iteration of run execution, the Modular Multiplication is made with two random elements of the JubJub base field (the same elements are used in both arithmetic systems for a fair comparison),
- the execution time and execution clock cycle numbers required by the modular multiplication operation are recorded for each iteration, the performance is the average of those iterations,
- the performance given in Table 6 is the average of 10 times the batch of 10000 iterations.

The execution time is obtained using the `std::time::{Duration, Instant}` library surrounding the multiplication. The clock cycle number is obtained using `std::arch::asm;` library to create the `rdtsc` instruction.

Our Rust implementations can be found in this GitHub repository:

https://github.com/PMNS-APPLICATION/Rust-code-jubjub

Table 6. Clock cycle number and execution time comparisons of Modular Multiplication for **JubJub** curve base field.

	PMNS		Classical	
	Clock cycle number	Execution time (ns)	Clock cycle number	Execution time (ns)
JubJub	723	313.5	1157	484.1

Thanks to PMNS, we also get in this case an implementation of the base field arithmetic which is more efficient than the one by default in the targeted library.

To complete the comparison, we also decided to compare the full scalar multiplication computation at the elliptic curve level. For this, we use the Zcash code [55] for the scalar multiplication (a constant-time double-and-add algorithm in extended projective coordinates [9,38]) on top of both their and our base field arithmetic. The group law formulas given in Subsect. 5.2 are naturally used, but in practice, in the Zcash implementation, the last line of the doubling is not performed and the point is stored as (U, V, Z, T_1, T_2). As the δ value of the PMNS basis is quite large in this case, we can easily avoid internal reduction after all the additions/subtraction operations involved in the group law formulas.

The comparison of the full scalar multiplication between the classical and PMNS arithmetic has been made in the same environment that the measurements of performance of the Modular Multiplication. The tests are made with a random multiple of the affine base point G and a random element of the JubJub scalar field. Of course the same elements are used for both side of the comparison and new ones are drawn at each iteration. The performance result are given in Table 7.

Table 7. Clock cycle number and execution time comparisons of Full Scalar Multiplication on **JubJub** elliptic curve.

	PMNS		Classical	
	Clock cycle	Execution time (ns)	Clock cycle number	Execution time (ns)
JubJub	2 992 436	1.1655	3 386 125	1.3185

It is not very surprising that these results confirm the ones obtained on the base field. But it shows that PMNS arithmetic can be easily used to replace classical Montgomery arithmetic on the base field and that it remains an interesting alternative at the elliptic curve level. Moreover, these results do not take into account the inherent properties of the PMNS arithmetic compared to classical ones (easy parallelisation, possibility of randomisation).

6   Conclusion

In this article, we illustrate how PMNS can be used for concrete cryptographic applications. We have chosen to work on cryptography based on elliptic curves because they are now essential in asymmetric cryptography and because, in some contexts, they require modular arithmetic modulo primes p that do not allow efficient specific arithmetic. PMNS arithmetic is an alternative to classical arithmetic for such primes. We consider the Brainpool curve (standardised and included in the widely deployed OpenSSL library), pairing-friendly elliptic curves for security level 128 (used in many advanced protocols), and the Jubjub elliptic curve (used in the Zcash cryptocurrency).

We compared our implementation on 64-bits architectures with the two mainstream libraries for cryptographers, GMP and OpenSSL. Both libraries rely on assembly code for optimisations. Our PMNS implementation was more naive, we implemented it in C in a sequential way without any assembly optimisations. We also compare a Rust version of our approach with the official Zcash library at both the finite field and elliptic curve levels. These implementations and test procedures can be checked out the following git:

https://github.com/PMNS-APPLICATION/

Our results are very promising, despite the lack of use of assembly code, and the extra machine word for the PMNS representation compared to the classical one. In many cases, our implementation outperformed OpenSSL, GMP and the Rust library for Zcash. This was not so obvious a priori because the addition of an extra machine word has an important impact when the total number of machine words is small, as it is the case for elliptic curve cryptography ($n=4$ to 8). This study then shows that the advantages of the PMNS representation (e.g. no carry propagation) compensate this drawback in practice. Note that this result must be put into perspective because, for our comparisons, we used general-purpose and widely deployed libraries which are not necessarily highly optimised for specific use cases (and our implementations either).

As a consequence, this work is the first step towards the introduction of PMNS arithmetic in cryptography. Further work on the implementation aspects, such as parallelisation or the introduction of some assembly routines, would be relevant to improve our PMNS implementation in the context of elliptic curve cryptography. It would certainly allow much better performances but also provide new opportunities inherent to PMNS properties, such as randomising the base field arithmetic against side channel attacks.

It would also be very interesting to complete this study in the context of post-quantum cryptography. In particular, the isogeny-based signature SQiSign makes intensive use of large prime field arithmetic and some important lattice-based cryptographic protocols use prime numbers (e.g. Dilithium or Fully Homomorphic Encryption).

Acknowledgments. This work was supported in part by French project ANR-11-LABX-0020-01 "Centre Henri Lebesgue". The authors thank Michael Scott for useful remarks and comments.

References

1. Bajard, J., Imbert, L., Plantard, T.: Arithmetic operations in the polynomial modular number system. In: 17th IEEE Symposium on Computer Arithmetic (ARITH-17 2005), 27–29 June 2005, pp. 206–213 (2005)
2. Bajard, J.-C., Imbert, L., Plantard, T.: Modular number systems: beyond the mersenne family. In: Handschuh, H., Hasan, M.A. (eds.) SAC 2004. LNCS, vol. 3357, pp. 159–169. Springer, Heidelberg (2004). https://doi.org/10.1007/978-3-540-30564-4_11
3. Barbulescu, R., Duquesne, S.: Updating key size estimations for pairings. J. Cryptol. **32**(4), 1298–1336 (2019). https://doi.org/10.1007/S00145-018-9280-5
4. Barbulescu, R., El Mrabet, N., Ghammam, L.: A taxonomy of pairings, their security, their complexity. IACR Cryptol. ePrint Arch. 485 (2019). https://eprint.iacr.org/2019/485
5. Barreto, P., Lynn, B., Scott, M.: On the selection of pairing-friendly groups. In: Matsui, M., Zuccherato, R.J. (eds.) SAC 2003. LNCS, vol. 3006, pp. 17–25. Springer, Heidelberg (2004). https://doi.org/10.1007/978-3-540-24654-1_2

6. Barreto, P., Naehrig, M.: Pairing-friendly elliptic curves of prime order. In: Preneel, B., Tavares, S. (eds.) SAC 2005. LNCS, vol. 3897, pp. 319–331. Springer, Heidelberg (2006). https://doi.org/10.1007/11693383_22

7. Barrett, P.: Implementing the Rivest Shamir and Adleman public key encryption algorithm on a standard digital signal processor. In: Odlyzko, A.M. (ed.) CRYPTO 1986. LNCS, vol. 263, pp. 311–323. Springer, Heidelberg (1987). https://doi.org/10.1007/3-540-47721-7_24

8. Ben-Sasson, E., Chiesa, A., Tromer, E., Virza, M.: Succinct non-interactive zero knowledge for a von neumann architecture. In: Proceedings of the 23rd USENIX Conference on Security Symposium, SEC'14, , pp. 781–796. USENIX Association (2014)

9. Bernstein, D.J., Duif, N., Lange, T., Schwabe, P., Yang, B.Y.: High-speed high-security signatures. J. Cryptogr. Eng. **2**, 77–89 (2012). https://doi.org/10.1007/s13389-012-0027-1

10. Bernstein, D.J., Lange, T.: Extended coordinates with a=-1 for twisted edwards curves. http://www.hyperelliptic.org/EFD/g1p/auto-twisted-extended-1.html

11. Bernstein, D.J., Lange, T.: Explicit-formulas database for elliptic curve cryptography. https://hyperelliptic.org/EFD

12. Bernstein, D.J.: Curve25519: new diffie-hellman speed records. In: Yung, M., Dodis, Y., Kiayias, A., Malkin, T. (eds.) PKC 2006. LNCS, vol. 3958, pp. 207–228. Springer, Heidelberg (2006). https://doi.org/10.1007/11745853_14

13. Bernstein, D.J., Lange, T.: Safecurves: choosing safe curves for elliptic-curve cryptography. https://safecurves.cr.yp.to

14. Bernstein, D.J., Lange, T., Niederhagen, R.: Dual EC: a standardized back door. In: Ryan, P., Naccache, D., Quisquater, J.-J. (eds.) The New Codebreakers. LNCS, vol. 9100, pp. 256–281. Springer, Heidelberg (2016). https://doi.org/10.1007/978-3-662-49301-4_17

15. Bonneau, J., Meckler, I., Rao, V., Shapiro, E.: Coda: Decentralized cryptocurrency at scale. Cryptology ePrint Archive, Paper 2020/352 (2020). https://eprint.iacr.org/2020/352

16. Brainpool: Ecc brainpool standard curves and curve generation (2005). http://www.ecc-brainpool.org/download/Domain-parameters.pdf

17. Checkoway, S., et al.: On the practical exploitability of dual EC in TLS implementations. In: Fu, K., Jung, J. (eds.) Proceedings of the 23rd USENIX Security Symposium, San Diego, CA, USA, 20–22 August 2014, pp. 319–335. USENIX Association (2014). https://www.usenix.org/conference/usenixsecurity14/technical-sessions/presentation/checkoway

18. Costello, C., et al.: Geppetto: Versatile verifiable computation. In: 2015 IEEE Symposium on Security and Privacy, pp. 253–270 (2015). https://doi.org/10.1109/SP.2015.23

19. Didier, L., Dosso, F., El Mrabet, N., Marrez, J., Véron, P.: Randomization of arithmetic over polynomial modular number system. In: 26th IEEE Symposium on Computer Arithmetic, ARITH 2019, pp. 199–206 (2019). https://doi.org/10.1109/ARITH.2019.00048

20. Didier, L.S., Dosso, F.Y., Véron, P.: Efficient modular operations using the Adapted Modular Number System. J. Cryptogr. Eng., 1–23 (2020)

21. Dosso, F.Y., Berzati, A., El Mrabet, N., Proy, J.: PMNS revisited for consistent redundancy and equality test. Cryptology ePrint Archive, Paper 2023/1231 (2023). https://eprint.iacr.org/2023/1231

22. Dosso, F.Y., El Mrabet, N., Méloni, N., Palma, F., Véron, P.: Friendly primes for efficient modular arithmetic using the polynomial modular number system. Cryptology ePrint Archive, Paper 2025/090 (2025). https://eprint.iacr.org/2025/090

23. Dosso, F.Y., Robert, J.M., Véron, P.: PMNS for efficient arithmetic and small memory cost. IEEE Trans. Emerg. Topics Comput. **10**(3), 1263–1277 (2022). https://hal.science/hal-03768546v1/file/TETC3187786.pdf

24. Dutta, R., Barua, R., Sarkar, P.: Pairing-based cryptographic protocols: a survey. IACR Cryptol. ePrint Arch. 64 (2004). http://eprint.iacr.org/2004/064

25. El Mrabet, N., Joye, M.: Guide to Pairing-Based Cryptography. Chapman & Hall/CRC, Boca Raton (2016)

26. Ethereum. https://ethereum.org/en/

27. Force, I.E.T.: Transport layer security. https://datatracker.ietf.org/wg/tls/about/

28. Freeman, D., Scott, M., Teske, E.: A taxonomy of pairing-friendly elliptic curves. J. Cryptol. **23**(2), 224–280 (2010). https://doi.org/10.1007/S00145-009-9048-Z

29. Garner, H.L.: The residue number system. IRE Trans. Electron. Comput. EL **8**(6), 140–147 (1959)

30. Gennaro, R., Gentry, C., Parno, B., Raykova, M.: Quadratic span programs and succinct NIZKs without PCPs. In: Johansson, T., Nguyen, P.Q. (eds.) EURO-CRYPT 2013. LNCS, vol. 7881, pp. 626–645. Springer, Heidelberg (2013). https://doi.org/10.1007/978-3-642-38348-9_37

31. GMP: The GNU Multiple Precision Arithmetic library. https://gmplib.org

32. Goldwasser, S., Micali, S., Rackoff, C.: The knowledge complexity of interactive proof systems. SIAM J. Comput. **18**(1), 186–208 (1989). https://doi.org/10.1137/0218012

33. Groth, J.: Simulation-sound NIZK proofs for a practical language and constant size group signatures. In: Lai, X., Chen, K. (eds.) ASIACRYPT 2006. LNCS, vol. 4284, pp. 444–459. Springer, Heidelberg (2006). https://doi.org/10.1007/11935230_29

34. Groth, J.: Short pairing-based non-interactive zero-knowledge arguments. In: Abe, M. (ed.) ASIACRYPT 2010. LNCS, vol. 6477, pp. 321–340. Springer, Heidelberg (2010). https://doi.org/10.1007/978-3-642-17373-8_19

35. Groth, J.: On the size of pairing-based non-interactive arguments. In: Fischlin, M., Coron, J.-S. (eds.) EUROCRYPT 2016. LNCS, vol. 9666, pp. 305–326. Springer, Heidelberg (2016). https://doi.org/10.1007/978-3-662-49896-5_11

36. Groth, J., Ostrovsky, R., Sahai, A.: Non-interactive zaps and new techniques for NIZK. In: Dwork, C. (ed.) CRYPTO 2006. LNCS, vol. 4117, pp. 97–111. Springer, Heidelberg (2006). https://doi.org/10.1007/11818175_6

37. Groth, J., Sahai, A.: Efficient non-interactive proof systems for bilinear groups. In: Smart, N. (ed.) EUROCRYPT 2008. LNCS, vol. 4965, pp. 415–432. Springer, Heidelberg (2008). https://doi.org/10.1007/978-3-540-78967-3_24

38. Hisil, H., Wong, K.K.-H., Carter, G., Dawson, E.: Twisted edwards curves revisited. In: Pieprzyk, J. (ed.) ASIACRYPT 2008. LNCS, vol. 5350, pp. 326–343. Springer, Heidelberg (2008). https://doi.org/10.1007/978-3-540-89255-7_20

39. Horner, W.G.: A new method of solving numerical equations of all orders, by continuous approximation. Phil. Trans. R. Soc. Lond. **109**, 308–335 (1819)

40. Software Foundation Inc: OpenSSL Library. https://openssl.org

41. Kachisa, E.J., Schaefer, E.F., Scott, M.: Constructing Brezing-Weng pairing-friendly elliptic curves using elements in the cyclotomic field. In: Galbraith, S.D., Paterson, K.G. (eds.) Pairing 2008. LNCS, vol. 5209, pp. 126–135. Springer, Heidelberg (2008). https://doi.org/10.1007/978-3-540-85538-5_9

42. Kim, T., Barbulescu, R.: Extended tower number field sieve: a new complexity for the medium prime case. In: Robshaw, M., Katz, J. (eds.) CRYPTO 2016. LNCS, vol. 9814, pp. 543–571. Springer, Heidelberg (2016). https://doi.org/10.1007/978-3-662-53018-4_20

43. Kosba, A.E., et al.: Cøcø: A framework for building composable zero-knowledge proofs (2016). https://api.semanticscholar.org/CorpusID:17760053

44. Méloni, N.: An alternative approach to polynomial modular number system internal reduction. IEEE Trans. Emerg. Top. Comput. (2022). https://doi.org/10.1109/TETC.2022.3190368

45. Merkle, J., Lochter, M.: Elliptic Curve Cryptography (ECC) Brainpool Standard Curves and Curve Generation. RFC 5639 (2010). https://doi.org/10.17487/RFC5639. https://www.rfc-editor.org/info/rfc5639

46. Montgomery, P.: Modular multiplication without trial division. Math. Comput. **44**(170), 519–521 (1985). https://doi.org/10.1090/S0025-5718-1985-0777282-X

47. Negre, C., Plantard, T.: Efficient modular arithmetic in adapted modular number system using lagrange representation. In: Mu, Y., Susilo, W., Seberry, J. (eds.) ACISP 2008. LNCS, vol. 5107, pp. 463–477. Springer, Heidelberg (2008). https://doi.org/10.1007/978-3-540-70500-0_34

48. NIST: The elliptic curve digital signature algorithm validation system. https://csrc.nist.gov/presentations/2004/the-elliptic-curve-digital-signature-algorithm-val

49. NIST: Digital signature standard (dss), nist fips 186-4 (2009). http://nvlpubs.nist.gov/nistpubs/FIPS/NIST.FIPS.186-4.pdf

50. Noyez, L., El Mrabet, N., Potin, O., Véron, P.: Modular multiplication in the AMNS representation: hardware Implementation. In: Selected Areas in Cryptography, Montréal (Québec), France (2024)

51. Sakemi, Y., Kobayashi, T., Saito, T., Wahby, R.S.: Pairing-Friendly Curves. Internet-Draft draft-irtf-cfrg-pairing-friendly-curves-11, Internet Engineering Task Force (2022). https://datatracker.ietf.org/doc/draft-irtf-cfrg-pairing-friendly-curves/11/

52. Schütze, T.: Requirements for standard elliptic curves position paper of the ecc brainpool (2014). https://api.semanticscholar.org/CorpusID:16091050

53. Solinas, J.A.: Pseudo-Mersenne Prime, pp. 992–992. Springer US, Boston (2011). https://doi.org/10.1007/978-1-4419-5906-5_42

54. Stein, W., al.: Sagemath (2005). http://www.sagemath.org/. Accessed 07 July 2022

55. Zcash: Rust implementation of the jubjub elliptic curve group. https://github.com/zkcrypto/jubjub/tree/main

56. Zcash: Zcash documentation. https://zcash.readthedocs.io/en/latest/

57. ZcashTeam: Zk snark in zcash. https://z.cash

Constant-Time Integer Arithmetic for SQIsign

Fatna Kouider[1]([⊠])(iD), Anisha Mukherjee[2](iD), David Jacquemin[2](iD), and Péter Kutas[1,3](iD)

[1] Eötvös Loránd University, Budapest, Hungary
fatnakouider@inf.elte.hu
[2] ISEC, Graz University of Technology, Graz, Austria
[3] University of Birmingham, Birmingham, UK

Abstract. SQIsign, the only isogeny-based signature scheme submitted to NIST's additional signature standardization call, achieves the smallest public key and signature sizes among all post-quantum signature schemes. However, its existing implementation, particularly in its quaternion arithmetic operations, relies on GMP's big integer functions, which, while efficient, are often not designed for constant-time execution.

In this work, we take a step toward side-channel-protected SQIsign by implementing constant-time techniques for SQIsign's big integer arithmetic, which forms the computational backbone of its quaternion module. For low-level fundamental functions including Euclidean division, exponentiation and the function that computes integer square root, we either extend or tailor existing solutions according to SQIsign's requirements such as handling signed integers or scaling them for integers up to ~12,000 bits. Further, we propose a novel constant-time modular reduction technique designed to handle dynamically changing moduli.

Our implementation is written in C without reliance on high-level libraries such as GMP and we evaluate the constant-time properties of our implementation using Timecop with Valgrind that confirm the absence of timing-dependent execution paths. We provide experimental benchmarks across various SQIsign parameter sizes to demonstrate the performance of our constant-time implementation.

Keywords: SQIsign · big integer arithmetic · constant-time implementation

1 Introduction

Post-quantum cryptography has gained significant attention due to the imminent threats posed by quantum computers to widely deployed public-key cryptographic systems. Many classical cryptographic schemes, including RSA and those based on ECC, rely on the hardness of problems such as integer factorization and the discrete logarithm problem, which can be efficiently solved using Shor's algorithm [20, 21] on a sufficiently large quantum computer. As a result, research

A. Nitaj et al. (Eds.): AFRICACRYPT 2025, LNCS 15651, pp. 192–215, 2026.
https://doi.org/10.1007/978-3-031-97260-7_10

in post-quantum cryptography (PQC) has explored alternative mathematical hard problems that remain secure against quantum attacks. Lattice-based, code-based, multivariate, hash-based, and isogeny-based cryptography have emerged as strong candidates in this domain, each offering unique trade-offs between security, efficiency, and key/signature sizes. Among these, isogeny-based digital signatures have attracted considerable interest due to its compact key sizes and reliance on the hardness of problems related to supersingular isogeny graphs.

SQIsign [1,6] is the only isogeny-based signature scheme submitted to the National Institute of Standards and Technology (NIST) "additional signatures" call [18], a standardization initiative for post-quantum digital signatures based on mathematical hardness assumptions beyond lattice-based cryptography. It is a promising candidate that provides the smallest public key and signature sizes among all known post-quantum signature schemes, signatures as small as just 148 bytes and public keys as small as 65 bytes for NIST-I security, making it particularly attractive for applications with stringent bandwidth or storage constraints.

To ensure a thorough and comprehensive evaluation of the submitted schemes beyond their theoretical security, NIST encourages submissions to also consider side-channel resistance and implement constant-time techniques to avoid potential timing attacks. While SQIsign [1,6] offers strong theoretical security guarantees, it lacks a fully constant-time implementation of its signing procedure.

Motivation for this Work: SQIsign relies on a complex framework that interpolates between supersingular elliptic curve arithmetic and its quaternion algebraic counterpart, facilitated by the Deuring correspondence. Efficient constant-time implementations for elliptic curve arithmetic have been widely explored in the literature, most recently in the context of SIKE [12], where extensive research has led to well-optimized and side-channel-resistant algorithms. However, the quaternion arithmetic involved in SQIsign is largely unexplored, as many of its computational techniques and algorithms are relatively novel and have not been extensively applied to other cryptographic constructions. This leaves significant room for further exploration, particularly in developing constant-time and efficient implementations of quaternion-based operations. Specifically, the most recent scheme specifications [1] submitted to Round-2 of the NIST call mentions that their current implementation, apart from elliptic curve and isogeny-based arithmetic, does not run in constant-time [1, Footnote-1, page-4]. Recently, [10,11] have proposed constant-time or time-independent alternatives for a selected few algorithms such as lattice reduction and GCD.

In this work, we take a step closer toward side-channel-protected implementations by introducing constant-time techniques, which form the foundation for secure cryptographic executions. The current implementation of SQIsign's quaternion arithmetic, encompassing all high-level algorithms within the quaternion module, relies on big integer arithmetic that is not inherently constant-time. To address this, we investigate the big integer functions for the source of non-constant time issues within them. We solve these issues one-by-one for all these functions within SQIsign's big integer arithmetic, as this constitutes the most fundamental computational layer upon which the higher-level quaternion arithmetic operations are built. Moreover, the big integer arithmetic in SQIsign presents unique challenges due to its specialized nature, requiring careful handling of operations such as modular reduction, multiplication, and exponentiation to ensure efficiency and side-channel resilience without compromising correctness.

1.1   Our Contributions

In this work, we present constant-time techniques for all the different integer arithmetic functions required in SQIsign, addressing several unique challenges posed by its parameter set, arithmetic structure, and lack of prior constant-time implementations. While constant-time multi-precision integer arithmetic libraries do exist in literature, SQIsign introduces specific challenges that necessitate new approaches.

Scalability to Large Integer Sizes: SQIsign requires handling integers of variable sizes, sometimes as large as $\sim 12,000$ bits due to the use of Hermite Normal Form (HNF) to perform operations with quaternion lattices. This scale raises questions about the efficiency and feasibility of existing constant-time big-integer implementations. We implement and analyze how available constant-time multi-precision arithmetic techniques scale up to such high parameters.

Handling Signed Integer Arithmetic: Many exiting cryptographic schemes such as SIKE [12], offer constant-time arithmetic techniques for several functions, but over modular arithmetic domains. SQIsign, on the other hand, operates on integer arithmetic, including signed integer representations, which introduces additional challenges. Our implementation extends constant-time techniques to handle signed integers efficiently while avoiding leakage from sign-dependent operations.

Constant-Time Implementations for Previously Under-explored Functions: Some integer functions (such as computing the nearest integer square root of a number, GCD or Euclidean division) are either very specific to SQIsign or rarely require constant-time solutions when used by other cryptographic primitives. To address such cases, we either develop constant-time versions of these functions tailored to SQIsign's specific requirements (e.g., for Euclidean division) or adapt the available constant-time solutions according to SQIsign (e.g., for GCD computation and integer square root function).

Modular Reduction with Dynamic Moduli: Unlike many cryptographic primitives that operate over a fixed modulus, for which efficient modular reduction techniques like Montgomery or Barrett reduction are well-optimized, SQIsign presents a unique challenge. During quaternion arithmetic, SQIsign involves ephemeral moduli that change dynamically throughout the signing procedure.

These moduli are not only variable but often random, making conventional optimizations ineffective. We develop a custom modular reduction technique that accounts for these changing moduli while maintaining constant-time guarantees.

Implementation and Benchmarks: The current SQIsign implementation heavily relies on GMP [9] functions, which, while efficient, do not guarantee constant-time execution. We provide a C implementation of the constant-time versions for the integer arithmetic functions required in SQIsign by completely eliminating such dependencies on high-level libraries. Furthermore, we conduct performance benchmarks across various SQIsign parameter sizes, including the largest configurations. To verify the constant-time nature of our implementation, we utilize Timecop with Valgrind, a tool which detects time-dependent branching and other execution variations. Additionally, we visually demonstrate the run-time behavior by plotting the average and median execution times (in CPU cycles) for the function implementations.

2   Background

In this section, we begin with a brief overview of SQIsign, followed by an analysis of the important integer functions, highlighting the non-constant time operations within them. Additionally, we discuss constant-time alternatives for some of these functions that are already available in the literature.

2.1   Notations

In this paper, we adopt the following notations for bitwise operations. Bitwise AND, OR and XOR operations are denoted by 'and', 'or' and 'xor', respectively. The operation of bitwise NOT is indicated using the overline notation, that is, $\bar{a}$ denotes the bitwise negation (complement) of a. Multiplication of two elements a and b is represented by $\cdot$, that is, $a \cdot b$. The expression $a \cdot (64)$ specifically represents the multiplication of a by $2^{64} - 1$. In this context, if $a = 1$, the result is a 64-bit value in which all bits are set to 1. Bitwise left and right shift operations of a by s positions are denoted by $a \ll s$ and $a \gg s$ respectively. The notation, '$==$' is used to compare the equality of two values.

We define the representation $\mathcal{D}(a)$ for a k-bit signed integer a as the following: $a = (a_{\text{sign}}, [a_{n-1}, a_{n-2}, \cdots, a_0])$, where a_{sign} is a bit value representing the sign of a and each a_i is a 64-bit word. The large integer a is a k-bit value, where the number of words satisfies $n \geq \lceil \frac{k}{64} \rceil$, and n is a fixed upper bound on the array size used for representing integers, we enforce $a_i = 0, \forall i \geq \lceil \frac{k}{64} \rceil$.

2.2   Supersingular Elliptic Curves, Isogenies and Quaternion Algebras

An isogeny between two elliptic curves is a rational map which is simultaneously a group homomorphism. The degree of the isogeny is its degree as a rational map, i.e., the degree of the field extension it induces between the function fields of the two curves. Isogenies from an elliptic curve E to itself are called endomorphisms. Endomorphisms together with the zero map form a ring under addition and composition called the endomorphism ring of the elliptic curve. Scalar multiplications are always endomorphisms thus $\mathbb{Z} \subseteq End(E)$. When elliptic curves are defined over finite fields then their endomorphism ring is always strictly larger than $\mathbb{Z}$. If $End(E)$ is commutative then E is called ordinary, otherwise it is called supersingular. In this paper we are always concerned with supersingular elliptic curves.

One can make a much more precise statement about the structure of the endomorphism ring of a supersingular elliptic curve. A quaternion algebra [22] is a central simple algebra of degree 2 over a field K. If $char(K) \neq 2$ then it is a four dimensional vector space over K with a basis $1, i, j, ij$ with the following properties: $i^2 = a, j^2 = b, ij = -ji$ where $a, b \in K^*$. One can thus write this quaternion algebra as $(a, b)_K$. A quaternion algebra is either isomorphic to $M_2(K)$ or is a division algebra (i.e., an algebra where every nonzero element has an inverse). In the context of supersingular elliptic curves the relevant quaternion is defined over $K = \mathbb{Q}$. Rational quaternion algebras can be classified by their local behavior,i.e., whether they are full matrix algebras or division algebras when you tensor them with a completion of $\mathbb{Q}$. This tensor product is almost always isomorphic to a full matrix algebra, except for finitely many cases which are places of ramification. Let p be the characteristic of the field of definition of the supersingular elliptic curve E. Then $B_{p,\infty}$ is the quaternion algebra ramified at p and infinity. When $p \equiv 3 \pmod 4$, then this simply means that $B_{p,\infty} \cong (-1, -p)_{\mathbb{Q}}$. A maximal order $\mathcal{O}$ in $B_{p,\infty}$ is a subring containing 1 which is a 4-dimensional lattice. The Deuring correspondence asserts that the endomorphism ring of a supersingular elliptic curve is a maximal order in $B_{p,\infty}$. An isogeny $E_1 \to E_2$ corresponds to a left ideal of $End(E_1)$ which is simultaneously a right ideal of $End(E_2)$. The norm of one-sided ideal is the greatest common divisor of the reduced norm of its elements and it corresponds to the degree of the corresponding isogeny.

2.3   The SQIsign Protocol

SQIsign's authentication mechanism is based on the following sigma protocol with the starting reference curve E_0, typically chosen as $y^2 = x^3 + x$. The secret isogeny is $\tau : E_0 \to E$ such that the supersingular elliptic curve E is the public key. The endomorphism rings of these curves, $\mathcal{O}_0 = \text{End}(E_0)$ and $\mathcal{O} = \text{End}(E)$, are linked through a hidden left ideal I_τ of large prime norm, corresponding to the secret isogeny τ. In the quaternion setting, the private key is represented by $\mathcal{O}$, the endomorphism ring of E.

– **Commitment:** The prover constructs an isogeny $\phi : E_0 \to E_1$ and sends the resulting curve E_1 to the verifier.
– **Challenge:** The verifier selects and sends a challenge isogeny $\psi : E_1 \to E_2$ to the prover.

– **Response:** The prover computes and returns an isogeny $\sigma : E \to E_2$ of degree l^e.

The verifier checks the validity of the response by ensuring that the isogeny correctly connects the expected curves and, when composed with the dual of the challenge isogeny, forms a cyclic structure. If these conditions hold, the response signature σ is accepted by the verifier as valid.

The interplay between isogenies and quaternions is fundamental to the SQIsign protocol and is evident throughout its execution. In particular, while the actual computations of the key generation and response phases in version-1 of the NIST submission [6, Algorithm 26] heavily rely on quaternion algebra arithmetic, such as those performed by the KLPT algorithm, the challenge phase predominantly involves elliptic curve arithmetic. The KLPT algorithm [6, Section 2.5.2] itself includes several key sub-routines such as the FullRepresentInteger [6, Algorithm 10], FullStrongApproximation [6, Algorithm 13] and EichlerModConstraint [6, Algorithm 11], all of which fundamentally rely on integer arithmetic including Euclidean division and GCD computations. The last step of the response however, invokes the IdealToIsogeny [6, Algorithm 18] algorithm which transitions from quaternion-based computations to explicit elliptic curve arithmetic. The most recent version submitted to round-2 of the NIST call [1] no longer uses the KLPT algorithm during the signing procedure [1, Algorithm 4.2]. However, the commitment and the response phases still include quaternion algorithms (such as a version of RepresentInteger) and hence require big integer arithmetic.

2.4   Big Integer Arithmetic in SQIsign

The elements of $B_{p,\infty}$ are represented as 5-tuples of integers $(a, b, c, d, r) \in \mathbb{Z}^5$, corresponding to the quaternion, $\alpha = \frac{a+bi+cj+dk}{r}$, with a canonical representation obtained via reducing by the common denominator r. This representation inherently requires efficient big integer arithmetic, as all operations on quaternions translate to computations involving large integers. Due to the variable sizes of these integers, a dynamic multi-precision integer library such as GMP is used in the reference implementation of SQIsign.

Such a library provides efficient implementations of these operations but they are not inherently designed to be constant-time as their execution times often depend on input values, conditional branching, or iterative computations. For example, such functions include basic arithmetic operations such as left or right shifts, addition, subtraction, multiplication, and division, all of which are essential for handling large integer representations of quaternions. Computing integer square roots, both approximate and exact, is another key requirement. Traditional algorithms, such as Newton's method or the binary search approach, involve iterative refinements that depend on the magnitude of the input, leading to variations in execution time. An important computational algorithm is the greatest common divisor (GCD) algorithm, which finds an integer g such that

$g = \text{GCD}(a, b)$ This classical Euclidean algorithm involves division and remainder operations whose iteration count depends on the values of the input numbers, leading to data-dependent execution times. Modular arithmetic, including modular reduction and exponentiation, is another fundamental operation. Techniques such as Montgomery [16] or Barrett [2] reduction algorithms which are commonly used to optimize modular reduction are most effective when the modulus remains fixed across multiple computations. However, in SQIsign, modular arithmetic within the quaternion algebra involves dynamically changing moduli rather than a single, fixed modulus and as a result, the pre-computation advantages that make Montgomery and Barrett reduction efficient in conventional settings do not directly apply to SQIsign. This makes it more challenging to design constant-time implementations, as optimizations that rely on fixed modular parameters cannot be utilized effectively. Another aspect of integer arithmetic in SQIsign is the representation and manipulation of lattices in the quaternion algebra $B_{p,\infty}$. Lattices in this algebra are defined by a basis $(\alpha_1, \alpha_2, \alpha_3, \alpha_4)$ of $\mathbb{Q}$-linearly independent quaternions, typically represented as columns of a matrix L, with the row vector description given by: $(\alpha_1 \; \alpha_2 \; \alpha_3 \; \alpha_4) = (1 \; i \; j \; k) \cdot L$ [6, Section 2.4.4.1]. For consistency and efficiency in representation, SQIsign enforces a canonical form for lattices by computing their Hermite Normal Form (HNF). The HNF of a lattice basis ensures uniqueness up to unimodular transformations. This normalization facilitates efficient comparison and manipulation of lattices within SQIsign. However, the conversion of a lattice basis to HNF leads to a significant increase in integer sizes. Since HNF enforces integer coefficients, any rational components arising from quaternion arithmetic must be cleared by multiplying through an appropriate denominator. This process can lead to very larger coefficients, resulting in a blow-up of integer sizes during operations. The increased bit-length of integers also increases the computational complexity of fundamental arithmetic operations. Many of the integer operations discussed earlier, such as GCD or Euclidean division are heavily involved in computing the HNF. Since these operations inherently depend on input values, the computation of HNF is not constant-time in standard implementations. The integer size explosion also affects performance, as the growth of coefficients increases the cost of subsequent reductions and multiplications.

2.5   Existing Constant-Time Alternatives for Integer Functions

The work by [3] proposes a constant-time GCD algorithm in which the iterations within the GCD algorithm no longer depend on the inputs but on auxiliary parameters. The algorithm depends on a function called the Divstep that takes a parameter δ as an input, which is the actual constant-time element in the algorithm. In this GCD implementation, the auxiliary parameter δ depends on the maximum of the two input sizes, d, i.e., for two inputs f (odd) and g, $|f| < 2^d, |g| < 2^d$. The algorithm is constant-time if d is constant. It then calculates an integer m under a special function of d, iteration(d). This integer m serves as an upper bound of the number of iterations, [3, Theorem 11.2]. It ensures that whenever Divstep is executed m times with initial inputs (f, g), the sequence of intermediate values f_i and g_i are updated in a way such that, $f_n \to \pm \mathrm{GCD}(f,g)$ and, $g_n \to 0$. The algorithm uses iterative shifts and subtraction-based steps for all its sub-functions. We provide the pseudo-code of this algorithm in Algorithm 9 in the Appendix A.

In the context of SQIsign, we introduce an additional parameter r at the beginning of the Algorithm 9 to handle the cases where f is even and adjust it to be odd before computing d and calling Divstep. This allows for handling all integers inputs without affecting the core computation process. We implement the algorithm entirely using our constant-time variants of the basic operations such as addition, subtraction, left/right shifts.

Korzilius and Schoenmakers in [14] present a constant-time integer square root algorithm based on the Newton-Raphson method and fixed-point arithmetic. They use the secure fixed-point arithmetic model introduced by Catrina et al. in [4,5] with parameterized precision expressed in terms of the number of fractional bits f. For $\ell > f \geq 0$, the set $\mathbb{Q}_{\ell,f}$ of ℓ-bit fixed-point numbers with f fractional bits and $e = \ell - f$ bits for the integer part is defined as, $\mathbb{Q}_{\ell,f} = \{\bar{x} \cdot 2^{-f} : \bar{x} \in \mathbb{Z}, -2^{\ell-1} \leq \bar{x} < 2^{\ell-1}\}$, with all $x \in \mathbb{Q}_{\ell,f}$ represented used two's complement binary representation:

$$x = (d_{\ell-1}, \ldots, d_0, d_1, \ldots, d_{-f})_2 = -d_{\ell-1} \cdot 2^{\ell-1} + \sum_{i=-f}^{\ell-2} d_i \cdot 2^i, \text{with } d_i \in \{0,1\}.$$

Their approach begins by computing the Newton-Raphson based reciprocal square root $x \approx 1/\sqrt{a}$ for an input value a where $-2^{\ell-1} \leq 0 < a < 2^{\ell-1}$ as described in [14, Algorithm 5] with an error bound that does not exceed $\delta_f = 2^{-f}$. The required number of iterations θ is independent of the input value a; a will be scaled to $b = a \cdot v$ with $b \in [0.5, 2)$ and $v = 2^{2 \cdot m}$ before the Newton-Raphson iterations and scaled back by $v^{1/2}$ at the end. To increase the precision of this computation and improve the accuracy of the final result x, additional bits n can be added. The final result x of the reciprocal square root is subsequently used to compute an integer value q such that $q \leq \sqrt{a} < q + 1$ in the integer square root computation [14, Algorithm 7].

For the SQIsign implementation, we introduce a constant-time 64-bit precision based square root Algorithm 10 (Appendix A) to handle integers up to 2^{64}. From our experiments, we concluded that for larger integers of size $k > 2^{64}$, a precision of at least $\log_2(k)$ bits is required. However, further analysis is required to determine the exact precision requirement for handling large integers.

3   Constant-Time Big-Integer Arithmetic

The standard set of bit-wise operations including AND, OR, XOR, NOT, Left shift ($\ll$) and Right shift ($\gg$) is available in the C programming language and is constant-time for manipulating individual bits within a standard data type like int or uint64_t. Similarly, the traditional arithmetic operations (addition, subtraction, negation and multiplication) are also considered $\mathcal{O}(1)$ because they are single CPU instructions. Handling more than 64 bits integers is not supported.

The current SQIsign implementation [15] relies on GMP's multi-precision integer library for big-integer arithmetic involving integers of varying sizes. For realizing a constant-time quaternion module it is natural to first eliminate the GMP-dependency from all fundamental multi-precision integer arithmetic functions. We elaborate on constant-time solutions in this section.

For constant-time alternatives of basic low-level functions, we consult methods developed in SIKE [12] and propose tweaks to adapt them for SQIsign. Further, for the higher-level integer functions build on these fundamental operations, we either propose constant-time solutions ourselves or modify those which do not have a directly applicable constant-time solution in literature. For all the following descriptions and implementation, we use the representation $\mathcal{D}(a)$ for a signed k-bit integer a, that is, $a = (a_{\text{sign}}, a_{\text{abs}}) = (a_{\text{sign}}, [a_n, a_{n-1}, \cdots, a_0])$.

3.1   Low-Level Functions

In this section, we provide pseudo-codes Table 1 for constant-time algorithms of fundamental functions such as addition, subtraction, multiplication, negation, computing absolute value and exponentiation.

SIKE [12] provides constant-time arithmetic implementation for various functions over modular arithmetic domains with unsigned integers. Inspired by their unsigned version, we adapt Multiplication, conditional move ct-cmov, Negation and Absolute value for compatibility with signed integers by adding slight modifications based on bit-wise operation to handle the sign. For Addition and Subtraction, we use the two's complement representation to manage the signed integers. We implement a constant-time version of Exponentiation function based on the Montgomery powering ladder algorithm discussed in [13,17] using constant-time Addition, Multiplication and bit-wise operations.

Table 1. Constant-time versions of basic functions in the integer module. We denote b in $\mathcal{D}(b)$ representation and the resultant big integer by c which has a representation $\mathcal{D}(c)$. Addition and subtraction are computed with integers represented in two's complement, while multiplication is based on SIKE's implementation [7,12].

Functions	Pseudocode
Addition(a, b)	$c_i = a_i + b_i + \text{carry}_{i-1}$
Subtraction(a, b)	$c_i = a_i + (-b_i)$
Multiplication(a, b)	$c_i = a_i \cdot b_i, \quad c_{\text{sign}} = a_{\text{sign}} \text{ xor } b_{\text{sign}}$
Negation(a)	$c_{\text{sign}} = 1 \text{ xor } a_{\text{sign}}, \quad c_{\text{abs}} = a_{\text{abs}}$
Absolute value(a)	$c_{\text{sign}} = 0, \quad c_{\text{abs}} = a_{\text{abs}}$
Exponentiation(a)	Montgomery ladder [13,17]
ct-cmov(a)	$c_i = -1 \text{ and } (a_i \text{ xor } c_i), \quad c_{\text{sign}} = a_{\text{sign}}$

Computing the Bit-Size of Small Integers: The $\mathsf{nbits}_{64}(x)$ Algorithm 1 computes the bit-size of an unsigned integer $x < 2^{64}$ in constant-time. We initialize the bit-size n to 0. The algorithm then iterates 64 times performing the following operations: Step 3 increments n if $x > 0$, step 4 eliminate the least significant bit of x by shifting right by 1 bit preparing for the next iteration. This algorithm ensures a fixed number of iterations independent of the value of x. Moreover, each iteration involves simple bit-wise operations of addition and right shifts, thereby making it constant-time.

Algorithm 1. $\mathsf{nbits}_{64}(x)$

Require: $x \in \mathbb{Z}, |x| < 2^{64}$.
Ensure: n the bit-size of x.
1: Set $n = 0$.
2: **for** $i \in [0, 63]$ **do**
3:     $n = n + (x \text{ or } (0 - x)) \gg 63$.   ▷ Using a constant-time right shift, see
    Algorithm 4
4:     $x = x \gg 1$.
5: **end for**
6: **return** n

3.2   Computing the Bit-Size of Big Integers

We implement a constant-time Bitsize function Algorithm 2 that computes the bit-size of a big integer. The function is specifically designed to eliminate iterative and conditional branches that depends on the input value or its size to avoid execution time variations.

In particular, the function computes the bit-size of a big integer a represented using $\mathcal{D}(a)$ by iterating from the most significant word a_{n-1} downward to the least significant word a_0. Once a nonzero word is found, the computation stops updating the result k. However, this does not imply breaking out of the loop. Instead, the algorithm continues to iterate, but during these iterations, it adds zeros to k, ensuring that the result remains unchanged. The final output k is the position of the most significant bit in a which also represents the bit length of a. Regardless of the value of a, the Algorithm 2 executes a fixed number of iterations depending on the upper bound on the array size n and performs the same sequence of operations in each iteration.

Theorem 1. *The algorithm* Bitsize(a) *is correct and terminates in constant-time for a fixed upper bound of* n.

Proof. For a fixed upper bound on the array size of n, the algorithm is trivially constant-time as it is always executed in n iterations with constant-time operations.

Algorithm 2. Bitsize(a)

Require: $a \in \mathbb{Z}$ is a k-bit integer represented using $\mathcal{D}(a)$ with n some pre-fixed upper
   bound on the array size.
Ensure: k the bit-size of a.
 1: Set $k = 0$
 2: **for** $i \in [n-1, 0]$ **do**
 3:     $s = \mathsf{nbits}_{64}(a_i)$
 4:     $r = 1 \text{ xor } (k > 0)$.
 5:     $t = r \cdot (64) \text{ and } s$
 6:     $m = (t > 0) \text{ and } (r > 0)$
 7:     $k = k + t + 64 \cdot i \cdot m$
 8: **end for**
 9: **return** k

Now we prove correctness. Let a be a k-bit integer represented as $\mathcal{D}(a)$.
Consider the index, $j = \lfloor \frac{k}{64} \rfloor$ which gives us the relation, $k = k \pmod{64} + j \cdot 64$.
Within the *for* loop in Step 2, Algorithm 2, we scan through all the a_i's for
comparing index i with j starting from $i = n - 1$ to 0 using Algorithm 1. Let,
$s_i = \mathsf{nbit64}(a_i)$.

There are three possibilities for s_i in Algorithm 1: if $i > j$, then $s_i = \mathsf{nbit64}(a_i) = 0$. If $i = j$, then $s_i = k \pmod{64}$ and we can then compute
$k = \mathsf{nbit64}(a_i) + j \cdot 64$ to get the correct bit-size of a. Lastly, if $i < j$, $\mathsf{nbit64}(a_i)$
is not useful and needs to be discarded. This process of segregating the required
output as per to the three conditions given above is carried out using three
variables r, t and m that take values (for every iteration i) according to the
definitions of the following three functions:

$$f : \mathbb{N} \to \{0, 1\} \text{ such that, } k \mapsto \begin{cases} r = 1, & \text{if, } k = 0 \\ r = 0 & \text{if, } k > 0 \end{cases}$$

$$g : \mathbb{N}^2 \to \mathbb{N} \text{ such that, } (r, s) \mapsto \begin{cases} t = s, & \text{if, } r = 1 \\ t = 0, & \text{otherwise} \end{cases}$$

$$h : \mathbb{N}^2 \to \{0, 1\} \text{ such that, } (k, t) \mapsto \begin{cases} m = 1, & \text{if, } k = 0 \text{ AND } t \neq 0 \\ m = 0, & \text{otherwise} \end{cases}$$

The constant-time expressions corresponding to the functions f, g and h are
given in Steps 4–6 of the algorithm respectively.

Set $k = 0$; in Step 7, for all $i > j$, $s_i = 0$, $r_i = f(k_{i-1}) = 1$, $t_i = g(r_i, s_i) = 0$
and $m_i = h(k_{i-1}, t_i) = 0$, and thus, $k_i = k_{i-1} + t_i + 64 \cdot i \cdot m_i = k_{i-1} + g(r_i, s_i) + h(k_{i-1}, t_i) \cdot 64 \cdot i = k_{i-1} + 0 + 0 \cdot 64 \cdot i = 0$.

When $i = j$, $s_i \neq 0$ while $k_{i-1} = 0$, so, $r_i = 1$, $t_i = g(r_i, s_i) = s_i$ and
$m_i = h(k_{i-1}, t_i) = 1$. Hence, $k_i = k_{i-1} + t_i + 64 \cdot i \cdot m_i = 0 + s_i + 64 \cdot j \cdot 1 = k$,
which is the required correct output.

Finally, when $i < j$, $k_{i-1} \neq 0$, thus, $r_i = f(k_{i-1}) = 0$, $t_i = g(r_i, s_i) = 0$ and
$m_i = h(k_{i-1}, t_i) = 0$. So, $k_i = k_{i-1} + t_i + 64 \cdot i \cdot m_i = k + 0 + 64 \cdot j \cdot 0 = k$. This
means that once $i < j$, the value of k_i is not updated anymore in the remaining
iterations. The output of this algorithm is therefore, $s_j + 64 \cdot j = k$.

3.3   Left and Right Shift Functions for Big Integers

As mentioned in Sect. 3, the standard set of bit-wise operations including Left/Right shift is available in the C programming language and are constant-time. However, shifts of more than 64 bits are not supported.

A left shift can be seen as a special case of multiplication. Shifting a number to the left by s bits is equivalent to multiplying it by 2^s. For example, $11_2 \ll 3 = 11000_2$ is equivalent to $3_{10} \cdot 2^3 = 24_{10}$. On the other hand, a right shift is a special form of division. Shifting a number to the right by s bits is the same as dividing it by 2^s. For example $11000_2 \gg 2 = 110_2$ is equivalent to $\frac{24_{10}}{2^2} = 6_{10}$, where the numbers in the subscript are the base of the representation.

While the basis of our proposed left/right shift algorithms are inspired from SIKE [12], we have modified them to remove some data dependencies which were present in the original constructions. These dependencies appeared because the input of the shift value s was also treated as a secret. We have redesigned the left shift operation (see Algorithm 3) to be constant-time w.r.t s as well. Additionally, we propose a constant-time right shift algorithm (Algorithm 4) similar to the constant-time left shift algorithm.

Algorithm 3. Left_Shift(a, s)

Require: $a, s \in \mathbb{Z}$, with a an k-bit integer represented using $\mathcal{D}(a)$ and $\mathsf{Bitsize}(\mathcal{D}(a)) \leq n \cdot 64$, $s < n \cdot 64$ with n some upper bound on the array size.
Ensure: $a = (a \cdot 2^s)$
1: $r = s \bmod 64$
2: $j = s \gg 6$
3: Set $l = 1$
4: **for** $i \in [n-1, 0)$ **do**
5:    $a_i = l \cdot a_i$
6:    $j = l \cdot j$
7:    $l = l$ and $(i > j)$
8:    $a_i = (a_{i-j} \ll r)$ xor $((a_{i-j-1} \cdot l) \gg (64 - r))$
9: **end for**
10: $a_0 = (a_0 \ll r) \cdot l$
11: **return** b

Theorem 2. *The algorithm* Left_Shift(a, s) *is correct and terminates in constant-time for fixed upper bounds of n and s.*

Proof. Let a be a k-bit integer represented using $\mathcal{D}(a)$ representation. For a fixed upper bound on the array size n and a shift value $s < n \cdot 64$, the algorithm performs $n - 1$ iterations, each involving constant-time operations, thus the overall execution time of the Algorithm 3 is constant-time regardless of the values of a and s.

Now we prove correctness. The goal of the algorithm is to compute the result of left shift of a by s, i.e., $a = a \cdot 2^s$. However, since the result is stored within the n-word array representation using $\mathcal{D}(a)$, the result is taken module $2^{64 \cdot n}$.

This can be expressed as: $a = (a \cdot 2^s) \pmod{2^{64 \cdot n}}$. Let, j, r be the quotient and remainder of s by 64, $s = r + 64 \cdot j$ with $r = s \pmod{64}$ and $j = s \gg 6$. The variable r handles shifts within a single 64-bit block, while j represents the number of 64-bit blocks that is modified by the shift s.

The *for* loop scans through all words of a, updating them according to their relative positions with respect to j. For each iteration i of the loop, we define l as an indicator variable, which determines whether the index i is within the shifted range or not. Then the transformation is applied to a_i using the shift logic in step 8.

In step 8, the left shift is performed by taking the relevant bits from a_{i-j} (shifted left by r positions) and the carry bits from a_{i-j-1}(shifted right by $64 - r$ positions). These two sets of bits will then be combined using a bit-wise xor operation to form the final result. This ensures that the shifted value and the carry bits are properly integrated. Furthermore, each bit that was originally at position x in a will be moved to position $x + s$ in the final result.

- If $(s = 64 \cdot j)$, then $(r = 0)$ and there is no within-block shift, thus, $a_i = a_{i-j}$ in the shifted range $i \in [n - 1, j]$ and a_i set to 0 outside this range.
- If $(s = 64 \cdot j + r), (r \neq 0)$, Step 8 correctly handles the shift operation and properly manages the carry bit from a_{i-j-1} within the shifted range, while a_i is set to 0 outside this range. The correctness condition depends on the following three cases of the relationship between i and j:

1. $i > j$ (case that handles most significant words beyond the shifted range): When $i > j$ we set $l = 1$, thus, $a_i = a_i$. The step 8 correctly shifts the bits left by s within this range, $i \in \{n - 1, \ldots, j + 1, j\}$, the step also manages the carry-over from the lower word. The updated words are, $a_i = (a_{i-j} \ll r)$ xor $((a_{i-j-1}) \gg (64 - r))$.
2. $i = j$ (case that handles the particular word a_i where the shift transitions occur): When $i = j$, we still have $l = 1$ from previous iterations, therefore $a_i = a_i$ and $j = j$. Now l will be set to 0 because $i = j$ and then Step 8 will perform a left shift operation. The updated word is given as, $a_i = (a_0 \ll r)$ xor 0.
3. $i < j, i \neq 0$ (case that handles least significant words that should be zeroed): When $i < j$, all bits in a_i must be discarded, so we enforce $a_i = 0$ using the indicator variable l, $a_i = l \cdot a_i = 0$ and $j = 0$, all updates to a_i become zero in this range $i \in [j-1, 0)$. The updated words are, $a_i = (a_i \ll r)$ xor $((a_{i-1} \cdot 0) \gg (64 - r))$.

Then for the first element a_0, when $i = 0$, we perform a left shift by r only if $s < 64$ represented by the equation, $a_0 = (a_0 \ll r) \cdot l$.

Theorem 3. *The algorithm* Right_Shift(a, s) *is correct and terminates in constant-time for fixed upper bounds of n and s.*

Proof. The proof of constant-time exactly follows the Proof 3.3 of Theorem 2. Again, the proof for correctness closely follows Proof 3.3 with suitable changes in steps 4, 7, 8 and 10.

Algorithm 4. Right_Shift(a, s)

Require: $a, s \in \mathbb{Z}$, a is k-bit integer represented using $\mathcal{D}(a)$ and Bitsize$(\mathcal{D}(a)) \leq n \cdot 64$, $s < n \cdot 64$ and n an upper bound on $\mathcal{D}(a)$'s array size.

Ensure: $a = \lfloor a \cdot 2^{-s} \rfloor$

1: $r = s \bmod 64$
2: $j = s \gg 6$
3: Set $l = 1$
4: **for** $i \in [0, n-1)$ **do**
5:      $j = j \cdot l$
6:      $a_i = a_i \cdot l$
7:      $l = l$ and $((i + j + 1) < n)$.
8:      $a_i = (a_{i+j} \gg r)$ xor $((a_{i+j+1} \cdot l) \ll (64 - r))$
9: **end for**
10: $a_{n-1} = (a_{n-1} \gg r) \cdot l$
11: **return** a

3.4 Constant-Time Euclidean Division

The work in [11] introduces a constant-time half-GCD algorithm. It employs the same technique as in [3], adapting it to the Euclidean algorithm. Specifically, the algorithm also uses two sequences, with one that converges to the required output and the other to zero, as explained in Sect. 2.5, ensuring both correctness and constant-time.

In our work, we build upon this concept with certain modifications to perform Euclidean division Algorithm 5 instead of half-GCD. By adjusting the stopping condition, we terminate the algorithm earlier while preserving the constant-time property.

Algorithm 5. Euclidean_division(a, b)

Require: $a, b \in \mathbb{Z}$

Ensure: $q, r \in \mathbb{Z}$ such as $a = b \cdot q + r$ with $0 \leq r < b$.

1: $m = a$
2: $q = 0$
3: $n = 2 \cdot ($Bitsize$(a) - $Bitsize$(b)) + 1$
4: **for** $i \in [0, n-1]$ **do**
5:      $s = b - m$
6:      sign $= (s_{sign}$ and $(b == m))$
7:      $u = b \cdot sign$.
8:      $\alpha = $ Bitsize$(m) - $Bitsize$(u) - 1$, or 0.
9:      $m = m - u \ll \alpha$ $\triangleright$ Using a constant-time left shift algorithm, see Alg. 3
10:      $q = q + sign \ll \alpha$
11: **end for**
12: Set $r = m$
13: **return** q, r

Theorem 4. *The algorithm* Euclidean_division(a, b) *is correct and terminates in constant-time for a fixed upper bound of n.*

Proof. Let a and b be atmost k-bit integers represented using $\mathcal{D}(a)$ and $\mathcal{D}(b)$. For a fixed upper bound on the array size n, the algorithm operates in exactly n iterations, each consisting of constant-time operations, making its execution constant-time.

Now we prove correctness. This division algorithm is derived from the constant-time half-GCD for Cornacchia's algorithm presented in [11]. Its correctness is closely related to that of the constant-time half-GCD algorithm. By modifying step 5, where the control variable is changed from $l = \sqrt{a}$ in [11] to b, we alter the point at which the algorithm stagnates. Consequently, the termination condition is adjusted to $m < b$. Since our algorithm follows the structure of the Euclidean algorithm, it produces $m = a \mod b$, where $m \in [0, b - 1]$.

As our algorithm follows the Euclidean algorithm, keeping a track of the number of times a is subtracted from b gives the quotient q of the Euclidean division. This is done in Step 10, by adding the left-shifted value of the variable 'sign' by α.

3.5   Constant-Time Modular Reduction for Varying Moduli

In most applications, the algorithms that are used for modular reduction are either the Barrett reduction or the Montgomery modular reduction. These techniques are particularly efficient when modular arithmetic is performed within a fixed prime field, as they allow certain constants derived from the modulus to be precomputed, significantly reducing the cost of division operations. For example, Barrett reduction approximates division by precomputing an estimate of the reciprocal of the modulus b. Specifically, for a fixed modulus b, one precomputes: $\mu = \left\lfloor \frac{2^{2k}}{b} \right\rfloor$, where k is chosen such that $2^k > b$. This method is efficient because it replaces costly division operations with multiplication and bit-shifting. However, it is only practical when b is fixed so that μ can be precomputed once and reused. Similarly, Montgomery reduction avoids explicit division by transforming numbers into a special representation known as the Montgomery domain, where modular multiplication is performed efficiently. The core idea is to precompute a constant Montgomery factor, $R = 2^k$, where k is chosen such that $R > b$. Additionally, the modular inverse of b with respect to R and the modular inverse of R with respect to b are also pre-computed and reused over multiple operations. This approach is particularly beneficial for modular exponentiation, as multiplication in the Montgomery domain avoids costly modular division. However that is not valid in SQIsign, specially for quaternion arithmetic which requires modular reduction of $a \mod b$, with both a and b as large integer variable inputs. One approach is to use a constant-time version of the Euclidean Algorithm (see Algorithm 5). We also propose a constant-time modular reduction for varying moduli, as given in Algorithm 6 based on table access, which would make it hardware friendlier.

Theorem 5. *The algorithm* Reduction(a, p) *is correct and terminates in constant-time for a fixed upper bound of k on the bit-size of the input a.*

Algorithm 6. Reduction(a, p)

Require: A k-bit integer a, an n-bit prime p, with $k > n$
Ensure: $b = a \pmod{p}$
1: Select a small integer r
2: Create the table T such that $T : s \in [0, 2^r - 1] \to s \cdot 2^n \mod p$
3: Set $b = a$
4: **for** $i \in [1, (k - n)/r + 1]$ **do**
5:      Set b_H as the r-MSB of b ▷ Can be done using Bitsize on b followed by a right shift operation.
6:      $c = b_H \cdot 2^{k-r \cdot i}$
7:      Generate $d = T[b_H] \cdot 2^{n-r \cdot i}$.   ▷ Using the table Algorithm 7
8:      $b = b - c + d \cdot 2^{n-r \cdot i}$ ▷ Reduction by $r - 1$-bit
9: **end for**
10: $b = \text{finalstep}(b, p, r)$ ▷ Done using a iterative subtraction Algorithm 8.
11: **return** b

Proof. Let a be a k-bit integer represented using $\mathcal{D}(a)$ and p be an n-bit prime. For a fixed value of r, k and n, the algorithm operates in exactly $(k - n)/r + 1$ iterations, with each iteration consisting of constant-time sub-operations such as constant-time addition, subtraction and shifts. Since the number of iterations is bounded for a fixed k, n and r, the overall execution steps remain constant relative to input variations within the bound.

Now, we prove correctness. Let, $l = (k - n)/r + 1$ and let $i \in \{1, 2, \ldots, l\}$. We define b_H as the most significant r bits of b and b_l the remaining bits of b, such that, $b = b_H \cdot 2^{k-n \cdot i}$. We set d as $T[b_H] \cdot 2^{n-r \cdot i}$. We prove that step 8 ensures that the remaining bits are correctly updated while reducing b by $(r - 1)$-bits modulo p. Suppose, $D = d \cdot 2^{k-n-r \cdot i}$ and $C = b_H \cdot 2^{k-r \cdot i} \pmod{p}$. Now, consider the following equation:

$$
\begin{aligned}
D - C \pmod{p} &= T[b_H] \cdot 2^{k-n-r \cdot i} - b_H \cdot 2^n \cdot 2^{k-n-r \cdot i} \\
&= (b_H \cdot 2^n \pmod{p} - b_H \cdot 2^n) \cdot 2^{k-n-r \cdot i} \pmod{p} \\
&= 0 \pmod{p}
\end{aligned}
$$

Subtracting by $C = b_H \cdot 2^{k-r \cdot i}$ refers to removing the r most significant bit of b, while adding $D = d \cdot 2^{k-n-r \cdot i}$ is used as a correction terms to ensure that the result is correctly reduced. This implies that the update maintains the correct modular equivalence at each step. The size of $(b - b_H \cdot 2^{k-r \cdot i})$ is $(k - r \cdot i)$-bit. However, $d \cdot 2^{k-n-r \cdot i}$ is also $(k - r \cdot i)$-bit. As a result, the addition of both is $(k - r \cdot i + 1)$-bit. Hence, the *for* loop in steps 4–9 updates b_i by b_{i+1} which are have the same value modulo p, but b_{i+1} is $(r-1)$-bit smaller than b_i. This means that after l iterations, the updated value of b_l is either the correct reduction of $a \pmod{p}$ or it is still a partial reduction of size at most $(n + r)$-bits.

Thus, the last step in 10 involves computing a conditional constant-time subtraction of b_l by p until $0 \le b < p$. This guarantees that the final result b is the correct reduction of a modulo p. The proof of the table generation Table_reduction and Final_Step is discussed later.

Remark 1. The proposed reduction method would be better suited for hardware implementations than for software ones. As shown in Table 2, its performance in software is slower compared to the Euclidean division method, which also performs a modular reduction.

Algorithm 7. Table_reduction(a, p)

Require: p and n-bit prime and $r > 1$ a small integer.
Ensure: A table T with $\forall i, T[i] = (i \cdot 2^n) \mod p$
1: Set $T[0] = 0$
2: Set $T[1] = 2^n - p$
3: $m = 2^r - 1$
4: **for** $i \in [2, m]$ **do**
5:      $a = i \cdot 2^n - i \cdot p$
6:      **for** $j \in [0, i]$ **do**
7:          $t = a - p$
8:          $s = t_{sign}$ ▷ Test to see if subtraction creates a negative integer
9:          $a = a - \bar{s} \cdot p$ ▷ Constant-time conditional subtraction
10:      **end for**
11:      $T[i] = a$
12: **end for**
13: **return** T

Theorem 6. *The algorithm* Table_reduction(a, p) *is correct and terminates in constant-time for a fixed r.*

Proof. For a fixed r, the algorithm operates in exactly $(2^r - 1) \cdot 2^{r-1}$ iterations, with each iteration consisting of constant-time sub-operations such as constant-time subtraction and shifts. Thus, it is naturally constant-time.

Now we prove by induction that $T[i]$ correctly stores intermediate modular values. $T[0] = 0$ and $T[1] = 2^n - p$ are initialized correctly. Suppose $T[i]$ is correct for all $i < m$. For $i = m$:

-   Compute $a = i \cdot 2^n - i \cdot p$.
-   Iteratively subtract p using a conditional subtraction until $a < p$, ensuring $T[i] = (i \cdot 2^n) \pmod p$.
-   Since $2^n > p$, this implies, $i \cdot 2^n - 2 \cdot i \cdot p < 0 \leq T[i] < i \cdot 2^n - i \cdot p$, and hence the computed value is valid.

Thus, the table is correctly generated.

Corollary 1. *The algorithm* Final_step(a, p) *is correct and terminates in constant-time for a fixed upper bound of r.*

Proof. The arguments for constant-time and correctness directly follow the proof of Theorem 6.

Algorithm 8. Final_step(a, p)

Require: An $n + r$-bit integer a, an n-bit prime p and a small integer r
Ensure: $b = a \pmod p$
 1: $m = 2^r - 1$
 2: **for** $i \in [0, m]$ **do**
 3:    $t = a - p$
 4:    $s = \overline{t_{sign}}$
 5:    $a = a - s \cdot p$
 6: **end for**
 7: Set $b = a$
 8: **return** b

4 Benchmarking Results

We conducted our experiments on a Linux-based system with Ubuntu 14.2.0 operating system equipped with an 11th Gen Intel(R) Core(TM) i5-1135G7 CPU, x64-based processor and 16 GB of RAM. All algorithms were implemented in C programming language and compiled using GCC version 14.2.0 with -march=native -O3 optimization flags, with Turbo Boost and Hyper-Threading disabled. Each benchmark was run and repeated 1000 times with random inputs, we measured and recorded the average and median execution times in terms of CPU cycles (cc) in Table 2.

Table 2. Average and median execution times for 1000 runs.

Size	Average (in cc)/Median (in cc)		
(bits)	320	640	12000
Addition	219/217	454/455	7015/6975
Subtraction	233/234	485/486	7181/7110
Multiplication	488/490	2126/2111	660028/654979
Euclidean division	3216/3195	7585/7541	767073/759785
Right shift	104/106	236/231	6665/6614
Left shift	116/117	254/253	6905/6874
Bitsize	478/478	925/928	17355/17246
GCD	1607482/1605695	5985343/5978259	$2.26 \cdot 10^9/2.26 \cdot 10^9$
Reduction	80623/79971	193507/192049	21102273/21098608

Following the summary of the execution times in Table 2, we present runs versus cycles plots that visually represent the performance of our algorithms across inputs of maximum bit-lengths of 320 and 640 bits. These plots illustrate the relationship between the input sizes and the execution time across 1000 runs, with the runs represented on the x-axis and the execution time (measured in CPU cycles) represented on the y-axis. The data points in each plot correspond to the average execution time in blue and median execution times in orange, derived from 1000 repeated runs with random inputs.

Linear Growth in Run-Time with Respect to Upper Bound on Input Array Size: The execution time is constant for a given upper bound n on the array size in the integer representation $\mathcal{D}(a)$ of a. It exhibits a linear scaling factor for addition, subtraction, left and right shifts algorithms, that is, the execution time for these operations increases proportionally as the upper bound n increases, as can be seen in Figs. 1, 2, 3a, 3b. Some variability due to measurement noise in a CPU and occasional outliers can be observed in the plots. Note, however, that these plots are not intended as a visual proof or evidence of constant-time behavior of our implementation. Instead, it was verified using Timecop and Valgrind.

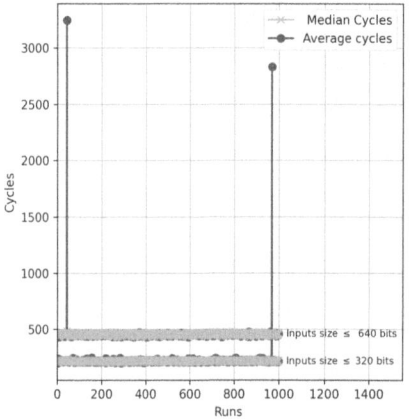
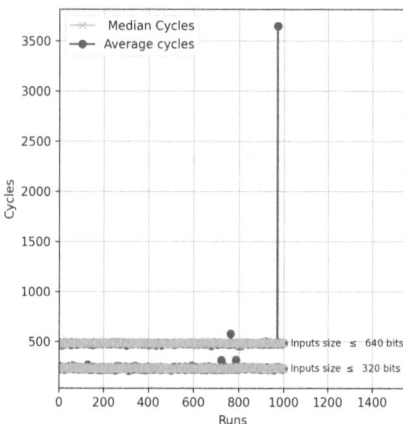

Fig. 1. Execution time of Addition.   **Fig. 2.** Execution time of subtraction.

Unscaled Constant Time Complexity: The execution time for multiplication, GCD, Euclidean division, modular reduction and bit-size algorithms also increases as the the upper bound n grows. However, unlike the other basic functions, the run-times for these functions do not follow a straightforward linear scaling relationship with respect to the value of n. This non-linear behavior is demonstrated in plots Figs. 4a, 4b for GCD, plots Figs. 5a, 5b for division computation results, followed by plot Fig. 6 and plot Fig. 7 for multiplication and modular reduction, respectively.

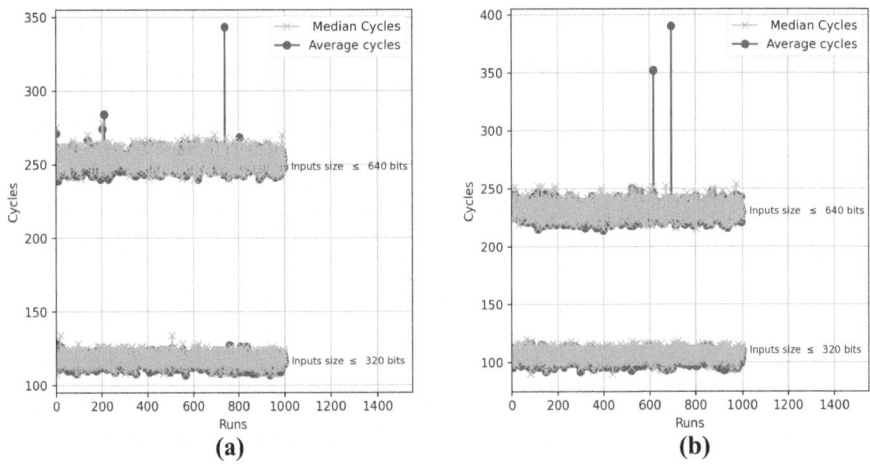

Fig. 3. Left and right shift benchmarks for different input sizes. (a) Execution time of Left shift. (b) Execution time of Right shift.

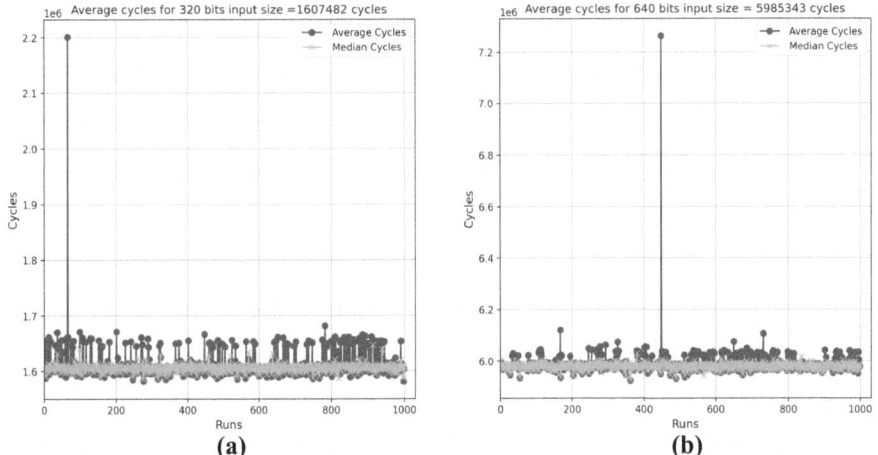

Fig. 4. GCD benchmarks for different input sizes. (a) GCD Benchmark for 320 bits input size. (b) GCD Benchmark for 640 bits input size.

Verification of the Constant Time Implementation: To verify that our implementation is constant time, we used the "TIMECOP" toolkit [8] which works in combination with the "Valgrind" analysis tool [19]. These tools are used to detect secret-dependent branching or other secret-dependent program behavior, which we run on all of our functions successfully.

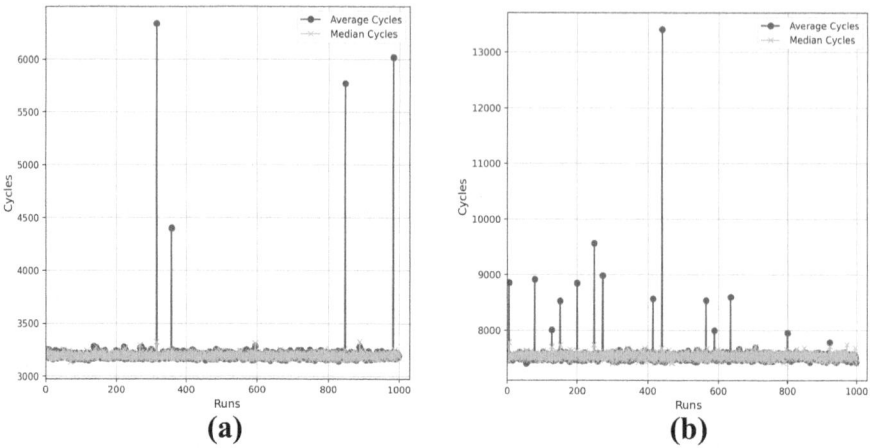

Fig. 5. Division benchmarks for different input sizes. (a) Division Benchmark for 320 bits input size. (b) Division Benchmark for 640 bits input size.

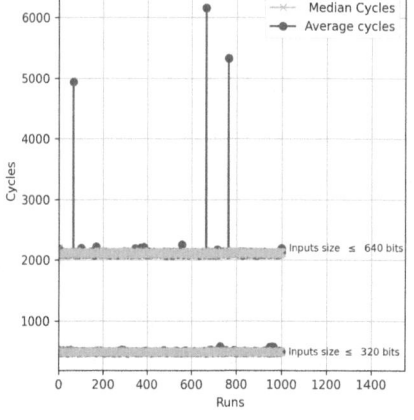

Fig. 6. Multiplication benchmark results.

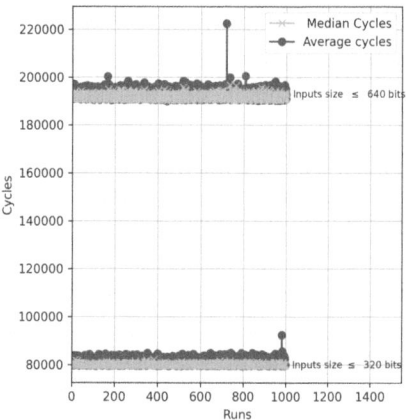

Fig. 7. Reduction benchmark results.

5   Conclusion

In this work, we analyzed and implemented constant-time alternatives for the main big integer functions that are used in SQIsign's quaternion arithmetic module. We modified and adapted already existing solutions according to specific requirements of quaternion arithmetic. Further, we also proposed a constant-time modular reduction algorithm that is useful when the moduli varies across operations. We implemented these functions in C programming language without depending on high-level libraries like GMP and also provided the average and median run-times of these implementations. We verified the constant-time behavior of the implementation using Timecop with Valgrind. The precision analysis for efficient implementation of the integer square root function for large integers is left for future exploration. Note that in this work, we aimed at resolving constant-time issues with the integer functions used in SQIsign's quaternion arithmetic. The next line of work in this direction would be to explore constant-time algorithms for the quaternion functions so that the implementation proposed in this work can be integrated with the quaternion module of SQIsign. With our work, we aim to contribute towards a secure and practical implementation of SQIsign, facilitating its deployment in post-quantum cryptographic applications.

Acknowledgement. Anisha Mukherjee is supported by the Austrian FWF grant PAT6402023. Péter Kutas is supported by the Hungarian Ministry of Innovation and Technology NRDI Office within the framework of the Quantum Information National Laboratory Program and by the grant "EXCELLENCE-151343". He is also supported by the János Bolyai Research Scholarship of the Hungarian Academy of Sciences and partly by EPSRC through grant number EP/V011324/1.

A   Pseudo-Codes for Constant-Time GCD and Square-Root Computations

In this section, we will present the constant-time GCD [3] as well as the Newton-Raphson-based square root [14] pseudo-codes outlined in Sect. 2.5.

The constant-time GCD Algorithm 9 presents a slightly modified version of the existing constant-time GCD from [3]. We extend its functionality by handling both odd and even integers, whereas the original version was restricted to the first input being odd. We introduce step 3 along with Bitzeros constant-time function to factor out powers of 2 from even input integers.

The Newton-Raphson-based square root Algorithm 10 was originally proposed in [14]. This algorithm is based on fixed point arithmetic for a precision dependent on the bit-size of the fractional part and some additional bits $f + n$ for better accuracy.

Algorithm 9. $\mathsf{GCD}(a, b)$

1: $\mathsf{ct} - \mathsf{cmov}(f, a)$.
2: $\mathsf{ct} - \mathsf{cmov}(g, b)$.
3: $r = \mathsf{Min}(\mathsf{Bitzeros}(f), \mathsf{Bitzeros}(g))$.▷ Bitzeros(a) returns the largest α s.t $a = 2^\alpha \cdot x$.
4: $\mathsf{Right\_Shift}(f, r)$.
5: $\mathsf{Right\_Shift}(g, r)$.
6: $\mathsf{d} = \mathsf{Max}(\mathsf{Bitsize}(f), \mathsf{Bitsize}(g))$.
7: $m = \mathsf{Iteration}(d)$.
8: **if** $(f_0$ and $1)$ **then**
9:     $\mathsf{Divstep}(m, m + d, 1, f, g)$.
10:     $\mathsf{ct} - \mathsf{cmov}(c, f)$.
11: **else**
12:     $\mathsf{Divstep}(m, m + d, 1, g, f)$.
13:     $\mathsf{ct} - \mathsf{cmov}(c, g)$.
14: **end if**

Algorithm 10. SQRT(a)

Require: $a \in \mathbb{Z}$, $-2^{f-1} \leq a < 2^{f-1}$, a is a 64-bit integer, represented using $\mathcal{D}(a)$ binary representation
Ensure: a boolean s if $q = \sqrt{a}$ exists and was computed .
1: $a = a \cdot 2^f$ $\triangleright$ Using constant time left shift
2: $v, v^{1/2} \leftarrow$ Scale(a) $\triangleright$ $v = \pm 2^k$, k is even integer
3: $b = 2^{-f+n} \cdot a \cdot v$
4: $\beta = (\sqrt{2} - 1)/4$
5: $\tau = 3/\sqrt{2}$
6: $\theta = \lceil log_2 \cdot log_{\tau \cdot \beta}(\tau \cdot 2^{-(f+n)}) \rceil$
7: $c_0 = 3/2 + \beta -$ Round$_1(b/2,$ deterministic$)$
8: **for** $i \in [1, \theta]$ **do**
9:     $z_1 =$ Round$_{f+n}(c_{i-1} \cdot b)$
10:    $z_2 = 3 -$ Round$_{f+n}(c_{i-1} \cdot z_1)$
11:    $c_i =$ Round$_{f+n+1}(\frac{1}{2} \cdot c_{i-1} \cdot z_2)$
12: **end for**
13: $w =$ Round$_{f-n}(a \cdot v^{\frac{1}{2}})$
14: $\tilde{q} =$ Round$_{f+2n}(c_\theta \cdot w,$ deterministic$)$ $\triangleright$ $-2^{\ell-1} \leq \tilde{q} < 2^{\ell-1}$
15: $\bar{q} =$ Round$_f(\tilde{q},$ deterministic$)$
16: $q = \bar{q} - (\bar{q}^2 > a)$
17: $s = (q^2 == a)$ **return** s, q.

References

1. Aardal, M.A., et al.: SQISIGN: algorithm specifications and supporting documentation. National Institute for Standards and Technology (2025)
2. Barrett, P.: Implementing the Rivest Shamir and Adleman public key encryption algorithm on a standard digital signal processor. In: Odlyzko, A.M. (ed.) CRYPTO 1986. LNCS, vol. 263, pp. 311–323. Springer, Heidelberg (1987). https://doi.org/10.1007/3-540-47721-7_24
3. Bernstein, D.J., Yang, B.Y.: Fast constant-time gcd computation and modular inversion. IACR Trans. Cryptogr. Hardw. Embed. Syst. **2019**(3), 340–398 (2019). https://doi.org/10.13154/tches.v2019.i3.340-398
4. Catrina, O., de Hoogh, S.: Secure multiparty linear programming using fixed-point arithmetic. In: Gritzalis, D., Preneel, B., Theoharidou, M. (eds.) ESORICS 2010. LNCS, vol. 6345, pp. 134–150. Springer, Heidelberg (2010). https://doi.org/10.1007/978-3-642-15497-3_9
5. Catrina, O., Saxena, A.: Secure computation with fixed-point numbers. In: Sion, R. (ed.) FC 2010. LNCS, vol. 6052, pp. 35–50. Springer, Heidelberg (2010). https://doi.org/10.1007/978-3-642-14577-3_6
6. Chavez-Saab, J., et al.: SQISIGN: algorithm specifications and supporting documentation. National Institute for Standards and Technology (2023)
7. Comba, P.G.: Exponentiation cryptosystems on the ibm pc. IBM Syst. J. **29**(4), 526–538 (1990). https://doi.org/10.1147/sj.294.0526
8. Crypto, P.A.: Timecop: automated dynamic analysis for timing side-channels. https://www.post-apocalyptic-crypto.org/timecop/
9. Granlund, T.: The GMP development team: GNU MP: The GNU Multiple Precision Arithmetic Library. https://gmplib.org/

10. Hanyecz, O., Karenin, A., Kirshanova, E., Kutas, P., Schaeffler, S.: Constant time lattice reduction in dimension 4 with application to sqisign. IACR Trans. Cryptogr. Hardw. Embed. Syst. (2024). https://eprint.iacr.org/2025/027

11. Jacquemin, D., Mukherjee, A., Kutas, P., ROY, S.S.: Ready to SQI? safety first! towards a constant-time implementation of isogeny-based signature, SQIsign. Cryptology ePrint Archive, Paper 2023/807 (2023). https://eprint.iacr.org/2023/807

12. Jao, D., et al.: Sidh-spec (2022). https://sike.org/files/SIDH-spec.pdf

13. Joye, M., Yen, S.-M.: The montgomery powering ladder. In: Kaliski, B.S., Koç, K., Paar, C. (eds.) CHES 2002. LNCS, vol. 2523, pp. 291–302. Springer, Heidelberg (2003). https://doi.org/10.1007/3-540-36400-5_22

14. Korzilius, S., Schoenmakers, B.: Divisions and square roots with tight error analysis from newton–raphson iteration in secure fixed-point arithmetic. Cryptography **7**(3), 43 (2023). https://doi.org/10.3390/cryptography7030043

15. Longa, P., Leroux, A.: sqisign-ec23 (2023). https://github.com/SQISign/sqisign-ec23

16. Montgomery, P.L.: Modular multiplication without trial division. Math. Comput. **44**(170), 519–521 (1985). https://www.ams.org/journals/mcom/1985-44-170/S0025-5718-1985-0777282-X/S0025-5718-1985-0777282-X.pdf

17. Montgomery, P.L.: Speeding the pollard and elliptic curve methods of factorization. Math. Comput. **48**(177), 243–264 (1987). https://wstein.org/edu/124/misc/montgomery.pdf

18. National Institute for Standards and Technology (NIST): Post-quantum cryptography: Additional digital signature schemes. https://csrc.nist.gov/projects/pqc-dig-sig/round-2-additional-signatures

19. Seward, J., Nethercote, N., et al.: Valgrind: a framework for heavyweight dynamic binary instrumentation. Website (2007). https://valgrind.org/

20. Shor, P.W.: Polynomial-time algorithms for prime factorization and discrete logarithms on a quantum computer. SIAM J. Comput. **26**(5), 1484–1509 (1997)

21. Shor, P.: Algorithms for quantum computation: discrete logarithms and factoring. In: Proceedings 35th Annual Symposium on Foundations of Computer Science, pp. 124–134 (1994). https://doi.org/10.1109/SFCS.1994.365700

22. Voight, J.: Quaternion Algebras, Graduate Texts in Mathematics, vol. 288. Springer, Heidelberg (2021). https://library.oapen.org/handle/20.500.12657/50018

FPTRU: Optimization of NTRU-Prime and TLS Performance Assessment

Xiaowen Hu[1], Hanyu Wei[1], Hengchuan Zou[1], Zhichuang Liang[1], Wenqian Li[1], and Yunlei Zhao[1,2(✉)]

[1] Department of Computer Science, Fudan University, Shanghai, China
ylzhao@fudan.edu.cn
[2] State Key Laboratory of Cryptology, Beijing, China

Abstract. The advent of quantum computers poses a significant threat to existing cryptographic systems, thereby affecting the confidentiality and integrity of communications. Among various post-quantum cryptographic schemes, those based on NTRU lattices have achieved considerable success. For example, NTRU-Prime has been implemented in network security protocols such as OpenSSH and OpenBSD, becoming a de facto standard. However, traditional NTRU key encapsulation mechanisms still suffer from poor computational efficiency, inability to compress ciphertexts, and a narrow range of secret values.

To address these challenges, an optimization of NTRU-Prime–FPTRU (Fast Prime NTRU) constructed on LPPNF (large-Galois-group prime-degree prime-ideal number field) is presented. It provides enhanced security assurances and support for lossy compression of ciphertexts. Pseudo-Mersenne reduction and pseudo-Mersenne incomplete NTT are used to accelerate polynomial multiplication in LPPNF. Considering the situation of batch key generation in practical applications, we apply Montgomery inversion to key generation of FPTRU and explore the optimal batch size. With a batch size of 32, FPTRU-761 achieves a $4.7\times$ efficiency improvement over serial key generation and an $80.7\times$ improvement over SNTRU-Prime-761 batch key generation. FPTRU-653 matches the classical and quantum security of SNTRU-Prime-761. Integrated into OpenSSL, FPTRU-653 outperforms SNTRU-Prime-761 in various network conditions. For example, with 15.458 ms latency and 15% packet loss, FPTRU-653 completes $1.2\times$ more handshakes than SNTRU-Prime-761.

Keywords: post-quantum cryptography · NTRU lattice · TLS

1 Introduction

With the development of quantum computing technology, traditional public key cryptosystems are facing significant threats. Consequently, the research on new public key cryptosystems that can withstand quantum attacks, i.e. post-quantum cryptography, has garnered extensive attention. The adoption of post-quantum

A. Nitaj et al. (Eds.): AFRICACRYPT 2025, LNCS 15651, pp. 216–241, 2026.
https://doi.org/10.1007/978-3-031-97260-7_11

cryptography will also depend on the successful transition of communication protocols and applications to use these new algorithms, such as integrating them into protocols like TLS (Transport Layer Security).

Designing post-quantum KEM(key encapsulation scheme) based on lattice (especially NTRU lattice) is one of the mainstream directions in lattice cryptography. [21] formally proposed the NTRU encryption scheme in 1998, and today NTRU has become one of the foundational components of various cryptographic primitives, such as Falcon, one of the proposed standardized digital signature schemes. Besides, schemes based on the NTRU lattice have long embarked on the path of standardization and commercialization. As early as 2008, IEEE Std 1363.1 standard included lattice-based cryptographic schemes including NTRU-Encrypt [23]. The international standard OpenSSH, in versions released after version 9.0 in April 2022, adopted a hybrid mode of NTRU-Prime combined with X25519 ECDH to resist "decrypt-then-capture" attacks [29]. However, the traditional NTRU KEM still suffers from drawbacks such as poor computational efficiency, inability for ciphertext compression, narrow secret value range, and weak starting point for CCA security reduction.

Besides, existing NTRU lattice-based cryptographic schemes, are based on the cyclotomic ring construction. However, the rich algebraic structure of cyclotomic rings makes these schemes vulnerable to attacks, as highlighted in literature [9,11,13,15,33]. Bernstein et al. [6] proposed LPPNF(large-Galois-group prime-degree primeideal number field), a foundational algebraic structure with high security, prime-degree, large Galois group, and inert modulus. Bernstein et al. [6] also recommended migrating existing foundational algebraic structures from cyclotomic rings to LPPNF to resist known and potential attacks against cyclotomic rings, thereby providing schemes with more conservative security. Thus, the NTRU-Prime scheme based on LPPNF was proposed in this context [6].

Thus, FPTRU (Fast Prime NTRU), a new NTRU lattice based cryptographic scheme, is presented. It is constructed on LPPNF to resist known and potential attacks against cyclotomic rings. FPTRU features support for lossy compression of ciphertexts, thereby bringing bandwidth advantages. It adopts E_8 lattice code known for robust error-correcting capability and efficient constant-time implementation, enabling a broader noise tolerance range.

1.1 Related Works

The NTRU lattice-based cryptographic scheme has become a popular research area in recent years. Stehlé et al. [36] were the first to design a NTRU lattice-based PKE (public key encryption) based on power-of-2 cyclotomic rings $\mathbb{Z}[x]/(x^{2k} + 1)$ and provided a rigorous security proof. However, the scheme has limited practicality due to its large public key size. Jarvis et al. [24] extended NTRU-type PKE to the Eisenstein integer ring $\mathbb{Z}[\omega]/(x^n - 1)$, where $\omega = exp(\frac{2\pi i}{3})$, achieving advantages in key size and performance. Hülsing et al. [22] improved key and ciphertext sizes as well as implementation efficiency of the classical NTRU encryption scheme. Their proposed NTRU-HRSS was one of the finalists in the third round of the NIST Post-quantum Cryptography Standardization project. Bernstein et al. [6] constructed the NTRU-Prime scheme based on a less algebraically structured LPPNF, which was also a candidate in the third round of the NIST Post-quantum Cryptography Standardization project.

The aforementioned NTRU schemes are all constructed based on the traditional NTRU framework and cannot compress ciphertexts. For example, Fouque et al. [18] proposed an NTRU-type KEM named BAT, based on power-of-2 cyclotomic rings $\mathbb{Z}_q[x]/(x^n+1)$ and an improved Babai rounding algorithm. Nonetheless, it mainly targets parameter sets with $n = 512, 1024$ and lacks support for the commonly used lattice cryptography parameter sets $n = 761, 768$. However, aforementioned NTRU-type KEMs are all constructed based on cyclotomic rings and susceptible to related attacks targeting these rings.

The protocol integration for cryptographic schemes is as crucial as their design. There are three major lines of work to prepare the TLS ecosystem for post-quantum cryptography. The first is (draft) specifications of how post-quantum algorithms could be integrated into existing protocol formats and message flows [20,32]. The second is prototype implementations demonstrating such integrations can be done [1,25] and whether they would meet existing constraints in protocols and software [16]. The third is performance evaluations in either basic laboratory network settings [12,35] or more realistic network settings [25]. For NTRU lattice-based schemes, there have been some works evaluating them in real-world protocols. [8] further optimized SNTRU-Prime and integrated the library sntrup761 into OpenSSL to explore its performance.

1.2 Contributions

In this paper, FPTRU based on LPPNF is presented. Our work is a network-oriented solution, targeting at challenges faced by NTRU-based cryptosystem in practical use. The key contributions of our work are summarized as follows:

- **Construction of FPTRU.** The specific construction and implementation of FPTRU is presented. Specifically ciphertext lossy compression is introduced and more robust error-correcting scalable E_8 lattice code is adopted. We also compare FPTRU with SNTRU-Prime implemented in [6]. Specifically, FPTRU-761 performs KeyGen, Encaps, and Decaps operations 16.1 times, 174.5 times, and 284.5 times faster than SNTRU-Prime-761, respectively.
- **Polynomial operator optimization.** Given that batching keys is a more interesting challenge in practical usage of KEMs, we apply Montgomery inversion to key generation of FPTRU and explore the optimal batch size theoretically and practically. For the batch size 32, FPTRU-761 batch key generation brings a $4.7\times$ efficiency improvement compared to serial key generation and an $80.7\times$ efficiency improvement compared to SNTRU-Prime-761 batch key generation. LPPNF is not NTT-friendly, making implementation of polynomial multiplication a challenge. So we design pseudo-Mersenne incomplete NTT based on optimized pseudo-Mersenne reduction.

– **TLS applications.** Considering practical application, we give a commonly
   used OpenSSL patches method and integrate FPTRU and its batch key generation version into OpenSSL. Our results show that FPTRU-653 outperforms
   SNTRU-Prime-761 on links with both low and high network latency. For
   example, when latency is 15.458 ms and packet loss is 15%, FPTRU-653 can
   complete 1.2× handshakes compared to SNTRU-Prime-761.

2 Preliminaries

2.1 Notations

The symbol $\mathbb{Z}$ represents the set of integers. $\mathbb{R}$ represents the set of real numbers.
For $x \in \mathbb{R}$, $\lfloor x \rceil$ represents the rounded value of x. n and q are positive integers.
$\mathbb{Z}_q = \mathbb{Z}/q\mathbb{Z} \cong \{0, 1, \ldots, q-1\}$ denotes the residue class modulo q, where $\mathbb{Z}_q^{\times}$
denotes the set of invertible elements in $\mathbb{Z}_q$. Elements of polynomial rings $R = \mathbb{Z}[x]/(x^n - x - 1)$ and $R_q = \mathbb{Z}_q[x]/(x^n - x - 1)$ are n-dimensional polynomials with
coefficients in $\mathbb{Z}$ or $\mathbb{Z}_q$. These polynomials are denoted by lowercase letters such
as f or $f(x)$, and $f(x)$ can be represented as a power series $f = \sum_{i=0}^{n-1} f_i x^i$ where
$f_i \in \mathbb{Z}$ or $\mathbb{Z}_q$. $r' = r \bmod \pm q$ represents the absolute smallest complete residue
of r, i.e. the representative of r falling in the interval $[-\frac{q}{2}, \frac{q}{2})$. $r' = r \bmod q$
represents the non-negative smallest complete residue of r, i.e. the representative
of r falling in the interval $[0, q)$.

   For $\omega \in \mathbb{R}$, its l_∞ norm is denoted as $||\omega||_{q,\infty} = |\omega \bmod \pm q|$. If ω is an
n-dimensional vector, its l_2 norm is $||\omega||_{q,2} = \sqrt{||\omega_0||_{q,\infty}^2 + \ldots + ||\omega_{n-1}||_{q,\infty}^2}$.

   If D is a set, $x \xleftarrow{\$} D$ indicates selecting x uniformly at random from D.
If D is a probability distribution, $x \leftarrow D$ indicates selecting x according to
the distribution D. The centered binomial distribution B_η with an integer
parameter η is defined as follows: randomly sample from $\{0, 1\}^{2\eta}$ uniformly
$(a_1, \ldots, a_\eta, b_1, \ldots, b_\eta)$ and output $\sum_{i=1}^{\eta}(a_i - b_i)$. Sampling a polynomial f from
B_η refers to sampling each coefficient of f independently according to the distribution B_η.

   Let Ψ be a distribution over R. $\mathrm{Adv}_{R,\Psi}^{\mathrm{NTRU}}(\mathcal{A})$ and $\mathrm{Adv}_{R,\Psi}^{\mathrm{RLWR}}(\mathcal{A})$ denote the
advantages of any probabilistic polynomial-time adversary $\mathcal{A}$ when facing the
NTRU and RLWR problems, respectively. $\mathrm{Adv}_{\mathrm{KEM}}^{\mathrm{IND\text{-}CCA}}(\mathcal{A})$ is the advantage of
any adversary $\mathcal{A}$ in distinguishing the KEM scheme under chosen-ciphertext
attacks. $\mathrm{Adv}_{\mathrm{PKE}}^{\mathrm{IND\text{-}CPA}}(\mathcal{A})$ is the advantage of any adversary $\mathcal{A}$ in distinguishing
the PKE scheme under chosen-plaintext attacks.

2.2 Hardness Assumptions
Definition 1 (NTRU assumption [21]). *According to the distribution Ψ,
sample polynomials f and g such that f needs to be invertible in R, and denote
$h = g/f$. The NTRU problem is to distinguish whether h is a uniformly random*

element in R. The NTRU problem is hard, meaning that the advantage of any probabilistic polynomial-time adversary $\mathcal{A}$ is negligible, where

$$Adv_{R,\Psi}^{NTRU}(\mathcal{A}) = \left| \Pr\left[b' = 1 : \begin{array}{c} f, g \leftarrow \Psi; f^{-1} \in R; \\ h = g/f \in R; b' \leftarrow \mathcal{A}(h) \end{array} \right] - \Pr\left[b' = 1 : \begin{array}{c} h \xleftarrow{\$} R; \\ b' \leftarrow \mathcal{A}(h) \end{array} \right] \right|$$

Definition 2 (RLWR assumption [5]). *Let $q > p \geq 2$ be positive integers. Let R be a polynomial ring. Denote $R_q = R/qR$ and $R_p = R/pR$ as quotient rings. The RLWR problem is to distinguish whether the tuple (h, c) is uniformly random in $R_q \times R_p$, where $h \leftarrow R_q, r \leftarrow \Psi, c = \lfloor \frac{p}{q} hr \rceil \mod p$. The RLWR problem is hard, meaning that the advantage of any probabilistic polynomial-time adversary $\mathcal{A}$ is negligible, where $Adv_{R,\Psi}^{RLWR}(\mathcal{A}) =$*

$$\left| \Pr\left[b' = 1 : \begin{array}{c} h \xleftarrow{\$} R_q; r \leftarrow \Psi; \\ c = \lfloor \frac{p}{q} hr \rceil \mod p; b' \leftarrow \mathcal{A}(h, c) \end{array} \right] - \Pr\left[b' = 1 : \begin{array}{c} h \xleftarrow{\$} R_q; c \xleftarrow{\$} R_p; \\ b' \leftarrow \mathcal{A}(h, c) \end{array} \right] \right|$$

2.3 TLS 1.3 Handshake

TLS is one of the most important protocols in our daily life. It operates on the TCP/IP protocol stack, providing end-to-end authentication and establishing encrypted communication tunnels between them, ensuring the confidentiality, integrity, and authenticity of communication data. It is widely used to protect web (HTTPS), file transfer (FTP), email (SMTP, POP) and many other applications. The handshake process and message formats of TLS 1.3 are fully described in [31].

2.4 Number Theoretic Transform (NTT)

The Number Theoretic Transform (NTT) is a special form of the Fast Fourier Transform (FFT) over finite fields. The main idea is to transform the polynomial coefficients into the NTT domain to perform faster polynomial multiplication operations. f, g and h are polynomials. To get $h = fg$, NTT computes $h = \mathsf{INTT}(\mathsf{NTT}(f) \circ \mathsf{NTT}(g))$, where NTT is forward transform , INTT is inverse transform and $\circ$ is element-wise product.

Bernstein [7] summarized a fast algorithm for computing NTT called FFT trick. Essentially, the FFT trick is based on the Chinese Remainder Theorem (CRT) in the form of polynomial rings, specifically for pairs of mutually coprime polynomials $g_1, g_2, \cdots, g_k$, $\mathbb{Z}_q[x]/(g_1, g_2, \cdots, g_k)$ is isomorphic to $\prod_{i=1}^{k} \mathbb{Z}_q[x]/(g_i)$ and f is mapped to $(f \mod g_1, f \mod g_2, \cdots, f \mod g_k)$. The forward FFT trick can utilize the Cooley-Tukey(CT) butterfly operation in [14], while the inverse FFT trick can utilize the Gentleman-Sande(GS) butterfly operation in [19]. For GS butterfly, lazy reduction can be used to optimize its implementation. Radix-N NTT is defined as $\mathbb{Z}_q[x]/(x^{Nm} - \zeta^N) \cong \prod_{i=0}^{N-1} \mathbb{Z}_q[x]/(x^m - \rho^i \zeta)$, where ρ represents the N-th primitive root of unity.

3   Construction and Analysis of FPTRU

In this section, we will give the specific scheme construction of FPTRU. It includes an IND-CPA secure public key encryption scheme called FPTRU.PKE and an IND-CCA secure key encapsulation scheme called FPTRU.KEM. Polynomial scalable E_8 lattice code is introduced firstly, which replaces the rough, error-prone plaintext encoding scheme used by traditional NTRU schemes. Besides, we provide detailed error rate calculation and security analysis of FPTRU.

3.1   Polynomial Scalable E_8 Lattice Code

The scalable E_8 lattice is constructed from the extended Hamming code in dimension 8, which is defined as $H_8 = \{\mathbf{c} \in \{0,1\}^8 \,|\, \mathbf{c} = \mathbf{z}\mathbf{H} \bmod 2, \mathbf{z} \in \{0,1\}^4\}$ where the binary matrix $\mathbf{H}$ is

$$\mathbf{H} = \begin{bmatrix} 1 & 1 & 1 & 1 & 0 & 0 & 0 & 0 \\ 0 & 0 & 1 & 1 & 1 & 1 & 0 & 0 \\ 0 & 0 & 0 & 0 & 1 & 1 & 1 & 1 \\ 0 & 1 & 0 & 1 & 0 & 1 & 0 & 1 \end{bmatrix}$$

Let $C = \{(x_1, x_1, x_2, x_2, x_3, x_3, x_4, x_4) \in \{0,1\}^8 \,|\, \sum x_i \equiv 0 \bmod 2\}$, where C is spanned by the up most three rows of H. Then the scalable E_8 lattice is constructed as $E_8 = \lambda \cdot [C \cup (C + \mathbf{c})] \subset [0, \lambda]^8$, where $\mathbf{c} = (0, 1, 0, 1, 0, 1, 0, 1)$ is the last row of $\mathbf{H}$, $\lambda \in \mathbb{R}^+$ is the scale factor and $\lambda \cdot C$ means that all the elements in C multiply by λ.

The encoding algorithm of the E_8 lattice (see Algorithm 1) is to calculate $\lambda \cdot (\mathbf{k}\mathbf{H} \bmod 2)$, given a 4-bit binary string $\mathbf{k}$.

Given any $x \in \mathbb{R}^8$, the decoding algorithm is to find the solution of the closest vector problem (CVP) of x in the E_8 lattice, which is denoted by $\lambda \cdot (\mathbf{k}\mathbf{H} \bmod 2)$, and it outputs the 4-bit string $\mathbf{k}$. The detailed algorithm is shown in Algorithm 2, along with Algorithm 3 as its subroutines. To solve the CVP of $x \in \mathbb{R}^8$ in the E_8 lattice, one need to address the CVP of x and $x - \lambda\mathbf{c}$ in the lattice $C' = \lambda \cdot C$ using Algorithm 3. The one having smaller distance is the final answer. Note that in Algorithm 3, given $x \in \mathbb{R}^8$, for every two components in x, determine whether they are close to $(0, 0)$ or (λ, λ). Assign the corresponding component of $\mathbf{k}$ to 0 if the former is true, and 1 otherwise. If $\sum k_i \bmod 2 = 1$, the second closest vector $\mathbf{k}$ is chosen.

Due to the fact that the dimension of the LPPNF is not a multiple of 8, it is not possible to directly use multiple E_8 lattices for encoding plaintext messages. Therefore, Algorithm 4 and Algorithm 5 are provided below.

The scaled E_8 lattice used in Algorithm 4 is constructed based on the scaling factor $\frac{q}{2}$, i.e. $E_8' = \frac{q}{2} \cdot [C \cup (C + \mathbf{c})]$. Note that, n', number of bits of plaintext, is a multiple of 8. PolyEncode takes 4 bits from plaintext m as input and outputs 8 coefficients for v. Thus, each plaintext m generates a total of $2n'$ coefficients for v. Since another $n - 2n'$ coefficients do not contain any information from the plaintext, to compute conveniently and avoid affecting the error rate, we assign them value 0.

Algorithm 1. Encode$_{E_8}$

Require: binary string $\mathbf{k} \in \{0,1\}^4$
Ensure: encoded result v
1: $\mathbf{v} = \lambda \cdot (\mathbf{kH} \bmod 2) \in [0, \lambda]^8$
2: **return v**

Algorithm 2. Decode$_{E_8}$

Require: $\mathbf{x} = (x_0, \ldots, x_7) \in \mathbb{R}^8$
Ensure: $\mathbf{k} \in \{0,1\}^4$
1: $\mathbf{c} = (0, 1, 0, 1, 0, 1, 0, 1)$
2: $(\mathbf{k_0}, TotalCost_0) = \mathsf{Decode}_{C'}(x)$
3: $(\mathbf{k_1}, TotalCost_1) = \mathsf{Decode}_{C'}(x - \lambda\mathbf{c})$
4: $b = \mathrm{argmin}\,\{TotalCost_0, TotalCost_1\}$
5: $(k_0, k_1, k_2, k_3) = \mathbf{k_b}$
6: $\mathbf{k} = (k_0, k_1 \oplus k_0, k_3, b) \in \{0,1\}^4$
7: **return k**

Algorithm 3. Decode$_{C'}$

Require: $\mathbf{x} = (x_0, \ldots, x_7) \in \mathbb{R}^8$
Ensure: $(\mathbf{k} \in \{0,1\}^4, TotalCost)$
1: $mind = +\infty$
2: $mini = 0$
3: $TotalCost = 0$
4: **for** i=0 to 3 **do**
5:     $c_0 = ||x_{2i}||_{2\lambda,2}^2 + ||x_{2i+1}||_{2\lambda,2}^2$
6:     $c_1 = ||x_{2i} - \lambda||_{2\lambda,2}^2 + ||x_{2i+1} - \lambda||_{2\lambda,2}^2$
7:     $k_i = \mathrm{argmin}\,\{c_0, c_1\}$
8:     $TotalCost = TotalCost + c_{k_i}$
9:     **if** $c_{1-k_i} - c_{k_i} < mind$ **then**
10:       $mind = c_{1-k_i} - c_{k_i}$
11:       $mini = i$
12:     **end if**
13: **end for**
14: **if** $k_0 + k_1 + k_2 + k_3 \bmod 2 = 1$ **then**
15:     $k_{mini} = 1 - k_{mini}$
16:     $TotalCost = TotalCost + mind$
17: **end if**
18: $\mathbf{k} = (k_0, k_1, k_2, k_3) \in \{0,1\}^4$
19: **return** $(\mathbf{k}, TotalCost)$

In Algorithm 5, the scaling factor is $\frac{q_2}{2}$ and the scaled E_8 lattice is $E_8'' = \frac{q_2}{2} \cdot [C \cup (C + \mathbf{c})]$. We use 8 coefficients of v to generate 4 bits and then combine $\frac{n'}{4}$ groups of 4 bits as output m in Algorithm 5.

Algorithm 4. PolyEncode

Require: plaintext $m = \sum_{i=0}^{n'} m_i x^i \in \mathcal{M}$
Ensure: encoded polynomial $v = \sum_{i=0}^{n-1} v_i x^i$
1: **for** $i = 0$ to $\frac{n'}{4} - 1$ **do**
2:    $\mathbf{k_i} = (m_{4i}, m_{4i+1}, m_{4i+2}, m_{4i+3}) \in \{0,1\}^4$
3:    $(v_{8i}, v_{8i+1}, \ldots, v_{8i+7}) = \mathsf{Encode}_{E_8'}(\mathbf{k_i})$
4: **end for**
5: **for** $i = 2n'$ to $n - 1$ **do**
6:    $v_i = 0$
7: **end for**
8: $v = \sum_{i=0}^{n-1} v_i x^i$
9: **return** v

Algorithm 5. PolyDecode

Require: polynominal $v = \sum_{i=0}^{n-1} v_i x^i$
Ensure: plaintext m
1: **for** $i = 0$ to $\frac{n'}{4} - 1$ **do**
2:    $\mathbf{x_i} = (v_{8i}, v_{8i+1}, \ldots, v_{8i+7})$
3:    $(m_{4i}, m_{4i+1}, m_{4i+2}, m_{4i+3}) = \mathsf{Decode}_{E_8''(\mathbf{x_i})}$
4: **end for**
5: $m = \sum_{i=0}^{n'-1} m_i x^i \in \mathcal{M}$
6: **return** m

3.2   PKE and KEM

FPTRU.PKE is shown in Algorithm 6, Algorithm 7 and Algorithm 8. q_2 is the ciphertext modulus, typically chosen as a power of 2 and less than q. p is the plaintext space modulus, and $gcd(p,q) = 1$. We focus on the case that q is an odd prime number and $p = 2$. Ψ_1 and Ψ_2 are two given distributions on $R = \mathbb{Z}[x]/(x^n - x - 1)$. For simplicity, in the following text, f', g are drawn from Ψ_1, and r is drawn from Ψ_2. In practice, Ψ_1 and Ψ_2 can be different distributions. $\mathcal{M} = \{0,1\}^{n'}$ represents the plaintext space, where each $m \in \mathcal{M}$ can be viewed as an n'-dimensional polynomial with each coefficient belonging to $\{0,1\}$.

The Fujisaki-Okamoto(FO) transform is one of the most effective methods for converting a CPA-secure PKE into a CCA-secure KEM. Key encapsulation mechanism of FPTRU is based on $FO_{ID(pk),m}^{\perp}$ transformation, proposed in [17], denoted as FPTRU.KEM = (Keygen, Encaps, Decaps). The pseudocode for the three algorithms of FPTRU.KEM can be found in Algorithm 9, Algorithm 10 and Algorithm 11 respectively.

$\mathcal{H} : \{0,1\}^* \to \mathcal{K} \times \mathcal{COINS}$ is a hash function, where $\mathcal{K}$ is shared key space exported by FPTRU.KEM and $\mathcal{COINS}$ is the random number space used by FPTRU.PKE. Function $\mathcal{H}(\cdot)$ can be divided into two parts: $\mathcal{H}_1(\cdot)$ denotes output mapped to $\mathcal{K}$, and $\mathcal{H}_2(\cdot)$ denotes output mapped to $\mathcal{COINS}$. In Algorithm 10, $\mathcal{H}_2$ can be firstly used in line 2 to generate the necessary coin for encryption. After computing the ciphertext c in line 3, $\mathcal{H}_1$ can be then used to derive the

---

Algorithm 6. FPTRU.PKE.Keygm

Require: security parameter 1^k
Ensure: public-private key pairs of public key encryption (pk, sk)
1: $f', g \leftarrow \Psi_1$
2: $f = pf' + 1$
3: $h = g/f$
4: **return** $(pk = h, sk = f)$

Algorithm 7. FPTRU.PKE.Enc

Require: public key pk, plaintext m
Ensure: ciphertext c
1: $r \leftarrow \Psi_2$
2: $\sigma = hr$
3: $c = \lfloor \frac{q_2}{q}(\sigma + \mathsf{PolyEncode}(m)) \rceil \bmod q_2$
4: **return** c

Algorithm 8. FPTRU.PKE.Dec

Require: secret key sk, ciphertext c
Ensure: plaintext m
1: $m' = cf \bmod {}^{\pm} q_2$
2: $m = \mathsf{PolyDecode}(m')$
3: **return** m

Algorithm 9. FPTRU.KEM.KeyGen

Require: security parameter 1^k
Ensure: public-private key pairs of key encapsulation mechanism (pk', sk')
1: $(pk, sk) \leftarrow \mathsf{FPTRU.PKE.KeyGen}(1^k)$
2: $z \xleftarrow{\$} \{0,1\}^l$
3: **return** $(pk' = pk, sk' = (sk, z))$

Algorithm 10. FPTRU.KEM.Encaps

Require: public key pk'
Ensure: ciphertext c, shared secret K
1: $m \xleftarrow{\$} \mathcal{M}$
2: $(K, coin) = \mathcal{H}(ID(pk), m)$
3: $c = \mathsf{FPTRU.PKE.Enc}(pk, m; coin)$
4: **return** (c, K)

---

shared key K. $ID : \mathcal{PK} \rightarrow \{0,1\}^\gamma$ is a function with fixed-length output, where γ is a positive integer and satisfies $\gamma \geq 256$.

Algorithm 11. FPTRU.KEM.Decaps

Require: secret key $sk' = (sk, z)$, ciphertext c
Ensure: shared secret K
1: $m' = $ FPTRU.PKE.Dec(sk, c)
2: $(K', coin') = \mathcal{H}(ID(pk), m')$
3: $\widehat{K} = \mathcal{H}_1(ID(pk), z, c)$
4: **if** $m' \neq \perp$ and $c = $ FPTRU.PKE.Enc$(pk, m'; coin)$ **then**
5:      **return** K'
6: **else**
7:      **return** $\widehat{K}$
8: **end if**

3.3   Error Rate Calculation

This section calculates the error rate of FPTRU and provides the specific form of polynomial product coefficients in LPPNF, which is used to compute the coefficient distribution of polynomial products during error rate calculation.

Theorem 3 (Correctness of FPTRU). *Let Ψ_1 and Ψ_2 be distributions over R and n, n', q, q_2 be the scheme parameters. $2n' \leq n$, q_2 is even and smaller than q. Let $f', g \leftarrow \Psi_1$ and $r \leftarrow \Psi_2$. Let $\epsilon \leftarrow \chi$, where χ is a distribution over R and defined as sampling $h \leftarrow \mathcal{R}_q$, $r \leftarrow \Psi_2$ and outputing $[\lfloor \frac{q_2}{q} hr \rceil - \frac{q_2}{q} hr]$ mod $^{\pm} q_2$. Let Err_i be i-th octuple of $gr + \frac{q}{q_2}\epsilon f$. Denote $1 - \delta = \Pr[\|Err_i\|_{q,2} < \frac{q}{2}, 1 \leq i \leq \frac{n'}{4}]$ then the error rate of FPTRU is δ.*

In Algorithm 7

$$
\begin{aligned}
c &= \lfloor \tfrac{q_2}{q}(\sigma + \mathsf{PolyEncode}(m)) \rceil = \lfloor \tfrac{q_2}{q} hr + \tfrac{q_2}{q} \cdot \tfrac{q}{2} s \rceil \\
&= \lfloor \tfrac{q_2}{q} hr \rceil + \tfrac{q_2}{2} s = \tfrac{q_2}{q} hr + \epsilon + \tfrac{q_2}{2} s \quad \text{mod } q_2,
\end{aligned}
\tag{1}
$$

where $s \in R_2$, and $\frac{q_2}{2}s$ is the lattice point of the encoded polynomial of m in E_8''. We have cf mod $^{\pm} q_2 = \frac{q_2}{q}((\frac{q}{q_2}c)f$ mod $^{\pm} q)$, thus

$$
\begin{aligned}
m &= \mathsf{PolyDecode}_{E_8''}(cf \quad \text{mod } ^{\pm} q_2) \\
&= \mathsf{PolyDecode}_{E_8'}((\tfrac{q}{q_2}c)f \quad \text{mod } ^{\pm} q)
\end{aligned}
\tag{2}
$$

Substituting the expression of c and $h = \frac{g}{f}$, we get $\left(\frac{q}{q_2}c\right) f$ mod $^{\pm} q = \frac{q}{2}s + gr + \frac{q}{q_2}\epsilon f$ mod $^{\pm} q$. $\frac{q}{2}s$ is the lattice point of the encoded polynomial of m in E_8'. Every octet group of it can be recorded as $\frac{q}{2}(\mathbf{k_i H}$ mod $2)$. To recover $\mathbf{k_i}$, Err_i must satisfy $\|Err_i\|_{q,2} < \frac{q}{2}$, where Err_i is the i-th octet group of $gr + \frac{q}{q_2}\epsilon f$, $1 \leq i \leq \frac{n'}{4}$. Moreover, only the first $\frac{n'}{4}$ octet groups need to be processed to recover the plaintext m, as the information of m is only encoded in the first $\frac{n'}{4}$ octet groups. In conclusion, Theorem 3 is proved.

Notably, since the coefficient distribution of the polynomial product depends on the distribution and number of coefficients of the multiplied polynomials, the exact number of terms in the polynomial product over LPPNF must also be specified. For polynomials $f = \sum_{i=0}^{n-1} f_i x^i, g = \sum_{i=0}^{n-1} g_i x^i \in R_q$, denote their product as $h = fg = \sum_{k=0}^{n-1} h_k x^k \in R_q$.

1. for $k = 0$, h_k has n terms of the form $f_i g_j$;

$$h_k = f_0 g_0 + \sum_{i=1}^{n-1} f_i g_{n-i} \tag{3}$$

2. for $1 \leq k \leq n - 2$, h_k has $2n - k$ terms of the form $f_i g_j$;

$$h_k = \sum_{i=0}^{k} f_i g_{k-i} + \sum_{i=k}^{n-1} f_i g_{n-1+k-i} + \sum_{i=k+1}^{n-1} f_i g_{n+k-i} \tag{4}$$

3. for $k = n - 1$, h_k has $n + 1$ terms of the form $f_i g_j$.

$$h_k = \sum_{i=0}^{n-1} f_i g_{n-1-i} + f_{n-1} g_{n-1} \tag{5}$$

Given the distribution of f_i and g_j, the distribution of h_k can be computed. The methodology and Python scripts for calculating the error rate of FPTRU are derived from references [4]. The related error rate calculation results can be seen in Table 1.

3.4   Security Analysis

PKE based on NTRU can naturally achieve OW-CPA security based on the security of NTRU. Besides achieving OW-CPA security, FPTRU.PKE can also achieve IND-CPA security based on the hardness assumptions of NTRU and RLWR.

Theorem 4 (IND-CPA security of FPTRU). *For any probabilistic polynomial-time adversary $\mathcal{A}$, there exist probabilistic polynomial-time adversaries $\mathcal{B}$ and $\mathcal{C}$ such that*

$$Adv_{\mathsf{FPTRU.PKE}}^{IND\text{-}CPA}(\mathcal{A}) \leq Adv_{\mathcal{R}_q, \Psi_1}^{NTRU}(\mathcal{B}) + Adv_{\mathcal{R}_q, \Psi_2}^{RLWR}(\mathcal{C}) \tag{6}$$

The proof will be completed through a sequence of games. $\mathcal{A}$ is a polynomial time adversary. Win_i is the winning event that $\mathcal{A}$ outputs a bit $b' = b$ in game G_i.

Game G_0 is the original IND-CPA security game of FPTRU.PKE. Therefore, $Adv_{\mathsf{FPTRU.PKE}}^{IND\text{-}CPA}(\mathcal{A}) = |\Pr[Win_0] - \frac{1}{2}|$.

Game G_1 is essentially the same as game G_0, except that in the key generation algorithm of game G_1, the public key $h = \frac{g}{f}$ is replaced by a randomly chosen element h from R_q. Therefore, distinguishing between game G_0 and game G_1 is equivalent to solving the decision NTRU hardness problem. That is, there exists an adversary $\mathcal{B}$, whose running time is comparable to $\mathcal{A}$, and $|\Pr[Win_0] - \Pr[Win_1]| \leq \mathrm{Adv}_{R_q, \Psi_1}^{\mathrm{NTRU}}(\mathcal{B})$.

Game G_2 is similar to game G_1 except that in game G_2, the ciphertext $c = \lfloor \frac{q_2}{q} hr \rceil + \frac{q_2}{2} s \mod q_2$, where $s \in R_2$. Additionally, game G_2 replaces $\lfloor \frac{q_2}{q} hr \rceil$ in $\lfloor \frac{q_2}{q} hr \rceil + \frac{q_2}{2} s \mod q_2$ with a uniformly random element in R_{q_2}. Thus distinguishing between game G_1 and G_2 is equivalent to solving the RLWR hardness problem. In other words, there exists an adversary $\mathcal{C}$, whose running time is comparable to $\mathcal{A}$, and $|\Pr[Win_2] - \Pr[Win_1]| \leq \mathrm{Adv}_{R, \Psi_2}^{\mathrm{RLWR}}(\mathcal{C})$.

In game G_2, the plaintext message m_b is perfectly hidden by the uniformly random element in R_{q_2}, and any probabilistic polynomial-time adversary has zero advantage, i.e., $\Pr[Win_2] = \frac{1}{2}$.

In conclusion, combining the above probability equations, we get

$$\mathrm{Adv}_{\mathsf{FPTRU.PKE}}^{\mathrm{IND\text{-}CPA}}(\mathcal{A}) \leq \mathrm{Adv}_{R_q, \Psi_1}^{\mathrm{NTRU}}(\mathcal{B}) + \mathrm{Adv}_{R_q, \Psi_2}^{\mathrm{RLWR}}(\mathcal{C}). \tag{7}$$

Since FPTRU.KEM is derived from FPTRU.PKE through $FO_{ID(pk),m}^{\not\perp}$ transformation, FPTRU.KEM also meets IND-CCA security under the classical random oracle model and quantum random oracle model based on the conclusion from [17]. The results presented in this section are most reproducrd from [26] for content self-containment and clear reference.

Theorem 5 (IND-CCA security of FPTRU).
Let ℓ be the minimum entropy of $ID(pk)$, where $(pk, sk) \leftarrow$ FPTRU.PKE. KeyGen. For any (quantum) adversary $\mathcal{A}$, if it can make at most q_D decapsulation queries and q_H (quantum) random oracle queries, then there exists an (quantum) adversary $\mathcal{B}$ with running time comparable to $\mathcal{A}$ such that

1. in the classical random oracle model, we have

$$Adv_{\mathsf{FPTRU.KEM}}^{IND\text{-}CCA}(\mathcal{A}) \leq 2 \left(Adv_{\mathsf{FPTRU.PKE}}^{IND\text{-}CPA}(\mathcal{B}) + \frac{q_H + 1}{|\mathcal{M}|} \right)$$
$$+ \frac{q_H}{2^\ell} + (q_D + q_H) \cdot \delta + \frac{1}{2^\ell}. \tag{8}$$

2. in the quantum random oracle model, let $q_{HD} = q_D + q_H + 1$, then

$$Adv_{\mathsf{FPTRU.KEM}}^{IND\text{-}CCA}(\mathcal{A}) \leq 2\sqrt{q_{HD} \cdot Adv_{\mathsf{FPTRU.PKE}}^{IND\text{-}CPA}(\mathcal{B})}$$
$$+ \frac{4q_{HD}}{\sqrt{|\mathcal{M}|}} + \frac{4(q_H + 1)}{\sqrt{2^\ell}} + 16q_{HD}^2\delta + \frac{1}{|\mathcal{M}|} + \frac{1}{2^\ell}. \tag{9}$$

We use the Python script provided by [3] to calculate the classical and quantum security strength using the core-SVP methodology. The results are shown in Table 1.

Table 1. FPTRU parameter set

	n	q	q_2	n'	(Ψ_1,Ψ_2)	$|pk|$	$|ct|$	B.W.	$NTRU(C,Q)$	$RLWR(C,Q)$	δ
FPTRU-653	653	4621	2^{11}	320	(B_3,B_3)	994	898	1892	(152,137)	(151,136)	2^{-166}
FPTRU-761	761	4591	2^{10}	376	(B_2,B_2)	1158	952	2110	(173,157)	(172,156)	2^{-167}
FPTRU-1277	1277	7879	2^{10}	632	(B_2,B_2)	2067	1597	3664	(299,271)	(297,269)	2^{-279}

3.5 FPTRU Parameter Set

Table 1 provides three sets of parameters for FPTRU: FPTRU-653, FPTRU-761, and FPTRU-1277.

$R_q = \mathbb{Z}_q[x]/(x^n - x - 1)$ is LPPNF used in FPTRU, where n is the dimension and q is the modulus, with the condition that $x^n - x - 1$ is irreducible in $\mathbb{Z}_q[x]$. q_2 is the ciphertext modulus. The plaintext space is $M = \{0,1\}^{n'}$, whose space modulus is fixed at $p = 2$. Ψ_1 and Ψ_2 represent probability distributions, and FPTRU only focus on the distribution B_η, which denotes the centered binomial distribution with integer η as a parameter. $|pk|$ denotes the size of the public key, $|sk|$ denotes the size of the ciphertext, and B.W. denotes the bandwidth, i.e. $|pk| + |sk|$, all measured in bytes.

4   Implementation of FPTRU

4.1   Optimized Pseudo-mersenne Reduction

Pseudo-mersenne numbers refer to values of the form $q' = 2^x - 2^y + 1$, where x and y are positive integers. Pseudo-mersenne primes are utilized in modular reduction via the property $2^x \equiv 2^y - 1 \bmod q'$. Traditional pseudo-Mersenne reduction [34] requires the input and output ranges to be positive integers and also necessitates additional correction steps. Our optimized version extend the input range and eliminate additional correction steps, using simple bitwise operations (logical AND, shifts) and addition/subtraction instead of multiplication or division and requiring no precomputed values.

Algorithm 12. Pseudo-Mersenne reduction (single round)

Require: pseudo-Mersenne number $q' = 2^x - 2^y + 1, y < \frac{x}{2}$, integer a, $-2^{2x-y} < a < 2^{2x-y}$

Ensure: $r = a \bmod q', -q' \leq r < q'$

1: $r = [a]_x - [a]^x + [a]^x << y - q'$

2: **return** r

Single round version is shown in Algorithm 12. It takes input $a \in (-2^{2x-y}, 2^{2x-y})$ and computes $r = a \bmod q' \in [-q', q')$, suitable for subsequent

---

Algorithm 13. Pseudo-Mersenne reduction (dual round)

Require: pseudo-Mersenne number $q' = 2^x - 2^y + 1, y < \frac{x}{2}$, integer a, $-2^{3x-2y} < a <$
  2^{3x-2y}

Ensure: $r = a \bmod q', -q' \le r < q'$
  1: $r = [a]_x - [a]^x + [a]^x << y$
  2: $r = [r]_x - [r]^x + [r]^x << y - q'$
  3: **return** r

FFT trick computations. Dual round version shown in Algorithm 13 is applicable to a larger input range with $a \in (-2^{3x-2y}, 2^{3x-2y})$ as input. It is suitable for computing modular multiplication $r = ab \bmod p'(a, b \in \mathbb{Z}_{q'})$ where the magnitude of ab often exceeds the effective representation range of current integer variables.

4.2 Pseudo-Mersenne Incomplete NTT

In FPTRU, there are two types of polynomial multiplications: $h = gf_{inv} \bmod q$ in R_q and $m' = cf \bmod {}^{\pm}q_2$ in R_{q_2}. However, due to the fact that both the parameters n and q chosen in FPTRU are prime and q_2 is a power of 2, the direct usage of length-n cyclic convolution NTT for computing these two types of polynomial multiplications is not feasible. We transform polynomial multiplication in $\mathbb{Z}_q[x]/(x^n - x - 1)$ to $\mathbb{Z}_{q'}[x]/(x^N - 1)$. The NTT operation in $\mathbb{Z}_{q'}[x]/(x^N - 1)$ is defined as pseudo-Mersenne incomplete NTT.

Table 2. Parameters of pseudo-Mersenne incomplete NTT

	(n, q, q_2, η)	(N, q')	order of FFT trick
FPTRU-653	(653,4621,2^{11},3)	(1344,16777153 $= 2^{24} - 2^6 + 1$)	5 radix-2 NTTs, 1 radix-3 NTT, 1 radix-2 NTT
FPTRU-761	(761,4591,2^{10},2)	(1536,33550337 $= 2^{25} - 2^{12} + 1$)	9 radix-2 NTTs
FPTRU-1277	(1277,7879,2^{10},2)	(2560,33550337 $= 2^{25} - 2^{12} + 1$)	9 radix-2 NTTs

Polynomial multiplication $h = fg \in R_q$ will be shown below as an example with the corresponding schematic diagram provided in Fig. 1. Firstly, extending n-dimensional polynomials f and g by padding zeros to the higher degree terms to obtain extended polynomials $f', g' \in \mathbb{Z}_{q'}[x]/(x^N - 1)$, where $N \ge 2n$ and q' is a sufficiently large prime number such that it exceeds the maximum coefficient value of the polynomials during the computation process. Secondly, utilizing the pseudo-Mersenne incomplete NTT of dimension N to perform forward NTT, point-wise multiplication, and inverse NTT sequentially on f' and g', resulting in $h' = f'g' \in \mathbb{Z}_{q'}[x]/(x^N - 1)$. Thirdly, Computing $h = (h' \bmod x^n - x - 1) \bmod q$, which is the result of multiplication of f and g in R_q.

The criteria for selecting N and q' is to maximize the inclusion of factors of 2 in N, while q' is chosen to be a pseudo-Mersenne prime. Table 2 shows the parameter selection and order of FFT trick for pseudo-Mersenne incomplete

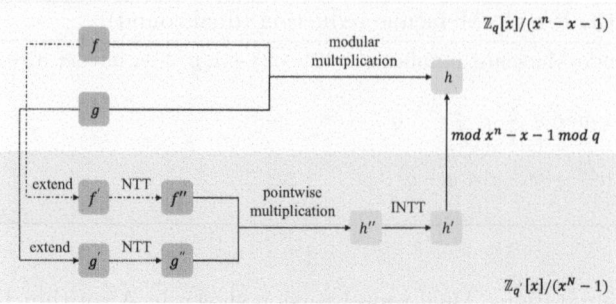

Fig. 1. Diagram of computing $h = fg \in R_q$.

NTT for different FPTRU parameters. For example, for FPTRU-653, since $N = 1344 = 2^6 \cdot 3 \cdot 7$, it can perform 6 radix-2 NTTs and 1 radix-3 NTT. To reduce the storage space required for primitive roots of unity, we first compute 5 layers of radix-2 NTT, then 1 layer of radix-3 NTT, and finally 1 layer of radix-2 NTT.

4.3   Batch Key Generation for FPTRU

The batch key generation method of FPTRU is based on the technique of Montgomery inversion proposed by [27]. This method is also applied to the batch key generation of SNTRU-Prime in [8]. In this section, we will present the main idea and pseudocode of FPTRU batch key generation.

Assuming $(f_1, f_2, \cdots, f_n)$ are n polynomials in $Z_q[x]/f(x)$, our goal is to compute the inverses of these polynomials, i.e. $(f_1^{-1}, f_2^{-1}, \cdots, f_n^{-1})$. Let $f_{mul} = \prod_{i=1}^{n} f_i$, then using one polynomial inversion, we obtain f_{mul}^{-1}. To get $f_k^{-1}, 1 \leq k \leq n$, we compute $f_{mul}^{-1} \cdot \prod_{i=1}^{k-1} f_i \cdot \prod_{i=k+1}^{n} f_i$.

Algorithm 14. BatchPolyInv: Batch Polynomial Inverse

Require: n polynomials $(f_1, f_2, \cdots, f_n)$ in $Z_q[x]/f(x)$
Ensure: $(f_1^{-1}, f_2^{-1}, \cdots, f_n^{-1})$
1: $f_{mul} = \prod_{i=1}^{n} f_i$
2: $f_{mul}^{-1} = \mathsf{PolyInverse}(f_{mul})$
3: **for** $i = n$ to 3 **do**
4:    $f_i^{-1} = f_{mul}^{-1} \prod_{j=1}^{i-1} f_j$
5:    $f_{mul}^{-1} = f_{mul}^{-1} f_i$
6: **end for**
7: $f_1^{-1} = f_{mul}^{-1} f_2$
8: $f_2^{-1} = f_{mul}^{-1} f_1$
9: **return** $(f_1^{-1}, f_2^{-1}, \cdots, f_n^{-1})$

Traditional methods require calling the polynomial inversion algorithm n times, whereas Algorithm 14 transforms n polynomial inversions into one polynomial inversion and $\frac{n^2}{2} + \frac{3n}{2} - 2$ polynomial multiplications. We define time

Algorithm 15. FPTRU.PKE.BatchKeygen

Require: security parameter 1^k
Ensure: n public-private key pairs of public key encryption (PK_s, SK_s)
1: $H = [\cdot], F = [\cdot], G = [\cdot]$
2: **while** $len(F) < n$ **do**
3:      $f', g \leftarrow \Psi_1$
4:      $f = pf' + 1$
5:      F.append(f)
6:      G.append(g)
7: **end while**
8: $F = \mathsf{BatchPolyInv}(F)$
9: **for** i=1 to n **do**
10:      $h = G[i] \cdot F[i]$
11:      H.append(h)
12: **end for**
13: **return** $(PK_s = H, SK_s = F)$

---

consume of PolyMul(polynomial multiplication) is a, then PolyInverse(polynomial inversion) is ra, where r is the the ratio of PolyInverse to PolyMul. Besides, let time consuming of other operations in key generation except PolyInverse and PolyMul is c. Then for batch size n, the average time is $\frac{a(\frac{n^2}{2} + \frac{3n}{2} - 2) + ra + nc}{n} = \frac{an}{2} + \frac{(r-2)a}{n} + \frac{3a}{2} + c$, where the minimum lies in $\sqrt{2(r-2)}$ theoretically. We implement PolyInverse based on the constant time algotithm proposed in [10] and PolyMul with pseudo-Mersenne incomplete NTT described in Sect. 4.2.

Algorithm 15 is the batch version of Algorithm 6. Three lists are used to store n batches of $f, g, h \in \mathbb{Z}_q[x]/(x^n - x - 1)$. The processing logic of Algorithm 6 and Algorithm 15 is roughly the same, the major difference is that n inversions is replaced by algorithm BatchPolyInv in line 8. The batch key generation is essentially an optimization of polynomial inversion. The processes associated with secret keys such as polynomial sampling are still carried out separately and independently. This ensures no correlation between keys and maintains their randomness.

5   TLS Application

To measure the performance of FPTRU in real-world environments, in this section, we will discuss the TLS integration of FPTRU and its batch key generation version and emulated network. Specifically, after integrating FPTRU into OpenSSL, we utilized a client program to simulate TLS interactions in real network environments with an nginx server loaded with patched OpenSSL.

5.1   OpenSSL Patches

We developed patches for OpenSSL 3.3 to test how FPTRU works in real protocols. Figure 2 depicts the architecture diagram of OpenSSL, highlighting with black dot line boxes inside the providers and liboqs modules, the patched OpenSSL components. Provider is a unit that provides one or more algorithm implementations. 3rd party providers enable any developer to inject any new algorithms they want to OpenSSL, one of which is oqs-provider using post-quantumn algorithms implemented in liboqs, an open source C library for quantum-safe cryptographic algorithms.

We inject FPTRU into liboqs and modify oqs-provider to support it, enabling OpenSSL to correctly utilize the integrated FPTRU algorithm. As described above, once application loads oqs-provider correctly, with the help of module EVP and Core, it can use FPTRU to complete key exchange. Here, we will provide a detailed explanation of the specific call process using Fig. 2. After the application sends an initialization request to the Core, the Core physically loads the module into memory and calls the oqs-provider's entry point for self-initialization, as depicted by the green solid line. Once the user application requests FPTRU algorithms, such as key generation, by calling a fetch routine, the task is handled by the EVP module. As indicated by the gray dashed line, EVP first searches the Core's cache for the target algorithm; if not found, it queries providers for support of the algorithm. When the user starts using the algorithm, the function pointer is invoked and ends up in the oqs-provider for the implementation in liboqs to perform the requested algorithm, as shown by the yellow dash and dot line. In liboqs, FPTRU is instantiated in `OQS_KEM_new`. And according to the specific requests, pointers in `OQS_KEM` of FPTRU are used.

To support the situation of batch key generation in practical applications, we also implement Algorithm 15 in OpenSSL. When the batch size is n, Algorithm 15 is invoked once to generate keys, and any unused keys are stored in the memory pool. Subsequent $n - 1$ requests will directly use the keys from the memory pool. We achieve this process by encapsulating a decision layer around Algorithm 15 and integrating it with the `OQS_KEM_keypair` interface.

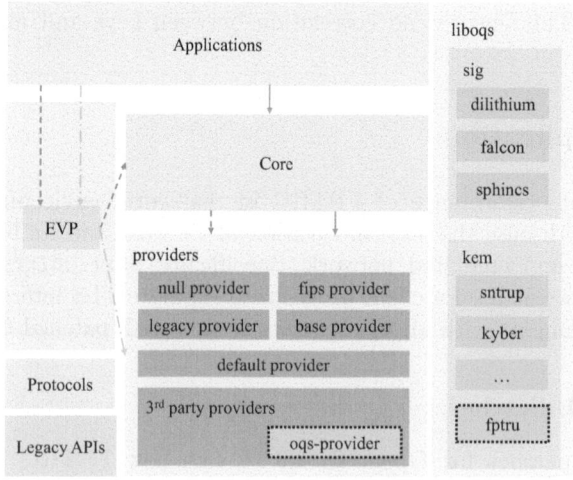

Fig. 2. OpenSSL structure and our patches.

5.2   Emulated Network

Based on [30] we conducted experiments on a single-link (client-server) topology, using netem to directly control network characteristics, allowing us to isolate the impact of individual network features on the different algorithm performance in TLS 1.3. The goal of the simulated network experiment is to measure the time required to complete a TLS handshake using FPTRU under various network conditions.

We first created two namespaces and connected them using veth pairs. One namespace serves as the client, and the other as the server. On the server side, an nginx server with the patched OpenSSL was run. On the client side, the `s_timer` program provided by OpenSSL was modified (named as `s_timers`) to record the TLS handshake time. Specifically, `s_timers` establishes multiple TLS connections with the nginx server. Once the connection is successfully established, it immediately terminates the connection and records the overall handshake time.

Network traffic within two namespaces can be controlled using netem. Netem simulates packet loss behavior by discarding packets sent by the kernel with a certain probability. Additionally, it provides functionality to delay packet transmission, thereby simulating transmission delay and queuing delay on the network. The delay on veth pairs is set to $\frac{x}{2}$ ms to simulate a round-trip delay of x ms. A packet loss rate of $y\%$ is set on each veth pair. Based on telemetry data collected by Mozilla in September and October 2019 from Firefox (Nightly 71) [28], we use a range of 0–15% to simulate different network qualities. Besides, using a pooling mechanism, we set different server loads to control the number of connections processed by the server at the same time.

6   Performance Analysis

The primary motivation behind the research on FPTRU is to design a scheme superior to SNTRU-Prime [6], so to demonstrate its superiority, we will compare it with SNTRU-Prime. We selected two C implementations of SNTRU-Prime, named SNTRUPA and SNTRUPB. The open-source project OpenQuantum-Safe [1] is dedicated to facilitating the migration to post-quantum cryptography, with SNTRUPA being its specific integrated implementation of the SNTRU-Prime algorithm. SNTRUPB is libsntrup761 [8], which not only includes a general implementation of SNTRU-Prime algorithm but also features batch key generation functionality. The experiments were run on a Linux(6.5.0-27-generic 22.04.1-Ubuntu) server, which has 3.2 GHz Intel(R) Core(TM) i9-14900K CPU and 62 GB RAM. The complier is gcc (Ubuntu 11.4.0-1ubuntu1 22.04) 11.4.0.

6.1   Polynomial Optimization

This section will present the test data for the pseudo-Mersenne reduction, pseudo-Mersenne incomplete NTT, and batch key generation, along with comparative experimental data with similar schemes.

Benchmarks for Pseudo-mersenne Reduction. In this section, we compare the single pseudo-Mersenne reduction with Barrett reduction because they have similar input-output ranges and dual pseudo-Mersenne reduction with Montgomery reduction for the same reason.

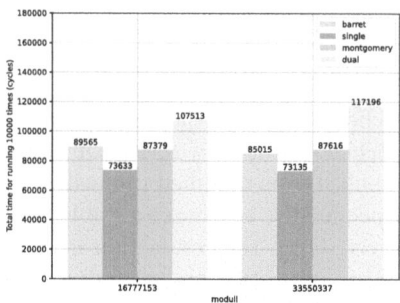

Fig. 3. Performance comparison of modular reduction algorithms for different pseudo-mersenne numbers.

As shown in the Table 2, in FPTRU two main pseudo-mersenne numbers are used, $16777153 = 2^{24} - 2^6 + 1$ and $33550337 = 2^{25} - 2^{12} + 1$. We run each reduction algorithms 10000 times and the results are shown in Fig. 3. For the two pseudo-mersenne numbers, single pseudo-Mersenne reduction outperforms barret reduction and Montgomery reduction outperforms dual pseudo-Mersenne reduction. We get the conclusion that in coefficient multiplication scenarios, Montgomery reduction should be used, while in scenarios where overflow is to be avoided after addition, single pseudo-Mersenne reduction should be employed.

Benchmarks for Pseudo-mersenne Incomplete NTT. This section will present a comparison of the polynomial multiplication in LPPNF using pseudo-Mersenne incomplete NTT with methods proposed in [2].

Due to the fact that [2] only optimizes NTT for polynomial multiplication over $\mathbb{Z}_{4591}[x]/(x^{761} - x - 1)$ in NTRU-Prime, lacking optimizations for $\mathbb{Z}_{4621}[x]/(x^{653} - x - 1)$ and $\mathbb{Z}_{7879}[x]/(x^{1277} - x - 1)$, Table 3 provides a comparison between the pseudo-Mersenne incomplete NTT and the three optimization strategies proposed by [2], i,e. Good's trick+NTT, mixed-radix NTT (strategy 1), and mixed-radix NTT (strategy 2), over $\mathbb{Z}_{4591}[x]/(x^{761} - x - 1)$. From Table 3, it can be observed that, compared to other algorithms, the pseudo-Mersenne incomplete NTT demonstrates advantages in single polynomial multiplication. Specifically, it requires 2.0–6.0 times fewer multiplications compared to Good's trick+NTT, mixed-radix NTT (strategy 1), and mixed-radix NTT (strategy 2). With the same dimension of extended ring, compared to Good's trick+NTT, the pseudo-Mersenne incomplete NTT consumes less multiplications.

Table 3. Comparison of the number of polynomial multiplications in $\mathbb{Z}_{4591}[x]/(x^{761} - x - 1)$

	extended ring	2 forward transform	inverse transform	pointwise multiplication	total
pseudo-Mersenne incomplete NTT	$\mathbb{Z}_{33550337}[x]/(x^{1536} - 1)$	10.8k	6.1k	3.6k	20.5k
Good's trick+NTT	$\mathbb{Z}_{6984193}[x]/(x^{1536} - 1)$	23.0k	17.7k	1.5k	42.2k
mixed-radix NTT (strategy 1)	$\mathbb{Z}_{4591}[x]/(x^{1620} - 1)$	24.3k	6.5k	11.3k	42.1k
mixed-radix NTT (strategy 2)	$\mathbb{Z}_{4591}[x]/(x^{1530} - 1)$	52.7k	52.7k	16.8k	122.2k

Benchmarks for Batch Key Generation. In this section, we will show how increasing n, the key generation batch size, amortizes the polynomial inversion cost.

Table 4. Average cpucycles of PolyInverse and PolyMul

	FPTRU-653	FPTRU-761	FPTRU-1277
PolyInverse	3411200.83	4642677.85	13088790.28
PolyMul	44692.42	46415.36	83567.38
$r = \frac{PolyInverse}{PolyMul}$	76.32	100.02	156.62

The essence of batch key generation lies in replacing the time-consuming polynomial inversion operation with less time-consuming polynomial multiplication. Specifically, batch key generation utilizes $\frac{n^2}{2} + \frac{3n}{2} - 2$ polynomial multiplications to replace $n - 1$ polynomial inversions. To understand the efficiency improvement brought by this operation, we first need to compare the efficiency of PolyInverse and PolyMul, which is shown in Table 4.

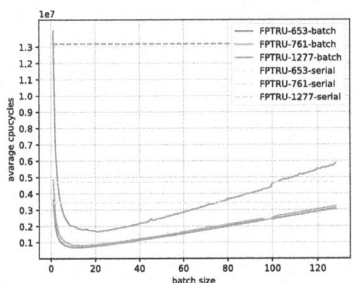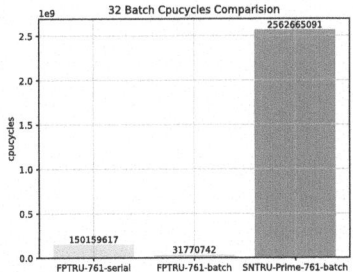

Fig. 4. BatchKeyGen metrics regarding various batch sizes (n).

We show the benchmark results for batch key generation (FPTRU.PKE.BatchKeyGen) in Fig. 4. All parameters of FPTRU outperforms its original implementation, which is shown with horizontal dashed line. The minimum average time is consistent with the theoretical analysis $\sqrt{2(r-2)}$ as described in Sect. 4.3, where r is the ratio of PolyInverse to PolyMul shown in the last row of Table 4. In conclusion, adopting batch processing for FPTRU key generation can provide throughput advantages.

Figure 4 also provides the cpucycles required for generating 32 sets of public-private keys under the batch size of 32 for various schemes. FPTRU-761-batch represents the scheme using batch key generation, while FPTRU-761-serial represents the scheme calling key generation 32 times serially. SNTRU-Prime-761-batch invokes SNTRUPB to complete batch key generation of SNTRU-Prime-761. It can be observed that batch key generation of FPTRU-761 brings a 4.7× efficiency improvement compared to serial key generation and an 80.7× efficiency improvement compared to batch key generation of SNTRU-Prime-761.

6.2   Overall Performance of FPTRU

Table 5 gives efficiency of all parameters of FPTRU and compares the efficiency of FPTRU-761 and SNTRU-Prime-761(implemented by SNTRUPB). Keygen, encaps and decaps respectively provide the avarage cpucycles for running the key generation algorithm, key encapsulation algorithm and key decapsulation algorithm 10000 times. We can get the conclusion that FPTRU-761 outperforms SNTRU-Prime-761. Specifically, for the keygen, encaps and decaps, FPTRU-761 is faster than SNTRU-Prime-761 by 16.1, 174.5 and 284.5 times respectively.

Table 5. Efficiency of FPTRU and comparison with SNTRU-Prime measured in cpucycles

	keygen	encaps	decaps
FPTRU-653	3453075	59367	110775
FPTRU-761	4691681	62533	116113
FPTRU-1277	13179118	109072	204742
SNTRU-Prime-761	75643460	10910838	33032824

Table 6 provides a performance comparison between FPTRU, SNTRU-Prime and Kyber. $|pk|$ denotes the public key size, $|ct|$ denotes the ciphertext size, and B.W. denotes the bandwidth, which is $|pk| + |ct|$, all measured in bytes. (C, Q) gives the security strength of the scheme, where C and Q measured in bits refer to the security strength under classical and quantum scenarios respectively. Under multiple hardness assumptions, the minimum security strength under different hardness assumptions is selected as the scheme's security strength. δ denotes the error rate of the scheme. In terms of bandwidth, although FPTRU and SNTRU-Prime have the same public key sizes, FPTRU-761/1277 exhibit smaller ciphertext sizes compared to SNTRU-Prime-761/1277 (reductions of 8.3% and

13.5% respectively) and FPTRU-653's ciphertext size is only one byte larger than SNTRU-Prime-653, which is practically negligible. Regarding security strength, all three parameter sets of FPTRU surpass SNTRU-Prime in both classical and quantum security strengths. Although SNTRU-Prime achieves zero error rate, error rates of FPTRU are practically negligible relative to its quantum security strengths, thus not impacting its security. For example, error rate of FPTRU-761 is 2^{-167} which is negligible and is smaller than 2^{-164} of Kyber-768, recommended as parameter of the ML-KEM standard.

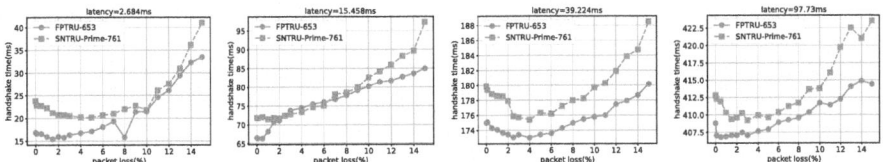

Fig. 5. Handshake completion time (median) vs. packet loss at different round trip times using FPTRU-653 and SNTRU-Prime-761.

6.3 TLS Performance

For various post-quantum key exchange algorithms, the differences in their bandwidth size and algorithmic performance yield varied impacts on TLS handshake time, as elucidated by the experimental findings from [30]. On high-quality links, TLS handshake time is significantly shaped by algorithmic performance, while on low-quality links, bandwidth constraints play a more important role.

In comparison to SNTRU-Prime-761, the classical and quantum security strengths of FPTRU-653 are already on par with it. From a security perspective, in real-world applications, FPTRU-653 can be considered as an alternative to SNTRU-Prime-761. Hence, in the context of TLS application, we compare FPTRU-653 with SNTRU-Prime-761.

Compared to SNTRU-Prime-761, FPTRU-653 achieves a reduction of 14.1% in public key size, 13.5% in ciphertext size, and an overall bandwidth reduction of 13.8%. We us SNTRUPA as an instantiation of SNTRU-Prime-761 and compare it with FPTRU-653. The results show that FPTRU-653 is 2 times faster in keygen, 7.8 times faster in encaps, and 11.5 times faster in decaps.

Based on emulated network described in Sect. 5.2, we set up 50 entities to attempt establishing connections with the server, with a maximum of 4 entities connecting simultaneously. Each entity attempts to perform 100 handshakes. We analyze the median of the 5000 handshake completion times.

Figure 5 shows handshake completion times of FPTRU-653 and SNTRU-Prime-761. On links with low network latency, exemplified by Fig. 5-1 and Fig. 5-2, FPTRU-653 consistently outpaces SNTRU-Prime-761 owing to its superior algorithmic performance. Consequently, it necessitates shorter handshake times,

Table 6. Performance comparison between FPTRU and SNTRU-Prime

	hardness assumption	algebraic structure	$|pk|$ (byte)	$|ct|$ (byte)	B.W. (byte)	(C, Q) (bit)	δ
FPTRU-653	NTRU+RLWR	LPPNF	994	898	1892	(151,136)	2^{-166}
FPTRU-761			1158	952	2110	(172,156)	2^{-167}
FPTRU-1277			2067	1597	3664	(297,269)	2^{-279}
SNTRU-Prime-653	NTRU-OW	LPPNF	994	897	1891	(129,117)	$2^{-\infty}$
SNTRU-Prime-761			1158	1039	2197	(153,137)	$2^{-\infty}$
SNTRU-Prime-1277			2067	1847	3914	(270,244)	$2^{-\infty}$
Kyber-768	MLWE	2^n-th cyclotomic ring	1184	1088	2272	(183,166)	2^{-164}
Kyber-1024			1568	1568	3136	(256,232)	2^{-174}

particularly when the packet loss rate is minimal (below 2%). For example, when latency is 2.684 ms and packet loss is 2%, FPTRU-653 can complete 1.3× handshakes compared to SNTRU-Prime-761. Nevertheless, as the packet loss rate increases, FPTRU-653's advantage gradually diminishes, tapering off to comparable handshake times with SNTRU-Prime-761. However, once the packet loss rate surpasses 10%, FPTRU-653's bandwidth efficiency shines through, showcasing a more pronounced superiority. Specifically, when latency is 15.458 ms and packet loss is 15%, FPTRU-653 can complete 1.2× handshakes compared to SNTRU-Prime-761. Conversely, on links with higher network latency, as illustrated in Fig. 5-3 and Fig. 5-4, FPTRU-653 demonstrates shorter handshake times than SNTRU-Prime-761 under minimal packet loss scenarios (below 2%). This aligns with the findings on links with lower network latency. However, as packet loss rate increases, the protracted transmission time between the client and server exacerbates the impact of packet loss on handshake time. Consequently, FPTRU-653's bandwidth advantage becomes more and more obvious and its superiority is more prominent with the increase of packet loss rate. Specifically, when latency is 39.224 ms, FPTRU-653 can complete 1.01× and 1.04× handshakes compared to SNTRU-Prime-761 when packet loss is 6% and 15% respectively.

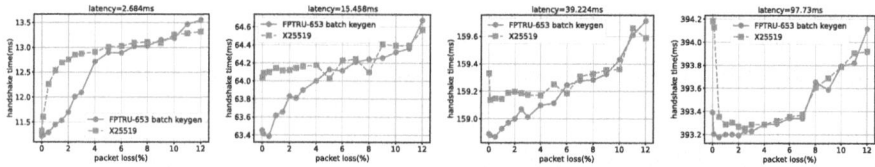

Fig. 6. Handshake completion time (median) vs. packet loss at different round trip times using FPTRU-653-batch-keygen and X25519.

Besides, we compare the runtime performance of the batch key generation version of FPTRU with non-quantum-safe techniques X25519. As shown in Fig. 6, under various link conditions, batch key generation of FPTRU-653 demonstrate better performance when packet loss smaller than 4% and similar performance of X25519 when packet loss larger than 4% with the difference in handshake times typically around 0.1 ms.

7   Conclusion

Traditional NTRU key encapsulation mechanisms exhibit shortcomings in computational efficiency, inability to compress ciphertexts, limited secret value range, and provide a weak foundation for CCA security reduction. Thus, FPTRU−−an optimization of NTRU-Prime is presented.

Firstly, ciphertext lossy compression is introduced in FPTRU to reduce bandwidth. Using the more robust error-correcting E_8 lattice code allows for a wider range of noise. Besides, optimized pseudo-Mersenne reduction is used to accelerate the process of reduction. Traditional NTT can not be applied in LPPNF, so pseudo-Mersenne incomplete NTT is used, which requires fewer multiplications.

Secondly, considering the situation of batch key generation in practical applications, we apply Montgomery inversion to key generation of FPTRU and explore the optimal batch size. For the batch size 32, FPTRU-761 batch key generation brings a 4.7× efficiency improvement compared to serial key generation and an 80.7× efficiency improvement compared to SNTRU-Prime-761 batch key generation.

Thirdly, FPTRU-653 is compared with SNTRU-Prime-761 in TLS 1.3 because they have same classical and quantum security length. Results show that FPTRU-653 outperforms SNTRU-Prime-761 on links with both low and high network latency. For example, when latency is 15.458 ms and packet loss is 15%, FPTRU-653 can complete 1.2× handshakes compared to SNTRU-Prime-761. Besides, our batch key generation of FPTRU demonstrate better performance when packet loss smaller than 4% and similar performance of X25519 when packet loss larger than 4% with the difference in handshake times typically around 0.1 ms.

References

1. Openquantumsafe, https://openquantumsafe.org/
2. Alkim, E., et al.: Polynomial multiplication in NTRU prime comparison of optimization strategies on cortex-m4. IACR Trans. Cryptogr. Hardw. Embed. Syst. **2021**(1), 217–238 (2021). https://doi.org/10.46586/TCHES.V2021.I1.217-238
3. Alkim, E., Ducas, L., Pöppelmann, T., Schwabe, P.: Post-quantum key exchange - A new hope. In: Holz, T., Savage, S. (eds.) 25th USENIX Security Symposium, USENIX Security 16, Austin, TX, USA, 10–12 August 2016, pp. 327–343. USENIX Association (2016). https://www.usenix.org/conference/usenixsecurity16/technical-sessions/presentation/alkim
4. Avanzi, R., et al.: Crystals-kyber algorithm specifications and supporting documentation. NIST PQC Round **2**(4), 1–43 (2019)
5. Banerjee, A., Peikert, C., Rosen, A.: Pseudorandom functions and lattices. In: Pointcheval, D., Johansson, T. (eds.) EUROCRYPT 2012. LNCS, vol. 7237, pp. 719–737. Springer, Heidelberg (2012). https://doi.org/10.1007/978-3-642-29011-4_42

6. Bernstein, D.J., Brumley, B., Chen, M.S., et al.: NTRU Prime: Round 3 (2020). https://csrc.nist.gov/projects/post-quantum-cryptography/round-3-submissions

7. Bernstein, D.J.: Multidigit multiplication for mathematicians. In: Advances in Applied Mathematics, pp. 1–19 (2001)

8. Bernstein, D.J., Brumley, B.B., Chen, M.S., Tuveri, N.: {OpenSSLNTRU}: faster post-quantum {TLS} key exchange. In: 31st USENIX Security Symposium (USENIX Security 22), pp. 845–862 (2022)

9. Bernstein, D.J., Lange, T.: Non-randomness of s-unit lattices. Cryptology ePrint Archive (2021)

10. Bernstein, D.J., Yang, B.Y.: Fast constant-time gcd computation and modular inversion. IACR Trans. Cryptogr. Hardw. Embed. Syst., 340–398 (2019)

11. Biasse, J.F., Song, F.: Efficient quantum algorithms for computing class groups and solving the principal ideal problem in arbitrary degree number fields. In: Proceedings of the Twenty-Seventh Annual ACM-SIAM Symposium on Discrete Algorithms, pp. 893–902. SIAM (2016)

12. Bos, J., ET AL.: Frodo: take off the ring! practical, quantum-secure key exchange from lwe. In: Proceedings of the 2016 ACM SIGSAC Conference on Computer and Communications Security, pp. 1006–1018 (2016)

13. Campbell, P., Groves, M., Shepherd, D.: Soliloquy: a cautionary tale. In: ETSI 2nd Quantum-Safe Crypto Workshop, pp. 1–9 (2014)

14. Cooley, J.W., Tukey, J.W.: An algorithm for the machine calculation of complex fourier series. Math. Comput. **19**(90), 297–301 (1965)

15. Cramer, R., Ducas, L., Wesolowski, B.: Mildly short vectors in cyclotomic ideal lattices in quantum polynomial time. J. ACM (JACM) **68**(2), 1–26 (2021)

16. Crockett, E., Paquin, C., Stebila, D.: Prototyping post-quantum and hybrid key exchange and authentication in tls and ssh. Cryptology ePrint Archive (2019)

17. Duman, J., Hövelmanns, K., Kiltz, E., Lyubashevsky, V., Seiler, G.: Faster lattice-based kems via a generic fujisaki-okamoto transform using prefix hashing. In: Proceedings of the 2021 ACM SIGSAC Conference on Computer and Communications Security, pp. 2722–2737 (2021)

18. Fouque, P.A., Kirchner, P., Pornin, T., Yu, Y.: Bat: Small and fast kem over ntru lattices. IACR Trans. Cryptogr. Hardw. Embed. Syst., 240–265 (2022)

19. Gentleman, W.M., Sande, G.: Fast Fourier transforms: for fun and profit. In: Proceedings of the 7–10 November 1966, Fall Joint Computer Conference, pp. 563–578 (1966)

20. Group, N.W., et al.: Design issues for hybrid key exchange in tls 1.3 (2019)

21. Hoffstein, J., Pipher, J., Silverman, J.H.: NTRU: a ring-based public key cryptosystem. In: Buhler, J.P. (ed.) ANTS 1998. LNCS, vol. 1423, pp. 267–288. Springer, Heidelberg (1998). https://doi.org/10.1007/BFb0054868

22. Hülsing, A., Rijneveld, J., Schanck, J., Schwabe, P.: High-speed key encapsulation from NTRU. In: Fischer, W., Homma, N. (eds.) CHES 2017. LNCS, vol. 10529, pp. 232–252. Springer, Cham (2017). https://doi.org/10.1007/978-3-319-66787-4_12

23. Jablon, D.: Ieee p1363 standard specifications for public-key cryptography. In: Proceedings of the IEEE NIST Key Management Workshop CTO Phoenix Technologies Treasurer, Gaithersburg, MD, USA, pp. 1–2 (2001)

24. Jarvis, K., Nevins, M.: Etru: Ntru over the eisenstein integers. Des. Codes Crypt. **74**(1), 219–242 (2015)

25. Kampanakis, P., Sikeridis, D.: Two post-quantum signature use-cases: non-issues, challenges and potential solutions. In: Proceedings of the 7th ETSI/IQC Quantum Safe Cryptography Workshop, Seattle, WA, USA, vol. 3 (2019)

26. Liang, Z., Zhao X, F.B.Z.Y.: An efficient and compact ntru-based key encapsulation mechanism over large-galoisgroup prime-degree prime-ideal number field. J. Softw. Chin

27. Montgomery, P.L.: Speeding the pollard and elliptic curve methods of factorization. Math. Comput. **48**(177), 243–264 (1987)

28. Mozilla: Telemetry portal (2020). https://telemetry.mozilla.org/

29. OpenSSH: Openssh release notes (2022). https://www.openssh.com/releasenotes.html

30. Paquin, C., Stebila, D., Tamvada, G.: Benchmarking post-quantum cryptography in TLS. In: Ding, J., Tillich, J.-P. (eds.) PQCrypto 2020. LNCS, vol. 12100, pp. 72–91. Springer, Cham (2020). https://doi.org/10.1007/978-3-030-44223-1_5

31. Rescorla, E.: The transport layer security (tls) protocol version 1.3. Technical report (2018)

32. Schanck, J.M., Whyte, W., Zhang, Z.: Quantum-safe hybrid (qsh) ciphersuite for transport layer security (tls) version 1.2. IETF, Internet-Draft draft-whyte-qsh-tls (2016)

33. Smart, N.P., Vercauteren, F.: Fully homomorphic encryption with relatively small key and ciphertext sizes. In: Nguyen, P.Q., Pointcheval, D. (eds.) PKC 2010. LNCS, vol. 6056, pp. 420–443. Springer, Heidelberg (2010). https://doi.org/10.1007/978-3-642-13013-7_25

34. Solinas, J.A.: Generalized mersenne numbers. J. Jishou Univ. (1999)

35. Stebila, D., Costello, C., Naehrig, M.: Post-quantum key exchange for the tls protocol from the ring learning with errors problem (2015)

36. Stehlé, D., Steinfeld, R.: Making NTRU as secure as worst-case problems over ideal lattices. In: Paterson, K.G. (ed.) EUROCRYPT 2011. LNCS, vol. 6632, pp. 27–47. Springer, Heidelberg (2011). https://doi.org/10.1007/978-3-642-20465-4_4

Side-channel Attacks

Simple Power Analysis Attack on SQIsign

Anisha Mukherjee[1]($\boxtimes$)(iD), Maciej Czuprynko[1](iD), David Jacquemin[1](iD),
Péter Kutas[2,3](iD), and Sujoy Sinha Roy[1](iD)

[1] ISEC, Graz University of Technology, Graz, Austria
{anisha.mukherjee,maciej.czuprynko,sujoy.sinharoy}@tugraz.at,
david.jacquemin@student.tugraz.at
[2] Eötvös Loránd University, Budapest, Hungary
kutasp@gmail.com
[3] University of Birmingham, Birmingham, England

Abstract. The isogeny-based post-quantum digital signature algorithm
SQIsign offers the most compact key and signature sizes among all candidates in the ongoing NIST call for additional post-quantum signature
algorithms. To the best of our knowledge, we present the first Simple
Power Analysis (SPA) side-channel attack on SQIsign, demonstrating
its feasibility for key recovery. Our attack specifically targets secret-
dependent computations within Cornacchia's algorithm, a fundamental
component of SQIsign's quaternion module. At the core of this algorithm, a secret-derived yet ephemeral exponent is used in a modular
exponentiation subroutine. By performing SPA on the modular exponentiation, we successfully recover this ephemeral exponent. We then
develop a method to show how this leaked exponent can be exploited
to ultimately reconstruct the secret signing key of SQIsign. Our findings
emphasize the critical need for side-channel-resistant implementations of
SQIsign, highlighting previously unexplored vulnerabilities in its design.

Keywords: Isogeny · SQIsign · Side-Channel Analysis · PQC

1 Introduction

Due to rapid advancements in the field of quantum computing in recent times,
cybersecurity experts recommend to shift from classical cryptographic primitives
to post-quantum alternatives. After the initial standardization effort for post-
quantum Key Encapsulation Mechanisms (KEMs) and digital signatures, the
National Institute of Standards and Technology (NIST) selected three digital
signature schemes: Dilithium [15], Falcon [20], and SPHINCS+ [4]. Since two
(Dilithium and Falcon) of these schemes rely on post-quantum lattice-based
hardness assumptions, recognizing the need for greater algorithmic diversity,
NIST announced a separate call for "additional digital signature" proposals in
2023 [34]. Interestingly, SQIsign is the only isogeny-based signature scheme that
has been submitted to this call.

A. Nitaj et al. (Eds.): AFRICACRYPT 2025, LNCS 15651, pp. 245–269, 2026.
https://doi.org/10.1007/978-3-031-97260-7_12

Isogeny-based cryptographic schemes date back to Couveignes's seminal paper [11] which was then rediscovered by Rostovtsev and Stolbunov [38]. Since then, quite a few different approaches have been used for designing isogeny-based signatures, including those that remain unaffected by recent SIDH attacks [5]. One such approach for constructing signatures from isogenies was proposed by Galbraith, Petit and Silva [21](GPS) that relies on the quaternion version of isogeny path-finding problem, referred to as the KLPT (Kohel, Lauter, Petit, Tignol) algorithm [28]. Proposed in 2020, SQIsign [13] improves upon GPS scheme by providing generalized version of the KLPT algorithm and introducing several other novel algorithms resulting in a practically feasible scheme with a much better performance. In fact, SQIsign stands out among all its isogeny-based predecessors and the rest of its NIST counterparts because it is the most compact post-quantum signature to date. Since the introduction of the first version in 2020, several follow-up variants[1] of the original scheme were proposed such as [18] and the higher-dimensional isogeny variants–SQIsignHD [12], SQIsign2D-West [2], SQIsign2D-East [33] and SQIPrime [16].

Along with theoretical security of the submitted schemes, NIST has broadened its assessment criteria [35] to also include implementation aspects such as performance, cryptanalysis and resistance to side-channel attacks (SCA). Since SQIsign relies on a combination of supersingular elliptic curve and quaternion arithmetic, it presents a broader cryptanalytic surface compared to purely elliptic curve-based schemes. While there are many elliptic curve-based side-channel literature such as [19, 36, 43], SQIsign is yet to undergo any rigorous cryptanalysis on its quaternion side, except the work by [29] that mounts a fault attack on [13]. Moreover, as stated in the NIST specifications document [6], SQIsign does not include a side-channel-resistant implementation, a critical requirement for practical applications.

Our Contributions: In this work, we analyze SQIsign's intricate mathematical framework to uncover side-channel vulnerabilities in its signing procedure. We make the following contributions towards side-channel assisted secret-key recovery of SQIsign.

1. **Identification of a Side-Channel Vulnerability:** As also mentioned by SQIsign in their most recent NIST submission [1, Section 1.1], signature generation in SQIsign follows a complex computational hierarchy involving multiple layers of mathematical function calls. This makes identifying side-channel vulnerabilities in SQIsign substantially non-trivial because, even if the attacker is able to recover an intermediate secret value via side-channels, the complete secret key recovery procedure using the obtained intermediate secret would also follow an intricate and complex back-tracking path.

---

[1] Recently, SQIsign successfully moved forward to the second round of the "additional signatures" call and the most recent update to the scheme has been described is the NIST Round-2 specifications [1].

In this work, through systematically analyzing this mathematical hierarchy, we identify Cornacchia's algorithm as a key vulnerable spot within SQIsign's quaternion module. This algorithm computes a square root with respect to an ephemeral modulus, say m, where m is derived from the secret signing key of SQIsign and is an input to Cornacchia's algorithm. We observe that the existing software implementation of SQIsign leaks m through power side-channels during the square root calculation. By exploiting this leakage, we successfully recover m, exposing a pathway to extract the secret key.

2. **Key Recovery via Backtracking:** We present a systematic framework for reconstructing SQIsign's secret signing key by leveraging side-channel-assisted recovery of the ephemeral input m in Cornacchia's algorithm. By tracing m through the computation path back to the KLPT algorithm, we formally establish its relationship with the secret key. We further prove the feasibility of polynomial-time key recovery through three theorems, demonstrating that once m is extracted, the full signing key can be efficiently reconstructed. We provide details about the key recovery attack for two versions of SQIsign, namely, [13,18] and discuss the possibilities for its extension and limitation with respect to the higher-dimensional variants.

3. **Practical Attack Demonstration:** We experimentally validate our attack using Simple Power Analysis (SPA) on a low-cost ChipWhisperer Nano board. By analyzing power traces of the modular square root computation in SQIsign's software implementation, we successfully recover the ephemeral secret input m to Cornacchia's algorithm. This empirical validation confirms that our attack is practical and capable of signing key extraction.

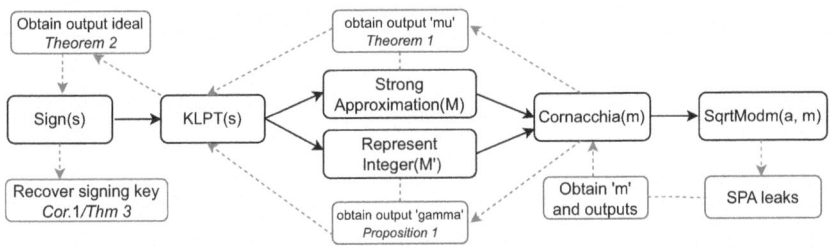

Fig. 1. Attack sketch in red: Steps for recovering the signing key s.

Attack Sketch: Figure 1 illustrates the high-level attack procedure, which consists of two main phases. In the first phase, the attacker exploits side-channel leakage by analyzing power traces from the signing procedure. By tracing through multiple levels of function calls down to the modular square root step, the attacker extracts the ephemeral secret-dependent modulus m using simple power analysis techniques. In the second phase, the attacker reconstructs the secret signing key through a purely computational process. By backtracking through the function call hierarchy, the attacker incrementally recovers intermediate secrets at each stage, ultimately deriving the full signing key.

In particular, our investigation begins with the signing process of SQIsign, where a significant portion of the computation involves processing the secret key through quaternion arithmetic enabled by the Deuring correspondence. The KLPT algorithm [28] (described in detail in Sect. 2.2) plays a central role in the signing procedure [13]. We recursively analyze its internal subroutines and identify Cornacchia's algorithm as a prime target for side-channel attacks. This algorithm is used to find a pair of integers (x, y) satisfying the equation $x^2 + d \cdot y^2 = m$ for co-prime integers d and m, where $d = 1$ in our case, and m is derived from the secret key s.

If the input m to Cornacchia's algorithm can be guessed correctly, it becomes possible to reconstruct the secret signing key efficiently. Having established a key recovery strategy under these conditions, we identify specific side-channel leakage points within Cornacchia's execution. A key insight of our work is that, deep down, Cornacchia's algorithm relies on a modular square root computation implemented via the *square-and-multiply* exponentiation method. Taking inspiration from side-channel attacks targeting modular exponentiation in RSA [10,23,24,27,31], we perform experimental Simple Power Analysis (SPA) on the exponentiation used inside Cornacchia's algorithm and successfully recover the exponent, which is a linear function of m. Thereafter, we perform backtracking, as shown in Fig. 1 to reconstruct the signing key of SQIsign.

Organization: The paper is organized as follows. In Sect. 2, we give all the important background information necessary for our paper. Section 3 presents a framework which can lead to a polynomial-time key recovery. We show that if an attacker is able to guess the input variables to Cornacchia, then it can successfully recover the signing key in polynomial time. We demonstrate an SPA-style attack on the modular exponentiation algorithm in Sect. 4.

2   Preliminaries

In this section we cover certain mathematical and algorithmic topics necessary to present our results. We use the notations $\mathbb{F}_q$, $\mathbb{Z}$ and $\mathbb{Q}$ to denote a finite field of order q, the set of integers and field of rational numbers respectively. Multiplication between integers, reals or quaternions is represented using the '·' operator, we omit the explicit use of '·' either to maintain readability or in contexts where this multiplication is obvious.

2.1   Supersingular Elliptic Curves and Quaternion Algebras

Let E_1 and E_2 be elliptic curves defined over some finite field $\mathbb{F}_q$. An isogeny is a non-zero rational map that sends the point of infinity of E_1 to the point of infinity of E_2. Being a finite map of curves, it induces a finite field extension on the function fields of the elliptic curves. The degree of the isogeny is defined as the degree of the field extension. An endomorphism of E is an isogeny from E to itself. Endomorphisms, including the zero map, form a ring under addition and composition. If the endomorphism ring of E is commutative, then we call E *ordinary*, otherwise E is *supersingular*. In this paper, we will only be looking at supersingular elliptic curves. Supersingular elliptic curves can all be defined over $\mathbb{F}_{p^2}$. Detailed discussion is available in [40].

A rational quaternion algebra H is a central simple algebra of dimension four over $\mathbb{Q}$. It always has a presentation $i^2 = a, j^2 = b, ij = -ji$ where $1, i, j, k = ij$ constitute a $\mathbb{Q}$-basis and $a, b \in \mathbb{Q}^*$: $H(a, b) = \mathbb{Q} + i\mathbb{Q} + j\mathbb{Q} + k\mathbb{Q}$. An order in a quaternion algebra is a subring that contains 1 and a $\mathbb{Q}$-basis of the algebra. An order is called maximal if it is maximal with respect to inclusion. To denote a quaternion algebra ramified at p and infinity, we use the notation, $B_{p,\infty}$. In the special case where $p \equiv 3 \pmod 4$ this just amounts to $i^2 = -1$ and $j^2 = -p$. The endomorphism ring of a supersingular curve over $\mathbb{F}_{p^2}$ is a maximal order in $B_{p,\infty}$. Furthermore, every maximal order in $B_{p,\infty}$ is the endomorphism ring of a supersingular elliptic curve. For more details, readers may refer to [42]. SQIsign [6] chooses primes p of size 254, 382 and 510 bits for NIST security levels I, III and V, respectively.

Connecting the World of Supersingular Elliptic Curves to Quaternions: The Deuring correspondence [14] is a correspondence between isomorphism classes of supersingular elliptic curves over $\mathbb{F}_{p^2}$ and isomorphism classes of maximal orders in $B_{p,\infty}$. The Deuring correspondence is two-to-one in most cases and one-to-one if and only if the curve can be defined over $\mathbb{F}_p$. We now define the quaternion analogue of an elliptic curve isogeny under this correspondence. The analogue of an isogeny with domain E is a left ideal I of $\text{End}(E)$. The norm of the ideal is defined as the greatest common divisors of all the norms in I and is equal to the degree of the associated isogeny. A natural question is how do we get the "codomain" for a given left ideal I. This is provided by the right order $\mathcal{O}_r(I) = \{\beta \in B_{p,\infty} | I\beta \subseteq I\}$. A connecting ideal between $\mathcal{O}_1$ and $\mathcal{O}_2$ is a left ideal of $\mathcal{O}_1$ whose right order is isomorphic to $\mathcal{O}_2$. An Eichler order is the intersection of two maximal orders. It encodes a particular connecting ideal as $\mathcal{O}_1 \cap \mathcal{O}_2 = \mathbb{Z} + I$ where I is a left ideal of $\mathcal{O}_1$ and a right ideal of $\mathcal{O}_2$. $\mathcal{O}_1 \cap \mathcal{O}_2$ is a $\mathbb{Z}$ sub-lattice of $\mathcal{O}_1$ and $\mathcal{O}_2$ of the same index (sometimes called the level) equal to the norm of the ideal I.

Remark 1. For the following three sections (2.2, 2.3, 2.4) of the necessary technical background, we adopt the following hierarchy for description:

-   We follow a left-to-right approach with respect to Fig. 1 and start with the description of the KLPT algorithm in Sect. 2.2. We provide a high-level idea of how it calls the two sub-algorithms RepresentInteger and StrongApproximation during computations. Note that, the description of these algorithms are necessary for the key recovery framework of Sect. 3.
-   Next, we move further right in Fig. 1 to describe Cornacchia's algorithm in Sect. 2.3. We defer the description of the specific lower-level constituent functions within Cornacchia until Sect. 3. The description of these algorithms

are important to understand the side-channel analysis of Sect. 4. Figure 3 visualizes the significance of these algorithms in the key recovery and side-channel attack.

– Finally, we provide a high-level sketch of the sigma protocol used by SQIsign. The secret signing key is the endomorphism ring of the public curve, E. The KLPT algorithm requires this secret endomorphism ring during a signature generation to compute the response isogenies, as we describe in Sect. 2.4.

We also highlight in red all those steps within an algorithm that involve the secret and are relevant for our attack.

2.2   The KLPT Algorithm

Isogeny-based cryptography relies on the mathematical problem of finding isogenies of very large smooth degrees d (usually, $d = l^k$ for a small prime l such as 2 or 3) between supersingular elliptic curves, which is presumed to be computationally infeasible even for a quantum computer. Interestingly, due to the Deuring correspondence, there is a natural quaternion analogue of this problem. Namely given two maximal orders, find a connecting ideal of norm l^e. Such a connecting ideal should exist for a large enough e. Although it is the exact analogue of a hard problem, it admits a polynomial time algorithm, discovered by Kohel, Lauter, Petit and Tignol (KLPT) [28, Section 4], discussed briefly here.

For simplicity we will assume that $p \equiv 3 \pmod 4$ (the general case is not much harder). The first observation is that if one wants to find a path between two maximal orders, then it is enough to connect both maximal orders to one specific order and concatenate the paths. This special order, denoted by $\mathcal{O}_0$ is the endomorphism ring of the elliptic curve $y^2 = x^3 + x$ and contains $1, i, j$ (it is actually generated as a $\mathbb{Z}$-module by $1, i, (1+j)/2$ and $(i+ij)/2$). From now on, we assume that we are looking for a connecting ideal between $\mathcal{O}_0$ and some other maximal order $\mathcal{O}$. One finds a connecting ideal I_0 using an algorithm of Kirschmer and Voight [26]. Naturally, the norm of this ideal is not likely to be of the form l^e, so our goal is to find an equivalent left ideal of $\mathcal{O}_0$ such that its norm is l^e. This is basically equivalent to finding some element in I_0 whose norm is $n(I_0) \cdot l^e$. The next important intermediate step is that one finds an equivalent ideal of prime norm N. This is easy as one just scans through elements of I_0 and since primes are relatively dense, one will find a suitable element very efficiently. This provides with an equivalent ideal I of prime norm N. So our goal is to find $\beta \in I$ such that $n(\beta) = Nl^e$.

KLPT in [13, Alg.9, Step-2] proceeds in two steps. First using RepresentInteger (Algorithm 1) it finds an element γ in $\mathcal{O}_0$ of norm Nl^{e_0}. Then it finds an element $\mu_0 \in j\mathbb{Z}[i]$ such that $\gamma(\lambda\mu_0 + N\mu_1)$ is in I for any $\lambda \in \mathbb{Z}$ and $\mu_1 \in O_0$. The final step, called StrongApproximation (Algorithm 2) is finding λ, μ_1 such that the norm of $\lambda\mu_0 + N\mu_1$ is l^{e_1}. Now it is clear that the norm of $\gamma(\lambda\mu_0 + N\mu_1)$ is Nl^e (with $e = e_0 + e_1$) and this is what we were looking for.

Require: $M \in \mathbb{Z}$ such that $M > p$.   ▷ p is a fixed SQIsign prime
Ensure: $\gamma = x + yi + zj + tij \in \mathcal{O}_0$ with $n(\gamma) = M$.
 1: Set $k = \left\lfloor \sqrt{\frac{M}{p \cdot (1+q)}} \right\rfloor$ and sample random integers $z, t \in [\![-k, k]\!]$.
 2: Set $M' = M - p \cdot f(z, t)$.   ▷ $f(z, t) = z^2 + t^2$
 3: **if** Cornacchia$(M') = \perp$ **then**
 4:     Go back to Step 1.
 5: **else**
 6:     $x, y \leftarrow$ Cornacchia(M').   ▷ Details in Sec. 2.3
 7: **end if**
 8: $\gamma = (x + iy + j(z + it))$.
 9: **return** γ.

Algorithm 1: RepresentInteger$_{\mathcal{O}_0}(M)$ [13]. It calls Cornacchia with the secret input M'. Recovering M' using SPA allows an attacker to guess the output γ by following Proposition 1.

Require: Prime N, l non quadratic residue modulo N, and $C, D \in \mathbb{Z}$.
Ensure: $\mu = \lambda \cdot \mu_0 + N \cdot \mu_1$, with $\mu_0 = j(C + iD)$, $\mu_1 \in \mathcal{O}_0$ such that $n(\mu) = l^{e_1}$
    for some $e_1 \in \mathbb{N}$.
 1: Select $e_1 \geq p \cdot N^4$ and adjust the parity so that $\frac{l^{e_1}}{p \cdot (C^2 + qD^2)}$ is a quadratic residue
    mod N. λ is its square root.
 2: Select z, t such as $l^{e_1} - p \cdot f(\lambda C + Nz, \lambda D + Nt) = 0 \mod N^2$.
 3: Set $M = \frac{l^{e_1} - p \cdot f(\lambda C + Nz, \lambda D + Nt)}{N^2}$.
 4: **if** Cornacchia$(M) = \perp$ **then**   ▷ Details in Sec. 2.3
 5:     Go back to Step 2.
 6: **else**
 7:     $x, y \leftarrow$ Cornacchia(M).   ▷ Details in Sec. 2.3
 8: **end if**
 9: **return** $\mu = \lambda j(C + iD) + N(x + iy + j(z + it))$.

Algorithm 2: StrongApproximation$_{l^{e_1}}(N, C, D, \lambda)$ [13]. It calls Cornacchia with the secret input M. Recovering M using SPA allows an attacker to guess the output μ by following Theorem 1.

2.3   Cornacchia's Algorithm

Cornacchia's algorithm [9] aims to find a pair of co-prime integers (x, y) as solutions to the quadratic diophantine equation, $x^2 + d \cdot y^2 = m$ where d and m are also co-prime integers. It takes as input m and applies the Euclid's division algorithm to the pair (u_0, m) where, $u_0^2 \equiv -d \pmod{m}$. The call to the Euclid's algorithm breaks when in the successive sequence (r_n) of remainders, it finds an r_k satisfying the relation, $r_k^2 < m \leq r_{k-1}^2$. This translates to employing the so-called 'half-GCD' algorithm in practical implementations. The solution is then, $\left(x = r_k, y = \sqrt{(m - r_k^2)/d} \right)$ if y is an integer, otherwise the process is repeated with another modular square root u_0' until all such roots get exhausted. In general, Cornacchia's algorithm applies to any integer d that is coprime to m, however, in the context of SQIsign [6], we are interested in the case of Cornacchia's algorithm when $d = 1$. We mention this algorithm in Algorithm 3. The sub-routine halfgcd (Steps 2–5 in Algorithm 3) is just the Euclid's GCD algorithm terminated 'half-way', that is, when the condition of $r_k < \sqrt{m}$ is met. We target the modular square root computation in Step 1 of Cornacchia. Hereafter, we use the representations Cornacchia or Cornacchia(m) (depending on whether the context requires the input to be specified) to specifically refer to Algorithm 3 ; otherwise we use the generic term 'Cornacchia's algorithm'.

Require: $m \in \mathbb{Z}$ such that d and m are co-prime in $x^2 + d \cdot y^2 = m$.
Ensure: $x, y \in \mathbb{Z}$ s.t. $x^2 + d \cdot y^2 = m$.
1: Compute $u_0 = \sqrt{-d} \bmod m$ and set $i, m_0 = 0, m$.   ▷ SqrtModm$(-d, m)$, see
   alg. 6
2: **while** $m_i > \lfloor \sqrt{m} \rfloor$ **do**   ▷ halfgcd algorithm [30]
3:     Compute $r_i = m_i \pmod{u_i}$.
4:     Set $m_{i+1}, u_{i+1}, i = u_i, r_i, i + 1$.
5: **end while**   ▷ End of halfgcd algorithm
6: Set $s_k = m_{i+1}$
7: Check, $\sqrt{(m - s_k^2)/d} \in \mathbb{Z}$.
8: **if** False **then**
9:     go to step 1 for a new u.
10: **else**
11:     $x = s_k, y = \sqrt{(m - s_k^2)/d}$.
12: **end if**
13: **return** x, y

Algorithm 3: Cornacchia(d, m) [9] requires the computation of the modular square root in Step-1. This computation is targeted via SPA.

Remark 2. In actual implementation [30], the authors use an 'extended' version of the algorithm referred to as ExtendedCornacchia(m_{ext}) whose steps are given in Algorithm 4. It ensures that the input m to Cornacchia is almost always a prime, definitely odd and has an easily computable modular square root. This is implemented using the following procedures: a check to ensure that m_{ext} is not congruent to 3 (mod 4) in Step 3, repeated divisions to remove all powers of primes which are less than 101 and congruent to 1 (mod 4) in Steps 1,4 and finally a probabilistic primality test. We experimentally observed that in many instances, $m_{\text{ext}} = k \cdot m$, with $k = 1$ or a 3 (mod 4) small prime, hence hereafter, for simplicity, we consider $m_{\text{ext}} = m$ for the following parts of the paper and do not distinguish between Cornacchia and its extended version.

Remark 3. We recall that Cornacchia's algorithm is called with the specific inputs M and M' whose explicit expressions are provided in Step 3 of StrongApproximation (Algorithm 2) and Step 2 of RepresentInteger(Algorithm 1) respectively.

Require: $m_{\text{ext}} \in \mathbb{Z}$.
Ensure: $x, y \in \mathbb{Z}$ such that $x^2 + d \cdot y^2 = m$ where m is computed from m_{ext}.
1: $h_1 = 2^{\nu_2} \cdot 5^{\nu_5} \cdot 13^{\nu_{13}} \cdots 101^{\nu_{101}}$ ▷ ν_j denotes the p-adic valuation of m_{ext} w.r.t j
2: $h_3 = 3 \cdot 7 \cdots 83$ ▷ Product of all 3 (mod 4) primes until 101
3: **if** $\gcd(m_{\text{ext}}, h_3) == 1$ **then**
4:    Compute $m = \frac{m_{\text{ext}}}{h_1}$.
5:    **if** m is a prime **then**
6:       Compute $x, y = \mathsf{Cornacchia}(1, m)$.   ▷ In SQIsign [6], $d = 1$
7:    **end if**
8:    **return** x, y
9: **end if**

Algorithm 4: ExtendedCornacchia(m_{ext}) as given in [30] acts as a pre-cursor to Cornacchia's algorithm.

2.4 The SQIsign Protocol

One way to interpret KLPT is that given two supersingular elliptic curves with known endomorphism rings, one can compute an isogeny between them (a task that is deemed hard otherwise). This motivates the following sigma protocol which is the high-level idea of SQIsign [13]. The public key is a supersingular elliptic curve E and let E_0 be the supersingular elliptic curve, $y^2 = x^3 + x$. Let, $\mathcal{O}_0 = \text{End}(E_0)$ and $\mathcal{O} = \text{End}(E)$ denote the endomorphism rings of E_0 and E, respectively. Here, $\mathcal{O}_0$ and $\mathcal{O}$ are connected by a secret left ideal I_τ of large prime norm corresponding to the secret isogeny τ. The quaternion secret key analogue is the endomorphism ring of E, that is, $\mathcal{O}$. This is visually represented in Fig. 2.

The main steps of the sigma protocol are the following. The prover computes an isogeny, $\phi : E_0 \to E_1$ and sends E_1 to the verifier. The verifier sends a challenge isogeny, $\psi : E_1 \to E_2$ to the prover. The prover responds with an isogeny σ between E and E_2 of degree l^e. The verifier accepts if the response isogeny σ is between E and E_2, has degree l^e, and $\hat{\psi} \circ \sigma$ is cyclic.

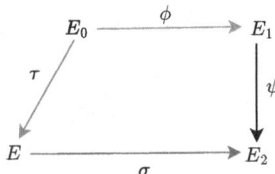

Fig. 2. The sigma protocol in SQIsign [13]. τ represents the secret, ϕ the commitment, ψ the challenge and σ the response isogenies.

Since one can translate endomorphism rings through isogenies [21], the endomorphism ring of E_2 can be computed by the prover. The naive approach here is to use the KLPT algorithm to provide an isogeny between E and E_2. However, the KLPT isogeny has the peculiar feature that it always goes through E_0. This reveals the secret key (i.e., the endomorphism ring of E) after one response. SQIsign uses a modified version of KLPT which connects E and E_2 in a direct fashion, not leaking (conjecturally) any information about the endomorphism ring of E. This can be done by deriving a quaternion analogue of commutative isogeny diagrams. One constructs a left $\mathcal{O}_0$-ideal of the correct norm and pushes it forward via I_τ to a left ideal of $\mathcal{O}$. Of course the difficulty here is to ensure that the right order of this left ideal is isomorphic to $\text{End}(E_2)$. This is ensured by using the Eichler order $\mathcal{O}_0 \cap \mathcal{O}$ and other techniques developed in KLPT.

To be able to respond to the verifier one has to translate the aforementioned ideal into an isogeny. There are two issues that arise in practice. First, the norm of the ideal obtained this way is large, hence its kernel will be defined over a large extension field. This issue is solved by breaking the ideal into smaller chunks, such that the kernel of every chunk is defined over a small extension field.

However, after evaluating the first chunk we need to have an efficient description of the new endomorphism ring (i.e., a way to evaluate every endomorphism of the curve efficiently). Indeed, the explicit Deuring correspondence requires that the kernels of the suitable endomorphisms appear as subgroups of the elliptic curve in order to get the kernels of the corresponding isogenies. This is needed as we have to proceed chunk-by-chunk (using the amount of rational torsion we can utilize). This issue is more complicated, furthermore, there is a difference between the original SQIsign construction [13] and the improved version [18]. We do not recall all the details here but the main concept is that [13] uses KLPT for each of these steps whereas [18] uses a different algorithm called SpecialEichlerNorm given in Algorithm 5.

Require: $\mathcal{O}$ a maximal order, I a $(\mathcal{O}_0, \mathcal{O})$-ideal and K a left $\mathcal{O}$-ideal of norm l.
Ensure: $\beta \in \mathcal{O} \backslash (\mathbb{Z} + K)$ of norm dividing T^2.
1: Set $L = \text{RandomEquivalentPrimeIdeal}(I)$, $N = n(L)$ and compute α such that $L = I\alpha$.
2: Compute $K' = \alpha^{-1} \cdot K \cdot \alpha$.
3: Compute $(C : D) = \text{EichlerModConstraint}(L, 1, 1)$.
4: Enumerate all possible solutions of $\mu = \text{FullStrongApproximation}(N, C, D)$ until $\mu \notin \mathbb{Z} + K'$. If it fails, go back to Step 1.
5: **return** $\beta = \alpha \cdot \mu \cdot \alpha^{-1}$

Algorithm 5: SpecialEichlerNorm$(\mathcal{O}, I, K)$ [18]. It calls a version of StrongApproximation so the recovery method from Theorem 1 can be extended to this algorithm.

The key idea of SpecialEichlerNorm is that one can give in a sense a simpler representation of the endomorphism rings throughout the isogeny path. This results in a considerable speed-up, mainly because a much better prime p (i.e., relaxed smoothness conditions on $p^2 - 1$) can be chosen this way.

3   The Key Recovery Attack

On the quaternion side, SQIsign represents elements of $B_{p,\infty}$ as a 5-tuple of integers in $\mathbb{Z}^5$ and hence, quaternion arithmetic boils down to linear algebra and integer arithmetic [6, Section 2.4]. We focus on integer arithmetic, especially within Cornacchia's algorithm. As a fundamental building block in SQIsign's quaternion arithmetic [6, Section 2.5.1], Cornacchia's algorithm directly interacts with derived (secret) values related to the secret $\mathcal{O}$. In this section, we first provide details of how we track the path of operations followed by the ephemeral secret, that is, the input to Cornacchia (see Algorithm 3). We investigate the modular square root function in Step 1 of the algorithm that ultimately leads us to the side-channel vulnerable *square-and-multiply* exponentiation algorithm. Then, provided that this input to Cornacchia is obtained via side-channel observations, we explain the steps that an attacker would back-track in order to recover the signing key.

3.1   Attack Localization Within Cornacchia

Cornacchia (Algorithm 3) requires the computation of the modular square root of $-d$ in Step 1. This modular square root u_0 is obtained using a modular exponentiation algorithm. In Algorithm 6, we give a pseudo-code of the modular square root function as provided in the reference implementation of [30]. We note from Algorithm 6 that, (1) the core principle of the algorithm relies on the *square-and-multiply* modular exponentiation algorithm, whose pseudo-code is given in Algorithm 7. Moreover, (2) the different exponents e (highlighted in red) in Algorithm 6 are linear functions of m derived based on the residue class of the prime m modulo 4 or 8. The "fast" cases correspond to $m \equiv 3 \pmod 4$ and $m \equiv 5 \pmod 8$ when the exponent is calculated as a linear expression in m. The case when $m \equiv 1 \pmod 8$ is handled using the Shanks-Tonelli algorithm [39,41]. Observations (1) and (2) together make Algorithm 7 a good target for side-channel analysis. The bit-dependent behavior of Square&MultiplyExponentiation(b, e, m) introduces a clear execution pattern that can be exploited in power-based side channel analysis that traces the different power consumption patterns of a squaring and a multiplication operation.

3.2   Signing Key Retrieval from Cornacchia

Let us assume that an attacker has observed side-channel leakage from Cornacchia and has guessed the input m correctly. Now, we show how the attacker can retrieve the outputs of StrongApproximation, RepresentInteger and eventually KLPT in the following part of the section.

Remark 4. In this paper, we consider both the original version [13] and the improved version [18] of SQIsign. Version-1 [6] submitted to NIST is, for our purposes, essentially the same as [18]. Nevertheless changes can be made (e.g., SQISignHD [12] is a somewhat different construction) and we would like to initiate new methods that might be interesting for future applications as well.

Require: a, m, where m is a prime
Ensure: $\sqrt{a} \pmod{m}$ if it exists, else the function returns failure
1: $a_{mod} = a \pmod{m}$
2: **if** $a_{mod} < 0$ **then**
3:     $a_{mod} = a_{mod} + m$
4: **end if**
5: **if** $\mathsf{Jacobi}(a_{mod}, m) \neq 1$ **then** $\triangleright$ computes the Jacobi symbol, $\left(\frac{a_{mod}}{m}\right)$
6:     **return** FAILURE
7: **end if**
8: **if** $m \equiv 3 \mod 4$ **then** $\triangleright$ branch-1 condition w.r.t m
9:     $e = (m+1)/4$
10:     $\sqrt{a} = a_{mod}^e \pmod{m}$
11: **else if** $m \equiv 5 \pmod{8}$ **then** $\triangleright$ branch-2 condition w.r.t m
12:     $e = (m-1)/4$
13:     $temp = a_{mod}^e \pmod{m}$
14:     **if** $temp \not\equiv 1 \pmod{m}$ **then**
15:         $e = (m+3)/8$
16:         $\sqrt{a} = a_{mod}^e \pmod{m}$
17:     **else**
18:         $e = (m-5)/8$
19:         $temp = (4 \cdot a_{mod})^e \pmod{m}$
20:         $\sqrt{a} = (2 \cdot a_{mod} \cdot temp) \pmod{m}$
21:     **end if**
22: **else** $\triangleright$ branch-3 condition w.r.t m
23:     $\sqrt{a} = \mathsf{ShanksTonelli}(a_{mod}, m)$ $\triangleright$ Shanks-Tonelli algorithm if $m \equiv 1 \pmod{8}$)

24: **end if**
25: **return** $\sqrt{a} \pmod{m}$

Algorithm 6: Modular Square Root Computation: $\mathsf{SqrtModm}(a, m)$

Proposition 1. *Suppose we have a way of retrieving the input and hence the outputs of* Cornacchia. *Then we can obtain a small set of valid outputs (amongst which is the actual output)* γ *of* RepresentInteger$_{\mathcal{O}_0}$ *in polynomial time if either of the following conditions is satisfied for the reduced norm of* γ, $n(\gamma) = M$:

- *M is of the form Nl^{e_0} where l, e_0 are known and $N < p$.*
- *$M < p \log(p)^c$ for some constant c.*

Proof. If one can obtain M', which is the input of Cornacchia in Step 3 of Algorithm 1, then we know x, y along with M' such that $x^2 + y^2 = M'$. Now, we split our algorithm into two cases depending on which condition is satisfied.

If the first condition is satisfied, then we know that $n(\gamma) = M = Nl^{e_0}$ where we know the value of l^{e_0} and $N < p$. We also have, $M = M' - p \cdot (z^2 + t^2)$ (Step 2, Algorithm 1) where we know p and M' but do not know z and t. This implies that we know M modulo p. Now as $M = Nl^{e_0}$ and l^{e_0} is known and coprime to p, we can obtain N modulo p by modular inversion. Since $N < p$, we have obtained the value of N exactly which implies that we have obtained M as well. This in turn implies that the value of $z^2 + t^2$ is known and finding

Require: Base, exponent and modulus given by $b, e, m \in \mathbb{Z}$ respectively. Also, let, $e = (e_{k-1}, \cdots, e_1, e_0)$ represent the bit decomposition of the exponent e.
Ensure: An integer $a = b^e \pmod{m}$ in $\mathbb{Z}_m$.
1: Set $a = 1$
2: **for** i from $k - 1$ to 0 **do**
3:     $a = a \cdot a \pmod{m}$ ▷ squaring step
4:     **if** $e_i = 1$ **then**
5:         $a = a \cdot b \pmod{m}$ ▷ multiplication step
6:     **end if**
7: **end for**
8: **return** a

Algorithm 7: Square&MultiplyExponentiation(b, e, m)

z, t boils down to the sum of two squares theorem which relates the number of solutions to the number of prime factors of $z^2 + t^2$. Since for a random integer N' (here, $N' = (M' - M)/p$) the number of distinct prime factors is typically $\log \log N'$ [22], this means that the solutions of the above equation are bounded by $O(\log{(N')}^c)$ choices where c is a small constant. Hence, we can enumerate over the possible solutions of z, t in polynomial time.

If the second condition is satisfied, then we can proceed in a similar fashion. Here, we just need to guess M in Step 2 of Algorithm 1. The condition $M < p \log(p)^c$ implies that the bound k in Step 1 of Algorithm 1 is small and thus we only have $O(\log(p)^c)$ choices for z, t.

Theorem 1. *Suppose we have a way of retrieving the input and hence the outputs of* Cornacchia. *Then we can obtain the output of* StrongApproximation *in KLPT if the output size l^{e_1} is known.*

Proof. The goal is to obtain μ by utilizing the input and outputs of Cornacchia. Having access to Cornacchia's input and outputs means we know M and x, y such that $M = x^2 + y^2$. From Step 3 of Algorithm 2 we have the equality,

$$MN^2 = l^{e_1} - p \cdot \left((\lambda C + Nz)^2 + (\lambda D + Nt)^2\right), \tag{1}$$

which simplifies to, $MN^2 \equiv l^{e_1} \pmod{p}$. Since M and l^{e_1} are known, we have two choices for the square root, N modulo p, of N^2. In KLPT, $N \approx \sqrt{p}$ which gives us the exact value of N in the following way: indeed, every residue has two square roots $(\pm a)$ modulo p (a and $p - a$). This implies that only one of the square roots of N^2 will be close to $\sqrt{p}$ and the other will be much larger than $p/2$, as $(\sqrt{p} \ll \frac{p}{2})$.

Next, knowing M, N and l^{e_1} in Eq. 1 implies that we know $(\lambda C + Nz)^2 + (\lambda D + Nt)^2$. From this we can solve the equation of the form, $N' = (\lambda C + Nz)^2 + (\lambda D + Nt)^2 = x_0^2 + y_0^2$ and compute all solutions x_0, y_0. The number of integer solutions to this equation is governed by the sum of two squares theorem, which relates the number of solutions to the number of prime factors of $(\lambda C + Nz)^2 + (\lambda D + Nt)^2$. Since for a random integer N' the number of distinct prime factors is typically $\log \log N$ [22], this means that the solutions of the above equation are bounded by $O(\log{(N')}^c)$ choices for a small constant c. Hence, by enumerating over all possible solutions, we can find $\lambda C + Nz$ and $\lambda D + Nt$. Since the output of StrongApproximation is $\mu = Nx + Nyi + (\lambda C + Nz)j - (\lambda D + Nt)ij$, we have found μ as we now know every coordinate of it.

Remark 5. In KLPT, l^{e_0} is mostly fixed and l^{e_1} is chosen in a way that StrongApproximation is solvable. For efficiency purposes one would like e_1 as small as possible which would leave only a constant number of choices (but definitely bounded by $\log p$) for e_1. Thus, in the statement of Theorem 1 we made this simplification that l^{e_1} is known which does not affect our attacks (furthermore, as part of the scheme, KLPT can easily be modified to return a fixed e_1).

Theorem 1 and Proposition 1 are the main building blocks that enable key recovery. We will provide two key recovery methods, one on the original SQIsign construction [13] and one on the newer version [18]. First we focus on the original construction.

Theorem 2. *Suppose we have a way of retrieving the input and hence the outputs of* Cornacchia. *Then we can retrieve the output ideal of the KLPT algorithm.*

Proof. The KLPT algorithm, as mentioned before (and described in [28]) has three main steps. The first step is computing γ which is the output of the RepresentInteger$_{\mathcal{O}_0}$ algorithm. Next comes computing a μ_0 such that $(\mathcal{O}_0\gamma)\mu_0 \equiv I$ (mod $N\mathcal{O}_0$) and then lifting μ_0 to μ whose norm is l^e. Then, $\gamma \cdot \mu$ will be an element of I of norm Nl^e which provides an equivalent ideal $I \sim J$ of norm l^e. Theorem 1 implies that we can obtain μ and Proposition 1 implies that we can obtain γ. Putting these together, we obtain $\gamma \cdot \mu$ which is exactly what we need to get the output of KLPT.

Remark 6. Proposition 1 might not be strictly necessary in certain contexts if the algorithm RepresentInteger$_{\mathcal{O}_0}$ is performed deterministically as one can just recompute the algorithm offline. The reason is that Theorem 1 also provides N (not just μ), hence if l^{e_0} is chosen deterministically one does not need to use the Cornacchia oracle again.

Corollary 1. *Suppose we have a way of retrieving the input and hence the outputs of* Cornacchia. *Then we can get the signing key in SQIsign [13] in polynomial time.*

Proof. We focus on [13, Algorithm 9] which provides the ideal-to-isogeny translation. In Step 2, KLPT is used to obtain an equivalent ideal J which is a connecting ideal between $\mathcal{O}_0$ and $\mathcal{O}$ where $\mathcal{O}$ is the endomorphism ring of the public curve. Theorem 2 implies that we can get J which immediately reveals $\mathcal{O}$ as the right order of J is isomorphic to $\mathcal{O}$.

Theorem 2 is not directly applicable to the new SQIsign version [18] as in the ideal-to-isogeny translation algorithm KLPT is no longer used. Instead of computing with entire endomorphism ring, the algorithm SpecialEichlerNorm is called which computes a well chosen endomorphism of the appropriate maximal order. In the next theorem, we show how to apply Theorem 1 to obtain the signing key.

Theorem 3. *Suppose we have a way of retrieving the input and hence outputs of* Cornacchia. *Then we can retrieve the signing key in the improved version of SQIsign [18] in polynomial time.*

Proof. In the improved version of SQIsign [18], we target Step 5 of SpecialEichler-Norm which is a direct call to StrongApproximation algorithm. Theorem 1 implies that we can obtain μ using our Cornacchia approach. Furthermore, the proof of Theorem 1 implies that we also retrieve $n(L) = N$ as $N < p$. Our goal is to compute generators for the ideal L as then the right order of L will be the required secret endomorphism ring $\mathcal{O}$ of the public curve (as the first input of SpecialEichlerNorm is the order $\mathcal{O}$). We outline the method to compute these generators in the following paragraph:

Note that, $\mu \in \mathbb{Z} + L$, so μ alone is not enough to retrieve L. Since $\mu \in \mathcal{O}_0$ one can write it as a 2×2 matrix with entries from $\mathbb{Z}/N\mathbb{Z}$ via the explicit isomorphism $\mathcal{O}_0/N\mathcal{O}_0 \cong M_2(\mathbb{Z}/N\mathbb{Z})$. Elements in L have the property that when they are written as 2×2 matrices, they are not invertible as their norms are divisible by N. Now, $\mu = \lambda + \sigma$, where $\lambda \in \mathbb{Z}$ and $\sigma \in L$ and hence we need to figure out the value of λ. Since $N\mathcal{O}_0$ is contained in L, actually, λ is only determined modulo N. Also, since elements in L correspond to matrices that are not invertible, $\mu - \lambda$ is not an invertible matrix which is equivalent to λ being an eigenvalue of μ. Eigenvalues can be computed efficiently as N is a prime number. In general μ has two eigenvalues which provides two possible choices λ_1 and λ_2 for λ. Elements in L correspond to a set of matrices in $M_2(\mathbb{Z}/N\mathbb{Z})$ whose kernel contains a particular cyclic subgroup of $(\mathbb{Z}/N\mathbb{Z})^2$ (or equivalently a point in $\mathbb{P}^1(\mathbb{Z}/N\mathbb{Z})$). Hence for both λ_i's we compute the kernel of $\mu - \lambda_i$ and compute the corresponding ideal L_i. By computing right orders we get two candidates $\mathcal{O}_1$ and $\mathcal{O}_2$ for $\mathcal{O}$. Then we compute the supersingular elliptic curves corresponding to these orders and choose the one whose j-invariant matches that of the public curve. The last step can be accomplished in polynomial time and is quite practical using the methods of SQIsign or that of [17].

Summarization of the Key Recovery Framework: An attacker obtains the input to Cornacchia $\xrightarrow{\text{Step-1}}$ finds a candidate output γ of RepresentInteger in Algorithm 1 using Proposition 1 $\xrightarrow{\text{Step-2}}$ finds a candidate output μ of StrongApproximation in Algorithm 2 using Theorem 1 $\xrightarrow{\text{Step-3}}$ (I) finds a candidate output KLPT using Theorem 2 $\rightarrow$ finds a candidate secret using Corollary 1 for [13] version or, (II) finds a candidate secret using Theorem 3 for [18] version of SQIsign. If the candidate secret does not match the actual secret, the attacker repeats Steps 1 to 3.I/3.II. These steps are shown in Fig. 3.

Remark 7. It would be interesting to attack SigningKLPT [6, Algorithm 17] using our methods as that is common in both versions as the difference lies in the ideal to isogeny translation algorithm. However, the StrongApproximation algorithms used there will reveal the endomorphism ring corresponding to the pushforward of the secret ideal hence it is not immediate how one would get

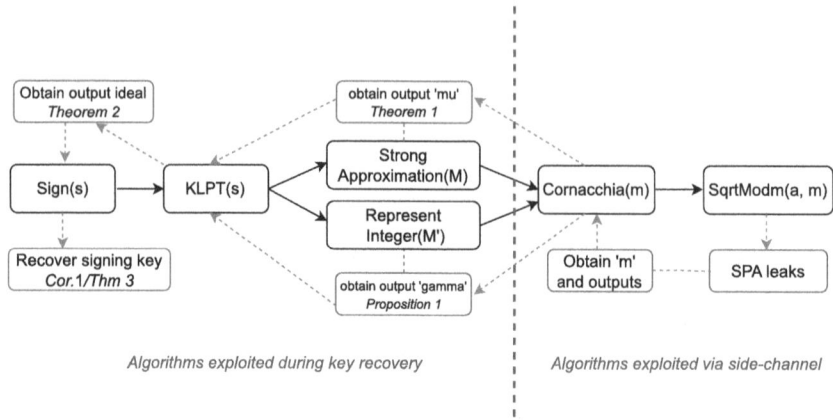

Fig. 3. Strategy for signing key recovery.

the signing key from that information. We leave this as an open problem for the future.

3.3 New Variants of SQIsign

Recently new variants of SQIsign were proposed essentially all leveraging techniques used in the SIDH attack [5]. A way of interpreting the attack is that one can represent an isogeny by providing evaluations of the isogeny on a sufficiently large subgroup. Verifying whether this representation indeed produces an isogeny between the correct curves of the correct degree can be accomplished by evaluating a chain of higher dimensional isogenies between principally polarized abelian surfaces. This idea was used in SQIsignHD [12] to significantly simplify the signing process of SQIsign but verification in SQIsignHD requires evaluating a chain of $(2, 2, 2, 2)$-isogenies between abelian surfaces which is much slower than verification in the original SQIsign protocol. However, several protocols emerged that modified SQIsignHD in a way that verification only requires 2-dimensional isogenies [2,16,33]. We will briefly discuss how our attacks generalize to these 2D variants.

SQIsign2D-East: SQIsign2D-East [33] has the most common algorithms with the original SQIsign protocol as it uses RepresentInteger and StrongApproximation. StrongApproximation is used in the response step as a subroutine of AuxiliaryPath [33, Algorithm 3]. Since it produces a quaternion in $\mathcal{O}_0 \cap \mathcal{O}$ where the level of this Eichler order can be computed as in Theorem 3, one similarly gets the endomorphism ring of the public curve. There is one small subtlety: in Theorem 3 when we invoke StrongApproximation, we know the output norm (as it is a fixed power of l), but, this is not apriori known in SQIsign2D-East. However, an attacker can obtain this value after observing a valid signature (this number actually changes every iteration, unlike in SQIsign). In conclusion, the attack from Theorem 3 can be applied in this context.

SQIsign2D-West: SQIsign2D-West [2] no longer uses StrongApproximation, only RepresentInteger. It is mainly used to evaluate a random isogeny both in the commitment and the response algorithm. However, the random isogeny evaluation algorithm takes an output of the RepresentInteger and then re-randomizes it internally. Due to this internal randomization step, our attacks, at the moment, cannot have a straightforward impact on SQIsign2D-West.

The most recent version of SQIsign [1] submitted to NIST round-2 adopts algorithms from SQIsign2D-West, hence, from a preliminary survey of the documentation, it appears that our key recovery attack is not directly applicable to this version. However, the modular square root algorithm presented in the document [1, Algorithm 3.1] is still essentially the same as presented in Algorithm 6 including the modular exponentiation, which leaves an opportunity open for a simple power analysis attack.

SQIPrime: Similar to SQIsign2D-West, SQIPrime [16] also only uses RepresentInteger. However, it doesn't mask using randomization which means our attacks could target the endomorphism ring of the commitment curve. One problem is that SQIPrime uses RepresentInteger on an unknown number, hence, Proposition 1 does not immediately apply. However, the secret integers whose values are required to be known appear in elliptic curve scalar multiplications in the commitment step. Thus, if implemented with a *double-and-add* algorithm, much like the *square-and-multiply* algorithm, this scalar multiplication could also be targeted as a separate but similar side-channel attack approach as in Sect. 4. Knowing the endomorphism ring of the commitment curve can be exploited in the following way: eventually, after a signature generation, one will have an isogeny representation of a non-smooth isogeny from the public curve to a curve of known endomorphism ring. Then, the attacker can use the quantum polynomial time attack against pSIDH [7] which recovers the secret endomorphism ring in quantum-polynomial time. Note however, that this is a significantly weaker attack compared to the attack presented in the paper as it would require extra information and has quantum polynomial time complexity.

4   Side-Channel Attack Experimentation

In the previous section, we demonstrated that if an attacker can guess the input to Cornacchia, they can reconstruct the secret signing key. The key question now is: How does the attacker determine this input? In this section, we outline our approach of recovering the input of Cornacchia's algorithm by analyzing side-channel leakage from the *square-and-multiply* modular exponentiation, i.e., Algorithm 7, used for square-root calculations in Algorithm 6. We infer the exponent, which has a linear relationship with Cornacchia's input. We keep in mind Remark 3.

In Sect. 3, we describe how the inputs to Cornacchia(m) are preprocessed using Algorithm 4 to ensure that the algorithm can find a solution to the given Diophantine equation. Notably, Step 2 of Algorithm 4 significantly reduces the likelihood of m being congruent to 3 (mod 4). In practice, we observe that values of m satisfying $m \equiv 1$ (mod 8) or $m \equiv 5$ (mod 8) are passed to Cornacchia(m). Consequently, either branch-2 or branch-3 is invoked in SqrtModm(a, m), Algorithm 6.

-   When branch-2 is invoked, the recovered exponent is one of the three forms given in Steps-12, 15 and 18. To validate a guess for the exponent and hence the signing key, the attacker follows the steps in Sect. 3, that is, from Theorem 1 until Corollary 1 or Theorem 3 depending on which variant of SQIsign being targeted. Thus, in the end the attacker computes the corresponding maximal order for each candidate guess and maps it to its associated supersingular elliptic curve representation. Since the j-invariant of the public curve is known, the attacker can verify the correctness of a guessed secret key by matching the computed j-invariant with the j-invariant of the public curve. A successful match confirms that the attacker has recovered the correct secret key.
-   When branch-3 is invoked, the Shanks-Tonelli algorithm involves iterative computations depending on the factorization of $m - 1$ and the structure of quadratic residues. Therefore, the exponent used in the exponentiation varies dynamically making it comparatively harder for a straight-forward inference of the exponent from the observed bits in a power trace. Furthermore, since m changes for every signature, each signing operation provides only one opportunity to collect a power trace for a given m.

Consequently, the success probability of the attack is 50% per Cornacchia call. In case of the two independent calls to Cornacchia, once within StrongApproximation 2 and the other within RepresentInteger 1 in the SQIsign version from [13], one out of the four pairs: $\left(m \equiv 5 \pmod 8 \text{ in Algorithm 2}, m \equiv 1 \pmod 8\right.$ in Algorithm 1$)$, $\left(m \equiv 1 \pmod 8 \text{ in Algorithm 2}, m \equiv 1 \pmod 8 \text{ in Algorithm 1}\right)$, $\left(m \equiv 1 \pmod 8 \text{ in Algorithm 2}, m \equiv 5 \pmod 8 \text{ in Algorithm 1}\right)$, $\left(m \equiv 5 \pmod 8 \text{ in Algorithm 2}, m \equiv 5 \pmod 8 \text{ in Algorithm 1}\right)$ is suitable for key recovery and since primes 5 (mod 8) and 1 (mod 8) are equally likely, the number of signature generations the attacker has to observe is at least four. In the case of the improved version [18] that calls only StrongApproximation, the number of signature generations for recovering m is two. Note that in case of a call to branch-1 if m is congruent to 3 (mod 4), the above-mentioned technique can also be utilized for recovery of m in the same way as branch-2.

4.1   Simple Power Analysis of Modular Exponentiation

Simple Power Analysis (SPA) is a widely used technique in side-channel attacks, where an adversary passively monitors a device's power consumption to infer secret information. Unlike more advanced techniques such as Differential Power

Analysis (DPA), SPA relies on directly interpreting power traces rather than statistical correlation. The underlying idea in SPA is quite simple: the power consumption of a device changes based on the functions or operations being executed at a point in time; a computationally expensive operation will consume more resources than a comparatively straightforward one. In our attack, we use SPA to observe power consumption patterns during modular square root computations, exploiting secret-dependent variations to recover secret information.

In Sect. 2.3 and specifically in Algorithm 7, we observed the bit-dependent behavior of Square&MultiplyExponentiation(b, e, m). At each step of the Algorithm, there is a squaring and when the processed exponent bit is 1, there is an additional multiplication. In SQIsign's implementation [30], the exponentiation algorithm contains specific squaring and multiplication functions along with modular reduction after every squaring and multiplication operation. Implementing these operations differently leads to distinct patterns in the power traces that let us use SPA and retrieve the secret exponent.

To demonstrate feasibility, we executed the attack on a ChipWhisperer Nano board featuring the STM32F030 microcontroller, using its built-in ADC for trace acquisition. The code for *square-and-multiply* exponentiation was compiled with arm-none-eabi version 10.2.1 with optimization level -O0. Due to the limited ROM and SRAM capacity of the microcontroller, we implemented the exponentiation for the 54 bit toy parameter set from [37]. Since this choice is a practical constraint imposed by hardware limitations, the attack can naturally be extended to actual NIST security level SQIsign parameters following our approach. The only difference will be that the execution time of the entire algorithm, and hence the trace, will be longer. We implemented the naive implementation described in Algorithm 7 with dedicated squaring and multiplication functions. As for the reduction modulo m, the Montgomery reduction was used, where the needed constants were precomputed before the start of the exponentiation.

We show part of the result of an exponentiation in Fig. 4. We highlight the visually distinguishable multiplications and squaring operations. Furthermore, we also distinguish the modular reduction which follows after both operations. In particular, we notice that the reduction contains two multiplications itself. In the given figure, we are able to 'read' the first four bits of the exponentiation which are 1001. By continuing this procedure for the whole exponentiation, we are able to retrieve the complete corresponding exponent with 100% success probability. The retrieved exponent would follow either of the branch conditions explained in the previous sub-section.

Indeed, when the prime m is congruent to 5 (mod 8), the attacker can link the retrieved exponent directly to either of the three forms given in Steps-12, 15 and 18 of SqrtModm 6. In the case of m being congruent to 1 (mod 8), the exponent obtained via observing the traces cannot be successfully used to get m. From the recovered exponent, the attacker can iterate over the three choices in Steps-12, 15 and 18 of Algorithm 6 one-by-one to compute the corresponding three candidates for m. These three candidates for m are in fact, the three possible choices for the input of Cornacchia. The attacker then repeats from

Steps 1 through 3.I/3.II depending on the SQIsign version until a match for the secret key is found based on the verification condition of Corollary 1 (or, Theorem 3). If, even after iterating through all the three possibilities, the attacker does not hit a match for the secret key, then Algorithm 6 executed branch-3 and m was congruent to 1 (mod 8). In such a scenario, the attacker has to repeat the process starting from power trace collection until Steps 1-3.I/3.II. In our SageMath implementation[2] of these steps with 54-bit parameter set, the time taken to find matches for γ and μ is in the order of 10^{-3} s.

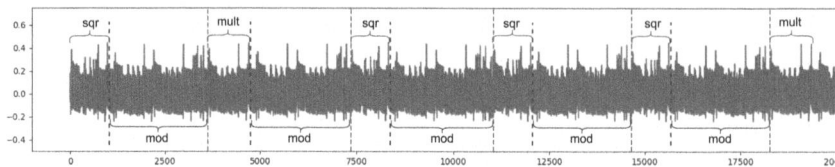

Fig. 4. SPA trace (power vs time) of the exponentiation showing the squaring, multiplication and modular reduction.

4.2   Countermeasures

As [24] discusses, there can be two broad approaches to prevent leakage of sensitive information through physical side-channel attacks such as an SPA. The first approach aims to remove or hide any correlation of the underlying secret-dependent operations from the observed side-channel patterns, while the second removes correlation of the side-channel from the secret data. [24] states that the latter approach is more hardware-oriented and aims to make the device more tamper-resistant. We discuss countermeasures related to the former approach. This approach works either by employing specific algorithmic tricks designed explicitly to make side-channel observations independent of the branch conditions related to the secret value, or introducing randomness to the secret-dependent parameters. Such countermeasures along this approach have been developed to protect the classical *square-and-multiply* exponentiation from SPA attacks.

Algorithmic Tweaks for Regularity of Operations: The usual *square-and-multiply* exponentiation contains conditional branches that either execute a squaring or a squaring followed by a multiplication depending on the exponent bit being 0 or 1. This "irregularity" in the sequence of operations are what allows an SPA attacker to distinguish between specific exponent bits. One intuitive way to alleviate this "irregularity" of operations can be circumvented by replacing the bit-dependent *square-and-multiply* exponentiation with algorithms that perform the same amount of computations irrespective of the secret exponent bit.

---

[2] https://github.com/anishamukh/Key-Recovery-of-SQIsign.

Two such widely-known algorithms are the *square-and-multiply always* exponentiation algorithm and the Montgomery ladder exponentiation [8,25,32]. The *square-and-multiply always* exponentiation performs both squaring and multiplication operations at every iteration, regardless of the exponent bit's actual value. When the exponent bit is 1, the multiplication step involves the intended operand, and when the exponent bit is 0, the algorithm multiplies by a dummy value. Consequently, each iteration follows a uniform operation sequence thereby producing consistent power consumption patterns that obscure secret-dependent information. The Montgomery ladder follows a similar algorithmic flow as the *square-and-multiply always* exponentiation but without dummy multiplications.

Note that in SQIsign, the ephemeral secret, that is, the input to Cornacchia changes with every signature execution. Thus, an attacker has only one chance at side-channel analysis for a particular value of the ephemeral secret. Using the aforementioned regular algorithms such as the Montgomery ladder, therefore, makes SPA essentially impractical. Moreover, it means that an attacker cannot collect enough traces with respect to that particular ephemeral secret value for mounting advanced attacks such as Differential Power Analysis. In [3], the authors consider the case of a scalar multiplication in ECC (elliptic curve cryptography) where the secret scalar is an ephemeral. They provide a list of the different types of possible passive attacks other than SPA such as horizontal (collision), horizontal correlation and template attacks that can still be exploited to recover the ephemeral scalar. Such alternative attacks could possibly also be explored w.r.t the *square-and-multiply* exponentiation as it is algorithmically similar to an elliptic curve scalar multiplication. Beyond using regular algorithms, [3] also suggests randomizing the secret value to protect against horizontal correlation attacks. In the following paragraph, we discuss a randomization method that can be applied to the secret exponent.

Exponent Randomization: In this technique [27], the exponent is randomized before performing the exponentiation operation. Specifically, the exponent e can be replaced by $e + r \cdot \phi(m)$ for some random integer r and Euler's totient function $\phi(m)$ that ensures correctness of the result modulo m. This randomization prevents an attacker from obtaining reliable leakage patterns since the observed power traces correspond to the randomized exponent instead of the fixed exponent value. A similar randomization technique could also be applied to the exponents of Algorithm 6 before the exponentiation step. It would require computing $\phi(m)$ when m is ephemeral secret. Observing the power consumption traces of the exponentiation algorithm would then provide an attacker with the corresponding bit representation of $e + r \cdot \phi(m)$ instead of e directly. Since the attacker only has one chance of collecting the power trace corresponding to the exponent, such a randomization would increase resistance to correlation attacks.

We note that in this paper, we explore one possible side-channel vulnerability in the signing procedure, namely, in the exponentiation operation within Cornacchia's algorithm. Accordingly, the aforementioned countermeasures provide SPA-resistant alternatives only for the *square-and-multiply* exponentiation in Cornacchia's algorithm. However, several other high-level algorithms involved in signing, or other subroutines within Cornacchia's algorithm, particularly those involving branch-dependent computations, still remain susceptible to side-channel attacks. Therefore, a comprehensive constant-time and side-channel-resistant implementation is necessary for all such algorithms, including Cornacchia's algorithm itself, whenever they process secret or secret-derived intermediate values in the signing procedure.

5 Conclusion

In this work, we presented the first Simple Power Analysis attack on SQIsign, demonstrating its feasibility for key recovery. Our attack exploited secret-dependent computations within Cornacchia's algorithm, a crucial component of SQIsign's quaternion module. By targeting the modular exponentiation used in the computation of modular square roots, we successfully extracted an ephemeral integer m, which is derived from the secret signing key.

Building on this leakage, we developed a systematic framework to trace m back through the KLPT algorithm, formally establishing its connection to the secret key. We showed that once m is recovered, the full signing key can be reconstructed efficiently in polynomial time. Our attack was validated experimentally using a low-cost ChipWhisperer Nano board, confirming its practical applicability. Furthermore, we analyzed the attack's implications across different versions of SQIsign, highlighting vulnerabilities in both the original and improved implementations. We also discussed potential generalizations to two higher-dimensional variants of SQIsign and also presented the limitations of our attack in case of the other variants.

To mitigate the observed side-channel vulnerability, we reviewed countermeasures such as constant-time exponentiation techniques (e.g., Montgomery ladder, square-and-multiply always) and exponent blinding, which prevent SPA leakage. Our findings emphasize the need for side-channel-resistant implementations of SQIsign to ensure its security in real-life applications. Future work includes analyzing advanced side-channel attacks, exploring comprehensive side-channel-resistant signing implementation, and evaluating the impact of countermeasures on performance.

Acknowledgements. Anisha Mukherjee, Maciej Czuprynko are supported by the Austrian FWF grant PAT6402023, and Sujoy Sinha Roy is partially supported by the State Government of Styria, Austria, through the Department Zukunftsfonds Steiermark. Péter Kutas is supported by the Hungarian Ministry of Innovation and Technology NRDI Office within the framework of the Quantum Information National Laboratory Program and by the grant "EXCELLENCE-151343", the János Bolyai Research Scholarship of the Hungarian Academy of Sciences and partly by EPSRC through grant number EP/V011324/1.

References

1. Aardal, M.A., et al.: SQISIGN: algorithm specifications and supporting documentation. In: Proposal to NIST Standardization of Additional Digital Signature Schemes, Round2. National Institute for Standards and Technology (2025)
2. Basso, A., et al.: SQIsign2D–west: the fast, the small, and the safer. In: International Conference on the Theory and Application of Cryptology and Information Security, pp. 339–370. Springer, Heidelberg (2024). DOI: https://doi.org/10.1007/978-981-96-0891-1_11
3. Batina, L., Chmielewski, L., Haase, B., Samwel, N., Schwabe, P.: Sok: Sca-secure ECC in software - mission impossible? IACR Trans. Cryptogr. Hardw. Embed. Syst. **2023**(1), 557–589 (2023). https://doi.org/10.46586/TCHES.V2023.I1.557-589
4. Bernstein, D.J., Hülsing, A., Kölbl, S., Niederhagen, R., Rijneveld, J., Schwabe, P.: The SPHINCS+ signature framework. In: Proceedings of the 2019 ACM SIGSAC Conference on Computer and Communications Security, CCS '19, pp. 2129–2146. Association for Computing Machinery, New York (2019). https://doi.org/10.1145/3319535.3363229
5. Castryck, W., Decru, T.: An efficient key recovery attack on SIDH. In: EURO-CRYPT 2023, Lyon, France, 23–27 April 2023, Part V, vol. 14008, pp. 423–447. Springer, Heidelberg (2023). https://doi.org/10.1007/978-3-031-30589-4_15
6. Chavez-Saab, J., et al.: SQISIGN: algorithm specifications and supporting documentation. In: Proposal to NIST Standardization of Additional Digital Signature Schemes, Round1. National Institute for Standards and Technology (2023)
7. Chen, M., Imran, M., Ivanyos, G., Kutas, P., Leroux, A., Petit, C.: Hidden stabilizers, the isogeny to endomorphism ring problem and the cryptanalysis of pSIDH. In: International Conference on the Theory and Application of Cryptology and Information Security, pp. 99–130. Springer, Heidelberg (2023). https://doi.org/10.1007/978-981-99-8727-6_4
8. Clavier, C., Feix, B., Gagnerot, G., Roussellet, M., Verneuil, V.: Square always exponentiation. In: Bernstein, D.J., Chatterjee, S. (eds.) INDOCRYPT 2011. LNCS, vol. 7107, pp. 40–57. Springer, Heidelberg (2011). https://doi.org/10.1007/978-3-642-25578-6_5
9. Cornacchia, G.: Su di un metodo per la risoluzione in numeri interi dell'equazione $\sum_{h=0}^{n} C_h x^{n-h} y^h = P$. Giornale di Matematiche di Battaglini **49**, 33–90 (1908)
10. Courrège, J.-C., Feix, B., Roussellet, M.: Simple power analysis on exponentiation revisited. In: Gollmann, D., Lanet, J.-L., Iguchi-Cartigny, J. (eds.) CARDIS 2010. LNCS, vol. 6035, pp. 65–79. Springer, Heidelberg (2010). https://doi.org/10.1007/978-3-642-12510-2_6
11. Couveignes, J.M.: Hard homogeneous spaces. IACR Cryptol. ePrint Arch. 291 (2006). http://eprint.iacr.org/2006/291
12. Dartois, P., Leroux, A., Robert, D., Wesolowski, B.: SQISignHD: new dimensions in cryptography. In: Annual International Conference on the Theory and Applications of Cryptographic Techniques, pp. 3–32. Springer, Heidelberg (2024). https://doi.org/10.1007/978-3-031-58716-0_1
13. De Feo, L., Kohel, D., Leroux, A., Petit, C., Wesolowski, B.: SQISign: compact post-quantum signatures from quaternions and isogenies. In: Moriai, S., Wang, H. (eds.) ASIACRYPT 2020. LNCS, vol. 12491, pp. 64–93. Springer, Cham (2020). https://doi.org/10.1007/978-3-030-64837-4_3

14. Deuring, M.: Die typen der multiplikatorenringe elliptischer funktionenkörper. Abh. Math. Semin. Univ. Hambg. **14**, 197–272 (1941)

15. Ducas, L., et al.: CRYSTALS-dilithium: a lattice-based digital signature scheme. IACR Trans. Cryptogr. Hardw. Embed. Syst. **2018**(1), 238–268 (2018). https://doi.org/10.13154/tches.v2018.i1.238-268

16. Duparc, M., Fouotsa, T.B.: SQIPrime: A dimension 2 variant of SQISignHD with non-smooth challenge isogenies. In: International Conference on the Theory and Application of Cryptology and Information Security, pp. 396–429. Springer, Heidelberg (2024). https://doi.org/10.1007/978-981-96-0891-1_13

17. Eriksen, J.K., Panny, L., Sotáková, J., Veroni, M.: Deuring for the people: supersingular elliptic curves with prescribed endomorphism ring in general characteristic. Cryptol. ePrint Arch. (2023)

18. Feo, L.D., Leroux, A., Longa, P., Wesolowski, B.: New algorithms for the deuring correspondence - towards practical and secure SQISign signatures. In: EUROCRYPT 2023, vol. 14008, pp. 659–690. Springer, Heidelberg (2023). https://doi.org/10.1007/978-3-031-30589-4_23

19. Feo, L.D., et al.: SIKE channels zero-value side-channel attacks on SIKE. IACR Trans. Cryptogr. Hardw. Embed. Syst. **2022**(3), 264–289 (2022). https://doi.org/10.46586/TCHES.V2022.I3.264-289

20. Fouque, P.A., et al.: FALCON: fast-fourier lattice-based compactsignatures over ntru. In: Proposal to NIST Standardization of Additional Digital Signature Schemes. National Institute for Standards and Technology (2023)

21. Galbraith, S.D., Petit, C., Silva, J.: Identification protocols and signature schemes based on supersingular isogeny problems. In: Takagi, T., Peyrin, T. (eds.) ASIACRYPT 2017. LNCS, vol. 10624, pp. 3–33. Springer, Cham (2017). https://doi.org/10.1007/978-3-319-70694-8_1

22. Hardy, G.H., Ramanujan, S.: The normal number of prime factors of a number n. Q. J. Math. **48**, 76–92 (1917)

23. Homma, N., Miyamoto, A., Aoki, T., Satoh, A., Shamir, A.: Comparative power analysis of modular exponentiation algorithms. IEEE Trans. Comput. **59**(6), 795–807 (2010). https://doi.org/10.1109/TC.2009.176

24. Joye, M., Olivier, F.: Side-channel analysis. In: van Tilborg, H.C.A., Jajodia, S. (eds.) Encyclopedia of Cryptography and Security, 2nd Ed, pp. 1198–1204. Springer, Heidelberg (2011). https://doi.org/10.1007/978-1-4419-5906-5_516

25. Joye, M., Yen, S.-M.: The montgomery powering ladder. In: Kaliski, B.S., Koç, K., Paar, C. (eds.) CHES 2002. LNCS, vol. 2523, pp. 291–302. Springer, Heidelberg (2003). https://doi.org/10.1007/3-540-36400-5_22

26. Kirschmer, M., Voight, J.: Algorithmic enumeration of ideal classes for quaternion orders. SIAM J. Comput. **39**, 1714–1747 (2010). https://doi.org/10.1137/080734467

27. Kocher, P.C.: Timing attacks on implementations of Diffie-Hellman, RSA, DSS, and other systems. In: Koblitz, N. (ed.) CRYPTO 1996. LNCS, vol. 1109, pp. 104–113. Springer, Heidelberg (1996). https://doi.org/10.1007/3-540-68697-5_9

28. Kohel, D., Lauter, K., Petit, C., Tignol, J.P.: On the quaternion-isogeny path problem. LMS J. Comput. Math. **17**(A), 418–432 (2014)

29. Lee, J., et al.: Fault attack on sqisign. In: Saarinen, M.O., Smith-Tone, D. (eds.) Post-Quantum Cryptography - 15th International Workshop, PQCrypto 2024, Oxford, UK, 12–14 June 2024, Proceedings, Part II. Lecture Notes in Computer Science, vol. 14772, pp. 54–76. Springer, Heidelberg (2024). https://doi.org/10.1007/978-3-031-62746-0_3

30. Longa, P.: sqisign-ec23 (2023) (2023). https://github.com/SQISign/sqisign-ec23
31. Messerges, T.S., Dabbish, E.A., Sloan, R.H.: Power analysis attacks of modular exponentiation in smartcards. In: Koç, Ç.K., Paar, C. (eds.) CHES 1999. LNCS, vol. 1717, pp. 144–157. Springer, Heidelberg (1999). https://doi.org/10.1007/3-540-48059-5_14
32. Montgomery, P.L.: Speeding the pollard and elliptic curve methods of factorization. Math. Comput. **48**, 243–264 (1987). https://api.semanticscholar.org/CorpusID:4262792
33. Nakagawa, K., et al.: SQIsign2D-east: a new signature scheme using 2-dimensional isogenies. In: International Conference on the Theory and Application of Cryptology and Information Security, pp. 272–303. Springer, Heidelberg (2024). https://doi.org/10.1007/978-981-96-0891-1_9
34. National Institute for Standards and Technology (NIST): Post-quantum cryptography: Additional digital signature schemes. https://csrc.nist.gov/projects/pqc-dig-sig/round-2-additional-signatures
35. National Institute for Standards and Technology (NIST): Call for proposals, post-quantum cryptography standardization (2016). https://csrc.nist.gov/csrc/media/projects/post-quantum-cryptography/documents/call-for-proposals-final-dec-2016.pdf
36. Park, D., Choi, M., Kim, G., Bae, D., Kim, H., Hong, S.: Stealing keys from hardware wallets: a single trace side-channel attack on elliptic curve scalar multiplication without profiling. IEEE Access **11**, 44578–44589 (2023). https://doi.org/10.1109/ACCESS.2023.3273150
37. Pope, G., Meyer, M., Santos, M.C., Eriksen, J.K.: Learningtosqi/sqisign-sagemath (2023). https://github.com/LearningToSQI/SQISign-SageMath.git
38. Rostovtsev, A., Stolbunov, A.: Public-key cryptosystem based on isogenies. IACR Cryptol. ePrint Arch. **2006**, 145 (2006)
39. Shanks, D.: Five number-theoretic algorithms. In: Congressus Numerantium 7, Utilitas Mathematica, pp. 51–70 (1973)
40. Silverman, J.H.: The arithmetic of elliptic curves, Graduate texts in mathematics, vol. 106. Springer, Heidelberg (1986)
41. Tonelli, A.: Bemerkung uber die au osung quadratischer congruenzen. In: Gottinger Nachrichten, pp. 344–346 (1891)
42. Voight, J.: Quaternion Algebras. Springer, Heidelberg (2021)
43. Zhang, F., et al.: Side-channel analysis and countermeasure design on ARM-based quantum-resistant SIKE. IEEE Trans. Comput. **69**(11), 1681–1693 (2020). https://doi.org/10.1109/TC.2020.3020407

Correlation Power Analysis of LESS and CROSS

Maciej Czuprynko$^{(\boxtimes)}$ ⓘ, Anisha Mukherjee ⓘ, and Sujoy Sinha Roy ⓘ

ISEC, Graz University of Technology, Graz, Austria
{maciej.czuprynko,anisha.mukherjee,sujoy.sinharoy}@tugraz.at

Abstract. This paper presents a side-channel attack targeting the LESS and CROSS post-quantum digital signature schemes, resulting in full key recovery for both. These schemes have advanced to the second round of NIST's call for additional signatures. By leveraging correlation power analysis and horizontal attacks, we are able to recover the secret key by observing the power consumption during the multiplication of an ephemeral secret vector with a public matrix. The attack path is enabled by the presence of a direct link between the secret key elements and the ephemeral secret, given correct responses. This attack targets version 1.2 of both schemes. In both settings we can recover the secret key in a single trace for the NIST's security level I parameter set. Additionally, we propose improvements to the existing horizontal attack on CROSS, reducing the required rounds that need to be observed by an order of magnitude for the same parameter sets.

Keywords: Side-channel attacks · Post-quantum cryptography · CROSS · LESS

1 Introduction

Current cryptographic primitives predominantly relying on the hardness of discrete logarithm and integer factorization problems face the threat to be rendered broken by Shor's algorithm [22,23], capable of factoring large integers—previously considered super-polynomially hard for classical computers—in polynomial time using quantum computing. In recent times, the potential emergence of large-scale quantum computers has driven extensive research in post-quantum cryptography. In 2016, the National Institute of Standards and Technology (NIST) initiated a process to standardize post-quantum Key Encapsulation Mechanisms (KEMs) and digital signature schemes. Along with theoretical security, NIST also considers practical aspects such as performance and resilience against side-channel attacks (SCA) in its evaluation framework. Until now, three digital signature schemes have been chosen for standardization: Dilithium [13], Falcon and SPHINCS+ [5]. Since two out of the three candidates (Dilithium and Falcon) rely on lattice-based hardness assumptions, in order to improve diversity, NIST announced a separate call for additional digital signatures in 2023.

© The Author(s), under exclusive license to Springer Nature Switzerland AG 2026
A. Nitaj et al. (Eds.): AFRICACRYPT 2025, LNCS 15651, pp. 270–295, 2026.
https://doi.org/10.1007/978-3-031-97260-7_13

In response to NIST's call for additional post-quantum digital signatures, many different constructions have been proposed which are based on a diverse range of mathematical hard problems. NIST has recently [18] announced the list of signatures that have successfully advanced to the second round of evaluation, which includes two novel code-based primitives, LESS [2,6] and CROSS [3,4]. LESS is constructed from a zero-knowledge identification protocol based on the hardness of the Linear Code Equivalence problem or LEP. Unlike most code-based cryptographic primitives based on the Syndrome Decoding Problem (SDP), LESS relies on the difficulty of determining the linear isometry between two codes. This allows LESS to choose smaller scheme parameters that minimizes key sizes while maintaining security and allows a well-balanced trade-off between the key/signature sizes and the efficiency of the signing/verification processes. On the other hand, the zero-knowledge identification protocol from which CROSS is constructed is based on the hardness assumption of Restricted-SDP or R-SDP.

An important consideration when implementing cryptographic schemes are side-channel attacks. These attacks exploit implementation-related leakage of the secret key using, for instance, timing variations or the power consumption. In the context of code-based cryptography, an extensive amount of work has been done for the KEMs in the 4th round of NIST [1,10,20]. In contrast, code-based signature schemes are relatively new and hence, have received less scrutiny. To the best of our knowledge, the fault injection attack presented in [17] is the only attack against LESS. The recent concurrent work by [21] is the only passive side-channel attack targeting CROSS.

1.1   Our Contribution

We summarize our contributions as follows:

Correlation Power Analysis on LESS-1.2: In this work, we introduce the first passive side-channel attack on version-1.2 of LESS [6]. This attack leverages correlation power analysis (CPA) by targeting the scaling of a set of public column vectors $\mathbf{g}_i$ by a set of ephemeral secret elements $\tilde{d}_i$ over the prime field $\mathbb{F}_q$. This is made possible by the fact that $\tilde{d}_i$ is directly related to a single element of the persistent secret key, $d_i \in \mathbb{F}_q$, through a correct signature. As such, a guess on the element d_i can be turned into a guess on a single element of the targeted ephemeral element $\tilde{d}_i$. Furthermore, we use the fact that a column scaling consists of multiple operations involving a single ephemeral secret to fully utilize a single trace. For certain parameter sets, the CPA attack leads to a full secret key recovery in a single trace.

A similar attack has been performed on the KEM Classical McEliece [10]. There, the authors describe a horizontal side-channel attack that targets a matrix-vector multiplication involving a secret vector and a public matrix. This operation is similar to our case because it can be seen as a column (or row) scaling followed by an accumulation. However, the operations in their case are performed over the field $\mathbb{F}_2$. Additionally, the targeted secret is ephemeral, meaning that the attack has to be performed in a single trace. In our case, we do not have this issue, even though we also target an ephemeral secret.

Extending Our Attack to CROSS: We showcase that our attack is applicable to another code based signature schemes CROSS. The fundamental side-channel attack stays the same. However, the secret key recovery technique from the ephemeral secret elements changes due to the differences in the scheme design. Furthermore, we show how our CPA attack is an extension to the horizontal attack introduced in the concurrent work [21]. In doing so, we report improvements to the existing attack methodology. In particular, we show how we are able to fully utilize the trace and hence, reduce the required number of signatures that have to be observed. Finally, we also present an alternative leakage model. Each of these improvements lead to a reduction in the required observed rounds by an order of magnitude.

2   Background

In this section we first introduce the notations used throughout this paper. We begin by covering the general concepts of code-based cryptography and then we present the scheme specific notions used in LESS and CROSS, respectively. For more details about the schemes as well as code based cryptography, we invite the readers to go to [2] and [3] for LESS and CROSS, respectively.

2.1   Notations

LESS works with elements in the field $\mathbb{F}_q$, while in CROSS, we use the field $\mathbb{F}_p$. Matrices in theses fields are denoted by bold uppercase letter (e.g., $\mathbf{A}$), vectors by bold lowercase letter (e.g., $\mathbf{a}$) and scalars by lowercase letters (e.g., a). For a matrix $\mathbf{A}$, the vector with the subscript $\mathbf{a}_i$ represents either the i-th column or the i-th row, as specified. An element of $\mathbf{A}$ at the i-th row and j-th column is denoted as $a_{i,j}$. For a vector $\mathbf{a}$, the subscript a_i indicates the i-th element. In contexts involving multiple matrices of a similar type, we use the superscript notation $\mathbf{A}^{(i)}$ to indicate the i-th matrix from that collection. Similar notations apply for vectors and scalars.

Furthermore, we denote $\mathbf{A}_J$ the matrix formed by the columns of $\mathbf{A}$ that are indexed by the elements in a set J. In the particular case that $\mathbf{A}$ is a square matrix, we abuse this notation to indicate a square matrix formed by keeping only the elements $a_{i,j}$ of $\mathbf{A}$ that satisfy $i \in J$ and $j \in J$.

Moreover, we typically use the usual implicit multiplication between the aforementioned objects, unless explicitly denoted by "·" for clarity. Finally, we denote the element wise multiplication of two vectors using the "$\star$" operator.

2.2   Linear Codes

In this section, we introduce the general notions used in linear codes.

An $[n, k]$-linear code $\mathcal{C}$ over the field $\mathbb{F}_q$ is a k-dimensional subspace of the vector space $\mathbb{F}_q^n$. This subspace can be represented by a full rank matrix $\mathbf{G} \in \mathbb{F}_q^{k \times n}$, which is called a generator matrix, where its rows form a basis of the subspace. As such, the elements $\mathbf{c} \in \mathcal{C}$, called code-words, are generated by vectors $\mathbf{u} \in \mathbb{F}_q^k$ such that $\mathbf{c} = \mathbf{u}\mathbf{G}$. Another way the linear code can be represented is through the kernel of the parity check matrix $\mathbf{H} \in \mathbb{F}_q^{(n-k) \times n}$ where $\mathcal{C} = \{\mathbf{x} \in \mathbb{F}_q^n : \mathbf{x}\mathbf{H}^\top = \mathbf{0}\}$. However, those representations are not unique since, given an invertible matrix $\mathbf{S}$ and a generator matrix $\mathbf{G}$ of a linear code $\mathcal{C}$, the generator matrix obtained as $\mathbf{S}\mathbf{G}$ defines the same code $\mathcal{C}$. This works similarly for the parity check matrix. To have a unique representation, the standard choice is to use the systematic form which is $\mathbf{G} = (\mathbf{I}_k | \mathbf{V})$ for a generator matrix, while the systematic form of the parity-check matrix is given by $\mathbf{H} = (\mathbf{W} | \mathbf{I}_{n-k})$.

2.3   Code-Based Hard Problems Underlying LESS and CROSS

The underlying problem in LESS focuses on finding a monomial transformation between two $[n, k]$-linear codes. Let M_n be the set of monomial transformation, then an element of this set can be represented as an $n \times n$ matrix $\mathbf{Q} \in \mathrm{M}_n$ such that $\mathbf{Q} = \mathbf{D}\mathbf{P}$, where $\mathbf{D}$ is an $n \times n$ diagonal matrix and its diagonal $\mathbf{d}$ is a vector of non-zero elements in $\mathbb{F}_q^*$. Furthermore, $\mathbf{P}$ is a permutation matrix with the corresponding permutation π of the indices $\{0, \ldots, n-1\}$. As such, a monomial matrix is characterized by the value pair $(\mathbf{d}, \pi)$. We highlight that a right or a left multiplication by $\mathbf{P}$ corresponds to a permutation of the columns or rows, respectively. Moreover, it has the property that its inverse is equal to its transpose, i.e. $\mathbf{P}^{-1} = \mathbf{P}^\top$. As such, we can define the underlying (computational) problem in LESS as:

Definition 1 (Linear Equivalence Problem (LEP) [2]). *Let RREF stand for the process of turning a matrix into its row reduced echelon form. Then, given two (systematic) generator matrices* $\mathbf{G}^{(0)}, \mathbf{G}^{(1)} \in \mathbb{F}_q^{k \times n}$, *find* $\mathbf{Q} \in \mathrm{M}_n$ *such that* $\mathbf{G}^{(1)} = RREF(\mathbf{G}^{(0)}\mathbf{Q})$.

Here, the row reduced echelon form is used to obtain a unique representation of the generator matrices. In most cases it is equivalent to the systematic form. However, it differs when the first k columns of a generator matrix $\mathbf{G} \in \mathbb{F}_q^{k \times n}$ are not invertible. In those cases, there are some columns that are not part of the identity matrix in-between the identity matrix of the systematic form. Furthermore, since the generator matrix after the RREF defines the same linear code, the RREF can be seen as the application of a change of basis matrix $\mathbf{S}$ such that $RREF(\mathbf{G}) = \mathbf{S}\mathbf{G}$.

On the other hand, CROSS is based on a different hard problem which is defined as follows:

Definition 2 (Restricted Syndrome Decoding Problem (R-SDP) [3]). *Let $\mathbb{E}$ be the cyclic subgroup of $\mathbb{F}_p$ generated by an element $g \in \mathbb{F}_p^*$ of multiplicative order z, such that $\mathbb{E} = \{g^i : i \in \{0, \ldots, z-1\}\}$. Then, given a parity check matrix*

$\mathbf{H} \in \mathbb{F}_p^{(n-k)\times n}$ and a vector $\mathbf{s} \in \mathbb{F}_p^{n-k}$ (called a syndrome vector), find $\mathbf{e} \in \mathbb{E}^n$ such that $\mathbf{s} = \mathbf{e}\mathbf{H}^\top$.

We note that an element $\mathbf{e} \in \mathbb{E}^n$ can be represented by a vector $\eta \in \mathbb{F}_z^{n\,1}$ such that $\mathbf{e} = (g^{\eta_0},\ldots,g^{\eta_{n-1}})$, where we use the Greek letters (except π which is used exclusively for permutations) to denote a vector with elements in $\mathbb{F}_z$. A variation of this problem that leads to smaller signature sizes is the Restricted Syndrome Decoding Problem with subgroup $\mathbb{G}$ (R-SDP(G)). In this setting, instead of requiring to find any vector $\mathbf{e} \in \mathbb{E}^n$, or the corresponding vector $\eta \in \mathbb{F}_z^n$, the search space is further restricted so that $\eta \in \mathbb{G}$. In particular, CROSS defines the subgroup $\mathbb{G}$ as a $[m,n]$-linear code over $\mathbb{F}_z$. As such, to sample η, a vector $\zeta \in \mathbb{F}_z^m$ is first uniformly sampled from $\mathbb{F}_z^m$ and then it is multiplied with the generator matrix of the linear code, denoted $\mathbf{M}_G$.

2.4   Correlation Power Analysis

Correlation power analysis (CPA) based attacks are powerful side-channel attacks that exploit the dependency between secret values and the power consumption during computations that are performed on them. This type of attack was investigated in [7,11,16] and is based on the differential power analysis introduced in [14].

A CPA-based attack, as described in [15], targets an intermediate computation, denoted as a function f, of the form $r = f(v, s)$ which is performed in a cryptographic algorithm, where r is the result of the computation, v is a known non-constant value and s is the targeted secret value. The general principle behind CPA is that the power consumption depends on the operation that is performed. A model that is commonly used is the Hamming weight (HW) model, where it assumed that the power consumption is proportional to the number of set bits in the binary representation of the result r, which we denote as $\mathrm{HW}(r)$. This leakage can be used to recover the secret over multiple executions of the algorithm.

To perform a CPA attack, an attacker first observes multiple executions of the algorithm, measuring the power consumption of the targeted device to obtain a power trace for each execution. The attacker then computes the intermediate values for each execution and for each possible secret value. These intermediate values are converted into hypothesized power consumption based on a chosen model. The Pearson correlation coefficient is then computed between the measured traces (at the time-step of the intermediate computation) and the hypothesized leakage for each possible secret value. This step is repeated for all possible secret values. If the selected model is sufficiently correct and enough traces are collected, the secret that leads to the highest correlation coefficient is the correct one. Usually, to obtain an accurate result a large amount of traces need to be collected.

---

[1] In the case of CROSS, the order z is always chosen to be a prime so that $\mathbb{F}_z$ is a field.

Horizontal Attacks. The presented CPA attack examines each time-step individually across multiple executions of the targeted algorithm. However, it is possible that multiple points within a single execution leak the secret. An example of this scenario is the repeated multiplication of a secret coefficient with a set of known values. In such cases, it can be beneficial to include multiple points from the same execution in the analysis. Attacks that utilize information from a single trace are referred to as horizontal attacks, in contrast to vertical attacks, which target the same point across multiple executions. This distinction was first proposed by the authors of [9]. As such, a CPA-style horizontal attack is a CPA based attack where the points come from the same trace instead of being gathered across multiple executions of the scheme.

Public Data	System parameters $q, n, k \in \mathbb{N}, \mathbf{G}^{(0)} = (\mathbf{I}_k|\mathbf{V}), \mathbf{V} \in \mathbb{F}_q^{k \times (n-k)}$ and hash function, 'Hash'.
Private Key	$\mathbf{Q} \in \mathrm{M}_n$.
Public Key	$\mathbf{G}^{(1)} = \mathrm{RREF}(\mathbf{G}^{(0)}\mathbf{Q})$.

PROVER		VERIFIER
$\tilde{\mathbf{Q}} \xleftarrow{\$} \mathrm{M}_n, \tilde{\mathbf{G}} \leftarrow \mathrm{RREF}(\mathbf{G}^{(0)}\tilde{\mathbf{Q}})$	$\xrightarrow{\mathrm{cmt}}$	
$\mathrm{cmt} \leftarrow \mathrm{Hash}(\tilde{\mathbf{G}})$		
	$\xleftarrow{\mathrm{ch}}$	$\mathrm{ch} \xleftarrow{\$} \{0,1\}$
$\mathrm{rsp} \leftarrow (1-\mathrm{ch})\tilde{\mathbf{Q}} + \mathrm{ch} \cdot \mathbf{Q}^{-1}\tilde{\mathbf{Q}}$	$\xrightarrow{\mathrm{rsp}}$	
		Accept if
		$\mathrm{Hash}(\mathrm{RREF}(\mathbf{G}^{(\mathrm{ch})} \cdot \mathrm{rsp})) = \mathrm{cmt}$

Fig. 1. Sigma protocol at the basis of LESS [6].

3 Correlation Power Analysis-Based Attack on LESS Sign

We begin with a simplified explanation of our attack technique on the identification scheme underlying LESS [2]. The scheme is recalled in Sect. 3.1. Our attack is based on a CPA-style horizontal attack which targets the multiplication of a public generator matrix $\mathbf{G}^{(0)} \in \mathbb{F}_q^{(n \times k)}$ in systematic form with an ephemeral secret monomial matrix $\tilde{\mathbf{Q}} \in \mathrm{M}_n$. We show in Sect. 3.2 that, using side-channel analysis, it is possible to recover the diagonal matrix $\tilde{\mathbf{D}}_J$, where $J = \{k, k+1, \ldots, n-1\}$, which forms the ephemeral monomial $\tilde{\mathbf{Q}} = \tilde{\mathbf{D}}\tilde{\mathbf{P}}$. Then, in Sect. 3.3, we present a method to convert the knowledge of $\tilde{\mathbf{D}}_J$ into partial knowledge of the secret $\mathbf{Q}$ given multiple responses of the form $\mathbf{Q}^{-1}\tilde{\mathbf{Q}}$. Concretely, the part we are able to recover is $\mathbf{Q}_J$. Finally, in Sect. 3.4, we show that knowing $\mathbf{Q}_J$ is sufficient to find a monomial $\mathbf{Q}' \in \mathrm{M}_n$ such that $\mathbf{G}^{(1)} = \mathrm{RREF}(\mathbf{G}^{(0)}\mathbf{Q}')$. We summarize the attack plan in Fig. 2.

In our context, executing the attack on the full scheme follows the same fundamental steps as those used in the identification scheme. The key differences,

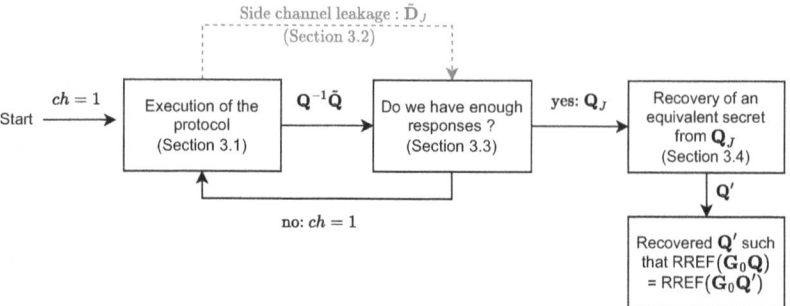

Fig. 2. Diagram representing the attack path.

particularly in the number of observed signatures required for LESS compared to the identification protocol, are discussed in the subsequent Sect. 3.5. Finally, in Sect. 3.6, we show how to turn the horizontal attack into a CPA attack. Furthermore, we mention how to deal with some difficulties arsing during the practical attack.

3.1 LESS Identification Scheme

The LESS signature scheme is based on a sigma protocol, which is a three-step interactive protocol enabling one party (the prover) to demonstrate their identity to another party (the verifier). In this protocol, the prover holds a secret key, while the verifier has access to the corresponding public key. The prover authenticates themself by convincing the verifier of their knowledge of the private key. Concretely, the LESS identification scheme proceeds in the following steps, which are summarized in the Fig. 1:

- **Key Generation:** The secret key is a monomial matrix $\mathbf{Q} \in M_n$. The corresponding public key is formed by a generator matrix in systematic form $\mathbf{G}^{(0)} = (\mathbf{I}_k | \mathbf{V})$ and the generator matrix $\mathbf{G}^{(1)}$ computed as $\mathbf{G}^{(1)} = \mathrm{RREF}(\mathbf{G}^{(0)}\mathbf{Q})$.
- **Commitment:** To prove the knowledge of $\mathbf{Q}$, the prover generates a random monomial matrix $\tilde{\mathbf{Q}} \in M_n$, applies it on the public generator matrix and computes the RREF obtaining $\tilde{\mathbf{G}} = \mathrm{RREF}(\mathbf{G}^{(0)}\tilde{\mathbf{Q}})$. The prover then commits to it by sending the hash $\mathrm{cmt} = \mathrm{Hash}(\tilde{\mathbf{G}})$ to the verifier.
- **Challenge:** The verify sends a challenge $ch \in \{0, 1\}$.
- **Response:** The prover responds with $\tilde{\mathbf{Q}}$ or $\mathbf{Q}^{-1}\tilde{\mathbf{Q}}$ if the challenge is equal to 0 or 1 respectively.
- **Verification:** In this step, the verifier is able to compute $\tilde{\mathbf{G}}$ as $\mathrm{RREF}(\mathbf{G}^{(0)}\mathbf{Q})$ or $\mathrm{RREF}(\mathbf{G}^{(1)}\mathbf{Q}^{-1}\tilde{\mathbf{Q}})$ depending if the challenge is equal to 0 or 1. Finally, they verify that $\mathrm{cmt} = \mathrm{Hash}(\tilde{\mathbf{G}})$.

To get an intuition on the attack, we notice that if a malicious verifier was able to know the ephemeral monomial $\tilde{\mathbf{Q}}$, they would be able to recover the secret key by sending the challenge equal to 1. Indeed, since they receives $\mathbf{Q}^{-1}\tilde{\mathbf{Q}}$ they are able to compute the secret key as:

$$\mathbf{Q} = \tilde{\mathbf{Q}}\left(\mathbf{Q}^{-1}\tilde{\mathbf{Q}}\right)^{-1}$$

As such, the target of the attack is the recovery of $\tilde{\mathbf{Q}}$. In the next section, we show how we are able to exploit the leakage during the matrix multiplication $\mathbf{G}^{(0)}\tilde{\mathbf{Q}}$, which is implemented as shown in Algorithm 1, to recover some of the ephemeral monomial. Unfortunately, the part that is learned is not sufficient to recover the secret in the straight forward way discussed in this section. The recovery is thus more involved and is the topic of the rest of the section.

Algorithm 1 GenMon_Mult($\mathbf{G}, \mathbf{Q}$)

Require: Matrix $\mathbf{G} \in \mathbb{F}_q^{k \times n}$, monomial matrix $\mathbf{Q} \in M_n$ represented by $(\mathbf{d}, \pi)$
Ensure: $\mathbf{A} = \mathbf{GQ}$
  for $i = 0$ to $n - 1$ **do**
    $\mathbf{t} \leftarrow d_i \cdot \mathbf{g}_i$ ▷ scaling of the i-th column of $\mathbf{G}$
    $\mathbf{a}_{\pi(i)} \leftarrow \mathbf{t}$ ▷ setting the $\pi(i)$-th column of $\mathbf{A}$, equivalent to applying

  the permutation π
  end for
  return A

3.2 Partial Recovery of Ephemeral $\tilde{\mathbf{Q}}$ Through Side-Channel Attack

In this section we demonstrate how we are able to partially recover the ephemeral secret monomial $\tilde{\mathbf{Q}} = \tilde{\mathbf{D}}\tilde{\mathbf{P}}$.

Recovering Elements of Ephemeral $\tilde{\mathbf{D}}_J$: To demonstrate the recovery of the ephemeral secret $\tilde{\mathbf{D}}$, we first note from the Algorithm 1 that the matrix multiplication $\mathbf{G}^{(0)}\tilde{\mathbf{Q}}$ can be split into the scaling of the columns of $\mathbf{G}^{(0)}$, represented by the application of the diagonal matrix $\tilde{\mathbf{D}}$, followed by a column permutation using the matrix $\tilde{\mathbf{P}}$, where $\tilde{\mathbf{Q}} = \tilde{\mathbf{D}}\tilde{\mathbf{P}}$.

In the rest of the section, we focus only on the scaling part of the operation, i.e. $\mathbf{G}^{(0)}\tilde{\mathbf{D}}$. Furthermore, taking into account the particular structure of $\mathbf{G}^{(0)}$, we have:

$$\mathbf{G}^{(0)}\tilde{\mathbf{D}} = (\mathbf{I}_k|\mathbf{V})\,\tilde{\mathbf{D}} = \left(\tilde{d}_0 \begin{bmatrix} 1 \\ \vdots \\ 0 \end{bmatrix}, \ldots, \tilde{d}_{k-1} \begin{bmatrix} 0 \\ \vdots \\ 1 \end{bmatrix}, \tilde{d}_k \begin{bmatrix} \mathbf{v}_0 \end{bmatrix}, \ldots, \tilde{d}_{n-1} \begin{bmatrix} \mathbf{v}_{n-k-1} \end{bmatrix}\right)$$

where $\mathbf{g}_j$ and $\mathbf{v}_j$ are the j-th columns of $\mathbf{G}^{(0)}$ and $\mathbf{V}$ respectively. The element $\tilde{d}_j$ is the j-th element of the diagonal of $\tilde{\mathbf{D}}$. The second part of the computation corresponding to the indices $J = \{k, \ldots, n-1\}$, i.e., the scaling of the columns of the dense matrix $\mathbf{V}$, consists in multiplying a single unknown secret $\tilde{d}_j, j \in J$ with a large number of public elements $v_{i,j-k}$. As such, this computation presents a good target for a CPA since we got an intermediate computation in the desired form that we can target as described in Sect. 2.4, albeit we are limited in the number of traces that we can use. We show how this issue is solved in Sect. 3.6. Thus, from the CPA, we are able to retrieve the value of $\tilde{d}_j$. Furthermore, in an implementation without shuffling countermeasures, the attacker also knows in which order each operation is performed, thus also revealing the index j.

The Challenge with Recovering Ephemeral $\tilde{\mathbf{D}}_{J'=\{0,\ldots,n-1\}/J}$**:** For the rest of the elements of the diagonal matrix (i.e. $\tilde{d}_j, j \in \{0, \ldots, n-1\}/J = \{0, \ldots, k-1\}$), the columns that are scaled are part of an identity matrix. As such, only a single multiplication by a non-zero value is performed. The leakage is thus considerably smaller compared to the leakage that can be observed during the scaling of a dense column. As such, this presents no practical opportunities to gain sufficient leakage to recover the values of $\tilde{d}_j$ for $j \in \{0, \ldots, k-1\}$. However, we show in Sects. 3.3 and 3.4 that knowing those elements is not needed for the full key recovery.

3.3   Partial Recovery of Fixed Secret Q

In this section, we move on to the next step and show how the knowledge of a part $\tilde{\mathbf{D}}_J$ of the ephemeral secret $\tilde{\mathbf{D}}$ can be used to recover the corresponding part of the long term secret $\mathbf{Q}_J = \mathbf{D}_J \mathbf{P}_J$.

To achieve this, we first notice that a relationship between $\tilde{\mathbf{Q}}$ and $\mathbf{Q}$ is needed since $\tilde{\mathbf{Q}}$ is randomly generated. In the identification protocol, we get such a thing when the challenge is equal to 1, corresponding to the case when the prover sends $\mathbf{Q}^{-1}\tilde{\mathbf{Q}}$. Hereafter, we consider that we get m such responses, which we denote as $\mathbf{Q}^{-1}\tilde{\mathbf{Q}}^{(i)}$ for $i \in \{0, \ldots, m-1\}$.

To understand the recovery process, we notice that $\mathbf{Q}^{-1}\tilde{\mathbf{Q}}^{(i)}$ can be represented as:

$$\mathbf{Q}^{-1}\tilde{\mathbf{Q}}^{(i)} = (\mathbf{DP})^{-1}\tilde{\mathbf{D}}^{(i)}\tilde{\mathbf{P}}^{(i)} \tag{1}$$

$$= \mathbf{P}^{-1}\mathbf{D}^{-1}\tilde{\mathbf{D}}^{(i)}\tilde{\mathbf{P}}^{(i)} \tag{2}$$

$$= \mathbf{P}^{\top}\mathbf{D}^{-1}\tilde{\mathbf{D}}^{(i)}\tilde{\mathbf{P}}^{(i)} \tag{3}$$

$$= \mathbf{P}^{\top}\mathbf{D}'^{(i)}\tilde{\mathbf{P}}^{(i)} \tag{4}$$

where we use the properties of the inverse of matrices to go from Eq. 1 to Eq. 2. Moreover, the multiplication of an inverse diagonal matrix $\mathbf{D}^{-1}$ with a diagonal matrix $\tilde{\mathbf{D}}^{(i)}$ gives another diagonal matrix $\mathbf{D}'^{(i)}$ where the elements on the diagonal are $d'_j = d_j^{-1} \cdot \tilde{d}_j^{(i)}$.

From Eq. 4, one can see that the multiplication between the matrices $\mathbf{Q}^{-1}$ and $\tilde{\mathbf{Q}}^{(i)}$ translates into two permutations of the diagonal matrix $\mathbf{D}'^{(i)}$. Concretely, the row permutation is given by a persistent and secret matrix $\mathbf{P}^{\top}$ while the column permutation is given by an ephemeral and also secret matrix $\tilde{\mathbf{P}}^{(i)}$. This can be summarized by:

$$q_{i',j'}^{(i)} = \begin{cases} d_j' = d_j^{-1} \cdot \tilde{d}_j^{(i)} & \text{if, } i' = \pi(j) \wedge j' = \tilde{\pi}^{(i)}(j) \\ 0 & \text{otherwise} \end{cases}$$

where $q_{i',j'}^{(i)}$ is the element of $\mathbf{Q}^{-1}\tilde{\mathbf{Q}}^{(i)}$ on the i'-th row and j'-th column. Moreover, π and $\tilde{\pi}^{(i)}$ are the permutation corresponding to the matrices $\mathbf{P}$ and $\tilde{\mathbf{P}}^{(i)}$ respectively.

A key observation is that the element d_j^{-1} of the secret key is always a factor of the signatures' non-zero element that lies in the i'-th row, regardless of the ephemeral column permutation $\tilde{\pi}^{(i)}$. This leads us to focus only on the rows of the elements $q_{i',j'}^{(i)}$, thus dropping the column index. We denote the obtained column vector as $\mathbf{c}^{(i)}$ such that[2]:

$$c_j^{(i)} = q_{i',j'}^{(i)} \text{ where } i' = \pi(j) \wedge j' = \tilde{\pi}^{(i)}(j).$$

Given this, we can retrieve the coefficients d_j and the permutation $i' = \pi(j)$, corresponding to the secret $\mathbf{Q}_J$, in the following way: we multiply the column vector $\mathbf{c}^{(i)}$ by the inverse of a retrieved element $\tilde{d}_j^{(i)}, j \in \{k, k+1, \ldots, n-1\}$. This gives us,

$$\mathbf{c}^{(i)} \cdot \left(\tilde{d}_j^{(i)}\right)^{-1} = \begin{pmatrix} c_0^{(i)} \\ \vdots \\ c_{\pi(j)}^{(i)} \\ \vdots \\ c_{n-1}^{(i)} \end{pmatrix} \cdot \left(\tilde{d}_j^{(i)}\right)^{-1} = \begin{pmatrix} d_{\pi^{-1}(0)}^{-1} \tilde{d}_{\pi^{-1}(0)}^{(i)} \cdot \left(\tilde{d}_j^{(i)}\right)^{-1} \\ \vdots \\ d_j^{-1} \tilde{d}_j^{(i)} \cdot \left(\tilde{d}_j^{(i)}\right)^{-1} \\ \vdots \\ d_{\pi^{-1}(n-1)}^{-1} \tilde{d}_{\pi^{-1}(n-1)}^{(i)} \cdot \left(\tilde{d}_j^{(i)}\right)^{-1} \end{pmatrix} = \begin{pmatrix} r_0^{(i)} \\ \vdots \\ d_j^{-1} \\ \vdots \\ r_{n-1}^{(i)} \end{pmatrix}$$

where $r_{j'}^{(i)} = d_{\pi^{-1}(j')}^{-1} \tilde{d}_{\pi^{-1}(j')}^{(i)} \cdot \left(\tilde{d}_{j'}^{(i)}\right)^{-1}, j' \in \{0, \ldots, n-1\}/\{\pi(j)\}$.

To make a pattern more apparent, we concatenate the products of each of the m responses to obtain,

$$\left(\mathbf{c}^{(0)} \cdot \left(\tilde{d}_j^{(0)}\right)^{-1} \middle| \ldots \middle| \mathbf{c}^{(m-1)} \cdot \left(\tilde{d}_j^{(m-1)}\right)^{-1}\right) = \begin{pmatrix} r_0^{(0)} & \cdots & r_0^{(m-1)} \\ \vdots & & \vdots \\ d_j^{-1} & \cdots & d_j^{-1} \\ \vdots & & \vdots \\ r_{n-1}^{(0)} & \cdots & r_{n-1}^{(m-1)} \end{pmatrix}.$$

---

[2] We are guaranteed that each row has only one non zero element since $\mathbf{Q}^{-1}\tilde{\mathbf{Q}}^{(i)}$ is the (row and column) permutation of a diagonal matrix.

Recovering Elements of $\mathbf{D}_J$ and $\mathbf{P}_J$ Simultaneously: We notice that the row $j' = \pi(j)$ is a sequence composed only of the element d_j^{-1}, since multiplying $c_j^{(i)} = d_j^{-1} \cdot \tilde{d}_j^{(i)}$ by the inverse of $\tilde{d}_j^{(i)}$ removes the ephemeral factor. On the other hand, given a row where $j' \neq \pi(j)$, the sequence of numbers will be made of random values $r_{j'}^{(i)}$. Indeed, for a given row j', each $r_{j'}^{(i)}$ is the product of a constant value $d_{\pi^{-1}(j')}^{-1}$ and two independent random values: $\tilde{d}_{\pi^{-1}(j')}^{(i)}$ and the inverse of $\tilde{d}_{j'}^{(i)}$.

As such, only the j'-th row contains a unique value, while the others can be made up of any value in $\mathbb{F}_q^*$. This enables us to identify the correct mapping of j by the permutation π, allowing us to deduce $j' = \pi(j)$. However, there exists a possibility that all values in a randomly generated sequence are identical, which stops us from distinguishing the correct result. This happens with probability

$$
\mathrm{P}\left(r_{j'}^{(i)} = r_{j'}^{(i')}, \forall i, i' \in \{0, \ldots, m-1\}\right) = \left(1/\left|\mathbb{F}_q^*\right|\right)^{m-1} = (1/126)^{m-1}.
$$

As such, we have to gather multiple responses to be certain that we can deduce the correct secret.

In the end, we are able to recover the value d_j^{-1} (and thus, d_j) corresponding to $\mathbf{D}_J$ and the result of $\pi(j) = j'$ corresponding to $\mathbf{P}_J$, where j is known from the CPA and j' is the row in which the element d_j^{-1} is identified. Doing this for each index $j \in \{k, k+1, \ldots, n-1\}$ leads to the knowledge of $\mathbf{Q}_J$.

On the Possibility of Extending the Attack to LESS 2.0: As explained in the aforementioned text, in order to recover an element d_j of $\mathbf{D}_J$ and the permutation $\pi(j) = j'$ in $\mathbf{P}_J$ using the partial matrix $\tilde{\mathbf{D}}_J$ retrieved through CPA, we utilize the response matrices of the form $\mathbf{Q}^{-1}\tilde{\mathbf{Q}}^{(i)}$ provided over multiple signatures. In particular, we need the pairs of values $(d_i^{-1}\tilde{d}_j^{(i)}, \pi(j))$ where $d_j^{-1}\tilde{d}_j^{(i)} = q_{\pi(j),\tilde{\pi}(j)}^{(i)} \in \mathbf{Q}^{-1}\tilde{\mathbf{Q}}^{(i)}$ (note that the index j is not known). However, in LESS 2.0 this attack path is no longer possible since we get less information from the signature. Concretely we only get to know which index is in the set $\pi(\tilde{\pi}^{-1}(\{0, \ldots, k-1\})^3$ and as such we cannot extend it to gain knowledge of $\tilde{d}_k$.

The next section covers a way to recover the full secret with this partial information and is the same for both the horizontal and CPA based attacks.

3.4 Full Secret Recovery

In [19], it was shown that LEP is equivalent to information-set LEP or IS-LEP. In the context of our attack, this means that knowing the action of an information set J (i.e. $\mathbf{Q}_J$) is enough to find the full monomial $\mathbf{Q}$, given $\mathbf{G}^{(0)}$ and $\mathbf{G}^{(1)}$ such that $\mathbf{G}^{(1)} = \mathrm{RREF}(\mathbf{G}^{(0)}\mathbf{Q})$. In this section, we show an algorithm which can be used to find the monomial even if the set that we get is not an information set.

---

[3] Note that we oversimplify this slightly by assuming that the first k columns of $\mathbf{G}^{(0)}\tilde{\mathbf{Q}}^{(i)}$ are invertible.

Concretely, during the SCA the set that we recover is $J = \{k, k+1, \ldots, n-1\}$ and the action $\mathbf{Q}_J$. This set is not an information set when $\mathbf{G}_J^{(0)} = \mathbf{V}$ is not invertible. To understand why it is possible, notice that we do recover an information set without the action (i.e. we do not get the one to one mapping of the permutation π nor the scaling elements). Indeed, we can recover the sets $\{0, \ldots, n-1\}/J = \{0, \ldots, k-1\}$ and $\pi(\{0, \ldots, k-1\}) = \{0, \ldots, n-1\}/J'$, where the first set corresponds to the column indices of the identity matrix which is always invertible and thus an information set. This knowledge is sufficient to recover $\mathbf{Q}$ as shown by the authors of [8].

To recover the secret $\mathbf{Q}$ using $\mathbf{Q}_J$, first notice that the RREF of $\mathbf{G}^{(0)}\mathbf{Q}$ can always be expressed as a matrix multiplication by an invertible matrix $\mathbf{S}$. As such, we have that $\mathbf{G}^{(1)} = \mathbf{S}\mathbf{G}^{(0)}\mathbf{Q}$. Next, let $J' = \pi(J)$ be the set of the indices after the column permutation and let $\{0, \ldots, n-1\}/J$ and $\{0, \ldots, n-1\}/J'$ be the set of column indices outside J and J', respectively. One can derive the following relations, which are adapted from [19]:

$$\mathbf{G}_{J'}^{(1)} = \mathbf{S}\mathbf{G}_J^{(0)}\mathbf{Q}_J, \quad \mathbf{G}_{\{0,\ldots,n-1\}/J'}^{(1)} = \mathbf{S}\mathbf{G}_{\{0,\ldots,n-1\}/J}^{(0)}\mathbf{Q}_{\{0,\ldots,n-1\}/J},$$

where $\mathbf{Q}_J \in M_k$ and $\mathbf{Q}_{\{0,\ldots,n-1\}/J} \in M_{n-k}$. Furthermore, given the parameter set of LESS, we have that $\mathbf{G}_{\{0,\ldots,n-1\}/J'}^{(1)} \in \mathbb{F}^{k \times k}$ is a square matrix and is invertible since it is a composition of invertible matrices. In particular, we always have that $\mathbf{G}_{\{0,\ldots,n-1\}/J}^{(0)} = \mathbf{I}_k$ since $\{0, \ldots, n-1\}/J = \{0, \ldots, k-1\}$ which corresponds to the indices of the identity matrix in $\mathbf{G}^{(0)}$. Thus, we can always derive the following relation:

$$\left(\mathbf{G}_{\{0,\ldots,n-1\}/J'}^{(1)}\right)^{-1}\mathbf{G}_{J'}^{(1)} = \left(\mathbf{S}\mathbf{G}_{\{0,\ldots,n-1\}/J}\mathbf{Q}_{\{0,\ldots,n-1\}/J}\right)^{-1}(\mathbf{S}\mathbf{G}_J\mathbf{Q}_J)$$

$$= \mathbf{Q}_{\{0,\ldots,n-1\}/J}^{-1}\left(\mathbf{G}_{\{0,\ldots,n-1\}/J}^{(0)}\right)^{-1}\mathbf{G}_J^{(0)}\mathbf{Q}_J$$

$$= \mathbf{Q}_{\{0,\ldots,n-1\}/J}^{-1}\mathbf{I}_k\mathbf{G}_J^{(0)}\mathbf{Q}_J$$

$$= \mathbf{Q}_{\{0,\ldots,n-1\}/J}^{-1}\mathbf{G}_J^{(0)}\mathbf{Q}_J.$$

After left multiplying both sides of the equation with $\mathbf{Q}_{\{0,\ldots,n-1\}/J}$, the result can be rearranged to obtain:

$$\mathbf{Q}_{\{0,\ldots,n-1\}/J}\left(\mathbf{G}_{\{0,\ldots,n-1\}/J'}^{(1)}\right)^{-1}\mathbf{G}_{J'}^{(1)} = \mathbf{G}_J^{(0)}\mathbf{Q}_J$$

$$\Longleftrightarrow \mathbf{Q}_{\{0,\ldots,n-1\}/J}\mathbf{A} = \mathbf{B}$$

where $\mathbf{A} = \left(\mathbf{G}_{\{0,\ldots,n-1\}/J'}^{(0)}\right)^{-1}\mathbf{G}_{J'}^{(0)}$ and $\mathbf{B} = \mathbf{G}_J^{(0)}\mathbf{Q}_J$ are known and the matrix $\mathbf{Q}_{\{0,\ldots,n-1\}/J}$ is the only unknown. To solve this system, one way is to right multiply both equation by the inverse of $\mathbf{A}$ which exists when J is an information set. In particular, it depends on the dense part of $\mathbf{G}^{(0)} = (\mathbf{I}_k|\mathbf{V})$ being invertible. For all the parameter sets in LESS, the probability that the matrix $\mathbf{V}$ is non invertible is approximately $1/|\mathbb{F}_q| = 1/126$. To take into account these cases, a more general approach is considered. Furthermore, this approach is also more suited for the practical attack as is shown in Sect. 3.6.

To consider a more general case, we replace $\mathbf{Q}_{\{0,\ldots,n-1\}/J}$ by $\mathbf{M}' \in M_{n-k}$. Indeed, it might be the case that the recovered monomial is not exactly the same as the one from the secret key. As such, we want to solve the system

$$\mathbf{M}'\mathbf{A} = \mathbf{B} \tag{5}$$

To recover the monomial $\mathbf{M}' = \mathbf{D}'\mathbf{P}'$, we can notice that each row $\mathbf{a}_{\pi'(i)}$ of the matrix $\mathbf{A}$ is related to a row $\mathbf{b}_i$ of the matrix $\mathbf{B}$ by the relation:

$$d'_{\pi'(i)}\mathbf{a}_{\pi'(i)} = \mathbf{b}_i \tag{6}$$

where d'_j is the j-th element of the diagonal matrix $\mathbf{D}'$ and π' is the permutation associated to the permutation matrix $\mathbf{P}'$. Even though both the permutation and the elements are unknown, this relation allows an efficient brute force search. Indeed, for each i-th row $\mathbf{a}_i$ of $\mathbf{A}$, we can multiply every element in each row of $\mathbf{B}$ by the inverse of the corresponding element in $\mathbf{a}_i$. Then, one of the results will be a vector containing only one constant a since we are guaranteed that for some row $\mathbf{b}_j$ the relation 6 holds. From this, we recover $\pi'(i) = j$ and $d'_j = a$. To complete this procedure, we also need to cover the case where one of the elements of $\mathbf{a}_i$ is equal to zero and thus does not have an inverse. In that case, the corresponding element of the row in $\mathbf{B}$ should also be equal to zero. Another case that has to be considered is when two or more rows of $\mathbf{B}$ are multiples of each other. This leads to multiple choices in vectors which have the same constant at the end of the procedure. However, it is not a problem since choosing either of them will lead to a solution $\mathbf{Q}'$ such that $\mathbf{G}^{(1)} = \mathrm{RREF}(\mathbf{G}^{(0)}\mathbf{Q}) = \mathrm{RREF}(\mathbf{G}^{(0)}\mathbf{Q}')$. This solution is not necessarily the same as the secret $\mathbf{Q}$, but can also be used in the identification protocol since both associated public keys are the same.

3.5 Extending the Attack from the ID Protocol to LESS-1.2

LESS is based on the identification protocol described in Fig. 1 and is obtained using the Fiat-Shamir transform. For the purpose of the SCA, there is no difference that fundamentally changes the procedure used for the attack. There are however differences that influence the expected minimum (without considering noise during the SCA) number of required signatures that need to be observed. The differences are as follows:

- For soundness reasons, the protocol is repeated multiple times. As such, one signature consists of multiple rounds. During these rounds, we are guaranteed to observe W responses of the form $\mathbf{Q}^{-1}\tilde{\mathbf{Q}}$, where W is a parameter defined by LESS.
- Depending on the parameter set of LESS, the prover generates from 1 to 7 private keys $\mathbf{Q}^{(i)}$ with the corresponding public key $\mathbf{G}^{(i)} = \mathrm{RREF}(\mathbf{G}^{(0)}\mathbf{Q}^{(i)})$, $i \in \{1,\ldots,7\}$. This is done in order to reduce the signature size, at the expense of the public key size.

– The responses of the form $\mathbf{Q}^{-1}\tilde{\mathbf{Q}}$ are compressed in such a way that only half of the elements and permutations are sent. Namely the action of $\mathbf{Q}^{-1}\tilde{\mathbf{Q}}$ on the first (for some ordering) information set of $\tilde{\mathbf{G}} = \mathrm{RREF}(\mathbf{G}^{(0)}\tilde{\mathbf{Q}})$ is sent.

The first point guarantees that we get W matrices of the form $\mathbf{Q}^{-1}\tilde{\mathbf{Q}}$ in a single signature, making single-trace attacks possible. On the other hand, points 2 and 3 increase the number of required values of the form $\mathbf{Q}^{-1}\tilde{\mathbf{Q}}$. Indeed, the former requires us to perform the attack on multiple secret keys while the latter reduces the information that is given to us in a signature.

3.6   CPA Attack in Practice

In this section, we focus on the practical aspect of the attack. First, we explain how to perform the horizontal attack on $\tilde{d}_i\mathbf{v}_{i-k}$. Then we explain how to turn it into a CPA. Finally, we highlight some issues arising from the choice of our power leakage model.

From a Horizontal Attack to a CPA Based Attack: In the setting presented before, we supposed that we get $\tilde{\mathbf{D}}_J$ through a CPA-based horizontal attack. There, we directly target the elements $\tilde{d}_i$ during the computation of $\tilde{d}_i\mathbf{v}_{i-k}$. To recover this element, we are limited to a single round since $\tilde{\mathbf{D}}_J$ is generated randomly each time. As such, while performing the correlation, we are limited to the number of elements in the vector $\mathbf{v}_{i-k}$ and thus only a small part of the trace is used. Another disadvantage is that, for a given response $\mathbf{Q}^{-1}\tilde{\mathbf{Q}}^{(j)}$, we have to go through all the possible elements $\tilde{d}_i^{(j)} \in \mathbb{F}_q^*$.

However, this is not optimal because we do not use the fact that, in a sequence of responses, some sequences of elements are not possible since they lead to mutually exclusive secret keys. Thus, rather than attacking the values of $\tilde{d}_i^{(j)}$, we propose to go one step further and attack the values of the secret key directly. In the case of LESS, this is possible since we can compute $\tilde{d}_i^{(j)}$ from the response by making an assumption on a small part of the secret. Concretely, for a given index $i \in \{k, k+1, \ldots, n-1\}$, we have to find $\pi(i) = i' \in \{0, \ldots, n-1\}$ and the value d_i, thus we have to verify only $n \cdot |\mathbb{F}_q^*|$ values pairs.

To explain how we perform the CPA attack, we focus on the recovery of a single pair of secret values $(d_k, \pi(k))$ corresponding to the index k. The same procedure can be then applied to other indices. As such, we first make a guess on the values of the secret, which we denote (d_k', k'). Next, we use signatures of the form $\mathbf{Q}^{-1}\tilde{\mathbf{Q}}^{(j)}$ to turn this guess into a sequence of elements from which we can compute a hypothesis on the power trace. To do this, recall from Sect. 3.3 that if we do not care about the column position, we can represent $\mathbf{Q}^{-1}\tilde{\mathbf{Q}}^{(j)}$ as a vector $\mathbf{c}^{(j)}$, where $c_{\pi(i)}^{(j)} = d_i^{-1}\tilde{d}_i^{(j)}$. Setting those vectors as the columns of a matrix we obtain:

$$
\left(\mathbf{c}^{(0)} \middle| \dots \middle| \mathbf{c}^{(m-1)} \right) = \begin{pmatrix} d_{\pi^{-1}(0)}^{-1} \tilde{d}_{\pi^{-1}(0)}^{(0)} & \cdots & d_{\pi^{-1}(0)}^{-1} \tilde{d}_{\pi^{-1}(0)}^{(m-1)} \\ \vdots & & \vdots \\ d_{\pi^{-1}(i)}^{-1} \tilde{d}_{\pi^{-1}(i)}^{(0)} & \cdots & d_{\pi^{-1}(i)}^{-1} \tilde{d}_{\pi^{-1}(i)}^{(m-1)} \\ \vdots & & \vdots \\ d_{\pi^{-1}(k-1)}^{-1} \tilde{d}_{\pi^{-1}(k-1)}^{(0)} & \cdots & d_{\pi^{-1}(k-1)}^{-1} \tilde{d}_{\pi^{-1}(k-1)}^{(m-1)} \end{pmatrix}
$$

where m is the number of collected responses. Given that, we take the k'-th row of this matrix and we multiply it by d_k'. This gives us:

$$
d_k' \cdot \left(d_{\pi^{-1}(k')}^{-1} \tilde{d}_{\pi^{-1}(k')}^{(0)}, \dots, d_{\pi^{-1}(k')}^{-1} \tilde{d}_{\pi^{-1}(k')}^{(m-1)} \right) = \left(\tilde{d}_k'^{(0)}, \dots, \tilde{d}_k'^{(m-1)} \right)
$$

where $\tilde{d}_k'^{(i)} = d_k' \cdot d_{\pi^{-1}(k')}^{-1} \tilde{d}_{\pi^{-1}(k')}^{(i)}$. We thus obtain a vector where the i-th element is a guess on the k-th element of the matrix $\tilde{\mathbf{D}}^{(i)}$. We then compare one by one the series of column scalings $\left(\tilde{d}_k'^{(0)} \mathbf{v}_k, \dots, \tilde{d}_k'^{(m-1)} \mathbf{v}_k \right)$ with the measured power leakage of the computations $\left(\tilde{d}_k^{(0)} \mathbf{v}_k, \dots, \tilde{d}_k^{(m-1)} \mathbf{v}_k \right)$, where $\mathbf{v}_k$ is the k-th column of the dense part of the public matrix $\mathbf{G}^{(0)}$. We then have 3 cases:

Case 1: $d_k' \neq d_{\pi^{-1}(k')}$

In that case, the sequence $\left(\tilde{d}_k'^{(0)}, \dots, \tilde{d}_k'^{(m-1)} \right)$ is random leading us to expect a low correlation between the power consumption and the hypothesized one.

Case 2: $d_k' = d_{\pi^{-1}(k')}$ but $k' \neq \pi(k)$

In that case, the sequence $\left(\tilde{d}_k'^{(0)}, \dots, \tilde{d}_k'^{(m-1)} \right) = \left(\tilde{d}_{\pi^{-1}(k'),0}, \dots, \tilde{d}_{\pi^{-1}(k'),m-1} \right)$. However, since $k' \neq \pi(k)$, it is still random compared to $\left(\tilde{d}_k^{(0)}, \dots, \tilde{d}_k^{(m-1)} \right)$ since each element of $\tilde{\mathbf{D}}$ is independently and randomly generated. Therefore, we also expect to obtain a low correlation.

Case 3: $d_k' = d_{\pi^{-1}(k')}$ and $k' = \pi(k)$

In that case, the sequence $\left(\tilde{d}_k'^{(0)}, \dots, \tilde{d}_k'^{(m-1)} \right) = \left(\tilde{d}_k^{(0)}, \dots, \tilde{d}_k^{(m-1)} \right)$ and we expect a high correlation since we have the correct values.

We repeat this procedure for each possible pairs of values (d_k', k'), keeping only the one which has the highest correlation. Given enough responses, we obtain the correct result. We do the same for the indexes in $\{k+1, \dots, n-1\}$.

In practice, this only ensures that the function π', which we reconstruct, has an image, i.e. $\forall i \in \{k, k+1, \dots, n-1\}, \exists j \in \{0, \dots, n-1\}$ such that $\pi'(i) = j$. But it does not ensure that it is a correct permutation since it might lead to collisions, thus mapping two different indices to the same index j. We resolve those collisions by choosing the mapping that has the highest correlation. For the other one, we take the second best choice and check again for collisions. We do this until the mapping is one to one.

Choice of the Power Leakage Model: To perform the CPA, we found out during experimentation that we get the best results when we target the output of the modular reduction of the multiplication between the secret elements of $\tilde{\mathbf{D}}_J$ and the elements of $\mathbf{G}_J^{(0)} = \mathbf{V}$. In particular, we use the Hamming weight of the output as our model for the power consumption. However, this choice does not let us distinguish between each value. Indeed, notice that for the prime field $q = 2^7 - 1$ used in LESS we have that:

$$\mathrm{HW}(x \mod q) = \mathrm{HW}(2x \mod q)$$

Since the only operations that are used during the computation of the hypothesis are multiplications and permutations, we cannot distinguish two elements if they are related by a power of 2. Thus, we get a set of possible values rather than a particular one[4]. To take this into account, the procedure of obtaining the full secret from Sect. 3.4 has to be slightly modified. We recall that, to obtain the secret, we had to solve the Eq. 5:

$$\mathbf{M'A} = \mathbf{B}$$

where $\mathbf{B} = \mathbf{G}_J^{(0)}\mathbf{Q}_J$. In this case, we do not have the exact value of $\mathbf{Q}_J$. Instead, we choose any value from the possible ones in the obtained sets. This gets us

$$\mathbf{Q}'_J = \mathbf{D''Q}_J$$

where the $\mathbf{D}''$ is a diagonal matrix with elements in the set $\{y : y = 2^x \mod q, x \in \mathbb{N}\}$.

As such, the new procedure involves a preprocessing step where we find the matrix $\mathbf{D}''$ up to a factor of 2. To do this, we begin by doing the same first step as in the original procedure. However, in this case we do not expect to find a row $\mathbf{r}$ containing the same element. Instead, we expect that each element is the same up to a power of 2. Concretely, we have that $\mathbf{r} = (c, \ldots, c) \star \mathbf{d}''$ where $c \in \mathbb{F}_q^*$ and $\mathbf{d}''$ are the elements on the diagonal of $\mathbf{D}''$[5]. This lets us recover $d_0''\mathbf{d}''^{-1} = 2^a\mathbf{d}''^{-1} = r_0^{-1}\mathbf{r}$, for some $a \in \mathbb{F}_q$. Then, we form our new matrix $\mathbf{B}' = \mathbf{B}(2^a\mathbf{D}''^{-1})\mathbf{Q}'_J$ and we continue with the normal procedure. At the end of it, we obtain a multiple of the original secret $\mathbf{Q}' = 2^a\mathbf{Q}$. This however is enough since our goal is not to obtain the exact secret but a monomial that matches the public key. Which is the case since $\mathrm{RREF}(\mathbf{G}^{(0)}\mathbf{Q}') = \mathrm{RREF}(\mathbf{G}^{(0)}2^a\mathbf{Q}) = \mathrm{RREF}(\mathbf{G}^{(0)}\mathbf{Q})$.

4   Extending the Attack to CROSS: Improvement on [21]

In this section, we begin by recalling the identification protocol underlying CROSS. We continue by briefly presenting the idea of the horizontal attack

---

[4] Another disadvantage is that it increases the required number of rounds since the probability that two sequences of guesses lead to the same power consumption is higher.

[5] For the sake of simplicity we omit the case where the row contains any zeros.

from [21], which targets the computations involving $\mathbf{u}$. The knowledge of this vector can be then used to recover the secret key η. Similarly to LESS, we apply the attack to the identification protocol, which can be generalized for the signature scheme by applying the Fiat-Shamir transform and by considering that multiple rounds of the scheme are executed during one signature.

Next, we show the improvements that can be applied to it. One of them is to turn the horizontal attack into a CPA and the other is a more optimal usage of the traces. Concretely, for the latter part, we will show how to reduce the number of elements of $\mathbf{u}$ that have to be recovered. Then, we propose a way to use all of the signature for the attack. Finally, we also propose a different intermediate computation to exploit the power traces. We note that we explain only the attack on the version of CROSS based on the R-SDP problem since the same attack can be applied on the R-SDP(G) one by considering that the secret key η is generated by a public generator matrix (in systematic form) $\mathbf{M}_G = (\mathbf{V}|\mathbf{I}_m)^6$, where $\mathbf{V} \in \mathbb{F}_z^{m \times (n-m)}$, and a secret vector $\zeta \in \mathbb{F}_z^m$ such that $\eta = \zeta \mathbf{M}_G$. Thus, the underlying secret can be recovered by noticing that $\zeta = (\eta_{n-m}, \ldots, \eta_n)$. Note that the major difference from R-SDP is that, in the R-SDP(G) setting, any vector that is taken from $\mathbb{F}_z^n$ is generated similarly to the secret key.

4.1   CROSS Identification Protocol

The CROSS signature scheme is based on a 5-pass protocol. Similarly to a sigma protocol, it is an interactive protocol enabling the prover to demonstrate their identity to the verifier. The key difference lies in an additional commitment and challenge phase (thus increasing the number of interactions from 3 to 5).

We continue by describing each of the steps in the rest of the section and summarize it in the Fig. 3. Note that this description of the identification protocol is presented in a different way than in [3] to make computations more explicit. As such, the protocol proceeds as follows:

- **Key generation:** The private key is a random vector $\eta \in \mathbb{F}_z^n$. The public key consists of a random parity check matrix in systematic form $\mathbf{H} = (\mathbf{W}|\mathbf{I}_{n-k})$ and the syndrome vector $\mathbf{s} = \mathbf{e}\mathbf{H}^\top$, where $\mathbf{e} = (g^{\eta_0}, \ldots, g^{\eta_{n-1}})$.
- **First Commitment:** The prover generates random vectors $\eta' \in \mathbb{F}_z^n$ and $\mathbf{u}' \in \mathbb{F}_p^n$. Then, they compute $\tilde{\mathbf{e}} = (g^{\sigma_0}, \ldots, g^{\sigma_{n-1}})$, where $\sigma = \eta - \eta'$. Next, the prover calculates $\mathbf{u} = \tilde{\mathbf{e}} \star \mathbf{u}'$ and the corresponding syndrome vector $\tilde{\mathbf{s}} = \mathbf{u}\mathbf{H}^\top$. The prover commits to theses results by sending the hashes $\text{Hash}(\tilde{\mathbf{s}}, \sigma) = c_0$ and $\text{Hash}(\mathbf{u}', \mathbf{e}') = c_1$, where $\mathbf{e}' = (g^{\eta_0'}, \ldots, g^{\eta_{n-1}'})$.
- **First challenge:** The verifier generates a random element $\beta \in \mathbb{F}_p$ and sends it to the prover.
- **Second Commitment:** The prover computes $\mathbf{y} = \mathbf{u}' + \beta\mathbf{e}'$ and commits to it by sending the hash $h = \text{Hash}(\mathbf{y})$.

- **Second challenge:** The verifier randomly selects $b \in \{0, 1\}$ and sends it to the prover.
- **Response:** The prover reveals either the pair of vectors $(\mathbf{y}, \sigma)$ or $(\mathbf{u}', \mathbf{e}')$, depending on whether the second challenge is 0 or 1, respectively.
- **Verification:** In the case the second challenge is equal to 0, the verifier computes the syndrome $\tilde{\mathbf{s}} = \tilde{\mathbf{y}}\mathbf{H}^\top - \beta\mathbf{s}$, where $\tilde{\mathbf{y}} = \tilde{\mathbf{e}} \star \mathbf{y}$ and $\tilde{\mathbf{e}}$ is obtained from σ. The verifier then checks if $\mathrm{Hash}(\mathbf{y}) = h$ and if $\mathrm{Hash}(\tilde{\mathbf{s}}, \sigma) = c_0$. On the other hand, if the second challenge is equal to 1, the verifier can compute $\mathbf{y} = \mathbf{u}' + \beta\mathbf{e}'$ and verifies that $\mathrm{Hash}(\mathbf{y}) = h$ and $\mathrm{Hash}(\mathbf{u}', \mathbf{e}') = c_1$.

Public Data	System parameters $p, n, k \in \mathbb{N}, g \in \mathbb{F}_p^*$ such that the order of g is z.
Private Key	$\eta \in \mathbb{F}_z^n$
Public Key	$\mathbf{H} \in \mathbb{F}_p^{(n-k) \times n}, \mathbf{s} = \mathbf{e}\mathbf{H}^\top \in \mathbb{F}_p^{n-k}$, where $\mathbf{e} = (g^{\eta_0}, \ldots, g^{\eta_{n-1}})$

PROVER		VERIFIER
$\mathbf{u}' \xleftarrow{\$} \mathbb{F}_p^n, \eta' \xleftarrow{\$} \mathbb{F}_z^n$		
$\sigma \leftarrow \eta - \eta', \tilde{\mathbf{e}} \leftarrow (g^{\sigma_0}, \ldots, g^{\sigma_{n-1}})$		
$\mathbf{u} \leftarrow \tilde{\mathbf{e}} \star \mathbf{u}'$		
$\tilde{\mathbf{s}} \leftarrow \mathbf{u}\mathbf{H}^\top$		
$\mathbf{e}' \leftarrow (g^{\eta'_0}, \ldots, g^{\eta'_{n-1}})$		
$c_0, c_1 \leftarrow \mathrm{Hash}(\tilde{\mathbf{s}}, \sigma), \mathrm{Hash}(\mathbf{u}', \mathbf{e}')$	$\xrightarrow{\ (c_0, c_1)\ }$	
	$\xleftarrow{\ \beta\ }$	$\beta \xleftarrow{\$} \mathbb{F}_p^*$
$\mathbf{y} \leftarrow \mathbf{u}' + \beta\mathbf{e}'$		
$h \leftarrow \mathrm{Hash}(\mathbf{y})$	$\xrightarrow{\ h\ }$	
	$\xleftarrow{\ b\ }$	$b \xleftarrow{\$} \{0, 1\}$
If $b = 0, f \leftarrow (\mathbf{y}, \sigma)$		
If $b = 1, f \leftarrow (\mathbf{u}', \mathbf{e}')$	$\xrightarrow{\ f\ }$	
		If $b = 0$
		$\quad \tilde{\mathbf{e}} \leftarrow (g^{\sigma_0}, \ldots, g^{\sigma_{n-1}})$
		$\quad \tilde{\mathbf{y}} \leftarrow \tilde{\mathbf{e}} \star \mathbf{y}, \tilde{\mathbf{s}} \leftarrow \tilde{\mathbf{y}}\mathbf{H}^\top - \beta\mathbf{s}$
		$\quad$ Accept if
		$\qquad \mathrm{Hash}(\mathbf{y}) = h$
		$\qquad \mathrm{Hash}(\tilde{\mathbf{s}}, \sigma) = c_0$
		$\qquad \sigma \in \mathbb{F}_z^n$
		If $b = 1$
		$\quad \mathbf{y} \leftarrow \mathbf{u}' + \beta\mathbf{e}'$
		$\quad$ Accept if
		$\qquad \mathrm{Hash}(\mathbf{y}) = h$
		$\qquad \mathrm{Hash}(\mathbf{u}', \mathbf{e}') = c_1$

Fig. 3. 5-pass protocol at the basis of CROSS [4].

4.2   Horizontal Attack on CROSS

Target of the Horizontal Attack: Similarly to LESS, it is possible to target the multiplication $\mathbf{u}\mathbf{H}^\top$ to recover $\mathbf{u}$ through side-channel analysis. Indeed, comparing Algorithm 1 with Algorithm 2, the later being implemented in CROSS, one can notice that the column scaling of a public matrix is also present there. As such, it presents a potential target for CPA. The remaining part is to show how to recover the secret given that $\mathbf{u}$ is known. While the relation between $\mathbf{u}$ and the secret η is not explicit, there is a straight forward way to compute it given a valid response, regardless of the second challenge. Concretely, there are two ways to achieve it, depending on which second challenge $b \in \{0,1\}$ was sent.

We show hereafter how to recover the secret from $\mathbf{u}$ element wise. Moreover we remind which data is shared. Let $\log_g : \mathbb{F}_p \to \mathbb{F}_z$ be the discrete logarithm in base g, which can be computed since p is small. We proceed with the recovery as follows:

Case where $b = 0$: known data β, $\mathbf{y}$, σ.
In this case, we are able to compute $u_i' = g^{-\sigma_i} u_i$ which lets us find $e_i' = \beta^{-1} \cdot (y_i - u_i')$. From this, we get $\eta_i' = \log_g(e_i')$ and finally the secret can be recover as $\eta_i = \sigma + \eta_i'$.

Case where $b = 1$: known data $\mathbf{u}'$ and $\mathbf{e}'$.
In this case, we first recover $\sigma_i = \log_g(u_i u_i'^{-1})$ from which we obtain the secret key as $\eta_i = \sigma_i + \log_g(e_i')$.

Algorithm 2 VecParity_Mult($\mathbf{u}, \mathbf{H}$)

Require: Matrix $\mathbf{H} = (\mathbf{W}|\mathbf{I}_{n-k})$, with $\mathbf{W} \in \mathbb{F}_q^{(n-k) \times k}$, vector $\mathbf{u} = (u_0, \ldots, u_{n-1}) \in \mathbb{F}_p^n$
Ensure: $\tilde{\mathbf{s}} = \mathbf{u}\mathbf{H}^\top$, where $\tilde{\mathbf{s}} \in \mathbb{F}_p^{n-k}$
    $\mathbf{a}^{(0)} \leftarrow (u_k, \ldots, u_{n-1})$
    for $i = 0$ to $k - 1$ **do**
        $\mathbf{t} \leftarrow u_i \cdot \mathbf{w}_i$ ▷ scaling of the i-th column of $\mathbf{W}$
        $\mathbf{a}^{(i+1)} \leftarrow (\mathbf{a}^{(i)} + \mathbf{t}) \mod p$ ▷ here the modular reduction is made explicit
    end for
    $\tilde{\mathbf{s}} \leftarrow \mathbf{a}^{(k)}$
    return $\tilde{\mathbf{s}}$

General Idea of the Horizontal Attack from [21]: The authors from [21] proceed in three steps, targeting the cases where the second challenge b is equal to 1:

Step 1: First, a horizontal attack on the computation of $u_i \mathbf{w}_i$ is performed. Thus, recovering each $u_i, i \in \{0, \ldots, k-1\}$.

Step 2: Then, the goal is to recover the rest of the vector $\mathbf{u}$. This is achieved by performing a horizontal attack on the intermediate values of the accumulator,

$$a_i^{(j)} = \left(u_{i+k} + \sum_{l=0}^{j-1} u_l w_{l,i} \right) \mod p$$

which are defined in Algorithm 2. For a given index i, the only unknown is u_{i+k} since the rest of the values where recovered during step 1.

Step 3: Recover the secret η from $\mathbf{u}$ and a valid signature where the challenge $b = 1$ using the procedure introduced in this section.

In the work [21], an optimization is introduced where the search space of $u_i \in \mathbb{F}_p$ is reduced by using the fact that most ephemeral values u_i together with a correct signature do not lead to a valid secret $\eta_i \in \mathbb{F}_z$. Concretely, there exists only one u_i for a given value η_i. Thus, the number of possibilities is reduced from $|\mathbb{F}_p|$ to $|\mathbb{F}_z|$, which is a reduction from 127 or 509 to 7 or 127 for R-SDP and R-SDP(G) versions of CROSS respectively.

Proposed Improvements of the Attack:

- First, we do not perform the second step of the attack since we can use the public key to recover the rest of the private key given the first k values of η. Indeed, we have that:

$$(e_k, \ldots, e_{n-1}) = \mathbf{s} - (e_0, \ldots, e_{k-1})\mathbf{W}^\top,$$

  where $\mathbf{e} = (g^{\eta_0}, \ldots, g^{\eta_{n-1}})$.
- Another improvement is that we are able to use every round, and thus all of the signature. Indeed, a link between η and $\mathbf{u}$ is shown in the previous part of this section for the cases where $b = 0$ and $b = 1$.
- Moreover, we apply the same idea as in LESS that leads us to the CPA attack, reducing the search space further. Concretely, we do not need to check each possible values of u_i each time for different rounds. Only an initial assumption on η_i is made from which the ephemeral secret u_i is computed.
- Finally, in Sect. 4.3 we show that the intermediate computation that is used for the attack in step 2 can be used to get better results, which are reported in Sect. 5.

4.3   Leakage Models in the Power Traces

In this section we present two leakage models. The first one is the same as in Sect. 4.2, i.e. we target the unreduced multiplication $u_i\mathbf{w}_i$. This can be used to target any round, no matter the value of the second challenge.

However, through testing we found out that there is a better leakage model. The computation that we target is the same as in step 2, i.e. the reduced accumulator $\mathbf{a}^{(j)}$, but rather than recovering $u_i, i \in \{k, k+1, \ldots, n-1\}$ we want to recover the other part of $\mathbf{u}$. One might notice that this cannot be done in a straight forward way because the accumulator is "masked" by the $n - k$ last elements of $\mathbf{u}$. This can be circumvented in the case that we target responses where the challenge is equal to 0. In that case, we are able to compute $\tilde{\mathbf{s}} \leftarrow \tilde{\mathbf{y}}\mathbf{H}^\top - \beta\mathbf{s}$ which is also the last value of the accumulator $\mathbf{a}^{(k)}$. To get the previous values, we can use the recursive formula:

$$\mathbf{a}^{(i)} = (\mathbf{a}^{(i+1)} - u_i\mathbf{w}_i) \mod p$$

One can see that to get the i-th value we need to know $u_j, i \leq j < k$. As such, we proceed by doing a CPA first on the accumulator $\mathbf{a}^{(k-1)}$ to get η_{k-1} to be able to correctly compute u_{k-1} for each response. We then continue with η_{k-2} and so one until we get η_1. We cannot get η_0 by targeting the modular reduction of the accumulator $\mathbf{a}^{(0)}$ since it is not performed. This, however, is not an issue since only one element in $\mathbb{F}_z$ is left unknown, leading to an efficient brute force attack.

5   Results and Discussion

We performed the attack on a ChipWhisperer Nano board equipped with the STM32F030 microcontroller where we used the onboard ADC for trace collection. The code was compiled using `arm-none-eabi` version 10.2.1. To be able to fit the computations in the small ROM and SRAM, we could only implement small parts of the computation. In the case of LESS, we implemented only the inner loop of the matrix multiplication, i.e. the column scaling. Furthermore, for the modular reduction we use the Barrett reduction provided in the reference implementation. As for CROSS, we implement only the vector matrix multiplication with accumulation as in the reference implementation. In this case we use the provided modular reductions.

We present the number of rounds required to fully recover the secret key in Table 1 for 10 different key pairs. We target a single parameter set of LESS, CROSS-R-SDP and CROSS-RSDP(G). The parameters sets that we use are the ones for NIST security level 1. In the case of LESS we target the "balanced" instantiation and for both instances of CROSS the "speed" one. Furthermore, for CROSS, we perform the attack assuming two different leakage models described in Sect. 4.3.

Table 1. Number of required rounds present in signatures for the full secret key recovery. The average is taken over 10 different key pairs.

Scheme	Leakage model	Required rounds			Required challenge value
		Minimum	Average	Maximum	
LESS	$HW(\tilde{d}_i \mathbf{v}_i)$	15	17.7	24	$ch = 1$
CROSS-R-SDP	$HW(\mathbf{a}^{(i)})$	1	1.4	2	$b = 0$
	$HW(u_i \mathbf{w}_i)$	15	20.2	28	$b = \{0, 1\}$
CROSS-RSDP(G)	$HW(\mathbf{a}^{(i)})$	4	4.7	6	$b = 0$
	$HW(u_i \mathbf{w}_i)$	14	24.6	30	$b = \{0, 1\}$

In the case of LESS, we were able to recover the full secret after at most 24 rounds where the challenge $ch = 1$ for the chosen parameter set, this corresponds to a key recovery in a single trace. We expect similar results for other parameter sets where there is a single secret monomial. On the other hand, when there are multiple secret monomials, the attack has to be performed on each of the keys separately, thus increasing the required rounds that have to be observed. Furthermore, this increase is not linear since the secret key that is used during a round is chosen randomly. As such, the underlying problem in estimating the number of necessary rounds is the coupon collector problem where multiple sets have to be completed [12]. Moreover, we present the evolution of the correlation coefficient for a full signature in Fig. 4 where we try to find for a fixed index i the corresponding index j such that $i = \pi(j), j \in \{k, k+1, \ldots, n-1\}$ and the element d_j. We do this for j where there is a solution and another where there is none. We note that the x axis has different maximums and it does not match the number of received rounds with ch $= 1$. This is due to the fact that we get only half of the elements, as described in Sect. 3.5, and are thus not always able to use a round.

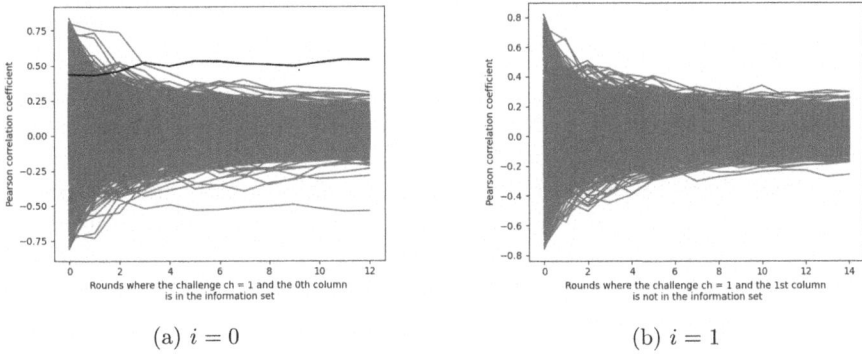

(a) $i = 0$ (b) $i = 1$

Fig. 4. Evolution of the correlation coefficient for the hypothesis where $\pi(\{k, k + 1, \ldots, n-1\}) = i$. For $i = 0$ there is an index that maps to it while for $i = 1$ there is not. The correct result is highlighted in red.

For CROSS, we tested two leakage models where we assumed either the HW of the accumulator $\mathbf{a}^{(i)}$ leaked or the HW of the unreduced multiplication $u_i \mathbf{w}_i$ leaked. In the former case we were able to recover the key after at most 2 or 6 rounds where the challenge was set to $b = 0$, for the R-SDP and R-SDP(G) variants respectively. In the other case we needed more rounds and we always had the correct key after at most 28 or 30 of them. We present the evolution of the correlation coefficient for both in Fig. 5. Note that in Fig. 5a the units of the x-axis are different from those in Fig. 5b; they represent respectively the number of individual multiplications and the number of rounds. We notice that the first strategy, targeting the reduced accumulator, converges faster, has a higher correlation for the correct value and is more pronounced compared to the incorrect ones. Individually, which strategy is better depends on how much of the signature has as the challenge $b = 0$ and thus how many rounds can be used from a single signature. An alternative idea is to combine both strategies.

Comparing this result with the work in [21] for the same parameter set of CROSS-R-SDP and CROSS-R-SDP(G), we require an order of magnitude less rounds to fully recover the secret key compared to their measurements. Concretely, we reduce the required rounds from 27 and 158 to 2 and 6 for R-SDP and R-SDP(G) respectively. We note that some of this discrepancy might be attributed to the different boards used. In any case, for the simulated noise free attack, we still have a reduction in the required rounds from 30 and 31 for R-SDP and R-SDP(G) respectively.

Comparing the attack on LESS and CROSS we notice that when we target a similar operation, i.e. the result of a computation after the modular reduction, we get noticeably different results even though in LESS we have more elements to work with. Concretely, we get a slower convergence for the correct value. This might come from the fact that different modular reductions are implemented. Furthermore, we require significantly more rounds to recover the secret key. We attribute this discrepancy to the fact that we receive only partial information in the signature, which is noted in Sect. 3.5. Another issue is that there is a non negligible probability that an incorrect assumption might be actually present in the trace, which is noted in Sect. 3.3, exacerbated by the choice of the leakage model where we are not able to distinguish values if they share the same hamming weight.

Finally, in both LESS and CROSS we notice that, usually, most of correct secret values are recovered early. Thus, the remaining rounds are collected in order to recover only a small part of the secret. If this part is small enough, an optimization can be investigated where the remaining elements of the secret are recovered using a brute force attack.

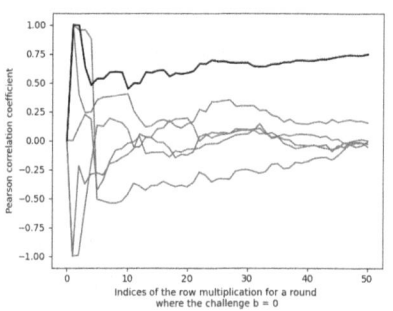
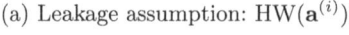
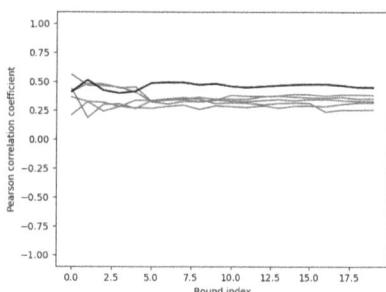

(a) Leakage assumption: $\mathrm{HW}(\mathbf{a}^{(i)})$ (b) Leakage assumption: $\mathrm{HW}(u_i\mathbf{w}_i)$

Fig. 5. Comparison of the evolution of the correlation coefficient for two different leakage models. Note that the units in the x axis and the scale of the y axis are different for the two figures. The correct results are highlighted in red. (Color figure online)

6   Conclusion

In this work, we present a complete key-recovery attack on the LESS and CROSS post-quantum digital signature schemes using CPA. This is achieved by building on previous horizontal attacks against code based schemes [10, 21]. Our attack exploits the direct dependency of the relatively small parts in the elements of the secret key and with the ephemeral secret. This allows us to mount a CPA-based attack targeting the multiplication of a secret ephemeral vector with a public matrix, leading to the full recovery of the secret key. This attack is applied to the versions 1.2 of both schemes, and leads to the recovery of the secret in a single trace for the parameter sets that are targeted. In the case of LESS the amount of traces that are required is expected to increase in the parameter sets where the number of secret keys is greater than one. On the other hand, for CROSS, the same result is expected for any parameter set. Furthermore, we show optimizations that require by an order of magnitude less rounds compared to existing attacks.

In the new 2.0 versions, it is still effective against CROSS, though it is no longer applicable for LESS. The later is due to the fact that the more recent version of LESS implements a compression technique of the signature which removes the required information for the attack to function.

This work underlines the importance of implementing countermeasures against side-channel attacks. We leave their implementation for future works.

Acknowledgement. This work was partially supported by the SINFONIA project, the FWF grant PAT6402023, and the State Government of Styria, Austria, through the Department Zukunftsfonds Steiermark. The SINFONIA has received funding from the Recovery and Resilience Facility (RRF) as the centrepiece of NextGenerationEU via the Austrian Research Promotion Agency (FFG) and Austria Wirtschaftsservice Gesellschaft mbH (aws) in the frame of the IPCEI ME/CT – Important Project of Common European Interest on Microelectronic and Communication Technologies under FFG project No 917423 and AWS project No P2431566.

References

1. Survey on side-channel attacks on code-based key encapsulation mechanism. Mor. J. Algebra Geom. Appl. (in press)
2. Baldi, M., et al.: LESS: linear equivalence signature scheme, version 1.2. National Institute for Standards and Technology (2023). https://www.less-project.com/LESS-2024-02-19.pdf
3. Baldi, M., et al.: CROSS: code and restricted object signature. National Institute for Standards and Technology (2023). https://csrc.nist.gov/csrc/media/Projects/pqc-dig-sig/documents/round-1/spec-files/CROSS-spec-web.pdf
4. Baldi, M., Bitzer, S., Pavoni, A., Santini, P., Wachter-Zeh, A., Weger, V.: Zero knowledge protocols and signatures from the restricted syndrome decoding problem. In: Tang, Q., Teague, V. (eds.) Public-Key Cryptography - PKC 2024 - 27th IACR International Conference on Practice and Theory of Public-Key Cryptography, Sydney, NSW, Australia, 15–17 April 2024, Proceedings, Part II. Lecture

Notes in Computer Science, vol. 14602, pp. 243–274. Springer (2024). https://doi. org/10.1007/978-3-031-57722-2_8

5. Bernstein, D.J., Hülsing, A., Kölbl, S., Niederhagen, R., Rijneveld, J., Schwabe, P.: The SPHINCS+ signature framework. In: Proceedings of the 2019 ACM SIGSAC Conference on Computer and Communications Security, CCS 2019, pp. 2129–2146. Association for Computing Machinery, New York (2019). https://doi.org/10.1145/ 3319535.3363229

6. Biasse, J., Micheli, G., Persichetti, E., Santini, P.: LESS is more: code-based signatures without syndromes. In: Nitaj, A., Youssef, A.M. (eds.) Progress in Cryptology - AFRICACRYPT 2020 - 12th International Conference on Cryptology in Africa, Cairo, Egypt, 20–22 July 2020, Proceedings. Lecture Notes in Computer Science, vol. 12174, pp. 45–65. Springer (2020). https://doi.org/10.1007/978-3-030-51938-4_3

7. Brier, E., Clavier, C., Olivier, F.: Correlation power analysis with a leakage model. In: Joye, M., Quisquater, J.J. (eds.) Cryptographic Hardware and Embedded Systems - CHES 2004, pp. 16–29. Springer (2004). https://doi.org/10.1007/978-3-540-28632-5_2

8. Chou, T., Persichetti, E., Santini, P.: On linear equivalence, canonical forms, and digital signatures. Cryptology ePrint Archive, Paper 2023/1533 (2023). https:// eprint.iacr.org/2023/1533

9. Clavier, C., Feix, B., Gagnerot, G., Roussellet, M., Verneuil, V.: Horizontal correlation analysis on exponentiation. Cryptology ePrint Archive, Paper 2010/394 (2010). https://eprint.iacr.org/2010/394

10. Colombier, B., Grosso, V., Cayrel, P.L., Drğgoi, V.F.: Horizontal correlation attack on classic McEliece. Cryptology ePrint Archive, Paper 2023/546 (2023). https:// eprint.iacr.org/2023/546

11. Coron, J.S., Kocher, P., Naccache, D.: Statistics and secret leakage. In: Frankel, Y. (ed.) Financial Cryptography, pp. 157–173. Springer (2001). https://doi.org/ 10.1007/3-540-45472-1_12

12. Doumas, A.V., Papanicolaou, V.G.: The coupon collector's problem revisited: generalizing the double dixie cup problem of newman and shepp (2015). https://arxiv. org/abs/1412.3626

13. Ducas, L., et al.: CRYSTALS-dilithium: a lattice-based digital signature scheme. IACR Trans. Cryptogr. Hardw. Embed. Syst. **2018**(1), 238–268 (2018). https:// doi.org/10.13154/tches.v2018.i1.238-268

14. Kocher, P.C., Jaffe, J., Jun, B.: Differential power analysis. In: Wiener, M.J. (ed.) Advances in Cryptology - CRYPTO 1999, 19th Annual International Cryptology Conference, Santa Barbara, California, USA, 15–19 August 1999, Proceedings. Lecture Notes in Computer Science, vol. 1666, pp. 388–397. Springer (1999). https:// doi.org/10.1007/3-540-48405-1_25

15. Mangard, S., Oswald, E., Popp, T.: Power analysis attacks - revealing the secrets of smart cards. Springer (2007)

16. Mayer-Sommer, R.: Smartly analyzing the simplicity and the power of simple power analysis on smartcards. In: Koç, Ç.K., Paar, C. (eds.) Cryptographic Hardware and Embedded Systems — CHES 2000, pp. 78–92. Springer. https://doi.org/10.1007/ 3-540-44499-8_6

17. Mondal, P., Adhikary, S., Kundu, S., Karmakar, A.: ZKFault: fault attack analysis on zero-knowledge based post-quantum digital signature schemes. Cryptology ePrint Archive, Paper 2024/1422 (2024). https://eprint.iacr.org/2024/1422

18. National Institute for Standards and Technology (NIST): Post-quantum cryptography: Additional digital signature schemes. https://csrc.nist.gov/projects/pqc-dig-sig/round-2-additional-signatures
19. Persichetti, E., Santini, P.: A new formulation of the linear equivalence problem and shorter less signatures. Springer (2023)
20. Schamberger, T., Renner, J., Sigl, G., Wachter-Zeh, A.: A power side-channel attack on the CCA2-secure HQC KEM. Cryptology ePrint Archive, Paper 2020/910 (2020). https://eprint.iacr.org/2020/910
21. Schupp, J., Sigl, G.: A horizontal attack on the codes and restricted objects signature scheme (CROSS). Cryptology ePrint Archive, Paper 2025/116 (2025). https://eprint.iacr.org/2025/116
22. Shor, P.W.: Polynomial-time algorithms for prime factorization and discrete logarithms on a quantum computer. SIAM J. Comput. **26**(5), 1484–1509 (1997)
23. Shor, P.: Algorithms for quantum computation: discrete logarithms and factoring. In: Proceedings 35th Annual Symposium on Foundations of Computer Science, pp. 124–134 (1994). https://doi.org/10.1109/SFCS.1994.365700

TPL: Power Leakage Model Based on Technology Library

Sumesh Manjunath Ramesh$^{(\boxtimes)}$ ⓘ and Hoda Alkhzaimi$^{(\boxtimes)}$

EMARATSEC, New York University Abu Dhabi, Abu Dhabi, UAE
r.sumesh.manjunath@nyu.edu, hoda.alkhzaimi@gmail.com

Abstract. In our increasingly interconnected world, the security of embedded devices plays a critical role in protecting sensitive information. Evaluating this security requires a meticulous examination of how cryptographic processes are implemented within the hardware of these devices. One widely employed technique for this purpose is Power Side Channel Analysis. At the heart of Correlation Power Side Channel Analysis lies the concept of the power consumption model, which helps to simulate power consumption while executing cryptographic operations on hardware. In this model, along with the hypothetical secret key, is correlated with the actual power consumption during the execution of a cryptographic operation under an unknown secret key. This approach enables the detection of potential vulnerabilities in cryptographic implementations. In this research, we introduce a novel power leakage model called the Technology library Power Leakage Model. This model is rooted in semiconductor technology. By aligning our model closely with specific semiconductor technology, we achieve a more realistic representation of power consumption. Our study provides compelling evidence for the effectiveness of the Power Leakage Model. We successfully extracted secret keys from an AES implementation using Correlation Power Analysis (CPA). Importantly, our Power Leakage Model can be adapted to accommodate various semiconductor technologies such as 55 nm or 14 nm technologies. In this work, we also compared the newly proposed leakage model with the Hamming Distance model and empirically evaluated that both models perform similarly when linear correlation techniques are used in CPA.

Keywords: Side Channel Analysis · Power Leakage Model · Correlation Power Analysis · Semiconductor Technology Library

1 Introduction

Cryptographic algorithms play a critical role in the security of a wide range of devices, including embedded devices and IoT devices. Consequently, safeguarding the implementation of these algorithms is of paramount importance to ensure the overall security of these devices. Historically, until the 1990s, the predominant focus was on meticulously analyzing cryptographic algorithms while leaving the implementation aspects to practitioners.

A. Nitaj et al. (Eds.): AFRICACRYPT 2025, LNCS 15651, pp. 296–316, 2026.
https://doi.org/10.1007/978-3-031-97260-7_14

However, the landscape changed significantly with the introduction of Differential Power Analysis (DPA) by Kocher in [4]. DPA ushered in a new era of side-channel attacks on cryptographic implementations, posing a substantial threat to device security. Various types and variants of side-channel analysis techniques emerged, with notable examples including the Template Attack [11] and the Correlation Power Analysis technique (CPA) [2]. The core premise underlying most power side-channel analysis methods involves modeling the leakage of power values using various techniques known as power leakage models. These models are instrumental in identifying vulnerabilities in cryptographic implementations. Although the literature predominantly relies on Hamming Distance or Hamming Weight leakage models [1], alternative models have also been proposed.

In the realm of related work, the Switching Glitch Leakage model [3] focus on modeling switching power and power consumption resulting from glitches within the cryptographic circuit. This model introduces a switching factor that accounts for different types of data transitions, distinguishes between $0 \rightarrow 1$ and $1 \rightarrow 0$ transitions, and addresses glitches. One limitation of this model is its reliance on a priori knowledge of the locations of the glitches. The Frequency Leakage model proposed in [13] transforms power traces from the time domain to the frequency domain and applies leakage analysis using Hamming Distance and Hamming Weight models. On the other hand, the Multivariate Leakage model introduced in [12] focuses on exploiting leakages occurring at various locations within power traces related to a single intermediate value computed during algorithm execution. This power leakage model exhibits enhanced performance even in the presence of noise within the power traces. In [7], the authors proposed Power Analysis framework using RTL only. Our work will complement this framework better. In [7], the framework applies Hamming distance and Hamming weight as the leakage models, assessing side channel analysis with the KullbackâĂŞLeibler (KL) divergence metric. Our suggested TPL model serves as a leakage model to achieve a maximum KL divergence for identifying the correct key. Our work, along with [8], employs dynamic power values for side channel analysis. The key distinction is that [8] demands the attacker to possess complete information about the logic circuit of the cryptographic algorithm, specifically the logic circuit of the targeted component (e.g., the AES S-box), to produce dynamic power values used as a leakage model for side channel analysis. By contrast, our approach only requires knowledge of the technology library used in hardware design, which is more accessible. Detailed internal circuit design information is unnecessary in our method.

Our work makes three significant contributions, including

1. *Proposing the Technology library Power Leakage (TPL) Model:* Our TPL model is based on total leakage power values obtained directly from the technology library of logic cells. We generate this model using both 55 nm and 14 nm technology libraries, and it is a variant of the Identity Leakage model.
2. *Conducting Correlation Power Analysis (CPA) with the TPL model:* We apply the TPL model in CPA experiments, focusing on an AES implemen-

tation. With 55 nm technology, we perform a CPA analysis for 100 random AES keys, each with 2000 power traces. Similarly, using 14 nm technology, we perform a CPA for one random key and 2000 power traces. In both cases, we achieve a 50% success rate with no more than 650 power traces and a 100% success rate with no more than 1500 power traces.

3. *Comparing the TPL Model with the Hamming Distance Model:* We conduct a comparative analysis to evaluate the performance of the TPL model against the widely used Hamming Distance model in terms of their success rates in side-channel analysis. Both models have similar performance.

The remainder of the paper is organized as follows. Section 2 offers a foundation by delving into preliminaries related to power consumption in hardware, power leakage models, Correlation Power Analysis and SCA performance metrics. Section 3 introduces the TPL model, elucidating its intricacies, the CAD flow process involved in generating essential power values, and valuable information about these power values. Section 4 outlines our approach to evaluate the proposed TPL model, including the defined criteria and methodologies and the evaluation results on 55 nm and 14 nm technology in Sect. 5. Finally, in Sect. 6, we present our concluding remarks and insights into potential future research directions.

2 Preliminaries

This section provides a concise overview of hardware power consumption, including discussions on power consumption models such as the Hamming Distance and Hamming Weight Models. Subsequently, we elucidate the Correlation Power Analysis technique and SCA performance metrics.

2.1 Power Consumption in Hardware

The embedded device (CMOS circuit) exhibits a total power consumption, denoted P_{cir}, which is the result of the cumulative power consumption of all logic cells within the circuit, as shown in Eq. (1). Logic cells are essential elements in digital circuits and encompass components such as logic gates, flip-flops, latches, and registers. This total power consumption can be subdivided into two components: static power consumption, known as P_{stat}, and dynamic power consumption, known as P_{dyn}. Static power denotes the energy drawn by the circuit in the absence of any switching activity within a logic cell, while dynamic power encompasses the power dissipated during switching activities within the logic cells, triggered by internal or external signals. In particular, dynamic power plays a predominant role in the total power profile and depends on the data processed by the logic cells [10].

$$P_{cir} = P_{stat} + P_{dyn} \tag{1}$$

A power trace comprises a collection of measurements representing the total power consumption during a cryptographic operation, recorded at regular intervals throughout the measurement period. As an illustration, consider an operation spanning one millisecond, with measurements sampled at a rate of 5 MHz, resulting in a power trace containing 5000 samples.

2.2   Power Consumption Model

In Power Side-Channel Analysis (SCA), the task often involves establishing a correlation between the data values manipulated during the cryptographic operation and the corresponding power consumption values. In this procedure, a hypothetical power trace is constructed on the basis of the data values, utilizing the power consumption model. The predominant models utilized in power SCA are the Hamming Distance, Hamming Weight, and Identity models.

Hamming Distance (HD) Model. The Hamming Distance Model [4,5,10] is employed to simulate dynamic power consumption, primarily targeting registers and buses within the hardware device. It operates under the assumption that all cells exhibit uniform power consumption characteristics, with no distinction between power consumption during $0 \rightarrow 1$ and $1 \rightarrow 0$ transitions. Additionally, this model presupposes that consecutive data values processed by the logic cell are available. *Hamming Distance*: Let V_{in} be the input data to the circuit and V_{out} be the output data from the circuit. Then the Hamming Distance is calculated using Eq. (2) below.

$$HD(V_{in}, V_{out}) = HW(V_{in} \oplus V_{out}) \tag{2}$$
$$HW(x) = \text{number of bits set to one in } x$$

Hamming Weight (HW) Model. The Hamming Weight (HW) Model [4,5, 10] offers a simpler alternative to the Hamming Distance (HD) model. In the HW model, it is assumed that power consumption is directly proportional to the number of bits set to one in the data processed within the targeted logic cell of the hardware device. It is important to note that the HW model is less precise than the HD model, primarily due to the fact that the dynamic power consumption of hardware devices is significantly influenced by data transitions within the logic cell, rather than the actual values of the data. Nevertheless, the HW model finds utility in situations where the HD model cannot be applied, often due to the unavailability of consecutive data values. Additionally, it is well-suited for scenarios where the circuit is pre-charged each time prior to data processing.

Identity Model. The Identity Leakage model stands out for its simplicity. In contrast to models like Hamming Weight or Hamming Distance, it assumes a direct correlation between the device's power consumption and the exact value of an intermediate data unit (like a register or a portion of a databus). This direct correlation allows for fine-grained analysis, potentially enabling the recovery of secrets with fewer traces (power measurements). The identity model is often the most powerful leakage model if it aligns accurately with the way a device leaks information. However, due to its association with specific values, the identity model tends to be highly device dependent, and its effectiveness relies on an accurate characterization of the target device's leakage behavior.

Let us assume that the power consumption of a cryptographic circuit depends on both the input data (V_{in}) and the output data (V_{out}) being processed. The leakage might then be represented as a function of these values:

$$L(V_{in}, V_{out}) = f(V_{in}, V_{out}) \tag{3}$$

where, f represents a potentially complex relationship between power consumption and processed data. It is rarely a simple linear combination.

In this work, the proposed leakage model is a variant of the Identity Leakage model. Instead of relying on complex mathematical representations, the model leverages actual power consumption values for each data transition using the technology library. That is, for each input and output transitions, is mapped to a power value generated empirically using a technology library.

2.3 Correlation Power Analysis (CPA)

Correlation Power Analysis is an important technique within power side-channel analysis, introduced in [2]. In CPA, the objective is to extract the secret key, K, used in the cryptographic operation executed on the hardware device. This extraction is achieved through the correlation between the actual power trace and a hypothetical power trace, which is constructed on the basis of a leakage model. Specifically, CPA targets the intermediate computations within the cryptographic operation, often focusing on non-linear operations such as S-Box transformations. To apply the HD model, it becomes necessary to have knowledge of both the input and output data values for the S-Box operation. Consequently, the plaintext or ciphertext, in conjunction with a portion of the guessed key, is employed within the HD model to formulate the hypothetical power trace.

In the context of explaining the Correlation Power Analysis (CPA) technique, let us consider the AES (Advanced Encryption Standard) operation. Specifically, we will focus on the last round of AES computation and the first byte of the unknown secret key, denoted by k_1, which is 8 bits in size.

Here is a step-by-step overview of the CPA process for this scenario:

1. *Data Collection:* Begin by selecting a set of N random plaintexts, each consisting of 128 bits. Execute the AES operation on a hardware device preloaded with an unknown secret key, K, using these N plaintexts. Capture the corresponding actual power traces and ciphertexts generated during these operations. Store these power traces in a matrix T. The matrix T will have N rows and s columns, where N represents the number of encryptions and s represents the sample size of the power trace.

2. *Hypothetical Power Traces:* To generate hypothetical power traces for each potential key byte value in the context of targeting the first byte of the secret key (with 256 possible values), we first calculate the intermediate state before the last AES round using the guessed key byte and the ciphertext. This involves inversion of the AES round function. Then, for each of the N ciphertexts, we have V_{in} and V_{out} of the target register. Now, based on the leakage model, the appropriate hypothetical power consumption for that specific ciphertext is calculated under the guessed key-byte value. Create a matrix, denoted by H, to store these hypothetical power consumptions. The matrix H will have N rows (corresponding to the N ciphertexts) and 256 columns (one column for each possible value of the guessed key byte). Each column in H will represent the hypothetical power trace generated for a specific value of the guessed keys byte. Among the 256 columns of the matrix H, one of these columns corresponds to the actual key byte, k_1.

3. *Correlation Analysis:* Calculate the Pearson Correlation Coefficient (PCC) between each column of matrix H and matrix T. Each column in H will have s PCC values for each column in T. The highest PCC value is the PCC for the column in H. Therefore, there is one PCC value for each column in H. The column in matrix H that has the highest PCC indicates the candidate key byte for k_1. This step is repeated for each of the remaining key bytes.

4. *Full Key Extraction:* Repeating the experiment for all key bytes and reversing the AES key-schedule algorithm, the complete 128-bit secret key,K, is extracted.

2.4   Guessing Entropy (GE) and Success Rate (SR)

In Side-Channel Analysis (SCA), Guessing Entropy (GE) and Success Rate (SR) provide rigorous metrics to quantify the effort required by an adversary to correctly identify the secret key [9]. GE and SR are crucial for evaluating and comparing SCA techniques, as they directly correlate with the computational complexity and resources involved in the successful recovery of keys. The Success Rate (SR) complements GE as a performance metric.

Consider an experiment δ, where Q traces are selected from N traces such that $Q \leq N$. Using these Q traces, Correlation Power Analysis is performed, which outputs a candidate key vector $\mathcal{G} = [g_1, g_2, ..., g_{|\mathcal{K}|}]$. Here, $|\mathcal{K}|$ denotes the size of the keyspace, and the guesses are arranged in descending order of the correlation coefficient values. Guessing Entropy is the average position of the correct subkey, k_a^*, in the output vector $\mathcal{G}$. If $g_1 = k_a^*$, then the experiment outputs 1; otherwise, it outputs 0.

After repeating the experiment E times, the Success Rate (SR) is calculated as

$$SR = \frac{1}{E}\sum_{i=1}^{E}\delta_i; \text{ where } \delta_i = \begin{cases} 1 & \text{if } g_1 = k_a^* \\ 0 & \text{otherwise} \end{cases} \tag{4}$$

In this work, the SCA is evaluated using the Success Rate as given in Eq. (4).

3   Technology Library Power Leakage (TPL) Model

The Technology library Power Leakage Model (TPL) is a variant of the Identity Leakage model tailored for side-channel analysis (SCA). This model leverages the power cell library technology to empirically generate a Power Table (P_{tech}) specific to a fixed input size. This table serves as a foundation for power leakage estimation in SCA techniques like Correlation Power Analysis (CPA). This section comprehensively details the TPL model alongside a step-by-step Computer-Aided Design (CAD) workflow for generating the Power Table using the technology library.

It is important to note that this table, P_{tech}, must be created only once for a given semiconductor technology. Once created, the table can be shared and reused for side-channel analysis (SCA) on any device manufactured using that technology. For example, if an adversary creates the table P_{55nm} for 55 nm technology, this table can then be used for SCA against all devices manufactured using 55 nm technology.

3.1   Description of the TPL Model

The total power consumption in a CMOS circuit includes combined power utilization of its logic cells, interconnecting wires, and the underlying technology. This total power consumption can be divided into two components: static power consumption and dynamic power consumption.

Static power consumption arises from the leakage current within the underlying logic cell component, persisting even in the absence of input and output signal transitions. However, dynamic power consumption occurs during input or output signal transitions within the logic cell. There are four possible transitions: $0 \rightarrow 0$, $0 \rightarrow 1$, $1 \rightarrow 0$, and $1 \rightarrow 1$. In fact, static power contributes to all four transitions, whereas dynamic power contributes exclusively to the second and third transitions [10].

In CMOS circuits, signals are typically stored using registers constructed from flip-flop logic cells, with each flip-flop holding a single bit of data. An 8-bit register is formed by logically interconnecting eight flip-flops. Many side-channel analysis (SCA) techniques targeting symmetric-key cryptographic primitives exploit a divide-and-conquer strategy, retrieving key values byte-by-byte (8 bits at a time). This approach aligns with the byte-oriented structure of common cryptographic operations and leverages the often significant power consumption impact of 8-bit registers within the device.

The Technology library Power Leakage (TPL) model tackles this issue by formulating a Power Table P_{tech} tailored for 8-bit registers, derived from the Technology Power Cell Library. Generally, this model can be adjusted for registers of varying sizes (n bits) depending on the computational resources accessible to the adversary constructing the table P_{tech}. However, there are constraints on computation and storage that limit the register sizes the TPL model can support effectively. In this study, our focus is on 8-bit registers only.

Within the TPL model, the technology power cell library serves as a crucial resource for estimating total power consumption. This estimation is deemed to be closer to the actual power consumption of cryptographic operations compared to the Hamming Distance (HD) and Hamming Weight (HW) models, which simulate power consumption and assume equal power consumption for both $0 \rightarrow 1$ and $1 \rightarrow 0$ transitions as well as for $0 \rightarrow 0$ and $1 \rightarrow 1$ transitions.

The TPL Model estimates the total power consumption for an 8-bit register following the computer-aided design (CAD) flow process, as detailed in Sect. 3.2. This process involves considering all possible transitions and generating a Power Table matrix (P_{tech}) for an 8-bit register, using a specific technology library. This matrix contains the total power consumption values for all 65536 data transitions. Importantly, this power table matrix needs to be created only once for a given technology. Once established, it can be used as a power leakage model for power side-channel analysis (SCA) on any device manufactured using that technology.

3.2   CAD Process for TPL Model

To create the power model from the technology library, we begin by generating a netlist consisting of eight D flip-flops. The design characteristics of these flip-flops (drive strength, threshold voltage, reset, $\bar{Q}$ pin, etc.) should be chosen to represent a typical implementation in the target technology. A testbench is then developed to treat this netlist as the Design Under Test (DUT). The testbench generates stimuli that drive the eight flip-flops through all possible byte-to-byte transitions, resulting in 2^{16} unique switching patterns. This switching activity is captured in a Value Change Dump (VCD) file.

Next, a power simulation utilizes the netlist and the VCD file, calculating the power consumption for each of the 2^{16} transitions. These power consumption data are then used to construct a power table, P_{tech} (dimension 256×256), which serves as the basis for Correlation Power Analysis (CPA) attacks. A high-level diagram of this workflow is presented in Fig. 1.

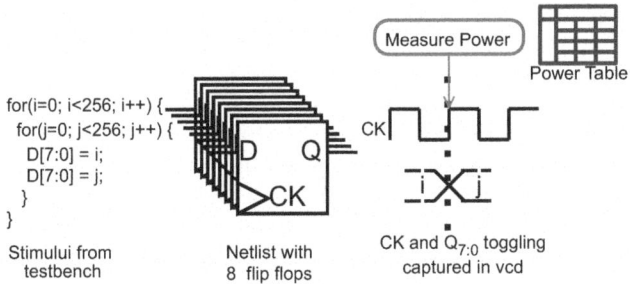

Fig. 1. Technology library power table generation flow.

3.3   Insights on TPL Model

Using a commercial library of 55 nm technology, we generated the Power Table P_{55nm} following the CAD flow process described in Sect. 3.2. A sample of power values from this table is provided in Table 2. The table contains 705 distinct power values ranging from 0.00007637 to 0.00554.

The power values are examined for each Hamming distance from 0 to 8, and these findings are displayed in Table 1. Empirically, it is observed that there is a range of power values corresponding to each Hamming distance leading to Observation 1. This variation underscores the influence of multiple factors, including input and output data, and the bit-transition positions within the 8-bit register, on power consumption. Furthermore, the gap between the highest and lowest power values for a given Hamming distance tends to widen as the Hamming distance increases.

Table 1. Power Leakage Model analysis with respect to Hamming Distance Values. The Min, Max and Difference power values are multiplied by $\times 10^{-5}$.

HD	Min	Max	Difference	Unique Pow Val
0	7.637	8.47	0.833	212
1	74.34	76.73	2.39	158
2	141	145	4	28
3	207.7	213.3	5.6	38
4	274.5	281.5	7	46
5	341.2	349.8	8.6	55
6	407.9	418	10.1	59
7	474.7	486.1	11.4	58
8	541.9	554	12.1	51

Observation 1. *The total power consumption due to the data transition in a register logic cell is not equal for all the data transitions with the same Hamming Distance.*

According to Observation 1, the TPL model provides a more accurate simulation of power consumption patterns compared to the hamming distance model. For instance, while two distinct data transitions with identical hamming distances will display different power consumption levels, the TPL model is capable of capturing this variation. In contrast, the hamming distance model treats both transitions as identical.

Consequently, based on these findings, we assume that the TPL power model, using the Power Table P_{55nm}, may offer greater efficiency in the correlation power analysis (CPA) compared to the Hamming Distance (HD) model.

4   Evaluation of TPL Model

In Sect. 3, we introduce the Technology library Power Leakage Model (TPL), a variant of the identity model that aims to generate simulation traces closer to real-world power measurements. To assess the effectiveness of the TPL model, we perform a comprehensive evaluation within the framework of a typical cryptographic primitive implementation. This evaluation concentrates on two key aspects:

1. *Validation:* We investigate whether the TPL model, when applied in the CPA analysis, can accurately extract the secret key from a cryptographic implementation, such as AES.
2. *Efficiency:* We assess whether the performance of the TPL model is similar to the HD model in the CPA analysis.

4.1   Model Validation

To evaluate the accuracy of the TPL model in the CPA technique, we tested on an AES implementation. The CPA analysis, as described in Sect. 2.3, utilizes the TPL model as a leakage model at the hypothetical step of power trace generation.

We initially have knowledge of the ciphertext byte and calculate the corresponding intermediate AES state byte before the last round of AES encryption using a guessed key byte, denoted k_{guess}. Let S_{out} represent the ciphertext byte, and let S_{in} represent the computed intermediate state byte. We recognize that the data in the S_{in} byte of the intermediate state are stored within an 8-bit register. Following the final round of AES execution, the data in S_{in} undergo a transition to S_{out} as dictated by the AES last round operations. Therefore, we look up the Power Table P_{55nm} to determine the power value associated with the data transition from S_{in} to S_{out}. This value represents the hypothetical power trace value for the key K_{guess} and the ciphertext (encryption). Subsequently, we proceed with the remaining steps as outlined in Sect. 2.3.

4.2   Model Efficiency

In the pursuit of model efficiency evaluation, we compare the TPL model and the HD model within the CPA technique, based on the minimum number of traces required to extract secret key bytes. Our CPA analysis experiment to assess efficiency follows the procedure detailed in Algorithm 1.

Specifically, we repeated CPA analysis using the TPL model and the HD model, utilizing subsets of power trace data, for a large number of random keys. We iteratively increase the subset size until the success rate in extracting the secret key reaches an optimal level. The power leakage model that achieves a higher success rate for a given number of power traces is considered to be more efficient in the context of CPA analysis applied to AES implementations.

Algorithm 1: Experiment for TPL Model Efficiency

Input : $Q = \{P_i, C_i, T_i | 1 \leq i \leq N\} \rightarrow$ power trace T_i, plaintext P_i and ciphertext C_i for i^{th} encryption, $N \rightarrow$ total encryptions;

$M \rightarrow$ number of iterations;

$K_{master} \rightarrow$ Master secret key of AES encryption;

$P_{tech} \rightarrow$ Procedure to output power value using TPL table;

$P_{HD} \rightarrow$ Procedure to output power values using Hamming Distance.

Output: $(S_{tech}, S_{HD}) \rightarrow S_{tech}, S_{HD}$ are arrays of size N.

1 **procedure Experiment** *(Q, N, M, K_{master}, P_{tech}, P_{HD})* **do**

2   Initialize: $S_{tech} = [], S_{HD} = [];$

3   **for** $i \leftarrow 1$ **to** N **do:**

4   **for** $j \leftarrow 1$ **to** M **do:**

5             $V_{tech} = 0, V_{HD} = 0;$

6             $Set_{test} \subseteq Q$, such that $|Set_{test}| = i$, elements are randomly selected;

7             $V_{tech} = V_{tech}+$ **CPA**$(Set_{test}, K_{master}, P_{tech});$

8             $V_{HD} = V_{HD}+$ **CPA**$(Set_{test}, K_{master}, P_{HD});$

9         $S_{tech}[i] = (V_{tech}/M \times 100);$

10        $S_{HD}[i] = (V_{HD}/M \times 100);$

11   **return** (S_{tech}, S_{HD})

12 **procedure CPA** *(Set_{test}, K_{master}, P_{model})* **do**

13     $success = 0$;

14   Run the CPA analysis as in Section 2.3 using $Set_{test}, K_{master}, P_{model}$;

15   Extract $K_{candidate}$ using above step ;

16   **if** $K_{candidate} = K_{master}$ **then**

17         $success = 1$

18   **return** *success*

4.3 CAD Flow for Leakage Evaluation

Our power analysis flow is designed to determine the minimum number of power traces needed to break a cipher and reveal the secret key. The high-level flow is depicted in Fig. 2. The process takes as input the register transfer level (RTL) of the cipher circuit, and the standard cell library of the target technology. We begin by synthesizing the cipher RTL using the selected target technology library. Then, a Gate-Level Simulation (GLS) of the post-synthesis netlist is performed. GLS generates sets of ciphertexts based on user-specified plaintexts and keys, and also a Value Change Dump (VCD) file, that captures the switching activity of every node within the netlist. Subsequently, power simulation is done using the VCD file, the post-synthesis netlist, and relevant libraries. Also, from the power simulation output, we extract the power values corresponding to the last-round operation of AES. Based on the output of GLS cipher texts, the power model gives different power values for all key guesses, and each of the power numbers corresponding to a guessed key is correlated with the last-round power of the AES extracted from the power simulation by calculating the Pearson

Correlation Coefficient (PCC). And if the correlation value is high, they are binned as a potential correct key candidate.

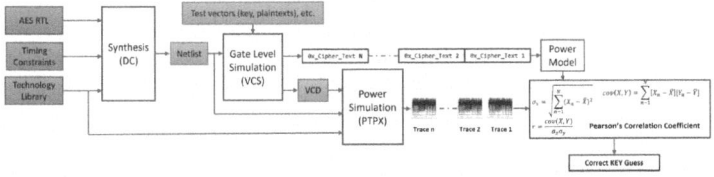

Fig. 2. CAD Flow for CPA Analysis.

5   Evaluation Results

This section provides a detailed account of our experimental setup, including data generation procedures. Subsequently, we present the results obtained for both the 55 nm and 14 nm technology libraries.

5.1   Experimental Setup

We adhered to industry-standard EDA (Electronic Design Automation) practices to generate simulated power traces. The workflow involved Synopsys Design Compiler (DC) for RTL synthesis, Synopsys VCS for gate-level simulation, and Synopsys PTPX for power simulation. Our AES implementation used a standard RTL design for AES-128, configured to execute a single encryption round ten times with appropriate round-specific inputs and keys. The substitution block used a lookup table implementation. Importantly, no side-channel countermeasures were included in this implementation.

For Correlation Power Analysis (CPA), we used a modified version of the open-source C/C++ framework originally presented in [6]. To facilitate optimal performance and resource utilization, all CPA executions were performed on a high performance computing (HPC) facility. This facility is equipped with 14-core Intel Broadwell processors (Xeon E5-2680) running at 2.4 GHz. The Slurm HPC scheduler ensured that each CPA run had dedicated access to 4 GB of RAM.

5.2   Dataset Generation

To thoroughly assess the performance of leakage models in the context of AES implementations, we generated a substantial dataset consisting of 2000 random 128-bit plaintexts and 100 random 128-bit AES master keys. This study aims to explore the applicability of leakage models in a range of process technologies commonly found in embedded systems. Although legacy embedded devices often use older technology libraries, devices that require enhanced performance or specialized features might leverage newer, more advanced libraries.

Our work focuses specifically on the 55 nm and 14 nm technology libraries as case studies. However, we emphasize that the methodologies and analysis presented can be readily adapted to investigate other libraries as well. This allows for a broader understanding of how leakage model performance might vary across different manufacturing processes and device generations.

5.3   Results on 55 nm Technology

In this section, we present the results obtained using the Global Foundries (GF) 55 nm technology library and the corresponding Power Table, denoted as P_{55nm}, as generated according to the procedure detailed in Sect. 3. A sample of power values for data transitions within the 8-bit register logic cell using the 55 nm library is displayed in Table 2.

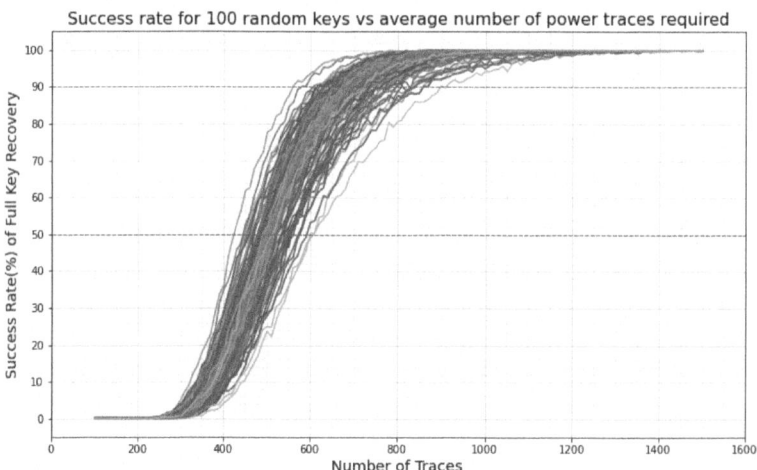

Fig. 3. 55 nm Technology Library: The success rate of secret key extraction for 100 keys vs required number of power traces.

Model Validation. We generate simulated power traces for AES encryptions using the 55 nm technology library, following the CAD flow detailed in Sects. 3.2 and 4.3. For each of the 100 random AES master keys (K_i), we encrypted 2000 unique plaintexts (P^j). This resulted in the corresponding ciphertexts (C^j) and simulated power traces (T_{55}^j), organized into datasets Q_{55}^i as follows:

$$Q_{55}^i = (P^j, C^j, T_{55}^j)|1 \le j \le 2000, 1 \le i \le 100$$

We then performed a CPA analysis on each dataset Q_{55}^i to extract the corresponding key, using the methodology outlined in Sect. 4.1. The accuracy of the extracted keys was determined by comparison with the original master key. This process was repeated for all 100 keys (generated as described in Sect. 5.2), and the results are presented in Fig. 3. These results confirm the successful extraction of secret keys using the TPL model in the context of the 55 nm technology library.

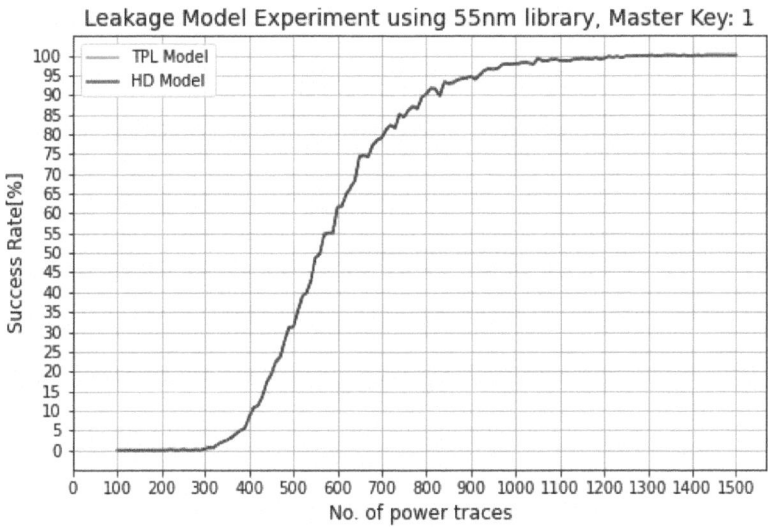

Fig. 4. CPA Experiment between 55 nm based TPL model and HD model for one key.

Model Efficiency. We evaluated the efficiency of the TPL model using the P_{55nm} power table compared to the Hamming Distance (HD) model. The metric for comparison was the success rate of secret key extraction using the minimum average number of power traces. This comparison followed Algorithm 1, with inputs including Q_{55}^i, K_i, the P_{55nm} power table and the HD calculation procedure for 8-bit data. To address the potential selection bias within the subset Set_{test} of Q_{55}^i, we performed $M = 1000$ iterations.

Figure 4 summarizes the success rate and the average minimum traces required to extract the secret key. For clarity, it displays results for the first 8 keys; however, the experiment comprehensively covered all 100 keys. This rigorous evaluation allows for a detailed analysis of the comparative performance between the TPL and Hamming Distance models.

Our analysis demonstrated that both the TPL and the HD model successfully extracted the entire 128-bit master key with a 100% success rate across all 100 keys. In particular, this was achieved with a maximum of 1500 power traces.

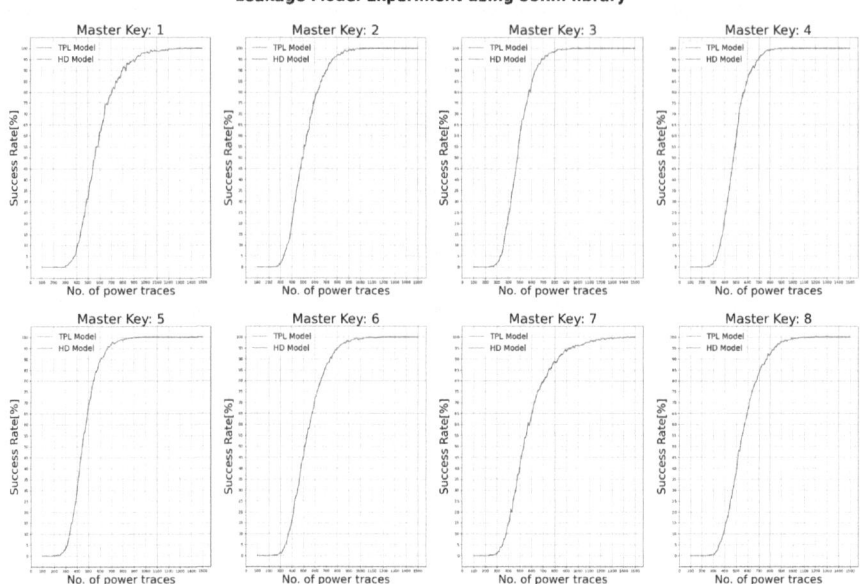

Fig. 5. CPA Experiment between 55 nm based TPL model and HD model for 8 keys.

Figure 4 and Fig. 5 illustrate the remarkably similar success rates of both models for any given subset of traces.

5.4   Results on 14 nm Technology

In this section, we present our findings on the TPL model's performance utilizing the 14nm technology library. We generate a power table, P_{14nm}, following the procedure in Sect. 3. This evaluation focuses on a single AES master key, K_1.

We simulate power traces for AES encryptions with the 14nm technology library, adhering to the CAD flow detailed in Sects. 3.2 and 4.3. Using 2000 unique plaintexts (P^j), we obtained the corresponding ciphertexts (C^j) and simulated traces (T_{14}^j). These were organized into the dataset:

$$Q_{14}^1 = (P^j, C^j, T_{14}^j)|1 \leq j \leq 2000$$

CPA analysis (Sect. 4.1) performed on Q_{14}^1 successfully extracted the correct key. This demonstrates the effectiveness of the TPL model in conjunction with the 14 nm technology library for CPA attacks.

We compared the TPL model (P_{14nm}) against the Hamming Distance (HD) model, focusing on their respective success rates in key extraction using the minimum average number of power traces (Algorithm 1). Figure 6 reveals a performance remarkably similar between the TPL and HD models, requiring a comparable minimum number of traces to achieve a given success rate.

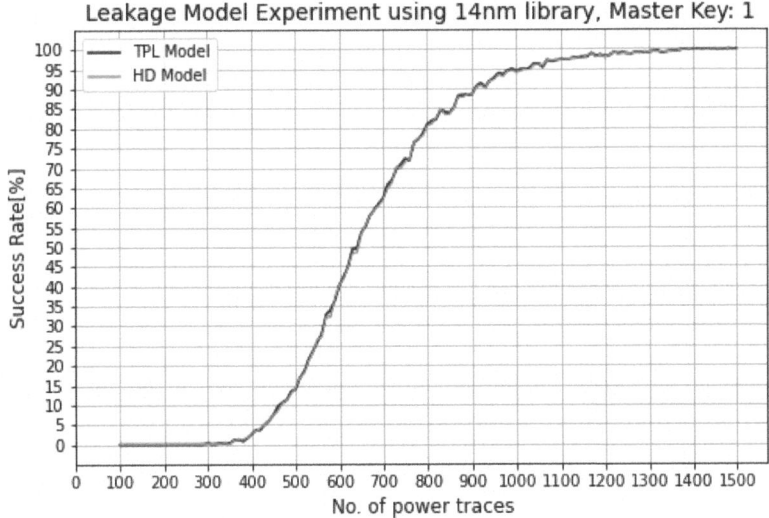

Fig. 6. CPA Experiment between 14 nm based TPL model and HD model for one key.

These results demonstrate that the TPL model, applied within the context of either the 55 nm or 14 nm technology libraries, exhibits a level of performance comparable to the Hamming Distance model in CPA attacks.

5.5 Discussion on the TPL Model

The successful validation of the TPL model in CPA-based key extraction highlights its potential as a power analysis tool. Despite our initial expectation that the TPL's detailed power modeling would surpass the Hamming Distance (HD) model, the observed performance parity warrants a deeper examination. This study emphasizes the interplay between leakage models and the attack methodology chosen. In a correlation power analysis, real power values are compared with those from a leakage model using the Pearson Correlation Coefficient. The relative covariance has more influence on the analysis than the absolute values themselves, resulting in the plotted graph having a consistent pattern with only amplitude variations, as illustrated in Fig. 7. For different inputs producing identical hamming distance leakage model values, the TPL model output will differ. This experiment focuses on the analysis of the AES algorithm's last round. The AES algorithm's inherent randomness in the last round results in diverse Hamming Distance values (0 to 8) for a target byte across power traces. This randomness limits the likelihood of many traces sharing the same HD value, potentially limiting the advantage of the TPL model's more granular power estimates.

These findings led us to consider several interesting avenues for further research. One direction is to explore alternative correlation metrics beyond the PCC that could reveal sensitivities that are better able to differentiate leakage

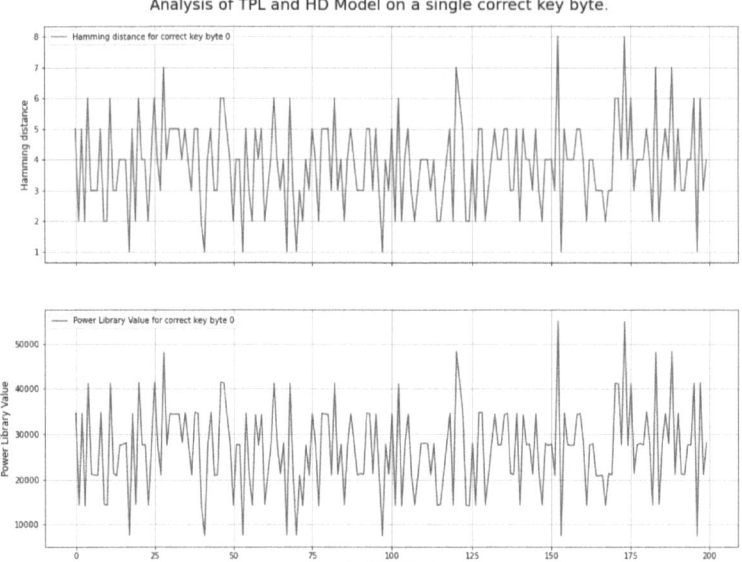

Fig. 7. Comparison of Hamming Distance values and 55 nm power table values with the correct key byte 1 of the master key K_1 for 200 power traces.

patterns captured by the TPL model. Metrics focusing on higher-order moments or non-linear relationships could be investigated. We could also consider modifications to the CPA approach itself, potentially targeting intermediate values across multiple rounds to better exploit the TPL's more granular leakage representation. Finally, examining the TPL model across different devices or cryptographic implementations could uncover scenarios where its advantages are more pronounced due to architectural differences in the target.

This study highlights the complex relationship between leakage modeling, attack techniques, and the characteristics of the target device. Although TPL shows promise, maximizing its impact on side-channel analysis likely requires a tailored approach that considers the intricate interplay of these factors.

5.6 Summary on TPL Model Complexities

This section summarizes key observations on the complexities involved in our analysis of AES implementation and the Technology library Power Leakage (TPL) model's evaluation:

- *Dataset Size*: Comprehensive evaluation of the TPL model required the use of a substantial dataset. We used a total of 200,000 power traces in our experiments, demonstrating the significant data requirements often associated with side-channel analysis. This dataset included 2000 traces for each of the 100 random AES master keys using the 55 nm library and another 2000 traces for a single key within the 14 nm library.

- *Success Rates*: Both the TPL and Hamming Distance (HD) models demonstrated high success rates across both the 55 nm and 14 nm technology libraries. This highlights the vulnerability of AES implementations to power-based side-channel attacks when appropriate countermeasures are absent. Both models consistently achieved a 50% key extraction success rate with at most 650 traces and reached a 100% success rate with no more than 1500 traces for all the analyzed keys.
- *Performance Similarity*: Interestingly, within the context of Correlation Power Analysis (CPA), the TPL and HD models exhibited remarkably similar performance. This was particularly evident in the minimum number of power traces that each model needed to achieve a given key extraction success rate.
- *Explaining Complexity*: Further investigation revealed a key contributor to this similarity: the Pearson Correlation Coefficient (PCC). It produced analogous results when correlating actual power traces with HD values or values from the TPL model. The inherent randomness of HD values across consecutive power traces appears to be a crucial factor in limiting the potential advantage of the more fine-grained TPL model within this CPA approach.
- *Implications*: This study emphasizes the intricate interconnections among leakage models, attack methods, and the characteristics of devices. It suggests that the choice of leakage model alone does not guarantee superior SCA performance and highlights the need to carefully consider the interplay between attack vectors and the target's implementation details.

6   Conclusion and Future Work

This study has presented a detailed investigation into the Technology library Power Leakage (TPL) model, a leakage model designed to provide a more accurate representation of actual power values in side-channel power analysis. We have meticulously described the model's creation, its theoretical underpinnings, and the practical workflow for its generation. Importantly, the TPL model's core principle is its direct reliance on empirical device power characteristics obtained from the underlying technology library thereby mimicking Identity Leakage model.

Our rigorous experimental evaluation provides significant evidence to validate the effectiveness of the TPL model. Through Correlation Power Analysis (CPA), we have demonstrated its ability to successfully extract secret keys from AES implementations in both 55 nm and 14 nm technology libraries. This not only confirms the soundness of the TPL model, but also highlights the vulnerability of cryptographic implementations to power-based side-channel attacks in the absence of countermeasures. A surprising finding emerging from our analysis was the performance parity of the TPL model with the established Hamming Distance (HD) model. Despite the more detailed power modeling of the TPL, the number of traces needed to achieve a specific success rate in key extraction remained strikingly similar for both models. This unexpected result underscores the crucial role that attack methodologies and analysis techniques play in determining the effectiveness of side-channel analysis, regardless of the leakage model used. Through careful analysis, we identified the core reason for this performance parity: the Pearson Correlation Coefficient (PCC). Used within the CPA approach, the PCC produced analogous values when correlating actual power traces with either HD values or the more fine-grained TPL power estimations.

The observations from this study point to intriguing areas for future investigation. Expanding the scope of analysis methods could unlock the full potential of the TPL model. Metrics focusing on higher-order moments, non-linear relationships, mutual information, or machine learning-based approaches might be able to better distinguish the nuances of power leakage captured by the TPL model. Developing CPA strategies specifically tailored to leverage the TPL's representation of intermediate values could lead to stronger attacks. Examining the TPL model on a wider variety of devices and cryptographic algorithms could reveal scenarios where its benefits are more pronounced. The TPL model offers a valuable tool for the assessment of countermeasures designed to thwart power analysis. By accurately modeling a device's leakage behavior, countermeasures can be both rigorously tested and fine-tuned under realistic conditions. Furthermore, the effectiveness of our TPL model can be assessed on other cipher implementations, such as ASCON and PQC algorithms, and its performance can be compared with other leakage models.

In summary, the TPL model represents significant progress in leakage modeling, offering potential advantages for side-channel analysis. However, this work emphasizes that the realization of its benefits requires a multifaceted strategy tailored to the target device and a critical examination of the SCA techniques employed.

Acknowledgment. This research was partially carried out on the High Performance Computing resources at New York University Abu Dhabi.

A   Sample 55 nm Leakage Table Entries

In this section, we give a few entries in the 55 nm leakage table in Table 2. The complete 55 nm leakage table along with 14 nm leakage table will be available at https://github.com/rsumeshmanjunath/TLPL-Leakage-Model.

Table 2. Sample entries in the 55 nm leakage table. Each value represents the power consumption value for data transition from input data (row) to output data (column).

	00	01	02	03	04	05	06	⋯⋯	⋯⋯	FE	FF
00	7.91E-05	7.62E-04	7.62E-04	1.44E-03	7.62E-04	1.44E-03	1.44E-03	⋯⋯	⋯⋯	4.86E-03	5.54E-03
01	7.46E-04	7.85E-05	1.43E-03	7.61E-04	1.43E-03	7.61E-04	2.11E-03	⋯⋯	⋯⋯	5.52E-03	4.86E-03
02	7.46E-04	1.43E-03	7.85E-05	7.61E-04	1.43E-03	2.11E-03	7.61E-04	⋯⋯	⋯⋯	4.17E-03	4.86E-03
03	1.41E-03	7.45E-04	7.45E-04	7.78E-05	2.10E-03	1.43E-03	1.43E-03	⋯⋯	⋯⋯	4.84E-03	4.17E-03
04	7.46E-04	1.43E-03	1.43E-03	2.11E-03	7.85E-05	7.61E-04	7.61E-04	⋯⋯	⋯⋯	4.17E-03	4.86E-03
05	1.41E-03	7.45E-04	2.10E-03	1.43E-03	7.45E-04	7.79E-05	1.43E-03	⋯⋯	⋯⋯	4.84E-03	4.17E-03
06	1.41E-03	2.10E-03	7.45E-04	1.43E-03	7.45E-04	1.43E-03	7.79E-05	⋯⋯	⋯⋯	3.49E-03	4.17E-03
07	2.08E-03	1.41E-03	1.41E-03	7.44E-04	1.41E-03	7.44E-04	7.44E-04	⋯⋯	⋯⋯	4.16E-03	3.49E-03
08	7.46E-04	1.43E-03	1.43E-03	2.11E-03	1.43E-03	2.11E-03	2.11E-03	⋯⋯	⋯⋯	4.17E-03	4.86E-03
09	1.41E-03	7.45E-04	2.10E-03	1.43E-03	2.10E-03	1.43E-03	2.78E-03	⋯⋯	⋯⋯	4.84E-03	4.17E-03
0A	1.41E-03	2.10E-03	7.45E-04	1.43E-03	2.10E-03	2.78E-03	1.43E-03	⋯⋯	⋯⋯	3.49E-03	4.17E-03
0B	2.08E-03	1.41E-03	1.41E-03	7.44E-04	2.76E-03	2.09E-03	2.09E-03	⋯⋯	⋯⋯	4.16E-03	3.49E-03
0C	1.41E-03	2.10E-03	2.10E-03	2.78E-03	7.45E-04	1.43E-03	1.43E-03	⋯⋯	⋯⋯	3.49E-03	4.17E-03
0D	2.08E-03	1.41E-03	2.76E-03	2.09E-03	1.41E-03	7.44E-04	2.09E-03	⋯⋯	⋯⋯	4.16E-03	3.49E-03
0E	2.08E-03	2.76E-03	1.41E-03	2.09E-03	1.41E-03	2.09E-03	7.44E-04	⋯⋯	⋯⋯	2.81E-03	3.49E-03
0F	2.75E-03	2.08E-03	2.08E-03	1.41E-03	2.08E-03	1.41E-03	1.41E-03	⋯⋯	⋯⋯	3.47E-03	2.81E-03
10	7.46E-04	1.43E-03	1.43E-03	2.11E-03	1.43E-03	2.11E-03	2.11E-03	⋯⋯	⋯⋯	4.18E-03	4.86E-03
⋯	⋯	⋯	⋯	⋯	⋯	⋯	⋯	⋯⋯	⋯⋯	⋯	⋯
⋯	⋯	⋯	⋯	⋯	⋯	⋯	⋯	⋯⋯	⋯⋯	⋯	⋯
FA	4.09E-03	4.77E-03	3.42E-03	4.10E-03	4.77E-03	5.45E-03	4.10E-03	⋯⋯	⋯⋯	7.67E-04	1.45E-03
FB	4.75E-03	4.09E-03	4.09E-03	3.42E-03	5.44E-03	4.77E-03	4.77E-03	⋯⋯	⋯⋯	1.43E-03	7.66E-04
FC	4.09E-03	4.77E-03	4.77E-03	5.45E-03	3.42E-03	4.10E-03	4.10E-03	⋯⋯	⋯⋯	7.67E-04	1.45E-03
FD	4.75E-03	4.09E-03	5.44E-03	4.77E-03	4.09E-03	3.42E-03	4.77E-03	⋯⋯	⋯⋯	1.43E-03	7.66E-04
FE	4.75E-03	5.44E-03	4.09E-03	4.77E-03	4.09E-03	4.77E-03	3.42E-03	⋯⋯	⋯⋯	8.35E-05	7.66E-04
FF	5.42E-03	4.75E-03	4.75E-03	4.09E-03	4.75E-03	4.09E-03	4.09E-03	⋯⋯	⋯⋯	7.50E-04	8.29E-05

References

1. Akkar, M.-L., Bevan, R., Dischamp, P., Moyart, D.: Power analysis, what is now possible... In: Okamoto, T. (ed.) ASIACRYPT 2000. LNCS, vol. 1976, pp. 489–502. Springer, Heidelberg (2000). https://doi.org/10.1007/3-540-44448-3_38
2. Brier, E., Clavier, C., Olivier, F.: Correlation power analysis with a leakage model. In: Joye, M., Quisquater, J.-J. (eds.) CHES 2004. LNCS, vol. 3156, pp. 16–29. Springer, Heidelberg (2004). https://doi.org/10.1007/978-3-540-28632-5_2
3. Liu, H., Qian, G., Tsunoo, Y., Goto, S.: The switching glitch power leakage model. J. Softw. **6**(9), 1787–1794 (2011). https://doi.org/10.4304/jsw.6.9.1787-1794
4. Kocher, P., Jaffe, J., Jun, B.: Differential power analysis. In: Wiener, M. (ed.) CRYPTO 1999. LNCS, vol. 1666, pp. 388–397. Springer, Heidelberg (1999). https://doi.org/10.1007/3-540-48405-1_25
5. Zhang, L., Vega, L., Taylor, M.B.: Power Side Channels in Security ICs: Hardware Countermeasures. CoRR abs/1605.00681 (2016). http://arxiv.org/abs/1605.00681

6. Northeastern University: Northeastern University TeSCASE dataset (2022). https://chest.coe.neu.edu/
7. Pundir, N., Park, J., Farahmandi, F., Tehranipoor, M.: Power side-channel leakage assessment framework at register-transfer level. IEEE Trans. Very Large Scale Integr. (VLSI) Syst. **30**(9) (2022). https://doi.org/10.1109/TVLSI.2022.3175067
8. Sadhukhan, R., Mathew, P., Roy, D.B., Mukhopadhyay, D.: Count your toggles: a new leakage model for pre-silicon power analysis of crypto designs. J. Electron. Test. **35**(5), 605–619 (2019). https://doi.org/10.1007/S10836-019-05826-8
9. Standaert, F.-X., Malkin, T.G., Yung, M.: A unified framework for the analysis of side-channel key recovery attacks. In: Joux, A. (ed.) EUROCRYPT 2009. LNCS, vol. 5479, pp. 443–461. Springer, Heidelberg (2009). https://doi.org/10.1007/978-3-642-01001-9_26
10. Mangard, S., Oswald, E., Popp, T.: Power Analysis Attacks - Revealing the Secrets of Smart Cards. Springer (2007)
11. Chari, S., Rao, J.R., Rohatgi, P.: Template attacks. In: Kaliski, B.S., Koç, K., Paar, C. (eds.) CHES 2002. LNCS, vol. 2523, pp. 13–28. Springer, Heidelberg (2003). https://doi.org/10.1007/3-540-36400-5_3
12. Hajra, S., Mukhopadhyay, D.: Multivariate leakage model for improving non-profiling DPA on noisy power traces. In: Lin, D., Xu, S., Yung, M. (eds.) Inscrypt 2013. LNCS, vol. 8567, pp. 325–342. Springer, Cham (2014). https://doi.org/10.1007/978-3-319-12087-4_21
13. Tiran, S., Ordas, S., Teglia, Y., Agoyan, M., Maurine, P.: A frequency leakage model for SCA. In: Koushanfar, F., Hsiao, M., Potkonjak, M. (eds.) 2014 IEEE International Symposium on Hardware-Oriented Security and Trust (HOST). IEEE (2014). https://doi.org/10.1109/HST.2014.6855577

Designs

Bivariate Proximity Test-Based Asynchronous Verifiable Secret Sharing

Daniel Augot[1,2], Olivier Blazy[1,2], Hugo Delavenne[1,2], and Lola-Baie Mallordy[1,2(✉)]

[1] LIX, École Polytechnique, Institut Polytechnique de Paris, Palaiseau, France
lola-baie.mallordy@inria.fr
[2] Inria, Le Chesnay-Rocquencourt, France

Abstract. We present an Asynchronous Verifiable Secret Sharing (AVSS) protocol leveraging Interactive Oracle Proofs of Proximity (IOPPs). By integrating an IOPP to the product of Reed-Solomon codes *i.e.,* to bivariate polynomials, we achieve strong agreement properties while maintaining efficiency: our scheme achieves a total communication complexity of $O(n^2)$ for the dealer and $O(n \log^2(n))$ per party, and a computational complexity of only $O(n \log(n))$ per party. It provides *optimal resilience* i.e., is secure against up to $t < n/3$ corrupted parties. Furthermore, our construction is resistant against post-quantum adversaries, as its security relies solely on the security of the underlying hash functions.

Keywords: Hash-based · Verifiable Secret Sharing · Asynchronous · Coding Theory · Multivariate IOPP · Polynomial Commitment Scheme

1 Introduction

1.1 Secret Sharing

Secret sharing is a fundamental cryptographic primitive that enables a dealer to distribute shares of a secret among a set of participants in such a way that only authorized subsets can reconstruct it, while unauthorized subsets gain no information from their shares. Introduced by Shamir and Blakley in 1979 [Sha79, Bla79], secret sharing schemes have become a cornerstone of secure multiparty computation (MPC), threshold cryptography, and distributed trust protocols.

However, classical secret sharing assumes an honest dealer who correctly distributes the shares. In real-world applications, this assumption is often unrealistic. An adversarial dealer might distribute incorrect or inconsistent shares, leading to undetectable failures in later reconstruction. This limitation motivated the introduction of Verifiable Secret Sharing (VSS) by Chor et al. in 1985 [CGMA85], which enhances secret sharing with a verification mechanism that ensures participants can detect and reject invalid shares before the reconstruction phase.

VSS is particularly crucial in adversarial settings, such as Byzantine fault-tolerant systems, secure distributed key generation, and blockchain protocols.

A. Nitaj et al. (Eds.): AFRICACRYPT 2025, LNCS 15651, pp. 319–342, 2026.
https://doi.org/10.1007/978-3-031-97260-7_15

A robust VSS scheme must satisfy two key properties: correctness, ensuring that honest participants can reconstruct the original secret, and verifiability, guaranteeing that any misbehavior by the dealer or dishonest participants can be detected and mitigated. Achieving these guarantees without hindering efficiency, especially in the presence of a computationally unbounded adversary, remains an active area of research.

It is also imperative to address the emerging challenges posed by advancements in quantum computing. Quantum computers have the potential to break many of the cryptographic schemes currently in use, rendering classical VSS protocols vulnerable. In response to this threat, research has been directed towards developing VSS schemes based on quantum-resistant assumptions. This has been via post-quantum hypotheses like isogeny-based cryptography [EB22], hybrid assumptions based on both discrete logarithm and lattice assumptions like [GHL22]; or purely-based on symmetric key cryptography as in [CCG24]. In this paper, we rather explore solutions which only rely on lightweight primitives such as hash functions.

Asynchronous Verifiable Secret Sharing (AVSS) [BCG93] extends traditional VSS to make it more suitable for the real-world setting where communication is asynchronous, meaning there is not a global clock or guaranteed message delivery within a fixed time. This model is particularly relevant in distributed systems such as blockchain networks, secure multiparty computation (MPC), and Byzantine fault-tolerant consensus protocols, where network delays and adversarial interference can disrupt protocol execution. An AVSS protocol must guarantee the additional properties that all honest parties obtain their shares even if they do not receive the message from the dealer in time, and that they are able to know when all honest parties have obtained their shares and are ready for a successful secret reconstruction.

Some AVSS protocols rely on polynomial commitment schemes to ensure that honest participants can verify their share consistency and correctly reconstruct the secret. In the sharing phase, the dealer commits to the polynomial that it will use in the sharing, using univariate [AVZ21] or bivariate [BDK13] polynomial commitment schemes. The parties can then assert whether their share is a correct evaluation of the committed polynomial. In this paper, we prove these kinds of statements by using *Proofs of Proximity* to a code.

1.2   Interactive Oracle Proof of Proximity

An *Interactive Oracle Proof of Proximity* (IOPP) [BCS16] is a protocol between a Prover and a Verifier in which the Prover aims to convince the Verifier that a given word $f \in \mathbb{F}^n$ is δ-close to a given code $C \subseteq \mathbb{F}^n$.

The Prover is given the word f as input while the Verifier is only given oracle access to f. That is, the Verifier can query any coordinate of f without having to read it entirely. During the protocol, the Prover can provide access to new oracles to the Verifier. Several complexity measures are considered for IOPPs:

– the computational complexity of the Prover,

- the computational complexity of the Verifier,
- the round complexity (the number of rounds of interaction),
- the query complexity (the number of queries done by the Verifier), and
- the proof length (the sum of the length of the oracles).

An IOPP must satisfy two properties.

- *Completeness*: there exists an honest Prover such that if $f \in C$ then the Verifier accepts with probability 1,
- *Soundness*: for any Prover, if the distance between f and C is large enough, the Verifier accepts with probability bounded by a soundness parameter,

where the probabilities are taken over the Verifier's internal randomness.

We require the protocols to be public-coin in order to apply the Fiat-Shamir heuristic to turn them into non-interactive proofs [FS87, BCS16]. The oracles are implemented as Merkle trees. The Prover provides an oracle by sending the root of a Merkle tree to the Verifier. When the Verifier queries to open a coordinate, the Prover only has to open the corresponding branch of the Merkle tree.

We use in particular the Fast Reed-Solomon IOPP (FRI) [BBHR18] that tests proximity to Reed-Solomon codes, and its bivariate equivalent [ABN23], that tests proximity to tensor products of Reed-Solomon codes.

1.3 Contributions

We leverage existing IOPP protocols to obtain a new efficient IOPP-based AVSS scheme. Let n be the total number of parties $P_1, \ldots, P_n$, and t be the maximum number of corrupted parties. Our protocol is secure when $n \geq 3t + 1$, which is the optimal resilience for asynchronous schemes.

Following the standard bivariate AVSS construction, our dealer commits to a (t, t)-degree polynomial $\varphi(X, Y)$ such that $\varphi(0, 0) = s$ the secret to be shared. It computes a bivariate IOPP [ABN23] on $\varphi(X, Y)$ and proves that its degree in both variables is not greater than t. Since this proximity proof is not zero-knowledge, the dealer samples another masking polynomial r of degree at most t in both variables, and proves the statement on a random linear combination $\psi := \varphi + \alpha r$, where α is derived with a hash function from both φ and r. The rest of the dealer operations are reduced to several univariate Merkle trees computations: its overall complexity comes from the evaluation of the bivariate polynomial ψ in n^2 points, which is in $O(n^2 \log(n))$, assuming the underlying field is FFT-friendly.

Each party P_i's share is a partial evaluation $\varphi(X, i)$ in one variable, which is verified with Merkle tree openings. This makes our protocol very efficient on each party P_i's side, since a Merkle tree opening has logarithmic complexity. In the reconstruction phase, each party computes a proof of univariate polynomial evaluation on its share using the dealer's polynomial commitment, and sends it to the other parties. We reduce this proof to a univariate IOPP [BGKS20], which has a quasi linear complexity for the prover.

Using these techniques, our IOPP-based AVSS scheme enjoys the following properties:

- **Efficiency:** our AVSS scheme has a state of the art dealer computational complexity of $O(n^2 \log(n))$, the same as Bingo [AJM+23] and FRISS [ZLG+24], and a better computational complexity per party of only $O(n \log(n))$. The only other scheme [YLF+21] with such a complexity on a party's side relies on the q-SDH assumption, which is not post-quantum.
- **Strong Agreement:** We use a bivariate IOPP to ensure that, if the reconstruction phase succeeds, all of the honest parties reconstruct the same secret $\varphi(0,0)$ where φ is a polynomial of degree at most t in both variables, without an honest dealer assumption. This is a stronger property than the agreement property that is proven in recent similar FRI-based AVSS protocols [ZLG+24].
- **Lightweight:** We only use *lightweight* cryptographic primitives such as hash functions, which makes our protocol resistant against quantum adversaries. We prove our security in the *Random Oracle Model* (ROM). Additionally, we obtain better computational complexity than those requiring *e.g.* exponentiations or pairings.

1.4   Related Work

Asynchronous VSS schemes allow parties to both recover their share even if they do not receive the message from the dealer in time, and know when all honest parties obtain their shares and are ready for reconstruction. A common approach in asynchronous secret sharing is to send to each P_i shares of every P_j's share, and let them redistribute each shares of share to the corresponding party P_j. This way, a party does not only depend on the dealer to receive its share, but needs only $t + 1$ messages out of the n participants.

The eAVSS scheme [BDK13] was the first one with $O(n^2)$ global communication complexity, using Pedersen bivariate polynomial commitments which would not be secure against quantum adversaries. Their dealer complexity is in $O(n^3)$. More recent works also rely on Pedersen commitments [DXT+23, LLS+24]. The former [DXT+23] uses only univariate polynomials, but their dealer needs to stay online until the sharing phase is over. The work of [AVZ21] also uses only univariate polynomials, but this yields a dealer complexity of $O(n^3)$.

The hbACSS scheme [YLF+21] uses a *encrypt-then-disperse* strategy to obtain quasi linear communication complexity on the parties side. However, as Bingo [AJM+23], they rely on pairings which does not provide security against a quantum adversary. The works of [SS24, CLL+24] also use this approach, relying only on *lightweight* cryptography, however their communication complexity in the worst case is in $O(n^3)$. The recent work of [CP23] also yields a communication complexity of $O(n^3)$, and provides information-theoretic security.

Most recently, FRISS [ZLG+24] also relies on code-based polynomial commitments. Their work has the same dealer complexity as ours, but they have a computational complexity of $O(n \log^2(n))$ per party, while we obtain a lower one. Unlike our present contribution, they do not prove the *Commitment* property introduced in [PCR09] *i.e.,* that if the reconstruction phase succeeds, all honest parties reconstruct the same secret. The work of [BCI+23] on IOPP for Reed-Solomon codes also proposed an application to verifiable secret sharing. However, they do not work in the asynchronous setting: they do not achieve the property that if an honest user completes the sharing phase, then all honest users will achieve the sharing phase.

Other asynchronous schemes also were designed in the particular setting of proactive secret sharing [GDKK22,LRU22]. We summarize these comparisons in Table 1.

Table 1. A comparison of the computation (for the dealer and each party) complexities, communication overhead and security assumptions of existing AVSS protocol, for a number of n parties. In our protocol, the dealer has a total communication complexity of $O(n^2)$ while each party only has one of $O(n \log^2(n))$.

	Dealer	Party	Comm.	Assumption
eAVSS [BDK13]	$O(n^3)$	$O(n)$	$O(n^2)$	q-SDH
hbACSS [YLF+21]	$O(n^2)$	$O(n \log(n))$	$O(n^2 \log(n))$	q-SDH
HAVEN-1 [AVZ21]	$O(n^3)$	$O(n)$	$O(n^2)$	q-SDH
Bingo [AJM+23]	$O(n^2 \log(n))$	$O(n^2)$	$O(n^2)$	q-SDH
HAVEN-2 [AVZ21]	$O(n^3)$	$O(n^2)$	$O(n^2 \log(n))$	DLog
FRISS [ZLG+24]	$O(n^2 \log(n))$	$O(n \log^2(n))$	$O(n^2 \log(n))$	ROM
Our Protocol	$O(n^2 \log(n))$	$O(n \log(n))$	$O(n^2)$	ROM

2   Preliminaries

2.1   Polynomial Commitment Schemes

A Merkle tree is a vector commitment scheme with linear prover time and logarithmic verifier time. In this paper, we use it to commit evaluations of polynomials p in one or two variables, at n points for $n > \deg(p)$ for univariate polynomials, or n^2 points for bivariate polynomials of p is of degree less than n in both variables.

Definition 1 (Merkle Tree [Mer87]). *It consists of three different algorithms:*

- MT.Commit$\big((p(x))_{x \in \mathcal{I}}\big) \rightarrow c$: *outputs the Merkle root for the vector of evaluations* $(p(x))_{x \in \mathcal{I}}$, *assuming that* $|\mathcal{I}| > \deg(p)$.
- MT.Open$(y, x, c) \rightarrow \pi$: *outputs the path* π *to the value* $y = p(x)$ *for the Merkle root* c.
- MT.Verif$(c, y, x, \pi) \rightarrow b \in \{0, 1\}$: *Checks whether the path to the Merkle root* c *is correct for the value* $y = p(x)$.

If one wants to produce evaluation proofs $p(x) = y$ at any point $x \in \mathbb{F}$, they must use polynomial commitment schemes.

Definition 2 (Polynomial Commitment [KZG10]). *A polynomial commitment scheme consists of the three following algorithms:*

- PC.Commit(p) → c: *outputs a commitment c to the polynomial p.*
- PC.Open(y, x, p, c) → π: *outputs a proof π that y is a correct evaluation of p at x.*
- PC.Verif(c, y, x, π) → $b \in \{0, 1\}$: *Checks whether the proof π is correct for the value y at x for commitment c.*

In our work, we use polynomial commitment schemes whose commit algorithm is a Merkle tree commitment, and then use it to produce more complex proofs.

2.2 Asynchronous Verifiable Secret Sharing

We denote by $[n]$ the set $\{1, \ldots, n\}$.

A (t, n)-AVSS scheme consists of two different phases, the sharing phase and the reconstruction phase. In the first phase, the dealer executes the algorithm Deal to distribute shares of a secret s to all n parties P_i for all $i \in [n]$. Then, the parties P_i communicate with each other to obtain their share s_i, and complete the GetShare algorithm. In the reconstruction phase, the honest parties can execute Recover to reconstruct the secret s provided that they know at least $t + 1$ valid shares. The parties are connected by an asynchronous channel providing authenticity and privacy. We furthermore assume the dealer can broadcast messages to all parties by reliable broadcast.

We denote by Hon the set of honest parties, and by Corr the set of corrupted parties. We denote by $\mathbb{F}_{\leq t}[X, Y]$ the set of polynomials of degree at most t in both X and Y.

Definition 3 (Asynchronous Verifiable Secret Sharing [BCG93]). *Assume that no adversary can corrupt more than t parties, and let $n > 3t$. A (t, n)-Asynchronous Verifiable Secret Sharing must verify the following properties:*

- Correctness: *If the dealer is honest, the reconstructed value is equal to the dealer's secret s.*
- Liveness: *If the dealer is honest, all the honest parties complete the GetShare algorithm.*
- Agreement: *If some $P_i \in$ Hon completes the GetShare algorithm, then all $P_j \in$ Hon will eventually complete the GetShare algorithm. Then if all $P_j \in$ Hon subsequently start the Recover protocol, they will all complete the Recover protocol.*
- Strong Agreement (Commitment in [PCR09]): *If the honest parties achieve the reconstruction phase, then they all reconstruct the same $\varphi(0, 0)$ with $\varphi \in \mathbb{F}_{\leq t}[X, Y]$.*

– Secrecy: *If the dealer is honest, any PPT adversary $\mathcal{A}$ cannot distinguish between the sharing of two messages.*

With the strong agreement property, we are ensured that there are only two scenarios possible: either none of the honest parties complete the sharing phase, or all the honest parties complete the sharing phase, and they all reconstruct the same $\varphi(0,0)$ with $\varphi \in \mathbb{F}_{\leq t}[X, Y]$.

2.3 IOPP-Based Low-Degree Commitment

We denote by Δ the relative Hamming distance.

Definition 4 (Relative Hamming distance). *For $u, v \in \mathbb{F}^n$, denote $\Delta(u, v) := \frac{1}{n}|\{i \in [n] \mid u_i \neq v_i\}|$ the relative Hamming distance between u and v. If $V \subseteq \mathbb{F}^n$, denote $\Delta(u, V) := \min_{v \in V}(\Delta(u, v))$.*

We fix n distinct values $x_1, ..., x_n \in \mathbb{F}$. For $k < n \in \mathbb{N}$, denote by $\mathsf{RS}[n, k]$ the Reed-Solomon code $\{(f(x_1), ..., f(x_n)) \mid f \in \mathbb{F}_{<k}[X]\}$, and denote by $\mathsf{RS}^2[n, k]$ the product $\mathsf{RS}[n, k] \otimes \mathsf{RS}[n, k]$.

Throughout the paper, whenever a word f is at unique decoding distance from a Reed-Solomon code (resp. product of Reed-Solomon codes), we denote by $\overset{\smallsmile}{f}$ the closest codeword. Recall that for the Reed-Solomon code $\mathsf{RS}[n, t+1]$, the unique decoding radius is $\frac{n-t-1}{2n}$, and for product of Reed-Solomon codes $\mathsf{RS}^2[n, t+1]$, the unique decoding radius is $\frac{(n-t)^2-1}{2n^2}$.

When $f = (f(x_i))_{i \in [n]}$ is a one-dimensional evaluation, we denote $\widehat{f}(X)$ the lowest degree polynomial such that $\widehat{f}(x_i) = f(x_i)$ for all $i \in [n]$. When $f = (f(x_i, x_j))_{i,j \in [n]}$ is a two-dimensional evaluation and $\Delta(f, \mathsf{RS}^2[n, t+1])$ is smaller than the unique decoding radius, we denote $\widehat{\overset{\smallsmile}{f}}(X, Y) \in \mathbb{F}_{\leq t}[X, Y]$ the polynomial such that $\widehat{\overset{\smallsmile}{f}}(x_i, x_j) = \overset{\smallsmile}{f}(x_i, x_j)$ for $i, j \in [n]$.

Fix $\delta_{\mathsf{Corr}} := \frac{(n-t)^2-1}{4n^2}$, $\delta_{\mathsf{BiFRI}} := \frac{(n-t)^2-1}{6n^2}$ and $\delta_{\mathsf{PC}} := \frac{n-t-1}{2n}$ the distance thresholds that we use throughout the paper.

3 Proximity Tests

3.1 Proximity Test to a Linear Combination

Since the FRI protocol, that we use for our proximity tests, leaks values of the word tested, we have to hide the values φ by adding another random polynomial r. In order for the proximity test on the combination ψ of φ and r to $\mathsf{RS}^2[n, t+1]$ to also prove proximity of φ and r to $\mathsf{RS}^2[n, t+1]$, we also require that this combination is a random linear combination $\psi := \varphi + \alpha r$, where α is given by the random oracle. As we show in Proposition 14, this masking technique does not leak any information on φ. The property that the proximity of

ψ also proves the proximity of φ and r with high probability on α is obtained by the correlated agreement from [BKS18], stated here in Lemma 1. Note that contrary to more regular uses of IOPP, we are here interested to prove proximity below the unique decoding radius and hence the soundness is lower than for instance [BKS18, Theorem 9].

Lemma 1 (Correlated agreement for linear codes [BKS18, Lemma 8]). *Let $C \subseteq \mathbb{F}^N$ be a linear code. Let $\delta < \frac{\Delta(C)}{2}$ and η such that $\delta - \eta < \frac{\Delta(C)}{3}$. Let $u_1, u_2 \in \mathbb{F}^N$. If $\underset{\alpha \in \mathbb{F}}{\mathbb{P}}(\Delta(u_1 + \alpha u_2, C) < \delta - \eta) > \frac{1}{\eta|\mathbb{F}|}$ then $\Delta(u_1, C) \leq \delta$ and $\Delta(u_2, C) \leq \delta$.*

Since $\delta_{\mathsf{BiFRI}} < \frac{(n-t)^2 - 1}{3n^2}$ we can apply Lemma 1, with $C := \mathsf{RS}^2[n, t+1]$, to obtain Corollary 1.

Corollary 1 (Correlated agreement for product of Reed-Solomon codes). *Let $\varphi, r : [n] \times [n] \to \mathbb{F}$. If*

$$\underset{\alpha \in \mathbb{F}}{\mathbb{P}}\left(\Delta(\varphi + \alpha r, \mathsf{RS}^2[n, t+1]) < \delta_{\mathsf{BiFRI}}\right) > \frac{1}{(\delta_{\mathsf{Corr}} - \delta_{\mathsf{BiFRI}})|\mathbb{F}|} = \frac{12n^2}{(n-t)^2|\mathbb{F}|} \quad (1)$$

then

$$\begin{cases} \Delta(\varphi, \mathsf{RS}^2[n, t+1]) \leq \delta_{\mathsf{Corr}} \\ \Delta(r, \mathsf{RS}^2[n, t+1]) \leq \delta_{\mathsf{Corr}}. \end{cases}$$

3.2   Bivariate Proximity Testing to Product of Reed-Solomon Codes

We define the function ProximityProof that takes as argument a bivariate polynomial $\psi \in \mathbb{F}[X_1, X_2]$ and an integer t, and that outputs a SNARK proof π. This SNARK proof is obtained by applying the transformation to non-interactive random-oracle proof from [BCS16, Section 6] to the Interactive Oracle Proof defined in Definition 5.

Definition 5 (Bivariate IOPP).
  Prover input: $\psi \in \mathbb{F}^{n \times n}$, $t \in \mathbb{N}$
  Verifier input: *oracle access to* $\psi \in \mathbb{F}^{n \times n}$, $t \in \mathbb{N}$
  Claim: $\Delta(\psi, \mathsf{RS}^2[n, t+1]) < \delta_{\mathsf{BiFRI}}$

 - *Prover and Verifier perform a bivariate FRI protocol defined in [ABN23, Section 7.3] to prove δ_{BiFRI}-proximity of ψ to $\mathsf{RS}^2[n, t+1]$.*

The protocol defined in Definition 5 has perfect completeness: if $\psi \in \mathsf{RS}^2[n, t+1]$ then the Verifier accepts with probability 1.

Proposition 1 (Bivariate FRI soundness [ABN23, Theorem 2]). *Let δ_{BiFRI} be defined as in Corollary 1. In the protocol defined in Definition 5, for* *any $0 < \eta < \delta_{\mathsf{BiFRI}}$, if $\Delta(\psi, \mathsf{RS}^2[n, t+1]) \geq \delta_{\mathsf{BiFRI}}$, with $\mu_{\mathsf{BiFRI}} \in \mathbb{N}$ a complexity parameter, the verifier accepts with probability at most*

$$\varepsilon_{\mathsf{BiFRI}} := \frac{4 \log n}{\eta^2 |\mathbb{F}|} + (1 - \delta_{\mathsf{BiFRI}} + 2\eta \log n)^{\mu_{\mathsf{BiFRI}}},$$

where the probability is taken over its internal randomness.

Our AVSS protocol also requires that the δ_{BiFRI}-proximity of ψ proves the δ_{Corr}-proximity of r to $\mathsf{RS}^2[n, t+1]$. We state that soundness in Proposition 2.

Proposition 2 (Correlated agreement and bivariate FRI soundness).
Let $\varphi, r \in \mathbb{F}^{n \times n}$. Let $\alpha \in \mathbb{F}$ be given by a random oracle. Let $\psi := \varphi + \alpha r$. The probability that the Verifier accepts the proof defined in Definition 5 while

$$\Delta(\varphi, \mathsf{RS}^2[n, t+1]) > \delta_{\mathsf{Corr}} \tag{2}$$

is at most

$$\varepsilon_{\mathsf{Corr}} := \varepsilon_{\mathsf{BiFRI}} + \frac{12n^2}{(n-t)^2 |\mathbb{F}|}, \tag{3}$$

where the probability is taken over the Verifier's internal randomness and the random oracle for α.

Proof. Let A denote the event "the Verifier accepts the proof" and B the event "$\Delta(\psi, \mathsf{RS}^2[n, t+1]) < \delta_{\mathsf{BiFRI}}$". Then by the law of total probability,

$$\mathbb{P}(A) \leq \mathbb{P}(B) + \mathbb{P}(A \mid \overline{B}). \tag{4}$$

Since we assume Eq. (2), by contrapositive of Corollary 1, we have that $\mathbb{P}(B) \leq \frac{12n^2}{(n-t)^2 |\mathbb{F}|}$. By Proposition 1, we have that $\mathbb{P}(A \mid \overline{B}) \leq \varepsilon_{\mathsf{BiFRI}}$. Combining these in Eq. (4) gives Eq. (3). □

Theorem 1 (Bivariate FRI complexity [ABN23, Theorem 2]). *The protocol defined in Definition 5, with the complexity parameter μ_{BiFRI} from Proposition 1, has the following complexity:*

- *Prover complexity: $< 8n^2$*
- *Verifier complexity: $< 24\mu_{\mathsf{BiFRI}} \log n$*
- *Round complexity: $< \log n$*
- *Query complexity: $< 4\mu_{\mathsf{BiFRI}} \log n + 1$*
- *Proof length: $< n^2/3$*

Using [BCS16, Theorem 7.1], we can compute the length of the proof π obtained after transforming this IOPP into a non-interactive proof of proximity.

Proposition 3 (Length of the proof of proximity). *The non-interactive proof π obtained from the IOPP defined in Definition 5 has length*

$$O(\mu_{\mathsf{BiFRI}} \log^2 n).$$

3.3   Evaluation IOP

We define the functions PC.Open and PC.Verif from Definition 2 as a SNARK proof and the verification of that SNARK proof. The function PC.Open takes as argument a vector $f \in \mathbb{F}^n$, the root of a Merkle tree of the values $(f(x_i))_{i \in [n]}$ and a value $y \in \mathbb{F}$, and outputs a SNARK proof π. PC.Open is obtained by applying the transformation to a non-interactive random-oracle proof [BCS16, Section 6] on the Interactive Oracle Proof defined in Definition 6. The function PC.Verif takes as argument the root of a Merkle tree of values $(f(x_i))_{i \in [n]}$, a SNARK proof π and a value $y \in \mathbb{F}$. PC.Verif is obtained by running the non-interactive verifier of the IOP defined in Definition 6.

In order to prove that $f(0) = y$, we prove instead that $f(X) - y$ can be divided by X as a polynomial, since $f(0) = y$ if, and only if, there exists $g \in \mathbb{F}_{\leq \deg f - 1}[X]$ such that $f(X) - y = Xg(X)$.

Proposition 4 (Reduction to proximity testing). *Let $\delta_{PC} \leq \frac{n-t-1}{2n}$. Let $(f(x_i))_{i \in [n]} \in \mathbb{F}^n$ and $(g(x_i))_{i \in [n]} \in \mathbb{F}^n$. Let $y \in \mathbb{F}$. Assume that*

$$\Delta(f, \mathsf{RS}[n, t+1]) < \delta_{PC} \tag{5}$$

$$\Delta(g, \mathsf{RS}[n, t]) < \delta_{PC} \tag{6}$$

$$\mathop{\mathbb{P}}_{i \in [n]} (f(x_i) - y = x_i g(x_i)) > \frac{t}{n} + 2\delta_{PC}. \tag{7}$$

Then

$$\widehat{\ddot{f}}(X) - y = X\widehat{\ddot{g}}(X). \tag{8}$$

Proof. The proof is done by contrapositive, by assuming Eqs. (5) and (6) and that

$$\widehat{\ddot{f}}(X) - y \neq X\widehat{\ddot{g}}(X) \tag{9}$$

There exists $D_0, D_1 \subseteq [n]$ such that $|D_i| > (1 - \delta_{PC})n$ for $i = 0, 1$, and $(\ddot{f}(x_j))_{j \in D_0} = (f(x_j))_{j \in D_0}$ and $(\ddot{g}(x_j))_{j \in D_1} = (g(x_j))_{j \in D_1}$. Let $D := D_0 \cap D_1$. Then $|D| > (1 - 2\delta_{PC})n$. Note that

$$\mathop{\mathbb{P}}_{j \in [n]} (f(x_j) - y = x_j g(x_j)) \leq \mathop{\mathbb{P}}_{j \in [n]} (f(x_j) - y = x_j g(x_j) \text{ and } j \in D) + \mathop{\mathbb{P}}_{j \in [n]} (j \notin D). \tag{10}$$

By Eq. (9) and by the Schwartz-Zippel lemma [Sch80] we have

$$\mathop{\mathbb{P}}_{j \in [n]} (f(x_j) - y = x_j g(x_j) \text{ and } j \in D) = \mathop{\mathbb{P}}_{j \in [n]} \left(\ddot{f}(x_j) - y = x_j \ddot{g}(x_j) \text{ and } j \in D \right)$$

$$\leq \mathop{\mathbb{P}}_{j \in [n]} \left(\ddot{f}(x_j) - y = x_j \ddot{g}(x_j) \right)$$

$$\leq \frac{t}{n}. \tag{11}$$

Furthermore, since $|D| > (1 - 2\delta_{PC})n$, we have $\mathbb{P}(j \notin D) < 2\delta_{PC}$. Thus, by Eqs. (10) and (11),

$$\underset{j \in [n]}{\mathbb{P}} \left(\widehat{f}(X) - y = X\widehat{g}(X) \right) \le \frac{t}{n} + 2\delta_{PC},$$

which concludes the proof. $\qquad\qquad\qquad\qquad\qquad\qquad\qquad\qquad\qquad\qquad\square$

We now define the IOP that proves this statement.

Definition 6 (Proof of evaluation IOP).
    Prover input: $f \in \mathbb{F}^n$, $t \in \mathbb{N}$, $y \in \mathbb{F}$
    Verifier input: *oracle access to* $f \in \mathbb{F}^n$, $t \in \mathbb{N}$, $y \in \mathbb{F}$

    Claim: $\Delta(f, \mathsf{RS}[n, t+1]) \le \delta_{PC}$ *and* $\widehat{f}(0) = y$

- *Prover provides an oracle access to* $(g(x_i))_{i \in [n]}$ *to Verifier*
- *Prover and Verifier perform a FRI protocol on* $(f(x_i))_{i \in [n]}$ *to prove* δ_{PC}-*proximity to* $\mathsf{RS}[n, t+1]$.
- *Prover and Verifier perform a FRI protocol on* $(g(x_i))_{i \in [n]}$ *to prove* δ_{PC}-*proximity to* $\mathsf{RS}[n, t]$.
- *Verifier chooses* ℓ *random values* $i_1, ..., i_\ell \overset{\$}{\leftarrow} [n]$, *and for* $j = 1, ..., \ell$, *Verifier queries* $f(x_{i_j})$ *and* $g(x_{i_j})$, *and checks that* $f(x_{i_j}) - y = x_{i_j} g(x_{i_j})$.

In Proposition 5, we state the completeness of the protocol defined in Definition 6 in the case where $f \in \mathsf{RS}[n, t+1]$.

Proposition 5 (Proof of evaluation completeness). *If the claim of Definition 6 holds, then there exists a prover that makes the Verifier accept with probability 1.*

Proof. Since $\deg \widehat{f} < t + 1$ and $\widehat{f}(0) = y$, there exists a polynomial $\widehat{g}$ of degree $\deg \widehat{f} - 1 < t$ such that $\widehat{f}(X) - y = X\widehat{g}(X)$. Hence the FRI protocol on $(\widehat{g}(x_i))_{i \in [n]}$ to $\mathsf{RS}[n, t]$ reaches perfect completeness, and for any $i \in [n]$, $f(x_i) - y = x_i g(x_i)$. Thus, the protocol has perfect completeness. $\qquad\qquad\qquad\qquad\qquad\qquad\square$

For the soundness, since our AVSS requires the unique decoding bound, we restate the FRI protocol soundness under the unique decoding bound, with $\delta_{PC} := \frac{n-t-1}{3n} < \frac{n-t-1}{2n}$.

Theorem 2 (FRI soundness [BKS18, Lemma 8 and Theorem 16]). *If* $\Delta(f, \mathsf{RS}[n, t+1]) > \delta_{PC}$, *with* μ_{FRI} *a complexity parameter, the verifier accepts with probability at most*

$$\varepsilon_{FRI} := \frac{\log n}{\eta |\mathbb{F}|} + (1 - \delta_{PC} + \eta \log n)^{\mu_{FRI}}.$$

Proposition 6 (Proof of evaluation soundness). *The soundness of the IOP defined in Definition 6 is*

$$\varepsilon_{PC} := \max \left(\left(\frac{t}{n} + 2\delta_{PC} \right)^\ell, \varepsilon_{FRI} \right). \qquad\qquad (12)$$

Proof. Let A denote the event "the Verifier accepts the proof" and B the event "$\Delta(f, \mathsf{RS}[n, t+1]) < \delta_{\mathsf{PC}}$ and $\Delta(g, \mathsf{RS}[n, t]) < \delta_{\mathsf{PC}}$". We have

$$\mathbb{P}(A) \le \max(\mathbb{P}(A \mid B), \mathbb{P}(A \mid \overline{B})). \tag{13}$$

By Theorem 2, we have that

$$\mathbb{P}(A \mid \overline{B}) \le \varepsilon_{\mathsf{FRI}}. \tag{14}$$

If B holds, then since the claim does not hold, we have that $\widehat{f}(X) - y \ne X\widehat{g}(X)$. Therefore, by contrapositive of Proposition 4, since Eqs. (5) and (6) hold but Eq. (8) does not hold, we have that Eq. (7) does not hold. Hence, using the notation of Definition 6, by independence,

$$\mathbb{P}_{i_1,\dots,i_\ell \in [n]} \left(\bigcap_{i=1}^{\ell} f(x_{i_j}) - y = x_{i_j} g(x_{i_j}) \right) = \prod_{i=1}^{\ell} \mathbb{P}_{j_i \in [n]} (f(x_{i_j}) - y = x_{i_j} g(x_{i_j}))$$

$$\le \left(\frac{t}{n} + 2\delta_{\mathsf{PC}} \right)^{\ell}. \tag{15}$$

By combining Eqs. (14) and (15) in Eq. (13), we obtain Eq. (12) as desired. □

As in Proposition 3, we use [BCS16, Theorem 7.1] to compute the length of the proof obtained after transforming this IOPP into a non-interactive random-oracle proof, in Proposition 8.

Proposition 7 (FRI complexity [BBHR18, Theorem 2]). *The protocol defined in Definition 6, with the complexity parameter μ_{FRI} from Theorem 2, has the following complexity:*

- *Prover complexity: $< 6n$*
- *Verifier complexity: $< 21\mu_{\mathsf{FRI}} \log n$*
- *Round complexity: $< \log n$*
- *Query complexity: $< 2\mu_{\mathsf{FRI}} \log n$*
- *Proof length: $< n/3$*

Proposition 8 (Length of the proof of evaluation). *The non-interactive proof obtained from the IOPP defined in Definition 6 has length*

$$O(\mu_{\mathsf{FRI}} \log^2 n + \ell).$$

3.4   Unicity of the Secret

In order to prove that a malicious dealer cannot generate shares that would recover to different secrets, we prove that under the validity of the bivariate proximity proof, any $2t + 1$ honest parties would recover the same secret.

Proposition 9 (Unique recovering). *Suppose that*

$$n = 3t + 1. \tag{16}$$

Let $\varphi \in \mathbb{F}^{n \times n}$. Assume that

$$\Delta(\varphi, \mathsf{RS}^2[n, t+1]) \le \delta_{\mathsf{Corr}}. \tag{17}$$

For any $H \subseteq [n]$ of size $2t + 1$, one can construct in polynomial time from $(\varphi(x_i, x_j))_{(i,j) \in H \times [n]}$ a set $I = \{\ell_1, ..., \ell_{t+1}\} \subseteq H$ of size $t + 1$ such that by denoting for $i, j \in [n]$, $f_i(x_j) := \varphi(x_i, x_j)$, we have

$$\forall i \in I, \Delta((f_i(x_j))_{j \in [n]}, \mathsf{RS}[n, t+1]) \le \frac{t}{n}, \tag{18}$$

and furthermore, with $L_{\ell_1}^I(X), ..., L_{\ell_{t+1}}^I(X)$ the degree t polynomials such that for $i, j \in I$, $L_i(x_j) = 1$ if $i = j$ and 0 otherwise, we have

$$\widehat{\breve{\varphi}}(X, Y) = \sum_{i \in I} L_i(X) \widehat{\breve{f}}_i(Y). \tag{19}$$

Proof. Let $H \subseteq [n]$ of size $2t + 1$. By Eq. (17), there exists $\breve{\varphi} \in \mathsf{RS}^2[n, t+1]$ such that $\Delta\left(\varphi, \breve{\varphi}\right) \le \delta_{\mathsf{Corr}}$. Let

$$R := \left\{ (x_i, x_j) \in H \times [n] \mid \varphi(x_i, x_j) \ne \breve{\varphi}(x_i, x_j) \right\}.$$

Then

$$|R| \le \delta_{\mathsf{Corr}} n^2. \tag{20}$$

For $i \in H$, let $R_i := \{j \in [n] \mid (i, j) \in R\}$, and let $B := \{i \in H \mid |R_i| > t\}$. Then

$$\bigsqcup_{i \in B} (\{i\} \times R_i) \subseteq R,$$

and therefore

$$|R| \ge \sum_{i \in B} |R_i| \ge t|B|. \tag{21}$$

Hence by Eqs. (16), (20) and (21), and since $\delta_{\mathsf{Corr}} \le \frac{1}{9}$,

$$\begin{aligned}
|B| &\le \frac{\delta_{\mathsf{Corr}} n^2}{t} \\
&= \delta_{\mathsf{Corr}} \frac{(3t+1)^2}{t} \\
&= 9\delta_{\mathsf{Corr}}(t + 1/3 + 1/9t) \\
&< t + 1. \tag{22}
\end{aligned}$$

Since $|H| \ge 2t + 1$, by Eq. (22) we have $|H \setminus B| \ge t + 1$.

By applying a decoding algorithm such as Berlekamp-Welch [WB86] to each element of H, it will succeed for $i \in H \setminus B$. Thus one can construct a set $I = \{\ell_1, ..., \ell_{t+1}\} \subseteq H \setminus B$ of size $t+1$. For $i \in I$, since $\Delta(f_i, \mathsf{RS}[n, t+1]) \leq \Delta(f_i, (\overset{\smallsmile}{\varphi}(x_i, x_j))_{j \in [n]})$, we have that f_i is at unique decoding radius from $\mathsf{RS}[n, t+1]$, and thus $\overset{\smallsmile}{f}_i$ is well-defined. Furthermore, we have $\widehat{\overset{\smallsmile}{f}}_i(Y) = \overset{\smallsmile}{\varphi}(x_i, Y)$.

By Eq. (17), $\widehat{\overset{\smallsmile}{\varphi}}(X, Y) \in \mathbb{F}_{\leq t}[X, Y]$ is well-defined. Since $L_{\ell_1}^I(X), ..., L_{\ell_{t+1}}^I(X)$ is a basis of $\mathbb{F}_{\leq t}[X]$, there exists polynomials $\widehat{g}_{\ell_1}(Y), ..., \widehat{g}_{\ell_{t+1}}(Y) \in \mathbb{F}_{\leq t}[Y]$ such that $\widehat{\overset{\smallsmile}{\varphi}}(X, Y) = \sum_{i \in I} L_i^I(X)\widehat{g}_i(Y)$. For $i \in I$, we have $\widehat{g}_i(Y) = \overset{\smallsmile}{\varphi}(x_i, Y) = \widehat{\overset{\smallsmile}{f}}_i(Y)$, and thus $\widehat{\overset{\smallsmile}{\varphi}}(X, Y) = \sum_{i \in I} L_i^I(X)\widehat{f}_i(Y)$, which concludes the proof. □

4   Asynchronous Verifiable Secret Sharing

4.1   Our AVSS Protocol

Let n be the number of parties $\{P_1, ..., P_n\}$ and $t < n$ a given threshold. We assume that $n \geq 3t+1$, which is the optimal threshold for asynchronous schemes. Our construction is similar to eAVSS [BDK13], using code-based polynomial commitments instead of KZG [KZG10].

We detail the dealer algorithm in Fig. 1 and the parties algorithms GetShare in Fig. 2 and Recover in Fig. 3. Let H be a pseudorandom one-way hash function.

Sharing Phase – Dealer's Side. The dealer samples a polynomial $\varphi \in \mathbb{F}_{\leq t}[X, Y]$ such that $\varphi(0, 0) = s$. Since our ProximityProof is not zero-knowledge, the dealer samples another polynomial $r \leftarrow_\$ \mathbb{F}_{\leq t}[X, Y]$ to perform the proof on the random linear relation $\psi = \varphi + \alpha r$ rather than on φ itself. The dealer commits to both $r(x_i, Y)$ and $r(X, x_i)$ for $i \in [n]$, and also to $\varphi(X, Y)$ using Merkle trees. The coefficient α is chosen to be the hash of those trees, to prevent the dealer from manipulating this value. Then, the dealer computes the Merkle trees commitments $c_{\psi(X, x_i)}, c_{\psi(x_i, Y)}$ of each $\psi(X, x_i)$ and $\psi(x_i, Y)$ for $i \in [n]$, and derives the Merkle tree c of ψ from them by using each $c_{\psi(X, x_i)}$ as its subbranches. This is depicted in Fig. 4. The dealer broadcasts the proximity proof and all the commitments, and sends to each party P_i their share $\{a_{i,j} = \varphi(x_i, x_j), b_{i,j} = r(x_i, x_j)\}_{j \in [n]}$.

Sharing Phase – Party's Side. Upon receiving its share, a party P_i will first check its validity by verifying the proximity proof. If the proof is not valid, it will immediately abort the protocol. Otherwise, P_i will compute the Merkle trees of its points $\{b_{i,j} = r(x_i, x_j)\}_{j \in [n]}$ and $\{w_{i,j} = a_{i,j} + \alpha b_{i,j} = \psi(x_i, x_j)\}_{j \in [n]}$. If the roots of the Merkle trees match the values $c_{r(x_i, Y)}$ and $c_{\psi(x_i, Y)}$ published by the dealer, and the commitment c_φ opens with path π_i to the points $\{a_{i,j}\}_{j \in [n]}$, the party P_i is ensured that it received correct shares. In this case, it sets the dealer as honest with $\mathsf{hon}_d \leftarrow 1$, and P_i can relay these shares to the corresponding parties. It sends an Echo message to each P_j containing the points $\{a_{i,j}, b_{i,j}\}$ along with the corresponding paths in the Merkle trees $c_{\psi(x_i, Y)}$ and $c_{r(x_i, Y)}$.

Deal($s \in \mathbb{F}$)

---

1 : $\varphi(X, Y) \leftarrow\!\!\!\!{}^\$ \ \mathbb{F}_{\leq t}[X, Y]$ s.t. $\varphi(0, 0) = s$

2 : $r(X, Y) \leftarrow\!\!\!\!{}^\$ \ \mathbb{F}_{\leq t}[X, Y]$

3 : $\forall i \in [n]$:

4 : $\forall j \in [n]: a_{i,j}, b_{i,j} \leftarrow \varphi(x_i, x_j), r(x_i, x_j)$

5 : $c_{r(X, x_i)} \leftarrow \mathsf{MT.Commit}(\{b_{j,i}\}_{j \in [n]})$

6 : $c_{r(x_i, Y)} \leftarrow \mathsf{MT.Commit}(\{b_{i,j}\}_{j \in [n]})$

7 : $c_{a(x_i, Y)} \leftarrow \mathsf{MT.Commit}(\{a_{i,j}\}_{j \in [n]})$

8 : $c_\varphi \leftarrow \mathsf{MT.Commit}(\{c_{a(x_i, Y)}\}_{i \in [n]})$

9 : $\forall i \in [n]: \pi_i \leftarrow$ Path to $c_{a(x_i, Y)}$ in c_φ

10 : $\alpha \leftarrow H(c_{r(x_1, Y)} || \dots || c_{r(x_n, Y)} || c_\varphi)$

11 : $\psi(X, Y) \leftarrow \varphi(X, Y) + \alpha r(X, Y)$

12 : $\forall i \in [n]$:

13 : $c_{\psi(X, x_i)} \leftarrow \mathsf{MT.Commit}(\psi(X, x_i))$

14 : $c_{\psi(x_i, Y)} \leftarrow \mathsf{MT.Commit}(\psi(x_i, Y))$

15 : $c \leftarrow \mathsf{MT.Commit}(\{c_{\psi(X, x_i)}\}_{i \in [n]})$

16 : $\pi \leftarrow \mathsf{ProximityProof}(\psi, t)$

17 : **Broadcast** $c, \pi, c_\varphi, \{c_{r(X, x_i)}, c_{r(x_i, Y)}, c_{\psi(X, x_i)}, c_{\psi(x_i, Y)}\}_{i \in [n]}$

18 : **Send** $\{a_{i,j}, b_{i,j}\}_{j \in [n]}, \pi_i$ to each P_i

---

Fig. 1. The dealer's algorithm Deal for our (t, n)-AVSS protocol, for a secret s.

Finally, upon receiving an Echo message from another P_j, P_i checks its validity using the received paths $\pi_{j,i}$ and $\pi'_{j,i}$ and the Merkle trees root $c_{r(x_j, Y)}$ and $c_{\psi(x_j, Y)}$ broadcast by the dealer. P_i can send a Ready message under two conditions: either it already received more than $2t$ valid shares and the dealer is honest, or it already received $t + 1$ Ready messages. When P_i has received at least $2t + 1$ Ready and at least $t + 1$ Echo messages, it can obtain its share $(\varphi(X, x_i), r(X, x_i))$ by interpolating the points $\{a_{j,i}\}_j$ and $\{b_{j,i}\}_j$.

Reconstruction Phase. Each P_i sends to each P_j an evaluation at 0 of their share polynomials $\varphi_i(X), r_i(X)$. If the dealer was honest in the sharing phase, P_i sends a Strong label along with a proof of evaluation using the polynomial commitments $c_{r(X, x_i)}$ and $c_{\psi(X, x_i)}$, otherwise it sends a Weak label without any proof. To recover the secret, each party needs either $t+1$ strong shares to interpolate, or fewer strong shares completed with weak shares such that the secret can be recovered using Reed-Solomon decoding algorithms *e.g.*, Berlekamp-Welch [WB86].

Complexity. In Deal, the dealer has to compute n^2 evaluations of the bivariate polynomials $\varphi(X, Y), r(X, Y)$, which as a complexity of $O(n^2 \log(n))$ with the Fast Fourier Transform. Using these evaluations, the dealer can compute the

GetShare for P_i

1:	$\text{hon}_d, V \leftarrow 0, \varnothing$
2:	Upon receiving $c, \pi, c_\varphi, \{c_{r(X, x_i)},$
	$c_{r(x_i, Y)}, c_{\psi(X, x_i)}, c_{\psi(x_i, Y)}\}_{i \in [n]}$
	and $\{a_{i,j}, b_{i,j}\}_{j \in [n]}, \pi_i$:
3:	if $\text{ProximityCheck}(c, t, \pi) = 0$:
4:	**abort**
5:	$\alpha \leftarrow H(c_{r(x_1, Y)} || \ldots || c_{r(x_n, Y)} || c_\varphi)$
6:	$w_{i,j} \leftarrow a_{i,j} + \alpha b_{i,j}$
7:	if $\text{MT.Verif}(c_\varphi, \{a_{i,j}\}_{j \in [n]}, \pi_i)$
	$\wedge \text{MT.Verif}(c_{r(x_i, Y)}, \{b_{i,j}\}_{j \in [n]})$
	$\wedge \text{MT.Verif}(c_{\psi(x_i, Y)}, \{w_{i,j}\}_{j \in [n]})$:
8:	$\text{hon}_d \leftarrow 1$
9:	$\pi_{i,j} \leftarrow \text{Path to } b_{i,j} \text{ in } c_{r(x_i, Y)}$
10:	$\pi'_{i,j} \leftarrow \text{Path to } w_{i,j} \text{ in } c_{\psi(x_i, Y)}$
11:	**Send** $(\text{Echo}, a_{i,j}, b_{i,j}, \pi_{i,j}, \pi'_{i,j})$
	to $P_j, \forall j \neq i$
12:	Upon receiving $(\text{Echo}, a_{j,i}, b_{j,i}, \pi_{j,i},$
	$\pi'_{j,i})$ from P_j for the first time:
13:	$w_{j,i} \leftarrow a_{j,i} + \alpha b_{j,i}$
14:	if $\text{MT.Verif}(c_{\psi(x_j, Y)}, \pi'_{j,i}, w_{j,i})$
	$\wedge \text{MT.Verif}(c_{r(x_j, Y)}, \pi_{j,i}, b_{j,i})$:
15:	$V \leftarrow V \cup \{a_{j,i}, b_{j,i}\}$
16:	if $|V| > 2t \wedge \text{hon}_d = 1$:
17:	**Send** Ready to all P_j
18:	Upon getting $t + 1$ Ready
	$\wedge$ Ready not sent yet:
19:	**Send** Ready to all P_j
20:	Upon getting $2t + 1$ Ready:
21:	Wait until $|V| > t$
22:	Interpolate V to get $(\varphi_i(X), r_i(X))$
23:	**return** $(\varphi_i(X), r_i(X))$

Fig. 2. The GetShare algorithm for our (t, n)-AVSS protocol.

Merkle Trees of $r(X, x_i), r(x_i, Y)$ and $\varphi(X, Y)$ all in $O(n)$. Additionally, deriving the Merkle Tree of $\psi(X, x_i), \psi(x_i, Y)$, and then ψ can also be done in linear time. The proximity proof has complexity $O(n^2)$ (*c.f.* Proposition 1). Hence, the total dealer complexity is in $O(n^2 \log(n))$. As for the communications, the dealer broadcast size is $(4n + 2)|H| + O(\log^2(n))$, with $|H|$ the size of the output of the hash function H. It sends $2n|\mathbb{F}| + \log(n)|H|$ bits to each party, with $|\mathbb{F}|$ the size of an element in $\mathbb{F}$.

In GetShare, each P_i verifies the proximity check, with complexity $\log(n)$. They open the Merkle tree roots $c_{r(x_i, Y)}, c_{\psi(x_i, Y)}$ and c_φ with their shares $\{b_{i,j}\}_{j \in [n]}, \{a_{i,j}\}_{j \in [n]}$ and the path π_i, which takes a linear complexity. They send the Merkle branches $\pi_{i,j}$ and $\pi'_{i,j}$ that they computed during the verifications in $c_{r(x_i, Y)}$ and $c_{\psi(x_i, Y)}$ to each party P_j. The Merkle tree verifications in step @refcheckspslinear2, which are repeated at most $n - 1$ times, have a $O(\log(n))$ complexity. Thus each party's complexity in the dealing phase is bounded by $O(n \log(n))$. As for communications, each party sends a total of $2n|\mathbb{F}| + 2n \log(n)|H|$ bits.

In Recover, each party computes one proof of evaluation for its share, with complexity $O(n \log(n))$. It verifies less than n other party's share, each of which has complexity $O(\log(n))$. Finally from Proposition 3 the proofs of evaluation have a size $O(\log^2(n))$, thus each party sends a total of $O(n \log^2(n))$ bits.

Recover($\text{hon}_d, \varphi_i(X), r_i(X)$) for P_i	
1 : $W, S \leftarrow \varnothing, \varnothing$	11 : Upon receiving $(\text{Strong}, (a_j, b_j), \pi_j, \pi'_j)$
2 : $\alpha \leftarrow H(c_{r(x_1, Y)} \| \dots \| c_{r(x_n, Y)} \| c_\varphi)$	from P_j for the first time :
3 : $\psi_i(X) \leftarrow \varphi_i(X) + \alpha r_i(X)$	12 : $w_j \leftarrow a_j + \alpha b_j$
4 : $a_i, b_i \leftarrow \varphi_i(0), r_i(0)$	13 : if PC.Verif($c_{r(X, x_j)}, \pi_j, b_j$)
5 : $w_i \leftarrow a_i + \alpha b_i$	$\wedge$ PC.Verif($c_{\psi(X, x_j)}, \pi'_j, w_j$) :
6 : if $\text{hon}_d = 1$:	14 : $W \leftarrow W \cup \{a_j\}$
7 : $\pi'_i \leftarrow \text{PC.Open}(\psi_i, c_{\psi(X, x_i)}, w_i)$	15 : $S \leftarrow S \cup \{a_j\}$
8 : $\pi_i \leftarrow \text{PC.Open}(r_i, c_{r(X, x_i)}, b_i)$	16 : Upon receiving $(\text{Weak}, s_j = a_j))$
9 : **Send** $(\text{Strong}, (a_i, b_i), \pi_i, \pi'_i)$	from P_j for the first time :
to each P_j	17 : $W \leftarrow W \cup \{a_j\}$
10 : **else send** (Weak, a_i) to P_j	18 : if $|W| + 2|S| \geq 3t + 1$
for all $j \neq i$	19 : **return** the decoding of $S \cup W$

Fig. 3. The Recover algorithm for our (t, n)-AVSS protocol.

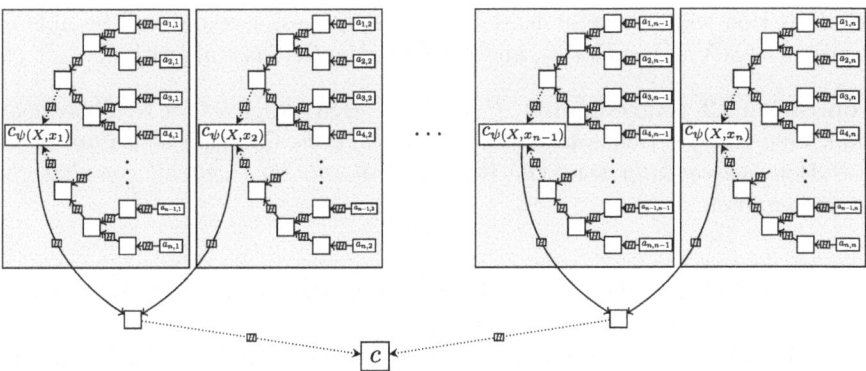

Fig. 4. The Merkle tree of $\psi(X, Y)$ computed by the dealer. The Merkle root c is computed from the n subbranches $c_{\psi(X, x_i)}$ for $i \in [n]$.

4.2   Security Analysis

We prove that our protocol achieves the correctness, liveness, agreement and secrecy properties. We consider the case where $n = 3t + 1$ where t is the maximum number of corrupted parties.

Proposition 10 (Correctness). *If the dealer is honest, the reconstructed value is equal to the dealer's secret s under the assumption that the proof PC.Open is sound.*

Proof. As the dealer is honest, the proximity proof is valid and all the commitments are consistent with the shares $\{a_{i,j} = \varphi(x_i, x_j), b_{i,j} = r(x_i, x_j)\}_{j \in [n]}$. Hence, all the $P_i \in \text{Hon}$ will send $(\text{Echo}, a_{i,j}, b_{i,j}, \pi_{i,j}, \pi'_{i,j})$ to each P_j. As the dealer is honest, each $P_i \in \mathsf{Hon}$ party will receive at least $|\mathsf{Hon}| \geq 2t + 1$ valid shares with proofs consistent with the dealer's commitments, and will send a Ready message. Thus, all $P_i \in \mathsf{Hon}$ are able to compute their share which is $(\varphi_i(X) = \varphi(X, x_i), r_i(X) = r(X, x_i))$.

In the reconstruction phase, the corrupted parties send at most t out of n wrong points for which they cannot forge false evaluation proofs consistent with the dealer's commitments under the soundness assumption of PC.Open. Hence, as the honest parties receive at least $2t + 1$ valid points $\varphi(0, x_i)$, they are able to decode the same secret, which is $\varphi(0, 0)$.   □

Proposition 11 (Liveness). *If the dealer is honest, all the honest parties complete the* GetShare *algorithm.*

Proof. If the dealer is honest, then the proximity proof is valid and the commitments are consistent with the shares $\{a_{i,j}, b_{i,j}\}_{j \in [n]}$. Hence, all the $P_i \in \mathsf{Hon}$ will send $(\mathsf{Echo}, a_{i,j}, b_{i,j})$ to each P_j. Thus, each honest party will receive at least $|\mathsf{Hon}| \geq 2t + 1$ correct shares, and will send a Ready message. Finally, each $P_i \in \mathsf{Hon}$ will receive at least $2t + 1$ Ready messages and will be able to reconstruct $(\varphi(X, x_i), r(X, x_i))$, and complete the GetShare algorithm.   □

Proposition 12 (Agreement). *If some $P_i \in \mathsf{Hon}$ completes the* GetShare *algorithm, then all $P_j \in \mathsf{Hon}$ will eventually complete the* GetShare *algorithm. If all $P_j \in \mathsf{Hon}$ subsequently start the* Recover *protocol, they will all complete the* Recover *protocol.*

Proof. First, assume that $P_i \in \mathsf{Hon}$ completes the GetShare algorithm. This means that P_i received at least $2t + 1$ Ready messages, with at least $t + 1$ of them resulting from honest parties that sent valid $w_{i,j}$. If an honesty party that has not sent Ready receives $t + 1$ Ready messages, it will also send Ready. Thus, every honest party will eventually receive $2t + 1$ Ready messages.

If all $P_j \in \mathsf{Hon}$ send Ready messages by step @refsendspsready2, that means that $t + 1$ Ready messages were sent by corrupted parties, which is impossible since $|\mathsf{Corr}| \leq t$. Hence, at least one honest party sent Ready by step @refsendspsready1, which means that at least $t + 1$ honest parties sent valid Echo messages. Hence, all honest parties will eventually complete GetShare.

Lastly, assume that all $P_j \in \mathsf{Hon}$ start the Recover protocol. As we saw above, at least $t + 1$ honest parties sent valid Echo messages, hence at least $t + 1$ honest parties will send Strong recovery messages. Hence, eventually all honest parties will receive at least $t + 1$ valid Strong messages. Assume that the t other honest parties only send valid Weak messages, each honest party will get

$$|S_{\mathsf{Weak}}| + 2|S_{\mathsf{Strong}}| \geq t + 2(t + 1) = 3t + 1,$$

thus all $P_i \in \mathsf{Hon}$ will be able to recover its secret.   □

Proposition 13 (Strong Agreement). *If the honest parties achieve the reconstruction phase, then they all reconstruct the same $\widehat{\overset{\leftrightarrow}{\varphi}}(0,0)$ with $\overset{\leftrightarrow}{\varphi} \in \mathbb{F}_{\leq t}[X,Y]$ with probability*

$$p_{\mathcal{A}} \leq t\varepsilon_{\mathsf{FRI}} + \varepsilon_{\mathsf{Corr}}$$

for $\varepsilon_{\mathsf{PC}}$ the soundness of PC.Open *and $\varepsilon_{\mathsf{Corr}}$ the soundness of the correlated proximity proof from Proposition 6.*

Proof. Assume that $\mathcal{A}$ breaks the strong agreement property of our scheme, we build a simulator $\mathcal{S}$ against the soundness of the proximity proof. Let $\varepsilon_{\mathsf{PC}}$ be the soundness of the proof PC.Open as defined in Proposition 6.

First, the simulator receives a proximity proof π and commitments from $\mathcal{A}$. Assuming that the proximity proof π is correct, from Proposition 2 we know that φ is also δ_{Corr}-close to $\mathsf{RS}^2[n, t+1]$.

Denote by A the event "some honest parties do not reconstruct $\widehat{\overset{\leftrightarrow}{\varphi}}(0,0)$" and denote by S the event "there exists a malicious party that created a false proof π_i". Then

$$p_{\mathcal{A}} = \mathbb{P}(A) \leq \mathbb{P}(S) + \mathbb{P}(A \mid \overline{S}). \tag{23}$$

We assume now that in the reconstruction phase, $\mathcal{A}$ succeeds and sends corrupted shares such that the recovered secret is $s' \neq \widehat{\overset{\leftrightarrow}{\varphi}}(0,0)$, while no malicious party could create a false proof π_i. Then by taking $H \subseteq [n]$ of size $2t+1$ that contains the corrupted shares and by denoting $\widehat{\varphi}'(X,Y) := \sum_{i \in I} L_i^I(X)\widehat{\overset{\leftrightarrow}{f}}_i(Y)$ the polynomial reconstructed using Proposition 9, we have that $\widehat{\varphi}'(0,0) \neq \overset{\leftrightarrow}{\varphi}(0,0)$ and therefore $\widehat{\varphi}'(X,Y) \neq \widehat{\overset{\leftrightarrow}{\varphi}}(X,Y)$, which contradicts the fact that φ is at unique decoding radius from $\mathsf{RS}^2[n, t+1]$. Therefore Eq. (17) does not hold, the proof of proximity π is false, and hence $\mathcal{A}$ managed to break the soundness of Proposition 2. Thus

$$\mathbb{P}(A \mid \overline{S}) \leq \varepsilon_{\mathsf{Corr}}. \tag{24}$$

By Proposition 6, we have

$$\mathbb{P}(S) \leq t\varepsilon_{\mathsf{FRI}}. \tag{25}$$

Combining Eqs. (24) and (25) in Eq. (23), it results that any adversary has a probability $p_{\mathcal{A}}$ to break the strong agreement property bounded by $p_{\mathcal{A}} \leq t\varepsilon_{\mathsf{FRI}} + \varepsilon_{\mathsf{Corr}}$. $\qquad\square$

Proposition 14 (Secrecy). *We model the hash function in the Merkle tree as a random oracle. Then, in the sharing phase, if the dealer is honest, any PPT adversary $\mathcal{A}$ can distinguish between the sharing of two messages with probability*

$$p_{\mathcal{A}} \leq n_q/|\mathbb{F}|^{t+1},$$

where n_q is the number of queries from $\mathcal{A}$ to the random oracle.

Proof. Let $\mathcal{C}$ be the challenger in the secrecy game. Let (m_0, m_1) be the challenge that $\mathcal{C}$ receives from $\mathcal{A}$. The adversary wins if it can guess which message m_b the challenger has shared, after the sharing phase is complete.

We modify the challenger in the following way. First, it samples $b \leftarrow\!\!\$ \{0,1\}$, $r \leftarrow\!\!\$ \mathbb{F}_{\leq t}[X,Y]$ and $(a_{i,j})_{j\in[n]} \leftarrow\!\!\$ \mathsf{RS}[n,t+1]$ for each $i \in \mathsf{Corr}$. Then, $\mathcal{C}$ sets φ to be the polynomial of degree t such that $\varphi(x_i, x_j) = a_{i,j}$ for all $i \in \mathsf{Corr}, j \in [n]$ and $\varphi(0,0) = m_b$. Using φ and r, the simulator computes $c_\varphi, \{c_{r(X,x_i)}, c_{r(x_i,Y)}\}_{i\in[n]}$ and $\{c_{\psi(x_i,Y)}\}_{i\in\mathsf{Corr}}$ honestly.

To prepare the Echo messages, $\mathcal{C}$ completes the set $(a_{j,i})_{j\in\mathsf{Corr}}$ with random values $(a_{j,i})_{j\in\mathsf{Hon}}$ for $i \in \mathsf{Corr}$ such that $(a_{j,i})_{j\in[n]} \in \mathsf{RS}[n,t+1]$. Due to the perfect secrecy of Shamir's secret sharing, these random points are indistinguishable from an honest sharing of m_b since $\mathcal{A}$ only learns at most t univariate polynomials $\varphi(X, x_i)$ and $\varphi(x_i, Y)$ for $i \in \mathsf{Corr}$, while $\varphi(X,Y)$ is of degree t in both variables. From these points $(a_{i,j})_{i,j}$, the previously chosen $(b_{i,j})_{i,j}$ and $\alpha = H(c_{r(x_1,Y)}||\ldots||c_{r(x_n,Y)}||c_\varphi)$, it derives the polynomial $\psi(X,Y)$. Then, $\mathcal{C}$ computes the rest of the Merkle trees $\{c_{\psi(x_i,Y)}\}_{i\in\mathsf{Hon}}$, $\{c_{\psi(X,x_i)}\}_{i\in[n]}$, c and the proximity proof π.

The challenger sends all the broadcast values $c, \pi, c_\varphi, \{c_{r(X,x_i)}, c_{r(x_i,Y)}, c_{\psi(X,x_i)}, c_{\psi(x_i,Y)}\}_{i\in[n]}$ to the adversary. Then, it sends Echo message to the adversary with the shares $(a_{j,i}, b_{j,i})$ for $j \in \mathsf{Hon}, i \in \mathsf{Corr}$ and their corresponding Merkle paths.

If $\mathcal{A}$ can answer with a bit $b' = b$ with non-negligible probability, considering that all values except c_φ were chosen independently of m_b, then $\mathcal{A}$ can distinguish between c_φ and the output of a random function. However, $\mathcal{A}$ lacks at least $t+1$ points in $\mathbb{F}$ (*i.e.*, at least one partial evaluation $\varphi(X, x_i)$ or $\varphi(x_i, Y)$) to entirely determine $\varphi(X,Y)$. Let n_q be the number of queries of $\mathcal{A}$ to the random oracle, its probability to guess these points is $n_q/|\mathbb{F}|^{t+1}$. $\qquad\square$

4.3   Choice of Complexity Parameters

In order to fix the parameters of the IOPPs used as a function of the security parameter λ, we compute the overall soundness of our protocol in the random-oracle model.

If $\lambda \in \mathbb{N}$ is a security parameter, by Proposition 13, we can choose $\mathbb{F}$, μ_{BiFRI}, ℓ and μ_{FRI} such that $t\varepsilon_{\mathsf{PC}} + \varepsilon_{\mathsf{Corr}} \leq 2^{-\lambda}$. Hence we can choose these parameters such that $\varepsilon_{\mathsf{PC}} \leq \frac{1}{t}2^{-\lambda-1}$ and $\varepsilon_{\mathsf{Corr}} \leq 2^{-\lambda-1}$. By Proposition 2, we can choose $\mathbb{F}$ and μ_{BiFRI} such that

$$\varepsilon_{\mathsf{BiFRI}} + \frac{12n^2}{(n-t)^2|\mathbb{F}|} \leq 2^{-\lambda-1},$$

and by Proposition 6, we can choose $\mathbb{F}$, ℓ and μ_{FRI} such that

$$\max\left(\left(\frac{t}{n} + 2\delta_{\mathsf{PC}}\right)^\ell, \varepsilon_{\mathsf{FRI}}\right) \leq \frac{1}{t}2^{-\lambda-1}.$$

Assume that $n = 3t + 1$. Let

$$|\mathbb{F}| \geq \begin{cases} 5184 \log^3 n \cdot 2^{\lambda+3} \approx \log^3 n \cdot 2^{\lambda+15.34} \\ 12t \log^2 n \cdot 2^{\lambda+2} \approx t \log^2 n \cdot 2^{\lambda+5.58}. \end{cases} \qquad (26)$$

- **Obtaining $\varepsilon_{\mathsf{BiFRI}} \leq 2^{-\lambda-2}$.** Since $t \geq 1$ we have $n \geq 4$ and therefore $2/27n + 8/27n^2 \leq 1/27$. Hence $\delta_{\mathsf{BiFRI}} = \frac{1}{2}\frac{(n-t)^2-1}{3n^2} = \frac{1}{2}\left(\frac{4}{27} - \frac{2}{27n} - \frac{8}{27n^2}\right) \geq \frac{1}{18}$. By Proposition 1 we have $\varepsilon_{\mathsf{BiFRI}} = \frac{4\log n}{\eta^2|\mathbb{F}|} + (1 - \delta_{\mathsf{BiFRI}} + 2\eta \log n)^{\mu_{\mathsf{BiFRI}}}$. Let $\eta = 1/72 \log n$. By Eq. (26), $|\mathbb{F}| \geq 5184 \log^3 n \cdot 2^{\lambda+3} \approx \log^3 n \cdot 2^{\lambda+15.34}$, therefore $\frac{4\log n}{\eta^2|\mathbb{F}|} \leq 2^{-\lambda-3}$. We can choose μ_{BiFRI} such that $(17/18 + 2\eta \log n)^{\mu_{\mathsf{BiFRI}}} \leq 2^{-\lambda-3}$, i.e.

$$\mu_{\mathsf{BiFRI}} \geq \frac{\lambda+3}{\log 36/35} \approx 24.6(\lambda+3). \qquad (27)$$

- **Obtaining $\frac{12n^2}{(n-t)^2|\mathbb{F}|} \leq 2^{-\lambda-2}$.** By Eq. (26), we have $|\mathbb{F}| \geq 27 \cdot 2^{\lambda+2}$. Therefore $\frac{12n^2}{(n-t)^2|\mathbb{F}|} = \frac{108}{4|\mathbb{F}|} \leq \frac{27}{|\mathbb{F}|} \leq 2^{-\lambda-2}$.

- **Obtaining $\left(\frac{t}{n}+2\delta_{\mathsf{PC}}\right)^\ell \leq \frac{1}{t}2^{-\lambda-1}$.** Since $\delta_{\mathsf{PC}} = \frac{n-t-1}{3n} < \frac{2n/3}{3n} = \frac{2}{9}$, we have $\frac{t}{n} + 2\delta_{\mathsf{PC}} < \frac{1}{3} + \frac{4}{9} = \frac{7}{9}$. Therefore, we can choose ℓ such that $\left(\frac{7}{9}\right)^\ell \leq \frac{1}{t}2^{-\lambda-1}$, i.e.

$$\ell \geq \frac{\log t + 1}{\log 9/7} \approx 2.76(\lambda + \log t + 1). \qquad (28)$$

- **Obtaining $\varepsilon_{\mathsf{FRI}} \leq \frac{1}{t}2^{-\lambda-1}$.** By Theorem 2 we have $\varepsilon_{\mathsf{FRI}} = \frac{\log n}{\eta|\mathbb{F}|} + (1 - \delta_{\mathsf{PC}} + \eta \log n)^{\mu_{\mathsf{FRI}}}$. Let $\eta = 1/12 \log n$. By Eq. (26), $|\mathbb{F}| \geq 12t \log^2 n \cdot 2^{\lambda+2}$ and therefore $\frac{\log n}{\eta|\mathbb{F}|} \leq \frac{1}{t}2^{-\lambda-2}$. Then we can choose μ_{FRI} such that $(11/12)^{\mu_{\mathsf{FRI}}} \leq \frac{1}{t}2^{-\lambda-2}$, i.e.

$$\mu_{\mathsf{FRI}} \geq \frac{\log t + 2}{\log 12/11} \approx 8(\lambda + \log t + 2). \qquad (29)$$

For instance, the Goldilocks field $\mathbb{F}_p$ for $p = 2^{64} - 2^{32} + 1$ [Ham15] could be considered. It is FFT-friendly since it has 2^{32} distinct 2^{32}-th roots of unity, hence allowing to use the FRI up to $t \leq 2^{32}$. By plugging $t = 2^{32}$ in Eq. (26), we get that taking a degree 3 extension of $\mathbb{F}_p$ suffices to achieve a security parameter $\lambda = 128$ even far beyond $n = 2^{64}$. Achieving 256 bits of security would require a degree 5 extension of $\mathbb{F}_p$ for a similar range of parameters n and t.

5   Conclusion

The AVSS protocol we propose achieves both low complexity parameters and strong post-quantum security thanks to the proximity test to products of Reed-Solomon codes. Lower complexity parameters could be achieved by using a correlated agreement (Corollary 1) under the unique decoding radius that is more specific to products of Reed-Solomon codes, like the one for univariate Reed-Solomon codes from [BCI+23, Lemma 4.2].

References

[ABN23] Augot, D., Bordage, S., Nardi, J.: Efficient multivariate low-degree tests via interactive oracle proofs of proximity for polynomial codes. Des. Codes Crypt. **91**(3), 1111–1151 (2023)

[AJM+23] Abraham, I., Jovanovic, P., Maller, M., Meiklejohn, S., Stern, G.: Bingo: adaptivity and asynchrony in verifiable secret sharing and distributed key generation. In: Handschuh, H., Lysyanskaya, A. (eds.) CRYPTO 2023, Part I. LNCS, vol. 14081, pp. 39–70. Springer, Cham (2023)

[AVZ21] AlHaddad, N., Varia, M., Zhang, H.: High-threshold AVSS with optimal communication complexity. In: Borisov, N., Diaz, C. (eds.) FC 2021. LNCS, vol. 12675, pp. 479–498. Springer, Heidelberg (2021). https://doi.org/10.1007/978-3-662-64331-0_25

[BBHR18] Ben-Sasson, E., Bentov, I., Horesh, Y., Riabzev, M.: Fast reed-solomon interactive oracle proofs of proximity. In: Chatzigiannakis, I., Kaklamanis, C., Marx, D., Sannella, D. (eds.) 45th International Colloquium on Automata, Languages, and Programming (ICALP 2018). Leibniz International Proceedings in Informatics (LIPIcs), Dagstuhl, Germany, vol. 107, pp. 14:1–14:17. Schloss Dagstuhl – Leibniz-Zentrum für Informatik (2018)

[BCG93] Ben-Or, M., Canetti, R., Goldreich, O.: Asynchronous secure computation. In: 25th ACM STOC, pp. 52–61. ACM Press (1993)

[BCI+23] Ben-Sasson, E., Carmon, D., Ishai, Y., Kopparty, S., Saraf, S.: Proximity gaps for reed-solomon codes. J. ACM **70**(5), 1–57 (2023)

[BCS16] Ben-Sasson, E., Chiesa, A., Spooner, N.: Interactive oracle proofs. In: Hirt, M., Smith, A. (eds.) TCC 2016. LNCS, vol. 9986, pp. 31–60. Springer, Heidelberg (2016). https://doi.org/10.1007/978-3-662-53644-5_2

[BDK13] Backes, M., Datta, A., Kate, A.: Asynchronous computational VSS with reduced communication complexity. In: Dawson, E. (ed.) CT-RSA 2013. LNCS, vol. 7779, pp. 259–276. Springer, Heidelberg (2013). https://doi.org/10.1007/978-3-642-36095-4_17

[BGKS20] Ben-Sasson, E., Goldberg, L., Kopparty, S., Saraf, S.: DEEP-FRI: sampling outside the box improves soundness. In: Vidick, T. (ed.) 11th Innovations in Theoretical Computer Science Conference, ITCS 2020, 12–14 January 2020, Seattle, Washington, USA, LIPIcs, vol. 151, pp. 5:1–5:32. Schloss Dagstuhl - Leibniz-Zentrum für Informatik (2020)

[BKS18] Ben-Sasson, E., Kopparty, S., Saraf, S.: Worst-case to average case reductions for the distance to a codeElectron. Colloquium Comput. Complex. TR18-090 (2018)

[Bla79] Blakley, G.R.: Safeguarding cryptographic keys. In: Proceedings of AFIPS 1979 National Computer Conference, vol. 48, pp. 313–317 (1979)

[CCG24] Cascudo, I., Cozzo, D., Giunta, E.: Verifiable secret sharing from symmetric key cryptography with improved optimistic complexity. In: Chung, K.-M., Sasaki, Yu. (eds.) ASIACRYPT 2024, Part VII. LNCS, vol. 15490, pp. 100–128. Springer, Singapore (2024)

[CGMA85] Choc, B., Goldwasser, S., Micali, S., Awerbuch, B.: Verifiable secret sharing and achieving simultaneity in the presence of faults (extended abstract). In: 26th FOCS, pp. 383–395. IEEE Computer Society Press (1985)

[CLL+24] Cheng, H., Li, J., Liu, Y., Lu, Y., Meng, W., Zhang, Z.: Resilience-optimal lightweight high-threshold asynchronous verifiable secret sharing. Cryptology ePrint Archive, Paper 2024/1761 (2024)

[CP23]   Choudhury, A., Patra, A.: On the communication efficiency of statistically secure asynchronous MPC with optimal resilience. J. Cryptol. **36**(2), 13 (2023)

[DXT+23] Das, S., Xiang, Z., Tomescu, A., Spiegelman, A., Pinkas, B., Ren, L.: Verifiable secret sharing simplified. Cryptology ePrint Archive, Paper 2023/1196 (2023)

[EB22]   Eslamia, K., Bahramiana, M.: An isogeny-based quantum-resistant secret sharing scheme. Filomat **36**(10), 3249–3258 (2022)

[FS87]   Fiat, A., Shamir, A.: How to prove yourself: practical solutions to identification and signature problems. In: Odlyzko, A.M. (ed.) CRYPTO 1986. LNCS, vol. 263, pp. 186–194. Springer, Heidelberg (1987). https://doi.org/10.1007/3-540-47721-7_12

[GDKK22] Günther, C.U., Das, S., Kokoris-Kogias, L.: Practical asynchronous proactive secret sharing and key refresh. Cryptology ePrint Archive, Paper 2022/1586 (2022)

[GHL22]   Gentry, C., Halevi, S., Lyubashevsky, V.: Practical non-interactive publicly verifiable secret sharing with thousands of parties. In: Dunkelman, O., Dziembowski, S. (eds.) EUROCRYPT 2022, Part I. LNCS, vol. 13275, pp. 458–487. Springer, Cham (2022)

[Ham15]   Hamburg, M.: ED448-goldilocks, a new elliptic curve. Cryptology ePrint Archive (2015)

[KZG10]   Kate, A., Zaverucha, G.M., Goldberg, I.: Constant-size commitments to polynomials and their applications. In: Abe, M. (ed.) ASIACRYPT 2010. LNCS, vol. 6477, pp. 177–194. Springer, Heidelberg (2010). https://doi.org/10.1007/978-3-642-17373-8_11

[LLS+24] Li, J., Lu, Z., Shen, R., Feng, Y., Lu, S.: Asynchronous verifiable secret sharing with elastic thresholds and distributed key generation. Cryptology ePrint Archive, Paper 2024/1463 (2024)

[LRU22]   Levrat, C., Rambaud, M., Urban, A.: Breaking the $t < n/3$ consensus bound: asynchronous dynamic proactive secret sharing under honest majority. Cryptology ePrint Archive, Paper 2022/619 (2022)

[Mer87]   Merkle, R.C.: A digital signature based on a conventional encryption function. In: Pomerance, C. (ed.) CRYPTO 1987. LNCS, vol. 293, pp. 369–378. Springer, Heidelberg (1988). https://doi.org/10.1007/3-540-48184-2_32

[PCR09]   Patra, A., Choudhary, A., Rangan, C.P.: Efficient statistical asynchronous verifiable secret sharing with optimal resilience. In: Kurosawa, K. (ed.) ICITS 2009. LNCS, vol. 5973, pp. 74–92. Springer, Heidelberg (2010). https://doi.org/10.1007/978-3-642-14496-7_7

[Sch80]   Schwartz, J.T.: Fast probabilistic algorithms for verification of polynomial identities. J. ACM **27**(4), 701–717 (1980)

[Sha79]   Shamir, A.: How to share a secret. Commun. Assoc. Comput. Mach. **22**(11), 612–613 (1979)

[SS24] Shoup, V., Smart, N.P.: Lightweight asynchronous verifiable secret sharing with optimal resilience. J. Cryptol. **37**(3), 27 (2024)

[WB86] Welch, L.R., Berlekamp, E.R.: Error correction for algebraic block codes. US Patent 4,633,470 (1986)

[YLF+21] Yurek, T., Luo, L., Fairoze, J., Kate, A., Miller, A.: hbACSS: how to robustly share many secrets. Cryptology ePrint Archive, Paper 2021/159 (2021)

[ZLG+24] Zhang, Z., et al.: Fast RS-IOP multivariate polynomial commitments and verifiable secret sharing. In: Balzarotti, D., Xu, W. (eds.) USENIX Security 2024. USENIX Association (2024)

Behemoth: Transparent Polynomial Commitment Scheme with Constant Opening Proof Size and Verifier Time

István András Seres[(✉)] and Péter Burcsi

Eötvös Loránd University, Budapest, Hungary
seresistvanandras@gmail.com

Abstract. Polynomial commitment schemes are fundamental building blocks in numerous cryptographic protocols, e.g., verifiable secret sharing, zero-knowledge succinct non-interactive arguments, and many more. The most efficient polynomial commitment schemes rely on a trusted setup, which is undesirable in trust-minimized applications, e.g., cryptocurrencies. However, transparent polynomial commitment schemes are inefficient (polylogarithmic opening proofs and/or verification time) compared to their trusted counterparts. It has been an open problem to devise a transparent, succinct polynomial commitment scheme or prove an impossibility result in the transparent setting. In this work, for the first time, we create a transparent, constant-size polynomial commitment scheme called Behemoth with constant-size opening proofs and a constant-time verifier. The downside of Behemoth is that it employs a cubic prover in the degree of the committed polynomial. We prove the security of our scheme in the generic group model and discuss parameter settings in which it remains practical even for the prover.

1 Introduction

A polynomial commitment scheme (PCS or **PC**) allows a prover to commit to a polynomial f of degree maximum d (typically over a finite field, i.e., $f \in \mathbb{F}_p^{\leq d}[x]$, and $p \approx 2^{256}, d \approx 2^{10} - 2^{30}$). Importantly, the prover can later open the committed polynomial at any point. Specifically, the prover can convince a verifier about evaluations of f at point $z \in \mathbb{F}_p$ of the polynomial f when the verifier is given only a short commitment to f and the statement $f(z) = s$. PCSs were first proposed by Kate, Zaverucha, and Goldberg (KZG) [32]. Since then, PCSs have become the cornerstone of many important cryptographic protocols, such as verifiable secret sharing, zero-knowledge sets, zero-knowledge succinct non-interactive arguments of knowledge (zkSNARKs) [9], Verkle trees [35] and many more. Therefore, it is of great interest to improve existing PCSs, as they directly translate to efficiency and trust assumption improvements in numerous applications. The most efficient PCSs are derived from the original KZG scheme [14,22,28]. The KZG scheme and its extensions offer short commitments, evaluation proofs (both one group element), and batching capabilities for the opening protocol at the expense of

A. Nitaj et al. (Eds.): AFRICACRYPT 2025, LNCS 15651, pp. 343–369, 2026.
https://doi.org/10.1007/978-3-031-97260-7_16

a *trusted setup* and a linear-sized (in the maximum degree d of the committed polynomials) common reference string.

A trusted setup requires private randomness to generate the public parameters necessary for the commitment scheme. The private randomness ("toxic waste") must be kept secret or discarded to maintain the soundness of the PCS. If the randomness used in the setup is known to an adversary, it is possible to break the binding property of the PCS or create invalid opening proofs. Therefore, a successful trusted setup is paramount for the security of the KZG PCS and its variants. Trusted setups are straightforward to perform if there exists a trusted third party who does not disclose private randomness. In the absence of a trusted party to distribute the trust in trusted setups, numerous multi-party protocols have been suggested for executing the KZG trusted setup [8,17,25,34,39]. However, trusted setups are usually undesirable in trust-minimized and decentralized applications, such as cryptocurrencies. To that end, significant efforts have been dedicated to devising transparent PCSs whose setup algorithm uses only public coins.

There is a multitude of transparent PCSs. They use various techniques and are instantiated under diverse cryptographic assumptions. FRI [7] and its variants [2,33] only assume the existence of one-way functions, hence post-quantum secure. Bootle et al. [16,49] and Bünz et al. [18] assume the discrete logarithm assumption in cyclic groups. Lee builds a transparent **PC** in groups with non-degenerate, efficiently computable, bilinear pairings [37]. A recent line of research designs PCSs [3,10,19,23] in groups of unknown order (GUO). An advantage of applying groups of unknown order in cryptographic applications is that some families of GUOs can be instantiated transparently [26]. Specifically, class groups of imaginary quadratic fields and Jacobians of hyperelliptic curves [48] can be sampled efficiently and transparently using only public randomness. For efficiency reasons, we focus mainly on instantiating our scheme in class groups. Currently, the best known algorithms can compute the order of an imaginary class group in subexponential time [30,45]. So far, all transparent **PC** schemes have had polylogarithmic evaluation proofs and/or verifiers.

Ideally, one wants to match the efficiency properties of the KZG **PC** scheme also in the transparent setting, i.e., both constant opening proofs and verifiers with possibly batching capabilities. Hence, a natural question arises:

Is there a transparent, succinct PCS that achieves constant-size *opening proofs and* constant-time *verifiers with possibly batching capabilities?*

In this work, we answer affirmatively. To our knowledge, we devise the first transparent PCS with *constant-size opening proofs and constant-time verifier*, i.e., the first transparent succinct polynomial commitment scheme.

Our Contributions. In this work, we make the following contributions.

We propose Behemoth,[1] the first succinct (constant opening proof size and verifier time), transparent polynomial commitment scheme. We prove its security in the random oracle and generic group models. Thus, we positively answer an open question by Nikolaenko et al. [39] about the existence of succinct, transparent polynomial commitment schemes.

As an application of our transparent **PC** scheme, we prove the existence of a transparent zkSNARK with constant proof size and verifier time, in the full version of this work. To our knowledge, this is the first such construction in the polynomial-IOP paradigm.

2 Technical Overview

This section presents the main ideas behind our polynomial commitment construction. Our end goal is to instantiate the KZG PCS in a group of unknown order and not to resort to techniques (e.g., inner product arguments or Merkle trees) that seem to inherently lead to (poly)logarithmic proofs and/or verifiers.

First, we recall the KZG polynomial commitment scheme. In the KZG scheme, the public parameters consist of the structured reference string produced by the trusted setup: $\mathsf{srs} = \{g^{\tau^i}\}_{i=0}^{\mathsf{d}}$ for $\tau \in_R \mathbb{F}_p^*$. The commitment to a polynomial $\mathsf{f} \in \mathbb{F}_p^{\leq \mathsf{d}}[x]$ is the evaluation of the polynomial at a random point τ not known even to the committer, i.e., $g^{\mathsf{f}(\tau)} \in \mathbb{G}$, for some prime-order elliptic curve group $\mathbb{G}$ ($|\mathbb{G}| = p$) with generator g. Furthermore, in the KZG scheme, we assume that $\mathbb{G}$ is equipped with an efficiently computable, non-degenerate bilinear pairing, i.e., $e : \mathbb{G} \times \mathbb{G} \to \mathbb{G}_T$. More interestingly, in the opening proof of KZG for the statement $\mathsf{f}(z) = s$, given the commitment $g^{\mathsf{f}(\tau)}$, the prover can convince the verifier by sending a commitment $g^{\mathsf{q}(\tau)}$ to the quotient polynomial $\mathsf{q}(x) := \frac{\mathsf{f}(x)-s}{x-z}$. This is correct because the verifier can check the equality of polynomials $\mathsf{q}(x)(x - z) = \mathsf{f}(x) - s$ in the exponent at the random point τ using the structured reference string and the bilinear pairing. The verification of the evaluation proof is achieved by checking $e(g^{\mathsf{q}(\tau)}, g^{\tau-z}) \stackrel{?}{=} e(g^{\mathsf{f}(\tau)-s}, g)$.

How can we possibly mimic the evaluation proof strategy of the KZG scheme in a group of unknown order $\mathbb{G}$? First, we observe that a KZG-style commitment $g^{\mathsf{f}(\alpha)} \in \mathbb{G}$ binds the prover to the value of $\mathsf{f}(\alpha)$, thanks to the unknown group order. We will show that *for a public and properly chosen α this also implies polynomial binding.*[2] Therefore, essentially, we have the same commitments to polynomials as the KZG scheme, i.e., $g^{\mathsf{f}(\alpha)}$ for a carefully chosen *public $\alpha \in \mathbb{Z}$.* Since we do not know the order of the group, we can only evaluate polynomials *over the integers* in the exponent. We denote the evaluation of a polynomial over the integers as $\widehat{\mathsf{f}(\alpha)}$ to disambiguate from the "regular" evaluation $\mathsf{f}(\alpha)$ over the finite field $\mathbb{F}_p$. We use integer representatives from $[0, p)$ to lift the polynomial.

---

[1] Behemoth is an enormous biblical monster described in the Book of Job. The name of the scheme alludes to the huge integers used in our scheme.

[2] We will make this precise later in Sect. 5.

The first challenge is to ensure polynomial binding by selecting α carefully. The intuition is that α must be large compared to $\mathbb{F}_p$ and d, so that $\widehat{\mathsf{f}(\alpha)}$ uniquely determines $\mathsf{f}(\alpha)$: the coefficients can be recovered from the base α representation of $\widehat{\mathsf{f}(\alpha)}$. If α is small, say $\alpha = 5$, then given a commitment $g^{127} = g^{\widehat{\mathsf{f}(\alpha)}}$, the prover can open this commitment to numerous polynomials, for instance, $\mathsf{f}_1 = 127, \mathsf{f}_2 = 6x + 97$ in fact for any $\mathsf{f}_2 = ax + b$ for any $(a, b) \in \mathbb{Z} \times \mathbb{Z} : 5a + b = 127$. We detail in Sect. 4.2, how to chose α properly to ensure polynomial and evaluation binding in $\mathbb{F}_p^{\leq \mathsf{d}}[x]$.

A major challenge that a (very) large value of α poses is constructing correct opening proofs. In the evaluation proofs, since we do not rely on private evaluation points, the verifier can check the equality $\widehat{\mathsf{q}(x)}(x - z) = \widehat{\mathsf{f}(x)} - \hat{s}$ in the exponent at the point α even without bilinear pairings. Specifically, given a commitment $g^{\widehat{\mathsf{q}(\alpha)}}$ to $\mathsf{q}(x)$, the verifier can compute $(g^{\widehat{\mathsf{q}(\alpha)}})^{\alpha - z}$ without a bilinear pairing, since α is public. A downside of this approach is that now, the right-hand side of the verification equation, $\widehat{\mathsf{f}(\alpha)} - \hat{s} \in \mathbb{Z}$ is a large integer with $\approx \mathsf{d} \log(p)$ bits. We describe in Sect. 4.3 the applied techniques that keep both our opening proofs and verifier constant, and the committer efficient. Moreover, along the way, we need to solve many technical challenges to preserve evaluation binding and the knowledge soundness properties of our proposed PCS. A major technical difficulty in proving knowledge soundness is to show that the protocols prevent adversarial provers from using integer polynomials that are not obtained by correctly lifting a modular polynomial. As mentioned above, one can only work over the integers in the exponent of a group of unknown order. This necessitates "projecting" statements over the integers back to finite fields. We achieve this by applying several non-interactive zero-knowledge proofs, cf. Sect. 3.5, to ensure the polynomial/evaluation binding and knowledge soundness of our PCS.

3   Background

3.1   Notations

In the following, we will use multiplicative notation to denote the group operation in the applied groups $\mathbb{G}$ (of unknown order). To sample x from a set S uniformly at random, we write $x \in_R S$. Some protocols need to sample random integers from the set of the first 2^λ primes that are denoted as $\mathsf{Primes}(\lambda)$, where λ is the security parameter. Let p denote a large odd prime. For an univariate polynomial $\mathsf{f}(x) \in \mathbb{F}_p^{\leq \mathsf{d}}[x]$ where $\mathsf{f}(z) = s$, let $\widehat{\mathsf{f}(z)} := \hat{s}$ denote the evaluation of f at z *over the integers*. We use a Python-like notation to index lists and arrays, i.e., we refer to the ith element of a list l as $l[i]$. Let

$$\mathcal{B} := \max_{x \in \mathbb{F}_p, \mathsf{f}(x) \in \mathbb{F}_p^{\leq \mathsf{d}}[x]} \widehat{\mathsf{f}(x)} = \sum_{i=1}^{\mathsf{d}+1} (p-1)^i = (p-1)\frac{1 - (p-1)^{\mathsf{d}+1}}{1 - (p-1)}. \tag{1}$$

$\mathcal{B}$ is a universal upper bound for the evaluation *over the integers* of polynomials from the polynomial ring $\mathbb{F}_p^{\leq \mathsf{d}}[x]$. Let $v_p(x)$ be the p-adic valuation of x, i.e., the (possibly negative) exponent of p in the factorization of x. The commitment of a polynomial f is denoted as $\boxed{f}$. The prover and the verifier are denoted as $\mathcal{P}$ and $\mathcal{V}$, respectively.

3.2   Polynomial Commitment Schemes

A polynomial commitment scheme $\mathbf{PC} = (\mathsf{GenSRS}, \mathsf{Com}, \mathsf{ComVerify}, \mathsf{Open}, \mathsf{OpenVerify})$ consists of five algorithms and allows to commit to a polynomial f and later "open" the commitment $\boxed{f}$ at point z by proving that for some value $s = f(z)$. More formally:

$\mathsf{GenSRS}(1^\lambda, \mathsf{d})$: The key generation algorithm takes in a security parameter λ and a parameter d which determines the maximal degree of the committed polynomial. It outputs a structured reference string srs (the commitment key). Note that srs implicitly determines λ and d.

$\mathsf{Com}(\mathsf{srs}, \mathsf{f}, \mathsf{d})$: The commitment algorithm $\mathsf{Com}(\mathsf{srs}, \mathsf{f}, \mathsf{d})$ takes in srs and a polynomial f with maximum degree d, and outputs a commitment $c(= \boxed{f})$ and a string hint $\in \{0, 1\}^*$ that aids the opening of the commitment c.

$\mathsf{ComVerify}(\mathsf{srs}, \mathsf{f}, \mathsf{hint}, c)$: checks the validity of the opening hint for the commitment c of $\mathsf{f} \in \mathbb{F}_p^{\leq \mathsf{d}}[x]$. If it is valid, it outputs 1; otherwise, it outputs 0.

$\mathsf{Open}(\mathsf{srs}, z, s, \mathsf{f}, \mathsf{d})$: The opening algorithm takes as input srs, an evaluation point z, a value s and the polynomial f of degree d. It outputs an opening proof π.

$\mathsf{OpenVerify}(\mathsf{srs}, c, \mathsf{d}, z, s, \pi)$: The verification algorithm takes in srs, a commitment c, the degree d of the claimed polynomial, an evaluation point z, a value s and an opening proof π. It outputs 1 if π is a valid opening for (c, z, s) and 0 otherwise.

If the possibly probabilistic $\mathsf{GenSRS}(\cdot)$ algorithm is a public coin algorithm, then we call the $\mathbf{PC}$ scheme a transparent $\mathbf{PC}$ scheme. Some formalizations of $\mathbf{PC}$s [15,19] define the Open and OpenVerify algorithms as interactive protocols.

A secure polynomial commitment $\mathbf{PC}$ should satisfy correctness, (polynomial) binding, evaluation binding, evaluation hiding, zero knowledge, and knowledge soundness as defined below. Additionally, a $\mathbf{PC}$ scheme might be succinct. The formal security definitions are deferred to the full version of this work. We remark that no known $\mathbf{PC}$ scheme in the transparent setting would be succinct before this work.

3.3   Generic Group Model Adversaries

We prove the security of our scheme in the generic group model introduced by Shoup [44]. The generic group model (GGM) is an abstraction of an adversary that does not use the representation of a cryptographic group. The generic group model was first applied to groups of unknown order in 2002 by Damgård and Koprowski in [24]. Since then, it has been extensively used [1,13,31,43] to show various reductions in groups of unknown order, e.g., the equivalence of the RSA and factoring assumptions [1].

3.4   Assumptions in Groups of Unknown Order

We build on standard cryptographic assumptions in groups of unknown order: the Strong RSA Assumption [6], the Order Assumption and the Adaptive Root Assumption [50]. It was shown in [13] that both the order and adaptive root assumptions hold in the generic group model. Similar reductions were proven in the algebraic group model [5].

3.5   Non-interactive Zero-Knowledge Proofs

We recall the relevant syntax of non-interactive zero-knowledge (NIZK) proofs following [11], and for the details and exact security requirements, we refer to [11]. NIZK arguments consist of four PPT algorithms that are defined with respect to a relation generator algorithm $\mathcal{R}$-Gen(1^λ) that, upon receiving some security parameter λ, outputs a polynomial time decidable relation $\mathcal{R} : \{0,1\}^* \times \{0,1\}^*$ for which in our case $(\phi, \mathsf{w}) \in \mathcal{R}$, where ϕ is typically an algebraic statement in a ring $\mathbb{F}_N$ or in a finite field $\mathbb{F}_p$ and w is a valid witness for the instance.

- NIZK.Setup$(\mathcal{R}) \rightarrow (\mathsf{crs}, \tau)$. For the relation $\mathcal{R}$, the setup produces a common reference string crs and a simulation trapdoor τ. This possibly randomized algorithm may use public coins (transparent setup) or private coins (trusted setup).
- NIZK.Prove$(\mathcal{R}, \mathsf{crs}, \phi, \mathsf{w}) \rightarrow \pi$. Upon the $(\phi, \mathsf{w}) \in \mathcal{R}$ and the common reference string crs, the prover returns an argument π.
- NIZK.Verify$(\mathcal{R}, \mathsf{crs}, \phi, \pi) \rightarrow \{0,1\}$. Upon the common reference string crs, the statement ϕ, and an argument π, the verification algorithm returns 0 or 1.
- NIZK.Sim$(\mathcal{R}, \tau, \phi) \rightarrow \pi$. Using the simulation trapdoor, τ, and statement ϕ, the simulator returns an argument π.

This paper relies on non-interactive zero-knowledge proofs built for the following NP languages in groups of unknown order. All of the corresponding proofs have a constant size and constant-time verifiers. They were shown to be proofs of knowledge in the GGM [13,47].

Chaum-Pedersen (also known as discrete logarithm equality (DLEq)) proof [21].

$$\mathcal{R}_{\mathsf{ChaumP}} = \{((s, t, u, v \in \mathbb{G}); x \in \mathbb{Z}) : s = t^x \wedge u = v^x\}. \tag{2}$$

Thakur showed how to instantiate the original Chaum-Pedersen discrete logarithm equality proof system in a group of unknown order setting soundly [47].

Proof of Exponentiation (PoE) [40,50].

$$\mathcal{R}_{\mathsf{PoE}} = \{((u, w \in \mathbb{G}, x \in \mathbb{Z}); \bot) : w = u^x \in \mathbb{G}\}. \tag{3}$$

Note there is no witness in the $\mathcal{R}_{\mathsf{PoE}}$ relation, i.e., the verifier knows the exponent x. The primary goal of the PoE proof system for the verifier is to outsource a possibly large exponentiation, i.e., for an exponent $x \in [2^{2^{30}}, 2^{2^{50}}]$ in a group $\mathbb{G}$ of unknown order.

Proof of Knowledge of Exponent (PoKE) [13].

$$\mathcal{R}_{\mathsf{PoKE}} = \{((u, w \in \mathbb{G}); x \in \mathbb{Z}) : w = u^x \in \mathbb{G}\}. \tag{4}$$

Note, unlike in the $\mathcal{R}_{\mathsf{PoE}}$ relation, the verifier does not know the exponent x in the $\mathcal{R}_{\mathsf{PoKE}}$ relation. We remark that a zero-knowledge variant of the PoKE proof system, ZKPoKE, exists due to Boneh, Bünz, and Fisch [13].

Proof of Knowledge of Exponent Modulo an odd integer (PoKEMon) [13].

$$\mathcal{R}_{\mathsf{PoKEMon}} = \{((w, g \in \mathbb{G}, \hat{x} \in [n]); x \in \mathbb{Z}) : w = g^x \in \mathbb{G}, x \bmod n = \hat{x}\}. \tag{5}$$

Proof of Knowledge of Squared Exponent (PoKSE) [3].

$$\mathcal{R}_{\mathsf{PoKSE}} = \{((w, g \in \mathbb{G}); x \in \mathbb{Z}) : w = g^{x^2} \in \mathbb{G})\}. \tag{6}$$

Proof of knowledge of positive exponent (PoKPE) [3].

$$\mathcal{R}_{\mathsf{PoKPE}} = \{((w, g \in \mathbb{G}); x \in \mathbb{Z}) : (w = g^x) \wedge (0 < x))\}. \tag{7}$$

We will denote the corresponding proofs as $\pi_{\mathsf{PoE}}, \pi_{\mathsf{PoKE}}, \pi_{\mathsf{PoKEMon}}, \pi_{\mathsf{PoKPE}}, \pi_{\mathsf{PoKSE}}$. For their proofs of security, the reader is referred to [3,13,40,50]. Some of these protocols were introduced as interactive proof systems. However, all of them were shown to be secure as non-interactive proof systems in the random oracle model (ROM) using the Fiat-Shamir transformation [29]. This work uses the non-interactive version of all the aforementioned (zero-knowledge) proof systems. Thus, we assume the ROM throughout.

4   Behemoth: A Transparent, Succinct PC Scheme

This section defines the univariate Behemoth, our polynomial commitment scheme. We formally describe our PC scheme in Fig. 1. Our Open protocol relies on two subprotocols. First, we ensure that the opening protocol is evaluation binding in the ProveEvaluation protocol; see Fig. 2. Afterwards, we build a protocol that guarantees that the Behemoth-committed polynomial is of bounded degree d, see Fig. 3.

4.1   Lifting Polynomials over a Finite Field to over the Rationals

We want to commit to polynomials $f \in \mathbb{F}_p^{\leq d}[x]$. However, we also want to work in a group of unknown order (GUO). Hence, we need to work over the integers in the exponent. A committer can represent every f in multiple ways. We call the canonical form of a $f \in \mathbb{F}_p^{\leq d}[x]$ polynomial, when all of its coefficients $\forall i \in [0, d] : f_i \in [0, p)$. Jumping ahead, an honest prover will always use the canonical representation of a committed polynomial. Still, we cannot force this behavior, i.e., a committer can represent internally their committed polynomial in any equivalent form. All of our protocols will work with the canonical representation of a polynomial. Let us consider the following example.

Example. Suppose we want to commit to univariate polynomials in $\mathbb{F}_7^{\leq 2}[x]$ in a group of unknown order $\mathbb{G}$. As we already alluded to, the Behemoth commitment to f will be $g^{\mathsf{f}(\alpha)} \in \mathbb{G}$ for $g \in_R \mathbb{G}$ and for a carefully chosen α. For the sake of concreteness, let $\alpha := 2^5 + 1 = 33$. Let us consider $\mathsf{f}(x) := 4(x^2 + x) \equiv \frac{x^2+x}{2} \equiv \frac{x^2+15x}{142} \bmod 7$. All of these polynomials are equivalent mod 7. Yet, there are crucial differences we must point out. The first polynomial $4(x^2 + x)$ is the canonical representation of the polynomial. The second representation of the polynomial $\frac{x^2+x}{2} \in \mathbb{Q}[x]$ is integer-valued everywhere and can be used to commit to the polynomial since it is an integer-valued polynomial. Note that the Behemoth commitments of $4(x^2 + x)$ and $\frac{x^2+x}{2}$ are different since $4(\alpha^2 + \alpha) \neq \frac{\alpha^2+\alpha}{2}$ even though the polynomials are equivalent mod 7. Nonetheless, we remark that the representation $\frac{x^2+x}{2}$ cannot be opened everywhere, as it will be apparent in Sect. 4.3 once we introduce our opening proofs. On the other hand, the third representation of the polynomial $\frac{x^2+15x}{142}$ is not integer-valued everywhere. In particular, $\frac{\alpha^2+15\alpha}{142} \notin \mathbb{Z}$. Specifically, suppose the committer "thinks of" the polynomial $4(x^2 + x)$ as $\frac{x^2+15x}{142}$. In that case, it cannot even commit to it unless it could compute arbitrary roots (142th roots in this example) in a group of unknown order $\mathbb{G}$, which is deemed to be computationally infeasible as long as the strong RSA assumption holds in $\mathbb{G}$, cf. Section 3.4. Motivated by this discussion, we define a homomorphism from rational polynomials to polynomials over finite fields, which maps polynomials to their canonical representations.

$$\mathsf{Project}(\cdot) : \mathbb{Q}^{\leq \mathsf{d}}[x] \cap \{\mathsf{f}|\forall i : v_p(\mathsf{f}_i) \geq 0\} \to \mathbb{F}_p^{\leq \mathsf{d}}[x];$$

$$\mathsf{Project}(\mathsf{f}^*(x)) := \sum_{i=0}^{d} \mathsf{f}_i x^i, \;\; such \; that \;\; \mathsf{f}_i \equiv \mathsf{f}_i^* \bmod p \wedge \mathsf{f}_i \in [0, p).$$

We remark that the requirement $\{\mathsf{f}|\forall i : v_p(\mathsf{f}_i) \geq 0\}$ is necessary for the polynomials in the domain of $\mathsf{Project}(\cdot)$. If $v_p(\mathsf{f}_i) < 0$ was for some i, then f_i could not be mapped to $\mathbb{F}_p$. Note that $\mathsf{Project}(\cdot)$ is a many-to-one projection, cf. the example above. Therefore, when one wants to define the "inverse" of this homomorphism, we select a canonical pre-image. This "inverse" mapping $\mathsf{Lift}(\cdot)$ is defined as follows.

$$\mathsf{Lift}(\cdot) : \mathbb{F}_p^{\leq \mathsf{d}}[x] \to \mathbb{Z}^{\leq \mathsf{d}}[x]; \mathsf{Lift}(\mathsf{f}) := \sum_{i=0}^{d} \mathsf{f}_i x^i, \;\; such \; that \;\; \forall i : \mathsf{f}_i \in [0, p). \quad (8)$$

Provers may proceed with different representations of a polynomial in different protocols of the Behemoth **PC** scheme. We only guarantee correctness for the canonical representation of committed polynomials. If provers represent internally polynomials in a non-canonical form, then our protocols (both the commitment Com and the Open protocols) may or may not work. However, (knowledge) soundness of the protocol is guaranteed to hold for *every representative of a committed* $f \in \mathbb{F}_p^{\leq d}[x]$ *polynomial* for which the prover has a non-negligible probability of successfully opening it.

4.2   Behemoth: a High-Level Description

The Behemoth univariate polynomial commitment scheme consists of the following five PPT algorithms, cf. Fig. 1. This high-level description contains two proof systems, i.e., ProveEvaluation and PoKDegUp, introduced formally in Sect. 4.3. These proof systems allow one to prove membership succinctly in the following NP relations.

$$\mathcal{R}_{\text{ProveEvaluation}}[f, z, s] = \{\boxed{f} \in \mathbb{G}, f(x) \in \mathbb{Q}[x], z, s \in \mathbb{F}_p : g^{\widehat{f(\alpha)}} = \boxed{f} \wedge f(z) = s\}.$$

$$\mathcal{R}_{\text{PoKDegUp}}[f, d] = \{\boxed{f} \in \mathbb{G}, f(x) \in \mathbb{Q}[x], d \in \mathbb{Z} : g^{\widehat{f(\alpha)}} = \boxed{f} \wedge deg(f) \leq d\}.$$

Remarks. First, note that in the GenSRS algorithm α is public. Hence, if the setup $GGen(\lambda)$ of the underlying group of unknown order $\mathbb{G}$ does not require a trusted setup, then our **PC** scheme can be instantiated with a transparent setup. For instance, this can be achieved with class groups of imaginary quadratic fields or hyperelliptic Jacobians [26]. Furthermore, it is important that α is large (i.e., $\alpha > p^d$), (see the toy attack example with small α in Sect. 2), and has a low Hamming weight for efficiency reasons. Note that α cannot be a power of two since an efficient algorithm exists in class groups to compute square roots due to Gauss. If α was a power of two, our Open protocol would not be sound. For more discussion on the choice of α, see Sect. 4.2. The public exponent α is large, specifically, α has $\mathcal{O}(d \log(p))$ bits, making the GenSRS algorithm a computationally heavy computation, i.e., $\mathcal{O}(d^2 \log p)$. In other words, for certain parameter settings, GenSRS essentially behaves as a verifiable delay function [12]. Practically speaking, this means that when $d \geq 2^{20}$ for larger finite fields ($p \approx 2^{256}$), the GenSRS(1^λ, d) algorithm of the Behemoth **PC** scheme becomes computationally heavy, i.e., finishing the transparent setup takes several months on specialized hardware.

The size of the srs is linear in the degree d of the committed polynomial. Note that the srs needs to contain negative degrees of α in the exponent of $g^{\alpha^{-i}}$ for $i \in [1, d]$. This seems unattainable since we cannot compute α-roots in a group of unknown order $\mathbb{G}$ (we can only compute roots of powers of two in class groups) as it would contradict the strong RSA assumption, see Appendix 3.4. In practice, one would compute the powers of α in the forward direction, i.e., $g, g^\alpha, \ldots, g^{\alpha^{2d}}$ and designate g^{α^d} as the "new" g. Lastly, one can attach PoE proofs [40,50] to convince resource-constrained devices that the transparent setup was computed correctly.

Once the srs is computed, committing to $f \in \mathbb{F}_p^{\leq d}[x]$ can be in $\mathcal{O}(d)$ time as it requires d "small" exponentiations, i.e., each exponent (coefficient of f) with bit-length $\approx \log(p)$. Additionally, this computation can be parallelized.

The Behemoth polynomial commitment scheme

GenSRS(1^λ, d): $\mathbb{G} \xleftarrow{\$} GGen(\lambda)$, $g_0 \in_R \mathbb{G}$. Let $\alpha := 2^{(d+1)(\lceil \log p \rceil + 1)} + 2^{d(\lceil \log p \rceil + 1)}$,
and $g := g_0^{\alpha^{d+1}}$. Then $\mathsf{srs}[i] := g^{\alpha^{i-(d+1)}} = g_0^{\alpha^i}$, where $i \in [0, 2(d+1)]$.

Com(srs, f, d): $\boxed{f}$ $:=$ $g^{\widehat{f(\alpha)}}$ $=$ $\prod_{i=0}^{d}(g^{\alpha^i})^{f_i} = \prod_{i=0}^{d} \mathsf{srs}[(d+1)+i]^{f_i}$, where

$f = \sum_{i=0}^{d} f_i x^i \in \mathbb{F}_p^{\leq d}[x]$.

Output: $\boxed{f}$.

ComVerify(srs, f, $\boxed{f}$): $\boxed{f} \stackrel{?}{=}$ Com(srs, f, d) $\wedge$ f $\stackrel{?}{\in} \mathbb{F}_p^{\leq d}[x]$.

Open(srs, f, d, z, s): The prover $\mathcal{P}$ convinces the verifier $\mathcal{V}$ that for $\boxed{f}$ it holds that f(z) = s $\wedge$ deg(f) $\leq$ d. $\mathcal{P}$ and $\mathcal{V}$ execute the following protocols.

1. $\mathcal{P}$ runs the ProveEvaluation(f, z, s) protocol and sends the $\pi_{\mathsf{ProveEvaluation}}^{f,z,s}$ to $\mathcal{V}$, see Figure 2. //This ensures that f(z) = s.
2. $\mathcal{P}$ samples $z' \in_R \mathbb{F}_p$ using the Fiat-Shamir transformation.
3. $\mathcal{P}$ runs the ProveEvaluation(f, z', s') protocol and sends the $\pi_{\mathsf{ProveEvaluation}}^{f,z',s'}$ to $\mathcal{V}$, see Figure 2. //This step is needed for knowledge soundness and ensures that f(z') = s'.
4. $\mathcal{P}$ runs the PoKDegUp(f(x), d) protocol with $\mathcal{V}$, see Figure 3. //This ensures that deg(f) $\leq$ d.
5. $\mathcal{P}$ runs the PoKDegUp(x^df(1/x), d) protocol with $\mathcal{V}$, see Figure 3. //This ensures that f(x) does not contain monomials of x^{-i} for any $i \in \mathbb{Z}$.

Output $\pi_{\mathsf{Open}} := (\pi_{\mathsf{ProveEvaluation}}^{f,z,s}, \pi_{\mathsf{ProveEvaluation}}^{f,z',s'}, \pi_{\mathsf{PoKDegUp}}^{f,d}, \pi_{\mathsf{PoKDegUp}}^{x^d f(1/x),d})$.

OpenVerify(srs, $\boxed{f}$, d, z, s, π_{Open}): Parse π_{Open} as π_{Open} = $(\pi_{\mathsf{ProveEvaluation}}^{f,z,s}, \pi_{\mathsf{ProveEvaluation}}^{f,z',s'}, \pi_{\mathsf{PoKDegUp}}^{f,d}, \pi_{\mathsf{PoKDegUp}}^{x^d f(1/x),d})$.

Output: NIZK.Verify($\mathcal{R}_{\mathsf{ProveEvaluation}}$, crs$_{\mathsf{ProveEvaluation}}$, $\phi_{\mathsf{ProveEvaluation}}$, $\pi_{\mathsf{ProveEvaluation}}^{f,z,s}$) $\wedge$
$\wedge$ NIZK.Verify($\mathcal{R}_{\mathsf{ProveEvaluation}}$, crs$_{\mathsf{ProveEvaluation}}$, $\phi_{\mathsf{ProveEvaluation}}$, $\pi_{\mathsf{ProveEvaluation}}^{f,z',s'}$) $\wedge$
$\wedge$ NIZK.Verify($\mathcal{R}_{\mathsf{PoKDegUp}}$, crs$_{\mathsf{PoKDegUp}}$, ϕ_{PoKDegUp}, $\pi_{\mathsf{PoKDegUp}}^{f,d}$) $\wedge$
$\wedge$ NIZK.Verify($\mathcal{R}_{\mathsf{PoKDegUp}}$, crs$_{\mathsf{PoKDegUp}}$, ϕ_{PoKDegUp}, $\pi_{\mathsf{PoKDegUp}}^{x^d f(1/x),d}$).

Fig. 1. The formal description of the five efficient algorithms (GenSRS, Com, ComVerify, Open, OpenVerify) of the Behemoth polynomial commitment scheme for univariate polynomials.

We remark that the evaluation proof has constant size; it is independent of the degree d of the committed polynomial. This holds, as we shall see because all the applied underlying zero-knowledge proofs have constant size. Moreover, the verifier also runs in constant time. To the best of our knowledge, this is the *first transparent polynomial commitment scheme with constant evaluation proofs and constant verifier*. The verifier's efficiency comes at the cost of a computationally heavy prover, i.e., a cubic prover. The bulk of the prover's work comes from the difficulty of finding the three (or four) squares decomposition of $\hat{s} = \widehat{f(z)} \approx \mathcal{B}$ over the integers. This results in a cubic computation using the state-of-the-art square decomposition algorithm of Pollack and Treviño [41]. To concretely reduce the prover's running time (unfortunately, the asymptotic complexity still remains cubic), in our construction, we decompose $\widehat{s} = \epsilon + q$ to the sum of a small positive integer ϵ and a prime q that can be further decomposed to two squares much faster than decomposing $\widehat{s}$ to the sum of three squares. Still, the cubic computational complexity constrains the prover to a specific range of parameters to preserve the practicality of our scheme. We further expand on our scheme's theoretical and practical performance in Sect. 6.

Strong Correctness. The original KZG commitment scheme satisfies the property of strong correctness, i.e., it is computationally infeasible to commit to polynomials of degrees larger than the maximum allowed degree d, i.e., the length of the srs, as long as the d-polyDH assumption holds. This property is beneficial and even wanted in certain applications, e.g., verifiable secret sharing. We note, however, that strong correctness is not satisfied by our polynomial commitment scheme as the srs is extensible by anyone. The possibility to extend the srs is valuable in certain applications, e.g., zkSNARKs. The extensible nature of the srs does not limit the complexity of the circuit one wants to prove statements about. It is conceivable that in the imminent future, when the community wants to support computational integrity proofs for statements with ever-increasing complexity (e.g., training or inference in zero-knowledge machine learning), then currently available srs strings with length $\approx 2^{28}$ will likely fall short in supporting such complex computations. Recall that the srs cannot be extended indefinitely without increasing α since that would forfeit evaluation binding, i.e., it must hold for d and p that $\mathcal{B} = \sum_{i=1}^{d+1} (p-1)^i \leq \alpha$. However, computing a larger, updated value of $\alpha' \geq \alpha$ and updating the srs $= \{g^{\alpha^{i-(d+1)}}\}_{i=0}^{2(d+1)}$ to srs$' := \{g^{\alpha'^{i-(d+1)}}\}_{i=0}^{2(d+1)}$ accordingly can be computed with much less effort than initializing a new **PC** instance. On the other hand, a malicious prover can use the extended srs to its favor, but we prove that this does not yield an attack on the security of our polynomial commitment scheme.

On the Choice of α in Class Groups. It is well-known that the ability to compute square roots in an RSA group, i.e., mod $N(= p \cdot q)$ with unknown factorization, is equivalent to factoring. However, in class groups, given $h_1 := g^x \in \mathsf{Cl}(\Delta)$, one can efficiently compute the "square root of h_1" given the factorization of Δ (in cryptographic applications of class groups $\Delta < 0$ and prime). Specifically, given a group element h_1, the algorithm outputs $h_2 = g^y$ such that $h_2^2 = g^{2y} = g^x$, or output $\bot$ if square roots do not exist [4]. This algorithm is due to Lagarias [36]. Assume for now that $\alpha = 2^k$.

We show next that such an α would render Behemoth insecure. If $\alpha = 2^k$, then for $z = 0$, $\forall s \in \mathbb{F}_p, \exists \pi_{\mathsf{Open},s} : \mathsf{OpenVerify}(\mathsf{srs}, \boxed{\mathsf{f}}, \mathsf{d}, 0, s, \pi_{\mathsf{Open},s}) = 1$ and such $\pi_{\mathsf{Open},s}$ can be found efficiently. In this case, the $\mathsf{OpenVerify}(\cdot)$ verification equation would be:

$$g^{\widehat{\mathsf{q}(\alpha)}(\alpha - z)} = \left(g^{\widehat{\mathsf{q}(\alpha)}}\right)^{2^k} \stackrel{?}{=} g^{\widehat{\mathsf{f}(\alpha)} - \widehat{s}}. \tag{9}$$

This check is vacuous if $\alpha = 2^k$ since the adversary can efficiently compute the 2^k-th root of any group element of $g^{\widehat{f(\alpha)} - \hat{s}}$ on the right-hand side of Eq. (9). Thus, if $\alpha = 2^k$ for any $k \in \mathbb{Z}$, the **PC** scheme's evaluation binding property would not hold.

Therefore, α cannot be a power of two, i.e., $\alpha \neq 2^k$. Similarly, α cannot be any value for which $\exists z \in \mathbb{F}_p$ such that $\alpha - \hat{z}$ is a power of two. For efficiency reasons, that is, to ensure a low Hamming weight for α, we set $\alpha = 2^k + 2^{k-1}$ for a $k \in \mathbb{Z}$ s.t. $\alpha \geq \mathcal{B}$.

4.3   Subprotocols of the Behemoth Open Protocol

Next, we detail the subprotocols of our Open protocol. First, we introduce a protocol called ProveEvaluation that allows the prover to convince the verifier that a Behemoth-committed polynomial f is evaluated to s at z. Second, we describe a protocol that allows the prover to show that a Behemoth-committed polynomial has degree maximum d.

The ProveEvaluation Protocol. In this protocol, we want to prove membership in the relation $\mathcal{R}_{eval} = \{(\boxed{\mathsf{f}}, z, s; \mathsf{f}) | \mathsf{f}(z) = s \wedge \mathsf{Com}(\mathsf{srs}, \mathsf{f}, \mathsf{d}) = \boxed{\mathsf{f}}\}$. The goal of the ProveEvaluation protocol is to mimic the KZG opening strategy soundly in the group of unknown order setting. Specifically, in the KZG opening proof to show that $\mathsf{f}(z) = s$, the prover demonstrates that $x - z$ divides $\mathsf{f}(x) - s$ by sending a commitment to $\mathsf{q}(x)$ such that the following verification equation is satisfied in the exponent

$$\mathsf{q}(x)(x - z) = \mathsf{f}(x) - s. \tag{10}$$

The challenge in our setting is that we need to work over the integers since the order of the group is hidden. This renders our statement to be $\widehat{\mathsf{f}(z)} = \hat{s}$. Therefore we check the KZG opening verification Eq. 10 in the exponent over the integers, i.e., we check polynomial equality in α:

$$\widehat{\mathsf{q}(\alpha)}(\alpha - z) = \widehat{\mathsf{f}(\alpha)} - \hat{s}. \tag{11}$$

This strategy entails several technical challenges that we solve with techniques mainly introduced in [3,13,50]. In particular, the following technical challenges arise when one translates the KZG opening strategy to the group of unknown order setting:

1. The prover can only compute $\widehat{\mathsf{q}(\alpha)}$ and not $\mathsf{q}(\alpha) \bmod p$ in the exponent. The prover sends $Q := g^{\widehat{\mathsf{q}(\alpha)}}$ as part of the opening proof. The prover uses the algorithm outlined in Fig. 4 to compute $g^{\widehat{\mathsf{q}(\alpha)}}$.
2. Due to efficiency reasons (recall $\alpha - z$ has $\approx \mathsf{d} \log p$ bits), the verifier cannot compute $Q^{\alpha - z}$ from the left-hand side of the verification Eq. 11 on its own, unlike in the bilinear pairing setting. This would entail a $\mathcal{O}(\log d + \log \log p)$ computation that would prevent us from achieving a constant-time verifier. Therefore, the verifier outsources this large exponentiation to the prover; that is, the prover needs to convince the verifier about the correctness of the exponentiation $Q^{\alpha - z}$ with a constant-size proof and in constant time [50].

3. On the right hand side of the verification Eq. 11, the prover computes $\widehat{s}$ in the exponent, i.e., $g^{\widehat{s}}$. The prover must convince the verifier with a constant proof in constant time that $\widehat{s}$ in $g^{\widehat{s}}$ has the same remainder mod p as s, i.e., $\widehat{s} \equiv s \bmod p$. This is achieved by the PoKEMon proof introduced in [13].

4. Finally, the prover shows that the exponent $\widehat{s}$ in $g^{\widehat{s}}$ lies in the appropriate range, i.e., $0 \leq \widehat{s} \leq \mathcal{B}$, recall that $\mathcal{B}$ is defined as a uniform upper bound on the integer evaluations at any polynomial, i.e., $\mathcal{B} := \max_{x \in \mathbb{F}_p, f(x) \in \mathbb{F}_p^{\leq d}[x]} \widehat{f(x)}$, cf. Sect. 3.1.

The ProveEvaluation(f, z, s) protocol

Statement: $\mathsf{f}(z) = s \land \mathsf{Com}(\mathsf{srs}, \mathsf{f}, d) = \boxed{\mathsf{f}}(= g^{\mathsf{f}(\alpha)})$.
Input: $\langle \mathcal{P}(\mathsf{srs}, \mathsf{f}, z, s), \mathcal{V}(g^\alpha, \boxed{\mathsf{f}}, z, s) \rangle$.

1. $\mathcal{P}$ sends $g^{\widehat{q(\alpha)}}$, where $\widehat{q(\alpha)} := \frac{\mathsf{f}(\alpha) - \widehat{s}}{\alpha - z}$, and $\widehat{s} := \widehat{\mathsf{f}(z)}$ over the integers. //$g^{\widehat{q(\alpha)}}$ is calculated using an algorithm in Figure 4.

2. $\mathcal{P}$ computes $g^{\widehat{q(\alpha)}(\alpha - z)}$ and obtains $\pi_{\mathsf{PoE}}^{\alpha - z} = \mathsf{NIZK.Prove}(\mathcal{R}_{\mathsf{PoE}}, \mathsf{crs}_{\mathsf{PoE}}, (g^{\widehat{q(\alpha)}}, g^{\widehat{q(\alpha)}(\alpha - z)}, \alpha - z), \perp)$.

   - In the verification of $\pi_{\mathsf{PoE}}^{\alpha - z}$, the verifier would need to compute $\alpha - z \bmod p' = \alpha \bmod p' - z \bmod p'$, where $p' \in_R \mathsf{Primes}(\lambda)$, see Wesolowski's proof of exponentiation protocol in [50]. Computing $\alpha \bmod p'$ would entail computing $\mathcal{O}(\log d)$ multiplications in $\mathbb{Z}_{p'}^*$. Hence, the verifier outsources this computation to the prover to avoid this logarithmic computation. The correctness of this outsourced computation is proved by $\pi_{\mathsf{PoKEMon}}^{\alpha, \alpha \bmod p'} := \mathsf{NIZK.Prove}(\mathcal{R}_{\mathsf{PoKEMon}}, \mathsf{crs}_{\mathsf{PoKEMon}}, (g^\alpha, g^{\alpha \bmod p'}), \alpha)$.

3. $\mathcal{P}$ sends $g^{\widehat{s}}$ to the verifier $\mathcal{V}$ and calculates $\pi_{\mathsf{PoKEMon}}^{s, \widehat{s}} := \mathsf{NIZK.Prove}(\mathcal{R}_{\mathsf{PoKEMon}}, \mathsf{crs}_{\mathsf{PoKEMon}}, (g^s, g^{\widehat{s}}), \widehat{s})$. //This ensures that $s \equiv \widehat{s} \bmod p$.

4. Let $J := g^{\mathcal{B}}/g^{\widehat{s}}$. The prover creates the proof $\pi_{\mathsf{PoKPE}}^{\mathcal{B} - \widehat{s}} := \mathsf{NIZK.Prove}(\mathcal{R}_{\mathsf{PoKPE}}, \mathsf{crs}_{\mathsf{PoKPE}}, J, \mathcal{B} - \widehat{s})$ and also computes $\pi_{\mathsf{PoKPE}}^{\widehat{s}} := \mathsf{NIZK.Prove}(\mathcal{R}_{\mathsf{PoKPE}}, \mathsf{crs}_{\mathsf{PoKPE}}, g^{\widehat{s}}, \widehat{s})$. //These proofs ensure that $0 \leq \widehat{s} \leq \mathcal{B}$.

The proof: $\pi_{\mathsf{ProveEvaluation}}^z := (\pi_{\mathsf{PoE}}^{\alpha - z}, \pi_{\mathsf{PoKEMon}}^{\alpha, \alpha \bmod p'}, \pi_{\mathsf{PoKEMon}}^{s, \widehat{s}}, \pi_{\mathsf{PoKPE}}^{\mathcal{B} - \widehat{s}}, \pi_{\mathsf{PoKPE}}^{\widehat{s}})$.
Verification: Parse the $\pi_{\mathsf{ProveEvaluation}}^z$ proof as the tuple $\pi_{\mathsf{ProveEvaluation}}^z = (\pi_{\mathsf{PoE}}^{\alpha - z}, \pi_{\mathsf{PoKEMon}}^{\alpha, \alpha \bmod p'}, \pi_{\mathsf{PoKEMon}}^{s, \widehat{s}}, \pi_{\mathsf{PoKPE}}^{\mathcal{B} - \widehat{s}}, \pi_{\mathsf{PoKPE}}^{\widehat{s}})$.
Output: $\mathsf{NIZK.Verify}(\mathcal{R}_{\mathsf{PoE}}, \mathsf{crs}_{\mathsf{PoE}}, \phi_{\mathsf{PoE}}, \pi_{\mathsf{PoE}}^{\alpha - z}) \land$
$\land \mathsf{NIZK.Verify}(\mathcal{R}_{\mathsf{PoKEMon}}, \mathsf{crs}_{\mathsf{PoKEMon}}, \phi_{\mathsf{PoKEMon}}, \pi_{\mathsf{PoKEMon}}^{\alpha, \alpha \bmod p'}) \land$
$\land \mathsf{NIZK.Verify}(\mathcal{R}_{\mathsf{PoKEMon}}, \mathsf{crs}_{\mathsf{PoKEMon}}, \phi_{\mathsf{PoKEMon}}, \pi_{\mathsf{PoKEMon}}^{s, \widehat{s}}) \land$
$\land \mathsf{NIZK.Verify}(\mathcal{R}_{\mathsf{PoKPE}}, \mathsf{crs}_{\mathsf{PoKPE}}, \phi_{\mathsf{PoKPE}}, \pi_{\mathsf{PoKPE}}^{\mathcal{B} - \widehat{s}}) \land$
$\land \mathsf{NIZK.Verify}(\mathcal{R}_{\mathsf{PoKPE}}, \mathsf{crs}_{\mathsf{PoKPE}}, \phi_{\mathsf{PoKPE}}, \pi_{\mathsf{PoKPE}}^{\widehat{s}})$.

Fig. 2. Behemoth ProveEvaluation protocol formal description. In the ProveEvaluation protocol, the prover convinces the verifier that $\mathsf{f}(z) = s$. It is a subprotocol of the Behemoth Open protocol, cf. Fig. 1.

Lemma 1. *The* ProveEvaluation *protocol (cf. Fig. 2) satisfies evaluation binding, i.e., it is not possible to show simultaneously that* $f(z) = s \wedge f(z) = s'$ *such that* $s \neq s'$ *for a Behemoth-committed polynomial* f.

The proof is provided in the full version of this work.

Note that at this point, we did not ensure that the committed polynomial f is in the desired polynomial ring $\mathbb{F}_p^{\leq d}[x]$. In particular, the committer might use polynomials of 1) higher degree than d, and 2) due to availability of negative powers of α in the exponent, i.e., $g^{\alpha^{-i}}$, in the srs, the committer might include monomials of x^{-i} in the committed polynomial. Next, we develop tools to prevent an adversarial prover from successfully opening such polynomials, i.e., with non-negligible probability.

Proving a Degree Bound of the Behemoth-Committed Polynomial. A crucial part of the Open protocol is to ensure that the committed polynomial $f \in \mathbb{F}_p^{\leq d}[x]$ has a degree less than or equal to d. This is not immediate in our setting, unlike in the KZG setting. Specifically, in the KZG PCS, if the srs has length d, then an efficient prover *cannot commit to polynomials of degree larger than* d as long as the d-polyDH assumption holds. This is because the exponents in the KZG srs are hidden, thanks to the trusted setup. However, in our setting, anyone can freely extend the srs to be able to support larger degree polynomials. Therefore, we must deal with malicious provers that can commit to arbitrarily large degree polynomials; $deg(f) \in \mathcal{O}(poly(\lambda))$. We follow the footsteps of Thakur and adapt his zero-knowledge proof systems about KZG-committed polynomials introduced in [46] to the group of unknown order setting.

*Proof of Knowledge of a Polynomial with a Degree Upper Bound (*PoKDegUp*).* The main goal of this subsection is to build a proof system that can show that a Behemoth-committed polynomial has degree most d using the previously introduced building blocks, i.e., PoKE, PoKPE, ProveEvaluation. We adapt Thakur's corresponding proof system for KZG-committed polynomials [46] to Behemoth-committed polynomials.

Thakur observes that $\forall d \in \mathbb{N}, \forall f \in \mathbb{Z}[x] : deg(f) \leq d \iff x | x^{d+1} \cdot f(x^{-1})$. Note the verifier already knows a commitment to x^{d+1} from the srs, i.e., let $a := \boxed{x^{d+1}}$ be the corresponding srs commitment to the monomial of degree $d+1$. The prover then sends a Behemoth-commitment to $b := \boxed{x^{d+1}f(x^{-1})}$ along with a PoKE(g^α, b) that shows that b is a commitment to a polynomial divisible by x. This is where it is important that α is not a power of two. Otherwise, this PoKE(g^α, b) proof is vacuous since, in class groups, it is possible to compute the roots of powers of two due to Lagarias [36]. We remark that we need the "negative" powers of α in the srs to commit to $f(1/x)$. Now, the prover shows the well-formedness of commitment b, i.e., that it is indeed a commitment to $x^{d+1}f(x^{-1})$. For a randomly generated challenge $\gamma \in_R \mathbb{F}_p^*$, the prover verifiably sends the element $g^{\widehat{f(\gamma)}}$, along with an evaluation proof that this is a commitment to the evaluation of $f(x)$ at γ, see the ProveEvaluation protocol at Fig. 2. The prover also sends the element $c := \boxed{x^{d+1}\widehat{f(\gamma)}} = g^{\alpha^{d+1}\widehat{f(\gamma)}}$ along with a Chaum-Pedersen proof [21] (also known as the discrete logarithm equality (DLEq) proof) to show that the discrete logarithms between the pair $(g, g^{\widehat{f(\gamma)}})$ and the pair $(g^{\alpha^{d+1}}, c)$ are the same, namely the common discrete logarithm is $\widehat{f(\gamma)}$. Next, the prover shows that the polynomial $h(x) := x^{d+1}f(x^{-1})$ committed in b satisfies the following relation:

$$\gamma h(x) \equiv \gamma x^{d+1} f(\gamma) \bmod (\gamma x - 1). \tag{12}$$

The prover does so by producing a $(\gamma\alpha - 1)$-th root of $b^\gamma \cdot c^{-\gamma} = g^{\gamma\alpha^{d+1}\widehat{f(1/\alpha)} - \gamma\alpha^{d+1}\widehat{f(\gamma)}}$. Since γ is randomly generated, this implies that with overwhelming probability, $h(x) = x^{d+1} \cdot f(x^{-1})$, due to the order assumption, see Sect. 3.4. Hence, the following proof system is an honest verifier zero-knowledge proof for the following relation:

$$\mathcal{R}_{\mathsf{PoKDegUp}}[f, d] = \{\boxed{f} \in \mathbb{G}, f(x) \in \mathbb{Q}[x], d \in \mathbb{Z} : g^{\widehat{f(\alpha)}} = \boxed{f}, deg(f) \leq d\}.$$

The PoKDegUp(f, d) protocol

Statement: The prover $\mathcal{P}$ knows a polynomial $f(x) \in \mathbb{Q}[x]$ such that $\boxed{f} = g^{\widehat{f(\alpha)}} \wedge deg(f) \leq d$.
Input: $\langle \mathcal{P}(\mathsf{srs}, f, d, \boxed{f}), \mathcal{V}(g^{\alpha^{d+1}}, d, \boxed{f}) \rangle$.

1. $\mathcal{P}$ sends the element $b := g^{\alpha^{d+1} \cdot f(1/\alpha)}$ with a proof for $\mathsf{PoKE}[g^\alpha, b]$.
2. $\mathcal{P}$ samples a challenge $\gamma \in_R \mathbb{F}_p^*$ using the Fiat-Shamir transformation.
3. $\mathcal{P}$ sends the elements $g^{\widehat{f(\gamma)}}$ and $c := g^{\alpha^{d+1}\widehat{f(\gamma)}}$ with a Chaum-Pedersen DLEq proof for the pairs $(g, g^{\widehat{f(\gamma)}})$ and $(g^{\alpha^{d+1}}, c)$.
4. $\mathcal{P}$ runs the protocol ProveEvaluation$(f, \gamma, f(\gamma))$, i.e., the prover convinces the verifier that $f(\gamma)$ evaluates to a certain value.
5. $\mathcal{P}$ sends proofs for $\mathsf{PoKE}[g^{\alpha-\gamma}, g^{\widehat{f(\alpha)}-\widehat{f(\gamma)}}]$ and $\mathsf{PoKE}[g^{\gamma\alpha-1}, b^\gamma c^{-\gamma}]$.

The proof: $\pi_{\mathsf{PoKDegUp}}^{f,d} := (\mathsf{PoKE}[g^\alpha, b], \mathsf{ChaumP}[g, g^{\widehat{f(\gamma)}}, g^{\alpha^{d+1}}, c]),$
ProveEvaluation$[f, \gamma, f(\gamma)], \mathsf{PoKE}[g^{\alpha-\gamma}, g^{\widehat{f(\alpha)}-\widehat{f(\gamma)}}], \mathsf{PoKE}[g^{\gamma\alpha-1}, b^\gamma c^{-\gamma}].$
Verification: $\mathcal{V}$ verifies the ProveEvaluation, PoKE, and the Chaum-Pedersen DLEq proofs.

Fig. 3. Proof of knowledge of f with degree upper bounded (PoKDegUp). The prover convinces the verifier that the degree of the committed polynomial f is upper bounded by an integer d. PoKDegUp is a subprotocol of the Behemoth Open protocol, cf. Fig. 1.

Example. What would constitute a soundness break of the PoKDegUp protocol? Consider the polynomial $f(x) = x^2 + 3\alpha^3$. This polynomial has the same Behemoth-commitment as $g(x) = 3x^3 + x^2$. From the verifier's perspective, it is indistinguishable which of these polynomials f or g are "in the prover's head". However, it is easy to see that the prover can only run successfully the ProveEvaluation(f, z, s) protocol for any $z \in \mathbb{F}_p$ with the evaluations of $s := g(z)$ due to the applied range checks in the ProveEvaluation protocol. We call such two polynomials *evaluation equivalent*, cf. Definition 1. Motivated by this discussion, we want the prover not to be able to prove that its committed polynomial f has $deg(f) \leq 2$. It is easy to see that this holds in this simple case. If the prover wants to show that $deg(f) \leq 2$ in the commitment $\boxed{f}$, then $f(1/x) = \frac{1}{x^2} + 3\alpha^3$. In the last step of the PoKDegUp protocol, the prover must show that $\gamma\alpha - 1|\gamma f_d \alpha^{d+1}\widehat{f(1/\alpha)} - \gamma f_d \alpha^{d+1}\widehat{f(\gamma)}$. In this particular example, this check entails to $\gamma\alpha - 1|\gamma\alpha^3(\frac{1}{\alpha^2} + 3\alpha^3) - \gamma\alpha^3(\gamma^2 + 3\gamma^3) = \gamma\alpha(1 + 3\alpha^5) - \gamma\alpha(\gamma^2\alpha^2 + 3\gamma^3\alpha^2)$. Since $gcd(\gamma\alpha - 1, \gamma\alpha) = 1$, therefore $\gamma\alpha - 1|3\alpha^5 - 3\alpha^2\gamma^3 - (\gamma\alpha + 1)(\gamma\alpha - 1) \iff \gamma\alpha - 1|3\alpha^5 - 3\alpha^2\gamma^3 = 3\alpha^2(\alpha^3 - \gamma^3) \iff (\gamma\alpha - 1)|(\alpha^3 - \gamma^3)$. Since $gcd(\gamma\alpha - 1, \alpha^3) = 1$, we have that $(\gamma\alpha - 1)|(\alpha^3 - \gamma^3) \iff (\gamma\alpha - 1)|\alpha^3(\alpha^3 - \gamma^3) = \alpha^6 - \gamma^3\alpha^3$. Because of $(\gamma\alpha - 1)|\gamma^3\alpha^3 - 1$, it suffices to show that $(\gamma\alpha - 1)|\alpha^6 - 1$, where the right-hand side does not contain γ anymore, that is chosen by the verifier uniformly at random. We conclude that the prover cannot convince the verifier that $f(x) = x^2 + 3\alpha^3$ is a quadratic polynomial. Next, we prove that the PoKDegUp protocol is secure in full generality.

Lemma 2. *The PoKDegUp protocol, see Fig. 3, is knowledge sound for the relation* $\mathcal{R}_{\text{PoKDegUp}} = \{(\boxed{f}, d; f)|f \in \mathbb{Q}[x] \wedge deg(f) \leq d\}$ *in the generic group and random oracle models.*

Proof. Suppose a PPT algorithm $\mathcal{A}$ outputs an accepting transcript. The extractability of the subprotocols PoKE$[g^{\alpha-\gamma}, g^{\widehat{f(\alpha)} - \widehat{f(\gamma)}}]$ and PoKE$[g^{\gamma\alpha-1}, b^\gamma c^{-\gamma}]$ imply that with overwhelming probability, $\mathcal{A}$ can output polynomials $f(x), g(x) = x^{d+1}f(\gamma), h(x) = x^{d+1}f(1/x)$ such that

$$g^{\widehat{f(\alpha)}} = \boxed{f}, g^{\widehat{g(\alpha)}} = g^{\alpha^d \widehat{f(\gamma)}} = b, g^{\widehat{f(\gamma)}}, g^{\widehat{h(\alpha)}} = c, \gamma h(x) \equiv \gamma g(x) \bmod (\gamma x - 1). \tag{13}$$

Since we do not assume the Knowledge of Exponent Assumption (KEA), we cannot immediately claim that such polynomials can be extracted from the prover. Instead, we argue as follows. Due to the extractability of the applied NIZK proof systems, the prover must *know* an integer in the exponent for every Behemoth commitment. Therefore, whenever we say that the prover knows a polynomial for a commitment, we refer to the unique polynomial that is derived from the α-adic representation of the integer known by the prover in the exponent. The Chaum-Pedersen DLEq proof implies that

$$g^{\alpha^{d+1}\widehat{f(\gamma)}} = a^{\widehat{f(\gamma)}} = c = g^{\widehat{h(\alpha)}} \tag{14}$$

Thus, the verifier checks in the exponent that

$$x^{d+1}f(x^{-1}) \equiv g(x) \bmod (\gamma x - 1), \tag{15}$$

and since γ was randomly and uniformly generated, this implies that with overwhelming probability $g(x) = x^{d+1}f(x^{-1})$ holds. This is because if it was the case that $g(x) \neq x^{d+1}f(x^{-1})$ and there was a non-negligible probability of finding a suitable γ for which $g(\gamma) \equiv \gamma^{d+1}f(\gamma^{-1}) \mod ord(\mathbb{G})$, then $g(\gamma) - \gamma^{d+1}f(\gamma^{-1}) \equiv 0 \mod ord(\mathbb{G})$ contradicting the order assumption, see Sect. 3.4. Finally, the sub-protocol $\mathsf{PoKE}[g^\alpha, b]$ implies that with overwhelming probability, $g(x)$ is divisible by x, hence it follows that $deg(\mathsf{f}) \leq \mathsf{d}$.

The only thing remaining to show is the case when the prover does not use the canonic α-adic polynomial representation of a polynomial. Let $deg_\alpha(\mathsf{f})$ be the degree of the canonical α-adic representation of the Behemoth-committed polynomial $\boxed{\mathsf{f}}$. On the other hand, let $deg^*(\mathsf{f})$ be the degree of the malicious prover's interpretation of $\boxed{\mathsf{f}}$, where $deg^*(\mathsf{f}) \neq deg_\alpha(\mathsf{f})$. Due to the correctness of this protocol, the following check for the honest prover needs to be satisfied,

$$(\gamma\alpha - 1)|\gamma\mathsf{h}(\alpha) - \alpha^{deg_\alpha(\mathsf{f})+1}\gamma\widehat{\mathsf{f}(\gamma)}. \tag{16}$$

Now, suppose that the prover applies a different polynomial h' in the check, that is,

$$(\gamma\alpha - 1)|\gamma\mathsf{h}'(\alpha) - \alpha^{deg^*(\mathsf{f})+1}\gamma\widehat{\mathsf{f}(\gamma)}. \tag{17}$$

If we subtract Eq. 17 from Eq. 16, then we find that the malicious prover must satisfy the following division,

$$(\gamma\alpha - 1)|\gamma(\mathsf{h}(\alpha) - \mathsf{h}'(\alpha)) - \gamma(\alpha^{deg_\alpha(\mathsf{f})} - \alpha^{deg^*(\mathsf{f})})\widehat{\mathsf{f}(\gamma)}, \tag{18}$$

where $gcd(\gamma\alpha - 1, \gamma) = 1$, thus we can eliminate γ. Note that $\widehat{\mathsf{f}(\gamma)}$ can be opened to a single evaluation due to the evaluation binding property of the ProveEvaluation protocol. Towards contradiction, assume that $\alpha^{deg_\alpha(\mathsf{f})} \neq \alpha^{deg^*(\mathsf{f})}$. We have the following congruence for $\widehat{\mathsf{f}(\gamma)}$,

$$\widehat{\mathsf{f}(\gamma)} \equiv \frac{\mathsf{h}(\alpha) - \mathsf{h}'(\alpha)}{\alpha^{deg_\alpha(\mathsf{f})} - \alpha^{deg^*(\mathsf{f})}} \mod (\gamma\alpha - 1). \tag{19}$$

Both the nominator $(\mathsf{h}(\alpha) - \mathsf{h}'(\alpha))$ and the denominator $\alpha^{deg_\alpha(\mathsf{f})} - \alpha^{deg^*(\mathsf{f})}$ are established before $\gamma \in_R \mathbb{F}_p$ is sent to the prover from the verifier or equivalently in the random oracle model, sampled via the Fiat-Shamir transformation [29]. Since $\widehat{\mathsf{f}(\gamma)}$ is proved by the committer to be the evaluation of f at γ, and the evaluation binding property of the ProveEvaluation protocol has been shown, we conclude that Eq. 19 can be satisfied only with negligible probability. ∎

Flexible Behemoth Open *Proofs over Multiple Fields.* Since the Behemoth-commitment of a polynomial f commits to it over the integers, one can reuse a commitment to later open the same commitment over different fields $\mathbb{F}_p$ and $\mathbb{F}_{p'}$. This flexibility might have several applications, as discussed next. Observe that all steps except one in the whole Open protocol are oblivious to the choice of the field $\mathbb{F}_p$ over which the committed polynomial is opened. The sole exception is the third step in the ProveEvaluation protocol, namely where the prover shows for the opening statement $f(z) = s$ that $\hat{s} \equiv s \mod p$ holds with a PoKEMon proof, cf. Fig. 2. If the p-dependent bound $\mathcal{B}$ for evaluations of polynomials (cf. Eq. 1) remains smaller than α, one can safely open a Behemoth-committed polynomial over that field $\mathbb{F}_p$ as well.

5   Security Proofs

In this section, we prove the security of our polynomial commitment scheme.

Theorem 1. *(Behemoth is a secure* **PC** *scheme) The Behemoth* **PC** *scheme satisfies correctness, evaluation binding, knowledge soundness, polynomial binding, and evaluation hiding in the generic group and random oracle models.*

Due to space constraints, we only include our knowledge soundness proofs. We refer the reader to the full version for the missing proofs.

5.1   Knowledge Soundness

Due to the transparent nature of our PCS, it is inherent that a prover is only bound to $\widehat{f(\alpha)}$ rather than a unique polynomial $f \in \mathbb{F}_p^{\leq d}[x]$. At first, this seems to violate knowledge soundness. However, since evaluation binding holds, see the full version of this work, the map $g : z \mapsto f(z) \bmod p$ is set to stone after committing to f. Below we show that the existence of this map g implies the knowledge of a   mod p polynomial f^* in the desired polynomial ring $\mathbb{F}_p^{\leq d}[x]$.

Consider $\boxed{f} := g^\alpha$, it may seem ambiguous whether it is a commitment to $f(x) = x$ or $f(x) = \alpha$. We remark that in the ProveEvaluation protocol, the prover can only open the $f(x) = x$ polynomial. This is because the applied range proofs in the ProveEvaluation protocol, i.e., the prover needs to show that at the evaluated point z, we have that $0 \leq \widehat{f(z)} \leq \mathcal{B}(< \alpha)$. Therefore, it is clear that the prover can only evaluate the $f(x) = x$ polynomial for every $z \in \mathbb{F}_p$. Note that without range proofs on $\widehat{f(z)}$ in the ProveEvaluation protocol, the prover could convince the verifier about the validity of any $\widehat{f(z)} + h(z)(\alpha - z)$ value evaluated of the committed polynomial at z. Thanks to the applied range proof, the committer can only evaluate the commitment $\boxed{f}$ as $f(z) = z$, this being the smallest positive representative of $\widehat{f(z)} \bmod \alpha - z$. This observation motivates the following definition.

Definition 1 (Evaluation Proxy). *The polynomial* $f_1 \in \mathbb{Q}^{\leq d}[x]$ *is an evaluation proxy for* $f_0 \in \mathbb{Q}^{\leq d}[x]$, *i.e.,* $f_0 \rightarrow_{Eval} f_1$ *if* $\forall z :$ OpenVerify$(srs, \boxed{f_0}, z, f_0(z), \pi_{Open}^{f_0,z}) = 1; \widehat{f_0(z)} \equiv \widehat{f_1(z)} \bmod \alpha - z$. *Put differently,* $\widehat{f_0(z)} = \widehat{f_1(z)} + h(z)(\alpha - z)$, *for some* $h(z) \in \mathbb{Z}$. *In other words, whenever* f_0 *is opened successfully at* z, *it has the same evaluation as* f_1 *at* z. *If* $f_0 \rightarrow_{Eval} f_1 \wedge f_1 \rightarrow_{Eval} f_0$ *holds, then we say that* f_0 *and* f_1 *are evaluation equivalent, i.e.,* $f_0 \equiv_{Eval} f_1$.

Example. $\alpha^2 + 3\alpha \rightarrow_{Eval} x^2 + 3x$. They are different polynomials   mod p, but they behave the same from an evaluation point of view. Even though the former polynomial can be considered a constant polynomial, anywhere the committer can open $\alpha^2 + 3\alpha$, it will "behave" as a polynomial $x^2 + 3x$. For every $z \in \mathbb{F}_p$, the committer can create convincing ProveEvaluation proofs such that $f(z) = z^2 + 3z$.

The previously proved evaluation binding property implies that this is the only way the prover can open a Behemoth commitment of a polynomial in $\mathbb{Q}[x]$. Similarly, it is easy to see that $x^2 + 3x \rightarrow_{\mathsf{Eval}} \alpha^2 + 3\alpha$ holds.

Example 2. $\frac{\alpha^2 + \alpha \cdot x}{2} \rightarrow_{\mathsf{Eval}} x^2$. One can only open successfully $\frac{\alpha^2 + \alpha \cdot x}{2}$ at points where $\alpha \equiv z \mod 2$. And at any successfully openable point z, $\frac{\alpha^2 + \alpha \cdot x}{2}$ has exactly the same evaluation as x^2. Observe that, on the other hand, $x^2 \not\rightarrow_{\mathsf{Eval}} \frac{\alpha^2 + \alpha \cdot x}{2}$, since there exist points z where x^2 can be opened, while for $\frac{\alpha^2 + \alpha \cdot x}{2}$ could not be opened.

Polynomials that can be opened at least at a single point z with non-negligible probability will play a crucial role in our knowledge soundness proof. Recall from Fig. 1, steps (2) and (3) in the Open protocol, this means that the prover can successfully run the ProveEvaluation protocol with non-negligible probability for a randomly chosen $z' \in \mathbb{F}_p$. We define openable polynomials formally as follows.

Definition 2 (Openable polynomials). *Given a valid* srs, *a polynomial* $\mathsf{f} \in (\mathbb{Q} \cap \mathbb{Z}_p)^{\leq \mathsf{d}}[x]$ *is said to be* openable *if*

$$\exists z \exists s \exists \pi_{\mathsf{Open}}^{*,\mathsf{f},z} \forall \mathsf{negl}(\lambda) \Pr[\mathsf{OpenVerify}(\mathsf{srs}, \boxed{\mathsf{f}}, \mathsf{d}, z, s, \pi_{\mathsf{Open}}^{*,\mathsf{f},z}) = 1] \geq \mathsf{negl}(\lambda) \quad (20)$$

where $\pi_{\mathsf{Open}}^{*,\mathsf{f},z}$ *a maliciously generated opening proof for* f, z, s.

As we saw in the proof of correctness in the full version, honest provers can always convince the verifier about correct openings. However, as noted above, we cannot force provers to use the canonical lifts of polynomials in $\mathbb{F}_p^{\leq \mathsf{d}}[x]$. For instance, consider the polynomial of $2x^3 - x + 7$. Due to its linear term $\mathsf{Lift}(\mathsf{Project}(2x^3 - x + 7)) \neq 2x^3 - x + 7$, but the prover can open everywhere the Behemoth commitment of $2x^3 - x + 7$. It is easy to argue that the opened values are always the same $\mod p$ as for $\mathsf{Lift}(\mathsf{Project}(2x^3 - x + 7)) = 2x^3 + (p-1)x + 7$, as expected. Thus, $\mod p$ knowledge soundness holds.

Definition 3 (p-faithful polynomial). *A polynomial* $\mathsf{f} \in \mathbb{Q}^{\leq \mathsf{d}}[x]$ *is said to be* p-faithful *if* $\forall z \in \mathbb{F}_p$ *where* f *can be opened with non-negligible probability, the evaluation* $\mathsf{f}(z) = s \equiv \mathsf{Project}(\mathsf{f})(z) \mod p$.

By the design of the ProveEvaluation protocol, all polynomials in $\mathbb{F}_p^{\leq \mathsf{d}}[x]$ are p-faithful. As the example above shows, there are polynomials in $\mathbb{Q}^{\leq \mathsf{d}}[x] \setminus \mathbb{F}_p^{\leq \mathsf{d}}[x]$ that are p-faithful. What poses a challenge to proving knowledge soundness is that not all openable polynomials are p-faithful polynomials.

Example. $\mathsf{f}(x) = \alpha$. Observe that f *is not* p-faithful. Although it is openable everywhere and its evaluations are congruent $\mod p$ to the $\mathsf{f}(x) = x$ polynomial. Yet, the commitment to the f polynomial could be viewed as a commitment to a constant polynomial. Even if the prover considers the committed polynomial a constant, it can only open it as the identity function of $\mathbb{F}_p$. This does not contradict knowledge soundness since the prover's behavior is identical to a prover who considers the committed polynomial as $f(x) = x$. As we shall show, the opening behavior of any openable polynomial can be reproduced by a p-faithful polynomial.

Lemma 3. *If $f_0 \in \mathbb{Q}^{\leq d}[x]$ is an openable polynomial, then there exists f^* such that $f_0 \rightarrow_{\mathsf{Eval}} f^*$ and f^* is p-faithful.*

Proof. If f_0 is an openable polynomial, we rewind $d+1$ times the execution of the Open protocol to immediately before step (2), cf. Fig. 1, with fresh randomness $z_i \in_R \mathbb{F}_p$ in each round $i \in [0, d]$. Every round $\forall i : i \in [0, d]$, the prover must also run the ProveEvaluation(f_0, z_i, s_i) protocol. Thus, the extractor obtains with non-negligible probability, two vectors $T := \{z_i\}_{i=0}^d$ and $\{s_i\}_{i=0}^d$ such that $\forall i \in [0, d] : f_0(z_i) = s_i$ holds. The soundness of the PoKDegUp protocol, cf. Sect. 4.3, ensures that f_0 is a maximum d degree polynomial. Therefore, next, the extractor Lagrange-interpolates a degree d polynomial $f^* \in \mathbb{Q}^{\leq d}[x]$ given the obtained valid evaluations from the rewinding process. These evaluations are unique due to evaluation binding proved in the full version. Hence, the Lagrange-interpolation f^* of f has the form:

$$f^*(x) := \sum_{i=0}^{d} s_i \mathcal{L}_i(x) = \sum_{i=0}^{d} s_i \prod_{j=0, j\neq i}^{d} \frac{x - z_j}{z_i - z_j} \leq (p-1) \sum_{i=0}^{d} \left| \prod_{j=0, j\neq i}^{d} \frac{x - z_j}{z_i - z_j} \right| =$$

$$= (p-1) \sum_{i=0}^{d} |\mathcal{L}_i(x)|,$$

(21)

where we call the polynomials $\{\mathcal{L}_i(x)\}_{i=0}^d$ as *Lagrange polynomials* or *Lagrange basis*. We want to obtain an upper-bound for the Lagrange-interpolation polynomial f^* on $[0, p)$ using Eq. 21. Let us divide the $[0, p)$ interval into 2d equal length intervals $S_i := \left[\frac{p \cdot i}{2d}, \frac{p \cdot (i+1)}{2d}\right)_{i=0}^{2d-1}$. For a better estimate on $\max_{x \in [0, p)} f^*(x)$, we slightly increase the running time of the extractor until we obtain sample points z_i that are sufficiently close to being equidistant. This helps us obtain a better upper bound on the Lagrange basis polynomials by avoiding "too small" denominators. Thus, the extractor selects uniformly at random interpolation points z_i from the interval $[0, p)$. According to the coupon collector's problem [27], the extractor must sample $\approx 2d \log 2d$ points on average to sample at least one interpolation point from every segment in $S^* := \{S_i : i \equiv 0 \mod 2\}$. Let the set of interpolation points, $T = \{z_i\}_{i=0}^d$, consisting of the $d + 1$ points chosen so that we choose one point from every segment in S^*. Note that points in T are close to be equidistant, i.e., $\forall i : \frac{p}{2d} \leq |z_i - z_{i+1}| \leq \frac{3p}{2d}$. We upper bound for these interpolation points $\max_{x \in [0, p)} f^*(x)$ as follows.

$$\max_{x\in[0,p)} \mathsf{f}^*(x) \leq (p-1)\sum_{i=0}^{\mathsf{d}} \left| \prod_{j=0,j\neq i}^{\mathsf{d}} \frac{x-z_j}{z_i-z_j} \right| \leq p\sum_{i=0}^{\mathsf{d}} \left| \frac{\prod_{j=0,j\neq i}^{\mathsf{d}} \frac{(j+1)p}{\mathsf{d}}}{\prod_{j=0,j\neq i}^{\mathsf{d}/2} (\frac{(2j+1)p}{2\mathsf{d}})^2} \right| \leq$$

$$\leq 2^{\mathsf{d}+1}p\sum_{i=0}^{\mathsf{d}} \left| \frac{\prod_{j=0,j\neq i}^{\mathsf{d}} (j+1)}{\prod_{j=0,j\neq i}^{\mathsf{d}/2} (2j+1)^2} \right| \leq 2^{\mathsf{d}+1}p(\mathsf{d}+1) \ll \alpha.$$

Next, we show that f^* is p-faithful, i.e., p-faithfulness is implied by the following:

$$\max_{x\in[0,p)} \mathsf{f}^*(x) \leq \alpha. \tag{22}$$

A successful evaluation of f^* at a point z means that $\mathsf{f}^*(z) - k(z-\alpha) \in [0, \mathcal{B}]$ for some $k \in \mathbb{Z}$. Equation 22 implies that this can only happen for $k = 0$. Therefore, since $k = 0$ for every opened evaluation point, the extracted polynomial gives the correct mod p evaluation, i.e., $\mathsf{f}^*(z)$. This concludes the proof of knowledge soundness as we showed that the extracted polynomial f^* behaves as f_0 from an evaluation point of view, more formally serves as an evaluation proxy for f_0, cf. Definition 1. Additionally, the extracted polynomial f^* has the property of p-faithfulness (which f_0 may lack), i.e., opening the integer substitution value at a point z and reducing it mod p yields the same result as taking all coefficients of f^* mod p.   ∎

6   Performance Analysis

6.1   Transparent Setup Efficiency

The $\mathsf{GenSRS}(1^\lambda, \mathsf{d})$ algorithm is transparent and somewhat time-sensitive as it incurs large exponentiations; computing $g^{\alpha^{\mathsf{d}}}$ entails $\mathsf{d}\log\alpha$ repeated squaring. Since $\alpha \approx p^{\mathsf{d}}$, the setup algorithm has a quadratic complexity $\mathcal{O}(\mathsf{d}^2\log p)$ in the degree d of the committed polynomial. This transparent setup only needs to be performed once. It is extensible in the sense that there is no limitation on the maximum degree of the committed polynomial. The extensibility of the srs might be valuable in certain applications, e.g., zkSNARKs. Whoever computes the Behemoth srs can also prove the correctness of the setup by proving that for every pair of neighboring elements in the srs, the exponentiation was done correctly. They can prove this by enclosing proofs of exponentiations for $\forall i$: $(g^{\alpha^i}, g^{\alpha^{i+1}})_{i=0}^{\mathsf{d}-1}$ [40,50]. In a typical parameters setting ($\mathsf{d} = 2^{20}, p \approx 2^{256}$), the setup algorithm entails computing $g^{\alpha^{\mathsf{d}}}$, i.e., one must compute $\approx \mathsf{d}^2\log p = 2^{48}$ repeated squarings to complete the transparent setup. This computation has a similar computational complexity to the LCS time-lock puzzle created by Rivest [42]. To compute the LCS time-lock puzzle, one needed to compute $\approx 2^{47}$ repeated squarings. Originally, the LCS time-lock puzzle was intended to last 35 years. However, on specialized hardware using novel techniques [38], it is possible to accomplish this computation in less than two months. Certainly, the complexity of the setup algorithm becomes more feasible for smaller polynomial commitment schemes, e.g., $d \in \{2^{12}, 2^{13}, 2^{14}, 2^{15}\}$. Such a shorter **PC** scheme has been recently deployed for a data availability application on the Ethereum blockchain [51] (Table 1).

Table 1. Comparing the performances of **PC** schemes. We only enclose the most efficient representative from each cryptographic approach to keep the table compact. Properties in red are undesirable or impractical, and properties in orange become an issue for polynomials with larger degrees d. Properties achieved in green indicate practical, efficient constructions or desirable characteristics. To account for the differences in the concrete efficiency of the applied groups, we denote the applied cryptographic groups differently. Specifically, schemes that are instantiated in groups equipped with bilinear pairings are denoted as $\mathbb{G}_P$, while groups of unknown orders are denoted as $\mathbb{G}_U$. Groups where one only needs to assume the discrete logarithm assumption or the existence of one-way functions are denoted as $\mathbb{G}$. Here, we report an optimized Behemoth proof size achieved by proof batching described in Sect. 6. Recall that Dew's verifier complexity is $\mathcal{O}(\log d)$ *field operations*, i.e., for practical parameter choices, logarithmic verifier complexity may be better than $\mathcal{O}(1)$ verifier complexity.

	|Com|	Open proof sizes $|\pi_{\mathsf{Open}}|$	Open time complexity Prove	Verify	|srs|	Setup
KZG [32]	$1\mathbb{G}_P$	$1\mathbb{G}_P$	$\mathcal{O}(d)$	$\mathcal{O}(1)$	$\mathcal{O}(d)\mathbb{G}_P$	Trusted
Bootle et al. [16]	$1\mathbb{G}$	$\mathcal{O}(\sqrt{d})\mathbb{G}$	$\mathcal{O}(d)$	$\mathcal{O}(\sqrt{d})$	$\mathcal{O}(\sqrt{d})\mathbb{G}$	Transparent
Bulletproofs [18]	$1\mathbb{G}$	$2 \log d\mathbb{G}$	$\mathcal{O}(d)$	$\mathcal{O}(d)$	$\mathcal{O}(d)\mathbb{G}$	Transparent
FRI [7]	$1\mathbb{G}$	$\lambda \log^2 d\mathbb{G}$	$\mathcal{O}(d \log d)$	$\mathcal{O}(\lambda \log^2 d)$		Transparent
DARK [19]	$1\mathbb{G}_U$	$2 \log d\mathbb{G}_U + 2 \log d\mathbb{F}_p$	$\mathcal{O}(d \log d)$	$\mathcal{O}(\log d)$		Transparent
Dory [37]	$1\mathbb{G}_P$	$6 \log d\mathbb{G}_P$	$\mathcal{O}(d^{1+\epsilon})$	$\mathcal{O}(\log d)$	$\mathcal{O}(d)\mathbb{G}_P$	Transparent
Dew [3]	$1\mathbb{G}_U$	$66\mathbb{G}$	$\mathcal{O}(d^3/\log d)$	$\mathcal{O}(\log d)$		Transparent
DewTwo [20]	$1\mathbb{G}_U$	$\mathcal{O}(\log \log d)$	$\mathcal{O}(d \log d)$	$\mathcal{O}(\log d)$		Transparent
Behemoth (this work)	$1\mathbb{G}_U$	$172\mathbb{G}_U + 64\mathbb{F}_p$	$\mathcal{O}(d^3/\log d)$	$\mathcal{O}(1)$	$\mathcal{O}(d)\mathbb{G}_U$	Transparent

6.2   Prover Efficiency

Committing to a polynomial f can be done by computing $g^{\widehat{f(\alpha)}}$. Though the size of $\widehat{f(\alpha)}$ is huge over the integers ($\approx p^{d+1}$), the prover can compute this exponentiation in $\mathcal{O}(d)$ time, since all the monomials g^{α^i} of α are provided in the srs. Hence, the prover only needs to compute d small exponentiations with exponents of length $\log p$.

Computing the opening proof for the statement $f(z) = s$ is more computationally heavy. First, the prover needs to compute $g^{\widehat{q(\alpha)}}$, where the quotient

---

Polynomial division algorithm for the ProveEvaluation **protocol.**

Input: $(\mathsf{srs}, \mathsf{f}(x) \in \mathbb{F}_p[x], z, s = f(z))$. $\mathcal{P}$ wants to compute $\widehat{\mathsf{q}(\alpha)} = \frac{\mathsf{f}(\alpha) - \hat{s}}{\alpha - z}$ in the exponent.

1. Let $Q := g^0$.
2. $\forall i \in [0, \mathsf{d}]$ do the following:
   - Compute $\mathsf{q}_{\mathsf{d}-i}$, i.e., the $(\mathsf{d} - i)$th coefficient of $\frac{\mathsf{f}(x) - \hat{s}}{x - z}$. Let $Q := Q \cdot (g^{\alpha^{\mathsf{d}-i}})^{\mathsf{q}_{\mathsf{d}-i}}$.

Output: $Q = g^{\widehat{\mathsf{q}(\alpha)}}$.

Fig. 4. Polynomial division algorithm to compute $\widehat{\mathsf{q}(x)} = \frac{\mathsf{f}(x) - \hat{s}}{x - z}$, and $g^{\widehat{\mathsf{q}(\alpha)}}$ in the exponent as part of the ProveEvaluation protocol. We note here that $\log_2(\mathsf{q}_{\mathsf{d}-i}) \approx i \log_2(p)$, hence, this is a quadratic algorithm in the degree of the committed polynomial.

polynomial $\mathsf{q}(x)$ is defined as $\mathsf{q}(x) := \frac{\mathsf{f}(x) - \hat{s}}{x - z}$. The prover computes directly this polynomial division using Horner's method. It computes $g^{\widehat{\mathsf{q}(\alpha)}}$ on a rolling basis, i.e., monomial by monomial, using the algorithm detailed in Fig. 4. This strategy leads to an $\mathcal{O}(\mathsf{d}^2)$ computation. Completing the opening proof (both to compute the ProveEvaluation and the PoKDegUp proofs) requires the computation of the following NIZKs.

π_{PoE}: using the techniques of Wesolowski [50], a PoE proof consists of a single group element. The biggest chunk of the prover's work in this NIZK is incurred by computing a large modular division: $x = ql + r$, where $x \approx p^{\mathsf{d}+1}$ and $l, r \approx \lambda$. Computing $q \in \mathbb{Z}$ takes quasi linear time in the number of digits of x, i.e., $\mathcal{O}(\mathsf{d} \log \mathsf{d} \log p)$.

π_{PoKEMon}: a PoKEMon proof consists of a single group element and a small integer r with size $\approx p$. The prover's work is quasi-linear, i.e., $\mathcal{O}(\mathsf{d} \log \mathsf{d} \log p)$.

π_{PoKPE}: Arguing about the positivity of $\hat{s}$ and $\mathcal{B} - \hat{s}$ for $\hat{s} = \widehat{f(z)}$ requires the prover to find three (four) squares that sum up to $\hat{s}$ and $\mathcal{B} - \hat{s}$, respectively. The size of both of these integers $\hat{s}, \mathcal{B} - \hat{s}$ is roughly $(\mathsf{d} + 1) \log p$ bits. The state-of-the-art algorithm by Pollack and Treviño finds the (three) four squares decomposition of an integer n in time $\mathcal{O}(\log^2 n / \log \log n)$. Hence, creating the PoKPE proof takes approximately $\mathcal{O}(\mathsf{d}^2 \log^2 p / (\log \mathsf{d} + \log \log p))$ arithmetic operations, i.e., quasi quadratic in the degree of the committed polynomial. Since the algorithm operates on integers of length $\mathsf{d} \log p$ bits, in practice, the computational complexity of creating the PoKPE proof via the three square decompositions is cubic. The proof consists of 6 group elements and 3 small ($\approx p$) integers.

π_{PoKE}: this proof system has the same complexity as the PoE proof that is $\mathcal{O}(\mathsf{d} \log \mathsf{d} \log p)$, though the proof consists of a group element from $\mathbb{G}$ and an integer in $\mathbb{F}_p$.

π_{ChaumP}: the Chaum-Pedersen DLEq proof has the same complexity as generating two PoKE proofs. It has a proof size of two group elements from $\mathbb{G}$ and two small integers from $\mathbb{F}_p$.

The ProveEvaluation protocol consists of 1 PoE, 2 PoKEMon, and 2 PoKPE proofs. The PoKDegUp proof consists of 3 PoKE, 1 Chaum-Pedersen DLEq, and 1 ProveEvaluation proof. Altogether the Open protocol requires the computation of 4 PoE, 8 PoKEMon, 8 PoKPE, 6 PoKE, and 2 Chaum-Pedersen DLEq proofs. Therefore, the unoptimized Behemoth Open proof size consits of $70\mathbb{G}$ and $42\mathbb{F}_p$ elements. Next, we mention techniques to shrink the proof size even further.

Batching the Applied NIZK Proofs. The Open protocol applies 24 instances of the PoKE, PoKPE, ChaumP, PoKEMon proofs where the verification equation checks that the prover knows a random prime x_i-root w_i of a public element a_i, i.e., $w_i^{x_i} = a_i$ for $i \in [0, 24]$. We have that with overwhelming probability for the λ-bit challenge primes: $\forall i, j (i \neq j) : gcd(x_i, x_j) = 1$. That makes the opening proof even more succinct by batching the underlying NIZK proofs due to the protocol PoKCR (aggregating knowledge of co-prime roots) introduced in [13].

6.3   Verifier Efficiency

The verifier runs in constant time. Verifying an opening proof entails verifying several NIZKs as subprotocols, i.e., PoE, PoKEMon, PoKPE, PoKE, ChaumP, all requiring constant time. The verifier needs to compute a constant number of group operations to verify a Behemoth Open proof. In particular, an unoptimized (without proof batching) version of the Open protocol requires the computation of 210 group operations.

7   Conclusion

In this work, to the best of our knowledge, we constructed the first transparent polynomial commitment scheme that achieves both constant-size opening proofs and verification time. The main idea of our construction is to instantiate the KZG opening strategy in a group of unknown order. Hence, our construction affirmatively answers the question of succinct, transparent polynomial commitment schemes raised in [39].

Acknowledgements. This research was supported by the Ministry of Culture and Innovation and the National Research, Development, and Innovation Office within the Quantum Information National Laboratory of Hungary (Grant No. 2022-2.1.1-NL-2022-00004).

References

1. Aggarwal, D., Maurer, U.: Breaking RSA generically is equivalent to factoring. IEEE Trans. Inf. Theory **62**(11), 6251–6259 (2016)
2. Ames, S., Hazay, C., Ishai, Y., Venkitasubramaniam, M.: Ligero: lightweight sublinear arguments without a trusted setup. In: Proceedings of the 2017 ACM SIGSAC Conference on Computer and Communications Security, pp. 2087–2104 (2017)

3. Arun, A., Ganesh, C., Lokam, S., Mopuri, T., Sridhar, S.: Dew: transparent constant-sized zksnarks. Cryptology ePrint Archive (2022)
4. van Baarsen, A.: Imaginary quadratic class groups and a survey of time-lock cryptographic applications (2023)
5. van Baarsen, A., Stevens, M.: On time-lock cryptographic assumptions in abelian hidden-order groups. In: Advances in Cryptology–ASIACRYPT 2021: 27th International Conference on the Theory and Application of Cryptology and Information Security, Singapore, 6–10 December 2021, Proceedings, Part II 27, pp. 367–397. Springer (2021)
6. Barić, N., Pfitzmann, B.: Collision-free accumulators and fail-stop signature schemes without trees. In: International Conference on the Theory and Applications of Cryptographic Techniques, pp. 480–494. Springer (1997)
7. Ben-Sasson, E., Bentov, I., Horesh, Y., Riabzev, M.: Fast reed-solomon interactive oracle proofs of proximity. In: 45th International Colloquium on Automata, Languages, and Programming (ICALP 2018). Schloss Dagstuhl-Leibniz-Zentrum fuer Informatik (2018)
8. Ben-Sasson, E., Chiesa, A., Green, M., Tromer, E., Virza, M.: Secure sampling of public parameters for succinct zero knowledge proofs. In: 2015 IEEE Symposium on Security and Privacy, pp. 287–304. IEEE (2015)
9. Ben-Sasson, E., Chiesa, A., Spooner, N.: Interactive oracle proofs. In: Theory of Cryptography Conference, pp. 31–60. Springer (2016)
10. Block, A.R., Holmgren, J., Rosen, A., Rothblum, R.D., Soni, P.: Time-and space-efficient arguments from groups of unknown order. In: Advances in Cryptology–CRYPTO 2021: 41st Annual International Cryptology Conference, CRYPTO 2021, Virtual Event, 16–20 August 2021, Proceedings, Part IV 41, pp. 123–152. Springer (2021)
11. Blum, M., Feldman, P., Micali, S.: Non-interactive zero-knowledge and its applications. In: Providing Sound Foundations for Cryptography: On the Work of Shafi Goldwasser and Silvio Micali, pp. 329–349. ACM (2019)
12. Boneh, D., Bonneau, J., Bünz, B., Fisch, B.: Verifiable delay functions. In: Annual International Cryptology Conference, pp. 757–788. Springer (2018)
13. Boneh, D., Bünz, B., Fisch, B.: Batching techniques for accumulators with applications to IOPs and stateless blockchains. In: Annual International Cryptology Conference, pp. 561–586. Springer (2019)
14. Boneh, D., Drake, J., Fisch, B., Gabizon, A.: Efficient polynomial commitment schemes for multiple points and polynomials. Cryptology ePrint Archive (2020)
15. Boneh, D., Drake, J., Fisch, B., Gabizon, A.: Halo infinite: proof-carrying data from additive polynomial commitments. In: Annual International Cryptology Conference, pp. 649–680. Springer (2021)
16. Bootle, J., Cerulli, A., Chaidos, P., Groth, J., Petit, C.: Efficient zero-knowledge arguments for arithmetic circuits in the discrete log setting. In: Annual International Conference on the Theory and Applications of Cryptographic Techniques, pp. 327–357. Springer (2016)
17. Bowe, S., Gabizon, A., Miers, I.: Scalable multi-party computation for ZK-snark parameters in the random beacon model. Cryptology ePrint Archive (2017)
18. Bünz, B., Bootle, J., Boneh, D., Poelstra, A., Wuille, P., Maxwell, G.: Bulletproofs: short proofs for confidential transactions and more. In: 2018 IEEE Symposium on Security and Privacy (SP), pp. 315–334. IEEE (2018)
19. Bünz, B., Fisch, B., Szepieniec, A.: Transparent snarks from dark compilers. In: Annual International Conference on the Theory and Applications of Cryptographic Techniques, pp. 677–706. Springer (2020)

20. Bünz, B., Mopuri, T., Shirzad, A., Sridhar, S.: Dewtwo: a transparent pcs with quasi-linear prover, logarithmic verifier and 4.5 kb proofs from falsifiable assumptions. Cryptology ePrint Archive (2025)
21. Chaum, D., Pedersen, T.P.: Wallet databases with observers. In: Annual International Cryptology Conference, pp. 89–105. Springer (1992)
22. Chiesa, A., Hu, Y., Maller, M., Mishra, P., Vesely, N., Ward, N.: Marlin: preprocessing zksnarks with universal and updatable SRS. In: Annual International Conference on the Theory and Applications of Cryptographic Techniques, pp. 738–768. Springer (2020)
23. Chu, H., Fiore, D., Kolonelos, D., Schröder, D.: Inner product functional commitments with constant-size public parameters and openings. Cryptology ePrint Archive (2022)
24. Damgård, I., Koprowski, M.: Generic lower bounds for root extraction and signature schemes in general groups. In: International Conference on the Theory and Applications of Cryptographic Techniques, pp. 256–271. Springer (2002)
25. Das, S., Xiang, Z., Ren, L.: Powers of tau in asynchrony. Cryptology ePrint Archive (2022)
26. Dobson, S., Galbraith, S.D., Smith, B.: Trustless unknown-order groups. Cryptology ePrint Archive (2020)
27. Erdős, P., Rényi, A.: On a classical problem of probability theory. Magyar Tud. Akad. Mat. Kutató Int. Közl **6**(1), 215–220 (1961)
28. Feist, D., Khovratovich, D.: Fast amortized KZG proofs. Cryptology ePrint Archive (2023)
29. Fiat, A., Shamir, A.: How to prove yourself: practical solutions to identification and signature problems. In: Conference on the Theory and Application of Cryptographic Techniques, pp. 186–194. Springer (1986)
30. Hafner, J.L., McCurley, K.S.: A rigorous subexponential algorithm for computation of class groups. J. Am. Math. Soc. **2**(4), 837–850 (1989)
31. Jager, T., Schwenk, J.: On the analysis of cryptographic assumptions in the generic ring model. J. Cryptol. **26**, 225–245 (2013)
32. Kate, A., Zaverucha, G.M., Goldberg, I.: Constant-size commitments to polynomials and their applications. In: International Conference on the Theory and Application of Cryptology and Information Security, pp. 177–194. Springer (2010)
33. Kattis, A., Panarin, K., Vlasov, A.: Redshift: transparent snarks from list polynomial commitment IOPs. Cryptology ePrint Archive (2019)
34. Kohlweiss, M., Maller, M., Siim, J., Volkhov, M.: Snarky ceremonies. In: International Conference on the Theory and Application of Cryptology and Information Security, pp. 98–127. Springer (2021)
35. Kuszmaul, J.: Verkle trees. Verkle trees **1** (2019)
36. Lagarias, J.C.: Worst-case complexity bounds for algorithms in the theory of integral quadratic forms. J. Algorithms **1**(2), 142–186 (1980)
37. Lee, J.: Dory: efficient, transparent arguments for generalised inner products and polynomial commitments. In: Theory of Cryptography Conference, pp. 1–34. Springer (2021)
38. Mert, A.C., Ozturk, E., Savas, E.: Low-latency ASIC algorithms of modular squaring of large integers for VDF evaluation. IEEE Trans. Comput. (2020)
39. Nikolaenko, V., Ragsdale, S., Bonneau, J., Boneh, D.: Powers-of-tau to the people: decentralizing setup ceremonies. Cryptology ePrint Archive (2022)
40. Pietrzak, K.: Simple verifiable delay functions. In: 10th Innovations in Theoretical Computer Science Conference (ITCS 2019). Schloss Dagstuhl-Leibniz-Zentrum fuer Informatik (2018)

41. Pollack, P., Treviño, E.: Finding the four squares in lagrange's theorem. Integers **18**, A15 (2018)
42. Rivest, R.L.: Description of the LCS35 time capsule crypto-puzzle (1999)
43. Rotem, L., Segev, G.: Generically speeding-up repeated squaring is equivalent to factoring: sharp thresholds for all generic-ring delay functions. In: Annual International Cryptology Conference, pp. 481–509. Springer (2020)
44. Shoup, V.: Lower bounds for discrete logarithms and related problems. In: Fumy, W. (ed.) EUROCRYPT 1997. LNCS, vol. 1233, pp. 256–266. Springer, Heidelberg (1997). https://doi.org/10.1007/3-540-69053-0_18
45. Sutherland, A.V.: Order computations in generic groups. Ph.D. thesis, Massachusetts Institute of Technology (2007)
46. Thakur, S.: Batching non-membership proofs with bilinear accumulators. Cryptology ePrint Archive (2019)
47. Thakur, S.: Arguments of knowledge via hidden order groups. Cryptology ePrint Archive (2020)
48. Thakur, S.: Constructing hidden order groups using genus three jacobians. Cryptology ePrint Archive (2020)
49. Wahby, R.S., Tzialla, I., Shelat, A., Thaler, J., Walfish, M.: Doubly-efficient zksnarks without trusted setup. In: 2018 IEEE Symposium on Security and Privacy (SP), pp. 926–943. IEEE (2018)
50. Wesolowski, B.: Efficient verifiable delay functions. In: Annual International Conference on the Theory and Applications of Cryptographic Techniques, pp. 379–407. Springer (2019)
51. Wood, G., et al.: Ethereum: a secure decentralised generalised transaction ledger. Ethereum Project Yellow Paper **151**(2014), 1–32 (2014)

Attribute-Based Encryption Using Sum-Product Decomposition of Boolean Functions

Arani Raychaudhuri[iD], Ramprasad Sarkar[(✉)][iD], and Mriganka Mandal[iD]

Cryptology and Security Research Unit, Indian Statistical Institute Kolkata,
Kolkata 700108, India
rayc.arani@gmail.com, {rpsarkar_p,mriganka}@isical.ac.in

Abstract. Attribute-based encryption (ABE) is an advanced crypto-graphic paradigm that enables access control over encrypted data based on users' attributes. In ABE, access to ciphertexts is governed by policies defined over a set of attributes associated with users. Since its introduction in 2007, ABE has gained significant attention, resulting in numerous constructions built upon various computationally hard problems. However, despite these advancements, none of the existing constructions have explored the integration of *logic optimization* with *consensual security* assumptions. In this paper, we propose an ABE scheme within the *symmetric key* framework, designed to enhance efficiency while ensuring strong access control security. Our approach introduces a hierarchical attribute management framework that leverages both an attribute group and an attribute tree, along with an optimization algorithm for logical access functions to enhance computational efficiency. To the best of our knowledge, we are the *first* to propose an ABE scheme based on consensual security assumptions. By substantially reducing key storage requirements, our scheme enhances scalability and practicality for real-world applications while maintaining robust security guarantees.

Keywords: Symmetric-Key Encryption · Attribute-based encryption · Boolean function · Access Control · Pseudorandom function

1 Introduction

Attribute-based encryption (ABE) [2,11,13] has emerged as one of the advanced cryptographic primitives that allow fine-grained access control over the encrypted data depending on the receivers' credentials (or attributes). This flexibility makes ABE a crucial tool in applications such as cloud security, healthcare systems, access control in distributed networks, etc. Depending on the strategies of access structure, ABE can be divided into two categories: *key-policy ABE (KP-ABE)* [13–15] and *ciphertext-policy ABE (CP-ABE)* [9,25]. In KP-ABE, the task of embedding the access structure into the user's secret keys goes to a trusted third party (aka the private key generation center), and any sender injects the attribute set of the users into the ciphertext during the encryption algorithm. On the other hand, in CP-ABE, the access structure is responsible for generating the ciphertext, and the attribute set is embedded in the user's secret key. In both cases, the attributes must satisfy the access policy to execute decryption.

In 2005, Sahai and Waters designed fuzzy identity-based encryption [22] in which each user can be identified with a certain set of attributes, and the sender employs a policy that helps to encrypt the plaintext. The receiver can decrypt the ciphertext only when the attribute set satisfies the policy. In recent years, fuzzy identity-based encryption has led to the design of the first concise construction of the fundamental cryptographic primitive ABE [13]. In the last decade, ABE has been extensively and intensively studied achieving various trade-offs between expressiveness, efficiency, security, and underlying assumptions [3,4,7,9,12,13,16–21,23,24,26] due to its various potential applications in one-to-many data transmission. Despite its strong theoretical foundations and practical potential, most existing ABE schemes operate within the traditional public-key encryption (PKE) framework and rely on hard number-theoretic problems. The main weakness of such schemes is that they rely on number-theoretic problems that can be solved in polynomial time using quantum computers. This raises a fundamental question:

Is it possible to construct a secure ABE scheme without relying on number-theoretic hardness assumptions?

To address this challenge, researchers have explored alternative postquantum security approaches, including lattice-based ABE constructions [2,27,28]. However, lattice-based schemes often suffer from large ciphertext sizes and computational overhead, making them impractical for real-life applications. Another promising direction is exploring symmetric-key cryptographic techniques for constructing ABE that rely on consensual security assumptions, such as pseudorandom functions (PRF).

Recently, Dupin et al. [10] proposed a broadcast encryption (BE) scheme based on the sum-product decomposition of boolean functions using the PRF within a symmetric key setting. Although their work demonstrates the feasibility of achieving fine-grained access control in symmetric key frameworks, their approach incurs high storage overhead. Since ABE is a more generalized form of BE, it is natural to investigate whether an efficient and secure symmetric-key ABE scheme can be designed. However, no such construction has been proposed so far in the literature.

1.1 Contribution

In this paper, we propose a new symmetric-key ABE scheme that integrates logic optimization techniques, extending ideas from the prior broadcast encryption scheme [10]. Our scheme offers various advantages with lower bandwidth requirements. The main contributions are given below:

- In this work, we introduce a structured approach to managing attributes through attribute groups, which allows us to work with smaller subsets of attributes rather than processing all attributes simultaneously. This framework enables the construction of an attribute tree, where user groups form the leaves of the tree. Our proposed assumptions on the attribute universe ensure that user groups are mutually exclusive while collectively covering the entire user set. This hierarchical organization improves efficiency in attribute management and encryption.

- We also present an algorithm to minimize the logic function f, significantly reducing its complexity. Since the number of attributes in real-world scenarios is typically much smaller than the number of users, this optimization leads to a more compact representation of f. The attribute groups play a crucial role in enabling this minimization. Although the algorithm incurs an initial computational cost, it substantially reduces the time required for four critical operations: encoding and decoding of f, as well as encryption and decryption of the message.

- This work is the *first* to propose an ABE scheme within the symmetric-key framework that relies on simple and consensual security assumptions. Although the work of [10] applies logic optimization within the BE framework, our work adapts and extends this approach to support attribute-based access policies, thereby enabling more fine-grained access control based on attributes rather than user indices. Our scheme allows encryption with respect to a logical access policy, ensuring that only authorized users possessing the appropriate keys can decrypt the ciphertext. Importantly, since the encoding and decoding of f is made public, additional encryption and decryption costs are eliminated without compromising security.

- More positively, unlike the recent broadcast encryption scheme by Dupin et al. [10], where each user is required to store a large number of keys, which is equal to the total number of users in the system, our approach drastically reduces the key storage overhead per user by leveraging the attribute tree structure. This improvement makes our scheme much more efficient and scalable for practical applications.

1.2   Overview of Our Techniques

Before presenting our construction in detail, we first introduce the fundamental concepts: Boolean and pseudorandom functions, the attribute universe, the attribute groups, and the attribute tree. The notion of Attribute Groups plays a pivotal role in our design, as it allows for a partitioning of the attribute universe into mutually exclusive and collectively exhaustive subsets. This partitioning enables a precise definition of attribute negation: the negation of an attribute within a group is defined as the union of all other attributes in that group. We model the hierarchical structure of attributes through an attribute tree AT, where each level corresponds to an attribute group. At each level, we select an attribute group AG, and nodes from the previous level are expanded by attaching child nodes corresponding to each attribute in the selected group. This ensures that every node at a given level branches into a number of children equal to the cardinality of the next attribute group.

A central component of our approach is a logic minimization algorithm (*cf.* Sect. 3), designed to optimize Boolean access policies expressed as combinations of AND and OR gates. The original logical expression is often too large to use directly for encryption and decryption. Our minimization algorithm reduces the size of this expression, improving efficiency for both the emitter and the users. This process leverages the structure of Attribute Groups to systematically reduce the logic expression by processing one group at a time and stopping when no further reduction is possible.

For construction, we assume that the attribute universe is given by $\{A_1, \ldots, A_a\}$, where a is the total number of attributes. These are divided into g disjoint attribute groups $\{AG_1, \ldots, AG_g\}$. In the Setup phase (*cf.* Sect. 4), the emitter selects a master secret key k_{PRF} from a key space. Each attribute A_i is assigned a unique and publicly known label $k_i = \langle i \rangle_a$, where $\langle i \rangle_a$ denotes a-bit binary representation of i. During the Join phase, a user $u \in \{A_{i_1}\} \cap \{A_{i_2}\} \cap \ldots \cap \{A_{i_g}\}$ receives a decryption key of the form $F(k_{PRF}, \|_{j \in S} k_{i_j})$, for all ordered $S \subseteq [g]$ to the corresponding user and F denotes the pseudorandom function.

Our proposed scheme is in the symmetric key framework. The emitter starts with the minimized logical function $f = P_1 \vee P_2 \vee \ldots$ where each P_i is a conjunction of attributes. For each such product term, a label is generated on the basis of the involved attributes. Then, in the Encrypt algorithm, the emitter computes a ciphertext component $C_i = E(F(k_{PRF}, \|_{\alpha \in S_i} k_\alpha), k_e)$ for each product term P_i, where k_e is a session key and E denotes a symmetric encryption function. The complete ciphertext includes multiple encryptions of k_e (one per product term), followed by encryption of the actual message using k_e. Only users whose attributes satisfy $f(u) = 1$ will be able to recover k_e and decrypt the message. The correctness of the scheme follows from the fact that a user can satisfy a product term if and only if they possess all attributes required by that term. The security of our symmetric-key ABE protocol relies on the pseudorandomness of the underlying PRF.

1.3   Organization

The rest of the paper is organized as follows: Sect. 2 provides the necessary cryptographic background for our construction and introduces the concepts of the attribute universe, attribute groups, etc. Section 3 describes the minimization algorithm for logic functions, along with the construction of f and its encoding and decoding process. Section 4 details the design of our proposed scheme, including its correctness and security analysis. Section 5 presents the key estimation and evaluates the efficiency of our protocol. Finally, Sect. 6 summarizes our findings and discusses potential directions for future research.

2 Preliminaries

In this section, we provide an overview of essential building blocks, including Boolean functions and pseudorandom functions. We define assumptions on the attribute universe, attribute trees, and attribute groups, which form the foundational basis for our constructions.

Notations: Throughout the paper, we use the following notation: we represent $[\![a]\!]$ as the set $\{1, 2, \ldots, a\}$, $\langle x \rangle$ as the binary expansion of x, and $(\!|x|\!)_2$ as the encoding representation of x. The notation $s \xleftarrow{\$} S$ signifies that an element s is uniformly randomly chosen from a set S, and $\$(\cdot)$ represents a random function oracle. Moreover, we use $\bar{A}$ to denote the negation of the attribute A and $\{A\}$ to denote the corresponding user set associated with attribute A.

Definition 1 (Negligible Function). *A function* $negl : \mathbb{N} \to \mathbb{R}$ *is said to be a negligible function in* λ *if for every positive integer* c, *there exists a* λ_c *such that for all* $\lambda > \lambda_c$, $\lambda^c \cdot |negl(\lambda)| < 1$.

2.1 Boolean Function [1,8]

Definition 2 (Boolean Function). *A function is said to be Boolean if for any input from its domain, it outputs only binary values, specifically 0 or 1.*

In our context, we define the Boolean function as $f : \{0, 1\}^n \to \{0, 1\}$, where the inputs to f are n-bit binary strings and the output belongs to the set $\{0, 1\}$. The function f is deterministic, meaning that for each input, the output is uniquely determined.

We will also consider the 'Don't care' values of f, denoted by $*$, which is given as if $f(x) = *$ for some $x \in \{0, 1\}^n$, then $f(x) = 0$ or $f(x) = 1$ of either of them, but not both. However, we are not concerned with the exact values of f at such points and this will not influence our construction.

Let x be a n-bit string. We can write $x = x_1 x_2 \cdots x_n$, where $x_i \in \{0, 1\}$ for each $i \in [\![n]\!]$. We also assume that each x_i is an independent variable.

Definition 3 (Product Term). *A Product Term is defined as conjunctions (AND) of a subset of these variables. Formally, a product term is a logical conjunction of the form:*

$$a_{i_1} \wedge a_{i_2} \wedge \ldots \wedge a_{i_k},$$

where $\{i_1, i_2, \ldots, i_k\} \subseteq [\![n]\!]$. *For simplicity, we denote this as* $a_{i_1} a_{i_2} \ldots a_{i_k}$.

Definition 4 (Sum-Product Form). *We define the Sum-Product Form as the disjunctions (OR operations) of such product terms. For example, it can be expressed as:* $x_1 x_2 x_3 \vee x_4 x_5 \vee x_6 x_7 x_8 \vee \ldots$

In this paper, we assume that the input x is an element of $\{0, 1\}^n$. To simplify notation, we represent x as

$$x = x_{i_1} x_{i_2} \dots x_{i_k}$$

such that $x_{i_j} = 1 \ \forall \ j \in [\![k]\!]$ and $x_m = 0 \ \forall \ m \in [\![n]\!] \setminus \{i_1, i_2, \dots, i_k\}$. For example, if $x = 10110$, we will denote x by $x_1 x_3 x_4$. In particular, this representation uniquely identifies each input, providing a compact form.

2.2   Pseudorandom Function [5,6]

Let $F : \mathcal{K} \times \mathcal{X} \to \mathcal{Y}$ is said to be an efficient keyed function if there is a polynomial-time algorithm that computes $F(k, x)$ for a given $k \in \mathcal{K}$ and $x \in \mathcal{X}$. F is a pseudorandom function (PRF) if the function $F(k, .)$ (for a uniform key k) is indistinguishable from a function chosen uniformly at random from the set of all functions having the same domain and range. In other words, for all probabilistic polynomial-time (PPT) adversary $\mathcal{A}$, there exists a negligible function negl such that

$$\left| Pr[\mathcal{A}^{F(k,.)}(1^\lambda) = 1 : k \xleftarrow{\$} \mathcal{K}] - Pr[\mathcal{A}^{\$(.)}(1^\lambda) = 1] \right| \leq \mathsf{negl}(\lambda),$$

where $k \xleftarrow{\$} \mathcal{K}$ denotes that k is uniformly randomly chosen from $\mathcal{K}$, λ denotes the security parameter of $\mathsf{len}(k)$, and $\$(.)$ represents a random function oracle.

It is important to note that the total number of possible functions mapping from $\mathcal{X}$ to $\mathcal{Y}$, where $|\mathcal{X}| = |\mathcal{Y}| = 2^m$, is $(2^m)^{2^m}$ when $\mathcal{X}$ and $\mathcal{Y}$ from $\{0, 1\}^m$. Handling such an enormous set of random functions is computationally infeasible. In contrast, the number of pseudorandom functions (PRFs) depends solely on the cardinality of the key space $\mathcal{K}$. If $|\mathcal{K}| = 2^k$ (in practice, $k \leq m$), the total number of PRFs is 2^k, which is significantly smaller than the number of random functions: $\#(\mathsf{PRF}) = 2^k \ll (2^m)^{2^m} = \#(\mathsf{Random\ function\ oracle})$.

2.3   Attribute Universe

We define a set containing all possible attributes and refer to this set as the Attribute Universe (AU). Each attribute is an element of this set and it is assumed that no attribute exists outside of it. Let $\mathsf{AU} = \{A_1, ..., A_a\}$, where $|\mathsf{AU}| = a$ denotes the total number of attributes in the universe. The following assumptions hold for the attribute universe:

(a) Every attribute in AU is satisfied by at least one user. If an attribute exists that is not satisfied by any user, it can be excluded, and the analysis can proceed with the updated AU.

(b) If an attribute is satisfied by all users in the user set U, it is universally true. Such attributes can also be excluded, and the modified AU can be utilized.

(c) The negation of any attribute can be represented using some of the other attributes within the attribute universe. For instance, in an institution, the negation of the attribute 'Student' does not need to be explicitly described as 'Not Student'. Instead, it can be expressed as a union of other attributes, such as

$$\overline{\text{Student}} = \text{'Teacher'} \cup \text{'Staffs'} \cup \ldots \cup \text{'Workers'}$$

By this argument, for any $A_i \in \mathsf{AU}$, the negation of A_i ($\bar{A}_i$) can be computed with respect to it's corresponding user set as

$$\{\bar{A}_i\} = \cup_{j \in J}\{A_j\}, \quad \text{for some } J \subseteq \llbracket a \rrbracket.$$

Attribute Groups. Based on assumption (c), attributes can be grouped so that attributes within each group are mutually exclusive and exhaustive with respect to the set of users they represent. These groups are formed on the basis of logical relationships among the attributes.

Consider an attribute universe $\mathsf{AU} = \{A_1, A_2, A_3, A_4, A_5, A_6, A_7, A_8, A_9, \ldots\}$, where the attribute groups are $\mathsf{AG}_1 = \{A_1, A_2, A_3\}$, $\mathsf{AG}_2 = \{A_4, A_5, A_6, A_7\}$, $\mathsf{AG}_3 = \{A_8, A_9\}$, etc. In this structure, each attribute group represents a partition of the entire user set U. Specifically, for each attribute group, the union of the attributes within the group encompasses the entire user set as follows:

$$\{A_1\} \cup \{A_2\} \cup \{A_3\} = U \text{ for } \mathsf{AG}_1,$$
$$\{A_4\} \cup \{A_5\} \cup \{A_6\} \cup \{A_7\} = U \text{ for } \mathsf{AG}_2,$$
$$\{A_8\} \cup \{A_9\} = U \text{ for } \mathsf{AG}_3, \quad \text{and so on.}$$

Moreover, this construction implies that the negation of any attribute in AU is represented by the union of all other attributes within the same group. For example, the negation of A_2 is given by Negation of $A_2 = \bar{A}_2 = U \setminus \{A_2\} = \mathsf{AG}_1 \setminus \{A_2\} = \{A_1\} \cup \{A_3\}$, where $\{A_i\}$ represents the user set associated with attribute A_i.

Assumption for AG. No user can possess two distinct attributes from the same attribute group. Specifically, for any pair of attributes A_{i_1} and A_{i_2} within the same group AG_i, the intersection of the corresponding user sets is empty, *i.e.*, $\{A_{i_1}\} \cap \{A_{i_2}\} = \emptyset$.

If not, we can introduce an additional attribute and redefine it to ensure mutual exclusivity as follows:

$$\{A_i^{'}\} = \{A_{i_1}\} \cap \{A_{i_2}\}$$
$$\{A_{i_1}^{'}\} = \{A_{i_1}\} \setminus \{A_i^{'}\}$$
$$\{A_{i_2}^{'}\} = \{A_{i_2}\} \setminus \{A_i^{'}\}$$

The new attributes $\{A_i^{'}, A_{i_1}^{'}, A_{i_2}^{'}\}$ will be replaced in the places of $\{A_{i_1}, A_{i_2}\}$. The new attributes easily follow assumptions (a) and (b). Then, the corresponding attribute group will be updated to $\mathsf{AG}_i^{'} = (\mathsf{AG}_i \setminus \{A_{i_1}, A_{i_2}\}) \cup \{A_i^{'}, A_{i_1}^{'}, A_{i_2}^{'}\}$.

Pictorially; it can be expressed as follows:

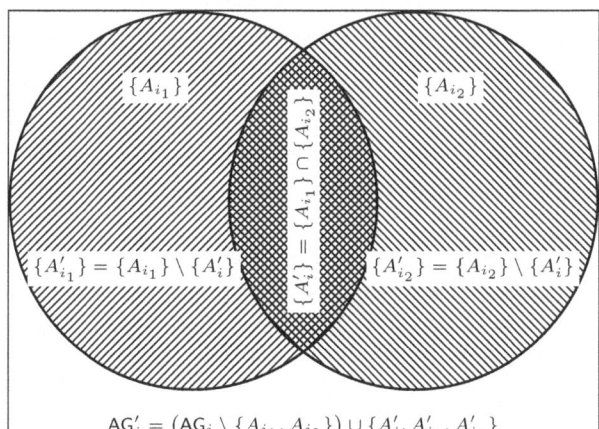

By applying all assumptions collectively, we can successfully construct attribute groups from the attribute universe that satisfy the mutually exclusive property within each group.

Construction of AG: The construction of attribute groups begins by selecting an initial attribute and considering its negation, which produces a complementary set of attributes. This set collectively spans the entire user space while preserving mutual exclusivity within the group. This initial group is designated as the first attribute group, characterized by the property that the negation of any attribute within it corresponds to the union of all other attributes in the same group. Subsequent attribute groups are constructed by selecting additional attributes not already included in previous groups and applying the same process. Given that the attribute universe is finite in practical application scenarios - determined by the specific logic function or application context - this procedure will eventually exhaust all available attributes. When new users are introduced after this point, it may become necessary to define new or synthetic attributes to accommodate them.

Assuming a well-defined attribute universe (AU), the above grouping method produces a unique set of AGs. This uniqueness arises from the fact that the negation of any attribute in an AG map precisely to the union of the remaining attributes in that group, according to the user sets they represent. Since all attributes in AU are consumed through this construction, it guarantees both the uniqueness and optimality of the resulting grouping. Furthermore, initiating the construction with an arbitrary attribute in AU still leads to an optimal grouping, thus improving time efficiency by eliminating the need to identify a specific starting element, a step often required in alternative approaches.

Lemma 1. *Any arbitrary combination of conjunctions ($\land$) and disjunctions ($\lor$) can be equivalently represented as disjunctions ($\lor$) of conjunctions ($\land$) only in the context of attribute combinations.*

378   A. Raychaudhuri et al.

Proof. Based on the assumptions, the attributes inherently correspond to specific user sets, and their combination will follow the set-theoretic properties. By applying De Morgan's Law, which states for any sets A, B, C, D

$$(A \cup B) \cap (C \cup D) = (A \cap C) \cup (A \cap D) \cup (B \cap C) \cup (B \cap D).$$

Then applying the same for the corresponding user sets $\{A_i\}$'s of attributes A_i's in attribute groups, we get our desired result.

Attribute Tree. To define the structure of the attribute tree AT, we proceed by selecting an attribute group AG at each level. As we move to the subsequent level, every component of the preceding level is expanded by incorporating all components from the next attribute group. This expansion ensures that the number of edges that originate from each node at the current level is precisely equal to the cardinality of the next-level attribute group.

For instance, consider the whole user set $U = \{AG_1, AG_2, AG_3\}$, where

$$AG_1 = \{A_1, A_2\}, \text{ satisfying } \{A_1\} \cup \{A_2\} = U,$$
$$AG_2 = \{A_3, A_4, A_5\}, \text{ satisfying } \{A_3\} \cup \{A_4\} \cup \{A_5\} = U,$$
$$AG_3 = \{A_6, A_7, A_8\}, \text{ satisfying} \{A_6\} \cup \{A_7\} \cup \{A_8\} = U.$$

This hierarchical construction, depicted in Fig. 1, ensures a systematic expansion of the tree, where the structure of each level is determined by the attributes of the corresponding group AG.

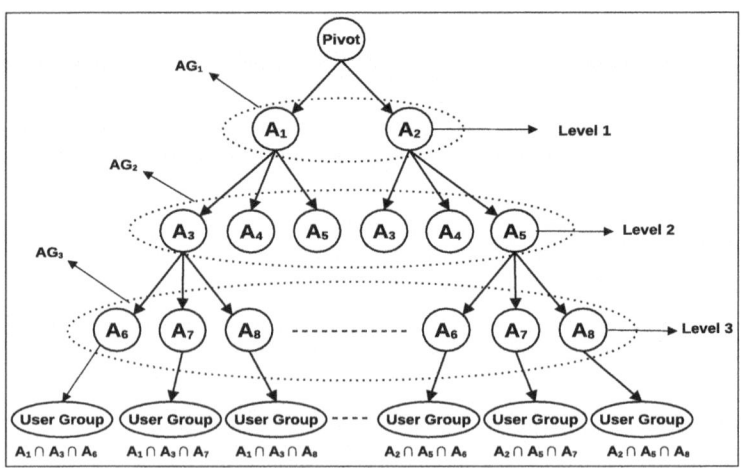

Fig. 1. Attribute Tree

Lemma 2. *If there are a total of g attribute groups $\{AG_1, \ldots, AG_g\}$, then for any two user sets located at depth $g + 1$ (i.e., the leaf nodes of the tree), their intersection must be the empty set $\emptyset$.*

Proof. Consider two user sets with a nonempty intersection, and assume that a user u belongs to two distinct user groups at depth $g + 1$ in the attribute tree AT. Then we have,

$$u \in \{A_{i_1}\} \cap \{A_{i_2}\} \cap \ldots \cap \{A_{i_g}\} \text{ and } u \in \{A_{j_1}\} \cap \{A_{j_2}\} \cap \ldots \cap \{A_{j_g}\},$$

where, $\{A_{i_m}, A_{j_m}\} \subseteq AG_m$ for $m \in \{1, 2, \ldots, g\}$. From the above equations, it follows that:

$$u \in \left(\{A_{i_1}\} \cap \{A_{i_2}\} \cap \ldots \cap \{A_{i_g}\}\right) \cap \left(\{A_{j_1}\} \cap \{A_{j_2}\} \cap \ldots \cap \{A_{j_g}\}\right) \neq \emptyset.$$

Rearranging the terms, we obtain $(\{A_{i_1}\} \cap \{A_{j_1}\}) \cap \ldots \cap (\{A_{i_g}\} \cap \{A_{j_g}\}) \neq \emptyset$.

This implies that none of the intersections $(\{A_{i_1}\} \cap \{A_{j_1}\}), \ldots, (\{A_{i_g}\} \cap \{A_{j_g}\})$ are empty. However, for any $(\{A_{i_m}\} \cap \{A_{j_m}\})$, for $m \in \{1, \ldots, g\}$, both A_{i_m} and A_{j_m} belong to the same attribute group AG_m.

By previous assumption, $\{A_{i_g}\} \cap \{A_{j_g}\}$ must be Φ for all $m \in \{1, \ldots, g\}$, leading to a contradiction. Therefore, no such user u exists. Thus, any two user groups at depth $g + 1$ in AT are mutually disjoint.

2.4   System of Symmetric-Key Attribute-Based Encryption

Syntax. A symmetric-key *attribute-based encryption* (ABE) scheme for an access policy f consists of four algorithms: (Setup, Join, Encrypt, Decrypt), where the first three algorithms are randomized and the last one is deterministic. The algorithms work as follows.

- **Setup.** Taking the security parameter λ as input, the setup algorithm generates the master secret key MSK and a set of public labels $\{k_i\}_{i \in AU}$ corresponding to the attribute universe AU.
- **Join.** The join algorithm takes as input the master secret key MSK and a user's attribute set. It outputs a secret key SK for the user associated with those attributes.
- **Encrypt.** The encryption algorithm takes as input the master secret key MSK, a message m, and an access policy f over the attribute universe AU. It outputs a ciphertext CT such that only users whose attributes satisfy the policy f can decrypt.
- **Decrypt.** The decryption algorithm takes as input a user's secret key SK and a ciphertext CT. If the user's attributes satisfy the policy f embedded in CT, it outputs the original message m; otherwise, it returns $\perp$.

Correctness. The above ABE scheme is said to be correct if for every security parameter λ, every message m, every access policy f, and every user attribute set $AS \subseteq AU$ satisfying $f(AS) = 1$, it holds that:

$$\Pr \left[m' = m : \begin{array}{l} (\mathsf{MSK}, \{k_i\}_{i \in \mathsf{AU}}) \leftarrow \mathsf{Setup}(\lambda), \ \mathsf{SK} \leftarrow \mathsf{Join}(\mathsf{MSK}, \mathsf{AS}); \\ \mathsf{CT} \leftarrow \mathsf{Encrypt}(\mathsf{MSK}, m, f); \\ m' \leftarrow \mathsf{Decrypt}(\mathsf{SK}, \mathsf{CT}) \end{array} \right] \geq 1 - \mathsf{negl}(\lambda)$$

Security. In contrast to public-key encryption (PKE) schemes, symmetric-key constructions generally lack well-established, provable security frameworks. While PKE protocols are typically supported by reductions to standard computational hardness assumptions - such as factoring, discrete logarithm, or lattice problems - symmetric-key schemes often rely on the security properties of underlying primitives without such reductions. In our case, the security of the proposed ABE framework is based on the pseudorandomness of the underlying pseudorandom function, which serves as the foundation for key generation and encryption algorithm. Moreover, a key security requirement in any ABE system is collusion resistance - ensuring that multiple users, each authorized under different attribute sets, cannot combine their keys to gain access to a ciphertext for which they are individually unauthorized.

3   Minimization Algorithm

The generic form of the function f includes all possible product terms in their most explicit form. Each product term consists of exactly one representative from each attribute group, ensuring that each product term uniquely corresponds to a specific user group (UG). This structure is derived by traversing a vertical path down in the attribute tree, crossing each level (representing an attribute group) exactly once. Our construction is well-defined for AND and OR gate. A logic function in our construction can be formed using these two gates with respect to attributes, which is a direct consequence of the Lemma 1. Although for a very high depth in AT, minimization of the function will require more time than desired, but in practice, it will be exceptional in real cases.

Since the generic form of f can be significantly large, minimizing it is crucial to reducing encoding and decoding times. This minimization not only optimizes the logic function f, but also enhances the efficiency in encryption and decryption within the proposed protocol. As a result, the overall computational costs for both the encoder and users are significantly reduced.

We propose a method to minimize the function f with respect to each attribute group. This technique involves the following steps given below:

- Selecting one attribute group at a time, fixing it, and considering a certain number of product terms, equal in number to the cardinality of that group.
- Upon checking whether the contribution of other attribute groups in that selected product term is equal or not, we stop minimization if the contributions are not the same.

- If they are the same, then we have to check that the attributes from our fixed attribute group are distinct (otherwise, two product terms will be the same), and they should exhaust all the attributes in the fixed attribute group.
- We can minimize and rewrite only one product term in place of all of them without writing the input from the fixed attribute group.

So, this process reduces the number of product terms significantly, as well as the length of the product term by one attribute, and to complete the minimization for that fixed attribute group, we have to check for all possible combinations of product terms, taking #(fixed attribute groups) the number of product terms at a time.

Algorithm 1

Require: $AG = \{AG_1, AG_2, \ldots, AG_g\}, f = \vee_{k=1}^{m} (\wedge_{i=1}^{g} A_{ik})$.
Ensure: Minimized function $f_{\min}$.
1: Initialize $f_{\min} \leftarrow f$.
2: **repeat**
3:     **for** each attribute group $AG_i \in AG$ **do**
4:         Let $n_i \leftarrow |AG_i|$.
5:         **for** each combination $C = \{P_1, P_2, \ldots, P_{n_i}\}$ of n_i product terms in $f_{\min}$ **do**
6:             Let $S_\alpha \leftarrow P_\alpha \setminus \{A_{ij}\}$, where $A_{ij} \in AG_i$ and $\alpha \in [\![n_i]\!]$.
7:             **if** $|S_1| = |S_2| = \ldots = |S_{n_i}|$ and $S_1 = S_2 = \ldots = S_{n_i} = S'$ **then**
8:                 **if** $\cup_{\alpha \in [\![n_i]\!]} P_\alpha \setminus S' = AG_i$ **then**
9:                     Replace $P_\alpha \setminus A_{ij} \leftarrow \vee_{\alpha \in [\![n_i]\!]} P_\alpha$.
10:                 **end if**
11:             **end if**
12:         **end for**
13:     **end for**
14: **until** no further minimization is possible
15: **Return** $f_{\min}$.

Stopping Condition. Suppose there are g attribute groups $\{AG_1, AG_2, \ldots, AG_g\}$. If the most recent minimization occurred for a specific group AG_i (where $1 \leq i \leq g$), we must continue to check for all other groups. This is because further minimization might still be possible for any group AG_j (where $1 \leq j \leq g$ and $j \neq i$), even if AG_j has already been minimized in any previous steps.

To ensure completeness, we follow the order of attribute groups as defined by the attribute tree. Starting from the group AG_i where the last minimization occurred, we check $AG_{i+1}, \ldots, AG_g$, and then loop back to $AG_1, \ldots, AG_{i-1}$. If no further minimization is found during this cycle, we stop and accept the current minimized form of the logic function f. However, if minimization is detected in any group, we fix the last minimized attribute group and repeat the process.

The stopping condition is met when no minimization is possible for the last $g - 1$ attribute groups checked in sequence. At this point, the minimized form of f is considered final. The pseudocode for this minimization algorithm for the logic function f is provided in Algorithm 1.

To illustrate the proposed minimization process, we present a detailed example. Consider three attribute groups $AG_1 = \{A_1, A_2, A_3\}, AG_2 = \{A_4, A_5, A_6, A_7\}$, $AG_3 = \{A_8, A_9\}$.The total number of possible product terms is determined by $|AG_1| \times |AG_2| \times |AG_3| = 3 \times 4 \times 2 = 24$. For a specific logic, the generic form of f may include a subset of these product terms. For instance, let

$$f = A_1 A_4 A_8 \vee A_2 A_4 A_8 \vee A_1 A_5 A_8 \vee A_1 A_6 A_8 \vee A_1 A_7 A_8 \vee A_2 A_4 A_9$$

We now proceed with minimization with respect to each attribute group:

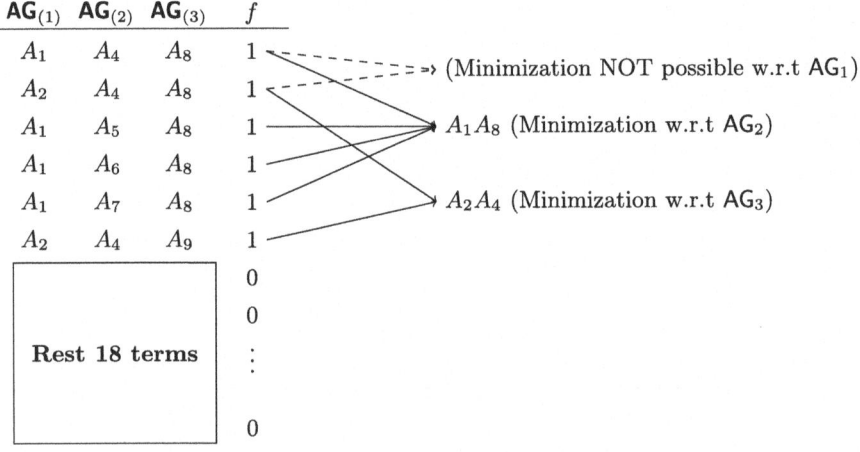

Fig. 2. Illustration of Minimization Algorithm

(a) **Minimization with respect to** AG_1: There are 3 attributes in $AG_1 = \{A_1, A_2, A_3\}$. Within f, the terms $A_1 A_4 A_8$ and $A_2 A_4 A_8$ share the same contributions from AG_2 and AG_3, namely $\{A_4 A_8\}$. However, the term $A_3 A_4 A_8$ is absent in f, meaning that all elements of AG_1 are not exhausted. Consequently, minimization is not possible for AG_1. A similar verification for the remaining terms confirms that no further reduction is feasible at this stage.

(b) **Minimization with respect to** AG_2: For minimization with respect to $AG_2 = \{A_4, A_5, A_6, A_7\}$, we consider four product terms at a time. The terms $A_1 A_4 A_8$, $A_1 A_5 A_8$, $A_1 A_6 A_8$ and $A_1 A_7 A_8$ exhibit identical contributions from AG_1 and AG_3, specifically $\{A_1 A_8\}$. Furthermore, these terms collectively exhaust all attributes in AG_2, allowing minimization:

$$A_1 A_4 A_8 \vee A_1 A_5 A_8 \vee A_1 A_6 A_8 \vee A_1 A_7 A_8$$
$$= A_1 A_8 \quad [\because \{A_4\} \cup \{A_5\} \cup \{A_6\} \cup \{A_7\} = U]$$

After this reduction, the simplified function is $f := A_2 A_4 A_8 \vee A_1 A_8 \vee A_2 A_4 A_9$.

Further minimization with respect to AG_2 is not possible.

(c) **Minimization with respect to AG_3:** For $AG_3 = \{A_8, A_9\}$, two product terms must be considered at a time. The terms $A_2 A_4 A_8$ and $A_2 A_4 A_9$ share identical contributions from AG_1 and AG_2, specifically $\{A_2 A_4\}$, and fully cover all attributes in AG_3. Thus, they can be minimized as follows:

$$A_2 A_4 A_8 \vee A_2 A_4 A_9 = A_2 A_4$$

After applying the minimization steps, the final reduced expression for f is

$$f := A_1 A_8 \vee A_2 A_4$$

To ensure completeness, we repeat the process for AG_1 and AG_2. No further reduction is possible, confirming that the form obtained is the minimal representation of f. Figure 2 illustrates the pictorial representation of this minimal form, where $AG_{(i)}$ denotes an arbitrary element of the attribute group AG_i, $i \in [\![3]\!]$.

Remark 1 (**Comparison with Quine-McCluskey algorithm**). The Quine-McCluskey algorithm, as employed in [10], operates strictly on Boolean variables, where the negation of a user is represented by a single binary input (either 0 or 1). The approach ultimately relies on Integer Linear Programming (ILP) to obtain an optimal minimization. However, ILP formulations are known to be computationally expensive, especially when used repeatedly for a *single minimization* task. To address this, [10] proposes using a near-optimal solution, which offers a good trade-off between performance and efficiency and can be obtained with significantly less computational effort.

In contrast, our proposed minimization algorithm is specifically designed to handle attribute-level negation. Unlike the binary case of the previous work [10], negation in our setting corresponds to a set of attributes that must be considered during minimization. To manage this, our algorithm processes one attribute group at a time and performs group-wise minimization as outlined in Algorithm 1. Although this method may incur slightly higher computational costs than the Quine-McCluskey approach, it produces an *optimal minimized logic function*. This optimality is particularly beneficial as it significantly reduces the size of the function and improves both the encoding/encryption time for the emitter and the decoding/decryption time for the users. Consequently, our algorithm offers a fundamentally different and more suitable minimization strategy for the proposed scheme, ensuring efficiency in all subsequent protocol steps.

3.1 Construction of f

By constructing the Attribute Tree (AT), we can uniquely identify each user group (UG) through distinct paths within the tree. The uniqueness is derived from the specific combinations of attributes that define each UG. Since a path from the root to a UG traverses each level exactly once, it precisely selects one attribute from each attribute group (AG), thereby covering all attribute groups.

To ensure a unique representation of each attribute, we introduce the Attribute Universe (AU), where each attribute is sequentially placed in a set. We then associate each attribute with a unique binary string. Specifically, the attribute at position i in the set is represented by a binary expansion of 2^{i-1}. For example,

$$AU = \{A_1, A_2, \ldots, A_6, A_7\}$$
$$A_3 = 100$$

Clearly, in this way, each attribute will be assigned to a unique binary string. Since each UG is defined by a unique combination of attributes, we can represent every UG using a binary string. If a UG consists of attributes $A_{i_1}, A_{i_2}, A_{i_3}, \ldots$, then its corresponding binary string is the binary expansion of $2^{i_1-1} + 2^{i_2-1} + 2^{i_3-1} + \ldots$. For example,

$$UG = \{A_2\} \cap \{A_4\} \cap \{A_7\} \text{ where } AU = \{A_1, A_2, ..., A_7\}$$
$$UG = \langle 2^1 + 2^3 + 2^6 \rangle = 1001010$$

This method allows any conjunction of attributes to be represented in a structured manner. Most importantly, each user in a particular user group takes the binary string assigned to its corresponding user group as its own input value. Whenever a user tries to verify its accessibility with respect to a logic function f, it uses that binary string as input.

Finally, to construct the function f, we express it in its minimal form as a disjunction of product terms. Using the previously described method, we assign a unique binary string to each product term. The function f is then defined such that it evaluates to 1 only for the binary strings corresponding to these product terms, while for all other binary strings of the same length, it outputs 0. Thus, f is given by $f : \{0,1\}^* \rightarrow \{0,1\}$. For example, if

$$AU = \{A_1, A_2, ..., A_7\}$$
$$AG_1 = \{A_1, A_2\}, AG_2 = \{A_3, A_4, A_5\} \text{ and } AG_3 = \{A_6, A_7\}$$
$$f = A_1 A_6 \vee A_2 A_3 A_7, \text{ (in the minimal form)}$$

then, we assign the values

$$f(x) = \begin{cases} 1, & x \in \{100001, 1000110\} \\ 0, & \text{otherwise} \end{cases}$$

3.2   Encoding and Decoding of f

In our construction, we employ a public encoding of the minimal form of f, which can be efficiently decoded by any user or an external entity. The minimal representation of f consists of disjunctions of multiple product terms. Let the minimal representation of f be $f = \vee_{k=1}^{m} P_k = \vee_{k=1}^{m} (\wedge_{i=1}^{g} A_{ik})$. However, the maximum number of product terms can be

$$|AG_1| \times |AG_2| \times \ldots \times |AG_g| = n_p \text{ (say)},$$

where $\{AG_1, AG_2, \ldots, AG_g\}$ denote the g attribute groups.

To encode the number of product terms in the minimal representation, a binary string of length $\lceil \log(n_p) \rceil$ is sufficient. However, to account for potential additions of attributes in some attribute groups (which will increase n_p exponentially), this length is extended to $\lceil \log(n_p) \rceil + \delta$, where δ is a small constant compared to n_p and we will take $\delta = \lceil \log(n_p)/2 \rceil$. This choice of δ ensures that the length of the representation of the function f does not need to be changed to add a large number of attributes to the scheme. Consider the case where a single attribute is added to an attribute group AG_g (without loss of generality). The total number of possible product terms will be $|AG_1| \times |AG_2| \times \ldots \times |AG_g + 1|$, which represents an increase of $|AG_1| \times |AG_2| \times \ldots \times |AG_{g-1}| \approx n_p/2$ in the worst-case scenario, where AG_g initially contained only two attributes. This increase will depend on the total number of product terms in the previous step. For example, if we add one more attribute to AG_g, the increase in the number of product terms with respect to starting n_p will be $(n_p + n_p/2) + \frac{(n_p + n_p/2)}{3} - n_p = n_p(\frac{1}{2} + \frac{1}{3} + \frac{1}{6})$ and so on. To efficiently manage this growth, our choice of δ guarantees that the number of binary strings available to represent product terms is at least

$$2^{\lceil \log(n_p) \rceil + \lceil \log(n_p)/2 \rceil} \geq 2^{log(n_p) + log(n_p)/2} = n_p \cdot \sqrt{n_p} = n_p^{\frac{3}{2}}.$$

Since $\lceil \log(n_p) \rceil \geq log(n_p)$, this bound is always valid. Importantly, $n_p^{\frac{3}{2}}$ is exponentially greater than n_p, which ensures that the representation can accommodate polynomial increases in product terms over time. Furthermore, as $log(n_p) \ll n_p$, the string length required for representation remains minimal. This efficiency translates directly into reduced computational costs for both encoding and decoding operations, making the scheme highly scalable and practical for large-scale deployments.

Then each product term is assigned to a binary string of length $|AU|$, following the same encoding method as before. The concatenation of all these binary representations follows the order of product terms in minimal form, prefixed by a binary string of length $\lceil \log(n_p) \rceil + \delta$, representing the number of product terms in decimal form. The final encoding of f is given by

$$\langle m \rangle \; (\!| P_1 |\!)_2 \; (\!| P_2 |\!)_2 \; \ldots \; (\!| P_m |\!)_2,$$

where $\langle m \rangle$ denotes $\lceil \log(n_p) \rceil + \delta$ bit binary string, representing decimal form of m and $(\!| \cdot |\!)_2$ denotes encoding representation. This encoding of f is then included in the header and transmitted along with the encrypted message. For example, if

$AU = \{A_1, A_2, ..., A_7\}, |AU| = 7$
$AG_1 = \{A_1, A_2\}, AG_2 = \{A_3, A_4, A_5\}, AG_3 = \{A_6, A_7\},$
$\lceil \log(n_p) \rceil + \delta = 6$, taking the value of $\delta = 2$ and $n_p = 2 \times 3 \times 2 = 12,$

then, the encoding of f will be 000010 100001 1000110.

Since the encoding of f is transmitted in the header, any user can efficiently decode it using the predefined values of $(\lceil \log(n_p) \rceil + \delta)$ and $|AU|$. Consequently, the binary strings corresponding to the product terms are readily accessible to all users. To verify whether a given user satisfies the function f, they begin with their assigned binary input, which corresponds to their user group UG. In the minimized representation, a product term may not necessarily include one attribute from each attribute group (AG), as the function is of minimal form. For a user to satisfy a product term, it must include only attributes possessed by the user, while excluding any attributes that the user does not have. Formally, if the user's binary string contains 1's at positions $\{i_1, i_2, \ldots, i_k\}$, then the corresponding product term must not have any 1's at positions $\{\llbracket |AU| + 1 \rrbracket \setminus \{j_1, j_2, ..., j_k\}\}$.

To optimize this aforementioned verification process, it is sufficient to check whether the binary representation of a product term has 0's in the places of $\{\llbracket |AU| + 1 \rrbracket \setminus \{j_1, j_2, ..., j_k\}\}$ or not. Upon checking if 1 appears in any of these places, the user rejects that product term and moves on to the next. If it satisfies one product term, then it does not need to check for other product terms as it will be able to decrypt with respect to that product term itself.

Consider an example from Sect. 3.1, where a user has the binary input 100101, indicating that they possess the attributes $\{A_1, A_3, A_6\}$. To verify access, the user examines whether the binary representation of the first product term contains 0 in the positions corresponding to absent attributes. If the first product term is represented as 100001 (corresponding to $A_1 A_6$), it satisfies the condition, allowing the user to proceed with decryption without evaluating the remaining product terms. In contrast, if a user has the binary input 1001010, corresponding to the attribute set $\{A_2, A_4, A_7\}$, verification reveals that none of the product terms satisfy this input. Consequently, the user cannot decrypt the message.

4   Proposed Protocol

We introduce a collusion-resistant scheme that prevents any group of unauthorized users from decrypting a valid logic function within an attribute-based access control system. The scheme is designed to ensure security against collusion attacks while maintaining efficient key management and scalability.

Let the complete set of attributes be represented as $\{A_1, \ldots, A_a\}$, where a denotes the total number of attributes. These attributes are organized into g distinct attribute groups, denoted $\{AG_1, \ldots, AG_g\}$, according to our previous assumptions. The algorithms for our proposed scheme are described below.

- **Setup**: The Setup algorithm is executed by the emitter, which selects a random element k_{PRF} from the key space $\mathcal{K}$ as the only secret key of the system. For each attribute A_i in the attribute set, a corresponding label k_i is generated. These labels may be publicly known and are not required to be random or secret. However, it is essential that each label k_i is unique, ensuring that no two attributes share the same label. This uniqueness is essential to maintaining the integrity and functionality of the scheme.

  For an example, the label k_i can be constructed as $k_i = \langle i \rangle_a$, where a represents the total number of attributes and $\langle i \rangle_a$ denotes the a-bit binary representation of i.

- **Join**: When a user u joins the system, the algorithm Join first checks in which user group u belongs to the depth $g+1$ in the attribute tree. For a given u, we assume $u \in \{A_{i_1}\} \cap \{A_{i_2}\} \cap \ldots \cap \{A_{i_g}\}$, the corresponding labels $k_{i_1}, \ldots, k_{i_g}$ are selected. The emitter then computes and transmits the following functions $F(k_{\mathsf{PRF}}, \|_{j \in S} \, k_{i_j})$, for all ordered $S \subseteq [g]$ to the corresponding user. Here, F denotes the pseudorandom function (PRF).

  For example, if $g = 3$, the associated labels assigned to the user will be $k_{i_1}, k_{i_2}, k_{i_3}$. The following set of keys is distributed to the user:

$$F(k_{\mathsf{PRF}}, k_{i_1}), F(k_{\mathsf{PRF}}, (k_{i_1} \| k_{i_2})), F(k_{\mathsf{PRF}}, (k_{i_1} \| k_{i_2} \| k_{i_3})),$$
$$F(k_{\mathsf{PRF}}, k_{i_2}), F(k_{\mathsf{PRF}}, (k_{i_2} \| k_{i_3})), F(k_{\mathsf{PRF}}, \Phi),$$
$$F(k_{\mathsf{PRF}}, k_{i_3}), F(k_{\mathsf{PRF}}, (k_{i_1} \| k_{i_3}))$$

  Consequently, for any user, g labels are required to generate the keys. Based on this construction, each user will receive a total of 2^g keys.

- **Encrypt**: We consider the minimal representation of the logic function, denoted by f. A user u is authorized to decrypt if and only if $f(u) = 1$; otherwise, $f(u) = 0$.

  The encryption header includes an encoded representation of f, which is described in Sect. 3.2. Now, consider the logic function that can be expressed as $f = P_1 \vee P_2 \vee \ldots$, where P_i's are the product terms.

  Let S_i be the set of the corresponding indices of attributes in P_i. During encryption, the emitter selects a randomly generated ephemeral key k_e from $\mathcal{K}$. The ciphertext consists of multiple encryptions of k_e corresponding to each product term, followed by encryption of the original message using k_e. The encryption of k_e with respect to each product term P_i is given by

$$C_i = E(\mathsf{key}_i, k_e), \text{ with } \mathsf{key}_i = F(k_{\mathsf{PRF}}, \|_{\alpha \in S_i} \, k_\alpha),$$

  where E is any known encryption scheme, k_α represents the labels associated with attributes in P_i and the concatenation should be taken in the ordered format.

  For example, if $P_i = A_{i_1} A_{i_2} A_{i_3}$, then the corresponding key key_i will be $F(k_{\mathsf{PRF}}, (k_{i_1} \| k_{i_2} \| k_{i_3}))$. Following this, the final ciphertext corresponds to the minimal representation of the logic function $E(\mathsf{key}_1, k_e) \| E(\mathsf{key}_2, k_e) \| \ldots \| E(k_e, m)$, where m is the message to be delivered.

- **Decrypt**: After extracting the function f from the header, the user u evaluates whether $f(u) = 1$. If $f(u) = 0$, the decryption process is immediately terminated.

  If $f(u) = 1$, the user determines which product term it satisfies by sequentially evaluating each term from left to right. Although a single user may satisfy multiple product terms, it selects the term most satisfied on the left during this process. For the corresponding product term, say $P_i(u) = 1$, the user u retrieves the associated key designated for that term, using the key provided by the emitter.

  Using this key, the user u decrypts the respective ciphertext block corresponding to the identified product term and extracts the ephemeral key k_e. Finally, employing k_e, the user u decrypts the final ciphertext block to recover the original message m.

Correctness: To verify the correctness of the proposed scheme, we must verify that every authorized user can successfully decrypt the ciphertext. Given the minimal representation of the function f, a user can verify a product term if and only if the attributes within that term form a subset of the attributes possessed by the user. Since the system distributes decryption keys corresponding to all relevant subsets of attributes held by each authorized user, the decryption key associated with any valid product term must have been provided at the time of joining by the emitter. Consequently, this guarantees the correctness of the proposed scheme.

Security Analysis: Unlike public-key encryption (PKE) schemes, traditional symmetric schemes often lack rigorous and well-defined provable security models. Additionally, while any public-key encryption protocol typically derives its security from well-studied hardness assumptions (*e.g.,* factoring, discrete logarithm, lattice-based problems), symmetric-key encryption schemes often do not offer such reductions. Although we do not provide a formal or game-based security proof for our construction, we highlight that the security of our scheme relies on the standard assumption that the underlying pseudorandom function. Under this assumption, any adversary who does not possess the correct attribute set cannot distinguish the encryption key or recover any information about the plaintext. Moreover, we can leave a more formal security model and proof framework for symmetric-key ABE as an open direction for future work, as the field currently lacks a standardized security model for such constructions. Every ABE scheme should satisfy the collusion-resistant property. Therefore, we analyze only the collusion-resistant property for our proposed attribute-based encryption scheme. This property ensures that no subset of unauthorized users can successfully decrypt the ciphertext. In our framework, collusion refers to any unauthorized subset of users.

Theorem 1. *Assuming the security of the underlying pseudorandom function, the proposed symmetric-key ABE scheme satisfies the collusion-resistant property.*

Proof. Let $\mathcal{S}$ denote the set of all authorized users, and let $\bar{\mathcal{S}} = U \setminus \mathcal{S}$ represents unauthorized users for some particular logic statement, where U is the whole set of users. The boolean function f associated with this policy satisfies $f(u) = 1 \ \forall \ u \in \mathcal{S}$ and $f(u) = 0 \ \forall \ u \in \bar{\mathcal{S}}$. As discussed previously, f is expressed in its minimal sum of products as $f = \vee_i P_i$.

It is evident that any collusion will be able to decrypt the ciphertext if and only if it can retrieve the key corresponding to any of the product terms in the minimal form of f. Each product term takes the form of $P_i = A_{i_1} \wedge A_{i_2} \wedge \ldots \wedge A_{i_m}$ and is encrypted using the key $\mathsf{key}_i = F(k_{\mathsf{PRF}}, \|_{j \in [\![m]\!]} \ k_{i_j})$, where k_{i_j}'s are the labels corresponding to the attributes of that product term. Although these labels are publicly known, k_{PRF} is securely maintained by the emitter and remains inaccessible to unauthorized users. A successful collusion attack would involve one of the following scenarios:

(a) At least one unauthorized user within the colluding group possesses the decryption key key_i corresponding to a product term. However, this contradicts the definition of f, which ensures that $f(u) = 0 \ \forall \ u \in \bar{\mathcal{S}}$. This would mean that the logical access policy is incorrectly defined, which is not the case.

(b) If colluding users could derive key_i using their own keys obtained during the user joining phase, this would contradict the security properties of the pseudorandom function F. Specifically, reconstructing key_i would imply the ability to distinguish F from a truly random function, violating its assumed cryptographic security guarantees.

Thus, under the assumption that F is a secure PRF, no unauthorized collusion can decrypt the ciphertext, ensuring the collusion resistance of our scheme.

Minimization of Re-formatting of Keys: Re-formatting of the entire key-storage per existing user can be minimized. Once an attribute tree is constructed for a user set, if we have to introduce new synthetic attributes for new users, then we keep the previous two attributes to their corresponding places in the modified attribute universe AU as before and add synthetic attributes one by one at the end of AU. As the binary expression of an attribute depends solely on the position of these attributes in AU, these new synthetic attributes will not change the binary expressions of the previous ones. As a result, Consequently, key updates are necessary only for those new user groups whose paths in the tree involve the newly introduced synthetic attributes. The key storage for all other user groups remains unchanged.

For example, consider an initial attribute universe $\mathsf{AU} = \{A_1, A_2, A_3, A_4, A_5\}$ with attribute groups defined as $\mathsf{AG}_1 = \{A_1, A_2\}, \mathsf{AG}_2 = \{A_3, A_4, A_5\}$. Suppose that to incorporate a new user, the mutual exclusivity of AG_1 is violated. To restore exclusivity, we introduce a synthetic attribute and redefine the group as $\mathsf{AG}_1 = \{A_1', A_2', A_6\}$ which makes the new $\mathsf{AU} = \{A_1', A_2', A_3, A_4, A_5, A_6\}$, where $\{A_1'\} = \{A_1\} \setminus \{\{A_1\} \cap \{A_2\}\}, A_2' = \{A_2\} \setminus \{\{A_1\} \cap \{A_2\}\}$ and $\{A_6\} = \{A_1\} \cap \{A_2\}$. In this example, two of the original attributes (A_1' and A_2') retain their positions in the updated AU, ensuring that the corresponding binary expressions remain unchanged. Consequently, only the keys for user groups that involve the new synthetic attribute - such as $\{A_6A_3, A_6A_4,$ and $A_6A_5\}$ - must be reformatted and redistributed, while the keys for all other user groups remain unaffected.

Moreover, we emphasize that once an attribute tree has been constructed for a sufficiently large user set, the addition of a new synthetic attribute will be significantly low. As a result, the probability of needing to reconstruct and redistribute keys accordingly decreases.

5   Key-Estimation Analysis

In this section, we analyze the total number of keys stored by each user and demonstrate that our scheme considerably lowers the key storage requirements per user compared to the recently proposed scheme [10]. Specifically, each user stores a total of 2^g keys (*cf.* Sect. 4), as the user groups are positioned at depth $g + 1$ in the attribute tree (AT) corresponding to the attribute groups $AG_1, \ldots,$ AG_g. Furthermore, our scheme has the following property.

Property 1. The number of keys per user will be exponentially less than the total number of users present in the system for any non-trivial (real) scenario.

Proof. Depending on the inclusion of new users or attributes, we divide the proof into four distinct cases.

(a) **Case-I** (Each user group consists of exactly one user, and each attribute group comprises exactly two attributes): We consider this case as the worst-case (trivial) scenario due to the following reasons:

- If a user group does not contain any users, we can discard that user group along with the path in the attribute tree that led to its creation.
- If an attribute group contains only a single attribute, our prior assumptions establish that this attribute is universally true. Consequently, it does not affect any logical statements, allowing us to eliminate the attribute and, subsequently, the corresponding attribute group.

For Case-I, the total number of users can be computed as follows:

$$\text{Total number of users} = \text{Total number of user groups} \times 1$$
$$= 2^{(\text{Total number of attribute groups})}$$
$$= 2^g$$

Since each user is required to store 2^g keys, the number of keys per user is equal to the total number of users.

(b) **Case-II** (User groups consist of multiple users, and each attribute group contains exactly two attributes): In Case-II, each user group consists of multiple users, whereas in Case-I, each user group contains exactly one user. However, the number of user groups in Case-II remains the same as in Case-I. Thus, the total number of user groups remains 2^g.

Since each user group contains at least one user for Case-II, the total number of users satisfies the following condition:

$$\text{Total number of users} \geq 2^g = \text{Number of keys per user}$$

(c) **Case-III** (Each user group has exactly one user, and each attribute group has ≥ 2 attributes): If an attribute group contains more than 2 attributes, say $(2+\alpha)$ attributes, where $\alpha \in \mathbb{Z}^+$, then the total number of user groups is given by

$$\text{Total number of user groups} = 2 \times \ldots 2 \times (2+\alpha) \times 2 \ldots \times 2$$
$$= 2^g + \alpha 2^{g-1}$$

Similarly, if each of the other attribute groups contains more than or equal to 2 attributes, the total number of user groups increases exponentially.

Let AG_i contains $(2+\alpha_i)$ attributes for all $i \in \{1, ..., g\}$, where $\alpha_i \in \mathbb{N}$. Then the total number of user groups can be expressed as:

$$\prod_{i=1}^{g} (2 + \alpha_i) = 2^g + o(2^g)$$

This represents the total number of users, which grows exponentially and is substantially larger than 2^g. Hence, the number of keys per user is significantly smaller than the total number of users.

(d) **Case-IV** (User groups contain multiple users, and each attribute group consists of more than two attributes): This case represents the most generalized scenario and is most likely to occur in real-world applications. Based on the calculations from Case-III, we obtain the following expression for the total number of users:

$$\text{Total number of users} = (\prod_{i=1}^{g}(2+\alpha_i))(1+o(1))$$
$$= 2^g + o(2^g) + o(1)$$
$$= 2^g + o(2^g)$$
$$\gg \text{Number of keys per user}$$

The above four cases cover all possible combinations of attribute groups and user groups. For most of these cases (generalizing to real world scenario), the number of keys per user is significantly smaller than the total number of users.

Property 2. The number of keys per user does not change even if (i) new users are added to the system or (ii) additional attributes are included within existing attribute groups. The number of keys per user only changes when (iii) a new attribute group is added to the attribute tree, without affecting Property 1.

Proof. (i) When a new user is added to the system, it is placed in an existing user group, assuming that the mutual exclusivity between attribute groups is maintained. Although this increases the total number of users, it does not alter the structure or depth of the attribute tree. Since each user group is defined by a unique vertical path through the tree, the number of attributes (*i.e.*, one per level) representing the user remains unchanged. Therefore, the key storage per user does not alter while increasing the total users.

(ii) If new attributes are introduced within one or more existing attribute groups, either to preserve mutual exclusivity or to accommodate users with distinct attribute values, the size (*i.e.*, the number of nodes) of the attribute tree increases. However, its depth - the number of levels corresponding to distinct attribute groups - remains unchanged. Since the number of keys per user depends solely on the number of attribute groups (*i.e.*, tree depth), this inclusion does not affect key storage per user.

(iii) The only scenario that increases the number of keys per user is the addition of a new attribute group, which extends the attribute tree by one level and increases its depth from g to $g + 1$. In this case, each user will require 2^{g+1} keys instead of 2^g. However, this transition is handled efficiently: users retain their existing keys, and only the additional 2^g keys corresponding to the new attribute group are distributed. As specified in the Join procedure of our proposed protocol (*cf.* Sect. 4), each user receives only those new keys relevant to their label in the newly added attribute group. Since each attribute in the new group appears in exactly half of the 2^{g+1} total combinations, the distribution is both optimized and non-redundant.

It is important to note that once the attribute tree is constructed to accommodate a sufficiently large user base, the addition of a new attribute group is a rare event. Furthermore, as demonstrated in Case IV of Property 1, even in this case, the number of keys required per user remains significantly smaller than the total number of users in the system.

*Remark 2 (**Comparative analysis**).* The collusion-resistant BE scheme presented in [10] requires each user to store n secret keys, where n corresponds to the total number of users in the system. In contrast, our work extends their approach to a more expressive ABE framework and still achieves significantly lower key storage per user. This improvement is formally shown in Properties 1 and 2, demonstrating the scalability and efficiency of our protocol. Moreover, our scheme is designed within the symmetric key framework, which fundamentally differs from the public key setting in terms of security assumptions, key distribution and performance goals. Therefore, in our work, a direct comparison with public-key ABE schemes is not considered.

6   Conclusion

This paper presented the first attribute-based encryption (ABE) scheme within the symmetric-key framework, built upon consensual security assumptions such as pseudorandom functions. Our approach integrates a hierarchical attribute management mechanism using attribute groups and an attribute tree, enhancing efficiency in access control. In addition, we propose a minimization algorithm to optimize the logic function, effectively reducing storage overhead and computational bandwidth. Exploring functional encryption within a symmetric key cryptographic framework based on such consensual assumptions presents a promising avenue for future research, potentially broadening the applicability of symmetric-key techniques in fine-grained access control.

Acknowledgement. This study was funded by the Science and Engineering Research Board (SERB), Department of Science and Technology (DST), Government of India under File No. EEQ/2023/000164 and the Information Security Education and Awareness (ISEA) Project Phase-III initiatives of the Ministry of Electronics and Information Technology (MeitY) under Grant No. F.No. L-14017/1/2022-HRD. The second author also gratefully acknowledges the support received from the ANRF International Travel Support (ITS) scheme, Government of India, under file number ITS/2025/002548.

References

1. Abhyankar, S.: Minimal sum of products of sums expressions of boolean functions. IRE Trans. Electron. Comput. **4**, 268–276 (1958)
2. Agrawal, S., Kumari, S., Yamada, S.: Attribute based encryption for turing machines from lattices. In: Annual International Cryptology Conference, pp. 352–386. Springer (2024)
3. Agrawal, S., Yamada, S.: Optimal broadcast encryption from pairings and LWE. In: Annual International Conference on the Theory and Applications of Cryptographic Techniques, pp. 13–43. Springer (2020)
4. Attrapadung, N., Tomida, J.: Unbounded dynamic predicate compositions in ABE from standard assumptions. In: International Conference on the Theory and Application of Cryptology and Information Security, pp. 405–436. Springer (2020)
5. Bogdanov, A., Rosen, A.: Pseudorandom functions: three decades later. In: Tutorials on the Foundations of Cryptography: Dedicated to Oded Goldreich, pp. 79–158. Springer (2017)
6. Boyle, E., Goldwasser, S., Ivan, I.: Functional signatures and pseudorandom functions. In: International Workshop on Public Key Cryptography, pp. 501–519. Springer (2014)
7. Brakerski, Z., Vaikuntanathan, V.: Lattice-inspired broadcast encryption and succinct ciphertext-policy ABE. In: 13th Innovations in Theoretical Computer Science Conference (ITCS 2022). Schloss Dagstuhl-Leibniz-Zentrum für Informatik (2022)
8. Crama, Y., Hammer, P.L.: Boolean Functions: Theory, Algorithms, and Applications. Cambridge University Press (2011)
9. Datta, P., Komargodski, I., Waters, B.: Decentralized multi-authority ABE for NC1 from computational-BDH. Cryptology ePrint Archive (2021)
10. Dupin, A., Abelard, S.: Broadcast encryption using sum-product decomposition of boolean functions. Cryptology ePrint Archive (2024)
11. Garg, S., Gentry, C., Halevi, S., Sahai, A., Waters, B.: Attribute-based encryption for circuits from multilinear maps. In: Annual Cryptology Conference, pp. 479–499. Springer (2013)

12. Gong, J., Wee, H.: Adaptively secure ABE for DFA from k-lin and more. In: Annual International Conference on the Theory and Applications of Cryptographic Techniques, pp. 278–308. Springer (2020)
13. Goyal, V., Pandey, O., Sahai, A., Waters, B.: Attribute-based encryption for fine-grained access control of encrypted data. In: Proceedings of the 13th ACM Conference on Computer and Communications Security, pp. 89–98 (2006)
14. Han, J., Susilo, W., Mu, Y., Yan, J.: Privacy-preserving decentralized key-policy attribute-based encryption. IEEE Trans. Parallel Distrib. Syst. **23**(11), 2150–2162 (2012)
15. Lai, J., Deng, R.H., Li, Y., Weng, J.: Fully secure key-policy attribute-based encryption with constant-size ciphertexts and fast decryption. In: Proceedings of the 9th ACM Symposium on Information, Computer and Communications Security, pp. 239–248 (2014)
16. Lewko, A., Okamoto, T., Sahai, A., Takashima, K., Waters, B.: Fully secure functional encryption: attribute-based encryption and (hierarchical) inner product encryption. In: Annual International Conference on the Theory and Applications of Cryptographic Techniques, pp. 62–91. Springer (2010)
17. Lewko, A., Waters, B.: New techniques for dual system encryption and fully secure hibe with short ciphertexts. In: Theory of Cryptography Conference, pp. 455–479. Springer (2010)
18. Lewko, A., Waters, B.: New proof methods for attribute-based encryption: achieving full security through selective techniques. In: Annual Cryptology Conference, pp. 180–198. Springer (2012)
19. Lin, H., Luo, J.: Compact adaptively secure ABE from k-lin: beyond NC1 and towards NL. In: Annual International Conference on the Theory and Applications of Cryptographic Techniques, pp. 247–277. Springer (2020)
20. Okamoto, T., Takashima, K.: Fully secure functional encryption with general relations from the decisional linear assumption. In: Annual Cryptology Conference, pp. 191–208. Springer (2010)
21. Okamoto, T., Takashima, K.: Fully secure unbounded inner-product and attribute-based encryption. In: International Conference on the Theory and Application of Cryptology and Information Security, pp. 349–366. Springer (2012)
22. Sahai, A., Waters, B.: Fuzzy identity-based encryption. In: Annual International Conference on the Theory and Applications of Cryptographic Techniques, pp. 457–473. Springer (2005)
23. Tomida, J., Kawahara, Y., Nishimaki, R.: Fast, compact, and expressive attribute-based encryption. Des. Codes Crypt. **89**(11), 2577–2626 (2021). https://doi.org/10.1007/s10623-021-00939-8
24. Tsabary, R.: Fully secure attribute-based encryption for t-CNF from LWE. In: Annual International Cryptology Conference, pp. 62–85. Springer (2019)
25. Waters, B.: Ciphertext-policy attribute-based encryption: an expressive, efficient, and provably secure realization. In: International Workshop on Public Key Cryptography, pp. 53–70. Springer (2011)
26. Waters, B.: Functional encryption for regular languages. In: Annual Cryptology Conference, pp. 218–235. Springer (2012)
27. Wee, H.: Optimal broadcast encryption and CP-ABE from evasive lattice assumptions. In: Annual International Conference on the Theory and Applications of Cryptographic Techniques, pp. 217–241. Springer (2022)
28. Wee, H.: Circuit ABE with poly (depth, λ)-sized ciphertexts and keys from lattices. In: Annual International Cryptology Conference, pp. 178–209. Springer (2024)

Simultaneously Simple Universal and Indifferentiable Hashing to Elliptic Curves

Dimitri Koshelev$^{(\boxtimes)}$ ⓘ

Department of Mathematics, University of Lleida, Lleida, Catalonia, Spain
dimitri.koshelev@gmail.com

Abstract. The present article explains how to generalize the hash function SwiftEC (in an elementary quasi-unified way) to any elliptic curve E over any finite field $\mathbb{F}_q$ of characteristic > 3. The new result apparently brings the theory of hash functions onto elliptic curves to its logical conclusion. To be more precise, this article provides compact formulas that define a hash function $\{0,1\}^* \to E(\mathbb{F}_q)$ (deterministic and indifferentible from a random oracle) with the same working principle as SwiftEC. In particular, both of them equally compute only one square root in $\mathbb{F}_q$ (in addition to two cheap Legendre symbols). However, the new hash function is valid with much more liberal conditions than SwiftEC, namely when $3 \mid q - 1$. Since in the opposite case $3 \mid q - 2$ there are already indifferentiable constant-time hash functions to E with the cost of one root in $\mathbb{F}_q$, this case is not processed in the article. If desired, its approach nonetheless allows to easily do that mutatis mutandis.

Keywords: absolute irreducibility · conics · hyperelliptic curves · hashing to elliptic curves · unirationality problem

1 Introduction

Hashing to an elliptic $\mathbb{F}_q$-curve E plays an important role in elliptic curve cryptography (ECC). To be exact, we are talking about a map $\mathcal{H}\colon \{0,1\}^* \to E(\mathbb{F}_q)$ from the set of binary strings of arbitrary length to the $\mathbb{F}_q$-point group of E. The given primitive already arose in Koblitz's pioneering work [14, Section 3] on ECC under the name "imbedding plaintext". It is not surprising, because

https://www.linkedin.com/in/dimitri-koshelev

This research is a result of the strategic project "Advances in post-quantum cryptography applied to the development of a coupon system" (C039/24), resulting from an agreement between the Spanish National Cybersecurity Institute (INCIBE) and University of Lleida. This initiative is carried out in the scope of the funds from the Recovery, Transformation and Resilience Plan, funded by the European Union (Next Generation). The paper is also part of the R&D+i project PID2021-124613OB-I00 funded by MICIU/AEI/10.13039/501100011033 and FEDER, EU.

A. Nitaj et al. (Eds.): AFRICACRYPT 2025, LNCS 15651, pp. 395–413, 2026.
https://doi.org/10.1007/978-3-031-97260-7_18

many classical public-key encryption schemes, including *Massey–Omura* and *El Gamal* ones (see, e.g., [14, Section 4]), represent a secret message $m \in \{0,1\}^*$ as an elliptic curve point $\mathcal{H}(m)$. Thus, the need for $\mathcal{H}$ appeared long before other more mainstream primitives on elliptic curves such as pairings and isogenies.

To prevent leakage of m, the running time of $\mathcal{H}$ must depend exclusively on the length of m, not on its content. In the early years of development of ECC, people did not know how to safely construct $\mathcal{H}$ unless the j-invariant $j(E) = 0$ and $3 \mid q - 2$ or, similarly, $j(E) = 1728$ and $4 \mid q - 3$ thanks to Kaliski Jr. [13, Section 3] in 1991. In both situations, E is necessarily a supersingular curve. In the same year it became clear [23] that supersingular curves are weaker for ECC than ordinary (a.k.a. non-supersingular) ones. Therefore, a large layer of cryptographic protocols based on the discrete logarithm problem (DLP) essentially remained for a long time untransferable to $E(\mathbb{F}_q)$ from the multiplicative group $\mathbb{F}_q^*$. Undoubtedly, constant-time hashing of the form $\{0,1\}^* \to \mathbb{F}_q^*$ does not present any difficulties. By contrast, a required hash function to ordinary elliptic curves was independently invented only in the mid-2000s by Skałba [29] and Shallue–van de Woestijne [28].

Since in some scenarios $\mathcal{H}$ is called many times, it is desirable that the given primitive be as cheap as possible. This is the case, e.g., for *incremental (i.e., homomorphic) multiset hashing* [21] and for numerous signature schemes among which a ring signature utilized in *CryptoNote cryptocurrencies* [26]. In the latter, a hash-to-curve function is the principal component of so-called *key image* [24]. For information, it is basically a non-homomorphic map from $E(\mathbb{F}_q)$ to itself designed to hide the discrete logarithm between input and output points. According to an established tradition in the research area under consideration, the operating time of $\mathcal{H}$ is measured in the number of radicals $\sqrt[n]{\cdot} \in \mathbb{F}_q$ (usually with an even $n \in \mathbb{N}$) contained in $\mathcal{H}$. Moreover, each of them is frequently expressed through one exponentiation in $\mathbb{F}_q$. By the way, hashing over highly 2-adic fields is discussed in [11,18], [20, Section 4].

Indifferentiability (from a random oracle) in the sense of [22] is yet another indispensable cryptographic property imposed on hash functions. The point is that this property periodically occurs in reliability proofs of cryptographic protocols and it is not always possible to get rid of it. That is why it is desirable for versatility of use that $\mathcal{H}$ maintain the indifferentiability. For instance, Kaliski Jr.'s hash functions are random oracles, because they are built upon specific readily computable bijective maps $\mathbb{P}^1(\mathbb{F}_q) \to E(\mathbb{F}_q)$ (see a detailed explanation in [30]).

For a long time, there was an open question about the existence of indifferentiable (and still deterministic) hash functions to ordinary elliptic curves with the cost of one root. The first example of such a hash function $\mathcal{H}_3$ was invented several years ago in [16] for curves of j-invariant 0 having, at the same time, an $\mathbb{F}_q$-point of order 3. Subsequently, a number of other constructions arose in the literature. Unfortunately, each of them is applicable solely under certain restrictions on E and $\mathbb{F}_q$. Indeed, $\mathcal{H}_3$ (as well as the hash function $\mathcal{H}_4$ from [17]) inherently exploits a non-trivial automorphism on curves of j-invariant 0 (1728, respectively). In turn, the hashing solution $\mathcal{H}_6$ from [20, Section 2.1] works whenever $3 \mid q - 2$ and, conversely, $j(E) \neq 0, 1728$. The index i in the notation $\mathcal{H}_i$ coincides with the degree of the root incorporated in $\mathcal{H}_i$.

Another indifferentiable deterministic hash function $\mathcal{H}_2$ (dubbed *SwiftEC*) was proposed in Chávez-Saab–Rodríguez-Henríquez–Tibouchi's paper [6]. It was recognized as one of the three best papers at Asiacrypt 2022, one of the three flagship cryptographic conferences under the auspices of IACR (International Association for Cryptologic Research). Apart from one square root, $\mathcal{H}_2$ has to determine the values of two Legendre symbols. Since recently, it is realized [2] that the Legendre symbol is a significantly faster operation than (square) root extraction even in the constant-time setting. As a consequence, $\sqrt{\cdot} \in \mathbb{F}_q$ is the unique bottleneck of $\mathcal{H}_2$, i.e., this function is computationally equivalent to the functions $\mathcal{H}_3$, $\mathcal{H}_4$, $\mathcal{H}_6$ that do not need to compute any (non-trivial) multiplicative characters $\mathbb{F}_q^* \to \mathbb{C}^*$.

The definitions of $\mathcal{H}_i$ are quite sophisticated and their implementation details may slightly vary. In a nutshell, we deal with the compositions $\mathcal{H}_i = h_i \circ \eta$, where $\eta \colon \{0,1\}^* \to (\mathbb{F}_q^*)^2$ is an auxiliary hash function and $h_i \colon (\mathbb{F}_q^*)^2 \to E(\mathbb{F}_q)$. Throughout the article, η is considered as deterministic and indifferentiable. Except for h_6, the other maps h_i are themselves the compositions $h_i = h_i' \circ \chi_i$ of a certain cornerstone map $h_i' \colon T_i(\mathbb{F}_q) \to E(\mathbb{F}_q)$ and of a rational $\mathbb{F}_q$-map $\chi_i \colon \mathbb{A}^2 \to T_i$ restricted on $(\mathbb{F}_q^*)^2$. Here, T_i is the three-dimensional quotient-variety with respect to a specific diagonal action of a finite group G_i on the direct product of three carefully selected (possibly trivial) twists of E.

In particular, SwiftEC is built upon the threefold $T = T_2 := E^3/G$, where $G = G_2 := \langle i_1, i_2 \rangle \simeq (\mathbb{Z}/2)^2$ is the group generated by $i_1 := (1, -1, -1)$ and $i_2 := (-1, 1, -1)$. By the way, $i_1 \circ i_2 = i_2 \circ i_1 = (-1, -1, 1)$. It is easily checked that an $\mathbb{F}_q$-point of T corresponds to the orbit having at least one vector $\overline{P} = (P_1, P_2, P_3) \in E^3$ with at least one $\mathbb{F}_q$-point P_i. The map $h' = h_2'$ is nothing but restoring P_i given $\overline{P}$. Furthermore, this can be done in constant time. A precise description of h' is contained, e.g., in [6, Section 3.1].

In their seminal paper [28] Shallue–van de Woestijne found an embedding $\varphi \colon S \hookrightarrow T$ of an $\mathbb{F}_q$-surface S equipped with a *conic bundle* structure $\pi \colon S \to \mathbb{A}^1$. This means that a general fiber of π is a smooth conic. Choosing in advance any non-degenerate fiber $\pi^{-1}(t)$ for $t \in \mathbb{F}_q$ and an $\mathbb{F}_q$-point on it, those researchers eventually obtained an $\mathbb{F}_q$-parametrization $\mathbb{A}^1 \to \pi^{-1}(t)$ and thereby a one-parametric $\mathbb{F}_q$-map $\mathbb{A}^1 \to T$. If the hash function $\mathcal{H}_2$ is not claimed to be indifferentiable, then it is sufficient to take the latter map (supplemented by $\{0,1\}^* \to \mathbb{F}_q^*$) instead of $\chi = \chi_2$.

The merit of Chávez-Saab et al. consists in that they analyzed the cases when the bundle π has an $\mathbb{F}_q$-section, that is, (the image of) an $\mathbb{F}_q$-map $s \colon \mathbb{A}^1 \to S$ such that $\pi \circ s = \mathrm{id}$. Its existence is known to give rise to a proper (i.e., birational) $\mathbb{F}_q$-parametrization $\psi \colon \mathbb{A}^2 \to S$, leading ultimately to the sought two-parametric $\mathbb{F}_q$-map $\chi := \varphi \circ \psi \colon \mathbb{A}^2 \to T$. Moreover, it is pretty easy to derive explicit formulas of ψ and hence of χ. In the language of algebraic geometry, the authors of SwiftEC established $\mathbb{F}_q$-*rationality* (see, e.g., [9]) of the surface S subject to the conditions represented in [6, Theorem 3]. Unfortunately, they are quite restrictive, although ordinary curves of j-invariant 0 (popular in practice) are completely covered.

1.1 New Contribution

This article aims to bring to life the idea of [20, Section 3], i.e., to concretize the hash function noted as "Shallue, van de Woestijne (modification)" in Table 1 of that article. The idea lies in the suggestion (correct as we will see) that for indifferentiability of $\mathcal{H}_2$, the $\mathbb{F}_q$-rationality condition of the surface S can be painlessly relaxed to $\mathbb{F}_q$-*unirationality* in the sense of [12, Section 4]. This means that an $\mathbb{F}_q$-parametrization $\psi : \mathbb{A}^2 \to S$ is allowed not to be invertible or, equivalently, not to have $\deg(\psi) = 1$. Incidentally, any $\mathbb{F}_q$-parametrization of a rational curve can be made proper (still over $\mathbb{F}_q$), e.g., with the help of [27, Section 6.1]. Thereby, the unirationality notion is meaningless as a separate notion in dimension one.

The new (quadratic) map ψ will be based on a so-called *bisection* of π (see, e.g., [9, Section 3.2]). By definition, this is a rational $\mathbb{F}_q$-curve $C \subset S$ intersecting twice (each) fiber of π, that is, the induced cover $\pi : C \to \mathbb{A}^1$ is two-sheeted. Unlike an $\mathbb{F}_q$-section, it turns out that an $\mathbb{F}_q$-bisection on S almost always exists and moreover has a simple equation. The formulas-free origin of ψ is explained in the proof of [12, Theorem 4.2]. As will become clear later, for more comfortable work with concrete formulas of ψ, it is reasonable to impose the restrictions $3 \mid q - 1$ (the first one for SwiftEC) and $j(E) \neq 0$. They do not affect the generality, bearing in mind Kaliski Jr.'s hash functions, $\mathcal{H}_4$, $\mathcal{H}_6$, and SwiftEC when $j(E) = 0$ (cf. Sect. 2.1).

As said at the end of [28, Section 5], the surface S is not $\mathbb{F}_q$-rational in general (maybe even under the introduced restrictions). So, the bisection-based map ψ appears to be an optimal $\mathbb{F}_q$-parametrization of S if one wants to deal with (pretty) universal formulas. Of course, in a series of situations (including those of SwiftEC) it is possible to replace ψ with a birational $\mathbb{F}_q$-map $\mathbb{A}^2 \to S$. Intuitively, the latter should possess slightly more compact formulas (as it turns out for $j(E) = 0$), albeit this does not formally follow from anywhere. In any case, such formulas can at best economize (during their evaluation) only a few multiplications in $\mathbb{F}_q$. As a downside, independent treatment of the opposite scenarios $\deg(\psi) \in \{1, 2\}$ will require additional work when implementing $\mathcal{H}_2$ in cryptographic software libraries.

It is impossible not to note that another quasi-universal $\mathbb{F}_q$-map to T was obtained in Skałba's article [29]. However, its formulas are more bulky compared to those of this article. In this regard, as far as the author knows, Skałba's formulas have never been implemented in practice. Much more importantly, their cumbersomeness is a substantial computational obstacle to a (simple) proof of a theorem (if any) analogous to Theorem 2 whose proof is itself not pleasant. This theorem is at the heart of why the hash function $\mathcal{H}_2$ is indifferentiable. Thus, security of Skałba's map is not confirmed (although not disproved), which is the prevailing applicability criterion in cryptography. It is also worth emphasizing that in Skałba's approach the requirement $j(E) \neq 0$ is crucial as opposed to the current approach.

To summarize, the new $\mathbb{F}_q$-map $\chi : \mathbb{A}^2 \to T$ enjoys the advantages (and does not have the drawbacks) of those from the all three previous articles [6, 28, 29] on hashing to elliptic curves via the threefold T, justifying the title of this article. In the author's taste, the proposed hashing solution is not very interesting from the mathematical viewpoint because of the remaining Legendre symbols in $\mathcal{H}_2$. Nonetheless, the practical significance of the result greatly outweighs this circumstance. That is why the author decided to share the given solution with the R&D community. Since cryptography is a pragmatic science (unlike pure mathematics), the stated view has a right to exist. It is hoped that the below formulas will be used sooner or later in real-world cryptosystems.

2 Formulas

Let's mainly stick to the notation of [20, Section 3]. Hereafter, the reader is invited to look in parallel at the program code [19] written in Magma to verify or leverage encountered (at least core) formulas. Implementers can skip the majority of the present section except for the resulting formulas (2) (cf. (3) when $j(E) = 0$) of the map χ.

Consider an elliptic curve $E : y^2 = f(x) := x^3 + ax + b$ over a finite field $\mathbb{F}_q$ of characteristic 5 or greater. Recall that the discriminant

$$D(E) = D(f) = -16(4a^3 + 27b^2) \neq 0.$$

Every specialist knows that $j(E) = 0 \Leftrightarrow a = 0$ and, similarly, $j(E) = 1728 \Leftrightarrow b = 0$.

The threefold T and Shallue–van de Woestijne surface S respectively have the equations

$$T : y^2 = f(x_1)f(x_2)f(x_3) \quad \subset \quad \mathbb{A}^4_{(x_1,x_2,x_3,y)}$$

and

$$S : y^2 + h(t)x^2 + f(t) = 0 \quad \subset \quad \mathbb{A}^3_{(x,y,t)},$$

where $h(t) := 3t^2 + 4a$. Let's borrow from [28, Section 5] the embedding

$$\varphi : S \hookrightarrow T \qquad (x, y, t) \mapsto \left(s, \; -t - s, \; r, \; \frac{f(r)g(t,s)}{2x} \right),$$

where

$$s := \frac{y - tx}{2x}, \qquad r := t + 4x^2, \qquad g := t^2 + ts + s^2 + a.$$

For the rest of the article, it is necessary to remember that $3 \mid q - 1$ if and only if the cubic root $\omega := \sqrt[3]{1}$ (such that $\omega \neq 1$) or, equivalently, the square root $\sqrt{-3} = 2\omega + 1$ belongs to $\mathbb{F}_q$.

Theorem 1. *Suppose that $a \neq 0$ or $3 \mid q - 1$. Then, the Shallue–van de Woestijne surface S is $\mathbb{F}_q$-unirational of degree at most 2.*

Proof. The other affine model

$$S' : y^2 + h(t) + f(t)z^2 = 0 \quad \subset \quad \mathbb{A}^3_{(y,z,t)}$$

of S is obtained by means of the transformation

$$\tau_2 \colon S' \to S \quad (y, z, t) \mapsto \left(\frac{1}{z}, \frac{y}{z}, t \right),$$
$$\tau_2^{-1} \colon S \to S' \quad (x, y, t) \mapsto \left(\frac{y}{x}, \frac{1}{x}, t \right).$$

The surface S' obviously inherits from S the conic bundle structure π. At the same time, there is the natural embedding

$$\iota \colon C \hookrightarrow S' \qquad (y, t) \mapsto (y, 0, t)$$

of the diagonal conic

$$C \colon y^2 + h(t) = 0 \quad \subset \quad \mathbb{A}^2_{(y,t)}.$$

Evidently, the intersection number $\iota(C) \cdot \pi^{-1}(t) = 2$. In the scenario $a = 0$ and $3 \mid q - 1$, the conic C is the union of the two $\mathbb{F}_q$-lines $L_\pm \colon y = \pm\sqrt{-3} \cdot t$. Each of them is the (usual) $\mathbb{F}_q$-section of π taken in the construction of SwiftEC (see [6, Section 5.1]), hence we literally rediscover Chávez-Saab et al.'s fact about $\mathbb{F}_q$-rationality of S in the given sporadic case. In the opposite one $a \neq 0$ (regardless of the remainder of q modulo 3), the conic C is non-degenerate. Since over finite fields there is no existence question of a rational point on C, it remains to apply [12, Theorem 4.2]. □

As a useful observation, when the theorem premise is not fulfilled (i.e., $a = 0$ and $3 \mid q - 2$), the lines $L_\pm$ are Frobenius-conjugate. Thereby, we do not have a clearly visible absolutely (i.e., geometrically) irreducible $\mathbb{F}_q$-(bi)section of π. But the surface S is still somehow $\mathbb{F}_q$-unirational owing to [15]. In the author's opinion, derivation of explicit formulas parametrizing S is a feasible task in all the cases.

Nonetheless, unless stated otherwise, it will be assumed that $a \neq 0$ **and** $3 \mid q - 1$. The reason is that by virtue of [6, Lemma 5], the weaker or-condition from the previous theorem is not sufficient (unlike the and-condition) for C to be a smooth conic enjoying an $\mathbb{F}_q(a)$-point. Of course, as well as in the above proof we could refer to the fact that $C(\mathbb{F}_q) \neq \emptyset$ for each fixed $a \in \mathbb{F}_q^*$. However, this would require involving two more dependent variables $(y_0, t_0) \in C$, cluttering the following formulas. As said in the introduction, this strategy is employed (for lack of an alternative) by Shallue–van de Woestijne.

To notice an announced $\mathbb{F}_q(a)$-point on C, it is proposed to switch to the affine model

$$C' : y^2 + 3 + 4av^2 = 0 \quad \subset \quad \mathbb{A}^2_{(y,v)}$$

via the transformation

$$\tau_1 : C' \to C \quad (y, v) \mapsto \left(\frac{y}{v}, \frac{1}{v}\right),$$

$$\tau_1^{-1} : C \to C' \quad (y, t) \mapsto \left(\frac{y}{t}, \frac{1}{t}\right).$$

As predicted, we have $P_1 := (\sqrt{-3}, 0) \in C'$. The projection from P_1 is the invertible map

$$pr_{P_1} : C' \to \mathbb{A}_{t_1}^1 \quad (y, v) \mapsto \frac{y - \sqrt{-3}}{v}$$

such that

$$\tau_1 \circ pr_{P_1}^{-1} : \mathbb{A}_{t_1}^1 \to C \quad t_1 \mapsto (f_y(t_1), f_t(t_1)),$$

where

$$f_y := \frac{t_1^2 - 4a}{2t_1}, \qquad f_t := \frac{t_1^2 + 4a}{-2\sqrt{-3}\cdot t_1}.$$

As usual, the surfaces S, S' can be interpreted as $\mathbb{F}_q(t)$-conics on $\mathbb{A}_{(x,y)}^2$, $\mathbb{A}_{(y,z)}^2$, respectively. There is the point $P_2 := (y_0, 0) \in S'$ over the quadratic extension $\mathbb{F}_q(t, y_0)$ generated by the root $y_0 := \sqrt{-h(t)}$. The composition of the inverse to the projection map

$$pr_{P_2} : S' \to \mathbb{A}_{t_2}^1 \quad (y, z) \mapsto \frac{y - y_0}{z}$$

and of the $\mathbb{F}_q(t)$-isomorphism $\tau_2 : S' \to S$ has the form

$$\psi := \tau_2 \circ pr_{P_2}^{-1} : \mathbb{A}_{t_2}^1 \to S \quad t_2 \mapsto (g_x(t, y_0, t_2), g_y(t, t_2)),$$

where

$$g_x := \frac{t_2^2 + f(t)}{-2y_0 t_2}, \qquad g_y := \frac{t_2^2 - f(t)}{2t_2}.$$

It is worth emphasizing that $(y_0 \circ f_t)(t_1) = f_y(t_1)$ if one looks at y_0 as a non-rational function in t. Realizing S again as an $\mathbb{F}_q$-surface in $\mathbb{A}_{(x,y,t)}^3$, we thus get the **rational** $\mathbb{F}_q$-parametrization

$$\psi : \mathbb{A}_{(t_1,t_2)}^2 \to S \quad (t_1, t_2) \mapsto \left(g_x\big(f_t(t_1), f_y(t_1), t_2\big), g_y\big(f_t(t_1), t_2\big), f_t(t_1)\right).$$

Explicitly,

$$\psi : \mathbb{A}_{(t_1,t_2)}^2 \to S \quad (t_1, t_2) \mapsto (\mathfrak{g}_x, \mathfrak{g}_y, f_t), \tag{1}$$

where $\mathfrak{g}_x = n_+/d_x$ and $\mathfrak{g}_y = n_-/d_y$,

$$n_\pm := t_1^6 + 2^3 3\sqrt{-3}\cdot b t_1^3 + 2^6 a^3 \pm 2^3 3\sqrt{-3}\cdot t_1^3 t_2^2$$

and

$$d_x := -2^3 3\sqrt{-3}(t_1^2 - 2^2 a) t_1^2 t_2, \qquad d_y := -2^4 3\sqrt{-3}\cdot t_1^3 t_2.$$

Everywhere below, $i \in \{1, 2, 3\}$ and $j \in \{1, 2\}$. Finally, we come to the two-parametric $\mathbb{F}_q$-map

$$\chi := \varphi \circ \psi \colon \mathbb{A}^2_{(t_1, t_2)} \to T \qquad (t_1, t_2) \mapsto (X_1, X_2, X_3, Y) \qquad (2)$$

whose x-coordinate functions $X_i = n_i/d_i$ possess the numerators

$$n_j := t_1^8 + 2^2\omega^{2j}at_1^6 + 2^33\sqrt{-3}{\cdot}bt_1^5 + 2^53\sqrt{-3}{\cdot}\omega^{2j}abt_1^3 + 2^6a^3t_1^2 + 2^8\omega^{2j}a^4$$
$$+ 2^33\sqrt{-3}(\omega^{2j}t_1^2 + 2^2a)t_1^3t_2^2,$$

$$n_3 := t_1^{12} + 2^43\sqrt{-3}{\cdot}bt_1^9 + 2^6(2a^3 - 3^3b^2)t_1^6 + 2^{10}3\sqrt{-3}{\cdot}a^3bt_1^3 + 2^{12}a^6$$
$$- 2^33\sqrt{-3}\Big(t_1^6 - 2^23at_1^4 - 2^43\sqrt{-3}{\cdot}bt_1^3 - 2^43a^2t_1^2 + 2^6a^3 - 2^33\sqrt{-3}{\cdot}t_1^3t_2^2\Big)t_1^3t_2^2$$

and the denominators

$$d_j := -2\sqrt{-3}{\cdot}\omega^j\Big(t_1^6 + 2^33\sqrt{-3}{\cdot}bt_1^3 + 2^6a^3 + 2^33\sqrt{-3}{\cdot}t_1^3t_2^2\Big)t_1,$$
$$d_3 := -2^43^3(t_1^2 - 2^2a)^2t_1^4t_2^2.$$

Given $x \in \mathbb{F}_q$, introduce the hyperplanes $\Pi_{i,x} \colon x_i = x$ in the space $\mathbb{A}^4_{(x_1, x_2, x_3, y)}$ as well as the curves

$$C_x^{(i)} := \varphi^{-1}(\Pi_{i,x}) \subset S, \qquad C_{i,x} := \chi^{-1}(\Pi_{i,x}) = \psi^{-1}(C_x^{(i)}).$$

The latter clearly have the equations $C_{i,x} \colon xd_i = n_i$ on the plane $\mathbb{A}^2_{(t_1, t_2)}$. Besides, we lack the infinity curve $C_\infty = C_{j,\infty} \colon d_j/t_1 = 0$. In a sense, it is $\chi^{-1}(\Pi_{j,\infty})$ up to the coordinate line $t_1 = 0$. It is readily seen that

$$\deg(C_{j,x}) = 8, \qquad \deg(C_{3,x}) = 12, \qquad \deg(C_\infty) = 6.$$

As a consequence, the arithmetic genera

$$p_a(C_{j,x}) = 21, \qquad p_a(C_{3,x}) = 55, \qquad p_a(C_\infty) = 10,$$

e.g., by virtue of [31, Theorem 2.3.18].

It is shown in [6, Section 3.2] that the curves $C_x^{(i)}$ are absolutely irreducible (of geometric genus 2) except for several values x. Nonetheless, this does not automatically result in the analogous statement for $C_{i,x}$ (not to mention C_∞), because the covers $\psi \colon C_{i,x} \to C_x^{(i)}$ are not birational, but only quadratic. Therefore, we are obliged to manually prove it.

Theorem 2. *As before, $a \neq 0$ by assumption. The curves $C_{i,x}$, C_∞ are absolutely irreducible whenever x is outside the degeneracy set*

$$\mathcal{D} := \left\{\pm\sqrt{\frac{a}{-3}}, \ \pm 2\sqrt{\frac{a}{-3}}, \ -\frac{b}{a}\right\} \cup x(E[2]).$$

Proof. Recall that absolute irreducibility of a plane curve $\subset \mathbb{A}^2_{(t_1, t_2)}$ (given by one polynomial) amounts to irreducibility of the corresponding univariate polynomial in t_2 over the field $\overline{\mathbb{F}_q}(t_1)$, where $\overline{\mathbb{F}_q}$ is the algebraic closure of $\mathbb{F}_q$.

For the sake of compactness, put

$$\rho_0 := t_1^6 + 2^3 3\sqrt{-3} \cdot bt_1^3 + 2^6 a^3, \qquad q_i := t_1^2 + 2\sqrt{-3} \cdot \omega^{2i} x t_1 + 2^2 \omega^i a.$$

First, there are the transformations

$$\sigma_{j,x} : C_{j,x} \to H_x \qquad (t_1, t_2) \mapsto (t_1,\ 2^2 3\omega^j q_j(t_1) t_1^2 t_2),$$

$$\sigma_{j,x}^{-1} : H_x \to C_{j,x} \qquad (t_1, t_2) \mapsto \left(t_1,\ \frac{t_2}{2^2 3 \omega^j q_j(t_1) t_1^2}\right)$$

between $C_{j,x}$ and the hyperelliptic curve

$$H_x : t_2^2 = h_x(t_1) := 2\sqrt{-3} \cdot \rho_0(t_1) q_1(t_1) q_2(t_1) t_1 \qquad \subset \mathbb{A}^2_{(t_1, t_2)}.$$

In particular, $C_{1,x} \simeq C_{2,x}$ with the help of $\sigma_{2,x}^{-1} \circ \sigma_{1,x}$. Since $\sigma_{j,x}$ are birational maps (constant on t_1), absolute (ir)reducibility of $C_{j,x}$, H_x takes place under the same circumstances. Looking ahead, this argument will be tacitly applied also to the transformations $\sigma_{3,x}$, σ_∞.

The discriminants

$$D(\rho_0) = 2^{18} 3^6 a^6 D(E)^3, \qquad D(q_i) = -2^2 \omega^i h(x).$$

In turn, the resultants

$$R(\rho_0, q_j) = -2^{12} 3^3 a^3 f(x)^2, \qquad R(q_1, q_2) = -2^4 3 a(a + 3x^2).$$

Besides, $(\rho_0 q_1 q_2)(0) = 0 \Leftrightarrow a = 0$. All this exactly means that the polynomial h_x has a multiple root only if $a = 0$ or $x \in \mathcal{D}$. Otherwise, h_x is certainly not a perfect square in $\overline{\mathbb{F}_q}(t_1)$. Incidentally, $\deg(h_x) = 11$, i.e., the geometric genus $g(C_{j,x}) = g(H_x) = 5$, albeit this fact will not be necessary for us.

By analogy,

$$\sigma_\infty : C_\infty \to H_\infty \qquad (t_1, t_2) \mapsto (t_1,\ -2^2 3 t_1^2 t_2),$$
$$\sigma_\infty^{-1} : H_\infty \to C_\infty \qquad (t_1, t_2) \mapsto \left(t_1,\ \frac{t_2}{-2^2 3 t_1^2}\right),$$

where

$$H_\infty : t_2^2 = h_\infty(t_1) := 2\sqrt{-3} \cdot \rho_0(t_1) t_1 \qquad \subset \mathbb{A}^2_{(t_1, t_2)}.$$

We already know that $D(\rho_0) \neq 0$. Furthermore, $\rho_0(0) = 0 \Leftrightarrow a = 0$. As a result, the curves C_∞, H_∞ are also absolutely irreducible. By the way, $\deg(h_\infty) = 7$, that is, $g(C_\infty) = g(H_\infty) = 3$.

It remains to analyze absolute (ir)reducibility of the last more awkward curve $C_{3,x}$. Below, we will meet the polynomials

$$\rho_\pm := t_1^6 \pm 2 \cdot 3\sqrt{-3} \cdot x t_1^5 \mp 2^2 3 a t_1^4 \mp 2^4 3\sqrt{-3}(ax + \delta_\mp b) t_1^3 \mp 2^4 3 a^2 t_1^2 \\ \pm 2^5 3\sqrt{-3} \cdot a^2 x t_1 + 2^6 a^3,$$

where $\delta_{\mp} := (3 \mp 1)/2$. It is convenient to simplify a little $C_{3,x}$ as follows:

$$\sigma_{3,x}: C_{3,x} \to C'_{3,x} \qquad (t_1, t_2) \mapsto (t_1, 2\sqrt{-3} \cdot t_1 t_2),$$
$$\sigma_{3,x}^{-1}: C'_{3,x} \to C_{3,x} \qquad (t_1, t_2) \mapsto \left(t_1, \frac{t_2}{2\sqrt{-3} \cdot t_1}\right).$$

The curve $C'_{3,x}$ is defined by the equation

$$C'_{3,x}: c_0(t_1) + c_1(t_1)t_2^2 + c_2(t_1)t_2^4 = 0 \quad \subset \quad \mathbb{A}^2_{(t_1,t_2)}$$

with the coefficients

$$c_0 := \rho_0(t_1)^2, \qquad c_1 := 2\sqrt{-3} \cdot \rho_+(t_1)t_1, \qquad c_2 := -2^2 3 t_1^2.$$

Consider the univariate quartic and quadratic $\overline{\mathbb{F}}_q(t_1)$-polynomials $Q_4(t_2) := C'_{3,x}(t_1)(t_2)$ and $Q_2(s_2) := Q_4(\sqrt{s_2})$, respectively. The second has the discriminant

$$D(Q_2) = 2^2 3^2 (t_1^2 - 2^2 a)^2 t_1^2 \cdot h_{3,x}(t_1)$$

with $h_{3,x}(t_1) := q_3(t_1)\rho_-(t_1)$. Therefore, the roots of Q_2 are nothing but

$$r_{\pm} = \frac{\rho_+(t_1) \pm \sqrt{-3}(t_1^2 - 2^2 a)s_1}{-2^2\sqrt{-3} \cdot t_1},$$

where s_1 is a square root of $h_{3,x}(t_1)$. The discriminant $D(q_3)$ was already determined earlier. Meanwhile,

$$D(\rho_-) = 2^{38} 3^{12} a^6 (ax + b)^2 f(x)^2 D(E), \qquad R(q_3, \rho_-) = -2^{16} 3^3 a^3 f(x)^2.$$

Thus, $D(Q_2)$ (i.e., $h_{3,x}$) is not a perfect square in $\overline{\mathbb{F}}_q(t_1)$ (as above, unless $a = 0$ or $x \in D$). Consequently, $r_{\pm}$ (i.e., s_1) do not belong to $\overline{\mathbb{F}}_q(t_1)$.

Let's involve the hyperelliptic curve $H_{3,x}: s_1^2 = h_{3,x}(t_1)$ on the plane $\mathbb{A}^2_{(t_1,s_1)}$. There is on $H_{3,x}$ the point $P_0 := (0, 2^4 a^2)$. The tangent line of $H_{3,x}$ at P_0 has the form

$$T_{P_0}: 2^5 a^2 (s_1 - 2^4 a^2) = h'_{3,x}(0)t_1.$$

Whenever $a \neq 0$, the left-hand side does not vanish, hence the line $t_1 = 0$ is different from T_{P_0}. As a result, t_1 (as a function on $H_{3,x}$) is known to be a uniformizing (a.k.a. local) parameter at P_0. Note that

$$(r_{\pm}t_1)(P_0) = \frac{2^5 a^3 \omega^{\delta_{\mp}}}{\sqrt{-3}} \neq 0, \infty.$$

We see that the order (a.k.a. valuation) $v_{P_0}(r_{\pm}) = -1$ is odd. At the same time, the theory of function fields says that $v_{P_0}: \overline{\mathbb{F}}_q(H_{3,x})^* \to \mathbb{Z}$ is a group homomorphism. So, neither of the roots of Q_4 (namely $\pm\sqrt{r_+}$ and $\pm\sqrt{r_-}$) lies in $\overline{\mathbb{F}}_q(H_{3,x}) = \overline{\mathbb{F}}_q(t_1, s_1)$.

To summarize, we demonstrated that

$$\overline{\mathbb{F}}_q(C'_{3,x}) \supsetneq \overline{\mathbb{F}}_q(H_{3,x}) \supsetneq \overline{\mathbb{F}}_q(t_1),$$

that is, $\overline{\mathbb{F}}_q(C'_{3,x}) = \overline{\mathbb{F}}_q(t_1, t_2)$ is a quartic extension of $\overline{\mathbb{F}}_q(t_1)$. This is possible if and only if Q_4 is an $\overline{\mathbb{F}}_q(t_1)$-minimal polynomial of t_2 as a function on $C'_{3,x}$. The theorem is proved. $\qquad \square$

2.1 The Case $a = 0$

Although we worked under the assumption $a \neq 0$ to avoid caveats, the formal substitution $a = 0$ into the formulas of the map ψ (Eq. (1)) gives rise to the equalities

$$\mathfrak{g}_x = \frac{-\mathfrak{g}_y + t_2}{\sqrt{-3} \cdot f_t}, \qquad \mathfrak{g}_y = \frac{f_t^3 + b - t_2^2}{-2t_2}, \qquad f_t = \frac{t_1}{-2\sqrt{-3}}.$$

They coincide with [6, Equalities (15)] up to the swap $x \leftrightarrow y$, the sign $-$ in front of $\mathfrak{g}_y$, and labeling the variables f_t, t_2. The proof of Theorem 1 predicts that ψ should be a birational map in the given sporadic case. For the sake of completeness, here is its inverse

$$\psi^{-1} \colon S \to \mathbb{A}^2_{(t_1, t_2)} \qquad (x, y, t) \mapsto (-2\sqrt{-3} \cdot t, \ \sqrt{-3} \cdot xt + y).$$

In turn, the formulas of the functions X_i (Eq. (2)) are not explicitly written out in [6]. It is useful to have them before our eyes, not pretending to their authorship:

$$X_i = \frac{\mathfrak{n}_i}{\mathfrak{d}_i}, \qquad \mathfrak{n}_j = \mathfrak{n}_j t_1^4, \qquad \mathfrak{n}_3 = \mathfrak{n}_3 t_1^6, \qquad \mathfrak{d}_j = \mathfrak{d}_j t_1^4, \qquad \mathfrak{d}_3 = \mathfrak{d}_3 t_1^6, \qquad (3)$$

where

$$\mathfrak{n}_j := \left(t_1^3 + 2^3 3\sqrt{-3} \cdot b + 2^3 3\sqrt{-3} \cdot \omega^{2j} t_2^2 \right) t_1,$$
$$\mathfrak{n}_3 := t_1^6 + 2^4 3\sqrt{-3} \cdot b t_1^3 - 2^6 3^3 b^2 - 2^3 3\sqrt{-3} \left(t_1^3 - 2^4 3\sqrt{-3} \cdot b - 2^3 3\sqrt{-3} \cdot t_2^2 \right) t_2^2$$

and

$$\mathfrak{d}_j := -2\sqrt{-3} \cdot \omega^j \left(t_1^3 + 2^3 3\sqrt{-3} \cdot b + 2^3 3\sqrt{-3} \cdot t_2^2 \right), \qquad \mathfrak{d}_3 := -2^4 3^3 t_1^2 t_2^2.$$

Formally speaking, Theorem 2 is not true when $a = 0$. However, this is just a reflection of the fact that the initial numerators n_i and denominators d_i of the functions X_i have common factors (namely powers of t_1) after specializing a in the given way. Since the map ψ is invertible and the curves $C_x^{(i)} \subset S$ remain generally absolutely irreducible, so are their inverse (i.e., direct) images $C_{i,x} = \psi^{-1}(C_x^{(i)})$. Their right equations on $\mathbb{A}^2_{(t_1, t_2)}$ are nothing but $C_{i,x} \colon x\mathfrak{d}_i = \mathfrak{n}_i$. By the way, the infinity curve $C_\infty = C_{j,\infty} \colon \mathfrak{d}_j = 0$ becomes a twist of E. To sum up, the situation encountered for elliptic curves E of j-invariant 0 degenerates, because it is even simpler.

3   Final Remarks

First of all, the function Y of the map χ (Eq. (2)) seemingly does not have (as opposed to X_i) a very short expression, using solely the variables t_1, t_2. Fortunately, evaluating Y is not required, since the map $h' \colon T(\mathbb{F}_q) \to E(\mathbb{F}_q)$ from the introduction in fact does not depend on the y-coordinate of T. Indeed, Y just has to constantly fall into $\mathbb{F}_q$ to be sure that at least one of the values $f(X_i)$ is a quadratic residue in $\mathbb{F}_q$. Besides, it is not important that X_3 structurally does not resemble X_1, X_2. The point is that an implementer must guarantee evaluating all the functions X_i despite a well-defined choice of $\sqrt{f(X_i)} \in \mathbb{F}_q$. Otherwise, constant-time behavior of the hash function $\mathcal{H}_2$ is not respected. Curiously, $X_i(t_1, t_2) = X_i(t_1, -t_2)$, hence the sign of t_2 can serve as the sign of the chosen $\mathbb{F}_q$-root $\sqrt{f(X_i)}$. This proposal is not consistent with [6, Section 3.1], where one additional bit is involved for the given purpose.

Clearly, the functions X_i are correctly defined outside the lines $t_j = 0$, $t_1 = \pm 2\sqrt{a}$ and the curve C_∞. Since the latter is an absolutely irreducible curve (due to Theorem 2) and its arithmetic genus is a small number independent of q, we conclude that $\#C_\infty(\mathbb{F}_q) = q + O(\sqrt{q})$. The remark concerning $p_a(C_\infty)$ is essential, because there are (e.g., in [10]) absolutely irreducible plane curves of degree $\geqslant q + 1$ (dubbed *plane-filling curves*) containing even the whole set $\mathbb{F}_q^2$. So, X_i are meaningful on a subset of $\mathbb{F}_q^2$ of cardinality $q^2 + O(q)$. The probability for a hash function $\eta \colon \{0, 1\}^* \to (\mathbb{F}_q^*)^2$ of falling into the undefined locus of X_i is thereby negligible for finite fields of cryptographic size. If desired, the map $h = h_2 \colon (\mathbb{F}_q^*)^2 \to E(\mathbb{F}_q)$ can be manually extended to $t_1 = \pm 2\sqrt{a}$ (of course, if $\sqrt{a} \in \mathbb{F}_q$) and $C_\infty(\mathbb{F}_q)$, leading to a little more complicated implementation.

Corollary 1. *The map h is ϵ-regular (i.e., statistically ϵ-indistinguishable from the uniform distribution on the codomain) with $\epsilon = O(q^{-1/2})$.*

It is enough to comment on this statement without a rigorous proof owing to the main work done by Chávez-Saab et al. Fix a non-zero point $P = (x, y) \in E(\mathbb{F}_q)$ such that $x \notin \mathcal{D}$ to be able to refer to Theorem 2. By analogy with C_∞, absolute irreducibility of the curves $C_{i,x}$ (as well as smallness of $p_a(C_{i,x})$) is responsible for the fact that $\#C_{i,x}(\mathbb{F}_q) = q + O(\sqrt{q})$. Taking into account the sign of y (i.e., of t_2) and the careful reasoning from [6, Section 3.2] (cf. [16, Section 4], [17, Section 4]), we easily establish that $\#h^{-1}(P) = q + O(\sqrt{q})$. This equality is indispensable for the resulting one $\epsilon = O(q^{-1/2})$.

Rigorously speaking, without absolute irreducibility one cannot resort to *Hasse–Weil* and *Perret bounds* [6, Lemmas 1, 2]. Fortunately, these bounds hold true for singular curves (as in our situation) if the geometric genus is replaced by the arithmetic one (see [3]). It is not superfluous to also stress that the curves $C_{i,x}$, C_∞ obviously have few $\mathbb{F}_q$-points on the coordinate lines $t_j = 0$ (and on the infinity line of $\mathbb{P}^2$) whose number is hidden in $O(\sqrt{q})$. Therefore, it does not matter that our h acts from $(\mathbb{F}_q^*)^2$ rather than from $\mathbb{F}_q^2$ as in the definition of SwiftEC. Thus, the above cardinality estimations of $C_{i,x}(\mathbb{F}_q)$, $C_\infty(\mathbb{F}_q)$, and $h^{-1}(P)$ are actually fair.

As usual in the theory of hash-to-curve functions, the degenerate elements $x \in \mathcal{D}$ (also as the zero point of E) do not play any (significant) role in estimating ϵ, since they constitute a negligible quantity with respect to q. Furthermore, the proof of [6, Lemma 4] (cf. [16, Corollary 2], [17, Corollary 2]) can be shortened without finding a more or less exact constant c in front of $q^{-1/2}$ in the O-notation. For SwiftEC, $c = 6 + o(1)$, while the current $c = O(1)$ should be a little bit greater, because the arithmetic genera of the curves $C_{i,x}$ slightly exceed those of $C_x^{(i)}$ (naturally, for $a \neq 0$). Nevertheless, this is absolutely not important for huge fields $\mathbb{F}_q$ used in ECC.

We eventually come to the next result identical to [6, Theorem 2].

Corollary 2. *The map h is ϵ-admissible with $\epsilon = O(q^{-1/2})$ and hence the hash function $\mathcal{H}_2 = h \circ \eta \colon \{0,1\}^* \to E(\mathbb{F}_q)$ is indifferentiable from a random oracle.*

In conclusion, we obtain the following eye-catching statement.

Corollary 3. *For every elliptic curve E (supersingular or ordinary) over a finite field $\mathbb{F}_q$ of characteristic > 3, there is an indifferentiable deterministic hash function $\{0,1\}^* \to E(\mathbb{F}_q)$ with the cost of one radical in $\mathbb{F}_q$ (and maybe two Legendre symbols).*

Its extension (mutatis mutandis) to the characteristics 2, 3 is seemingly just the question of necessity, because most of the preliminary work was already done in Shallue–van de Woestijne's original paper [28]. To the author's knowledge, elliptic curves over finite fields of characteristic 3 are not utilized at all in today's real world cryptography. In turn, binary (even ordinary) curves were and continue to be suspicious, despite the fact that they are as a rule faster than prime curves. For example, there is the speed-record curve GLS254 [1,25] preferable (among other things) for multiset hashing [21]. It is remarkable that binary curves are deprecated in the last version of the NIST (National Institute of Standards and Technology) standard [5, Section 3.3] on ECC. In addition, there are quasi-polynomial in ℓ algorithms of solving the DLP in $\mathbb{F}_{2^\ell}^*$. As an illustration, the paper [8] computes a discrete logarithm for $\ell = 30750$, which is today the largest bit length $\ell = \lceil \log_2(q) \rceil$ of a field $\mathbb{F}_q$ with a successfully attacked DLP instance in $\mathbb{F}_q^*$. That is why binary pairing-friendly curves (including supersingular ones) are unsafe, although that cannot be said for plain curves.

Appendix. How to Avoid Legendre Symbols in Hashing to Elliptic Curves

As earlier, let E be an elliptic curve over a finite field $\mathbb{F}_q$ (of characteristic > 3). In the main part of the present article we established that there is always an *admissible* (in the sense of [6, Definition 4]) map $h \colon \mathbb{F}_q^2 \to E(\mathbb{F}_q)$ underlying an indifferentiable deterministic hash function $\mathcal{H} \colon \{0,1\}^* \to E(\mathbb{F}_q)$. Moreover, h requires to compute only one root in $\mathbb{F}_q$ and at worst two instances of the Legendre symbol $\left(\frac{\cdot}{q}\right)$. Unfortunately, fast constant-time algorithms (such as in [2]) of determining $\left(\frac{\cdot}{q}\right)$ are pretty complicated. Hence, being improperly implemented, they may be a potential source of leaking secret information inputted to $\mathcal{H}$. In this connection, it is desirable to completely avoid $\left(\frac{\cdot}{q}\right)$ (if possible) in the structure of $\mathcal{H}$.

It is worth emphasizing once again that admissible maps h (collected in [20, Table 1]) without Legendre (and any other) symbols have quite severe applicability restrictions. The current appendix explains how to circumvent them (almost for free) in the situation when after $\mathcal{H}$ comes a scalar multiplication on E. In other words, the overall computational task is to evaluate the function $[m] \circ \mathcal{H}$ for some scalar m (constant or variable, public or secret) of considerable size. This task arises when producing numerous cryptographic objects among which BLS signatures [7, Section 1.4.3] and key images [26, Section 4.4]. That is why the given batching strategy is really justified.

As is customary, E is of interest for ECC solely if there is a subgroup $G \subset E(\mathbb{F}_q)$ of large prime order r and of cofactor c such that $r \nmid c$. Typically, $c \leqslant 8$ for real-world non-pairing friendly curves, including the NIST standardized ones from [5, Section 3]. Clearly, the hash function $[c] \circ \mathcal{H} \colon \{0,1\}^* \to G$ is still indifferentible and deterministic (with a proper implementation of $[c]$). Therefore, it is usually enough to deal with hashing to E, abstracting from its concrete subgroup. Nevertheless, the below material concerns direct hashing to G because of inevitable technical details. Looking ahead, this material is relevant provided that c is moderate, namely $c = O(\sqrt{q})$. Curiously, the new batching technique partially resembles that of [20, Section 1.2] valid if E is a pairing-friendly curve and, conversely, c is huge, namely $c = \Omega(r)$.

Instead of h, it is suggested to consider a map of the form $e \colon \mathbb{F}_q \to E(\mathbb{F}_q)$. Let's suppose that it is α-*weak* (for $\alpha \in \mathbb{N}$) in accordance with [4, Definition 5] (see also [21, Definition 4.1]). In particular, e is α-*bounded* (i.e., $\#e^{-1}(Q) \leqslant \alpha$ for each $Q \in E(\mathbb{F}_q)$) and so the image cardinality $\#\mathrm{Im}(e) \geqslant q/\alpha$. A state-of-the-art classification of such weak maps is exhibited in [20, Table 2], although there the weakness notion is not explicitly addressed. They are free of $\left(\frac{\cdot}{q}\right)$ in most cases, but still dependent on one radical in $\mathbb{F}_q$. Importantly, α is a small number for all maps from that classification. Whenever $j(E) \neq 0, 1728$, it is possible to take as e the *simplified Shallue–van de Woestijne(–Ulas) map* e_{sSWU} appeared originally in [4, Section 7] and optimized in [32, Section 4]. In the case of e_{sSWU}, the bound $\alpha = 8$ according to [4, Lemma 6] and, in fact, $\alpha = 4$ if the sign of the resulting y-coordinate is taken into account.

As we know from [30], maps e are not itself *regular* unless E is a supersingular curve. We are thus forced to search for an alternative for e to serve ordinary curves. There is a series of widespread regular (mostly $\left(\frac{\cdot}{q}\right)$-free) maps to G:

$$
\begin{aligned}
F_0 \colon \mathbb{F}_r \to G & \qquad n \mapsto [n]P_0, \\
F_1 \colon V \to G & \qquad (t,n) \mapsto [c]e(t) + [n]P_0, \\
F_2 \colon \mathbb{F}_q^2 \to G & \qquad (t_1, t_2) \mapsto [c]\big(e(t_1) + e(t_2)\big),
\end{aligned}
$$

where $P_0 \in G$ is a non-zero fixed point and $V := \mathbb{F}_q \times \mathbb{F}_r$. These maps can be found in any detailed survey of hash-to-curve functions, for example in [4, Section 1]. Note that the index i in the notation F_i means the copy number of e in the structure of F_i.

Consider the one more map

$$
F \colon V \to G \qquad (t,n) \mapsto [nc]e(t).
$$

Despite its simple shape, the author has never met this map anywhere in the literature. For compactness, let's also label the infinity point $\mathcal{O} := (0 : 1 : 0)$ and the complementary subgroup $G' := E(\mathbb{F}_q)/G$ of order c.

Theorem 3. *If e is an α-bounded map, then F is an ϵ-regular map with $\epsilon = 2c\alpha/q$.*

Proof. Given $P \in G$ and $n \in \mathbb{F}_r$, the inverse image

$$[nc]^{-1}(P) = \begin{cases} [(nc)^{-1}]P + G' & \text{if} \quad n \neq 0, \\ \emptyset & \text{if} \quad n = 0 \text{ and } P \neq \mathcal{O}, \\ E(\mathbb{F}_q) & \text{if} \quad n = 0 \text{ and } P = \mathcal{O}. \end{cases}$$

Consequently,

$$U := \bigcup_{n \in \mathbb{F}_r} [nc]^{-1}(P) = \begin{cases} E(\mathbb{F}_q) \setminus G' & \text{if} \quad P \neq \mathcal{O}, \\ E(\mathbb{F}_q) & \text{if} \quad P = \mathcal{O} \end{cases}$$

and thereby

$$e^{-1}(U) = \begin{cases} \mathbb{F}_q \setminus e^{-1}(G') & \text{if} \quad P \neq \mathcal{O}, \\ \mathbb{F}_q & \text{if} \quad P = \mathcal{O}. \end{cases}$$

It is readily seen that U is in reality a disjoint union $\bigsqcup$ when $P \neq \mathcal{O}$. In other words, the projection $V \to \mathbb{F}_q$ is bijective between the sets $F^{-1}(P)$ and $e^{-1}(U)$. Note that

$$0 \leqslant \#e^{-1}(G') \leqslant c\alpha \qquad \text{and so} \qquad q - c\alpha \leqslant \#F^{-1}(P) \leqslant q.$$

Meanwhile, $[nc]^{-1}(\mathcal{O}) = G'$ for each $n \in \mathbb{F}_r^*$, which leads to

$$F^{-1}(\mathcal{O}) = \left(\mathbb{F}_q \times \{0\}\right) \sqcup \left(e^{-1}(G') \times \mathbb{F}_r^*\right), \qquad q \leqslant \#F^{-1}(\mathcal{O}) \leqslant q + c\alpha(r - 1).$$

This means that

$$\left|\#F^{-1}(P) - q\right| \leqslant \begin{cases} c\alpha & \text{if} \quad P \neq \mathcal{O}, \\ c\alpha(r - 1) & \text{if} \quad P = \mathcal{O}. \end{cases}$$

As a result, the sum of

$$\delta(P) := \left| \frac{\#F^{-1}(P)}{\#V} - \frac{1}{\#G} \right| = \frac{\left|\#F^{-1}(P) - q\right|}{qr}$$

is equal to

$$\sum_{P \in G} \delta(P) = \sum_{P \neq \mathcal{O}} \delta(P) + \delta(\mathcal{O}) \leqslant 2(r - 1)\frac{c\alpha}{qr} \leqslant 2\frac{c\alpha}{q}.$$

This fits the regularity definition represented, e.g., in [4, Equality (3)].   □

Corollary 4. *Assume that* $c = O(\sqrt{q})$, $\alpha = O(1)$, *and* e *is an* α-*weak map. Then,* F *is an admissible map and hence the hash function* $\mathcal{H} = F \circ \eta \colon \{0,1\}^* \to G$ *is indifferentiable whenever so is* $\eta \colon \{0,1\}^* \to V$.

Proof. By virtue of the last theorem, F is ϵ-regular with $\epsilon = O(q^{-1/2})$ (cf. Corollary 1) for the assumed values c, α. This is a sufficient bound on ϵ to satisfy the inequality $\log_2(\epsilon) \lesssim -\lambda$ in view of the classical one $\log_2(q) \gtrsim 2\lambda$, where λ (typically, ≈ 128) is a desirable security level. The given formalization of negligibility for ϵ is first introduced in [20, Section 1.2]. Besides, F is obviously computable in constant time, since weakness of e includes this aspect.

In a nutshell, samplability of F follows from that of e. To be definite, suppose that a point $P \in G$ is different from $\mathcal{O}$. Nothing prevents from sampling uniformly at random $n \in \mathbb{F}_r^*$ and $Q \in [nc]^{-1}(P)$. This is readily done, because it is elementary to determine (in precomputations) at most two generators of G' (and thereby of $E(\mathbb{F}_q) = G \times G'$). Therefore, $Q - [(nc)^{-1}]P$ is one of their linear combinations with samplable coefficients.

At worst, the whole subgroup G' lies in $\mathrm{Im}(e)$, hence

$$\#\big(U \cap \mathrm{Im}(e)\big) \geqslant \#\mathrm{Im}(e) - \#G' \geqslant \frac{q}{\alpha} - c.$$

With the (large) probability

$$\frac{\#\big(U \cap \mathrm{Im}(e)\big)}{\#U} \geqslant \frac{q/\alpha - c}{\#E(\mathbb{F}_q)} = \frac{q - c\alpha}{\alpha\big(q + O(\sqrt{q})\big)} \approx \frac{1}{\alpha},$$

the point $Q \in \mathrm{Im}(e)$. Otherwise, one just tries the other n and Q. It remains to pick uniformly at random $t \in e^{-1}(Q)$, getting ultimately $(t, n) \in F^{-1}(P)$.

The above reasoning can be evidently formalized by analogy with [4, Algorithm 1]. Without any obstacles, the case $P = \mathcal{O}$ is processed separately in a similar way. This finishes the proof of admissibility for F, which as usual implies (see, e.g., [4, Theorem 1]) indifferentiability for $\mathcal{H}$.   □

It is time to discuss advantages of the new construction F compared to the previous ones F_i. Clearly, F is a modification of F_0 in which the base point is variable. The fixed point P_0 is responsible for why F_0 is vulnerable to a catastrophic attack mentioned in [7, Section 8.1] and at the end of [11, Section 1.1]. It is easily checked that (at least) this attack does not work at all for F. Moreover, the map F_0 is not admissible (namely not samplable), because the discrete logarithm $\log_{P_0}(P) \in \mathbb{F}_r$ is unknown for a general point $P \in G$.

In turn, the maps F_1, F_2 are admissible and widely recognized to be reliable. Nonetheless, they cannot be efficiently batched with a subsequent scalar multiplication $[m]$ in G, where $m \in \mathbb{F}_r$. Meanwhile, for computing $[m] \circ F(t, n)$, it is enough to perform one additional (cheap) multiplication $N := m(nc)$ in the field $\mathbb{F}_r$, since the sought point is expressed as $[N]e(t)$. Thus, we manage to get by with only one scalar multiplication.

In conclusion, it is worth stating explicitly that the new map F is itself an order of magnitude slower than the SwiftEC(-like) map $[c] \circ h_2$, because the same holds true when comparing $[n]$ with two $\left(\frac{\cdot}{q}\right)$. As a result, F is meaningless if a hash function $\mathcal{H}$ is a standalone primitive (or m is small) in a cryptographic scheme. This is the case, e.g., for multiset hashing. However, it is in reality sufficient (owing to [21, Section 4.1, Appendix A]) for this hashing type to employ a weak map e instead of an admissible one. Offhand, it is hard to remember a scheme that requires $\mathcal{H}$ to be simultaneously indifferentiable, deterministic, and not followed by a scalar multiplication. By reason of F, the SwiftEC(-like) map is thereby a slightly less significant achievement than it seems at first glance.

References

1. Aardal, M.A., Aranha, D.F.: 2DT-GLS: faster and exception-free scalar multiplication in the GLS254 binary curve. In: Smith, B., Wu, H. (eds.) SAC 2022. LNCS, vol. 13742, pp. 53–74. Springer, Cham (2024). https://doi.org/10.1007/978-3-031-58411-4_3

2. Aranha, D.F., Salling Hvass, B., Spitters, B., Tibouchi, M.: Faster constant-time evaluation of the Kronecker symbol with application to elliptic curve hashing. In: CCS 2023: ACM Conference on Computer and Communications Security, pp. 3228–3238. ACM Press, New York (2023). https://doi.org/10.1145/3576915.3616597

3. Aubry, Y., Perret, M.: A Weil theorem for singular curves. In: Pellikaan, R., Perret, M., Vlăduţ, S.G. (eds.) Arithmetic, Geometry, and Coding Theory, pp. 1–7. Proceedings in Mathematics. De Gruyter, Berlin (1996). https://doi.org/10.1515/9783110811056.1

4. Brier, E., Coron, J.-S., Icart, T., Madore, D., Randriam, H., Tibouchi, M.: Efficient indifferentiable hashing into ordinary elliptic curves. In: Rabin, T. (ed.) CRYPTO 2010. LNCS, vol. 6223, pp. 237–254. Springer, Heidelberg (2010). https://doi.org/10.1007/978-3-642-14623-7_13

5. Chen, L., Moody, D., Regenscheid, A., Robinson, A., Randall, K.: Recommendations for discrete logarithm-based cryptography: elliptic curve domain parameters (NIST Special Publication 800-186) (2023). https://csrc.nist.gov/publications/detail/sp/800-186/final

6. Chávez-Saab, J., Rodríguez-Henríquez, F., Tibouchi, M.: SwiftEC: Shallue-van de Woestijne indifferentiable function to elliptic curves. In: Agrawal, S., Lin, D. (eds.) ASIACRYPT 2022. LNCS, vol. 13791, pp. 63–92. Springer, Cham (2022). https://doi.org/10.1007/978-3-031-22963-3_3

7. El Mrabet, N., Joye, M. (eds.): Guide to pairing-based cryptography. Cryptography and Network Security Series. Chapman and Hall/CRC, New York (2017). https://doi.org/10.1201/9781315370170

8. Granger, R., Kleinjung, T., Lenstra, A.K., Wesolowski, B., Zumbrägel, J.: Computation of a 30750-bit binary field discrete logarithm. Math. Comput. **90**(332), 2997–3022 (2021). https://doi.org/10.1090/mcom/3669

9. Hassett, B.: Rational surfaces over nonclosed fields. In: Darmon, H., Ellwood, D.A., Hassett, B., Tschinkel, Y. (eds.) Arithmetic Geometry. Clay Mathematics Proceedings, vol. 8, pp. 155–209. Clay Mathematics Institute, Cambridge (2009). https://www.math.brown.edu/bhassett/papers/Claylecture/CMIPhassett.pdf

10. Homma, M.: Fragments of plane filling curves of degree $q+2$ over the finite field of q elements, and of affine-plane filling curves of degree $q+1$. Linear Algebra Appl. **589**, 9–27 (2020). https://doi.org/10.1016/j.laa.2019.12.012

11. Icart, T.: How to hash into elliptic curves. In: Halevi, S. (ed.) CRYPTO 2009. LNCS, vol. 5677, pp. 303–316. Springer, Heidelberg (2009). https://doi.org/10.1007/978-3-642-03356-8_18

12. Iskovskikh, V.A.: Rational surfaces with a pencil of rational curves. Math. USSR-Sbornik **3**(4), 563–587 (1967). https://doi.org/10.1070/sm1967v003n04abeh002769

13. Kaliski, B.S., Jr.: One-way permutations on elliptic curves. J. Cryptol. **3**(3), 187–199 (1991). https://doi.org/10.1007/bf00196911

14. Koblitz, N.: Elliptic curve cryptosystems. Math. Comput. **48**(177), 203–209 (1987). https://doi.org/10.1090/s0025-5718-1987-0866109-5

15. Kollár, J., Mella, M.: Quadratic families of elliptic curves and unirationality of degree 1 conic bundles. Am. J. Math. **139**(4), 915–936 (2017). https://doi.org/10.1353/ajm.2017.0024

16. Koshelev, D.: Indifferentiable hashing to ordinary elliptic $\mathbb{F}_q$-curves of $j = 0$ with the cost of one exponentiation in $\mathbb{F}_q$. Des. Codes Crypt. **90**(3), 801–812 (2022). https://doi.org/10.1007/s10623-022-01012-8

17. Koshelev, D.: The most efficient indifferentiable hashing to elliptic curves of j-invariant 1728. J. Math. Cryptol. **16**(1), 298–309 (2022). https://doi.org/10.1515/jmc-2021-0051

18. Koshelev, D.: Hashing to elliptic curves through Cipolla–Lehmer–Müller's square root algorithm. J. Cryptol. **37**(2), article 11 (2024). https://doi.org/10.1007/s00145-024-09490-w

19. Koshelev, D.: Magma code (2024). https://github.com/Dimitri-Koshelev/Simultaneously-simple-universal-and-indifferentiable-hashing-to-elliptic-curves

20. Koshelev, D.: Some remarks on how to hash faster onto elliptic curves. J. Comput. Virol. Hack. Tech. **20**(4), 593–605 (2024). https://doi.org/10.1007/s11416-024-00514-4

21. Maitin-Shepard, J., Tibouchi, M., Aranha, D.F.: Elliptic curve multiset hash. Comput. J. Sect. D: Secur. Comput. Syst. Netw. **60**(4), 476–490 (2017). https://doi.org/10.1093/comjnl/bxw053

22. Maurer, U., Renner, R., Holenstein, C.: Indifferentiability, impossibility results on reductions, and applications to the random oracle methodology. In: Naor, M. (ed.) TCC 2004. LNCS, vol. 2951, pp. 21–39. Springer, Heidelberg (2004). https://doi.org/10.1007/978-3-540-24638-1_2

23. Menezes, A.J., Vanstone, S.A., Okamoto, T.: Reducing elliptic curve logarithms to logarithms in a finite field. In: STOC 1991: ACM Symposium on Theory of Computing, pp. 80–89. ACM Press, New York (1991). https://doi.org/10.1145/103418.103434

24. Noether, S.: Understanding ge fromfe frombytes vartime. https://www.getmonero.org/ru/resources/research-lab/pubs/ge_fromfe.pdf

25. Pornin, T.: Faster complete formulas for the GLS254 binary curve (2023). https://eprint.iacr.org/2023/1688

26. van Saberhagen, N.: CryptoNote v 2.0 (2013). https://bytecoin.org/old/whitepaper.pdf

27. Sendra, J.R., Winkler, F., Pérez-Díaz, S.: Rational algebraic curves: a computer algebra approach. Algorithms Comput. Math. **22** Springer, Heidelberg (2008). https://doi.org/10.1007/978-3-540-73725-4

28. Shallue, A., van de Woestijne, C.E.: Construction of rational points on elliptic curves over finite fields. In: Hess, F., Pauli, S., Pohst, M. (eds.) ANTS 2006. LNCS, vol. 4076, pp. 510–524. Springer, Heidelberg (2006). https://doi.org/10.1007/11792086_36

29. Skałba, M.: Points on elliptic curves over finite fields. Acta Arith **117**(3), 293–301 (2005). https://doi.org/10.4064/aa117-3-7
30. Tibouchi, M.: Impossibility of surjective Icart-like encodings. In: Chow, S.S.M., Liu, J.K., Hui, L.C.K., Yiu, S.M. (eds.) ProvSec 2014. LNCS, vol. 8782, pp. 29–39. Springer, Cham (2014). https://doi.org/10.1007/978-3-319-12475-9_3
31. Tsfasman, M.A., Vlăduţ, S.G., Nogin, D.Y.: Algebraic geometric codes: basic notions. In: Mathematical Surveys and Monographs, vol. 139. American Mathematical Society, Providence (2007). https://doi.org/10.1090/surv/139
32. Wahby, R.S., Boneh, D.: Fast and simple constant-time hashing to the BLS12-381 elliptic curve. IACR Trans. Cryptogr. Hardw. Embed. Syst. (CHES) **2019**(4), 154–179 (2019). https://doi.org/10.13154/tches.v2019.i4.154-179

Cryptanalysis

Conjunctive Dynamic SSE Schemes Under Scrutiny: Exposing Privacy Issues in SDSSE-CQ-S and VCDSSE

Bibhas Chandra Das[1,2]($\boxtimes$) (iD)

[1] Institute for Advancing Intelligence, TCG CREST, Kolkata, India
`bibhaschandra.das@tcgcrest.org`
[2] Chennai Mathematical Institute, Chennai, India
`https://www.tcgcrest.org/institutes/iai/`, `https://www.cmi.ac.in/`

Abstract. Designing an efficient conjunctive dynamic searchable symmetric encryption (DSSE) scheme with forward and backward privacy is a crucial and rapidly growing area of research. Recently, Zuo et al., in PETs'25, proposed two state-of-the-art forward and backward private conjunctive dynamic SSE schemes, namely **SDSSE-CQ** and **SDSSE-CQ-S**. **SDSSE-CQ** is an efficient construction with minimal communication and computation overhead, but could achieve only a weaker notion of backward privacy. On the contrary, **SDSSE-CQ-S** surpasses **SDSSE-CQ** by offering a stronger backward privacy guarantee, however, at the cost of additional communication and computation overhead. Further to address the challenge in a potentially malicious server setting, Lu et al., in TCJ'22, proposed the first verifiable conjunctive dynamic SSE scheme, dubbed **VCDSSE**, offering forward and backward security along with verifiable search results. This paper revisits the state-of-the-art constructions, **SDSSE-CQ-S** and **VCDSSE**, and reports fatal privacy issues. First, we have attacked **SDSSE-CQ-S** and disproved its stronger privacy claim, reducing its privacy guarantee to an unarguably weaker level. The novelty of our attack lies in its simplicity; it relies only on tricky but elementary algebraic calculations, yet remains highly effective. Next, we have attacked **VCDSSE** and shown that **VCDSSE** fails to provide forward privacy. We have also identified the flaw in the design of **VCDSSE**, causing the privacy loss, and argued that there is no immediate solution. We have explained both the issues through respective prototype examples. We strongly believe that our attacks will inspire researchers to design efficient dynamic conjunctive SSE schemes that provide proper strong privacy guarantees.

Keywords: Dynamic SSE · Conjunctive Queries · Forward Privacy · Backward Privacy · Verifiable

1 Introduction

With the advancements in digital technology, high-speed internet, and affordable third-party cloud storage have significantly increased. As a result, storing huge

A. Nitaj et al. (Eds.): AFRICACRYPT 2025, LNCS 15651, pp. 417–440, 2026.
https://doi.org/10.1007/978-3-031-97260-7_19

amounts of data in the cloud has become highly convenient for users, enabling easy access and efficient data management. However, it is essential to remember that much of this data is sensitive and confidential.

Necessarily, to protect our data from malicious servers and third-party attackers, we need some encryption mechanism. Conventional encryption methods can not serve the purpose since they do not support querying the encrypted information. Generic cryptographic tools like *fully homomorphic encryption* (FHE) and *oblivious RAM* (ORAM) can potentially mitigate this issue by enabling users to search on encrypted data. However, these tools are very costly in terms of space and time complexity, and hence impractical for large databases. Therefore, the need for an alternative solution is evident, which will simultaneously allow clients to perform keyword-efficient search over an encrypted database and minimize information leakage to the cloud. *Searchable Symmetric Encryption* (SSE) [8,9,16,21] serves as the solution to this problem, which provides a trade-off between the efficiency of searching over encrypted data and minimal information leakage to the cloud.

1.1   Searchable Symmetric Encryption

In SSE, a database is abstracted as a collection of documents, each containing certain keywords. Each document is associated with a unique identifier. So, one can view the database as a collection of keyword-identifier pairs. The first SSE scheme was proposed by Song et al. [21], followed by a similar work by Goh [12]. Curtmola et al. [9] laid the foundational framework for SSE schemes, which has since become the de facto standard for SSE.

Most of the initial works [5,9] on SSE were designed explicitly for static databases, where modification is not allowed. However, in a practical scenario, we need constructions that allow adding or deleting keywords to or from documents, even when they are already stored in the cloud. In [16], the first definition and security notion of *dynamic SSE* (DSSE) scheme was introduced. Since then, numerous DSSE schemes have been proposed in [1,3,10,15]. Incorporating the update feature with SSE introduced a new information leakage scenario. Adversaries may exploit this information leakage to compromise data privacy as shown in [4,13]. In this regard, Cash et al. introduced the notion of forward privacy in [4]. Informally, forward privacy requires that updating a file should not reveal whether it contains keywords that have been previously searched for. Bost [1] formally defined this privacy notion and proposed the first scheme achieving forward privacy. Concurrently, Stefanov et al., in [22], introduced another important property privacy notion, dubbed *"backward privacy"*. Informally, backward privacy requires that in a search query for keyword w, the scheme should not reveal any information about the files that once contained w, but later w has been deleted from those files. In [3], Bost et al. formally defined this privacy notion and proposed four schemes that achieve backward privacy. Since then, forward and backward privacy have been essential requirements for an SSE scheme.

1.2   Conjunctive Dynamic Searchable Symmetric Encryption

The works mentioned above are all designed to allow search queries with only one keyword at a time. However, in a practical scenario, SSE must accommodate a richer set of search queries, such as conjunctive keyword searches. In conjunctive search, given a set of keywords $w_1, w_2, \ldots, w_n$, the result should return the set of file identifiers containing all the searched keywords. One naive solution for conjunctive searches can be to make n distinct single keyword queries for the n searched keywords. In that case, the cloud would respond with a large number of matching records. Now the client would need to download all those returned records and filter out the result set locally. This simple solution, however, significantly increases communication overhead and introduces extra leakages. In this regard, a new research direction has emerged in the name of *Conjunctive Searchable Symmetric Encryption*. In [5], Cash et al. proposed the first scheme, dubbed *Oblivious Cross-Tag* (OXT), enabling conjunctive search. This is the first sub-linear conjunctive SSE scheme for arbitrarily structured data. The authors introduced the idea of cross-tags, which are pre-computed during the update protocol and stored on the server. During the search protocol, the client sends some pointers, computed only with information on the searched keywords, to unlock these pre-computed tags and check for the required conjunction without revealing all updates of all the searched keywords to the server. This construction and a follow-up work by Lai et al. [18] work only for static databases. The first dynamic SSE scheme with support for conjunctive queries was proposed by Kamara et al. [14].

All the conjunctive DSSE schemes discussed above only ensure forward privacy. Designing a conjunctive DSSE scheme with both forward and backward privacy remained open until the work of Patranabis et al. [20]. Inspired by OXT [5], the authors proposed a new conjunctive DSSE scheme, dubbed *Oblivious Dynamic Cross-Tags* (ODXT). The authors emulated the idea of cross-tags for the dynamic database and introduced the novel notion of dynamic cross-tags. ODXT computes the cross tags through an oblivious computation achieved through blinded exponentiation in a cyclic group of prime order. Authors have proved that ODXT achieves backward privacy with update pattern when the conjunctive search gets boiled down to a single keyword search. Concurrent to this work, Zuo et al. [26] proposed two forward and backward secure DSSE schemes for conjunctive queries, dubbed FBDSSE-CQ and SFBDSSE-CQ. However, these two constructions, built upon the extended bitmap index data structure, incur a high communication overhead and have practicality issues.

In [25], Zuo et al. identified a serious forward privacy issue of the ODXT scheme from [20]. In this regard, they proposed two new conjunctive DSSE schemes, dubbed SDSSE-CQ and SDSSE-CQ-S, based on a similar framework as ODXT. Contrary to ODXT, both SDSSE-CQ and SDSSE-CQ-S use a forward and backward private DSSE scheme for single keyword search, as example Aura [23] in their case, to encrypt the update tokens before storing them at the server. Moreover, the authors introduced two new notions of backward privacy for conjunctive DSSE schemes to quantify the leakages of the proposed schemes. The weaker notion, dubbed Type-O, informally leaks (a) *result pattern* : the files matching the current query $q = w_1 \wedge w_2 \wedge \cdots \wedge w_n$, (b) *time* : the total number of updates and corresponding update times for each w_i and (c) *size* : the number of matching files of each $w_1 \wedge W$ pair, where W is the conjunction of any subset of $\{w_2, \ldots, w_n\}$. For the stronger notion, dubbed Type-O$^-$, the first two leakages are the same as before only exception being: in place of the number of matching files of each $w_1 \wedge W$ pair, it only leaks the number of matching files of each $w_1 \wedge W_{w_1}$ pair, where W_{w_1} is the conjunction of any subset of $\{w_2, \ldots, w_n\}$ corresponding to the current least frequent keyword w_1, i.e., the keyword with the least number of updates on it. To understand the difference, consider the following instance of some database: file f_1 contains keywords w_1 and w_3. Now, on this, the client performs the following sequence of queries: first, search for the conjunction $w_1 \wedge w_2$, then add keyword w_2 to file f_1, and finally search for the conjunction $w_3 \wedge w_2$. Clearly here $W = \{w_2\}$ and $W_{w_3} = \phi$. Hence, after responding to the final search query, the server learns $size(w_1 \wedge W) = 1$ whereas $size(w_1 \wedge W_{w_3}) = 0$. The authors have proved that, while SDSSE-CQ achieves the weaker Type-O backward privacy, SDSSE-CQ-S achieves stronger Type-O$^-$ backward privacy.

1.3 Verifiable Conjunctive Dynamic SSE

All the above schemes are designed in an *honest but curious* server model: the server follows the protocol precisely, providing accurate responses to search and update queries without tampering with results. However, it attempts to infer information about the user data from the elements it observes while processing these queries. However, in practice, this assumption is weak as the server could be fully dishonest, trying not only to infer about the user data but also to deviate from the protocol and provide incorrect results. This describes an *malicious* server model. A *verifiable* SSE (VSSE) scheme generates a *proof* alongside each search result, which allows the user to verify the correctness of those results.

The first *verifiable dynamic* SSE (VDSSE) scheme was proposed in [17]. However, the scheme was not forward private. The first VDSSE scheme achieving forward privacy was proposed in [2], followed by another forward private scheme by Zhang et al. [24]. However, both of these constructions require high client-side storage. Further to reduce this storage overhead, Zhang et al. [11] proposed a novel data structure called *Accumulative Authentication Tag*. While all these VDSSE schemes only dealt with single keyword search queries, designing a conjunctive VDSSE scheme remained open until the work of Lu et al. [19]. In this work, the authors proposed a conjunctive VDSSE scheme, claiming that the scheme achieves both forward and backward privacy. They incorporate the concept of Homomorphic MACs [6] for the verifiability of search results; however, this approach significantly increases client-side storage overhead, sometimes even in the order of the number of files in the database.

1.4   Our Contribution

In this paper, we revisit the state-of-the-art conjunctive DSSE and VDSSE schemes and identify some serious privacy issues in those schemes.

Attack on Backward Privacy SDSSE-CQ-S: The first scheme under scrutiny is SDSSE-CQ-S, proposed by Zuo et al. [25], which provides the strongest privacy guarantee, surpassing previous conjunctive DSSE schemes such as ODXT [20] and SDSSE-CQ [25]. While in SDSSE-CQ, one conjunctive search query could directly be linked to a different previous conjunctive search query even when they have only one keyword in common, Type-O$^-$ backward privacy guarantee of SDSSE-CQ-S, reduces this leakage profile by incorporating additional randomness during the generation of update and search tokens. This paper refutes their claim of improved backward privacy in SDSSE-CQ-S. Specifically, we have shown that SDSSE-CQ-S is still Type-O backward private, i.e., leaks the same information as SDSSE-CQ. We have also shown that, for the attack, the adversarial server only needs some additional algebraic calculations on the elements observed while processing responses to the search queries. We explain the issue in detail with a prototype example in Sect. 3 and provide an algorithmic description of the main attack in the same section.

Attack on Forward Privacy of VCDSSE: The second scheme under scrutiny is VCDSSE proposed by Lu et al. [19]. The authors proposed the first verifiable DSSE scheme that supports conjunctive queries and claimed that VCDSSE achieves both forward and backward privacy. While studying the scheme closely, we observed that an update query in VCDSSE can be linked to a previous search query if the update is involved in any keyword from that search query, except the least frequent one. In other words, VCDSSE does not provide a full forward privacy guarantee. We have elaborated on this issue with a suitable prototype example in Sect. 4.

ROAD MAP: We discuss all the notations, necessary background, and security definitions in Sect. 2. We have presented the attack on the Type-O$^-$ backward privacy of SDSSE-CQ-S in Sect. 3. Next, in Sect. 4, we discuss the attack on the forward privacy of VCDSSE in detail. Finally, we conclude with some open research directions in Sect. 5.

2   Preliminaries

For any natural number $n \in \mathbb{N}$, we write $[n]$ to denote the set $\{1, \ldots, n\}$. For a variable x and some set X, we write $x \xleftarrow{\$} X$ to denote the random selection of an element from set X and assign it to the variable x. Similarly, for two variables x and y, we write $x \leftarrow y$ to denote the assignment of the value in y to the variable x.

Database: Let $\mathcal{W} = \{w_1, \ldots, w_n\}$ be the set of all distinct keywords, which we call the *dictionary of keywords*. Let $\mathcal{F} = \{f_1, \ldots, f_s\}$ be a collection of files such that each file f_i is associated with an identifier id. Let $\mathcal{ID}$ be the set of all identifiers and $\mathsf{DB} = \{(w, id) : w \in \mathcal{W}, \ id \in \mathcal{ID}\}$ be the set of all keyword-identifier pairs such that a given pair $(w, id) \in \mathsf{DB}$ if and only if the keyword w is in a file having the identifier id. For a given keyword $w \in \mathcal{W}$, $\mathsf{DB}(w)$ denotes the set of all file identifiers containing w as a keyword. Let, $|\mathcal{W}|$ denote the number of keywords in DB. Similarly, $|\mathsf{DB}(w)|$ denotes the number of files that contain the keyword w and $|\mathsf{DB}|$ denotes the number of distinct keyword-identifier pairs. Finally, $|\mathsf{Upd}(w)|$ be the number of times update queries have been made involving the keyword w.

Conjunctive Queries: We represent a conjunctive search query over n distinct keywords $w_1, w_2, \ldots, w_n$ as $q = w_1 \wedge w_2 \wedge \ldots \wedge w_n$ and define the set $\mathsf{DB}(q) = \cap_{i=1}^{n} \mathsf{DB}(w_i)$ to be the result of the conjunctive search query which returns all the files having $w_1, \ldots, w_n$ as their keywords. Depending on the context, we assume that the keyword w_1 is the least frequent keyword, i.e. it has the least number of updates among all keywords in the conjunction q. We refer to this least frequent keyword as *sterm* and all the other keywords in the conjunction are called *xterm*.

2.1   Dynamic Searchable Symmetric Encryption Schemes

A dynamic searchable symmetric encryption(DSSE) scheme consists of three algorithms, namely Setup, Update, and Search. Following Chamani et al. [7], we define DSSE as follows:

Setup$(1^\lambda, \mathsf{DB})$: A probabilistic algorithm takes as input the security parameter λ and the database DB. It outputs a state σ, a secret key sk, which is kept secret, and an encrypted database EDB, which is made public.

Update$(op, (w, id))$: An interactive algorithm. First, the client takes as input the current state σ, the operation $op \in \{add, del\}$ and a keyword-identifier pair $\{w, id\}$ and outputs an update token UT. UT is then sent to the server. On input UT, the server updates the encrypted database EDB and the client state σ also gets updated.

Search(q): Again an interactive algorithm. Here the client first takes as input the current state σ and a query q and outputs a search token ST, which is sent to the server. The server uses this search token ST to retrieve the desired encrypted identifiers from the encrypted database EDB. The encrypted identifiers are then sent to the client. The client decrypts those encrypted identifiers and finally outputs the list of file identifiers belonging to the result set.

2.2   Security Model of DSSE Scheme

The security model of a DSSE scheme is defined in terms of leakage functions related to the scheme. Formally, given a DSSE, the leakage function is given by

$$\mathcal{L} \triangleq \left(\mathcal{L}^{\mathsf{SetUp}}, \mathcal{L}^{\mathsf{Update}}, \mathcal{L}^{\mathsf{Search}}\right),$$

where $\mathcal{L}^{\mathsf{SetUp}}$, $\mathcal{L}^{\mathsf{Update}}$ and $\mathcal{L}^{\mathsf{Search}}$ denotes the leakage to an adversarial server $\mathcal{A}$ during the Setup, Update and Search algorithms respectively.

For these leakage functions the security model of a DSSE scheme is given by two experiments, namely Real and Ideal. The experiments are defined as follows:

Real World: On input the security parameter λ and a database DB, the real challenger first returns an encrypted database EDB following the SetUp algorithm. Then adversarial server $\mathcal{A}$ interacts with the real challenger with update or search queries in an adaptive manner. The interaction follows the real Update and search algorithms of the scheme. Finally $\mathcal{A}$ outputs a single bit b.

Ideal World: Despite the real challenger, here the encrypted database EDB is simulated by a stateful probabilistic polynomial time simulator $\mathcal{S}$ following the setup leakage function $\mathcal{L}^{\mathsf{SetUp}}$. To respond to the update and search queries of the adversary $\mathcal{A}$, the simulator $\mathcal{S}$ uses the update leakage function $\mathcal{L}^{\mathsf{Update}}$ and the search leakage function $\mathcal{L}^{\mathsf{Search}}$, respectively. Finally, $\mathcal{A}$ outputs a single bit b.

A DSSE scheme is adaptively secure for a leakage function $\mathcal{L}$ if for every probabilistic polynomial time algorithm adversarial server $\mathcal{A}$, for every positive polynomial $p()$, and all sufficiently large security parameter λ, there exists an efficient simulator $\mathcal{S}$ such that:

$$|\Pr[\mathsf{Real}_{\mathcal{A}}(\lambda) = 1] - \Pr[\mathsf{Ideal}_{\mathcal{A},\mathcal{S}} = 1]| \leq \frac{1}{p(\lambda)}.$$

2.3 Forward and Backward Privacy of Conjunctive DSSE

The first formal definitions of forward and backward privacy for single keyword DSSE schemes were provided in [1] and [3] respectively. Later researchers, in [20,25,26], have extended those definitions for conjunctive DSSE schemes in a context-specific manner. Among these notions, we focus only on those which are relevant to our work.

Leakage Functions for Conjunctive DSSE: Let $\mathcal{Q}$ be the list of queries. Note that queries can be of the following two types: search queries (t, q) and update queries $(t, op, (w, id))$, where t is the timestamp, $op \in \{\mathsf{add}, \mathsf{del}\}$, and $q = w_1 \wedge w_2 \wedge \cdots \wedge w_n$. We define the following leakage functions from [25].

- $\mathsf{sp}(q)$: The search pattern leakage for a search query q is defined as:

$$\mathsf{sp}(q) = \{t : \{\mathsf{sp}(w)\}_{w \in q}\}_{q \in \mathcal{Q}}.$$

  where, $\mathsf{sp}(w)$ leaks all the timestamp where the keyword w as been searched for, i.e.,

$$\mathsf{sp}(w) = \{t : \exists (t, q') \in \mathcal{Q} | w \in q'\}.$$

- $\mathsf{rp}(q)$: The result pattern leakage for a search query q is defined as:

$$\mathsf{rp}(q) = \{\mathcal{I}\}_{q \in \mathcal{Q}}.$$

  where, $\mathcal{I}$ returns all the identifiers matching the conjunctive query q, i.e. $\mathsf{DB}(q)$.

- Time(q): For a conjunctive query q, Time(q) captures all the update times-tamps for each keyword $w \in q$. Formally,

$$\text{Time}(q) = \{t : \{(t, op, (w, id)) \in \mathcal{Q}\}_{w \in q}\}.$$

- size($w^* \wedge W$) and size($w_1 \wedge W$): The leakage functions size($w^* \wedge W$) and size($w_1 \wedge W$) capture the number of matching files for any conjunctive sub query of the form $w^* \wedge W$ and $w_1 \wedge W$, where W is the collection of any subset of $\{w_2, w_3, \cdots, w_n\}$.

$$\text{size}(w^* \wedge W) = \{|\text{DB}(w \wedge W)|\},$$
$$\text{size}(w_1 \wedge W) = \{|\text{DB}(w_1 \wedge W)|\}.$$

Using these leakage functions, we will now define the following notions of forward privacy [1] and backward privacy [25]. For any two leakage functions $\mathcal{L}_1$ and $\mathcal{L}_2$ we write $\mathcal{L}_1 \preceq \mathcal{L}_2$ to denote $\mathcal{L}_1$ leaks at most as $\mathcal{L}_2$ leaks.

Definition 1 (Forward Privacy). *A DSSE scheme Σ with leakage function $\mathcal{L}_\Sigma = \left(\mathcal{L}_\Sigma^{SetUp}, \mathcal{L}_\Sigma^{Update}, \mathcal{L}_\Sigma^{Search} \right)$ is called* forward private *if the leakage function $\mathcal{L}_\Sigma$ can be written as follows:*

$$\mathcal{L}_\Sigma^{Update}(op, (w, id)) \preceq \mathcal{L}'(op, id),$$

for any stateless function $\mathcal{L}'$.

Definition 2 (Type-O and Type-O⁻ Backward Privacy). *A conjunctive DSSE scheme Σ with leakage function $\mathcal{L}_\Sigma = \left(\mathcal{L}_\Sigma^{SetUp}, \mathcal{L}_\Sigma^{Search}, \mathcal{L}_{Sigma}^{Update} \right)$ is called* Type-O *(respectively,* Type-O⁻ *) backward private if the leakage function $\mathcal{L}_\Sigma$ can be written as follows:*

$$\text{Type-O} : \mathcal{L}_\Sigma^{Update}(op, (w, id)) \preceq \mathcal{L}'(op),$$
$$\mathcal{L}_\Sigma^{Search}(q) \preceq \mathcal{L}''(sp(q), rp(q), \text{Time}(q), \text{size}(w^* \wedge W)),$$
$$\text{Type-O}^- : \mathcal{L}_\Sigma^{Update}(op, (w, id)) \preceq \mathcal{L}'(op),$$
$$\mathcal{L}_\Sigma^{Search}(q) \preceq \mathcal{L}''(sp(q), rp(q), \text{Time}(q), \text{size}(w_1 \wedge W)),$$

for any stateless functions $\mathcal{L}'$ and $\mathcal{L}''$.

3   Attack on Backward Privacy of SDSSE-CQ-S

Zuo et al. in [25] alleviated SDSSE-CQ in SDSSE-CQ-S to achieve stronger backward privacy, namely Type-O⁻. We have identified that the Type-O⁻ privacy claim for SDSSE-CQ-S is faulty[1]. We will elaborate on the issue here through a prototype example. Before that, let us revisit the alleviation of SDSSE-CQ in SDSSE-CQ-S.

---

[1] Note that the issue we have identified in this paper is all about the Type-O⁻ backward privacy claim of the construction SDSSE-CQ-S, but not about the definition of Type-O⁻ backward privacy.

3.1 Overview of **SDSSE-CQ-S**

Both the schemes, SDSSE-CQ and SDSSE-CQ-S are designed over the framework of OXT. As mentioned in [25], SDSSE-CQ guarantees a weaker notion of backward privacy, dubbed Type-O. To demonstrate, let us consider there are two conjunctive queries q_1 and q_2 with some cross-term in common (say $q_1 = w_1 \wedge w_2$ and $q_2 = w_3 \wedge w_2$, where w_2 is the common cross-term). Also, consider there are some updates for the *xterm* between these two searches. Then an adversary can combine the query q_1 with the xtag values obtained while handling the XSet for the query q_2 and infer some critical information about the relation of the intermediate updates with the first search q_1. To reduce this leakage, in SDSSE-CQ-S, the client introduces additional randomness in the form of $F_p(K'_x, w \| c)^{-1}$, where c is the current update counter of w, while computing the cross tags (wxtag). Then, during any search query $q = w_1 \wedge w_2 \wedge \cdots \wedge w_n$, where w_1 is the least frequent keyword, the client computes search tokens (wxtoken$[i, j]$) for each $i \in [0, c_{w_1}]$ and for each $j \in [2, n]$ accordingly. In addition to this, it also computes:

$$\mathsf{wxt}[j][k] = F_p(K'_x, w_j \| k) \cdot F_p(K'_z, w_1), \quad \forall\, j \in [2, n],\ k \in [0, c_j].$$

Next in a joint computation, the client and the server populate WXSet with the values (wxtag)$^{\mathsf{wxt}[j][c_j]}$ for all $j \in [2, n]$. During the second round of the search protocol, to identify the files in conjunction the server only checks whether (wxtoken$[c, j]$)$^y \in$ WXSet or not for all $j \in [2, n]$. We refer the readers to Appendix A for the concrete formal specification of SDSSE-CQ-S.

3.2 Issue with **Type-O⁻** Backward Privacy of **SDSSE-CQ-S**

For SDSSE-CQ the authors showed that a newly searched xtag can always be used by previously issued search queries. Although SDSSE-CQ-S is claimed to achieve stronger backward privacy by introducing an additional keyword dependent randomness, we claim that a similar leakage profile is associated with SDSSE-CQ-S also. To demonstrate the additional leakage, we mounted an attack on SDSSE-CQ-S. Our attack follows the same setup as in [25], which was used to explain the weakness of SDSSE-CQ. To elaborate, let us consider the following example.

Concrete Example: Consider a DB contains four files f_1, f_2, f_3 and f_4 with corresponding set of keywords $\{w_1, w_3\}$, $\{w_2, w_3\}$, $\{w_1, w_2\}$ and $\{w_2\}$ respectively. Now the client performs the following sequence of queries on this DB:

1. Search: $(q_1 = w_1 \wedge w_2)$.
2. Update: $(add, (w_2, f_1))$.
3. Search: $(q_2 = w_3 \wedge w_2)$.

We can easily verify that the result of q_1 is $\{f_3\}$ whereas the result of q_2 is $\{f_1, f_2\}$. Now we claim that an adversarial server interacting with the client through update and search algorithms of SDSSE-CQ-S, can figure out that the file f_1 from the intermediate update $(add, (w_2, f_1))$ is involved in the first search q_1. However, this information is not immediately obvious to the server. This is because, after intermediate update query, the only generated search tokens belong to a different search query, namely to q_2. This contradicts the definition of Type-O$^-$ backward privacy. For better understanding, we have illustrated the issue in Fig. 1.

3.3   Technical Details and Formal Attack

Now let us dive into the technical details of the attack. Consider the above mentioned files f_1, f_2, f_3 and f_4 with respective set of keywords: $\{w_1, w_3\}$, $\{w_2, w_3\}$, $\{w_1, w_2\}$ and $\{w_2\}$. Without loss of generality we can assume that the sequence of update operations on the DB are as follows:

$$(t_1, add, (w_1, id_1)), (t_2, add, (w_2, id_2)), (t_3, add, (w_1, id_3)), (t_4, add, (w_2, id_3)),$$
$$(t_5, add, (w_3, id_1)), (t_6, add, (w_2, id_4)), (t_7, add, (w_3, id_2)).$$

First Search Query: Consider at the next timestamp t_8, the client performs search query for the conjunction: $q = w_1 \wedge w_2$. For this search, w_1 is the least frequent keyword with $c_{w_1} = 2$. So, during this search query, the following wxtoken and wxt values will be communicated from the client to the server:

$$\mathsf{wxtoken}^1[0,2] = g^{F_p(K_z, w_1\|0)\cdot F_p(K_x, w_2)\cdot F_p(K'_z, w_1)},$$
$$\mathsf{wxtoken}^1[1,2] = g^{F_p(K_z, w_1\|1)\cdot F_p(K_x, w_2)\cdot F_p(K'_z, w_1)},$$
$$\mathsf{wxt}^1[2][0] = F_p(K'_x, w_2\|0) \cdot F_p(K'_z, w_1),$$
$$\mathsf{wxt}^1[2][1] = F_p(K'_x, w_2\|1) \cdot F_p(K'_z, w_1),$$
$$\mathsf{wxt}^1[2][2] = F_p(K'_x, w_2\|2) \cdot F_p(K'_z, w_1).$$

In the next step, the client and the server jointly perform two instances of the search protocol of the underlying forward private DSSE scheme Aura [23], one each for w_1 and w_2. At the end of the search for cross-term w_2, the server gets the sequence of $\mathsf{wxtag}\|c_j^1$ values corresponding to all updates of w_2. To be specific, the server gets the following information:

$$\mathsf{wxtag}_0^1 = g^{F_p(K_x, w_2)\cdot F_p(K_i, id_2)\cdot F_p(K'_x, w_2\|0)^{-1}},$$
$$\mathsf{wxtag}_1^1 = g^{F_p(K_x, w_2)\cdot F_p(K_i, id_3)\cdot F_p(K'_x, w_2\|1)^{-1}},$$
$$\mathsf{wxtag}_2^1 = g^{F_p(K_x, w_2)\cdot F_p(K_i, id_4)\cdot F_p(K'_x, w_2\|2)^{-1}}.$$

Moreover, after the other search involving the *sterm* w_1, the server gets the sequence of $e_i^1\|y_i^1\|c_i^1$ values corresponding to all updates of w_1. To be specific, the server gets the following information:

$$e_0^1 = \mathsf{SE.Enc}(K_{w_1}, id_1), \qquad y_0^1 = F_p(K_i, id_1) \cdot F_p(K_z, w_1\|0)^{-1},$$
$$e_1^1 = \mathsf{SE.Enc}(K_{w_1}, id_3), \qquad y_1^1 = F_p(K_i, id_3) \cdot F_p(K_z, w_1\|1)^{-1}.$$

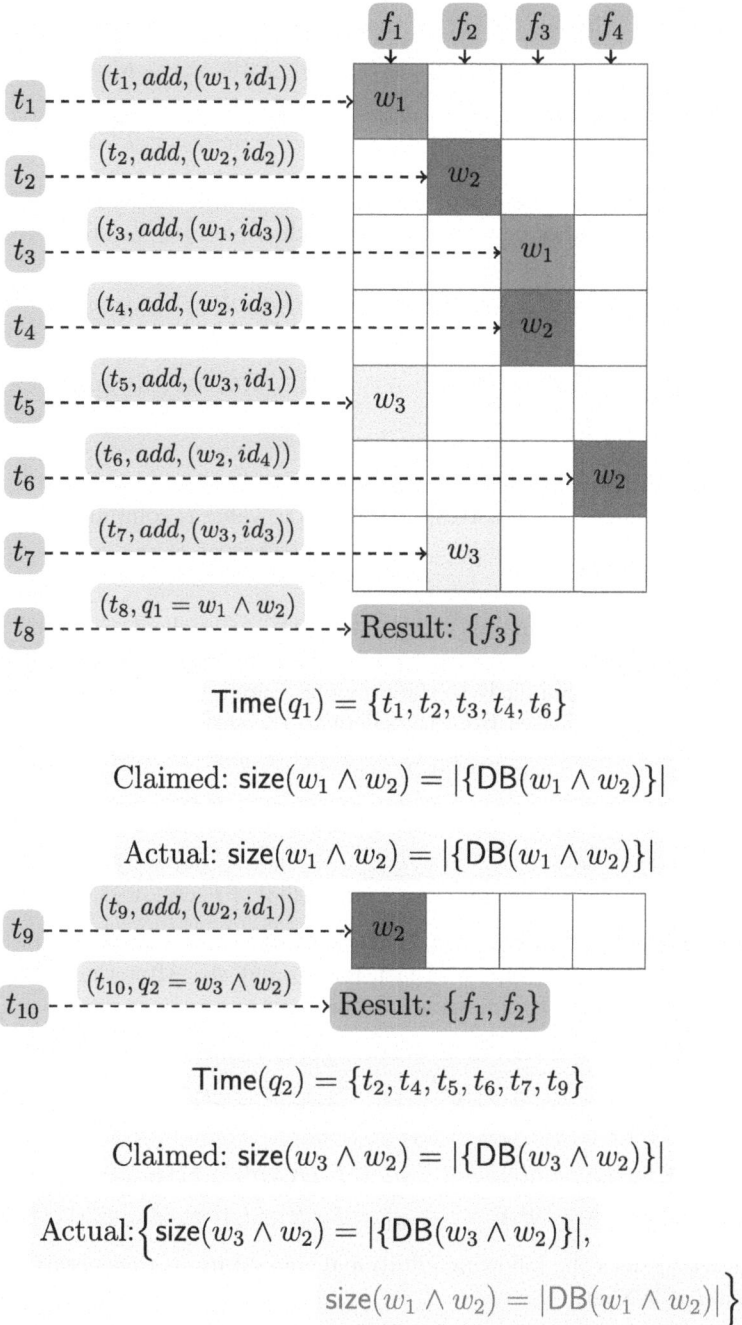

Fig. 1. Issue with Type-O⁻ backward privacy of SDSSE-CQ-S. The quantity marked in red in the size leakage of q_2 is the additional leakage for SDSSE-CQ-S than originally claimed in [25].

With these values in hand, the server then generates the WXSet as follows:

$$\text{WXSet} = \begin{cases} (\text{wxtag}_0^1)^{\text{wxt}^1[2][0]} = g^{F_p(K_x,w_2) \cdot F_p(K_i,id_2) \cdot F_p(K_z',w_1)}, \\ (\text{wxtag}_1^1)^{\text{wxt}^1[2][1]} = g^{F_p(K_x,w_2) \cdot F_p(K_i,id_3) \cdot F_p(K_z',w_1)}, \\ (\text{wxtag}_2^1)^{\text{wxt}^1[2][2]} = g^{F_p(K_x,w_2) \cdot F_p(K_i,id_4) \cdot F_p(K_z',w_1)}. \end{cases}$$

Finally to compute the result set, the server will only have to check: $\text{wxtoken}^1[c_i^1, 2]^{y_i^1} \in \text{WXSet}$ or $\notin \text{WXSet}$, for each tuple $e_i^1 \| y_i^1 \| c_i^1$ retrieved from small-term. Note that at this point:

$$\text{wxtoken}^1[0, 2]^{y_0^1} = g^{F_p(K_x,w_2) \cdot F_p(K_i,id_1) \cdot F_p(K_z',w_1)} \notin \text{WXSet}$$

whereas,

$$\text{wxtoken}^1[1, 2]^{y_1^1} = g^{F_p(K_x,w_2) \cdot F_p(K_i,id_1) \cdot F_p(K_z',w_1)} \in \text{WXSet}.$$

Hence e_0^1 will not feature in the final result set.

Intermediate Update Query: Followed by this, in timestamp t_9, the client inserts w_2 to the file f_1. The corresponding wxtag value is computed as:

$$\text{wxtag}^* = g^{F_p(K_x,w_2) \cdot F_p(K_i,id_1) \cdot F_p(K_x',w_2\|3)^{-1}}.$$

Final Search Query: Finally, at timestamp t_{10}, the client performs search query for the conjunction $q = w_3 \wedge w_2$. For this search, w_3 is the least frequent keyword with $c_{w_3} = 2$. Similarly to the previous search, first the following search tokens will be communicated from the client to the server:

$$\text{wxtoken}^2[0, 2] = g^{F_p(K_z,w_3\|0) \cdot F_p(K_x,w_2) \cdot F_p(K_z',w_3)},$$

$$\text{wxtoken}^2[1, 2] = g^{F_p(K_z,w_3\|1) \cdot F_p(K_x,w_2) \cdot F_p(K_z',w_3)},$$

$\text{wxt}^2[2][0] = F_p(K_x', w_2\|0) \cdot F_p(K_z', w_3)$, $\text{wxt}^2[2][1] = F_p(K_x', w_2\|1) \cdot F_p(K_z', w_3)$,
$\text{wxt}^2[2][2] = F_p(K_x', w_2\|2) \cdot F_p(K_z', w_3)$, $\text{wxt}^2[2][3] = F_p(K_x', w_2\|3) \cdot F_p(K_z', w_3)$.

Again the client and the server will jointly perform two instances of the search protocol of Aura [23], this time one each for w_2 and w_3. After the searches are over, the server will get the following information:

$\text{wxtag}_0^2 = g^{F_p(K_x,w_2) \cdot F_p(K_i,id_2) \cdot F_p(K_x',w_2\|0)^{-1}}$, $\text{wxtag}_1^2 = g^{F_p(K_x,w_2) \cdot F_p(K_i,id_3) \cdot F_p(K_x',w_2\|1)^{-1}}$,

$\text{wxtag}_2^2 = g^{F_p(K_x,w_2) \cdot F_p(K_i,id_4) \cdot F_p(K_x',w_2\|2)^{-1}}$, $\text{wxtag}_3^2 = g^{F_p(K_x,w_2) \cdot F_p(K_i,id_1) \cdot F_p(K_x',w_2\|3)^{-1}}$.

$$e_0^2 = \text{SE.Enc}(K_{w_3}, id_1), \qquad y_0^2 = F_p(K_i, id_1) \cdot F_p(K_z, w_3\|0)^{-1},$$
$$e_1^2 = \text{SE.Enc}(K_{w_3}, id_2), \qquad y_1^2 = F_p(K_i, id_2) \cdot F_p(K_z, w_3\|1)^{-1}.$$

Then the server does the following additional computations to generate the current version of WXSet:

$$\text{WXSet} = \begin{cases} (\text{wxtag}_0^2)^{\text{wxt}^2[2][0]} = g^{F_p(K_x,w_2) \cdot F_p(K_i,id_2) \cdot F_p(K_z',w_3)}, \\ (\text{wxtag}_1^2)^{\text{wxt}^2[2][1]} = g^{F_p(K_x,w_2) \cdot F_p(K_i,id_3) \cdot F_p(K_z',w_3)}, \\ (\text{wxtag}_2^2)^{\text{wxt}^2[2][2]} = g^{F_p(K_x,w_2) \cdot F_p(K_i,id_4) \cdot F_p(K_z',w_3)}, \\ (\text{wxtag}_3^2)^{\text{wxt}^2[2][3]} = g^{F_p(K_x,w_2) \cdot F_p(K_i,id_1) \cdot F_p(K_z',w_3)}. \end{cases}$$

So, the final check for the server will be: whether $\mathsf{wxtoken}^2[c_i^2, 2]^{y_i^2} \in \mathsf{WXSet}$ or $\notin \mathsf{WXSet}$ for each $e_i^2 \| y_i^2 \| c_i^2$ retrieved for w_3. Note that the server will see that:

$$\mathsf{wxtoken}^2[0,2]^{y_0^2} = g^{F_p(K_x, w_2) \cdot F_p(K_i, id_1) \cdot F_p(K_z', w_3)} \in \mathsf{WXSet},$$

$$\mathsf{wxtoken}^2[1,2]^{y_0^2} = g^{F_p(K_x, w_2) \cdot F_p(K_i, id_2) \cdot F_p(K_z', w_3)} \in \mathsf{WXSet}.$$

Hence both e_0^2 and e_1^2 will be included in the final result set.

Final Attack Strategy: We can see that, unlike SDSSE-CQ, the server does not directly learn anything new about the earlier search query q_1 after processing the new search query q_2. However, we will show that with some tricky algebraic calculations, the server can still figure out the same useful information about q_1 and the intermediate update query as in SDSSE-CQ, where this information is directly leaked. Precisely, the server will do the following:

Algorithm 1. Attack on SDSSE-CQ-S

1: $j \xleftarrow{\$} \{0, 1, \cdots, c_{w_2} - 1\}$.
2: Compute $\mathsf{temp} \leftarrow \mathsf{wxt}^2[2][j]^{-1}$
3: Compute $\Delta \leftarrow \mathsf{wxt}^1[2][j] \times \mathsf{temp}$
4: **for** $k = 0, 1, \cdots, c_{w_2}$ **do**
5:     $\mathsf{wxt}^*[2][k] \leftarrow \Delta \times \mathsf{wxt}^2[2][k]$
6: **end for**

Now, take a close look at the resulting $\mathsf{wxt}^*[2][k]$ values. These are simply the wxt values the client would have generated for the search query $q_1 = w_1 \wedge w_2$ but in the current scenario. Also, note that for other search tokens, the $\mathsf{wxtoken}$ values remain unaffected by the number of updates on cross-term w_2. This means the server already holds the likely search token values for the very first search q_1 but in the current scenario. Hence, for the current DB, the server will be able to compute the response of the search query $q_1 = w_1 \wedge w_2$ even if it is not the current search query of the client. In the following, we describe the server's respective computations.

- From the first search query the server has the $\mathsf{wxtoken}^1$ values $\mathsf{wxtoken}^1[0,2]$, $\mathsf{wxtoken}^1[1,2]$ and the update token values $(e_0^1, y_0^1), (e_1^1, y_1^1)$.
- Whereas from the second search query the server has the wxtag^2 values $\mathsf{wxtag}_0^2, \mathsf{wxtag}_1^2, \mathsf{wxtag}_2^2, \mathsf{wxtag}_3^2$.
- Last but not least, the server has the wxt^* values $\mathsf{wxt}^*[2][0], \mathsf{wxt}^*[2][1], \mathsf{wxt}^*[2][2], \mathsf{wxt}^*[2][3]$ from Algorithm 1.

The server now computes WXSet^* as:

$$\mathsf{WXSet}^* = \begin{cases} (\mathsf{wxtag}_0^2)^{\mathsf{wxt}^*[2][0]} = g^{F_p(K_x, w_2) \cdot F_p(K_i, id_2) \cdot F_p(K_z', w_1)}, \\ (\mathsf{wxtag}_1^2)^{\mathsf{wxt}^*[2][1]} = g^{F_p(K_x, w_2) \cdot F_p(K_i, id_3) \cdot F_p(K_z', w_1)}, \\ (\mathsf{wxtag}_2^2)^{\mathsf{wxt}^*[2][2]} = g^{F_p(K_x, w_2) \cdot F_p(K_i, id_4) \cdot F_p(K_z', w_1)}, \\ (\mathsf{wxtag}_3^2)^{\mathsf{wxt}^*[2][3]} = g^{F_p(K_x, w_2) \cdot F_p(K_i, id_1) \cdot F_p(K_z', w_1)}. \end{cases}$$

And finally, the server gets:

$$\text{wxtoken}^1[0,2]^{y_0^1} = g^{F_p(K_x,w_2) \cdot F_p(K_i,id_1) \cdot F_p(K_z',w_1)} \in \text{WXSet}^*$$

and,

$$\text{wxtoken}^2[0,2]^{y_0^1} = g^{F_p(K_x,w_2) \cdot F_p(K_i,id_3) \cdot F_p(K_z',w_1)} \in \text{WXSet}^*.$$

Hence the server learns that at this point both e_0^1 and e_1^1 belong to the result set of $w_1 \wedge w_2$, i.e. $\text{size}(w_1 \wedge w_2) = |\text{DB}(w_1 \wedge w_2)| = 2$. However, this information should not have been revealed to the server if SDSSE-CQ-S were Type-O$^-$ backward private.

4   Attack on Forward Privacy of VCDSSE

VCDSSE [19] is the first proposed verifiable conjunctive DSSE scheme, designed on the basic OXT framework and uses the idea of Homomorphic MACs [6] for verifiability. Despite having such a nice idea, careful observation reveals that VCDSSE often fails to provide the forward privacy guarantee. We will elaborate on the issue here using a prototype example. But before that, let us recall the core idea of the construction first.

4.1   Overview of VCDSSE

The central tool of VCDSSE is the notion of cross-tag, dubbed xtag, adopted from [5]. The xtag values are precomputed during update queries and then retrieved during conjunctive search queries. To enable this, the authors have used the *blinded exponentiation* in a cyclic group of prime order along with a blinding factor y for every update of $(t, op, (w, id))$ of a keyword w. The blinding factor is a product of two entities: (a) the first one masks the information about the file identifier id and corresponding update operation op ("*add*" or "*del*") and (b) the other one keeps the information about the updated keyword w. During any conjunctive search query, the client generates a set of cross-tokens, dubbed xtoken, for the *xterms* corresponding to all *sterm*'s updates and sends them to the server. These tokens incorporate the oblivious shared recomputation of the xtags between the server and the client. To be precise, after receiving the xtoken values, the server retrieves the blinded factors y corresponding to each update operation of the *sterm*. With the xtokens and the corresponding y values, the server computes the possible xtag values. For the efficient verification of search results, the authors have used the idea of Homomorphic MAC from [6]. The algorithmic description of VCDSSE is given in Appendix B.

4.2   Issue with Forward Privacy of VCDSSE

It is important to note that the construction of xtag values for VCDSSE is deterministic, i.e. does not depend on whether it is computed for an update query or recomputed for a search query. As a result, the server always has an opportunity to associate a given update xtag with a previous search query where it was computed for the first time by the server. This is clearly against the requirement of forward privacy. Here we provide a concrete example demonstrating this issue.

Concrete Example: Consider a database DB containing three files f_1, f_2, and f_3 with corresponding set of keywords $\{w_1\}$, $\{w_2, w_3\}$, and $\{w_2\}$, respectively. Now consider the following sequence of operations on DB:

1. Search: $(w_1 \wedge w_2)$.
2. Update: $(add, (w_2, f_1))$.

An adversarial server here processes the client update and search queries while complying with VCDSSE. Once the server completes responding to the latest update, it can easily determine that this update involves some keyword-identifier pair that was searched during the previous query. However, forward privacy demands that updates must not be linkable to prior search queries. Hence we conclude that VCDSSE does not guarantee the forward privacy. The technical details and underlying reasons for this issue are discussed in the following sections.

4.3   Technical Details

Consider a DB that contains three files f_1, f_2, and f_3 with respective set of keywords: $\{w_1\}$, $\{w_2, w_3\}$, and $\{w_2\}$. Now, without loss of generality, we can assume that the sequence of update operations on the database DB is as follows:

$$(t_1, add, (w_1, id_1)), (t_2, add, (w_2, id_2)), (t_3, add, (w_3, id_2)), (t_4, add, (w_2, id_3)).$$

We also consider all the corresponding y values stored in the EDB at the server:

$$y_1^1 = F_p(K_Y, id_1\|add) \cdot F_p(K_Z, w_1\|1)^{-1}, \ y_1^2 = F_p(K_Y, id_2\|add) \cdot F_p(K_Z, w_2\|1)^{-1},$$
$$y_1^3 = F_p(K_Y, id_2\|add) \cdot F_p(K_Z, w_3\|1)^{-1}, \ y_2^2 = F_p(K_Y, id_3\|add) \cdot F_p(K_Z, w_2\|2)^{-1}.$$

First Search Query: Consider the next query on DB to be the search query for the conjunction $q = w_1 \wedge w_2$. Note that w_1 is the least frequent keyword with $c_1 = 1$. So, during this search query, the following xtoken value will be communicated to the server along with the keyword-dependent hash key t_{w_1}, current state $st_{c_1}^1$, and c_1.

$$\mathsf{xtoken}_{2,1} = g^{F_p(K_X, w_2) \cdot F_p(K_Z, w_1\|1)}.$$

Upon receiving these values, the server first computes TSet location UT and retrieves the corresponding update token as the following:

$$\mathsf{UT}_1^1 = H_1(t_{w_1}\|st_1^1), \ (e_1^1, C_{st_0^1}, y_1^1) \leftarrow \mathsf{TSet}[\mathsf{UT}_1^1].$$

Finally to compute the result set, the server checks for $\mathsf{xtoken}_{2,1}^{y_1^1} \in \mathsf{XSet}$, or $\notin \mathsf{XSet}$. For our purpose we denote this value as xtag'. Currently:

$$\mathsf{xtag}' = \mathsf{xtoken}_{0,2}^{y_1^1} = \left(g^{F_p(K_X, w_2) \cdot F_p(K_Z, w_1 \| 1)}\right)^{F_p(K_Y, id_1 \| add) \cdot \left(F_p(K_Z, w_1 \| 1)\right)^{-1}}$$

$$= g^{F_p(K_X, w_2) \cdot F_p(K_Y, id_1 \| add)} \notin \mathsf{XSet}$$

Next Update Query: The next query on DB is an update query: adding w_2 to the file f_1. Along with the other values, a new xtag value is generated and sent to the server as a part of the current update token.

$$\mathsf{xtag} = g^{F_p(K_x, w_2) \cdot F_p(K_y, id_1 \| add)}.$$

Final Attack: Once the server receives the xtag value from the client during the latest update, it will easily identify that:

$$\mathsf{xtag} = g^{F_p(K_x, w_2) \cdot F_p(K_y, id_1 \| add)} = \mathsf{xtag}'.$$

Consequently, the server can quickly deduce that the keyword-identifier pair in this update query matches the previous search. However, generating such one-to-one correspondence is against the requirement of forward privacy.

4.4   Reason and Possible Solution

The precise reason behind this issue with VCDSSE is that during any update query involving some (w, id) pair, the client consistently generates the same xtag value, regardless of whether the pair was previously searched for or not. If there was an earlier search for this pair, the server can easily detect that this update xtag matches one of the xtag' values from that earlier search. Consequently, the server can deduce that the keyword, currently being updated in a file, was part of the previous conjunctive search query.

The discussion above suggests that xtag values should be generated carefully. Specifically, if an xtag value for a (w, id) pair appears in a search query, then in any future update involving the same pair, the update xtag value must be different from the one used during the previously issued search. Hence, a straightforward solution to this problem would be to arrange the updates for the same keyword based on the timestamps they appear. While performing such an update, one should include the corresponding update counter in the xtag computation. A modified xtag for an update query $(t, op, (w, id))$ could be:

$$\mathsf{xtag} = g^{F_p(K_x, w \| c) \cdot F_p(K_y, id \| op)}.$$

The generation of the corresponding xtoken value would also be modified accordingly. Precisely, for a search query $q = w_s \wedge w_x$ with $sterm$ w_s and $xterm$ w_x, one should have:

$$\mathsf{xtoken} = g^{F_p(K_x, w_x \| i) \cdot F_p(K_Z, w_s \| j)} \ \forall \ i \in [1, c_{w_x}] \ and \ \forall \ j \in [1, c_{w_s}].$$

This introduces additional computational overhead, as now for each $xterm$ w_x and each update of $sterm$ w_s, the client needs to generate c_{w_x} many xtokens in place of only one xtoken in VCDSSE. Thus, modifying the current VCDSSE scheme to ensure forward privacy with similar computational and communication overhead may be highly challenging.

5   Conclusion

In this paper, we examined the two state-of-the-art conjunctive DSSE schemes that provide forward and backward privacy, SDSSE-CQ-S in the honest but curious server model, and VCDSSE in the malicious server model. First, we mounted an attack on the Type-O$^-$ backward privacy guarantee of SDSSE-CQ-S. Next, we attacked the forward privacy guarantee of VCDSSE. The findings of our paper show that, in either server setting whether honest but curious or malicious there is currently no efficient forward private conjunctive DSSE scheme with a strong backward privacy guarantee. This leads us to reconsider the goal of designing a conjunctive DSSE scheme that offers both forward and backward privacy in both settings. Also developing a formal definition of backward privacy for conjunctive DSSE schemes remains a challenging open research problem.

Acknowledgments. I would like to express my sincere gratitude to my Ph.D. advisor, Dr. Nilanjan Datta, for his continuous guidance, insightful suggestions, and generous support throughout the development of this paper. His helpful advice, especially on the technical parts, played an important role in shaping this work.

Appendix

A   Specification of SDSSE-CQ

We present an algorithmic description of the update protocol for SDSSE-CQ-S in Algorithm 2 and the search protocol for SDSSE-CQ-S in Algorithm 3 and 4 respectively. In this algorithm, Σ is assumed to be a forward secure symmetric searchable encryption scheme with support for single keyword query only, Aura, for example, as mentioned in [23].

Algorithm 2. Update SDSSE-CQ-S $(sk, st, op, id, w; \text{EDB}_T, \text{EDB}_X)$

1: **function** CLIENT
2:     $sk = (K, K_x, K_i, K_z, K'_x, K'_z)$
3:     $st = (\text{UpdateCnt}, \text{EDB}_T, \text{EDB}_X)$
4:     $c \leftarrow \text{UpdateCnt}[w]$
5:     **if** c is NULL **then** set $c = -1$
6:     **end if**

7:     Set $c = c + 1$, $\text{UpdateCnt}[w] \leftarrow c$
8:     $K_w = F(K, w), e \leftarrow \text{SE.Enc}(K_w, id)$
9:     Set $\text{xid} = F_p(K_i, id), z \leftarrow F_p(K_z, w\|c), y \leftarrow \text{xid} \cdot z^{-1}$
10:    Set $\text{wxtag} = g^{F_p(K_x, w) \cdot \text{xid} \cdot F_p(K'_x, w\|c)^{-1}}$
11: **end function**

1: **function** CLIENT $\Leftrightarrow$ SERVER
2:     Run $\Sigma.\textbf{Update}(op, (w, e\|y\|c), \sigma_T, \text{EDB}_T)$
3:     Run $\Sigma.\textbf{Update}(op, (w, \text{wxtag}\|c), \sigma_X, \text{EDB}_X)$
4: **end function**

Algorithm 3. Search (Round I) SDSSE-CQ-S $(sk, st, q = (w_1, w_2, \ldots, w_n);$ $\mathsf{EDB}_T, \mathsf{EDB}_X)$

1: **function** CLIENT
2:     $sk = (K, K_x, K_z)$
3:     $st = (\mathsf{UpdateCnt}, \mathsf{EDB}_T, \mathsf{EDB}_X)$
4:     Initialize $\mathsf{Res}_T, \mathsf{Res}_X, \mathsf{Res}$ to an empty list.
5:     $c \leftarrow \mathsf{UpdateCnt}[w_1], K_{w_1} \leftarrow F(K, w_1)$
6:     **if** $c = \bot$ **then**
7:         **return** $\emptyset$
8:     **end if**
9:     **for** $i = 0$ to c **do**
10:         **for** $j = 2$ to n **do**
11:             $\mathsf{wxtoken}[i, j] \leftarrow g^{F_p(K_z, w_1 \| i) \cdot F_p(K_x, w_j) \cdot F_p(K_z', w_1)}$
12:         **end for**
13:     **end for**
14:     **for** $j = 2$ to n **do**
15:         $c_j \leftarrow \mathsf{UpdateCnt}[w_j]$
16:         **if** $c_j = \bot$ **then**
17:             **return** $\emptyset$
18:         **end if**
19:         **for** $k = 0$ to c_j **do**
20:             $\mathsf{wxt}[j][k] \leftarrow F_p(K_x', w_j \| k) \cdot F_p(K_z', w_1)$
21:         **end for**
22:     **end for**
23:     **Send** the list of $(\mathsf{wxtoken}, \mathsf{wxt})$ to the server
24: **end function**

1: **function** CLIENT $\Leftrightarrow$ SERVER
2:     $\mathsf{Res}_T \leftarrow \Sigma.\, \mathrm{Search}(w_1, \sigma_T; \mathsf{EDB}_T)$
3:     **if** $\mathsf{Res}_T = \bot$ **then**
4:         **return** $\emptyset$
5:     **end if**
6:     Set $\mathsf{WXSet} \leftarrow \emptyset$
7:     **for** $j = 2$ to n **do**
8:         $\mathsf{Res}_{X,j} \leftarrow \Sigma.\, \mathrm{Search}(w_j, \sigma_X; \mathsf{EDB}_X)$
9:         **if** $\mathsf{Res}_{X,j} = \bot$ **then**
10:             **return** $\emptyset$
11:         **end if**
12:         **for** each $(\mathsf{wxtag} \| c_j) \in \mathsf{Res}_{X,j}$ **do**
13:             Set $\mathsf{WXSet} \leftarrow \mathsf{WXSet} \cup \mathsf{wxtag}^{\mathsf{wxt}[j][c_j]}$
14:         **end for**
15:     **end for**
16: **end function**

Algorithm 4. Search (Round II) SDSSE-CQ-S $(sk, st, q = (w_1, w_2, \ldots, w_n);$ $\mathrm{EDB}_T, \mathrm{EDB}_X)$

```
1: function SERVER
2:     for each (e‖y‖c) ∈ Res_T do
3:         flag ← 1
4:         for j = 2 to n do
5:             if wxtoken[c, j]^y ∉ WXSet then
6:                 flag ← 0
7:             end if
8:         end for
9:         if flag = 1 then
10:            Res ← Res ∪ {e}
11:        end if
12:    end for
13:    Send Res to the client
14: end function
```

B   Specification of VCDSSE

This subsection provides the formal specification of the VCDSSE scheme. To be precise, we present the update algorithm for VCDSSE in Algorithm 5. The search algorithm is depicted in Algorithm 6 and 7. Since we have nothing to do with the verification algorithm of VCDSSE, we have skipped that here.

Algorithm 5. Update-VCDSSE (w, ind, op, W, K; TSet, XSet)

```
1: function CLIENT
2:     Let K = (K_t, K_g, sk, ek, K_X, K_Y, K_Z)
3:     t_w ← F_t(K_t, w)
4:     (st_c, c, Tag_w) ← W[w]
5:     if (st_c, c) = ⊥ then
6:         c = 0, st_c ← ⊥, Tag_w ← Φ
7:     end if
8:     σ_{c+1} ← HomMAC.Auth(sk, τ, ind)
9:     if op = add then
10:        Tag_w = Tag_w ∪ {σ_{c+1}}
11:    else
12:        Tag_w = Tag_w \ {σ_{c+1}}
13:    end if
14:    st_{c+1} ←$ {0,1}^λ
15:    W[w] ← (st_c, c, Tag_w)
16:    UT_{c+1} ← H_1(t_w‖st_{c+1})
17:    Set e_{c+1} ← R_1(K_g, op‖ind)
18:    C_{st_c} ← H_2(t_w‖st_{c+1}) ⊕ st_c
19:    y ← F_p(K_Y, ind‖op) · (F_p(K_Z, w‖c + 1))^{-1}
20:    xtag = g^{F_p(K_X, w) · F_p(K_Y, ind‖op)}
21:    Send (UT_{c+1}, (e_{c+1}, C_{st_c}, y); xtag) to Server
22: end function

1: function SERVER
2:     TSet[UT_{c+1}] ← (e_{c+1}, C_{st_c}, y)
3:     XSet ← XSet ∪ xtag
4: end function
```

Algorithm 6. Search-VCDSSE $(w_1 \wedge w_2 \wedge \cdots \wedge w_n,$ W, K; TSet, XSet)

1: **function** CLIENT
2:     $K = (K_t, K_g, sk, ek, K_X, K_Y, K_Z)$
3:     $t_{w_1} \leftarrow F_t(K_t, w_1)$
4:     $(st_{c_1}, c_1, \mathsf{Tag}_{w_1}) \leftarrow W[w_1]$
5:     **if** $(st_{c_1}, c_1) = \perp$ **then**
6:         **return** $\emptyset$
7:     **end if**
8:     **for** $j = 1$ to c_1 **do**
9:         **for** $i = 2$ to n **do**
10:             Set $\mathsf{xtoken}_{i,j} = g^{F_p(K_X, w_i) \cdot F_p(K_Z, w_1 \| j)}$
11:         **end for**
12:         $\mathsf{xtokenList}_j \leftarrow \{\mathsf{xtoken}_{2,j}, \mathsf{xtoken}_{3,j}, \cdots, \mathsf{xtoken}_{n,j}\}$
13:     **end for**
14:     $\mathsf{xtoken} \leftarrow (\mathsf{xtokenList}_1, \mathsf{xtokenList}_2, \cdots, \mathsf{xtokenList}_{c_1})$
15:     **Send** $(t_{w_1}, st_{c_1}, c_1, \mathsf{xtoken})$ to Server
16: **end function**

1: **function** SERVER
2:     $R \leftarrow \emptyset$
3:     **for** $j = c_1$ to 1 **do**
4:         $\mathsf{ct}_j = 1$
5:         $UT_j \leftarrow H_1(t_{w_1} \| st_j)$
6:         $(e_j, \mathsf{C}_{st_{j-1}}, y_j) \leftarrow \mathsf{TSet}[UT_j]$
7:         **for** $i = 2$ to n **do**
8:             **if** $\mathsf{xtoken}_{i,j}^{y_j} \in \mathsf{XSet}$ **then**
9:                 $\mathsf{ct}_j = \mathsf{ct}_j + 1$
10:             **end if**
11:         **end for**
12:         $R \leftarrow R \cup \{(e_j, \mathsf{ct}_j)\}$
13:         **if** $\mathsf{C}_{st_{j-1}} = \perp$ **then**
14:             break
15:         **end if**
16:         $st_{j-1} \leftarrow H_2(t_{w_1} \| st_j) \oplus \mathsf{C}_{st_{j-1}}$
17:     **end for**
18:     **Send** R to Client
19: **end function**

Algorithm 7. Search Continued

1: **function** CLIENT
2:     $R_s \leftarrow \emptyset$
3:     **for** $j = 1$ to c_1 **do**
4:         $(e_j, \mathsf{ct}_j) \leftarrow R$
5:         $(op_j \| ind_j) \leftarrow R_1^{-1}(K_g, e_j)$
6:         **if** $op_j = add \wedge \mathsf{ct}_j = n$ **then**
7:             $R_s = R_s \cup \{ind_j\}$
8:         **else if** $op_j = del \wedge \mathsf{ct}_j > 0$ **then**
9:             $R_s = R_s \setminus \{ind_j\}$
10:         **end if**
11:     **end for**
12: **end function**

References

1. Bost, R.: Σοφος: forward secure searchable encryption. In: Weippl, E.R., Katzenbeisser, S., Kruegel, C., Myers, A.C., Halevi, S. (eds.) Proceedings of the 2016 ACM SIGSAC Conference on Computer and Communications Security, Vienna, Austria, 24–28 October 2016, pp. 1143–1154. ACM (2016). https://doi.org/10.1145/2976749.2978303

2. Bost, R., Fouque, P., Pointcheval, D.: Verifiable dynamic symmetric searchable encryption: optimality and forward security. IACR Cryptol. ePrint Arch. 62 (2016). http://eprint.iacr.org/2016/062

3. Bost, R., Minaud, B., Ohrimenko, O.: Forward and backward private searchable encryption from constrained cryptographic primitives. In: Thuraisingham, B., Evans, D., Malkin, T., Xu, D. (eds.) Proceedings of the 2017 ACM SIGSAC Conference on Computer and Communications Security, CCS 2017, Dallas, TX, USA, 30 October–03 November 2017, pp. 1465–1482. ACM (2017). https://doi.org/10.1145/3133956.3133980

4. Cash, D., Grubbs, P., Perry, J., Ristenpart, T.: Leakage-abuse attacks against searchable encryption. In: Ray, I., Li, N., Kruegel, C. (eds.) Proceedings of the 22nd ACM SIGSAC Conference on Computer and Communications Security, Denver, CO, USA, 12–16 October 2015, pp. 668–679. ACM (2015). https://doi.org/10.1145/2810103.2813700

5. Cash, D., Jarecki, S., Jutla, C., Krawczyk, H., Roşu, M.-C., Steiner, M.: Highly-scalable searchable symmetric encryption with support for Boolean queries. In: Canetti, R., Garay, J.A. (eds.) CRYPTO 2013, Part I. LNCS, vol. 8042, pp. 353–373. Springer, Heidelberg (2013). https://doi.org/10.1007/978-3-642-40041-4_20

6. Catalano, D., Fiore, D.: Practical homomorphic MACs for arithmetic circuits. In: Johansson, T., Nguyen, P.Q. (eds.) EUROCRYPT 2013. LNCS, vol. 7881, pp. 336–352. Springer, Heidelberg (2013). https://doi.org/10.1007/978-3-642-38348-9_21

7. Chamani, J.G., Papadopoulos, D., Papamanthou, C., Jalili, R.: New constructions for forward and backward private symmetric searchable encryption. In: Lie, D., Mannan, M., Backes, M., Wang, X. (eds.) Proceedings of the 2018 ACM SIGSAC Conference on Computer and Communications Security, CCS 2018, Toronto, ON, Canada, 15–19 October 2018, pp. 1038–1055. ACM (2018). https://doi.org/10.1145/3243734.3243833

8. Chang, Y.-C., Mitzenmacher, M.: Privacy preserving keyword searches on remote encrypted data. In: Ioannidis, J., Keromytis, A., Yung, M. (eds.) ACNS 2005. LNCS, vol. 3531, pp. 442–455. Springer, Heidelberg (2005). https://doi.org/10. 1007/11496137_30

9. Curtmola, R., Garay, J.A., Kamara, S., Ostrovsky, R.: Searchable symmetric encryption: improved definitions and efficient constructions. In: Juels, A., Wright, R.N., di Vimercati, S.D.C. (eds.) Proceedings of the 13th ACM Conference on Computer and Communications Security, CCS 2006, Alexandria, VA, USA, 30 October–3 November 2006, pp. 79–88. ACM (2006). https://doi.org/10.1145/ 1180405.1180417

10. Etemad, M., Küpçü, A., Papamanthou, C., Evans, D.: Efficient dynamic searchable encryption with forward privacy. CoRR abs/1710.00208 (2017). http://arxiv.org/ abs/1710.00208

11. Ge, X., et al.: Towards achieving keyword search over dynamic encrypted cloud data with symmetric-key based verification. IEEE Trans. Dependable Secur. Comput. **18**(1), 490–504 (2021). https://doi.org/10.1109/TDSC.2019.2896258

12. Goh, E.: Secure indexes. IACR Cryptol. ePrint Arch. 216 (2003). http://eprint. iacr.org/2003/216

13. Islam, M.S., Kuzu, M., Kantarcioglu, M.: Access pattern disclosure on searchable encryption: ramification, attack and mitigation. In: 19th Annual Network and Distributed System Security Symposium, NDSS 2012, San Diego, California, USA, 5–8 February 2012. The Internet Society (2012). https://www. ndss-symposium.org/ndss2012/ndss-2012-programme/access-pattern-disclosure-searchable-encryption-ramification-attack-and-mitigation/

14. Kamara, S., Moataz, T.: Boolean searchable symmetric encryption with worst-case sub-linear complexity. In: Coron, J.-S., Nielsen, J.B. (eds.) EUROCRYPT 2017, Part III. LNCS, vol. 10212, pp. 94–124. Springer, Cham (2017). https://doi.org/ 10.1007/978-3-319-56617-7_4

15. Kamara, S., Papamanthou, C.: Parallel and dynamic searchable symmetric encryption. In: Sadeghi, A.-R. (ed.) FC 2013. LNCS, vol. 7859, pp. 258–274. Springer, Heidelberg (2013). https://doi.org/10.1007/978-3-642-39884-1_22

16. Kamara, S., Papamanthou, C., Roeder, T.: Dynamic searchable symmetric encryption. In: Yu, T., Danezis, G., Gligor, V.D. (eds.) the ACM Conference on Computer and Communications Security, CCS 2012, Raleigh, NC, USA, 16–18 October 2012, pp. 965–976. ACM (2012). https://doi.org/10.1145/2382196.2382298

17. Kurosawa, K., Ohtaki, Y.: How to update documents *verifiably* in searchable symmetric encryption. In: Abdalla, M., Nita-Rotaru, C., Dahab, R. (eds.) CANS 2013. LNCS, vol. 8257, pp. 309–328. Springer, Cham (2013). https://doi.org/10.1007/ 978-3-319-02937-5_17

18. Lai, S., et al.: Result pattern hiding searchable encryption for conjunctive queries. In: Lie, D., Mannan, M., Backes, M., Wang, X. (eds.) Proceedings of the 2018 ACM SIGSAC Conference on Computer and Communications Security, CCS 2018, Toronto, ON, Canada, 15–19 October 2018, pp. 745–762. ACM (2018). https:// doi.org/10.1145/3243734.3243753

19. Lu, H., Chen, J., Ning, J., Zhang, K.: Verifiable conjunctive dynamic searchable symmetric encryption with forward and backward privacy. Comput. J. **66**(10), 2379–2392 (2023). https://doi.org/10.1093/COMJNL/BXAC084

20. Patranabis, S., Mukhopadhyay, D.: Forward and backward private conjunctive searchable symmetric encryption. In: 28th Annual Network and Distributed System Security Symposium, NDSS 2021, Virtually, 21–25 February 2021. The Inter-

net Society (2021). https://www.ndss-symposium.org/ndss-paper/forward-and-backward-private-conjunctive-searchable-symmetric-encryption/

21. Song, D.X., Wagner, D.A., Perrig, A.: Practical techniques for searches on encrypted data. In: 2000 IEEE Symposium on Security and Privacy, Berkeley, California, USA, 14–17 May 2000, pp. 44–55. IEEE Computer Society (2000). https://doi.org/10.1109/SECPRI.2000.848445

22. Stefanov, E., Papamanthou, C., Shi, E.: Practical dynamic searchable encryption with small leakage. In: 21st Annual Network and Distributed System Security Symposium, NDSS 2014, San Diego, California, USA, 23–26 February 2014. The Internet Society (2014). https://www.ndss-symposium.org/ndss2014/practical-dynamic-searchable-encryption-small-leakage

23. Sun, S., et al.: Practical non-interactive searchable encryption with forward and backward privacy. In: 28th Annual Network and Distributed System Security Symposium, NDSS 2021, Virtually, 21–25 February 2021. The Internet Society (2021). https://www.ndss-symposium.org/ndss-paper/practical-non-interactive-searchable-encryption-with-forward-and-backward-privacy/

24. Zhang, Z., Wang, J., Wang, Y., Su, Y., Chen, X.: Towards efficient verifiable forward secure searchable symmetric encryption. In: Sako, K., Schneider, S., Ryan, P. (eds.) ESORICS 2019. LNCS, vol. 11736, pp. 304–321. Springer, Cham (2019). https://doi.org/10.1007/978-3-030-29962-0_15

25. Zuo, C., et al.: Searchable encryption for conjunctive queries with extended forward and backward privacy. Proc. Priv. Enhanc. Technol. **2025**(1), 440–455 (2025). https://doi.org/10.56553/POPETS-2025-0024

26. Zuo, C., Sun, S., Liu, J.K., Shao, J., Pieprzyk, J., Wei, G.: Forward and backward private dynamic searchable symmetric encryption for conjunctive queries. IACR Cryptol. ePrint Arch. 1357 (2020). https://eprint.iacr.org/2020/1357

Efficient and Optimized Modeling
of S-Boxes

Anirudh Aitipamula[1], Debranjan Pal[2(✉)], and Dipanwita Roy Chowdhury[1]

[1] Indian Institute of Technology Kharagpur, Kharagpur, India
`anirudhaitipamula@gmail.com`, `drc@cse.iitkgp.ac.in`
[2] Indian Institute of Technology Kanpur, Kanpur, India
`debranjan.crl@gmail.com`

Abstract. This paper presents a systematic exploration of the evolution of algorithms for S-Box modeling, tracing their progression from foundational techniques, such as the greedy algorithm by Sun et al., to state-of-the-art methods like the SuperBall approach by Li and Sun. Through a detailed comparative analysis, we examine these methodologies, highlight their key differences, and provide insightful observations. Early approaches, such as the greedy algorithm, relied on mathematical tools like SageMath, while more recent advancements leverage Mixed Integer Linear Programming (MILP) to model S-Box inequalities more effectively. Building on these developments, we introduce novel algorithms that utilize MILP techniques to enhance both the efficiency and accuracy of S-Box inequality generation. Our first algorithm, direct inequality generation, constructs the final set of inequalities directly using MILP models. The second, greedy generation and reduction, generates an expanded inequality set, which is then refined using the Sasaki and Todo reduction algorithm to obtain the final result. Both approaches employ the method of undetermined coefficients, similar to the SuperBall approach. Our comparative analysis demonstrates that the proposed algorithms not only meet cryptographic standards but also deliver comparable results to existing models. We further enhance the greedy algorithm proposed by Sun et al. through key modifications, while a novel iterative inequality augmentation technique based on convex hull methods improves the results introduced by Boura and Coggia. Additionally, we identify a lower bound in the SuperBall approach, enabling faster convergence to optimal results. We also suggest methods for deriving a minimal set of inequalities associated with the LAT, BCT, and DPT, as well as the DDT for any given S-box. These methods are useful for enhancing cryptanalysis techniques such as linear cryptanalysis, boomerang attacks, and division property-based attacks on ciphers.

Keywords: MILP · S-Box · Inequality · DDT · LAT · BCT

1 Introduction

In modern cryptography, symmetric key ciphers are very useful to protect sensitive information and ensure data privacy. A critical part of these ciphers is the

© The Author(s), under exclusive license to Springer Nature Switzerland AG 2026
A. Nitaj et al. (Eds.): AFRICACRYPT 2025, LNCS 15651, pp. 441–469, 2026.
https://doi.org/10.1007/978-3-031-97260-7_20

substitution box (S-Box) which are responsible for non-linear transformations that make the ciphers more secure.

MILP models are often used to analyze and break cryptographic systems. These were first used by researchers Mouha et al. [9], Wu and Wang [21] to find the minimum number of active S-Boxes that exhibit differential and linear properties. The goal is to demonstrate the cipher's resistance to these traditional cryptanalytic techniques. Sun et al. proposed two techniques in [16,17], their goal was to automate the process of identifying differential characteristics, which are crucial in various cryptanalytic attacks. Following this pioneering work, MILP methods have gained widespread adoption in the field of cryptanalysis. These MILP techniques have been successfully applied to different types of attacks, including differential attacks proposed in [4,23], as well as impossible differential attacks proposed in [13]. Additionally, MILP methods have proven valuable in the analysis of cube attacks, as demonstrated in [6,7,15,18,20,22]. It is important to make these MILP models more effective. However, it's not clear what kind of comprehensive model would work best. Therefore, various models must be created and carefully studied to solve this problem.

An S-Box model contains a set of linear inequalities describing the differential properties of the S-Box. Researchers aim to reduce the number of inequalities by at least one. Even a decrease of one in the number of inequalities is considerably good. This number may seem small, but for analyzing full encryption systems, reducing the number of inequalities decreases the model size, thereby enabling the solver to reach the optimal solution more efficiently, whereas previously, the computation time may have been prohibitive, leading to the acceptance of a sub-optimal result.

In simple terms, the goal is to find ways to model S-Boxes using the smallest possible number of mathematical inequalities, while satisfying the differential properties of the S-Box. Doing so makes the analysis easier, faster, and more scalable to larger systems. Another direction is to consider a minimal set of inequalities corresponding to the Linear Approximation Table (LAT), Boomerang Connectivity Table (BCT), and Differential Propagation Table (DPT), along with the Difference Distribution Table (DDT) for any given S-box. This comprehensive set of inequalities will be beneficial for facilitating cryptanalysis techniques such as linear cryptanalysis, boomerang attacks, and division property-based attacks on ciphers. All source codes of the algorithms in this paper, the final inequalities modeling the S-Boxes can be found at https://github.com/Non-Linear-Optimization/Efficient-and-Optimized-Modeling-of-S-Boxes.

1.1   Related Works

We start our analysis from the greedy and conditional differential behaviour approaches given by Sun et al. [16,17] in 2014. The greedy approach uses a mathematical tool (SageMath [1]) to generate the H-representation of the convex hull corresponding to the Difference Distribution Table [2] (DDT) for an S-Box.

Boura and Coggia [3] generates new inequalities by the summation of some specific k inequalities. The new inequality needs to be validated by checking whether it is indeed a useful or a redundant one. This validation step involves a comprehensive examination of the inequality to determine whether it removes a different and larger set of inequalities. Pal et al. [10] proposed a similar algorithm where the new inequality need not remove a different set of impossible transitions; rather, it suffices to remove at least as many points compared to the inequalities in consideration. The inequalities thus obtained are called the candidate inequalities. After obtaining the candidate inequalities, the reduction algorithm given by Sasaki and Todo [12] is used to produce the final set of inequalities. Their approach in reducing the number of inequalities is to model the reduction problem as an MILP problem. The SuperBall approach [8] uses the method of undetermined coefficients to generate a set of candidate inequalities, then reduce this set to obtain the final inequalities. Udovenko also proposed an idea independently, similar to SuperBall approach in his work [19] around the same time. We compare our results with Superball approach.

1.2 Contribution

The five key contributions are as follows,

- **Modified greedy approach** In the greedy approach proposed by Sun et al. [17], inequalities are first generated using SageMath [1]. A smaller subset of inequalities is then selected in a greedy manner, where the inequality that eliminates the maximum number of impossible transitions is added to the final set. However, in cases of ties between multiple inequalities, the final result depends on which inequality is chosen, introducing variability into the outcome. Here we consider different techniques to break the ties and get new results for different 4-bit S-Boxes.
- **Iterative inequality augmentation** In the convex hull techniques outlined by Boura and Coggia [3], the criterion for selecting useful inequalities is modified to ensure that newly added inequalities exclude points not already excluded by previous ones. This adjustment broadens the scope of candidate inequalities, allowing for a more robust and versatile final set. Our approach involves systematically iterating over subsets of inequalities. We applied the approach to different 4 and 5-bit S-Boxes to get improved results over Boura and Coggia [3].
- **Lower bound optimization in SuperBall Approach** [8] The SuperBall approach, introduced by Li and Sun [8], generates inequalities using MILP models. This method introduces the concept of a pattern, which imposes specific conditions on the coefficients of the generated inequalities. Based on our analysis of 4-bit and 5-bit S-Boxes, we provide a lower bound on the number of inequalities required per pattern to achieve optimal solutions.
- **Direct inequality generation** This method employs MILP models to directly generate inequalities, where each inequality generated in an iteration becomes part of the final set. Unlike previous methods, this approach eliminates the need for a reduction algorithm, streamlining the process. We have applied this method on 4-bit S-Boxes, varying the range of coefficients and the constant term.

– **Greedy generation and reduction** This approach also uses MILP models. We produce a large set of candidate inequalities then use the reduction algorithm [12] to reduce the set, thus obtaining the final inequalities. This approach has been applied on various 4-bit S-Boxes to produce comparable results with the SuperBall approach [8]. Additionally, in our approach we used a much smaller range for the coefficients and the constant term compared to the results given in the SuperBall approach. This facilitates better running times when applying these inequalities in full ciphers.
– **Modeling LAT, BCT and DPT** We also provided minimum set of inequalities corresponding to LAT, BCT and DPT along with DDT for any S-Box. The will be beneficial for linear cryptanalysis, boomerang attack and division property based attack on a cipher.

The execution environment for our algorithms is provided in Appendix A.

1.3   Organization

The basic notations and definitions are presented in Sect. 2. Next the modified greedy approach is described in Sect. 3. Section 4 demonstrates the iterative inequality augmentation approach. Then, the lower bound optimization for the SuperBall approach is presented in Sect. 5. Next, the direct inequality generation approach is explained in Sect. 6. Section 7 describes greedy generation and reduction approach. Finally, we conclude and give some possible future directions in Sect. 8.

2   Preliminaries and Background

Notations

– **Point/Transition** $2n$-bit numbers (for an n-bit S-Box) formed by appending the input and output differences of the DDT.
– **Possible Transitions** $(\mathcal{T})$ The numbers formed by appending input and output differences of DDT where cells have non-zero values.
– **Impossible Transitions** $(\mathcal{D})$ The numbers formed by appending input and output differences where cells have zero value.
– **Inequality/Function** (f) It is a linear polynomial consisting of 8 ($2n$ for an n-bit S-Box) coefficients and 1 constant term whose value upon substitution of a possible transition is non-negative.

Definition 1. *(S-Box modeling)* *The objective of our S-Box modeling is to obtain a set of inequalities.*

1. *Taking any inequality from the set should satisfy all the possible transitions i.e. $\{f(v) \geq 0 \ \forall \ v \in \mathcal{T}\}$.*
2. *Given any impossible transition, there should be at least one inequality that invalidates the impossible transition i.e. $\{\forall \ x \in \mathcal{D} \ \exists \ f \mid f(x) < 0\}$*

The set of inequalities satisfying the above criteria is called a valid set of inequalities.

Algorithm 1. Modified Greedy Algorithm.

Input: The set of possible transitions $(\mathcal{T})$, impossible transitions $(\mathcal{D})$
Output: The set of final inequalities $(\mathcal{R})$ modeling the particular S-Box.

1: $\mathcal{H} \leftarrow ConvHull(\mathcal{T})$ ▷ H-Representation of Convex Hull of Possible Transitions
2: $\mathcal{H}^* \leftarrow \mathcal{H}, \mathcal{X} \leftarrow \mathcal{D}, \mathcal{R} \leftarrow \emptyset$
3: **while** $\mathcal{X} \neq \emptyset$ **do**
4:     $l = \begin{cases} \text{Choose the First inequality from } L_{\max} \\ \qquad\qquad \text{or} \\ \text{Choose the Last inequality from } L_{\max} \\ \qquad\qquad \text{or} \\ \text{Choose the Middle inequality from } L_{\max} \\ \qquad\qquad \text{or} \\ \text{Choose a random inequality from } L_{\max} \end{cases}$
5:     $\mathcal{X} = \mathcal{X}-$ impossible transitions removed by l
6:     $\mathcal{H}^* \leftarrow \mathcal{H}^* - \{l\}$
7:     $\mathcal{R} \leftarrow \mathcal{R} \cup \{l\}$
8: **end while**
9: **return** $\mathcal{R}$

3   Modified Greedy Algorithm

The main idea behind the greedy approach is to generate the convex hull of the possible transitions and then iteratively select the inequality that removes the maximum number of impossible transitions from the set of impossible transitions that are yet to be removed. This gives us a set of inequalities that satisfy the two criteria (see Definition 1) for a valid set of inequalities.

Table 1. Results of Modified Greedy approach varying based on the strategy chosen for 4-bit S-Boxes. A dash indicates that the original work did not provide results for this S-Box.

S-Box	# Transitions		Sun et al. [17]	Modified Greedy Approach			
	Impossible	Possible		First Max	Last Max	Mid Max	Random Max
PRESENT	159	97	22	23	30	29	30
GIFT	157	99	-	24	31	30	31
KLEIN	150	106	22	24	28	32	28
LBLOCK_S0	159	97	28	28	30	28	25
LBLOCK_S1	159	97	27	26	29	31	29
LBLOCK_S2	159	97	28	27	33	28	25
LBLOCK_S3	159	97	26	27	31	29	23
LBLOCK_S4	159	97	29	27	30	29	22
LBLOCK_S5	159	97	28	28	29	29	22
LBLOCK_S6	159	97	26	26	29	31	26
LBLOCK_S7	159	97	25	26	29	31	27
LBLOCK_S8	159	97	28	28	31	31	24
LBLOCK_S9	159	97	29	27	29	28	24
LILLIPUT	150	106	-	28	28	30	28
MIBS	150	106	27	26	30	31	30
MIDORI_S0	159	97	-	23	26	28	26
MIDORI_S1	150	106	-	26	28	32	28
MINALPHER	150	106	-	26	27	27	27
PICCOLO	159	97	23	24	27	31	27
PRIDE	159	97	-	22	27	28	27
PRINCE	150	106	26	28	29	35	29
RECTANGLE	159	97	-	23	26	25	26
SERPENT_S0	168	88	23	27	27	29	27
SERPENT_S1	168	88	24	26	27	31	27
SERPENT_S2	168	88	25	27	28	30	31
SERPENT_S3	166	90	31	24	26	30	31
SERPENT_S4	162	94	26	26	29	31	32
SERPENT_S5	166	90	22	24	28	31	33
SERPENT_S6	166	90	22	21	26	26	32
SERPENT_S7	168	88	30	24	25	29	30
SKINNY	159	97	-	24	27	31	27
TWINE	150	106	23	26	27	29	27

3.1   An Interesting Observation in Greedy Approach

In the greedy approach [16,17], when selecting the inequality that removes the maximum number of impossible transitions, what if multiple inequalities remove the same number of maximum impossible transitions? When two or more inequalities are removing the same number of maximum impossible transitions, it is observed that the final set of inequalities obtained depends on the inequality chosen at each step.

Definition 2. Let $\mathcal{H}^* = \{l_1, l_2, ..., l_k\}$ be the inequalities available, and $\mathcal{D}$ is the set of impossible transitions that are yet to be removed. Define L_{max} as the set of inequalities (or inequality) that invalidates the highest number of points from $\mathcal{D}$.

The Algorithm 1 presents the implementation of the above described method. We begin by generating the convex hull (using SageMath [1]) and storing all the inequalities that remove the maximum number of impossible transitions in a list. From this list, we select one inequality based on one of four selection strategies: choosing the first maximum-removing inequality, the last maximum-removing inequality, the middle maximum-removing inequality, or a randomly selected maximum-removing inequality. Once an inequality is selected, it is applied to remove the impossible transitions from the total set. This process is repeated until all impossible transitions are removed. The final result $\mathcal{R}$ of the Algorithm 1, depends on which strategy we choose at Step 7 in each iteration. This is because the set $\mathcal{X}$ changes when a different inequality is chosen, as a different inequality would (possibly) remove a different set of impossible transitions. Although the number of impossible transitions removed by all inequalities in $L_{\max}$ will be the same, the set removed may vary.

3.2   Results of the Modified Greedy Algorithm

The data in Table 1 clearly shows that the greedy approach [16,17] is highly sensitive to the specific inequalities chosen at each step. This sensitivity directly influences the modeling outcomes in S-Box, as different selections from $L_{\max}$ lead to varied results. This emphasizes the complexity of the greedy approach and the importance of carefully considering inequality selection strategies to optimize the algorithm's performance. The results for the greedy Approach applied to LAT, BCT and DPT is described in Table 2 and Table 3. Now, we step into methods that use MILP models.

4   Iterative Inequality Augmentation (IIA)

In this section, we discuss about a criterion improvement in the algorithm given by Boura and Coggia [3]. The algorithm, similar to the approach in Sect. 3, starts by generating the convex hull of the possible transitions. Once the convex hull is obtained, look at each possible transition point and identify the inequalities from the convex hull that evaluate to zero at this point. Then, for each transition point, consider all subsets of these zero-equal inequalities, taking groups of size k (a chosen parameter) as potential subsets. Each such subset would contain k inequalities, adding up these k inequalities would give us a new inequality. Since all these k inequalities are satisfied by the possible transitions as they are

Table 2. Results of Modified Greedy approach for LAT, BCT and DPT of various 4-bit S-Boxes.

S-Box	LAT				BCT				DPT			
	# Imp	# Pos	# Inqs	Run time (s)	# Imp	# Pos	# Inqs	Run time (s)	# Imp	# Pos	# Inqs	Run time (s)
PRESENT	123	133	29	0.6	107	149	28	0.7	49	207	4	0.08
GIFT	123	133	19	0.6	102	154	26	0.4	68	188	5	0.09
KLEIN	105	151	29	0.5	112	144	32	0.8	41	215	6	0.04
LBLOCK_S0	123	133	18	0.3	103	153	25	0.3	69	187	8	0.05
LBLOCK_S1	123	133	18	0.4	103	153	26	0.4	69	187	7	0.07
LBLOCK_S2	123	133	18	0.8	103	153	26	0.6	69	187	7	0.07
LBLOCK_S3	123	133	19	0.4	103	153	25	0.5	69	187	7	0.04
LBLOCK_S4	123	133	19	0.5	103	153	26	0.4	69	187	8	0.04
LBLOCK_S5	123	133	18	0.4	103	153	25	0.5	69	187	7	0.08
LBLOCK_S6	123	133	18	0.5	103	153	26	0.4	69	187	7	0.08
LBLOCK_S7	123	133	18	0.5	103	153	26	0.4	69	187	7	0.07
LBLOCK_S8	123	133	18	0.3	103	153	25	0.3	69	187	7	0.04
LBLOCK_S9	123	133	19	0.3	103	153	25	0.3	69	187	7	0.04
LILLIPUT	105	151	32	0.5	120	136	28	0.8	48	208	6	0.05
MIBS	105	151	36	0.5	120	136	29	1.0	36	220	4	0.03
MIDORI_S0	123	133	28	0.3	107	149	26	0.6	47	209	6	0.03
MIDORI_S1	105	151	32	0.4	105	151	32	0.7	43	213	8	0.04
MINALPHER	105	151	31	0.8	112	144	31	1.1	41	215	4	0.05
PICCOLO	123	133	16	0.3	103	153	22	0.3	68	188	5	0.04
PRIDE	123	133	16	0.3	103	153	25	0.4	69	187	7	0.08
PRINCE	105	151	31	0.5	105	151	31	0.7	42	214	7	0.04
RECTANGLE	123	133	17	0.5	107	149	24	0.3	67	189	8	0.08
SERPENT_S0	119	137	32	0.4	97	159	28	0.4	52	204	7	0.05
SERPENT_S1	119	137	31	0.4	97	159	30	0.4	45	211	5	0.03
SERPENT_S2	119	137	33	0.5	97	159	30	0.4	50	206	5	0.05
SERPENT_S3	127	129	28	0.5	92	164	30	0.4	53	203	7	0.05
SERPENT_S4	115	141	24	0.4	104	152	27	0.5	60	196	9	0.07
SERPENT_S5	127	129	22	0.5	100	156	31	0.6	59	197	6	0.08
SERPENT_S6	127	129	25	0.5	104	152	26	0.4	54	202	5	0.05
SERPENT_S7	113	143	38	0.5	100	156	29	0.6	61	195	8	0.08
SKINNY	123	133	16	0.3	103	153	22	0.3	68	188	5	0.04
TWINE	105	151	32	0.6	120	136	28	1.0	48	208	6	0.05

part of the convex hull, addition of these inequalities would also satisfy for all possible transitions. For each new inequality, check which impossible transitions it removes. If the set of transitions removed by this new inequality is different (potentially larger) from those removed by the existing inequalities within the subset, add this new inequality as a candidate that might be included in the final set of valid inequalities. Once all the candidate inequalities are obtained, the candidate set is reduced using the reduction algorithm given by Sasaki and Todo [12] to obtain the final set of valid inequalities.

Definition 3. *For a possible transition v, let $C = \{c_1, c_2, \ldots, c_n\}$ (with $n \geq k$) be the set of inequalities in the convex hull that evaluate to zero, i.e., $c_i(v) = 0$ for all $i = 1, 2, \ldots, n$. Take a k-element subset of C, say $\{c_1, c_2, \ldots, c_k\}$, and let $\{S_1, S_2, \ldots, S_k\}$ represent the sets of impossible transitions invalidated by each inequality, where S_i is the set of impossible transitions invalidated by c_i. Generate a new inequality by summing all the inequalities in the chosen subset, defined as $c_{new} = c_1 + c_2 + \cdots + c_k$, and let S_{new} represent the set of impossible transitions invalidated by c_{new}. This new inequality is considered **useful** if it removes a different set of transitions than any of those in the subset, i.e., $S_{new} \not\subseteq S_i$ for all $i = 1, 2, \ldots, k$.*

Table 3. Results of Modified Greedy approach for LAT, BCT and DPT of various 5-bit S-Boxes.

S-Box	LAT				BCT				DPT			
	# Imp	# Pos	# Inqs	Run time (s)	# Imp	# Pos	# Inqs	Run time (s)	# Imp	# Pos	# Inqs	Run time (s)
$SC2000\_5$	527	497	91	57.5	465	559	102	54.4	192	832	15	0.96
$KECCAK$	647	377	66	8.1	445	579	57	14.1	381	643	20	1.58
$ICEPOLE$	497	527	81	16.1	425	599	72	37.6	61	963	2	0.09
$FIDES\_5$	527	497	95	55.2	465	559	95	49.4	205	819	16	1.95
$ASCON$	647	377	71	83.1	445	579	65	28.6	260	764	16	1.63
APN_S4	527	497	94	66.2	465	559	90	60.9	184	840	16	1.38
APN_S3	527	497	91	52.0	465	559	88	51.9	196	828	17	1.57
APN_S2	527	497	97	68.3	465	559	100	67.1	191	833	14	1.29
APN_S1	527	497	92	73.0	465	559	94	65.8	195	829	18	1.76
APN_S0	217	807	88	7.0	465	559	96	90.6	88	936	8	0.27

4.1   Inequality Augmentation

Whenever a new inequality is generated, it should be added to the set of candidate inequalities if it removes a distinct set of impossible transitions compared to the original inequalities. Here, distinct means that the transitions removed by this new inequality should not be a subset of those removed by any of the original inequalities. This is an improved criterion, where we are only adding new inequalities that remove unique sets of transitions. In contrast, in [3], the authors considered a new inequality useful if it removed a larger, but not necessarily unique set of transitions than the original inequalities. The approach in [3] might not always be helpful, as a new inequality doesn't necessarily have to remove a larger set of transitions to be useful; it can still be valuable if it eliminates a unique set of transitions that none of the original inequalities addressed. This refined criterion ensures we identify inequalities that contribute unique information, helping to build a more diverse and effective set of candidate inequalities. As a result, we end up with a larger, more robust pool of inequalities from which the final set will be selected.

The algorithm (Algorithm 2) takes as input $\mathcal{T}$, the set of possible transitions; $\mathcal{D}$, the set of impossible transitions; and a parameter k, which specifies the number of inequalities to combine in each iteration. Here, $\mathcal{P}(\mathcal{H})$ denotes the power set of $\mathcal{H}$. The algorithm begins by generating the convex hull $\mathcal{H}$ for the set $\mathcal{T}$. Next, for each possible transition in $\mathcal{T}$, it identifies all inequalities that evaluate to zero. These inequalities are used to construct useful inequalities, as described in Definition 3. All useful inequalities obtained through this process are added to the set of candidate inequalities, $\mathcal{C}$. Finally, the reduction algorithm by Sasaki and Todo [12] is applied to $\mathcal{C}$ to determine the final set of valid inequalities.

4.2   Comparison with Boura and Coggia's Approach [3]

Compared to Boura and Coggia [3], we make a better choice in each step, considering an inequality is useful if it removes a unique set of impossible transitions compared to the original inequalities. This unique set need not to be larger than the set of impossible transitions removed by each of the k inequalities. This improved criterion for useful inequality is more robust as it considers inequalities useful even if the removed points form a different set.

In [3], it is mentioned that, for PRESENT S-Box around 500 and 700 candidate inequalities are generated for $k = 2$ and $k = 3$ respectively. In the case of our criterion, we have 2587 and 52641 candidate inequalities respectively. The larger sets of candidate inequalities provide more freedom in the selection of final inequalities and hence give better results in some cases. We compare our best results (see Table 4) with those provided in [3].

In the case of 5-bit S-Boxes (see Table 5), our method typically generates **1 less inequality** compared to Boura and Coggia's [3] approach, which indicates an optimization in the modeling process. However, what stands out from the results is the significant difference in running times, especially for larger S-Boxes.

Table 4. Results for IIA based modeling for 4-bit S-Boxes, $k=3$.

S-Box	# Sage generated Inequalities ($\mathcal{H}$)	# Obtained Inequalities ($\mathcal{C}$)	Boura and Coggia [3]	Ours	Running time (in sec) (Our Approach)
$PRESENT$	327	52641	17	17	599.614
$GIFT$	237	56979	17	17	436.123
$KLEIN$	311	35875	19	19	381.671
$LBLOCK\_S0$	205	53545	17	16	317.195
$LBLOCK\_S1$	205	53545	17	16	312.487
$LBLOCK\_S2$	205	53545	17	16	312.553
$LBLOCK\_S3$	205	53545	17	16	303.584
$LBLOCK\_S4$	205	53545	17	16	299.501
$LBLOCK\_S5$	205	53545	17	16	299.439
$LBLOCK\_S6$	205	53545	17	16	299.675
$LBLOCK\_S7$	205	53545	17	16	299.193
$LBLOCK\_S8$	205	53545	17	16	296.871
$LBLOCK\_S9$	205	53545	17	16	305.384
$LILLIPUT$	324	47778	19	19	457.801
$MIBS$	378	45932	20	20	615.892
$MIDORI\_S0$	239	55096	16	16	357.451
$MIDORI\_S1$	367	112822	20	20	863.173
$MINALPHER$	338	47869	19	18	524.583
$PICCOLO$	202	51381	16	16	251.908
$PRIDE$	194	43703	16	17	244.286
$PRINCE$	300	50263	19	18	472.876
$RECTANGLE$	267	75001	17	16	602.021
$SERPENT\_S0$	410	94423	17	17	1169.586
$SERPENT\_S1$	409	94817	17	18	1247.040
$SERPENT\_S2$	408	99503	18	17	1207.549
$SERPENT\_S3$	396	121856	20	14	1302.355
$SERPENT\_S4$	328	96987	19	19	814.327
$SERPENT\_S5$	336	89965	19	17	818.247
$SERPENT\_S6$	382	141502	17	16	1264.136
$SERPENT\_S7$	470	126124	20	16	1771.794
$SKINNY$	202	51381	16	16	235.568
$TWINE$	324	47778	19	19	428.312

Algorithm 2. Iterative inequality augmentation based modeling algorithm.

Input: The set of possible transitions $(\mathcal{T})$, impossible transitions $(\mathcal{D})$, parameter deciding the size of the subset (k)

Output: The set of candidate inequalities $(\mathcal{C})$

1: $\mathcal{H} \leftarrow \mathrm{Hull}(\mathcal{T})$ ▷ H-Representation of Convex Hull of Possible Transitions
2: $\mathcal{C} \leftarrow \mathcal{H}$
3: **for all** $v \in \mathcal{T}$ **do**
4:    **for all** $\{c_1, c_2, ..., c_k\} \in \mathcal{P}(\mathcal{H}) \mid c_i(v) = 0 \ \forall \ i = 1, 2, ..., k$ **do**
5:       $c_{\mathrm{new}} = c_1 + c_2 + ... + c_k$
6:       **if** c_{new} removes a different set of impossible transitions **then**
7:          $\mathcal{C} \leftarrow \mathcal{C} \cup \{c_{\mathrm{new}}\}$
8:       **end if**
9:    **end for**
10: **end for**
11: return $\mathcal{C}$

Table 5. Iterative inequality augmentation based modeling: 5-bit S-Boxes, $k=2$. A dash indicates that the original work did not provide results for this S-Box.

S-Box	# Sage generate-dInequalities ($\mathcal{H}$)	# Obtained Inequalities ($\mathcal{C}$)	Boura and Coggia [3]	Ours	Running time (in sec) (Our Approach)
$KECCAK$	316	6561	34	34	284.874
$ASCON$	2415	298179	32	31	20509.450
$FIDES\_5$	910	10703	64	63	622.786
$SC2000\_5$	908	8919	66	65	564.596
APN_S0	1725	20811	-	70	1823.938
APN_S1	979	10593	-	62	643.379
APN_S2	890	9035	-	62	550.687
APN_S3	939	10028	-	61	681.495
APN_S4	893	9904	-	63	594.356
$ICEPOLE$	4997	≈ 670000	-	-	>37 h

Notably, for the ICEPOLE (5-bit) S-Box, our algorithm ran for approximately 37 h without producing any results. This highlights the computational challenges and time complexity involved in modeling large S-Boxes. The results for IIA Approach applied to LAT, BCT and DPT is described in Table 6 and Table 7.

5   Lower Bound Optimization (LBO) for the SuperBall Approach [8]

Till now, the inequalities used are generated by a mathematical tool (Sage-Math [1]) taking the possible transitions as input. We have no control what-

Table 6. Results of IIA approach for LAT, BCT and DPT of various 4-bit S-Boxes.

S-Box	LAT				BCT				DPT			
	# Imp	# Pos	# Inqs	Run time (s)	# Imp	# Pos	# Inqs	Run time (s)	# Imp	# Pos	# Inqs	Run time (s)
PRESENT	123	133	17	14.1	107	149	24	14.9	49	207	3	7.0
GIFT	123	133	13	39.7	102	154	19	9.9	68	188	5	12.9
KLEIN	105	151	23	12.3	112	144	23	16.2	41	215	4	4.3
LBLOCK_S0	123	133	12	20.6	103	153	18	8.6	69	187	5	4.5
LBLOCK_S1	123	133	12	19.1	103	153	18	9.0	69	187	5	4.4
LBLOCK_S2	123	133	12	17.9	103	153	18	8.8	69	187	5	4.4
LBLOCK_S3	123	133	12	20.7	103	153	18	8.5	69	187	5	4.5
LBLOCK_S4	123	133	12	20.2	103	153	18	8.5	69	187	5	4.3
LBLOCK_S5	123	133	12	23.3	103	153	18	8.6	69	187	5	4.3
LBLOCK_S6	123	133	12	17.3	103	153	18	8.6	69	187	5	4.4
LBLOCK_S7	123	133	12	16.8	103	153	18	9.1	69	187	5	4.4
LBLOCK_S8	123	133	12	16.3	103	153	18	8.5	69	187	5	4.3
LBLOCK_S9	123	133	12	16.4	103	153	18	8.6	69	187	5	4.3
LILLIPUT	105	151	22	10.9	120	136	22	26.8	48	208	5	5.1
MIBS	105	151	26	9.8	120	136	23	28.5	36	220	3	2.6
MIDORI_S0	123	133	16	8.3	107	149	18	15.0	47	209	4	2.5
MIDORI_S1	105	151	22	8.4	105	151	28	15.0	43	213	4	3.3
MINALPHER	105	151	23	13.1	112	144	26	17.7	41	215	3	4.7
PICCOLO	123	133	11	8.8	103	153	16	8.5	68	188	4	4.3
PRIDE	123	133	11	8.5	103	153	16	7.2	69	187	4	4.0
PRINCE	105	151	20	9.5	105	151	23	14.8	42	214	4	4.6
RECTANGLE	123	133	12	31.2	107	149	18	10.6	67	189	5	13.8
SERPENT_S0	119	137	23	12.2	97	159	20	9.3	52	204	4	6.8
SERPENT_S1	119	137	24	9.8	97	159	22	9.4	45	211	4	4.3
SERPENT_S2	119	137	26	13.0	97	159	22	7.9	50	206	4	6.0
SERPENT_S3	127	129	19	13.8	92	164	23	8.1	53	203	4	6.6
SERPENT_S4	115	141	14	14.0	104	152	20	10.7	60	196	5	8.2
SERPENT_S5	127	129	13	22.2	100	156	25	9.9	59	197	4	17.9
SERPENT_S6	127	129	16	17.0	104	152	18	10.1	54	202	4	10.6
SERPENT_S7	113	143	24	11.4	100	156	22	10.7	61	195	6	9.7
SKINNY	123	133	11	11.2	103	153	16	8.9	68	188	4	4.3
TWINE	105	151	22	13.5	120	136	22	27.0	48	208	5	5.5

Table 7. Results of IIA approach for for LAT, BCT and DPT of various 5-bit S-Boxes.

S-Box	LAT				BCT				DPT			
	# Imp	# Pos	# Inqs	Run time (s)	# Imp	# Pos	# Inqs	Run time (s)	# Imp	# Pos	# Inqs	Run time (s)
$SC2000\_5$	527	497	63	1409.5	465	559	70	1143.3	192	832	10	395.1
$KECCAK$	647	377	38	588.9	445	579	41	755.7	381	643	10	594.7
$ICEPOLE$	497	527	64	513.9	425	599	50	1898.0	61	963	2	16.2
$FIDES\_5$	527	497	62	1768.3	465	559	66	1067.2	205	819	10	1173.2
$ASCON$	647	377	44	15179.9	445	579	42	1110.4	260	764	10	542.8
APN_S4	527	497	64	998.9	465	559	69	1093.9	184	840	10	435.2
APN_S3	527	497	61	963.6	465	559	66	1026.6	196	828	11	1059.8
APN_S2	527	497	65	963.8	465	559	68	1018.8	191	833	9	431.2
APN_S1	527	497	64	1081.5	465	559	68	1050.9	195	829	12	673.1
APN_S0	217	807	74	68.4	465	559	74	1540.1	88	936	5	69.2

soever on the coefficients of inequalities obtained. The upcoming approaches use the method of undetermined coefficients to calculate the coefficients of the inequalities. In other words, from now on, we generate our own inequalities using MILP models.

The SuperBall approach [8] tries to generate functions (linear polynomials) which are later used to model a particular S-Box. For say, a 4-bit S-Box, we would have the possible/impossible transition point's size to be 8-bit. Now, the method tries to generate functions with 8 coefficients and a constant term which are satisfied by the possible transitions and are dissatisfied by the impossible transitions as a whole. Given below is one such function,

$$f(x) = a_0 x_0 + a_1 x_1 + a_2 x_2 + a_3 x_3 + a_4 x_4 + a_5 x_5 + a_6 x_6 + a_7 x_7 + b$$
$$f(v) \geq 0 \text{ for } v \in \mathcal{T}$$

$a_0, a_1, \ldots, a_7$ are the coefficients and b is the constant term of the function f.

Definition 4. *To address the ambiguity in generating inequalities without specific information on the coefficients, the authors of SuperBall [8] introduced the concept of a **pattern**. A pattern is defined as an n-bit binary number (for an m-bit S-Box, $n = 2\,m$) that provides structure for generating functions by specifying constraints on the coefficients.*

Example 1. For example, if the pattern is 11001010, the coefficients $a_0, a_1, \ldots, a_7$ are constrained as follows,

Pattern $= 11001010,$
$$\implies a_0 \leq 0, \quad a_1 \leq 0, \quad a_2 \geq 0, \quad a_3 \geq 0, \quad a_4 \leq 0, \quad a_5 \geq 0, \quad a_6 \leq 0, \quad a_7 \geq 0$$

Algorithm 3. Lower Bound Optimization

Input: The set of possible transitions $(\mathcal{T})$, constants (α, β, k), a pattern signifying the sign of coefficients.

Output: The set of k polynomials generated for this pattern.

 1: *Region, Border, miniBorder* ← RegionAndBorder(S)

 2: M = *Optimizer.createmodel*()   ▷ Create an Optimizer Model

 3: M.*addvar*() : a_j, integer in $\begin{cases} [0, R] \text{ if } j^{th} \text{ bit of pattern} = 0 \\ [-R, 0] \text{ if } j^{th} \text{ bit of pattern} = 1 \end{cases}$ ▷ Coefficients

 4: M.*addvar*() : b, int in range $[-nR, 0]$ ▷ Constant term variable

 5: M.*addvar*() : $y_\mathbf{v}$, binary , for $\mathbf{v} \in Region$ ▷ Auxiliary variables

 6: M.*addvar*() : $z_\mathbf{v}$, binary , for $\mathbf{v} \in Border$ ▷ Auxiliary variables

 7: M.*addcon*() : $f(\mathbf{v}) \geq 0$, for $\mathbf{v} \in miniBorder$ ▷ Satisfy the *miniBorder*

 8: M.*addcon*() : $f(\mathbf{v}) - (nR + 1) \cdot (1 - y_\mathbf{v}) \leq -1$, for $\mathbf{v} \in Region$ ▷ Point removal

 9: M.*addcon*() : $f(\mathbf{v}) - (nR + 1) \cdot (1 - z_\mathbf{v}) \leq 0$, for $\mathbf{v} \in Border$ ▷ Strength Criteria

10: M.*addobj*() : $maximize(\alpha(\sum_{\mathbf{v} \in Region} y_\mathbf{v}) + \beta(\sum_{\mathbf{v} \in Border} z_\mathbf{v}))$ ▷ Objective

11: M.*optimize*()   ▷ Optimize the model

12: *Result* ← ∅

13: **while** M *is not infeasible* and *Result*.size()< k **do**

14:      *Result* ← *Result* ∪ Function from the current optimization.

15:      M.*addcon*() : $\sum_{y_\mathbf{v}=0} y_\mathbf{v} + \sum_{z_\mathbf{v}=0} z_\mathbf{v} \geq 1$ ▷ Add new constraint

16:      M.*optimize*()   ▷ Obtain the next function

17: **end while**

18: return *Result*

In this way, each bit in the pattern determines the sign constraint on the corresponding coefficient: a 1 imposes a non-positive constraint (≤ 0), while a 0 imposes a non-negative constraint (≥ 0).

By altering the patterns, we modify the constraints applied to the coefficients. These patterns can represent any vector in $\mathbf{F}_2^n$. Each variation in the pattern leads to a new set of inequalities, which we determine by solving a MILP problem using an optimizer tool, such as Gurobi [5].

Once the model is optimized, it returns the optimal values for the variables. These include the coefficients $a_j \ \forall \ j \in \{0, \ldots, 7\}$ and the constant term b that best satisfy the objective function for the defined constraints.

Definition 5. *To effectively impose constraints on the possible and impossible transitions, we introduce auxiliary binary variables, denoted as y_v and z_v, for each point v in $\mathbf{F}_2^n$. These auxiliary variables help determine how each point v interacts with the function $f(v)$. R is a natural number that defines the ranges as $a_j \in [0, R]$ or $a_j \in [-R, 0]$ (depending on the pattern) $\forall j \in \{0 \ldots n - 1\}$ and $b \in [-nR, 0]$. The definitions of y_v and z_v are as follows:*

$$y_v = 1 \quad \textit{indicates that the function inval'idates } \boldsymbol{v},$$
$$\textit{i.e., } f(\boldsymbol{v}) < 0,$$
$$z_v = 1 \quad \textit{indicates that the function is zero for } \boldsymbol{v},$$
$$\textit{i.e., } f(\boldsymbol{v}) = 0.$$

These binary variables are used in formulating the constraints as follows:

- *If $y_v = 1$, the constraint $f(\boldsymbol{v}) - (nR + 1) \cdot (1 - y_v) < 0$ becomes active, enforcing $f(\boldsymbol{v}) < 0$ since the term $(nR + 1) \cdot (1 - y_v)$ vanishes.*
- *If $y_v = 0$, then $f(\boldsymbol{v}) - (nR + 1) < 0$ holds trivially, meaning this constraint does not impact the values of the coefficients a_j and b.*

This setup allows us to selectively enforce constraints on the function values for different points $\mathbf{v}$ in $\mathbf{F}_2^n$. The definitions and uses of $y_{\mathbf{v}}$ and $z_{\mathbf{v}}$ variables are referenced throughout this paper to control and model the behavior of $f(\mathbf{v})$ as needed.

5.1   Lower Bound Optimization

Algorithm 3 is adapted from a part of the complete algorithm provided in Super-Ball [8]. Although we do not follow the exact notation used in SuperBall, the original concept also involves reprocessing the coefficients of the generated functions. Our main idea is to introduce a lower bound on the number of inequalities generated per pattern to ensure an optimal solution. The motivation for finding this lower bound k is the potential reduction in runtime, which might be helpful when applying the method to larger S-Boxes. Certain elements, such as strength criteria (involving parameters α and β), are omitted here. For a more comprehensive and detailed explanation, please refer to the SuperBall approach [8]. Algorithm 3 generate functions according to a specified pattern. The terms Region, Border, and miniBorder are obtained using specific transformations outlined in the SuperBall approach. However, to provide an analogy suited to our current context, the definitions are summarized in Table 9.

Figure 1 gives a visual representation of the definitions of Region, Border and miniBorder. Introducing the lower bound value k, it's significance being the number of inequalities generated per pattern in the Algorithm 3 reduces the runtime by huge margins. Although this reduces the runtime, there is a risk of losing some inequalities if the chosen value of k is very low.

Table 8. Results LBO approach: 4-bit S-Boxes, $k=7$ inequalities generated per pattern.

S-Box	# Impossible Transitions	# Possible Transitions	SuperBall Approach	Running time (in sec)	Our Approach	Running time (in sec)
PRESENT	159	97	16	623.187	16	158.411
GIFT	157	99	16	1066.333	17(+1)	170.135
KLEIN	150	106	18	712.204	19(+1)	149.165
LBLOCK_S0	159	97	15	1052.457	15	177.718
LBLOCK_S1	159	97	15	1184.995	15	181.600
LBLOCK_S2	159	97	15	586.533	15	164.074
LBLOCK_S3	159	97	15	825.473	15	174.060
LBLOCK_S4	159	97	15	1117.161	15	177.216
LBLOCK_S5	159	97	15	991.940	15	178.439
LBLOCK_S6	159	97	15	1010.115	15	179.593
LBLOCK_S7	159	97	15	1131.192	15	185.270
LBLOCK_S8	159	97	15	796.194	15	177.685
LBLOCK_S9	159	97	15	690.946	15	162.779
LILLIPUT	150	106	19	466.458	19	143.635
MIBS	150	106	20	384.708	20	141.748
MIDORI_S0	159	97	16	769.201	17	158.902
MIDORI_S1	150	106	20	720.191	21	154.465
MINALPHER	150	106	18	780.266	18	148.895
PICCOLO	159	97	14	743.813	14	170.537
PRIDE	159	97	16	905.742	16	171.970
PRINCE	150	106	18	580.034	19(+1)	149.264
RECTANGLE	159	97	15	990.732	15	171.735
SERPENT_S0	168	88	16	?	17(+1)	164.001
SERPENT_S1	168	88	16	?	18(+1)	158.519
SERPENT_S2	168	88	17	725.031	17	161.668
SERPENT_S3	166	90	20	766.648	20	164.636
SERPENT_S4	162	94	18	777.704	18	158.107
SERPENT_S5	166	90	18	785.437	18	161.492
SERPENT_S6	166	90	16	941.360	16	162.095
SERPENT_S7	168	88	20	897.842	20	178.517
SKINNY	159	97	14	810.512	14	165.703
TWINE	150	106	19	543.430	19	144.971

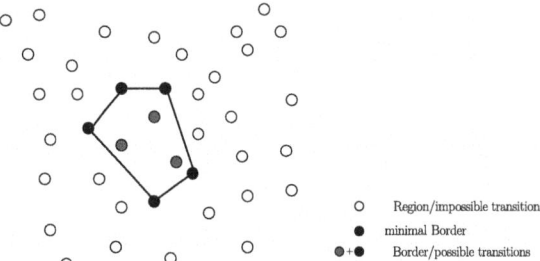

Fig. 1. Example figure showing *Region*, *Border* and *miniBorder*

Table 9. Analogy of terms used in SuperBall approach [8]

Term	Analogy
Region	Impossible transitions
Border	Possible transitions
miniBorder	The minimal set of points that suffices to model the possible transitions (also known as minimal border)

Table 10. Results for LBO approach: Minimum required number of inequalities per pattern for 4-bit S-Boxes

S-Box	# Impossible Transitions	# Possible Transitions	SuperBall Approach	Running time (in sec)	Our Approach	# Ineq. per pattern (k)	Running time (in sec)
$MIDORI\_S0$	159	97	16	769.201	16	8	198.656
$GIFT$	157	99	16	1066.333	16	9	205.737
$MIDORI\_S1$	150	106	20	720.191	20	9	257.590
$PRINCE$	150	106	18	580.034	18	10	291.399

5.2   Inference from the Results

The value k, referred to as the lower bound, represents the minimum number of inequalities that must be generated per pattern to achieve an optimal solution. We start with a small initial value for k and test whether it produces optimal results. For some S-Boxes, this initial value is sufficient, while for others it is not. We then incrementally increase k until optimal results are achieved across all S-Boxes. Once this occurs, k is considered as the lower bound, indicating that at least this many inequalities are necessary per pattern to obtain an optimal solution for an S-Box of the given size. This lower bound specially helps in reducing the runtime of the algorithm. Table 8 infers that for most of the 4-bit S-Boxes, taking 7 inequalities per pattern, the optimal result can be found. Based on Table 10, for $MIDORI\_S0$ S-Box, at least 8 inequalities are to be generated per pattern to obtain the optimal result. For the S-Boxes $GIFT$ and $MIDORI\_S1$, 9 inequalities per pattern are required for the optimal result. $PRINCE$ S-Box requires 10 inequalities per pattern for the optimal result. However, for S-Boxes $SERPENT\_S0$ and $SERPENT\_S1$ we were unable to verify the results (indicated by "?" in Table 8) given in SuperBall [8]. This is probably due to the range we provided for the coefficients and the constant term. In Tables 8 and 10, the running time provided is for our implementation of the SuperBall Approach. For S-Boxes $SC2000\_5$ and $FIDES\_5$ (see Table 11), taking 8 inequalities per pattern suffices to produce the optimal result. Whereas, S-Boxes $KECCAK$ and $ASCON$ need 11 inequalities per pattern for the optimal result. Based on the results, we belive that for an m-bit S-Box ($n = 2m$) a value of $k \geq n + 2$ should be a safe consideration for the optimal result.

Table 11. LBO approach: Minimum required number of inequalities per pattern for 5-bit S-Boxes. A dash indicates that the original work did not provide results for this S-Box.

S-Box	# Impossible Transitions	# Possible Transitions	SuperBall Approach	Our Approach	# Ineq per pattern (k)	Running time (Our Approach) (in hrs)
$SC2000\_5$	527	497	60	60	8	1.412
$FIDES\_5$	527	497	57	57	8	1.438
$ICEPOLE$	687	337	-	36	8	15.949
APN_S4	527	497	-	60	8	1.433
APN_S3	527	497	-	59	8	1.431
APN_S2	527	497	-	59	8	1.417
APN_S1	527	497	-	60	8	1.452
APN_S0	527	497	-	70	8	1.534
$KECCAK$	707	317	26	26	11	43.588
$ASCON$	707	317	27	27	11	22.237

6   Direct Inequality Generation (DIG)

From the method in Sect. 5, we achieve some customization on the coefficients of the inequalities. Moving forward, our focus will be on constructing simpler MILP models. By simplifying the model structure, we create formulations that are not only effective but also easier to interpret and analyze. First generate an inequality that eliminates the maximum number of impossible transitions while ensuring that all possible transitions remain satisfied. Once an inequality is created, remove from the set of impossible transitions those that is invalidated by this inequality.

To generate the next inequality, adjust the constraints and objectives to continue satisfying all possible transitions while targeting the removal of the maximum number of remaining impossible transitions in the updated set. With a suitable range for the coefficients, our results suggest that it is always feasible to find an inequality that meets these criteria. This process is repeated until there are no impossible transitions left in the set. We call this method direct inequality generation in the sense that this approach does not involve a reduction step rather the final result itself is produced step by step.

Definition 6. *Let us define the following sets:*

- ***RemovedSet*** *The set of points from the impossible transitions removed so far by the generated inequalities.*
- ***RemainingSet*** *The group of points that are yet to be removed from the complete set of impossible transitions.*
- ***Result*** *The set of inequalities currently used to model the S-Box.*

Algorithm 4. Direct Inequality Generation

Input: The set of possible transitions ($\mathcal{T}$), impossible transitions ($\mathcal{D}$), the upper bound of coefficients (A) and upper bound of constant term (B).

Output: The set of final inequalities ($\mathcal{R}$) modeling the particular S-Box.

 1: $RemovedSet \leftarrow \emptyset$
 2: $\mathcal{R} \leftarrow \emptyset$
 3: **while** $RemovedSet \neq \mathcal{D}$ **do**
 4:     $RemainingSet \leftarrow \mathcal{D} - RemovedSet$
 5:     M = $Optimizer.createmodel()$ ▷ Create an Optimizer Model
 6:     M.$addvar()$: a_j, integer in range $[-A, A]$, for $0 \leq j < n$ ▷ Coefficient variables
 7:     M.$addvar()$: b, integer in range $[0, B]$ ▷ Constant term variable
 8:     M.$addvar()$: $y_\mathbf{v}$, binary, for $\mathbf{v} \in RemainingSet$ ▷ Auxiliary variables
 9:     M.$addcon()$: $f(\mathbf{v}) \geq 0$, for $\mathbf{v} \in \mathcal{T}$ ▷ Satisfy the possible transitions
10:     M.$addcon()$: $f(\mathbf{v}) - (A \cdot n + B + 1) \cdot (1 - y_\mathbf{v}) \leq -1$, for $\mathbf{v} \in RemainingSet$
11:     M.$addobj()$: $maximize(\sum_{\mathbf{v} \in RemainingSet} y_\mathbf{v})$ ▷ Remove maximum points
12:     M.$optimize()$ ▷ Optimize the model
13:     $\mathcal{R} \leftarrow \mathcal{R} \cup f$ ▷ f is the function from current optimization
14:     **for** $\mathbf{v} \in RemainingSet$ **do**
15:         **if** $y_\mathbf{v} = 1$ **then**   ▷ Point being removed by the current function
16:             $RemovedSet \leftarrow RemovedSet \cup \{\mathbf{v}\}$ ▷ Update $RemovedSet$
17:         **end if**
18:     **end for**
19: **end while**
20: return $\mathcal{R}$

6.1   Algorithm to Directly Generate the Final Inequalities

Algorithm 4 uses a greedy approach in the optimizer to generate the functions of a particular S-Box. The algorithm tries to generate functions in each step. The generated function should remove the maximum number of points from the remaining set of impossible transitions. The objective function in Step 11 demonstrates the greedy nature of the generated function. In this algorithm, the three sets (see Definition 6) are necessary and sufficient for the generation of an inequality. A new MILP model is used every time, only the sets are updated. Since a new model is created after every iteration, the model has to remember only the constraints about the current function hence requiring less memory to run the algorithm. At the beginning of the algorithm, the $RemainingSet$ is the set of impossible transitions and the $RemovedSet$ is empty. Over each iteration of the algorithm, generate a function which removes the maximum number of points from the $RemainingSet$. The removed points are discarded from the $RemainingSet$. These discarded points are added to the $RemovedSet$. The key parameters in this algorithm are the bounds for the coefficients and the constant term, denoted as A and B, both positive integers, respectively. The coefficients are allowed to vary within the range $[-A, A]$, while the constant term ranges from $[0, B]$. Adjusting the values of A and B can significantly impact the results. These parameters play a critical role in shaping the behavior and effectiveness of the generated inequalities. Since the points get transferred from $RemainingSet$

Table 12. Results for DIG approach: 4-bit S-Boxes, $A = 256$ and $B = 256$

S-Box	# Impossible Transitions	# Possible Transitions	Inequalities Obtained	Running time (in sec)
PRESENT	159	97	20	70.182
GIFT	157	99	19	121.404
KLEIN	150	106	20	155.735
LBLOCK_S0	159	97	17	69.453
LBLOCK_S1	159	97	19	63.507
LBLOCK_S2	159	97	16	65.864
LBLOCK_S3	159	97	19	57.532
LBLOCK_S4	159	97	17	69.427
LBLOCK_S5	159	97	17	52.421
LBLOCK_S6	159	97	19	46.529
LBLOCK_S7	159	97	19	60.727
LBLOCK_S8	159	97	16	81.404
LBLOCK_S9	159	97	17	62.455
LILLIPUT	150	106	23	120.404
MIBS	150	106	24	91.501
MIDORI_S0	159	97	20	84.632
MIDORI_S1	150	106	24	55.559
MINALPHER	150	106	21	53.306
PICCOLO	159	97	18	61.343
PRIDE	159	97	19	81.894
PRINCE	150	106	20	74.395
RECTANGLE	159	97	18	131.040
SERPENT_S0	168	88	21	186.681
SERPENT_S1	168	88	22	135.565
SERPENT_S2	168	88	21	144.272
SERPENT_S3	166	90	16	142.080
SERPENT_S4	162	94	22	112.827
SERPENT_S5	166	90	20	121.294
SERPENT_S6	166	90	20	132.750
SERPENT_S7	168	88	19	179.004
SKINNY	159	97	18	72.574
TWINE	150	106	23	76.838

to *RemovedSet* and in each iteration at least one point is transferred, eventually all the points are moved from *RemainingSet* to *RemovedSet* thereby reaching the end of the algorithm.

Table 13. Results for DIG approach: 4-bit S-Boxes, $A = 500$ and $B = 500$

S-Box	# Impossible Transitions	# Possible Transitions	Inequalities Obtained	Running time (in sec)
PRESENT	159	97	20	48.283
GIFT	157	99	21	86.054
KLEIN	150	106	21	102.963
LBLOCK_S0	159	97	16	60.357
LBLOCK_S1	159	97	18	73.558
LBLOCK_S2	159	97	16	68.712
LBLOCK_S3	159	97	17	73.219
LBLOCK_S4	159	97	17	67.435
LBLOCK_S5	159	97	18	54.509
LBLOCK_S6	159	97	18	51.664
LBLOCK_S7	159	97	18	52.139
LBLOCK_S8	159	97	18	42.980
LBLOCK_S9	159	97	16	66.954
LILLIPUT	150	106	24	97.353
MIBS	150	106	25	78.328
MIDORI_S0	159	97	19	69.577
MIDORI_S1	150	106	24	62.805
MINALPHER	150	106	24	74.823
PICCOLO	159	97	18	76.102
PRIDE	159	97	19	60.922
PRINCE	150	106	22	31.199
RECTANGLE	159	97	18	77.805
SERPENT_S0	168	88	21	146.061
SERPENT_S1	168	88	23	128.148
SERPENT_S2	168	88	22	149.352
SERPENT_S3	166	90	18	104.871
SERPENT_S4	162	94	21	83.852
SERPENT_S5	166	90	19	109.755
SERPENT_S6	166	90	20	111.834
SERPENT_S7	168	88	19	184.492
SKINNY	159	97	18	61.968
TWINE	150	106	21	70.129

The final result of our algorithm is valid subject to satisfying the two criteria in Definition 1. Firstly, we impose the constraint that the generated function has to satisfy all the possible transitions, hence satisfying our first criterion.

Secondly, the constraint on an impossible transition is removed only after it has been removed by some inequality this clears the second criterion. For a good range of coefficients, the model is always able to produce some function which is trivial as the optimizer finds a solution maximizing the objective function and satisfying the constraints. Every impossible transition, at some point will be removed by an inequality. Therefore, the final set of inequalities obtained is a valid set of inequalities.

6.2   Results

The results show the impact of the values of A and B in the number of final inequalities. Table 12 uses $A = 256$ and $B = 256$ whereas for Table 13 $A = 500$, $B = 500$ is considered. However, a definite statement cannot be made say, given a larger range, lesser inequalities are generated. Take the S-Box $GIFT$ for example, 19 inequalities are required when values of A and B are both 256 to model the S-Box. Although the constraint $A = 500$ and $B = 500$ increases the freedom of the coefficient values, this produces 21 inequalities. This effect may occur because a larger range allows more optimal solution at an intermediate step. However, this intermediate solution can restrict the optimizer's flexibility, potentially blocking many better solutions later in the process and ultimately leading to less optimal overall result. The results for DIG Approach applied to LAT, BCT and DPT is described in Table 14.

The results of direct inequality generation, while not yielding optimal solutions, provide valuable insights into the structure and behavior of MILP models. This method offers a simpler and more intuitive understanding of how the models function. Moreover, it underscores the significance of the ranges assigned to the coefficients and the constant term in shaping the model's performance and accuracy. Although the results are sub-optimal, this approach serves as a foundational step that paves the way for the development of more refined techniques. In particular, it inspires our subsequent method, the greedy generation and reduction approach. In this approach, the greedy generation component retains a similar core methodology as the direct inequality generation. However, the inclusion of a reduction step ensures a more systematic refinement of the inequalities, aiming for enhanced efficiency and effectiveness.

7   Greedy Generation and Reduction (GGR)

We feel the direct inequality generation approach imposes too much constriction but the model always generates some inequality at each step. Therefore, rather than directly removing the impossible transitions invalidated by the current inequality from the total set of impossible transitions, we propose a more refined modification of the constraints. This produces a large set of candidate inequalities from which the final inequalities are selected. When applying these final inequalities to a full cipher, it is preferable to have the coefficients of these inequalities as small as possible. Although the authors of SuperBall mention

Table 14. Results of DIG approach for LAT, BCT and DPT of various 4-bit S-Boxes.

S-Box	LAT				BCT				DPT			
	# Imp	# Pos	# Inqs	Run time (s)	# Imp	# Pos	# Inqs	Run time (s)	# Imp	# Pos	# Inqs	Run time (s)
PRESENT	123	133	20	60.8	107	149	24	33.4	49	207	5	0.8
GIFT	123	133	17	70.3	102	154	23	27.3	68	188	6	1.5
KLEIN	105	151	27	22.4	112	144	22	68.8	41	215	5	0.6
LBLOCK_S0	123	133	12	29.9	103	153	16	38.7	69	187	5	1.0
LBLOCK_S1	123	133	13	34.6	103	153	16	34.9	69	187	5	2.4
LBLOCK_S2	123	133	12	26.6	103	153	16	24.6	69	187	5	1.3
LBLOCK_S3	123	133	12	24.5	103	153	17	31.3	69	187	5	1.2
LBLOCK_S4	123	133	12	15.0	103	153	17	21.1	69	187	5	0.6
LBLOCK_S5	123	133	13	17.2	103	153	16	19.8	69	187	5	0.6
LBLOCK_S6	123	133	13	20.4	103	153	16	23.2	69	187	5	0.7
LBLOCK_S7	123	133	13	20.9	103	153	16	21.9	69	187	5	0.7
LBLOCK_S8	123	133	12	20.2	103	153	18	25.6	69	187	5	0.6
LBLOCK_S9	123	133	11	14.2	103	153	17	19.9	69	187	5	0.6
LILLIPUT	105	151	24	26.2	120	136	25	50.5	48	208	6	1.0
MIBS	105	151	28	19.0	120	136	25	74.0	36	220	4	0.4
MIDORI_S0	123	133	18	12.0	107	149	18	33.0	47	209	4	0.5
MIDORI_S1	105	151	24	14.1	105	151	29	31.4	43	213	5	0.6
MINALPHER	105	151	26	16.7	112	144	28	41.1	41	215	4	0.3
PICCOLO	123	133	11	40.3	103	153	19	15.3	68	188	4	1.1
PRIDE	123	133	11	15.9	103	153	16	16.1	69	187	5	1.6
PRINCE	105	151	22	23.3	105	151	27	25.9	42	214	4	0.5
RECTANGLE	123	133	12	33.4	107	149	18	20.5	67	189	5	0.5
SERPENT_S0	119	137	25	28.6	97	159	20	24.6	52	204	6	0.8
SERPENT_S1	119	137	26	38.6	97	159	26	20.9	45	211	4	0.6
SERPENT_S2	119	137	27	31.1	97	159	25	22.7	50	206	4	0.6
SERPENT_S3	127	129	20	40.9	92	164	25	18.6	53	203	4	0.4
SERPENT_S4	115	141	15	28.1	104	152	21	24.2	60	196	5	1.3
SERPENT_S5	127	129	14	33.0	100	156	26	27.8	59	197	5	0.9
SERPENT_S6	127	129	18	47.6	104	152	19	30.2	54	202	4	0.5
SERPENT_S7	113	143	23	24.5	100	156	23	31.0	61	195	7	3.1
SKINNY	123	133	11	40.1	103	153	19	15.4	68	188	4	1.4
TWINE	105	151	23	20.5	120	136	24	45.9	48	208	6	1.1

using a smaller range of coefficients for generating inequalities, their results rely on a much larger range. In contrast, we have utilized a very small range for the coefficients, which is particularly advantageous when integrating these inequalities into complete cipher implementations.

7.1 Method of Greedy Generation

In this approach, instead of the complete removal of the impossible transitions invalidated by the current inequality from the total set of impossible transitions, generate inequalities by slowly imposing more and more constraints. Start by generating the inequality that removes the maximum number of impossible transitions. To get the next inequality, we again want it to remove the maximum number of impossible transitions (hence greedy) but, the constraints imposed now are such that,

---

Algorithm 5. Greedy Generation

Input: The set of possible transitions ($\mathcal{T}$), impossible transitions ($\mathcal{D}$), the upper bound of coefficients (A) and upper bound of constant term (B).
Output: A set of large inequalities ($\mathcal{R}$) which can be reduced.

1: $\mathcal{R} \leftarrow \emptyset$
2: M $= Optimizer.createmodel()$ ▷ Create an Optimizer Model
3: M.$addvar()$: a_j, int in range $[-A, A]$, for $0 \le j < n$ ▷ Coefficient variables
4: M.$addvar()$: b, int in range $[0, B]$, for $0 \le j < n$ ▷ Constant term variable
5: M.$addvar()$: $y_{\mathbf{v}}$, binary , for $\mathbf{v} \in \mathcal{D}$ ▷ Auxiliary variables
6: M.$addcon()$: $f(\mathbf{v}) \ge 0$, for $\mathbf{v} \in P$ ▷ Satisfy the possible transitions
7: M.$addcon()$: $f(\mathbf{v}) - (A \cdot n + B + 1) \cdot (1 - y_{\mathbf{v}}) \le -1$, for $\mathbf{v} \in \mathcal{D}$ ▷ Point removal
8: M.$addobj()$: $maximize(\sum_{\mathbf{v} \in \mathcal{D}} y_{\mathbf{v}})$ ▷ Remove maximum points
9: M.$optimize()$ ▷ Optimize the model
10: **while** M *is not infeasible* **do**
11:     $\mathcal{R} \leftarrow \mathcal{R} \cup f$ ▷ f is the function from current optimization
12:     $RemovedSet \leftarrow \emptyset$
13:     **for** $\mathbf{v} \in \mathcal{D}$ **do**
14:        **if** $y_{\mathbf{v}} = 1$ **then**   ▷ Point being removed by the current function
15:           $RemovedSet \leftarrow RemovedSet \cup \{\mathbf{v}\}$ ▷ Update $RemovedSet$
16:        **end if**
17:     **end for**
18:     $RemainingSet \leftarrow \mathcal{D} - RemovedSet$ ▷ Update $RemainingSet$
19:     M.$addcon()$: $\sum_{\mathbf{v} \in RemovedSet} y_{\mathbf{v}} \le$ **sizeof**($RemovedSet$) $- 1$ ▷ Remove new set
20:     M.$addcon()$: $\sum_{\mathbf{v} \in RemainingSet} y_{\mathbf{v}} \ge 1$ ▷ Remove at least one new point
21: **end while**
22: **return** $\mathcal{R}$

---

1. The new inequality should not remove the same set of impossible transitions removed by the previous inequality.
2. This new inequality must remove at least one new impossible transition that has not been removed by the previous inequality.

It is essential to note that, all the new constraints are dynamically added to the same model and thus the model never generates the same inequality. The reason is, as more constraints are being added while still holding the previous constraints. Due to this addition of constraints, the size of the model increases enormously therefore requiring more and more memory to store the model.

These inequalities are generated till the model is no longer feasible. Since we always add the constraint that the inequality should remove at least one new impossible transition and it cannot remove any subset of the points once removed (by a single inequality), we always observe that the model stops. Once this generation is complete, we have with us a large set of candidate inequalities, among which a few are to be selected for finally modeling the S-Box.

Description of the Algorithm The Algorithm 5 involves some similar steps as Algorithm 4, the main difference between the two algorithms is that, each

Table 15. Results of GGR algorithm for 4-bit S-Boxes,

S-Box	# Impossible Transitions	# Possible Transitions	SuperBall Approach	Our Approach	Running time (Our Approach) (in hrs)
PRESENT	159	97	16	16	35.917
GIFT	157	99	16	16	109.847
KLEIN	150	106	18	18	13.485
LILLIPUT	150	106	19	19	12.138
MIBS	150	106	20	20	11.843
MINALPHER	150	106	18	18	18.024
PRINCE	150	106	18	18	26.724
PICCOLO	159	97	14	14	124.832
PRIDE	159	97	16	16	136.273
MIDORI_S0	159	97	16	16	135.416
MIDORI_S1	150	106	20	20	15.902
LBLOCK_S0	159	97	15	15	130.751
RECTANGLE	159	97	15	15	131.214
SERPENT_S0	168	88	16	16	256.647
SERPENT_S1	168	88	16	16	281.314
SERPENT_S2	168	88	17	17	304.214
SERPENT_S3	166	90	20	17	248.352
SERPENT_S4	162	94	18	18	196.924
SERPENT_S5	166	90	18	18	208.653
SERPENT_S6	166	90	16	16	193.842
SERPENT_S7	168	88	20	18	237.489
SKINNY	159	97	14	14	186.357
TWINE	150	106	19	19	22.582

inequality/function generated in Algorithm 4 is a part of the final inequalities, whereas Algorithm 5 generates a larger set of inequalities among which we select a few as our final inequalities. Algorithm 5 follows a greedy approach when generating a function. The lines $18 - 19$ are crucial in the algorithm, where we dynamically update the constraints. The constraint added in Line 18 is to make sure that the next generated function does not remove the exact same set of points as the previous function. This constraint prevents redundancy and ensures that each new function contributes a unique set of points to the overall solution. The constraint in Line 19 ensures that the next function generated removes at least one new point that was not covered by the previous functions. This constraint is essential for making progress towards the desired solution and ensuring that the algorithm does not stagnate by repeatedly generating functions that cover the same points. These two constraints are the key to generating meaningful inequalities, as they guarantee that each new inequality introduces a novel and non-redundant contribution to the solution space. After obtaining the set $\mathcal{R}$ i.e. candidate inequalities, we use the reduction algorithm given by Sasaki and Todo in [12].

This approach increases the constriction of the model slowly, generating a vast number of inequalities. The constraint that every inequality should satisfy all possible transitions always exists, clearing the first criterion from Definition 1 for valid inequalities. Then, we try to generate inequalities that remove different sets of impossible transitions, each more constrained than the previous. The reduction algorithm by Sasaki and Todo [12] ensures that each impossible transition is dissatisfied by at least one inequality.

7.2 Results

Table 15 shows the application of our approach on various 4-bit S-Boxes. Improved results are observed for S-Boxes $SERPENT\_S3$ and $SERPENT\_S7$. The rest of the S-Boxes exactly match to the results of SuperBall approach. The huge running times of our algorithm is due the optimization required for generation of each inequality. The optimizer always starts the optimization from the start and hence in some cases several days are required to obtain all the candidate inequalities of a particular S-Box.

8 Conclusion

In this research, we have explored different approaches to represent S-Boxes using linear inequalities. Our observations revealed that the results of the greedy approach depend on the intermediate steps taken during the algorithm's execution. To enhance the performance of algorithm by Boura and Coggia [3], we improved the new inequality selection criterion that allows a larger set of candidate inequalities. The bound offered by this approach can potentially improve the efficiency of the algorithm by reducing the computational complexity. The direct inequality generation approach is very fast, it may not produce optimal results. The speed of this approach comes at the cost of potentially sacrificing the quality or accuracy of the generated inequalities. The greedy generation and reduction approach produces better results compared to the other two approaches. However, it requires more computational power and resources. Although the results are more accurate or optimal, the increased computational demands may be a trade-off to consider. The direct inequality generation approach prioritizes speed over optimality, and the greedy generation and reduction approach delivers better results at the expense of higher computational requirements. The choice of approach depends on the specific requirements, such as runtime constraints, accuracy needs, or available computational resources.

A System Configuration

Lenovo IdeaPad Gaming 3 15IAH7 laptop, equipped with an 12th Gen Intel Core i5-12450H (12 cores, 2 threads per core) processor, 16 GB of DDR3 RAM.

- Operating System: Ubuntu [14] 22.04.3 LTS
- Python [11] version: 3.10.12
- Sagemath [1] version: 9.5
- Gurobi [5] version: 10.0.3

References

1. The sage developers. Sagemath, the sage mathematics software system (version 9.0) (2020)
2. Biham, E., Shamir, A.: Differential cryptanalysis of DES-like cryptosystems. In: Menezes, A., Vanstone, S.A. (eds.) Advances in Cryptology - CRYPTO 1990. LNCS, vol. 537, pp. 2–21. Springer, Cham (1990)
3. Boura, C., Coggia, D.: Efficient MILP modelings for sboxes and linear layers of SPN ciphers. IACR Trans. Symmetric Cryptol. **2020**(3), 327–361 (2020)
4. Fu, K., Wang, M., Guo, Y., Sun, S., Hu, L.: MILP-based automatic search algorithms for differential and linear trails for speck. In: Peyrin, T. (ed.) FSE 2016. LNCS, vol. 9783, pp. 268–288. Springer, Heidelberg (2016). https://doi.org/10.1007/978-3-662-52993-5_14
5. Gurobi Optimization, LLC: Gurobi Optimizer Reference Manual (2023). https://www.gurobi.com
6. Hao, Y., Leander, G., Meier, W., Todo, Y., Wang, Q.: Modeling for three-subset division property without unknown subset. In: Canteaut, A., Ishai, Y. (eds.) EUROCRYPT 2020. LNCS, vol. 12105, pp. 466–495. Springer, Cham (2020). https://doi.org/10.1007/978-3-030-45721-1_17
7. Hu, K., Wang, M.: Automatic search for A variant of division property using three subsets (full version). IACR Cryptology ePrint Archive, p. 1187 (2018)
8. Li, T., Sun, Y.: Superball: a new approach for MILP modelings of Boolean functions. IACR Trans. Symmetric Cryptol. **2022**(3), 341–367 (2022)
9. Mouha, N., Wang, Q., Gu, D., Preneel, B.: Differential and linear cryptanalysis using mixed-integer linear programming. In: Wu, C.-K., Yung, M., Lin, D. (eds.) Inscrypt 2011. LNCS, vol. 7537, pp. 57–76. Springer, Heidelberg (2012). https://doi.org/10.1007/978-3-642-34704-7_5
10. Pal, D., Chandratreya, V.P., Chowdhury, D.R.: Efficient algorithms for modeling sboxes using MILP. CoRR abs/2306.02642 (2023)
11. Python Software Foundation: Python package index - pypi (2021). https://pypi.org/
12. Sasaki, Yu., Todo, Y.: New algorithm for modeling S-box in MILP based differential and division trail search. In: Farshim, P., Simion, E. (eds.) SecITC 2017. LNCS, vol. 10543, pp. 150–165. Springer, Cham (2017). https://doi.org/10.1007/978-3-319-69284-5_11
13. Sasaki, Yu., Todo, Y.: New impossible differential search tool from design and cryptanalysis aspects. In: Coron, J.-S., Nielsen, J.B. (eds.) EUROCRYPT 2017. LNCS, vol. 10212, pp. 185–215. Springer, Cham (2017). https://doi.org/10.1007/978-3-319-56617-7_7

14. Sobell, M.G.: A Practical Guide to Ubuntu Linux. Pearson Education (2015)
15. Sun, L., Wang, W., Wang, M.: Automatic search of bit-based division property for ARX ciphers and word-based division property. In: Takagi, T., Peyrin, T. (eds.) ASIACRYPT 2017. LNCS, vol. 10624, pp. 128–157. Springer, Cham (2017). https://doi.org/10.1007/978-3-319-70694-8_5
16. Sun, S., et al.: Towards finding the best characteristics of some bit-oriented block ciphers and automatic enumeration of (related-key) differential and linear characteristics with predefined properties. Cryptology ePrint Archive, Paper 2014/747 (2014)
17. Sun, S., Hu, L., Wang, P., Qiao, K., Ma, X., Song, L.: Automatic security evaluation and (related-key) differential characteristic search: application to SIMON, PRESENT, LBlock, DES(L) and other bit-oriented block ciphers. In: Sarkar, P., Iwata, T. (eds.) ASIACRYPT 2014. LNCS, vol. 8873, pp. 158–178. Springer, Heidelberg (2014). https://doi.org/10.1007/978-3-662-45611-8_9
18. Todo, Y., Isobe, T., Hao, Y., Meier, W.: Cube attacks on non-blackbox polynomials based on division property. IEEE Trans. Comput. **67**(12), 1720–1736 (2018)
19. Udovenko, A.: MILP modeling of Boolean functions by minimum number of inequalities. IACR Cryptology ePrint Archive, p. 1099 (2021)
20. Wang, S., Hu, B., Guan, J., Zhang, K., Shi, T.: MILP-aided method of searching division property using three subsets and applications. In: Galbraith, S.D., Moriai, S. (eds.) ASIACRYPT 2019. LNCS, vol. 11923, pp. 398–427. Springer, Cham (2019). https://doi.org/10.1007/978-3-030-34618-8_14
21. Wu, S., Wang, M.: Security evaluation against differential cryptanalysis for block cipher structures. IACR Cryptology ePrint Archive, p. 551 (2011)
22. Xiang, Z., Zhang, W., Bao, Z., Lin, D.: Applying MILP method to searching integral distinguishers based on division property for 6 lightweight block ciphers. In: Cheon, J.H., Takagi, T. (eds.) ASIACRYPT 2016. LNCS, vol. 10031, pp. 648–678. Springer, Heidelberg (2016). https://doi.org/10.1007/978-3-662-53887-6_24
23. Zhou, C., Zhang, W., Ding, T., Xiang, Z.: Improving the milp-based security evaluation algorithm against differential/linear cryptanalysis using a divide-and-conquer approach. Cryptology ePrint Archive, Paper 2019/019 (2019)

Tearing Solutions for Tree Traversal in Stateful Hash-Based Cryptography

Solane El Hirch[1,2]([✉]), Frank Custers[2], and Christine van Vredendaal[2]

[1] Radboud University, Nijmegen, The Netherlands
solane.elhirch@ru.nl
[2] NXP Semiconductors, Eindhoven, The Netherlands
{frank.custers_1,christine.cloostermans}@nxp.com

Abstract. Stateful hash-based signature schemes are a family of post-quantum signature schemes. XMSS and LMS, two digital signature schemes standardized by NIST, belong to this family. Both are structured as a collection of one-time signature key pairs, which are combined using Merkle binary tree. They rely on tree traversal algorithms to optimize time versus memory efficiency, reducing the signing time of the schemes at the cost of managing a larger amount of auxiliary data (i.e., state). In this paper, we focus on XMSS with the `BDS` algorithm when used in a practical setting on an embedded device. One challenge on such devices is that they can experience a loss of power unexpectedly. For instance, an NFC chip might be torn away from its power source In the case of such a tearing event, the validity of the state can be impacted: the algorithm does not update the state correctly if such an event occurs. We propose an algorithm based on `BDS` that we call `BDSFix`. This algorithm recovers the BDS state following a tearing event. Our algorithm either equals (for a single tearing event) or outperforms recovering the state through `BDS` for any number of tearings larger than 1. This ranges from a 9% speed-up for six subsequent tearing events to improvements by factors of up to 8 for a large number of tearing events.

Keywords: Stateful hash-based cryptography · Tree traversal · BDS algorithm · Tearing

1 Introduction

Current digital infrastructures heavily rely on cryptographic primitives, such as cryptographic signatures for their security. However, traditional public-key cryptography, such as RSA and ECC, which is being used today, is at risk of experiencing a loss in security with the realization of a cryptographically-relevant quantum computer. To mitigate this threat, decades of research have gone into Post-Quantum Cryptography (PQC) schemes. These schemes are based on different security assumptions than RSA or ECC and therewith assumed to be secure even against attacks utilizing a quantum computer. The National Institute of Standards and Technology (NIST) has published four PQC standards,

A. Nitaj et al. (Eds.): AFRICACRYPT 2025, LNCS 15651, pp. 470–492, 2026.
https://doi.org/10.1007/978-3-031-97260-7_21

and more are likely to follow. In 2020 a standard [CAD+20] for stateful hash-based signatures (sHBS) was released, containing standardized parameter sets for LMS [MCF19] (and its multi-tree version HSS) and XMSS [HBG+18] (and its multi-tree version XMSS-MT). In 2024 three more followed for key encapsulation mechanism ML-KEM [NIS23b], and digital signature standards ML-DSA [NIS23a] and SLH-DSA [NIS23c].

This work focuses on the stateful hash-based signature schemes LMS and XMSS. In the embedded context, these have the advantage of being based on the evaluation of hash functions SHA2 or SHAKE256. Especially for the former, many embedded devices already contain hardware acceleration. Additionally, sHBS signature verification is very fast and sHBS can be implemented using very little volatile memory: only a few hash values need to be stored at the time. Especially for small embedded devices RAM is usually not available in large amounts. While storing this information is not strictly necessary, memory tampering is easier in non-secure memory. Additionally, not all platforms support an API that retrieves the key partially from secure memory and partially from insecure Flash.

A disadvantage of these schemes lies in their stateful-ness. The underlying idea of sHBS schemes is that they are built by combining the key pairs of many one-time signature (OTS) key pairs into a single sHBS key pair. A signature is generated by using one of these key pairs at a time, usually in order, and its security degrades if a key pair is used for multiple signatures.

Currently, XMSS and LMS are recommended by the National Security Agency for software and firmware signing [CNS23]. In the embedded context, this usually means that a firmware package is signed by the owner of an embedded device in the back-end and then distributed to the device, which can verify the integrity and/or authenticity of the firmware before installation. More importantly, it means that only signature verification needs to be supported on the device side. This leaves the state management fully up to the back-end.

In the future, however, there might be settings where it is desirable to perform sHBS signing on a device because hardware acceleration is readily available, the available RAM is low, or there is a preference to utilize only one signature algorithm on the device. Compared to ECDSA or ML-DSA, this does come with challenges. For instance, the possibility of signature depletion needs to be taken into account. The largest challenge, however, is the maintenance of the state.

In its simplest form, the state consists of just the sHBS private key and the index of the next signature stored. However, in this case a signature operation will take as long as key generation, which for larger parameter sets can take years on an embedded device. An alternative is to store additional (public) information to increase signing performance, the *Merkle tree*. This however also has large drawbacks;

– Storing the Merkle tree of sHBS schemes requires tens of kBs up to tens of MBs of storage, depending on the parameter set. This can be infeasible for constrained devices.

– Even if it is feasible, it is then often stored in insecure memory like Flash. This is more easily tampered with in an embedded device setting. Having to recompute a Merkle tree again leaves us with slow signature operations.

Tree traversal algorithms such as BDS [BDS08] and the fractal tree algorithm [JLMS03] offer a trade-off in storage versus signing time to make it feasible on an embedded device. For the former, on which we focus in this work, the *BDS* state stores auxiliary data on top of the signature index to speed up the generation of a signature, which requires only a fraction of the storage of a Merkle tree. It can be stored in Flash but, due to its smaller size, might also fit more secure memory regions.

During a signing operation with state counter s, the signature counter should be increased from s to $s+1$ *and* computations performed to update the BDS state corresponding to signature s to that of signature $s+1$. This requires careful consideration, since generating two signatures with the same state degrades security. Therefore it is good practice when signing with state s and current BDS state aux_s, (s, key, aux_s), to firs update the state counter, $(s+1, key, aux_s)$, and then only after signing the message updating the BDS state to $(s + 1, key, aux_{s+1})$. This prevents an attacker from tampering with the state counter update after signature generation and thus risk multiple messages being signed with the same state.

A contactless smart card is an embedded device without the capability to generate its own power. It instead operates only when it is powered by an external RF field generated by a reader. Examples include payment cards (bank or credit), many types of transit cards and building access cards.

The reader application does not control the user holding the card. The user can move it away from the reader at any time and interrupt the operations that were being performed on the card. This phenomenon is called *tearing*. If the power source disappears while the chip is writing data to a non-volatile memory like Flash or EEPROM, the memory being written to would have been incompletely written or even corrupted. This problem is also present in contact cards, like a pin machine slot, but occurs less often.

If a tearing event occurs during the signing operation or update of the BDS state it would result in an incorrect key, e.g. $(s + 1, key, aux_s)$, for the next transaction and, therefore, invalid signatures. The BDS state can be recovered by recomputing it from scratch. However, this is a time-intensive process that is, in most cases, infeasible on a small embedded device.

Anti-tearing methods exist to protect memory from corruption. These methods consist of card countermeasures, such as copying each piece of data before it is written, in order to prevent tearing from resulting in corruption of the content stored in the memory. However, this does not necessarily solve the problem with the BDS state: with this technique, "preventing" a tear at signature s, the BDS state in memory will still be the one corresponding to state s while the next signature would be signed with state $s + 1$. Even in cases where the signature was not released and therefore the state s theoretically could be used again, it is desirable to move on to signature $s + 1$ instead to defend against side-channel attacks.

Although less likely, it is a realistic scenario that multiple tearing events occur in a row. For instance, a frustrated customer might attempt to perform multiple payment attempts with a contactless debit card, a software error or power problem on the side of the other party might be starting and aborting a protocol, or a malicious entity can be performing multiple attacks. In this case, j tearing events can occur in a row resulting in the BDS state in memory corresponding to state s, while the state counter has already advanced to state $s + j$ for some integer $j \geq 0$. Especially in the case of power problem or an attack, which are common considerations in an embedded context, it is not unthinkable that j can grow quite large.

Contributions. In this paper we present a novel algorithm to recover a valid BDS state in case of skipped update steps or corruption. More concretely,

- We present BDSFix, an algorithm that, given a BDS state corresponding to signature s, can efficiently compute the BDS state signature $s + j$. Depending on the value of j this algorithm is equally or up to 8 times faster than the straightforward method of applying a single signature update step of the BDS state j times in sequence.
- We show that BDSFix can generate a new signature in case of tearing much more efficiently than known methods can. In case of two subsequent tearing events, it can generate the next signature a factor 10 faster than traditional methods can.
- We propose methods as possible future extensions of BDSFix that still recover the BDS state in case the tearing corrupted the BDS state (partially). This is particularly useful if anti-tearing measures are not in place.
- We provide simulation data to support our claims: it shows that BDSFix for a single tearing event equals the performance, i.e. performs the same operations (for a single tearing event), of recovering the state through BDS. For any number of tearing events larger than 1, BDSFix outperforms BDS. This varies from a 9% speed-up for six subsequent tearing events to improvements by factors of up to 8 for a large number of tearing events. This shows that in a scenario with multiple subsequent tearing events, BDS becomes significantly less efficient compared to BDSFix.

Other Applications. We note that although our paper is focused on the (anti-)tearing case, our work has broader applicability. Domains where BDS state recovery can be useful:

- **Power-loss during Signature Generation.** In case a device that does have its own power source loses power, it can have similar consequences as a tear of a contact-less smart card. Although it is less likely to happen multiple times in a row, in cases of a (temporarily) unstable power source it can happen that multiple BDS state updates are interrupted.

- **Distributed Signatures.** Currently NIST SP 800-208 prohibits the export of sHBS private keys to prevent key re-use. For use cases like HSMs, where multiple devices sign with the same key pair, this is a prohibitive restriction and an adaptation to the standard is under consideration. One option is to allow segmentation of the states into intervals, where each interval can only be used by 1 HSM. Updating a BDS state from the first interval to the next will require less computing power than computing it from scratch.
- **Fault Attacks.** Active physical attacks on an embedded device aim to introduce faults (e.g. power glitches) during a cryptographic operations to reveal internal private data. Such a glitch can corrupt a memory value in a similar manner as a tear would. Additionally, a fault may occur between the counter update and the BDS update without a signature being produced, as the updates are performed sequentially in this order for security reasons.

Outline. In Sect. 2 we first recall some concepts about hash-based signatures (HBS) schemes, as well as necessary background on tree traversal algorithms. In Sect. 3, we introduce BDSFix and show its correctness. Finally, we present experimental support for our results in Sect. 4 and in Sect. 5 we provide conclusions and open problems.

2   Preliminaries

In this section, we first describe stateful hash-based signatures (HBS) schemes, of which LMS [MCF19] and XMSS [HBG+18] are standardized. Multi-tree versions of both algorithms exist, but for the clarity of our contributions, we focus on the single-tree versions. Secondly, we recall tree traversal algorithms, and more specifically, the details of the BDS algorithm [BDS08], which efficiently manages auxiliary data, the *BDS state* to improve the performance of signature generation.

2.1   Stateful Hash-Based Signatures Schemes

The idea of hash-based signatures (HBS) dates back to a proposal by Ralph Merkle [Mer89] in the late 1970s. The security of this approach relies on the cryptographic strength of the used hash function and the pseudo-random function family: cryptographic primitives which are well-studied, understood, and not known to be broken by quantum computers.

In essence, HBS schemes combine a one-time signature scheme with a Merkle hash tree to sign multiple messages with one key pair. XMSS is a NIST standardized hash-based scheme (original publication [HRS16]), resulting in the scheme described in RFC 8391 [HBG+18]. It uses WOTS+ [Hul13] as underlying One-Time Signature (OTS). Another standardized hash-based scheme is LMS, which is described in RFC 8554 [MCF19]. XMSS uses a variant of W-OTS [Mer89,DSS05], namely W-OTS$^+$, as a subroutine with a Merkle tree construction while LMS uses another variant of W-OTS, namely LM-OTS.

W-OTS. W-OTS is defined by multiple key parameters. Firstly, the security parameter n corresponds to the length in bits of the hash function output. The Winternitz parameter w controls the efficiency and security trade-offs by defining the length of chains of hashes underlying the W-OTS computations. Length parameters ℓ_1 and ℓ_2 correspond respectively to the number of hash chains needed to represent an n-bit message in base w and the the number of segments required for checksum values. Let F be a hash function, and let $c^i(x)$ denote the chaining function defined as follows. For $i = 0$, $c^i(x) = x$, and for $i > 0$, $c^i(x)$ is defined as $c^i(x) = F(c^{i-1}(x))$. Let sk $= (\mathrm{sk}_1, \ldots, \mathrm{sk}_\ell)$ be a randomly generated secret key, where $\ell = \ell_1 + \ell_2$. The corresponding public key is given by: pk $= (\mathrm{pk}_1, \ldots, \mathrm{pk}_\ell) = (f^{w-1}(\mathrm{sk}_1), \ldots, f^{w-1}(\mathrm{sk}_\ell))$. To sign an m-bit message M given in base-w representation, i.e., $M_i \in \{0, \ldots, w - 1\}$ for $i = 0, \ldots, \ell_1$, we begin by computing the checksum $C = \sum_{i=1}^{\ell_1}(w - 1 - M_i)$. Since $C < \ell_1(w - 1)$, its base-w representation is at most ℓ_2. The checksum is concatenated to M so that $B = (b_1, \ldots, b_\ell) = M \,\|\, C$. The signature corresponds then to $\sigma = (\sigma_1, \ldots, \sigma_\ell) = (f^{b_1}(\mathrm{sk}_1), \ldots, f^{b_\ell}(\mathrm{sk}_\ell))$. To verify the signature, the verifier computes: $(f^{w-1-b_1}(\sigma_1), \ldots, f^{w-1-b_\ell}(\sigma_\ell))$. If the result matches the public key $(\mathrm{pk}_1, \ldots, \mathrm{pk}_\ell)$, then the signature is valid. In this paper we will focus on XMSS, but all results apply to LMS as well.

Merkle Tree. At the core of both these schemes lies the Merkle binary-tree-graph structure in which leaf-nodes (the lowest layer) correspond to public keys of OTS scheme. In XMSS, for instance, the secret key can correspond to the concatenated secret key of all underlying OTS key pairs. However, as outlined in [CAD+20], it is recommended that the secret key corresponds instead to a seed that generates all the OTS secret keys pseudorandomly. These OTS public keys are in turn constructed from the OTS secret keys using a specific series of hash function computations. Such a tree corresponding to 16 OTS key pairs is depicted in Fig. 1. Generally, the *height* H corresponds to the number of vertical layers of the Merkle tree. The nodes of a Merkle tree consist of n-bit hash values. The lowest layer (the *leaves* of the tree) consists of the hashed OTS public keys of the OTS key pairs. The public key of the Merkle-tree scheme is then the root node of the Merkle tree, which is constructed by taking pair-wise hashes

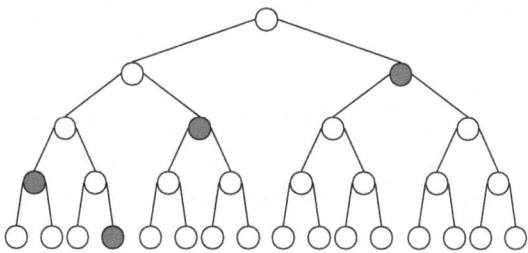

Fig. 1. The authentication path for a leaf i

of Merkle tree nodes, starting from the leaves, until one node remains at, for example, height $H = 4$ (the top node in Fig. 1).

XMSS Signatures. When signing a message the signer signs with a (previously unused) OTS key pair, and sends the OTS signature of their message, along with the corresponding *authentication path* to the verifier. This authentication path ensures a verifier can verify an OTS signature against the public key of the Merkle-tree-based scheme instead of the OTS public key. An example for the authentication path of the second OTS key pair is depicted in Fig. 1.

Given the signature, the verifier can then compute the candidate root key as follows. First they compute the OTS PK from the OTS signature, and apply a hash to construct the corresponding Merkle tree leaf. Then they can apply in order a pairwise hash with the elements of the provided authentication path. If the result matches the public key, the signature is verified. The Merkle tree is therefore used to authenticate the OTS public keys, supporting efficient generation and verification of multiple signatures. The authenticity of all OTS verification keys is reduced to the authenticity of the single XMSS public key corresponding to the root of the Merkle tree.

For the signer, computing the authentication path is a computation-intensive task. If they start from their XMSS secret key, they have to re-compute almost all Merkle tree leaf nodes to be able to compute the authentication path. This is therefore almost equivalent to repeating the key generation for that secret key. To give an idea, for a tree of height h, key generation amounts to computing 2^h OTS public keys from their secret key counterparts. For common parameter sets ($h = 10$, 15 or even 20) the computation of the authentication path would take millions of hash operations, while the WOTS+ signature generation only takes hundreds of hash operations.

An alternative is to store the entire Merkle tree in memory. For the parameter sets of interest this means storing more than 50 Kbyte, or even megabytes, which is infeasible on constrained devices, especially in secure memory.

2.2   Tree Traversal in Stateful Hash-Based Signature Schemes

To reduce the signing time, previous works propose sophisticated time/memory trade-off algorithms like the fractal tree algorithm [JLMS03] and log tree traversal algorithm [BDS08]. These algorithms focus on minimizing asymptotic costs, constant time signing and averaging over all 2^h signatures. The idea is to not store the entire Merkle tree, but strategic parts (i.e. auxiliary data) of it. Instead of storing a key as $(s, SEED)$, it is now stored as $(s, SEED, aux_s)$. After each signature generation, additional operations update the stored auxiliary data aux_s to aux_{s+1} for the next signature. Storing a few thousand bytes allows the authentication paths to be computed in the order of magnitude of thousands of hash operations instead of millions. For instance for parameters $H = 10, w = 4, n = 32$ and BDS parameter $K = 4$, we can see the trade-offs in Table 1.

Table 1. Impact of tree traversal utilization in XMSS. Here *hashes sign* indicates the number of applications of the WOTS+ functions H and F [HBG+18]. MT denotes storing the entire Merkle tree structure.

State storage	$(s, SEED)$	$(s, SEED, aux_s)$	$(s, SEED, MT)$
Storage in bytes	52B	1184B	65kB
Hashes sign [BDS09, Thm. 5.2]	1 million	4029	1005

We can now also see why tearing at signature s is an issue for tree traversal implementations. While in an implementation where no auxiliary information is stored the next signature can simply be signed with signature $(s + 1, SEED)$, in a tree traversal implementation the tearing might occur after the update of the state, but before or during the update of the auxiliary data. This would lead to an invalid key $(s + 1, SEED, aux_s)$, or even a corrupted state $(s + 1, SEED, aux_{corr})$. One solution is to first re-compute the auxiliary data, but this can take more time than is allotted. In this paper we will present BDSFix, which updates aux_s efficiently.

2.3   The BDS Algorithm

In this paper we focus on the log tree traversal algorithm [BDS08] of Buchmann, Dahmen and Schneider (i.e. 'BDS' algorithm).

In a Merkle tree of height H, the authentication path differs for each leaf of the tree. An efficient algorithm to compute the authentication path for each leaf without recomputing the entire tree is the BDS algorithm [BDS08] which relies on the algorithm treehash, described in Algorithm 1, as a subroutine. The treehash algorithm uses the function leafcalc(s) to compute the Merkle tree leaf s and the hash function F as subroutines to compute a specific node v at height h of the tree. It then uses the pop and push functions to push and pop the nodes required to compute v in an orderly fashion, pushing them onto and popping them from the stack. This allows the computation of v in a memory-efficient way. The methodical order also allows the computation of the treehash algorithm, a treehash instance TREEHASH$_h$, to be distributed over multiple sessions, i.e. signature operations. Such a TREEHASH$_h$ stores the stack of nodes that already have been computed, such that computation can be resumed at a later time. The BDS algorithm is designed to balance memory usage and run time to efficiently update the authentication path as new leaves are processed thus reducing the signing time.

The authentication path from a leaf to the root can be encoded in binary. In fact, each node within the tree has a unique position which can be represented by its path from the root node. A binary string that encodes the path indicates which side (left or right) the path takes in the Merkle tree: a 0 in the binary position means a transition to the left child from a parent node, while a 1 indicates a transition to a right child. Regarding the computation of a node, the computation of right and left authentication nodes differs, as with the stored state of BDS the computation of left nodes is much cheaper than right nodes. The BDS algorithm takes this into account and performs three key tasks.

The first key idea is that a node that is a left child can be computed using a right node that appeared in a previous authentication path which results in one hash function evaluation. Therefore, the BDS algorithm stores those authentication nodes in a KEEP array. We denote by $v_h[j]$ a node in the Merkle tree at height h, where $h = 0, \ldots H$, and j represents the position of the node at that height, counted from left to right. As right nodes need to be computed from scratch, the second task is to store a fixed number of right nodes, determined by the BDS parameter k, during the key generation. Those nodes correspond to the right nodes close to the root $v_h[3], \ldots, v_h[2^{H-h} - 1]$ with $H - k \leq h \leq H - 2$ and are stored in a stack RETAIN$_h$. Finally, the generation of the remaining right authentication nodes is distributed across previous authentication paths computation. This is done by scheduling one instance of treehash per tree level. This instance TREEHASH$_h$ compute and stores exactly one right authentication node on height h with $h < H - k$, as part of the BDS algorithm. A description of the BDS algorithm is given in Algorithm 2.

Algorithm 1. treehash

    Input: Stack **Stack**, leaf index s
    Output: Updated stack **Stack**

1: node $N = $ leafcalc(s)
2: **while** top node on **Stack** has same height h as N **do**
3:     $N \leftarrow$ F(**Stack**.pop $\parallel N$)   ▷ N has now height $h + 1$
4: **Stack**.push(N)
5: **return Stack**

Right Nodes Computation. Regarding the generation of right authentication nodes, a fixed budget is allocated to their computation in each round. This budget corresponds to $(H - k)/2$ leaf computations and evaluation of treehash. Each treehash instance is either pending, in progress, or finished with varying levels of attention allocated to each. One key feature of the BDS algorithm is the use of a stack shared by all treehash instances.

A treehash instance that is underway stores one tail node per level at a time on the stack. A treehash update consists of generating one leaf and its parent nodes using the tail nodes present on the stack. The selection of the instance that is updated is done using the function TREEHASH$_h$.height(). This function returns the height of the lowest tail node stored on the stack by the instance. In the case that no such node exists then the function returns the height h of the instance if it is neither finished nor initialized. Otherwise, it returns ∞. The treehash update gives priority to the instance that returns the smallest value through TREEHASH$_h$.height(). On the occasion that more than one treehash instance

---

Algorithm 2. BDS

    Input: BDS state, leaf index s
    Output: BDS state updated

1: Let $\tau = 0$ if s is a left leaf or let τ be the height of the first left parent node of s:
    $\tau \leftarrow \max\{h : 2^h | (s+1)\}$
2: If the parent of s on height $\tau + 1$ is a left node then store the current authentication node on height τ in $\mathtt{KEEP}_\tau$:
    if $\lfloor s/2^{\tau+1} \rfloor$ is even **and** $\tau < H - 1$ **then** $\mathtt{KEEP}_\tau \leftarrow \mathtt{AUTH}_\tau$
3: If s is a left node, it is one of the authentication nodes of leaf $s + 1$:
    if $\tau = 0$ **then** $\mathtt{AUTH}_0 \leftarrow \mathtt{leafcalc(s)}$
4: Otherwise, s is a right node and the authentication path for $s+1$ changes on height $0, \ldots, \tau$:
    if $\tau > 0$ **then**
    (a) Compute the new left node on height τ using the current authentication node on height $\tau - 1$ and the node on height $\tau - 1$ stored in $\mathtt{KEEP}_{\tau-1}$. The node in $\mathtt{KEEP}_{\tau-1}$ is then removed:
        $\mathtt{AUTH}_\tau \leftarrow H(\mathtt{AUTH}_{\tau-1} \| \mathtt{KEEP}_{\tau-1})$
    (b) Update the right authentication nodes on height $h = 0, \ldots, \tau - 1$ using the nodes saved in $\mathtt{TREEHASH}_h$ or in $\mathtt{RETAIN}_h$ depending on the value of h:
        for $h = 0$ **to** $\tau - 1$ **do**
            if $h < H - k$ **then** $\mathtt{AUTH}_h \leftarrow \mathtt{TREEHASH}_h.\mathtt{pop}$
            if $h \geq H - k$ **then** $\mathtt{AUTH}_h \leftarrow \mathtt{RETAIN}_h.\mathtt{pop}$
    (c) For $h = 0$ to $h = \min\{\tau - 1, H - k - 1\}$, initialize the treehash instances using the leaf index s:
        for $h = 0$ **to** $\min\{\tau - 1, H - k - 1\}$ **do**
            if $s + 1 + 3 \cdot 2^h < 2^H$ **then** $\mathtt{TREEHASH}_h.\mathtt{initialize}(s + 1 + 3 \cdot 2^h)$

5: Use the budget of $(H - k)/2$ updates on the treehash instances:
    repeat $(H - k)/2$ **times**
    (a) Select the treehash instance whose lowest tail node has the lowest height. If there is more than one instance, select the one with the lowest index. Let k be the index of the selected instance:
        $k \leftarrow \min\left\{h : \mathtt{TREEHASH}_h.\mathtt{height}() = \min_{j=0,\ldots,H-k-1}\{\mathtt{TREEHASH}_j.\mathtt{height}()\}\right\}$
    (b) One update is given to the treehash instance with index k:
        $\mathtt{TREEHASH}_k.\mathtt{update}()$
6: **return** $\mathtt{AUTH}_0, \ldots, \mathtt{AUTH}_{H-1}$

---

returns the same smallest value then the priority is given to the instance with the smallest index.

Single Stack. The BDS algorithm computes nodes when they are needed: instead of computing right nodes all at once they are incrementally built. As each treehash instance compute their target nodes, intermediate nodes for the target node are temporarily stored in the stack. To minimize memory usage and optimize computational efficiency, all the treehash instances share a stack to manage the intermediate nodes. To compute the authentication node on height h, up to h tail nodes at different heights can be stored on the stack by an instance TREEHASH$_h$. The stack holds those nodes until they are ready to be combined, i.e., when two tail nodes can form a higher-level node.

While an instance TREEHASH$_h$ is updated and thus stores tail nodes on the stack, it is possible that instances on lower heights $i \in \{0, \ldots, h-1\}$ are initialized and therefore receive updates. Those instances will thus store intermediate nodes on the stack. Since the height of the lowest tail node in TREEHASH$_h$ is greater than i, TREEHASH$_i$ will be completed before TREEHASH$_h$ receive another update. Therefore, tail nodes of higher treehash instances will not interfere with tail nodes of lower instances.

2.4   Assumptions

In the next section, we will assume that when a tearing event happens the BDS state is not corrupted, it just has not been updated. I.e., if a tear occurs while signing signature s with $(s, SEED, aux_s)$, then the resulting state will be $(s, SEED, aux_{s+1})$. If j tears happen in a row, which can happen in the case of a user presenting their NFC card too quickly to a terminal multiple times, or a faulty power supply, then our assumption is that the resulting state will be $(s + j, SEED, aux_s)$. Furthermore, we assume that the BDS state has its own index which corresponds to the index of the signature, i.e. it can be detected that $s + j$ and aux_s are a mismatch. This index is associated with all the elements of the BDS state and is updated after a complete BDS update to match the next signature index.

This assumption is realistic for many microcontroller settings that have anti-tearing countermeasures in place. A simple example of such a countermeasure is the mirroring technique, where twice the memory is allocated for writing the BDS state to storage. After updating, the BDS state is first written to the first half of the memory, and then to the second. If a sudden power-loss were to occur, then one of the two parts of the memory will have the valid state. Another example is to protect the card writing operations with a hardware tool. For instance, if the chip has a capacitor and buffer memory, then the to-be-written state can be calculated and stored in the buffer memory and once the operation is finished, the capacitor is first checked on whether it has enough power stored to complete the write operation. This ensures that an incomplete write operation cannot occur.

Note that in both cases the index s is assumed to be updated (and stored in memory) before any signature generation or BDS operations take place. This is an essential protection to ensure that no double signing with the same state can occur. We also assume that in the application of our algorithm the same techniques are applied: we replace the invalid BDS state with the result BDSFix so that only a guaranteed writing operation succeeds.

In the case anti-tearing protections are not in place, then the situation can occur that the state in memory has been partially updated, i.e. containing part of aux_s and aux_{s+j}, or even containing a corrupted node written to memory that is correct for neither the old state aux_s nor the new state aux_{s+j}. In this case `BDSFix` cannot be straightforwardly applied. We discuss options for this situation in Sect. 3.3.

3   Recovering a BDS State

The BDS state aux_s consists of 4 components that are initialized during key generation.

- AUTH: after the BDS update of aux_s to aux_{s+1}, AUTH contains the correct authentication path of the signature with index $s + 1$. It is initialized by storing the authentication path of signature 0.
- KEEP: stores the nodes that leave the current authentication path, which can be used to efficiently calculate a left-node of a future authentication path. It is initialized as an empty array.
- RETAIN: stores right nodes not in AUTH that are computationally most expensive to re-compute due to them needing to be computed from scratch. Note that RETAIN is stored during the key generation phase and is not updated after that.

The BDS algorithm updates the BDS state after each signature to reduce the signing time per signature. The algorithm is designed to ensure that the authentication path is precomputed and available when the signature is required. However, it is designed to be updated after each signature. Therefore, if a signature is skipped then the BDS state is incorrect which leads to an incorrect authentication path as well as the signature.

We now present our algorithm to recover aux_{s+j} from aux_s efficiently, for any signature s and any j subsequent tearing events.

3.1   The Algorithm

Although a BDS state could be recomputed from the secret $SEED$, this is not very efficient since it would take approximately the same time as an XMSS key generation. Instead, with `BDSFix`, the valid BDS state can be recovered with the current signature index $s + j$ and the information from the last BDS state aux_s stored in memory. At a high level, our algorithm works in three steps.

1. **Re-use:** Unless the signatures are very far apart, nodes of the BDS state s in the memory can still be re-used for the computation of BDS state $s + j$. From the new index value and the one associated with the BDS state in memory, we first derive which nodes should be kept for the new state.
2. **Determine:** Next is to determine which nodes are missing. This includes determining whether nodes stored in aux_s can be used for the computation of aux_{s+j}. For instance a node in the KEEP of aux_s can often be used for a node of the AUTH of aux_{s+j}.
3. **Compute:** Efficiently compute the nodes. Computing the authentication path can also be used to compute Keep nodes.

We describe the algorithm that recovers the valid BDS state using the current data in memory in Algorithm 3.

Algorithm 3. BDSFix

Input: BDS state $aux_s = (\text{AUTH}, \text{KEEP}, \text{RETAIN}, \text{treehash})$
Output: Updated BDS state for index $(s + j)$ stored in aux'_{s+j}

1: $aux'_{s+j} =(\text{AUTH'}, \text{KEEP'}, \text{RETAIN}, \text{treehash'}0$
2: **for** $h = H - 1$ to 1 **do**
3:     **if** $\text{AUTH}_h \in aux'_{s+j}$ **then** $\text{AUTH'}_h = \text{AUTH}_h$
4:         **if** AUTH_h is right child-node with a left parent-node **then** $\text{KEEP'}_h = \text{KEEP}_h$
5:     **else** break   ▷ h is the height from which AUTH' and AUTH differ
6: AuthPathUpdate(h)
7: TreehashUpdate$()$
8: **return** aux'_{s+j}
9:
10: **function** AUTHPATHUPDATE(h) ▷ compute the remaining AUTH and KEEP nodes
11:     Compute AUTH'_h using $\text{KEEP}_{\max(i:i<h)}$
12:     **for** $i \in \{0, \ldots, h - 1\}$ **do**
13:         Compute AUTH'_i
14:         **for** $k \in \{0, \ldots, i - 1\}$ **do**
15:             **if** node at position $\frac{s+j}{2^k}$ is right node child of a left node **then** store in KEEP'
16:         **if** AUTH_h is right node child of left node **then** store in KEEP'_h
17: **end function**
18:
19: **function** TREEHASHUPDATE
20:     **for** $0 \leq h < H - k$ **do**
21:         **if** $\text{TREEHASH}_h \in aux'_{s+j}$ **then** $\text{TREEHASH'}_h = \text{TREEHASH}_h$
22:         **else** TREEHASH'_h.initialize$(2^{h+1} \cdot \lfloor \frac{s}{2^{h+1}} \rfloor + 3 \cdot 2^h)$
23:         Compute the budget allocated to the instance
24:     **for** $h = H - k - 1$ to 0 **do**
25:         Loop on the allocated budget for TREEHASH'_h: TREEHASH'_h.update$()$
26: **end function**

3.2   Correctness of the Algorithm

In this section, we show the correctness of Algorithm 3. Using the binary representation of the authentication path, we first show that authentication nodes stored in the last BDS state aux_s may be relevant for the BDS state aux_{s+j}. Then we show that we can recover the KEEP nodes of aux_{s+j} during the generation of the remaining authentication path nodes of aux_{s+j}. For treehash we first show that we can retrieve the exact initialization indices with the index of the current signature, and secondly we can recover the specific number of updates, i.e. budget, that each treehash instance requires to match the expected value of aux_{s+j}.

Overlap of Authentication Paths. Authentication path nodes only change value at height h every 2^h signatures. Therefore the authentication paths for the signature with index s and index $s + j$ have nodes in common as long as $s < 2^{h-1}$

and $s + j > 2^{h-1}$ does not hold. To determine the overlap, we compare the binary representation of the two indices. Since their respective authentication paths are the complements of their index representations, a comparison gives the exact nodes that are common between signature s and $s + j$. An example of two authentication paths that overlap is depicted in Fig. 2 where common nodes are represented in gray. Note that a non-equal authentication path node for s and $s + j$ at height h implies non-equal authentication nodes at heights $0, 1, \ldots, h - 1$ as well: the authentication paths live in different subtrees of the binary Merkle tree. The first diverging bit in the binary representation of s and $s+j$ therefore identifies the exact position in the tree where the binary representations differ. Therefore s and $s + j$ share the same $\texttt{AUTH}_i$ for $i \in \{1, \ldots, h - 1\}$ if $\left(\frac{s}{2^i} \oplus 1\right) = \left(\frac{s+j}{2^i} \oplus 1\right)$.

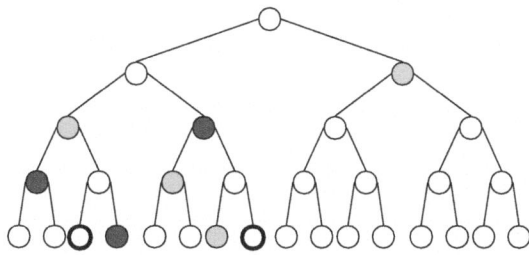

Fig. 2. Example of an authentication path a (bolded) leaf s (in red) and (bolded) leaf $s + j$ (in green). Common authentication path nodes are marked in gray. (Color figure online)

It therefore suffices to determine the bit h at which the binary representation of s and $s + j$ deviate (counting downwards from the most significant bits), which identifies correctly where the path for two different leaves diverges. This height h is determined in Line 5 in Algorithm 3. The nodes that appear on the authentication paths from the Merkle tree root down to the level position $h - 1$ are shared, see Algorithm 3 Line 3, and do not need to be recomputed while the nodes from level h to the leaf $s+j$ need to be computed in Line 7 of Algorithm 3. KEEP *Nodes Are Detected during the Authentication Path Generation.* As can be seen in Algorithm 2, Line 1/2, at each signature at most one node of the authentication path is stored in KEEP. Specifically, the authentication node is stored in KEEP if the authentication path node is a right node that, when combined with its sibling left node results in a parent node that is a left node. By construction, this parent node is not in the authentication path for signature s, but since it is a left node, it will be includes in future authentication paths and it can be used to compute this node more efficiently. KEEP nodes thus correspond to right authentication nodes of AUTH that are not immediately relevant for the authentication path of s, but are reused in future BDS updates to generate a left authentication node. In Fig. 3, the KEEP node and the previous authentication node are combined to generate the new left authentication node depicted in orange. We first look at the case where only 1 signature or BDS update was skipped. In this case, the difference between the binary representations of s and $s+1$ provides the potential keep node after round s. Just as in the authentication path recovery process, the level h that indicates where the authentication paths diverge determines if a node was stored in KEEP. The first differing authentication node for $s+1$ indicates the potential keep node: if it is a left child of a right authentication node then its sibling was stored in the KEEP array. Indeed, the node at level h stored in keep will be concatenated to the current left authentication node at the same level to generate a future left authentication node as described in the BDS algorithm.

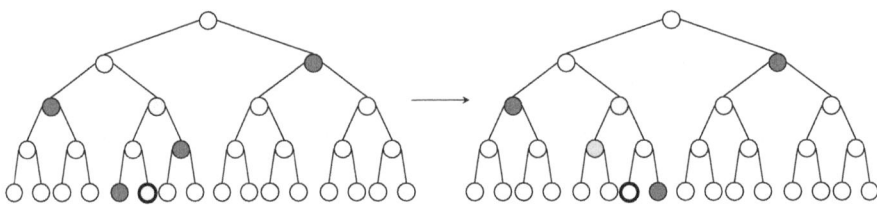

Fig. 3. Depiction of the generation of the next state's authentication path (in red, right tree) using previous state's keep node (in yellow) and authentication path (computed node in orange). (Color figure online)

Similarly, the keep nodes found in the shared path between round s and round $s + j$ are present in round $s + j$. It follows that during the generation of unique nodes, if the authentication node is a left node and its parent is a left node then the sibling of the authentication node is stored in the KEEP array. This step corresponds to Line 4 of Algorithm 3.

Keep Node to Compute the First New Authentication Node. The first diverging authentication node between AUTH and AUTH$'$ is a left node at height h (see Line 5 of Algorithm 3). This node can be efficiently computed by combining a keep node of aux_s with the left authentication node at height h, AUTH$_h \in aux_s$. The keep node of aux_s which has the largest height is used to compute this new authentication node. This new authentication node corresponds to the root of the subtree of the Merkle Tree that contains all the AUTH nodes in aux_s irrelevant for the computation of AUTH in aux_{s+j}. The combination of the keep node and left authentication node either directly generates an authentication node of aux_{s+j} or is used to build up the subtree using the irrelevant authentication nodes to compute the root of this subtree. We give an example of such a usage of a keep node to compute the highest authentication node in Fig. 4: the blue nodes represent nodes of aux_s (either the keep node or the authentication nodes) that are used to generate the largest height differing authentication node between aux_s and aux_{s+j} (in orange). If no such keep node exists, such as the yellow node in Fig. 4, then the left leaf is computed instead.

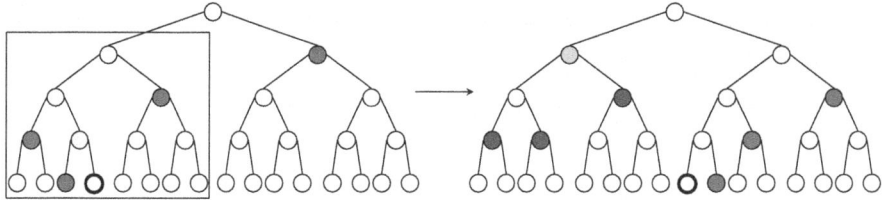

Fig. 4. Generation of the highest height ($h = 3$) authentication node (in orange) using the highest height ($h = 1$) keep node (in yellow on the left-hand side) and authentication nodes (represented in red). (Color figure online)

Shared Treehash Instances. Treehash instances are responsible for computing the next required right authentication nodes at specific heights in the tree. Nodes at higher levels are used in the authentication path of multiple signatures and once a right authentication node is computed, it can be reused by any signature that has an authentication paths that pass through it. For each such right node at height h, a treehash instance TREEHASH$_h$ is created 2^h signatures before the node is required for an authentication path, and its computation is distributed over the 2^h signatures, or more accurately the 2^h BDS updates. Since an instance TREEHASH$_h$ is common in the BDS states aux during a specific number of signatures depending on the height h, the instance can be both in aux_s and aux_{s+j}, although at a different stage of computation. In this case, instead of recomputing the instance from scratch, it can be reused and its computation can be continued from $s + j$. In Fig. 5, we illustrate of two BDS states aux_3 and aux_5 sharing the same treehash instance TREEHASH$_1$, where the purple nodes represent the leaves needed to compute the target pink node of the instance.

Treehash Instance Starting Point Determined from Signature Index. For the treehash instances that are not common between two different BDS states aux_s and aux_{s+j}, the starting leaf of an instance can be determined by the current state $s + j$. It corresponds to the leaf position $2^{h+1} \cdot \lfloor \frac{s+j}{2^{h+1}} \rfloor + 3 \cdot 2^h$ where $s + j$ is the current leaf index. In fact, as in the initialization step in BDS algorithm where each TREEHASH$_h$ is initialized with the leaf at position $s + 3^h$ where s corresponds to 0, we simply need to find the leaf index before the starting point of the subtree of height h with the current leaf index $s + j$. From there, we can then compute the starting leaf of the instance as if it is done in the initialization step of BDS. The treehash is initialized at this position and it determines all the Merkle tree leaves needed to compute the target right authentication node.

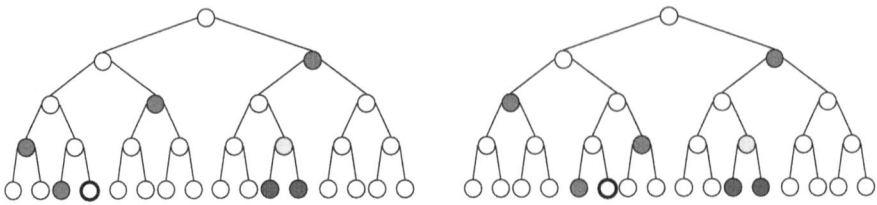

Fig. 5. BDS states corresponding to signatures S and $s + j$ (nodes with bold border) sharing the same treehash instance depicted in pink which is constructed from leaves in purple. (Color figure online)

Treehash Instances Are Given a Specific Budget per Signature. Treehash instances are updated with each signature generated. In each round, a budget of $(H - K)/2$ leaf computations is allocated for the update of the instances, see Line 5 of Algorithm BDS. A treehash instance for height h that is initialized in round s requires 2^h updates to be completed and must be completed before signature $s + 2^{h+1}$ [BDS09, Thm. 5.2], where its root is an authentication node. During the 2^{h+1} BDS updates where the treehash instance can be updated, a number of $2^{h+1}/2^{i+1}$ treehash instances are initialized on heights $i = 0, \cdots, h - 1$. The strategy of the BDS algorithm is to use the budget of $(H - K)/2$ leaf node computations to treehash instances with the lowest tail node first. This means that the instances created at heights 0 through $h - 1$ are always finalized before updating the newly created instance at height h. To explain this further, as mentioned earlier a treehash instance TREEHASH$_i$ requires 2^i leaf computations. However, if this instance was initialized during signature s, or even before, and has been updated but is still incomplete by signature $s + j$, then it did $2^r < 2^i$ leaf computations. The exact number of leaf computations that has been performed by signature $s + j$ can be computed by looking at its position on the stack. In fact, tail nodes stored in the stack correspond to nodes at specific height and therefore give us the exact number of leaf operations computed for this instance so far. Thus, if a lower instance TREEHASH$_i$ is still valid for the new signature and was not completed, it means that it did not use 2^i leaf computations but instead the real budget used for this instance comes from the information obtained by looking at the stack and corresponds to 2^r. Since the total budget available for those rounds is $j \cdot \frac{H-K}{2}$ then the instance TREEHASH$_h$ has $j \cdot \frac{H-K}{2} - \sum_{i=0}^{h-1} (\lceil \frac{j}{2^{i+1}} \rceil \cdot 2^i)$ required leaf computations for its completion. However, if one of the instances TREEHASH$_i$ is still valid but incomplete and only performs 2^r leaf computations then we adjust the operations accordingly. The allocated budget per round for TREEHASH$_i$ is fixed and computable. It differs for every instance and varies depending on the position of the leaf's position in the tree.

Reordering of the Stack. Since instances with lower heights have priority during the update phase, tail nodes of higher treehash instances, if they exist, are stored first in the stack so as not to interfere with the tail nodes of lower instances when the stack is updated in last-in-first-out order. Therefore, in our algorithm we recover the correct stack by processing the recovery in decreasing order: from the highest height treehash instance to the lowest. First, if a treehash instance of aux_s is still present in aux_{s+j} for the current signature $s + j$ and has tail nodes stored in the stack, they are recovered for the computation of the corresponding treehash in aux_{s+j}. Then, if this instance has a budget, it is updated with it before moving to the lower instance due to the stack being ordered by always having incomplete treehash instances with higher height before the incomplete instances with lower height.

3.3   The Corrupted Case

Lastly, we want to mention the broader application of our BDSFix algorithm in case the assumptions we made in Sect. 2.4 are not true, i.e. after a tearing event the BDS state is either partially updated (consisting of elements of aux_s and aux_{s+j}) or even has a corrupted node that was being written during the tearing event that belongs to neither aux_s nor aux_{s+j}.

The reference implementation of XMSS updates and stores nodes of the BDS state aux_s during its computation. Therefore, if a tearing event occurs during the BDS update, it can corrupt a specific part of the state, whether it is a common authentication node, a treehash instance or even the last tail node on the stack, and leave the rest of the state intact.

To still apply an adapted version of BDSFix, a solution could be to add an additional information associated to the signature index to each element of the BDS state, at the expense of the BDS state size, and to update it along with each node being computed. This information could indicate whether nodes in aux belong to aux_s or aux_{s+j} and if a node has been corrupted. If the latter is the case it should not be considered it during the recovery of the BDS state. For corrupted information, it is therefore necessary to recompute it as if its corresponding element in the BDS state is not relevant anymore.

Depending on how many cases the implementer wants to cover, BDSFix can be adapted to first do additional checks on the nodes. It might even be faster since the partially computed aux_{s+j} nodes do not have to be re-computed. However, in some situations there are too many options or there is the possibility that it is not possible to determine which nodes are corrupted. In this case it might very well be that a straightforward re-computation of the BDS state from scratch is necessary. You can still utilize the techniques BDSFix to do that faster than generating the initial BDS state and applying consecutive updates by only computing the nodes necessary for aux_{s+j} of the current signature.

4   Experiments

We implement BDSFix by adapting the reference implementation of XMSS [Xms] which includes the BDS algorithm. We compile the code using gcc 16.0.0, with the compiler optimization flag -O3 and execute on a 2 GHz Quad-Core Intel Core i5 processor.

Throughout the experiments, we verify correctness of the recovered BDS state of BDSFix (after one or multiple tearing events) by comparing it to the BDS state recovered by using updates of the BDS algorithm. In all cases, the BDS states obtained through both methods are identical. BDSFix is implemented in XMSS instantiated with SHA2-256 as specified in RFC 8391, Winternitz parameter $w = 16$, BDS parameter $k = 2$, and tree height $H = 10$. It is also designed to generalize to larger parameters.

We first compare the performances in terms of the number of required hash operations for recovering the correct state with both BDS and BDSFix. For BDS the state of $s + j$ is recovered from a aux_s by subsequently applying the BDS update steps j times. We count the number of SHA2-256 call in both algorithms and exclude the number of hash calls for computing the message hash as this step is independent and irrelevant to the BDS algorithm.

We report our experimental results in Table 2 showing the average number of hash computations across $(2^H - \text{jump} - 1)$ signatures. We report the average signing time in nanoseconds as well. It first shows that if one tearing event occurs, i.e. one signature is skipped, then we obtain the same average number of hash computations for both the BDS and BDSFix. In fact in all cases, it confirms that BDS and BDSFix do the same number of hash operations. If more than one tearing event occurs, i.e. 2 or 10 signatures are skipped, then BDSFix reduces the average total computational cost of hash evaluation. In this case for a distance 2 between the previous state of signature s and the desired state $s + 2$, BDSFix requires 0.04% fewer hash operations on average. For 6 subsequent tearing events, this increases to a 9% performance gain of BDSFix over using BDS. The larger the number of tearing events, the better BDSFix performs comparatively to obtain the correct BDS state.

Table 2. Average total hash count in BDSFix and BDS.

H	Algorithm	jump	# hash	sign (ns)
10	BDSFix	1	13425	954414
10	BDS	1	13425	7671124
10	BDSFix	2	26035	1426629
10	BDS	2	26870	15090421
10	BDSFix	6	61467	7162518
10	BDS	6	67322	51350121

To further illustrate the use of BDSFix, we also add the minimum signing time in Table 2. In the case of a single or multiple tearing events after signature s, one of the priorities for the signer might be to deliver the signature $s + j$ as quickly as possible, and performing further computation to recover the

BDS state thereafter. With BDS, it is not feasible to independently recover the authentication path without also performing treehash instance-computations: in BDS the treehash instances are used to compute the next right authentication nodes and irrelevant instances for the computation of signature $s + j$ are still instantiated and updated. Conversely, BDSFix allows for this separation. BDSFix first updates the treehash instances and keep nodes relevant to the recovery of the authentication path of $s + j$ and only thereafter performs computations on the keep nodes and treehash instances relevant for signatures $s + j + 1$ and further. For this reason, we measure and report in Table 2 the average time, in nanoseconds, required to recover the authentication path.

We see that if we compare time to signature delivery, BDSFix performs relatively even better compared to BDS. For 2 subsequent tearing events, BDSFix can deliver signature $s + 2$ over 11 times faster then with the state recovery of BDS. For 10 subsequent tearing events, where more work is necessary to compute authentication path nodes, it is still almost 6 times faster. Note that for a single tearing event BDS could be adapted to also release the signature at the same speed, but for a larger number of tearing events, this is not possible. Also note that an alternative strategy of computing the authentication path from scratch (and computing the BDS state later) can become faster than subsequent application of BDS, but will never outperform BDSFix. This is due to BDS inherently computing some nodes double or triple in different signature generations, while BDSFix avoids computing any irrelevant nodes.

Next, we illustrate the efficiency comparison between BDS and BDSFix across all signatures of an XMSS instance. The results are shown in Fig. 6.

These figures reveal clear trends in how the value of the signature indices s and $s + j$ impact the performance of BDSFix compared to BDS. The first figure shows the sharp contrast in the efficiency ratio depending on which height $H - 1$ subtree $s+j$ belongs to. We see for each signature s (state idx) what the overhead cost is to recover signature 511 (in blue) and signature 512 (in orange) with BDS compared to BDSFix. It shows that at the boundary signature 2^{H-1}, BDS becomes significantly less efficient compared to BDS. This is due to BDS still performing a lot of computations to compute nodes in the left subtree of height $H - 1$, while this subtree is irrelevant for authentication paths of signatures after state 511, save for the root of that tree.

The right figure in Fig. 6 is a heatmap that highlights a larger number of tearing events results in higher inefficiency for BDS. On the x-axis we plot the signature state at which the sequence of tearing events (jump) occurs. On the y-axis we indicate how many tearing events occur. As seen in the yellow high efficiency ratios, larger numbers of tearing events lead to BDSFix gaining performance over BDS by a factor of over 8. Note that outside of a faulty power wire, this is quite an unrealistic setting in many cases. We see however that with smaller jumps BDSFix also has a significant performance gain.

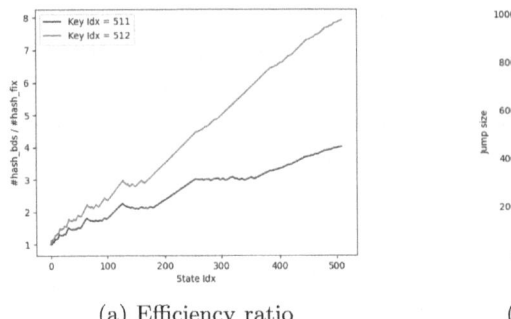
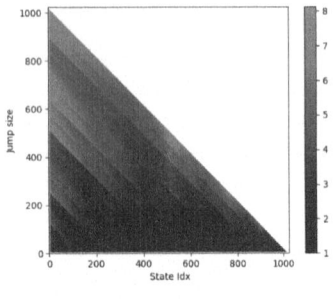

(a) Efficiency ratio   (b) Behavior of the algorithms

Fig. 6. Efficiency comparison between `BDS` and `BDSFix`. On the left: ratio of `BDS` and `BDSFix` running time as a function of the current state index s with the target state index $s + j = 511$ respectively $s + j = 512$. On the right: ratio of `BDS` and `BDSFix` running time as a function of the current state index s and target index $s + j$ (where j is indicated as the jump size). Yellow indicates a high ratio, and dark blue indicates (near-)equal running time. (Color figure online)

5   Conclusion

The `BDS` algorithm is an highly efficient algorithm that manages Merkle tree authentication paths for balanced runtime and memory usage for signature generation with stateful hash-based cryptography. It assumes the careful maintenance of a state consisting of a set of Merkle tree nodes, that are updated in order with each signature generated. In this paper we look at a setting where a loss of power, as can occur with removing a smart card too soon from its power source (a 'tear') can interfere with the update of the BDS state. Since `BDS` does not have a recovery mechanism when one or more BDS updates do not occur due to a power-loss, it can only recover by simply reapplying itself the appropriate number of times. This comes with overhead: computations are included in the update that are irrelevant for future signature. In this work we present `BDSFix`, a dedicated algorithm for the update of the BDS state if a tearing event occurs. `BDSFix` is an adaptation of the techniques of `BDS`, and improves the computational cost compared to the classical `BDS`. We show `BDSFix` for a single tearing event equals the performance, i.e. performs the same operations (for a single tearing event), of recovering the state through `BDS`. For any number of tearing events larger than 1, `BDSFix` outperforms `BDS`. This ranges from a 9% speed-up for six subsequent tearing events to improvements by factors up to 8 for a large number of tearing events. Additionally, we show it can be used to deliver the required XMSS signature after multiple tearing events faster than `BDS` can deliver it.

Outside of the discussion in Sect. 3.3, this paper does not investigate different types of memories that can cause a BDS state to be partially updated or even partially corrupted at a tearing event. Methods to recover from a corrupted BDS state with `BDSFix` would likely require storing additional information in the BDS state and would increase the complexity of the algorithm. How this impacts the running time of both BDS and BDSFix is left as future work. This paper also does not cover alternative tree traversal techniques such as Fractal tree traversal [JLMS03]. This would also be an interesting direction for future work.

Acknowledgements. Solane El Hirch is supported by the Cryptography Research Center of the Technology Innovation Institute (TII), Abu Dhabi (UAE), under the TII-Radboud project with title *Evaluation and Implementation of Lightweight Cryptographic Primitives and Protocols*. Part of this work was performed at NXP Semiconductors, Eindhoven (The Netherlands).

References

[BDS08] Buchmann, J., Dahmen, E., Schneider, M.: Merkle tree traversal revisited. In: Buchmann, J., Ding, J. (eds.) PQCrypto 2008. LNCS, vol. 5299, pp. 63–78. Springer, Heidelberg (2008). https://doi.org/10.1007/978-3-540-88403-3_5

[BDS09] Buchmann, J., Dahmen, E., Szydlo, M.: Hash-based digital signature schemes. In: Bernstein, D.J., Buchmann, J., Dahmen, E. (eds.) Post-Quantum Cryptography, pp. 35–93. Springer, Heidelberg (2009). https://doi.org/10.1007/978-3-540-88702-7_3

[CAD+20] Cooper, D., Apon, D., Dang, Q., Davidson, M., Dworkin, M., Miller, C.: Recommendation for stateful hash-based signature schemes (2020)

[CNS23] National Security Agency. Announcing the Commercial National Security Algorithm Suite 2.0 (2023). https://media.defense.gov/2022/Sep/07/2003071834/-1/-1/0/CSA_CNSA_2.0_ALGORITHMS_.PDF

[DSS05] Dods, C., Smart, N.P., Stam, M.: Hash based digital signature schemes. In: Smart, N.P. (ed.) Cryptography and Coding 2005. LNCS, vol. 3796, pp. 96–115. Springer, Heidelberg (2005). https://doi.org/10.1007/11586821_8

[HBG+18] Hülsing, A., Butin, D., Gazdag, S.-L., Rijneveld, J., Mohaisen, A.: XMSS: Extended Hash-Based Signatures. RFC 8391 (2018)

[HRS16] Hülsing, A., Rijneveld, J., Song, F.: Mitigating multi-target attacks in hash-based signatures. In: Cheng, C.-M., Chung, K.-M., Persiano, G., Yang, B.-Y. (eds.) PKC 2016. LNCS, vol. 9614, pp. 387–416. Springer, Heidelberg (2016). https://doi.org/10.1007/978-3-662-49384-7_15

[Hul13] Hülsing, A.: W-OTS+ – shorter signatures for hash-based signature schemes. In: Youssef, A., Nitaj, A., Hassanien, A.E. (eds.) AFRICACRYPT 2013. LNCS, vol. 7918, pp. 173–188. Springer, Heidelberg (2013). https://doi.org/10.1007/978-3-642-38553-7_10

[JLMS03] Jakobsson, M., Leighton, T., Micali, S., Szydlo, M.: Fractal Merkle tree representation and traversal. In: Joye, M. (ed.) CT-RSA 2003. LNCS, vol. 2612, pp. 314–326. Springer, Heidelberg (2003). https://doi.org/10.1007/3-540-36563-X_21

[MCF19] McGrew, D., Curcio, M., Fluhrer, S.: Leighton-Micali Hash-Based Signatures. RFC 8554 (2019)

[Mer89] Merkle, R.C.: A certified digital signature. In: Brassard, G. (ed.) CRYPTO 1989. LNCS, vol. 435, pp. 218–238. Springer, New York (1990). https://doi.org/10.1007/0-387-34805-0_21

[NIS23a] National Institute of Standards and Technology. Module-Lattice-Based Digital Signature Standard (ML-DSA) (2023). Federal Information Processing Standards Publication 204 (Initial Public Draft). https://doi.org/10.6028/NIST.FIPS.204.ipd

[NIS23b] National Institute of Standards and Technology. Module-Lattice-Based Key-Encapsulation Mechanism Standard (ML-KEM) (2023). Federal Information Processing Standards Publication 203 (Initial Public Draft). https://doi.org/10.6028/NIST.FIPS.203.ipd

[NIS23c] National Institute of Standards and Technology. Stateless Hash-Based Digital Signature Standard (2023). Federal Information Processing Standards Publication 205 (Initial Public Draft). https://doi.org/10.6028/NIST.FIPS.205

[Xms] XMSS. XMSS/XMSS-reference: Repository for the XMSS reference code, accompanying RFC 8391, XMSS: Extended Merkle signature scheme

Author Index

A. Nitaj et al. (Eds.): AFRICACRYPT 2025, LNCS 15651, pp. 493–494, 2026.
https://doi.org/10.1007/978-3-031-97260-7

The manufacturer's authorised representative in the EU is Springer
Nature Customer Service Centre GmbH, Europaplatz 3, 69115 Heidelberg,
Germany. If you have any concerns regarding our products, please
contact ProductSafety@springernature.com

Printed and bound by CPI Group (UK) Ltd, Croydon, CR0 4YY

29/04/2026

02099511-0008